Ninth Edition

Family Communication

Cohesion and Change

Kathleen M. Galvin

Northwestern University

Dawn O. Braithwaite

University of Nebraska-Lincoln

Carma L. Bylund

Hamad Medical Corporation

Routledge
Taylor & Francis Group

LONDON AND NEW YORK

First published 2015, 2012, 2008 by Pearson Education, Inc.

Published 2016 by Routledge

2 Park Square, Milton Park, Abingdon, Oxon OX14 4RN

711 Third Avenue, New York, NY 10017, USA

Routledge is an imprint of the Taylor & Francis Group, an informa business

ISBN : 9780205790760 (pbk)

Cover Designer: Bruce Kenselahar

Library of Congress Cataloging-in-Publication Data
Galvin, Kathleen M.
   Family communication : cohesion and change / Kathleen M. Galvin, Northwestern University, Carma L. Bylund, Hamad Medical Center, Doha, Qatar, Memorial Sloan-Kettering Cancer Center, Dawn O. Braithwaite, University of Nebraska.
      pages cm.
   Includes bibliographical references and index.
   ISBN-13: 978-0-205-94523-8
   ISBN-10: 0-205-94523-6
   1. Communication in families—United States.   2. Interpersonal communication—United States.   I. Title.
   HQ734.G19 2015
   306.85—dc23
                                                                        2013047760

DEDICATION

To my family: the Galvins, Wilkinsons, Nicholsens, and Sullivans, plus the special friends I consider as my family.   KMG

To all my families—adoptive, stepfamily, voluntary, beagle— and especially my husband, Chuck. Thanks to all of you, it's a wonderful life.   DOB

To the many people I am privileged to call family, especially Greg, Thurman, Nicholas, and Madeline.   CLB

BRIEF CONTENTS

CONTENTS

PREFACE

It is with amazement and a deep sense of gratitude that we introduce the ninth edition of *Family Communication: Cohesion and Change*. The first edition, published over 30 years ago, represented the first textbook to explore the family from a communication perspective. At that time few communication classes addressed the subject, and only a small number of communication scholars conducted research in the area. Currently, most communication departments in colleges and universities offer one or more courses on the subject at both the undergraduate and graduate levels. The field has progressed from an early period when marital communication dominated the research agenda to the present when scholars address interaction within multiple family forms; there is a research journal devoted to family communication scholarship, and the number of family communication scholars and students is at an all-time high.

The authorship team has changed over these years. Kathleen M. Galvin initiated the book project in 1980 and the first copy was published in 1982. Bernard J. Brommel served as coauthor on the first five editions; Carma L. Bylund assumed that role for the next three editions. Dawn O. Braithwaite joined Galvin and Bylund as the second author for this ninth edition.

Historically, family interactions have received scholarly attention from family therapists, academic psychologists, and sociologists, who studied family issues at the macro level. Today, family scholars rely on a wide range of theories developed within the family communication field and in areas of social sciences. Contemporary scholars address questions related to family members' interactions within a wide range of family forms and address interactions across the life span and within multiple cultures, relying on theories developed within the social sciences as well as those developed by family communication researchers. Today's scholars undertake their studies using multiple quantitative and qualitative methodologies that have grown increasingly sophisticated with each passing decade. As an increasing number of communication scholars focus on family interaction, their findings contribute increased depth and insight to each edition of the book.

Our basic premise remains the same—communication processes create and reflect family systems and family identity. Relying on a range of theoretical perspectives, we examine the communication patterns enacted within families to demonstrate how these patterns affect, and are affected by, family life in the twenty-first century. Our objective focus remains to describe family interaction patterns rather than to prescribe specific interaction practices because we believe there are multiple ways to be a well-functioning family. We believe that readers will be in the best position to make their own choices about family communication when they have in-depth and up-to-date information on family interactions processes.

Throughout the book we present a range of family experiences, including introductory case examples that open each chapter, and de-identified real-life examples appear throughout the text. These are first-person examples provided by our students, friends, and family members. These personal examples ground the theory and research in real-life experiences.

New to This Edition

We made multiple changes in this edition based on feedback from instructors using this book as well as from thoughtful reviewers and comments from our students. Each chapter has been revised to keep pace with changes in the discipline and the state of everyday family life. More specifically we have developed sections that address the following topics: communication challenges in military families, the increasing impact of new technologies on family interaction, shifts in structured aging patterns to highly flexible ones. We have also paid increased attention to international and ethnic families as well as to national crisis situations.

In addition to updating the research base in every chapter, we now begin each chapter with learning objectives readers can expect to address. Other changes include the following:

> Chapter 1: Expanded the "Families: current status" section and the discussion of emerging family forms
> Chapter 2: Updated the primary and secondary functions framework
> Chapter 3: Updated the description of theories with a special focus on advances in relational dialectics theory
> Chapter 4: Added a new mediated section to networks and expanded the narrative section addressing varied family forms and storytelling practices
> Chapter 5: Added a section on respect and expanded the rituals section
> Chapter 6: Expanded the treatment of diversity and sexuality
> Chapter 7: Explored the increasing complexity of family and gender roles
> Chapter 8: Developed the focus on power as negotiated in interaction across different family forms
> Chapter 9: Expanded the discussion of conflicts as managed rather than resolved and the characteristics of negotiating conflict as an interpersonal family process
> Chapter 10: Enlarged the discussion of the role of communication in life stages and across the life course
> Chapter 11: Added a section on communication challenges in military families
> Chapter 12: Revised and updated the discussion of genetics and family communication

Features

As in earlier editions, the first three chapters establish the theoretical foundations of the text. Chapter 1 presents an introduction to communication, discourse-dependent families, and family concepts as well as an elaborate overview of the current state of the family. Chapter 2 depicts and discusses a framework for analyzing family communication that threads through the remaining chapters. It also includes a discussion of family-of-origin patterns because they link directly to the framework patterns. Chapter 3 examines key theories emphasizing systems theory, which undergirds the text, as well as social constructionism/symbolic interaction, relational dialectics theory, narrative theory, and communication privacy management theory. Chapter 4 explores the communicative construction of family identity through family patterns and meanings, including communication rules, family secrets, communication networks, and narratives. Chapter 5 addresses partner and family relational maintenance strategies; these include confirmation, respect, rituals, and relational currencies. Chapter 6 focuses on developing intimacy; topics include commitment, self-disclosure, sexuality, other factors including forgiveness, and barriers to intimacy. Chapter 7 discusses the nature and enactment of family roles and of family typologies. Chapter 8 focuses on power and decision-making, while Chapter 9 discusses conflict, including conflict models and patterns, both destructive and constructive. Chapters 10 and 11 focus on both predictable and unpredictable family stresses. Predictable stress includes managing family developmental stages and the transitions between these stages; unpredictable stress refers to coping with the unforeseen, and usually negative, challenges including death, illness, divorce, and separation due to military deployment, as well as social support. Finally, Chapter 12 examines physical and psychological aspects of family well-being and discusses three emerging areas of future research. The first section examines communication about family health, followed by a discussion of the capacity to hold difficult dialogues, and, finally, psychological well-being and approaches to improving family communication.

Instructor and Student Resources

Please visit the companion website at www.routledge.com/9780205945238

Acknowledgments

We continue to be grateful to Pearson editors and editorial staff, specifically Melissa Mashburn, Amanda Zagnoli, Maggie Brobeck, George Jacob, and, as always, Karon Bowers. We thank our insightful reviewers who provided highly detailed and thoughtful feedback on the last edition and we applaud them: Vickie Harvey, California State University, Stanislaus; Jennifer T. Isaac, Normandale Community College; Daniel M. Paulnock, Saint Paul College; Julie Simanski, Des Moines Area Community College; Joseph Velasco, Sul Ross State University. We are also grateful for the contributions of those who reviewed earlier editions. For this edition we are most grateful to Haley Kranstuber Horstman, University of Missouri, for her development of this edition's excellent Instructor's Manual and Test Bank. In addition, we relied heavily on the creative and organized support of Madaline Goldstein, a Northwestern University student; Kathy Thorne, University of Nebraska-Lincoln, for her substantial work on the bibliographic citations in the book; and Kaitlin Phillips, University of Nebraska-Lincoln, for her highly detailed revision of the bibliography. Finally, we remain thankful to all our students, colleagues, and friends who continue to expand our horizons in discussions regarding the fascinating subject of family communication.

Our own family lives have changed significantly over the past decades, a reality that continually teaches us the importance of understanding family communication including basic interaction patterns in family systems, relationship maintenance and intimacy, conflict management, developmental and unpredictable changes, and adapting to societal changes. To our growing number of family members, related to us by biological, legal, and discursive ties, we express our continued gratitude for their patience, support, and unwitting contributions to some examples in the book! Through our ongoing interactions with our students and our own research projects, we continue to learn firsthand about family interaction patterns in multiple contexts. As each year passes we increasingly appreciate what it means to function as members of complex family systems.

We hope that you will be captured by the importance and complexity of family communication and that you will find the study of family interactions to be a thought-provoking and meaningful experience.

Kathleen M. Galvin
Northwestern University

Dawn O. Braithwaite
University of Nebraska-Lincoln

Carma L. Bylund
Hamad Medical Corporation

CHAPTER 1

Introduction to the Family

LEARNING OBJECTIVES

- Create a personal definition of family and provide reasons for this definition
- Explain what it means to be a discourse and dependent family
- Provide examples of external and internal boundary management strategies for multiple types of discourse and dependent families
- Identify key demographic trends that impact contemporary families
- Describe economic and ethnic trends that affect contemporary families
- Explain how communication serves to construct family relationships
- Explore the implications of ongoing changes in family forms

Angela and her sister Gwen were born to Staci and Mike soon after he returned from combat in Operation Desert Storm. Mike was ten years older than Staci and uncertain about fatherhood. She persuaded him that children would bring joy and meaning to their lives and he reluctantly agreed to her dreams of having children. Soon after the marriage, Angela was born, followed quickly by Gwen. At this time Mike was struggling with uncertainty about his career path and confronting periods of severe depression. Within two years he asked Staci for a divorce, citing her complete devotion to the girls and distance from him, as well as his need for independence. After two years Staci started to date Adam, a colleague at work who had never married. Six months later Staci and the girls moved in with Adam; Mike seldom contacted the girls, who became attached to Adam and his extended family. Staci and Adam worked long hours while Adam's mother cared for the girls when they were not in school. Staci's career flourished and she moved quickly up the corporate ladder. After two years Adam proposed, indicating how much he loved Staci and the girls and how he happily anticipated adding more children to their lives. He was devastated to hear that Staci had no interest in having more children and, although they tried to continue their living arrangement, Adam's pressured pleas for a new family led Staci to announce that she and the girls were leaving. The girls were distraught at losing Adam and, although he tried to maintain contact, Staci discouraged the connection. After six years of career success and struggles as a single parent, Staci married Angelo, a widower with two grown sons, whom she met online. Although he treated the girls well, it was clear he could not wait until they would leave home so he and their mother could begin a life involving just the two of them.

Last week Lacy's boss announced a company-wide cutback in hours and selected benefits due to poor sales figures in the faltering economy. Lacy felt like she had been punched in the stomach. As a 27-year-old wife, the mother of an autistic son (Sean), and an economic support for her mother, who suffered from multiple sclerosis, any drop in income would create major family challenges. Her husband Will's position at a local factory paid less than her income; both incomes were necessary to keep the family afloat. On top of the income loss, the company dropped the tuition benefit that Lacy had used to take classes in respiration therapy at the local community college. She had four more classes to complete before finishing the program and starting on a career track. Eventually Lacy hoped to earn her RN and work in pediatrics. Graduation would represent a major life milestone; she had been struggling to complete the program for five years as she attempted to balance Sean's needs and therapy, her work, and school, with little support. A teenage pregnancy had derailed her successful high school career, although she received her GED and took college classes whenever possible. Although Lacy could not bear to tell her mother the news, she decided to talk with her godmother, Belle, a preschool teacher who had been married to her Uncle Jack. Although Jack died in a car accident more than a decade ago, Belle remained strongly connected to Lacy, serving as a loving aunt and sounding board for her as she grew up. Whenever things piled up, Lacy knew she could count on Belle to talk her through the problem and to give her pragmatic advice. After two hours of talking and five cups of coffee, Lacy left with some ideas about government-supported tuition programs and the promise of loans to finish her course work.

W e are born into a family, mature in a family, form new families, and leave our families upon death. Family life is a universal human experience. Yet, no two individuals share the exact same experience, partly because of the unique communication patterns in each family system. Because the family is such a powerful influence in our lives, we need to examine family relationships to understand ourselves better as members of one of the most complex and important societal groups. Family communication patterns serve to construct as well as reflect familial experience. We create our families just as we are created by these families.

As you read this text, you will encounter some content about which you have some expertise, because you have spent your life in some type or types of family arrangements. Yet, because you have lived in only one or a small number of family structures, your experience is limited compared to the range of potential family experiences. Your reading and reflections should expand your understanding of many families' communication patterns and life experiences, such as the families you meet in the opening of each chapter.

You will encounter a framework for examining communication within families that addresses primary family functions (managing cohesion and change) and secondary functions (family images, themes, boundaries, and biosocial issues). You will encounter this framework as well as systems theory throughout the book. Eventually, you should be able to apply the framework to an unknown family and analyze it as a communication system. We also hope that you will apply what you learn about communication dynamics to your own family or others' family experiences.

Throughout this book, you will find cases at the beginning of chapters and narratives written in first person within the text itself. You will also find short first-person family examples, provided by friends and students, which illustrate many of the concepts discussed in the text. (The names of the characters have been altered to provide anonymity.) These cases should enable you to understand and apply the concepts more completely. Some of the narrative comments will remind you specifically of your own family experiences, whereas others will seem quite different from your background. What we hope these narratives demonstrate the multiple ways to live a functional family life, as in the following example:

I guess you could say I've had three "moms" and two-and-a-half "dads." My parents divorced when my twin brother and I were about three years old. My dad remarried and, after two more sons, got divorced again. Then he remarried and now I have a baby sister young enough to be my daughter. My mom remarried and got divorced again when we were about seven. The "half-father" that we had was a man who lived with us for ten years who recently moved out at my mother's request. The reason my brother and I are still sane is because our mom and dad have always remained friends. We were never treated like pawns in the middle of a battle.

As family members, teachers, and family researchers, we hold certain basic beliefs that undergird our writings. Our backgrounds have given us particular perspectives that affect how we view families and their communication patterns. Our perspectives may be very similar to or quite different from yours. Because our backgrounds influence our thinking and writing, we wish to share these beliefs with you in order to establish a context for understanding.

1. There are many ways to be a family. Family life is as diverse as the persons who create families.
2. The "perfect" family does not exist. Each family must struggle to create its own identity as it experiences good times and stressful times over many years. All families are influenced by the larger context in which they exist.
3. Communication serves to *construct* as well as *reflect* family relationships. It is through talk that persons define their identities and negotiate their relationships with other family members and with the rest of the world. In addition, talk serves to indicate the state of family relationships to family members and, sometimes, to others.
4. Communication serves as the process by which family members create and share their meanings with each other. Members develop a relational culture, or a shared worldview, that contributes to creating a relatively unique communication system.
5. Families socialize members to their underlying values and beliefs about significant life issues, such as gender, health, love, and religion, to name a few.
6. Families involve multigenerational communication patterns. Members are influenced by the patterns of previous generations even as they create their own patterns, which, in turn, influence future generations. The family serves as each person's first communication classroom, teaching members about managing relational closeness and distance in relationships, as well as change.
7. Families reflect cultural communication patterns. Racial and ethnic backgrounds influence lifestyle and behavior, as well as communication norms that affect future generations unless they are consciously altered.

8. In well-functioning families members work at understanding and managing their communication patterns; they recognize that developing and maintaining relationships takes effort. Members develop the capacity to adapt, create connections, and manage conflict. Finally, members are self-aware; most strive to achieve the goal of effective communication.

This text avoids presenting prescriptive solutions for family problems; rather, it introduces you to the diverse world of families and their complex communication patterns. We believe the ideas and examples presented will help you develop your observational and analytical skills. We hope your increased understanding of family communication will give you an increased appreciation for complexities and variations inherent in today's **diverse family forms**. We also hope you will find the study of family communication as fascinating and challenging as we do.

As an introduction to the family, in this chapter we will discuss definitional issues and family status. The next section establishes an understanding of the concept of the family that will be used throughout the rest of the book. We invite you to read these pages with your heart as well as your head.

Families: Definitional Issues

What does the word *family* mean to you? Reaching agreement on the meaning of the word *family* presents a greater challenge than you might suspect. In this subsection, you will encounter the variations implied in the simple term *family*. Today, no widely agreed upon definition of the term *family* exists. Over the past three decades families have been described according to biological ties and legal ties, as networks of persons who live together over periods of time supporting each other, and as groups of people who have ties of marriage and/or kinship to one another.

Even today, after many academic disagreements, the question of how best to define family remains inherently problematic. Many family scholars believe that *the* American family does not exist. Family historian Tamara Harevan (1982) expressed her concern with the idealized family, claiming that U.S. society always has contained "great diversities in family types and family behavior that were associated with the recurring entrance of new immigrant groups into American society. Ethnic, racial, cultural class differences have also resulted in diversity in family behavior" (p. 461). Another family historian, Stephanie Coontz (1999), believes that most Americans move in and out of a variety of family experiences across their lifetimes. Factors such as finances and individual educational levels significantly affect the different paths of family formation and dissolution (Cherlin, 2010). In other words, "Families change their size and shape throughout their histories...but throughout these changes we recognize them still as families, and as whole ones at that" (Stewart, Copeland, Chester, Malley, & Barenbaum, 1997, pp. 245–246).

Today, a family may be viewed more broadly as a group of people with a past history, a present reality, and a future expectation of interconnected mutually influencing relationships. Members often, but not necessarily, are bound together by heredity, legal marital ties, adoption, or committed voluntary ties. Wamboldt and Reiss (1989) developed a process definition of the family as "a group of intimates who generate a sense of home and group identity; complete with strong ties of loyalty and emotion, and experience history and future" (p. 728). In her essay on redefining families, the legal scholar Martha Minow (1998) argued that it is not important whether a group fits a formal legal definition; instead, what is important is "whether the group of people function as a family: do they share affection and resources, think of one another as family members, and present themselves as such to neighbors and others?" (p. 8). Clearly, these definitions emphasize the personal, voluntarily connected relationships among family members instead of relying solely on blood ties or legal agreements as the basis for a family.

Recently, Floyd, Mikkelson, and Judd (2006) offered three frames or lenses for crafting family definitions—a *role* lens, a *sociolegal* lens, and a *biogenetic* lens. Looking through the role lens, "relationships are familial to the extent that relational partners feel and act like family" (p. 27); this establishes social behavior and emotion as the defining characteristics. The sociolegal lens relies on the enactment of laws and regulations, defining family relationships as those formally sanctioned by law. The biogenetic lens depends on two criteria: the extent to which the relationship is directly reproductive, at least potentially, and whether or not the relational partners share genetic material (p. 33). The latter point reflects findings that humans have an evolved motivation to be conscious of their levels of genetic relatedness with others. These approaches represent the complexity of defining a family that challenges everyone, from researchers to each individual family's members.

In addition to the family systems framework that undergirds our view of families in this book, you will see a second perspective appearing in the pages to come. This perspective is important as it highlights the central role of communication in all aspects of family life. One of your authors, Kathleen Galvin (2006), argued that contemporary families depend, in part or in whole, on communication to define themselves, calling this "discourse-dependency." That is, families depend on communication to develop, identify as a family, and carry out being a family over the life course. We will talk more about the central role of communication in families in Chapter 2.

The family is becoming less "traditional," given the growth of the number of single-parent families, stepfamilies, adoptive families, and families headed by lesbian or gay partners. This is important, as we will see in some of the statistics to follow that discourse-dependent families are becoming the norm. Today, many diverse family forms, previously referred to as "non-traditional," appear increasingly normative. Yet, some members face unsettling challenges to their family's authenticity. Therefore, many family members depend, in part or in whole, on communication to "define themselves for themselves" as they interact with outsiders, and even each other, about their family identity.

The more **discourse dependent** a family is, the more members rely on communication strategies to manage their family boundaries. They need to do this with those outside the family and, at certain time, with those inside the family. **External boundary management** involves using communication strategies to reveal or conceal information about the family to outsiders. These strategies include labeling, explaining, **legitimizing**, and defending. In contrast, **internal boundary management** refers to the use of communication strategies to create maintain members' internal sense of we-ness or being a family. These strategies include naming, discussing, narrating, and ritualizing (Figure 1.1).

External Boundary Management

When families appear different to outsiders, questions and challenges arise. Members reveal or conceal relevant family information.

<u>Labeling</u>

Titles and positions provide an orientation to a situation; labeling frequently involves identifying the familial tie when introducing or referring to another person.

- I want you to meet...my (options) stepfather, Bill, my mother's husband, my pops
- Maggie is...(options) my mother's friend, my mother's partner, my stepmother

<u>Explaining</u>

Explaining involves making a labeled family relationship understandable, giving reasons for it, or elaborating on how it works. Usually this is a response to non-hostile inquiry.

- My sister used a sperm donor and her eggs. I was the gestational carrier.
- We adopted him from Vietnam when he was eight months old.

<u>Legitimizing</u>

Legitimizing invokes the sanction of law or custom: it positions relationships as genuine and conforming to recognized standards.

- My mother and Don have been together for 14 years. He functions as my father.
- I adopted my husband's son after his former wife died. He calls me "Moms."

<u>Defending</u>

Defending involves shielding oneself or a familial relationship from attack, justifying it or maintaining its validity against opposition. This is a response to hostility or a direct challenge.

- My mother gets enraged when people ask if I'm her "real daughter."
- When someone tells me my mothers will go to hell, I tell them off.

Internal Boundary Management

<u>Naming</u>

Naming plays a significant role in the development of internal family identity as members struggle to indicate their familial status and connections.

- We call my birth mother Aunt Carrie or Carrie.
- My step-grandmother goes by "Nona Pat."

<u>Discussing</u>

Discussing reflects the degree of difference among family members that affects the amount of ambiguity in their family situation. This occurs when members see few role models for their family form.

- We talk about Karin's anonymous sperm donor and his musical talents.
- Jack asked how he thought he should address his birth mother whom he located.

<u>Narrating</u>

Narrating involves the emergence of family stories; they represent the family's definition of itself. Members tell and retell, to themselves and to others, the story of who they are and how they got there.

- Let's get out the scrapbook with your adoption story.
- Tell Uncle Jack about the first time I introduced you to your stepmother.

Ritualizing

Ritualizing allows families to accomplish their "emotional business" as they enact their identity. Family rituals include major celebrations and mundane routines.

- Our family celebrates "Gotcha Days," or the days on which they adopted each of us.
- My father and stepfather agreed to walk me down the aisle together.

FIGURE 1.1

Discourse-dependent families: Constructing and deconstructing family identity

Source: From Galvin, K. M. (2006). Diversity's impact on the family: Discourse-dependence and identity. In L. H. Turner & R. West (Eds), *The Family Communication Sourcebook* (pp. 3–19). Thousand Oaks, CA: Sage.

We believe that families define themselves, for themselves, through their interactions. At the same time, longevity, legal flexibility, personal choice, ethnicity, gender, geographic distance, and reproductive technology impact traditional biological and legal conceptions of family. Society has passed the point of distinguishing between traditional and nontraditional family categories as functional, because what were once thought of as nontraditional families are emerging as normative family forms (Le Poire, 2006). Fitzpatrick (1998) argued that society needs to "employ definitions of the family that depend on how families define themselves rather than definitions based on genetic and sociological criteria" (p. 45). From this perspective "families are constituted by the very communication processes one seeks to study as being 'within a family'" (Steier, 1989, p. 15). Many scholars are concerned with how family members define themselves as families—in other words, how they use communication to define their family for themselves. For example, think about how

Two-parent biological families are one of many forms.

two single-parent families must communicate to define themselves as a stepfamily when the parents marry. This **constitutive approach** to creating family challenges the conception of one dominant form of family life.

As we talk about families, we will take a broad, inclusive view. Therefore, if the members consider themselves to be a family, and appear to function as a family, we accept the members' self-definition. From this perspective, we refer to families as *networks of people who share their lives over long periods of time bound by ties of marriage, blood, law, or commitment, legal or otherwise, who consider themselves as family and who share a significant history and anticipated future of functioning as a family*. Such a definition encompasses countless variations of familial forms and numerous types of interaction patterns.

In contemporary society, family diversity abounds. One indication of the complexities of today's families may be found in a review of current literature, which includes such categories as large, extended, blood-related groups; formal and informal communal groups; stepfamilies; single-parent families; and gay and lesbian partnerships. These families reflect multiple cultural and socioeconomic situations.

Your Authors   We want to tell you a bit about the current authors of this book as we represent three very different family experiences and have experienced first-hand family diversity and how families are constituted in communication. Kathleen Galvin grew up in New York City as an only child of Irish immigrants. After her parents died, she acquired an adoptive Norwegian-German family with three siblings. Currently she is married, a parent to three adult children, one of whom was adopted from Korea, and a grandmother of three. Dawn Braithwaite was born in urban Chicago and adopted by a couple in the suburbs. After her adoptive mother died, her family became a stepfamily. She has been married for a long time and she and her husband are a family that is childless by choice. The third, Carma Bylund, is the oldest of seven children and grew up in a university town in Missouri. After a short first marriage, she is currently married and the mother of two energetic school-aged boys and their baby sister. Although our biological and/or adoptive relatives are important to each of us, we also want to note that each of us has friends whom we consider as family members.

What about you? You may have grown up in a small family or a large four-generation household. Your brothers and sisters may be blood related, step, or adopted. Some of you may be *married parents*, single parents, stepparents, or foster parents. And some of you may have experienced one committed marriage or single

My family consisted of a mother and brother only, but lacked a father. Due to this fact, my mother brought us together ideologically with a strong focus on being one as a group, but lacking strength when separated. Her comments strongly suggested this when, in time of crisis, she always said, "As long as we pull together and believe in one another, we'll be okay." Physical proximity also played a role in this togetherness through attending church together on Sundays, and trying to speak to our mother at least once a day. Due to the fact that she worked 13-hour days, she normally arrived home after we had fallen asleep.

lifestyle, whereas others may have experienced divorce and remarriage, or life in a committed partnership. No one-size-fits-all family pattern exists.

Family Types This diverse family reality creates a challenge for texts such as this one. We wish to represent the multiple ways families are formed and enacted, yet much of the research still focuses on a small number of family forms. In the following pages we will address these more established family forms more frequently because that reflects the information we have available from research. However, we do need to recognize that families represent multiple overlapping structural forms. Our category system encompasses the following styles of family formation: the two-parent biological family, single-parent family, stepfamily, extended or intergenerational family, GLBT partners and parents, and **committed partners** or small groups. The last category represents a family formed solely through language. These are not discrete categories; many families reflect more than one variation. And it is important to note here that there is no longer a majority family form in the United States.

A *two-parent biological family* consists of parents and the children who result from the union of these parents. Thus, full-blood ties characterize this family; the majority of parents are married but increasingly many are cohabiters.

Traditionally the term "married partners" referred to heterosexual couples who legally marry but do not serve as parents due to choice or infertility. Members of such partnerships continue to serve as children to the previous generation and as siblings and extended family members to other generations, while providing loyalty and affection to one another. Many find themselves deeply involved with extended family members such as nieces and nephews. Today the term also includes many gay and lesbian couples who have legally married in certain states in the United States or other countries.

Committed partners include adult pairs (heterosexual or homosexual) who cannot or choose not to marry or parent who consider each other to be family. They may become actively involved with extended family members. Families with these relationships include those who may choose to remain child-free or are infertile, cohabiting heterosexual couples, and gay male and lesbian partners who consider themselves a family.

A *single-parent family* consists of one parent and one or more children. This formation may include an unmarried man or woman and his or her offspring; a man or a woman who lost his or her partner through death, divorce, or desertion, and the children of that union; a single parent and his or her adopted or foster children or a child conceived with technological assistance. For some children, life in a single-parent system is temporary until the parent marries or remarries; however, many children will live in a one-parent family if their parent stays single.

Although the term *single parent* is commonly used, we will alternate that term with *solo parent*, which describes one parent carrying out all parental obligations while ongoing involvement with the other parent is precluded. This occurs most frequently in cases of death, desertion, and single-parent adoption. When two parents take some, usually unequal, responsibility for children, the custodial parent is referred to as the primary parent. When both adults remain involved, they are referred to as co-parents.

The *stepfamily* or **blended family** refers to families formed through merging existing family units. The stepfamily consists of two adults and children, not all of whom are from the union of the adults' relationship. Most often two families are blended through remarriage or re-partnering, a situation that brings two smaller units into a new familial relationship. The most common stepfamily formation pattern occurs when a two-parent family becomes a single-parent family for a period of time, after which certain members become part of a stepfamily. Some or all members bring past family history from a relationship that has changed or ended. The couple does not begin as a dyad but, rather, the parent-child relationship predates the partnership bond. Many of these individuals experienced a sense of loss after a first family ended but some stepfamilies are formed by one or both single parents.

The stepfamily has a complex extended family network and children may function as members of two or more households. Many of these family relationships began as "not-so-freely-chosen" or involuntary relationships, as children, stepparents, and siblings most often not choose each other but come together because of the relationship of the parent and stepparent (Braithwaite, Schrodt, & Baxter, 2006; Coleman, Fine, Ganong, Downs, & Pauk, 2001; Pasley & Lee, 2010). Children may have a primary residence in one home or co-reside in both parents' homes. In many cases, no legal relationship automatically exists between the stepparent and stepchild. An increasing number of stepfamilies are headed by gay or lesbian partners. Today many individuals find themselves part of a second stepfamily before they die due to the remarriage of older adults.

Adoption creates another type of blended family—a family "that is connected to another family, the birth family, and often to different cultures and to different ethnic and national groups as well" (Bartholet, 1993, p. 186). Constructing families through adoption is a centuries-old process, evolving from a responsibility managed within family bloodlines to practices of matching personal characteristics, such as ethnicity or religion, to an open style of connections crossing religious, racial, and international lines. In contrast to earlier practices, in recent decades an increasing number of adoptions are transnational, transracial, and involve older children or children with disabilities, and involve single parents or gay male and lesbian parents. Today almost all domestic adoptions are "open," reflecting allowing long-term connections between birth mothers and adoptive parents, creating new types of extended families with communication challenges (Galvin & Colaner, 2014). Today, approximately half of domestic adoptions involve children moving from the foster care system.

Foster families serve children who cannot remain living with their biological relatives at a given period of time because the adult parental figure(s) is incapable of safe and appropriate parenting. They provide a substitute family experience until such time as children can return to biological relatives or are adopted by another family or enter a group home at an older age. State-approved individuals and families serve as surrogate parents for indefinite periods of time. Foster families are temporary for some children, while others remain in adoptive families, or group homes, until they "age out" of the system at 18 or 21.

The terms *extended* or *intergenerational family* traditionally refer to that group of relatives living within a nearby geographic area. It may be more narrowly understood as the presence of blood or adoptive relatives, other than the parents, in the everyday life of a child. For example, an extended family may be a cross-generational form, including grandparents who live with a parent-child system or who take on exclusive parenting roles for grandchildren. Given increasing longevity, more families will include four and five generations of relatives who may maintain active contact, as the following indicates:

I grew up in an extended family. My great-grandparents were the dominant figures. Most of us lived with our grandparents at one time or another. There were six different households in the neighborhood I grew up in. My great-grandmother, referred to as "Mother," babysat for all the kids while our parents were at work.

The *intentional* family involves a pair or a group of people, all or most of whom are unrelated biologically or legally, who share a commitment to each other, may live together, and consider themselves to be a family. These relationships are sometimes called *fictive*, *voluntary*, or *chosen family*. Formal examples of these family types are found in communal situations such as an Israeli kibbutz. Other intentional families are formed through friendship or common interests or commitments. Two neighboring families may share so many experiences that, over time, both sets of children and parents begin to talk of each other as "part of the family," or a family relationship may grow from common experiences, such as being lesbian or gay. Intentional families may form when the **family of origin** is estranged, does not share values, or does not meet needs, or when there is a death in the family that leaves a void to be filled. In this case people will create family relationships as substitute or supplemental (Braithwaite et al., 2010). Families formed through intentional ties are highly discourse dependent to define and defend this family type, and members rely heavily on the strategies described earlier in Figure 1.1.

Families formed by *same-sex partners* continue to rise as increasing numbers of gay and lesbian couples marry or commit to long-term partnerships. Many of these couples also become parents through adoption or procreation. More than 700,000 same-sex households existing in the United States are male-male partners, 13 percent of whom have at least one child living with them. Overall 25.7 percent of all members of same-sex couple households reported that they were spouses (Lofquist, 2011), and this number will undoubtedly rise as marriage becomes legal for lesbian and gay couples in more states.

This last category represents a growing change in thinking regarding family membership. We leave it to you to decide how to consider this idea. Pets, or companion animals, are viewed increasingly as family members. As families become smaller, stresses multiply and more individuals live alone; some scholars argue that "For many people, pets are already functioning as family members" (Cohen, 2002, p. 635). Individuals who see their pets as companion animals experience a psychological bond and mutual relationship (Kurdek, 2009; Walsh, 2009a). Research suggests that children living in single-parent homes bond more strongly with pets than those in two-parent families and that only children bond with household pets more strongly than do those with siblings (Walsh, 2009b). Finally, numerous romantically involved young adults choose to raise pets together before raising children; other pairs raise pets instead of raising children.

Most people experience family life in an evolutionary manner, moving through different family forms over time, experiencing changes due to factors such as aging, death of a family member, or unpredictable stresses. In addition, most persons experience life with one or more biological and adopted siblings, or step-siblings. For most people sibling ties are the longest-lasting family relationships due to age similarity. Sibling relationships are significant sources of information on communication patterns such as family stories, rituals, and memories, specifically in adulthood (Mikkelson, 2006).

It is important to distinguish between two types of family experiences: current families and families of origin. Families beget families through the evolutionary cycles of individuals coming together and separating. Each person experiences family life differently, starting with his or her family of origin. The term, *family of origin,* refers to the family, or families, in which one grows up. Pioneering family therapist Virginia Satir (1988) depicts the family of origin as the blueprint for people-making, stating, "Blueprints vary from family to family. I believe some blueprints result in nurturing families, some result in troubled ones" (p. 210). Multigenerational patterns, those of more than two generations, are considered as part of the blueprint. As you will discover, family-of-origin and multigenerational experiences influence the development of communication patterns in current families.

Families: Current Status

Demographic Trends

The composition and shape of the contemporary family is constantly changing. In order to understand family interaction fully, it is necessary to examine the current status of family life in the United States. No matter how old you are, you have lived long enough to witness major changes in your family or in the families around you—changes that bear witness to an evolving national and international picture. American families continue to reflect greater racial and ethnic diversity with each passing decade, and rising numbers of families face increasing economic stress or poverty. Although there are numerous similarities in family communication patterns across large groups, differences in family forms, composition, and culture affect members' interactions.

A key baseline is the average number of people per household, which was 2.60 in between 2007 and 2011 (United States' Census Bureau, 2013). Although research figures shift constantly and various sources provide slightly different numerical data, the overall picture emerges. As you read the following demographic trends, think about how they might affect the ways in which family members communicate with each other.

The American family continues to undergo dramatic changes in the twenty-first century, as indicated by the following trends:

- *The profile of marriage continues to change.* Americans are less likely to marry than in previous decades and most couples live together before marrying for the first time (Wilcox & Marquardt, 2009). Currently couples are marrying later and less as the number of cohabiting couples has risen steadily (Angier, 2013).

Slightly more than half (51 percent) of all U.S. adults are married and this is a record low (Cohn, Passel, Wang, & Livingston, 2011). This does not mean that marriage is unimportant in America. In fact, over 90 percent of Americans will marry at least once. Current trends indicate that first marriages are taking place later in life. Due to rising life expectancies, American marriages are more likely to reach a 40th wedding anniversary than ever before. The odds of remaining in a first marriage until the death of one spouse depend on multiple factors including higher levels of education, parents who remained married, a decent income, marrying after the age of 25, becoming a parent after marriage, and having a religious affiliation (Wilcox & Marquardt, 2009).

The divorce rate is stabilizing. The United States has the highest divorce rate in the world (NCMFR, 2012), although the divorce rate continues to drop. This drop may be explained by the rise of long-term cohabiters, many of whom split up, but this is not included in the national divorce statistics. Divorce rate figures also vary by race and age. First marriages that end in divorce lasted a median of eight years although separation occurred around the seventh year (Kreider & Ellis, 2011).

- *The majority of people who divorce eventually form new partnerships either through remarriage or through cohabitation.* Almost 30 percent of marriages in 2010 were remarriages for at least one person; the remarriage rate is much higher for men than for women (NCMFR, 2012). Multiple remarriages are becoming more common. Approximately 50 percent of people who divorce remarry within four years. About one in five men and women ages 50 to 69 has remarried twice (Kreider & Ellis, 2011). Childless divorced women under 30 years old are most likely to remarry, followed by divorced women under age 30 with children. Older women are the least likely to remarry.

- *The number of single-parent families continues to increase.* Americans are witnessing the continuing rise of single-parent or *primary parent* systems. Recent data reveal that 48 percent of first U.S. births (the mother's first child) were to unmarried women (Hymowitz, Carroll, Bradford & Kaye, 2013). Single parents maintained 28 percent of U.S. households with children under 18, with 24 percent of these households headed by single mothers (Federal Interagency Forum on Child and Family Statistics Forum, 2013). These single-parent figures vary by ethnicity. For example, only 34.5 percent of black children live in married households (Wilcox, 2009). In 2011 25 percent of white children, 67 percent of black or African American children, 42 percent of Hispanic/Latino children, and 17 percent of Asian children lived in single-parent homes (Kids Count, 2013).

Stepfamilies continue to increase through remarriage and cohabitation. *The stepfamily* remains a vital family form, although exact figures are difficult to use because of variations in custodial arrangements. Thirteen hundred stepfamilies are forming every day according to Stepfamily Solutions (2010). More than 40 percent of American adults have at least one step-relative in their family ("A Portrait of Stepfamilies," 2011). Most children in remarried households live with their biological mother and stepfather.

- *Fewer families have children under 18.* As the large baby boomer population ages and fertility rates decline, the percentage of families with their own child living at home decreased to 46 percent in 2008 (Edwards, 2009). To some extent this figure represents the increase in the number of women who are voluntary childless (i.e., child-free) or involuntary childless, often due to attempt to become pregnant at a later age (McQuillan et al., 2012).

Birthrates are dropping in western nations. The U.S. birthrate reached a record low as the overall U.S. birthrate decreased 8 percent from 2007 to 2010. The birthrate for foreign-born women plunged 14 percent although these women continue to give birth to large share of babies. Hispanics experienced the largest percentage declines (Livingston & Cohn, 2012).

- *Families continue to be constructed through adoption and foster care.* Two percent of U.S. children are adopted; 9,000 were adopted in 2011 (CCAI, 2011). Adoption includes "related" and "non-related" children. The past decades have witnessed a significant increase in transracial adoption and adoption of older children and those with special needs. International adoption is declining as adoption becomes more normative around the world and adoption regulations have become more stringent. Currently, the vast majority of domestic adoptions are *open adoptions*. Each year the Internet plays a greater role in the adoption process and adoption reunions.

  Foster care provides temporary alternative families for many children. Approximately 408,000 children (average age of nine) lived within the foster care system in 2010. Almost half lived in a non-relative foster family and a quarter lived with a relative. Approximately 50 percent of children exit foster care each year; many return to their biological families while others are adopted and some remain within the system until they age out. Older foster children confront significant challenges as they try to establish an adult identity and a supportive community (Evan B. Donaldson Institute, 2011).

- *Some families are constructed or expanded through scientific technologies.* The number of babies born through reproduction technologies, across the globe, has reached an estimated 5 million (American Society for Reproductive Medicine, 2013). Although the numbers are small, certain individuals and couples are achieving parenthood through anonymous or known donor insemination due to lifestyle choice or infertility. Infertility affects about 12 percent of reproductive-age women and men (National Health Statistics Report, 2013). Although success rates remain low for infertile individuals, multiple attempts and scientific advances are making this possibility more viable (Smock & Greenland, 2010). Often this process remains shrouded in secrecy.

  Many lesbian or gay individuals or couples turn to new technologies in order to achieve parenthood. Many gay males achieve parenthood through the use of a surrogate who carries a baby to term using her eggs or an implanted embryo. Some single or partnered women achieve parenthood through sperm donated by a known or unknown sperm donor.

- *More adult children are living at home.* Young adult children tend to remain at home until an older age and are more likely to return after departures from the parental home. Many college graduates, often referred to as "boomerang kids," live with their parents (Vogt, 2009). Among the three-in-ten young adults (ages 25 to 34) who experienced this, a large majority are satisfied with their living arrangements (Parker, 2012). Although reasons vary, common explanations for this change include growing economic pressures, cultural norms, and returning young divorced mothers with small children.

- *A recent study indicates that 48 percent of women interviewed between 2006 and 2010 cohabited with a partner as a first union, as compared to 43 percent in 2002.* This represents another increase in the growing trend of cohabitation for race and ethnic groups except Asians (Copen, Daniels, & Mosher, 2013). For never-married young adults it is frequently a stage before marriage, but for others it is an end in itself. Traditionally cohabitation was frequently perceived as less of an investment in the relationship due to the lack of a formal ceremony and legal complications. Yet, cohabiters today are more likely to bear children than in previous times. Nearly 20 percent of these women experience a pregnancy in the first year of their premarital cohabitation (Copen et al., 2013).

- *Families formed by lesbians and gay males continue to increase.* Gay male and lesbian committed couples are more visible due, in part, to a greater willingness of same-sex partners to identify their lifestyle as well as to the growth in same-sex parenting, which makes their partnered or marital status more visible. Recent data releases, one by the Census Bureau and one by the American Community Survey, address this issue. The former estimated same-sex married couple households with children at 131,729 and the same-sex unmarried partners at 514,735. The latter estimated same-sex married couples at 152,335 and the same-sex unmarried partners at 440,989. Children included biological step, adopted, non-related, or a combination of types of children.

- *Interracial and interethnic families continue to grow.* Marriages and partnerships among individuals of different races or ethnicities have increased to 10 percent in 2010 (Kreider, 2012). Within three decades the United States will become a plurality nation. The non-Hispanic whites will lose their majority status by 2050 if not before; this population will still remain the largest group but no majority group will exist (Taylor & Cohn, 2012). As a result, the rise of interracial and interethnic families will continue (Powell, Bolzendahl, Geist, & Steelman, 2010).

- *Multigenerational households continue to increase due to changes in ethnicity patterns and recent economic downturns.* In 2012 5.6 percent of family households were multigenerational versus 3.7 percent over a decade ago (Blumenthal, 2012). This was the highest number of multigenerational family households since the 1950s. Due to the economic downturn many young people (25 to 34) are living with their parents, a large majority of whom (75 percent) viewed this arrangement as acceptable or good for the family members involved (Parker, 2012). Many other families are surrounded by relatives in nearby neighborhoods or communities.

As American families become more culturally diverse through immigration, the extended family has reemerged in importance (Bush, Bohon, & Kim, 2010). The African American tradition of extended kinship, as well as the values of recent Asian immigrants, reinforces the central importance of biological or fictive kin (Lee & Mock, 2005).

Grandparents play an increasingly significant role in the family households of many children even when a parent is present. A major study of grandparent child-care responsibilities over a ten-year period found that more than 60 percent of grandparents provided grandchild care and more than 70 percent of them provided it for more than two years (Luo, LaPierre, Hughes, & Waite, 2012). When children live in households without either of their parents, close to half lived in their grandparent's household.

- *Families increasingly represent four and five generations.* Individuals continue to live longer. According to the CDC, U.S. life expectancy for someone born in 2005 was 77.9 years for all races. Gender differences do exist, however. U.S. males have a life expectancy of 75.3 years, whereas women have an expectancy of 80.4 years (CDC, 2010).

  This longevity results in four- and five-generation households. Increasing numbers of children are living in grandparent-headed households with or without a parent. In addition, more middle-aged persons are taking on caregiver roles for elderly parents and grandparents. Considering that most people marry for the first time before age 30, a continuous marriage might well be expected to last 45 to 50 plus years. The number of married couples without children at home continues to rise as people live longer and as women bear a smaller number of children in the early years of marriage. On a somber note, widowhood has become an expected life event for the majority of older married women. Since women have a longer life expectancy than men, two-thirds of persons who die at age 85 or older are females.

As you can see, family demographics reveal an increasingly complex set of family structures and characteristics. At the same time it is important to understand that these statistics do not represent all families. Some families are "counted out" or not considered within the census and other statistics. For example, as we discussed earlier, many individuals with no legal or blood ties are creating intentional voluntary kin family systems that provide emotional and economic support over many decades (Braithwaite et al., 2010), and these families are not accounted for in national statistics.

Other families do not "fit" easily on a family tree due to the use of new technologies to achieve parenthood. Not long ago the sister of a woman who could not conceive a child became pregnant with a donor's sperm and gave birth to a female child who was adopted by her childless sister and her husband. For medical purposes the baby's aunt is also her biological mother (Holson, 2011). Every year more families add children through the use of technology.

Economic Issues

All these demographic changes are intertwined with economic and cultural realities. Working mothers are commonplace and are now the primary wage earners in 40 percent of single-parent and married households (Wang, Parker, & Taylor, 2013). Many couples view a dual income as a necessity or highly desirable. Currently, almost half of parents who live with their children believe they spend too little time, and desire to spend more time, with their children (EHRC, 2009); more fathers report their greater commitment to family than in previous decades (Duckworth & Buzzanell, 2009). In many cases, dual-earner couples with children are working shift schedules for economic or personal reasons. Due to economic realities for American families, members experience great pressures. Some preteens and teenagers are expected to contribute to the successful running of the household. Young children may spend many waking hours with babysitters or in day-care centers, encountering their parents only a few hours a day. Research on negative spillover between work and family concludes that negative stress from work-family overlap begins in young adulthood and continues through midlife (Grzywacz, Almeida, & McDonald, 2002).

Another economic reality with a direct impact on family life is poverty. Children have replaced seniors as the poorest segment of the population. Children comprise 34 percent of all people in poverty; 45 percent of children live in low-income families; and 22 percent live in poor families (Addy, Engelhardt, & Skinner, 2013). Over the past 15 years young adolescents who did not live with two parents were less likely to move up to a high-income group 12 years later (DeParle, 2012).

Over one-third of the homeless are families with children—a figure that is rising rapidly. More than 1.6 million (1 in 45) children under the age of 18 were homeless in the United States during 2010 (The National Center on Family Homelessness, 2013). Although a large number of poor families contain two parents, about one quarter of single-parent families have incomes below the poverty level (Grall, 2009). Economic pressures add significant stress to the lives of poor family members, and this stress affects the ways family members relate to each other.

Other factors cause economic stress in families. The recent economic downturns have affected family members of all ages and varying economic levels. As noted above, many young adults, with or without partners and children, have returned to live with their parents due to economic pressures. The PEW Research Center reported that three in ten adult children lived with their parents in the last several years (Parker, 2012).

The stresses of poverty increase family tensions.

Racial/Ethnic Issues

No examination of family status is complete without a discussion of ethnicity's impact on family functioning. Within the past decades, several forces have combined to bring issues of ethnicity and race to the attention of family scholars. First, the overall ethnic composition of U.S. families is changing as the number of African American, Hispanic American, Asian American, and Native American families increases. Second, scholars are recognizing the long-term effect of ethnic heritage on family functioning.

American society represents a rapidly changing and diverse set of ethnic and cultural groups, according to recent predictions. Hispanics will soon represent the largest minority group, followed by African Americans and Asians. Small percentages of Native American Indians and Alaska Natives and Native Hawaiians and Other Pacific Islanders round out the population (Taylor & Cohn, 2012). The result will include a significant generational ethnic shift as the Caucasian population both ages and decreases.

Significant differences in race and ethnicity are reflected in family structures. Asians report one of the highest percentages of currently married individuals and the lowest proportion of separated or divorced individuals. Black men and women reported the lowest percentage of currently married, although there were distinct gender differences—42 percent of black men were married, while 31 percent of black women were married. American Indians and Alaska Natives reported the highest divorce rate, whereas, among women, blacks and Hispanics had the highest separation rates (Kreider & Simmons, 2003). Families with children vary greatly by ethnicity. Whereas 35 percent of black children under two years old and 42 percent of black adolescents lived with a solo parent, findings for Asian children indicate 1 percent for toddlers and 9 percent for teenagers. These figures were 6 percent for

© Olesia Bilkei / shutterstock.com

Increasingly, single men and women or gay and lesbian partners are having or adopting children.

white children, 17 percent for white teenagers, 10 percent for Hispanic children, and 22 percent for Hispanic teenagers (Kreider & Elliott, 2009). In 2010, nearly 40 million foreign-born (13 percent of the population) resided in the United States. The largest group (53 percent) was from Latin America followed by immigrants from Asia (Acosta & de la Cruz, 2011). Traditionally, these families report strong grandparent and extended family ties.

As a result of current Hispanic and Asian immigration patterns, many family members have difficulty speaking a second language, English, or do not speak English at home. Twenty-eight percent of immigrants live in households where no one older than age 13 speaks English "very well" or "well" (Hill, 2011). The number of people, ages five and older, who speak a language other than English at home has more than doubled in the past three decades although the majority of these individuals report speaking English "very well" (Shin & Kominski, 2010). The majority of these children are of Hispanic or Asian origin.

Classification systems based on race and ethnicity categories are becoming less useful as people form relationships, marry, and adopt across cultures. In the future, categorization of family race and ethnicity will change as intermarriage, adoption, and cohabitation increase the population of mixed-ethnicity families. Interracial or interethnic opposite-sex married couple households grew by 28 percent over the decade from 7 percent in 2000 to 10 percent in 2010. The number of African American and white interracial married couples has almost doubled in the past two decades. The number of persons who reported multiple races grew by 32 percent between 2000 and 2010 (Jones & Bullock, 2012).

Although generalizations about cultural groups must always be accompanied by an indication of exceptions, a consideration of family ethnicity provides a critical perspective from which to examine communication patterns. This perspective will receive increased attention by the middle of the twenty-first century, Americans of European ancestry will be in the minority. This shift will influence underlying assumptions about what it means to be a family.

Family ethnicity deserves attention because, contrary to popular myth, Americans have not become homogenized in a "melting pot" where cultural identity is discarded; instead, various cultural and ethnic heritages are maintained across generations. There is increasing evidence that ethnic identification and values are retained for many generations after immigration and play a significant role in family life and personal development throughout the life cycle, as second-, third-, and even fourth-generation Americans reflect their original cultural heritage in lifestyle and behavior (McGoldrick, Giordano, & Garcia-Preto, 2005b), as indicated by the following comment:

My parents' marriage reflected an uneasy blend of Italian and Norwegian cultures. My mother included her Italian relatives on many issues my father considered private. He was overwhelmed by her family's style of arguing and making up and would retreat to the porch during big celebrations. I came to realize that cultural tension was reflected in many of their differences, including their child-rearing patterns. I carry pieces of those conflicting patterns within me today.

Ethnicity affects family traditions, celebrations, occupations, values, and problem-solving strategies. Strong variations appear across cultures and family issues, such as age at first marriage, single parenthood, older marriages, changing marital partners, and male-female roles. Even the definition of the concept *family* may differ across ethnic groups. For example, whereas the majority "white Anglo-Saxon" definition focuses on the intact nuclear unit, African American families focus on a wide kinship network, and Italians function within a large, intergenerational, tightly knit family that includes godparents and old friends. Most Chinese family members include all ancestors and descendants in the concept of family. Each of these differences impacts communication within the family.

Economic factors also affect multiethnic families. Families are more likely to be poor if they are of African American, Hispanic, or Native American background. Pressures that plague higher percentages of certain ethnic groups, such as unemployment, low wages, and poverty, discourage or erode marriage, and further confound economic well-being and daily life experiences for family members (Simms, Fortuny, & Henderson, 2009).

Changes in family forms, accompanied by economic and cultural variations, affect the ways family members communicate with each other and create needs for families to manage their relationships. For example, the rise of two-career families alters the amount of time parents and children experience direct, face-to-face contact. Economic stress results in escalating family stress. The high divorce rate increases the chances that all family members will undergo major stressful transitions, including changes in their communication patterns. The growth in single-parent families and dual-career couples increases a child's interpersonal contact with a network of extended family or professional caregivers. Most children in stepfamilies function within two different family systems, each with its own communication patterns. As U.S. families reflect greater ethnic diversity, family life will be characterized by a wider range of communication patterns.

Increased reliance on communication technologies impacts family communication patterns. Working parents use cell phones to check on their children home alone, while nonresidential parents and geographically dispersed transnational family members may keep up with each other's lives through social media and communication technologies, such as Skype. For example, geographically separated Filipino mothers and children maintain their close ties through technology (Madianou, 2012).

Functional Families

It is important to forecast the families we will discuss in the upcoming chapters. Historically, most literature on family interaction has focused on struggling or pathological families (Fincham & Beach, 2010) as researchers are often drawn to trying to understand the problems that are visible and create negative attention. Early studies examined families with one or more severely troubled member—a trend that was followed by attempts to characterize "normal" families. As you may imagine from the previous description of the definitions and the status of families, there is little agreement on what is "normal." Currently, many studies focus on the characteristics of well-functioning families.

The following four perspectives on so-called normal families represent the evolution of family studies on family functioning (Walsh, 1993):

1. *Normal families as asymptomatic family functioning*—implies that family members exhibit no major symptoms of psychopathology.
2. *Normal families as average*—addresses families that appear typical or fit common patterns.
3. *Normal families as optimal*—describes ideal or positive characteristics, sometimes reflecting members' accomplishments.
4. *Normal family processes*—assumes a systems perspective addressing adaptation across the life cycle and management of stresses and diversity contexts.

The first three perspectives quickly prove unworkable because of the static nature of each explanation. The fourth perspective provides a sense of variation and adaptation that captures the dynamic nature of family experiences.

Current scholarship focuses on family strengths in addition to helping families navigate problems (DeFrain & Stinnett, 2007). Recent studies of well-functioning families highlight the tremendous diversity of families that appear to be functional, even as they struggle with predictable and unpredictable changes (Price, Price, & McKenry, 2010). A recent call for a focus on **relationship flourishing** reinforces this commitment to understanding well-functioning families—those that exhibit relationship strengths—in order to understand how they enact such strengths in the face of life stresses (Fincham & Beach, 2010). Members of these families exhibit intimacy, growth, and resilience; they balance focusing on familial relationships with engaging the larger community.

As it is impossible to talk about what a "normal" family is or should be, in this text, we will focus on *communication within functional families*, because this constitutes the primary experience for most individuals, most of the time. We hold two basic assumptions about families: (1) *there is no one right way to be a family* and (2) *there is no one right way to communicate within a family*. The following pages address a wide variety of family structures and communication behaviors. We take a descriptive approach to families in order to increase your understanding and appreciate the wide range of family life. And we focus on the dynamics of family communication in order to help you appreciate the many different ways to interact within a family.

We hope that you experience some personal benefit, rather than just academic benefit, from reading these pages. Most of you grew up in and live within families that experienced their share of pain and problems as well as joys and successes. May these pages provide you with new insights into those people with whom you share your lives as well as others who live in your communities. As you read, think about your own family and other real, fictional, or media families with which you are familiar. We hope your study of family communication will assist you to make wise choices as you apply what you learn to your own family life and the lives of families you encounter in your careers or communities. We close this chapter with the words of one previous reader who described how she approached the study of family communication:

Analyzing my own family has not been an easy process. As I began, my entire soul cried out, "How do I begin to unravel the web of rules, roles, and strategies that make up our family system?" I do not claim to have all possible answers; certainly my opinions and attitudes are different from those of the others in my family. I also do not claim to have the answers to all our problems. But I have tried to provide answers to my own confusion and to provide some synthesis to the change and crises that I have experienced. And I have grown from the process.

Conclusion

This chapter provides an overview of what it means to be a family and the importance of understanding communication processes in families, and illustrates the enormous diversity of family life. We shared some of our basic beliefs about families and communication, and examined a range of family definitions. We also depicted the current status of the American family through an overview of trends in marriage and partnering, divorce, remarriage, and the formation of families though birth, adoption, and stepfamily relations, as well as ongoing single-parent families. In addition, we addressed issues of economic pressures and cultural diversity. The chapter concluded with a discussion of issues related to "normal" family functioning. Each of these issues will thread through the following chapters.

In Review

1. At this point in your life, what is your definition of a family? To what extent has it changed in the past five years?
2. Describe how your own family members, or those in another actual or media family, manage their (internal and external) boundaries as they define or defend their family form.
3. Describe ways in which you have heard (real or fictional) family members address their identity.
4. Select two demographic trends and discuss how they are impacting family ties and communication patterns.
5. Discuss how the recent economic climate impacted a real or media family and how family members communicated about these issues.
6. Identify the family systems of two friends. Compare them in terms of family types as well as socioeconomic status and ethnicity. Explain how these descriptors appear to influence members' interactions.
7. At this point in your life, how would you describe a well-functioning family?

Key Words

CHAPTER 2

Framework for Family Communication

Bruce grew up in a household where he learned not to trust anyone who was not a member of the family because "There's always somebody out to get you." His grandfather, swindled twice by trusted business partners, taught his children to be wary of outsiders, a belief passed down to his son, and eventually to his grandchildren. When Bruce finished high school he joined the family business in order to maintain the company run by relatives. At age 22 he met and married Melissa, a warm, friendly, and trusting person. Unfortunately, their core worldview differences haunted their marriage. Bruce would say to his children, "Don't depend on anyone else. Take care of problems yourself" and "You can only depend on your family." Melissa thought Bruce would realize how narrow his perspective was as he grew older. She had grown up in a family surrounded by the warmth of adult friends and close neighbors; she made good friends in high school that she remained close to even though Bruce did not like them. Although Bruce was a distant son-in-law, the couple created a good life despite their fundamental worldview differences—until the children arrived.

As the children aged, Bruce insisted that they could not sleep over at other people's houses, join organized sports, or loan money to anyone. Close friends were discouraged; siblings and cousins were expected to meet each other's needs for companionship. Although Melissa tried to convince Bruce that he was overreacting, his position never changed. In fact, he became increasingly angry when she would get involved with neighborhood female friends, friends at work, or spend time on social media sites. After years of struggling with her husband about his need for total control, her need for friends, and the children's need for outside companionship and participation in a larger world, Melissa chose to end the marriage.

Mark grew up in a family in which his father worked outside the home while his mother stayed home to raise Mark and his two younger sisters. Mark's father was in the insurance industry and traveled a lot for work. Consequently, Mark didn't see his father very often. Yet, Mark's father was the disciplinarian in the family. Whenever Mark or his sisters were misbehaving, his mother would say things like, "You better stop it, or I will tell your father." The threat of having his father discipline him was often enough to make Mark shape up. When he was young, his father would spank him; as he became older, his father would ground him or take away other privileges. Mark's father tended toward bursts of anger and verbal attacks, using words like "dumb," "bad," "irresponsible," and "worthless." After such incidents, Mark's father would never apologize, but seemed to go out of his way to be nicer toward him. Mark assumed his father loved him, even though he never said the words.

Later in life, Mark married Julie and a few years later their first child, Alex, was born. Mark loved being a father. But as Alex entered the "terrible twos," he became a challenging child. Mark relied on what he had learned from his father about discipline, spanking Alex and calling him a "bad boy." Such behavior caused a great deal of tension between Mark and his wife Julie. Julie had been raised in a family where milder disciplinary tactics were used; neither she nor her siblings had ever been spanked. Her parents were soft-spoken, patient people who doled out more love and empathy than punishment. Julie preferred these tactics and was shocked the first time Mark spanked their son. These struggles continued until Alex was 6, when Julie insisted they talk with a counselor because the disagreements were affecting their marriage. During their marital counseling Mark realized he had "become" his father—that he was recreating the unhealthy communication patterns in his relationship with Alex.

Families repeat themselves within and across generations. Members become caught up in predictable and often unexamined life patterns that are created, in part, through their interactions with other family members. This text explores the family as a communication system, concentrating on processes by which communication patterns serve to create and reflect family relationships. Within the framework of shared cultural communication patterns, each family has the capacity to develop its own communication codes based on the experiences of individual members as well as the collective family experience. Individuals develop their communication competencies within the family context, learning both the general cultural language(s) and specific familial communication patterns. Since most people take their personal backgrounds for granted, you may not be aware of the context your family provided for learning how to communicate. For example, when you were a child, your family members taught you acceptable ways of expressing intimacy and conflict, how to relate to other family members, how to make decisions, and how to share information inside and outside the family boundaries. Other families may have taught their members different lessons. From our perspective, families are defined primarily through their interaction patterns rather than through their structures (Whitchurch & Dickson, 1999). In other words, "Through their communicative practices, parties construct their social reality of who their family is and the meanings that organize it" (Baxter & Braithwaite, 2002, p. 94). Communication serves a constitutive function, thereby placing interaction at the core of familial experience.

In order to understand the family as an interactive system you need to explore key communication concepts and understand how they can be applied to family patterns. This chapter will (1) provide an overview of the communication process, including the development of interpersonal meanings; (2) explain a set of primary and secondary family functions that influence communication; (3) introduce the concept of transgenerational communication patterns; and (4) present a framework for analyzing family communication patterns.

The Communication Process

We view **communication** as a symbolic, transactional process of creating and sharing meanings. The claim that communication is symbolic implies that symbols are used to create meaning and messages. Words or verbal behavior represent the most commonly used symbols, but the whole range of nonverbal behavior—including facial expressions, eye contact, gestures, movement, posture, appearance, and spatial distance—also occurs symbolically. Symbols may represent things, feelings, or ideas. Many families use kisses, special food, teasing, or poems as symbols of love, and silence or yelling as symbols of anger. The symbols must be mutually understood for the meanings to be shared. For example, if family members do not agree on how much is "a lot" of money to spend on a gift or vacation or how to express and recognize anger, confusion will result. If meanings are not mutually shared, confusion develops. The result appears in the following example of misunderstanding:

In my first marriage, my wife and I often discovered that we had very different meanings for the same words. For example, we agreed we wanted a "large" family but I meant three children and she meant seven or eight. I thought "regular" sex meant once a day and she thought it meant once a week. I thought spending "a lot" of money meant spending over $1,000; she thought it meant spending over $100. In my second marriage, we talk very frequently about what our words mean so we don't have so many disagreements.

Viewing communication as "transactional" means that communication involves mutual influence and interaction. In relationships, participants are affecting and being affected by others. The focus is placed on the relationship, not on individual participants. Participation in an intimate relationship transforms fundamental relational definitions for both partners and in so doing transforms the partners themselves (Baxter, 2004). The joint actions of family members contribute to the development of private relational realities as reflected in the unique relationships of the pair or family. Siblings may create teasing patterns that allow them to feel connected, but no one else could joke that way without creating tension. Every day family members engage in symbolic interaction or creating joint meanings within their relationships.

A **transactional communication perspective** and the family systems perspective, which will be explained in Chapter 3, complement each other because both share a relational focus. In other words, when trying to understand family dynamics, relationships take precedence over individuals. A transactional communication perspective focuses on the interaction between two or more persons. Each individual communicates within an interpersonal context, and each communication act reflects the nature of those relationships. In addition, as relational partners interact, they change the relationship, creating context for the other and relating to the other within that context. For example, you may perceive a brother-in-law as distant and relate to him in a very polite but restrained manner. In turn, he may perceive your politeness as formal and relate to you in an even more reserved manner. A similar situation is demonstrated here.

My father and brother had a very difficult relationship for many years, although both of them had excellent relationships with everyone else in the family. Daniel saw Dad as repressive and demanding, although I would characterize him as serious and concerned. Dad viewed Daniel as careless and uncommitted, although no one else saw him that way. Whenever they tried to talk to each other, each responded to the person he created in his mind, and it was a continual battle.

In the previous example, knowing Daniel or his father separately does not account for their interactional behaviors. Each influences the other's actions and reactions. Each creates a context for the other and relates to the other within that framework. It is as if one says to the other, "You are sensitive," or "You are repressive," and "that's how I will relate to you." The content and style of messages vary according to how each person sees himself or herself and how each predicts the other individual will react.

The transactional perspective stresses the importance of the communicators' perceptions and actions in influencing the outcome of interactions. Relationship patterns, not specific acts, become the focal point. One's perception of another and one's subsequent behavior can actually change the behavior of the other. An aunt who constantly praises her nephew for his thoughtfulness and sensitivity may help him change his perception of himself and his subsequent behavior with her and other relatives. A husband who constantly complains about his wife's parenting behavior may contribute to lowering her self-esteem and affect her subsequent behavior toward him and their children. Thus, in relationships, each person (1) creates a context for the other, (2) simultaneously creates and interprets messages and, therefore, (3) simultaneously affects and is affected by the other.

To view communication as a process implies that it is continuously changing. Communication is never static; rather, it develops over time. Relationships, no matter how committed, change continuously, and communication both affects and reflects these changes. The passage of time brings with it predictable and unpredictable crises, which take their toll on family regularity and stability. Yet it is not just the big life events but also everyday moods, minor pleasures, or irritations that may shift the communication patterns on a day-to-day basis. As time passes, family members subtly renegotiate their relationships. Today, you may be in a bad mood and family members may respond to your personal state. Next week, a parent's major job change may affect all your relationships. Over time, families change as they pass through stages of growth; members are born, age, leave, and die. Communication patterns impact and reflect these developments in the family system.

As indicated earlier, communication may be viewed as a symbolic, transactional process of creating and sharing meanings. Communication serves to create a family's social reality. Effective communication depends on the members' shared reality, or sets of meanings.

Meanings and Messages

How often do people in close and committed relationships find themselves saying "That's not what I mean" or "What do you mean by that?" Even in the most mundane interchanges, participants' messages convey meanings or their visions of the nature of social and physical reality as well as their values, beliefs, and attitudes. Communication involves the negotiation of shared meanings; if meanings are not shared by the speakers, confusion or misunderstanding results. A primary family task involves "meaning-making," or the "co-creation of meanings." In other words, as we interact, we are continually offering definitions of ourselves and reacting to definitions of others (Stewart, 1999). In their classic work, Berger and Kellner (1964) captured the sense of creating meanings within a marriage, suggesting, "Each partner's definition of reality must be continually correlated with the definitions of the other" (p. 224). Such correlation requires regular communication and ongoing coordination of meanings. In families, we are continually co-creating meanings. Think about how you and your parents have negotiated meanings in your relationship across the years; this process is in continual flux. Symbolic interaction, a theory discussed in Chapter 3, provides one lens through which family communication will be viewed. This meaning-centered theory positions communication as central to the process of creating a family's social reality.

Worldviews reflect one's fundamental beliefs about issues, such as the nature of change and the nature of human beings; these are the unspoken presuppositions a person brings to each interpersonal encounter.

My mother and stepfamily clash regularly because they hold divergent views about human nature. My mother believes people are inherently good and should be trusted. My stepfather Jack assumes that people seldom tell the truth or the whole truth in difficult situations. Whereas my mother tends to believe what people tell her, Jack looks for the holes in every story. This drove me crazy when I was a teenager. Jack would grill me constantly about my activities whereas my mother would accept my explanations or excuses, and this often caused a lot of tension between them as well.

Development of Meanings   How does a person develop a set of meanings? Imagine each person has lenses, or perceptual filters, through which to view the world. Everyone views the world within personal contexts such as age, race, ethnicity, gender, health status, religion, and national culture. In addition, views of reality are affected by family history and traditions across generations and even influences like birth order. These factors combine uniquely for each individual, impacting how

Family members negotiate meanings in a variety of family activities.

that person perceives and interacts with the members of his or her family system. Although this sounds like a very individualistic process, remember the transactional perspective. Each communicator constantly affects and is affected by the other; thus, perceptions are co-created within the context of a relational system and are constantly influenced by that system.

Meanings emerge as information passes through each person's perceptual filters. One's physical state, based on human sensory systems of sight, hearing, touch, taste, and smell, constitutes the first set of filters. Perceptions reflect the social system including a person's language, accepted worldview, family culture, and class status. An individual shares common meanings for certain verbal and nonverbal symbols with those around him or her. Each individual shares some general experiences with many people and more specific experiences with a smaller number of individuals, such as a family.

Social experiences frame your world. The language you speak limits and shapes your meanings. For example, the move to replace the term "ex-spouses" with "co-parents" reflects a focus on the present working relationship rather than the previous marital relationship. Current terminology limits easy discussion of increasingly complex family relationships, such as "my half-brother's grandfather on his mother's side." Yet, although language may limit meanings, people are capable of broadening such perspectives by creating and learning new terminology and opening themselves to new experiences.

The immediate groups to which a person belongs exert a strong influence on the individual's perceptions. The family group provides contextual meaning and influences the way one gives meaning to sensory data. If one considers handmade gifts as a special sign of caring, a hand-knitted scarf may be valued, whereas an expensive necklace may not convey strong affection. Although physical and social systems combine to provide perceptual filters, specific constraints and experiences influence an individual's meanings. Individual constraints refer to the interpretations you create for your meanings based on your own personal history. Although you may have similar elements of your personal history as others, each person develops a unique way of dealing with sensory information, and therefore develops his or her way of seeing the world and relating to others. This concept is captured in the expression "No two children grow up in the same family." For example, many siblings disagree on the kind of family life they experienced together. One sister may state, "Mom was very nurturing," whereas her brother asserts, "Mom only really cared about her work." Meanings change over time as well; for example, an oldest sibling may have experienced more cautious and strict parents, whereas the youngest child may experience parents who are less strict and more relaxed. Each person experiences "family" differently, as indicated in the following example:

In our house, my sister Diane was considered the "problem child." As far as psychologists can determine, her emotional difficulties stemmed from an unknown trauma when she was age 3, when they suggest she was rejected by my parents at a time when she needed love. The reality was that Diane functioned as a scapegoat for all of us. Although Diane and I are close in age, we experienced a different family because of the negative way she perceived the family and family members perceived her.

Over time, individuals negotiate their shared meanings. "People may not see the same meanings, but meanings do become coordinated, so that meaning for one family member elicits complementary meanings for other family members" (Breunlin, Schwartz, & Kune-Karrer, 2001, p. 52). The greater the repetition of interaction, the greater the probability of a similar meaning for an event. Enduring relationships are characterized by agreements between members as to the meaning of things. These persons develop a relationship worldview reflecting the members' symbolic interdependence.

Eventually you learn to interpret and understand the meanings within your family. As a child, when you heard your mother yell "Jonathan" or "Kyung Chu," you were able to tell from her tone of voice just what to expect. Today, if you hear your younger sister say, "I just hate that Brett Holland," you know that she has just broken up with another boyfriend. Meanings are renegotiated over time as children move into adolescence, as adults witness the death or decline of their parents and grandparents, and as world events force people to reevaluate their values and beliefs. For example, after events that shattered complacency, such as 9/11, some long-term cohabiting couples decided to marry and other individuals attempted to repair ruptured family ties.

Levels of Meaning and Metacommunication   Understanding what others mean requires that you analyze their messages on two levels—the content level and the relationship level. The content level contains information, whereas the relationship level indicates how the information should be interpreted or understood. The relationship level involves more nonverbal messages. When your older sister says, "When are you going to pick up those clothes?" it appears to be an informational question, but there may be another level of meaning. It is up to you to determine if, by her tone of voice, she is really questioning at what time of day you will remove the dirty socks and jeans, or if she is telling you to remove them in the next 30 seconds. Relational pairs develop their own interpretation of symbols. When a father puts his arm on his daughter's shoulder, it may mean "I support you" or "Slow down, relax." Over time, the daughter will understand the intended message. Three siblings may develop a code system for alerting each other to their mother's presence in the area.

Metacommunication   This occurs when people communicate about their communication—for example, when they give verbal and nonverbal indications about how their messages should be understood. Remarks such as "I was only kidding," "This is important," or "Talking about this makes me uncomfortable" signal how another should interpret certain comments. Nonverbal cues, such as facial expressions, gestures, or vocal tones, indicate if a comment is humorous or serious. This is especially important to understand when communicating via technology such as on the phone, text messaging, or online as so many of these nonverbal cues that help us interpret a message are missing. It may be hard to tell if someone is joking or serious, for example.

Sometimes relational parties will try to come to agreement about metacommunication. For example, family members may spend hours talking about how they might engage in conflict or express affection in a more desirable way. Metacommunication serves an important function within families because it allows members to state their needs, clarify confusion, and establish more constructive relational patterns. If distressed members find themselves continually fighting over the meaning of the messages, the need to engage in metacommunication becomes commonplace. Meanings serve a central function in all family communication processes. The next section examines the role communication plays in forming, maintaining, and changing family systems as families enact key functions.

Communication Patterns and Family Functions

When you encounter other families, you may notice how their communication practices differ from those of your family. Everyday ways of relating, making decisions, sharing feelings, and handling conflict vary from your personal experiences. Communication provides form and content to a family's life as its members engage in family-related functions. From a technical perspective, a function is simply something a system must do, or an operation it must perform, in order to avoid a breakdown. The following section examines two primary family functions and four supporting functions that affect and are affected by communication and taken together form a family's collective identity.

Primary Functions

In their attempt to integrate the numerous concepts related to marital and family interaction, researchers Olson, Sprenkle, and Russell developed what is known as the circumplex model of marital and family systems (Olson, 2000; Olson, Russell, & Sprenkle, 1983; Olson, Sprenkle, & Russell, 1979). This model bridges family theory, research, and practice. Two central dimensions of family behavior, or family opera-tions are at the core of the model: family cohesion and family adaptability (see Figure "Cohesion continuum" p.33). Each of these dimensions is divided into four levels matched on a grid to create 16 possible combinations. The four types in the center of the grid are called balanced; the types at the extremes are seen as dysfunctional. The theorists suggest moderate scores represent reasonable functioning, whereas the extreme scores represent family dysfunction.

Over time the model evolved to include three dimensions: (1) cohesion, (2) adaptability, and (3) communication. The two central dimensions remain fam-ily cohesion and family adaptability, which are perceived as the intersecting lines of an axis. The third dimension is family communication, a facilitating dimension that enables couples and families to move along the cohesion and adaptability dimen-sions, but because it is a facilitating dimension, it is seldom included in the model diagrams. We do not present the entire circumplex model here; rather, we have adapted the dimensions of cohesion and adaptability as primary family functions.

The concepts of cohesion and change form a framework through which to view communication within various types of families. From this perspective, two primary family functions involve (1) establishing a pattern of cohesion, or separateness and connectedness and (2) establishing a pattern of adaptability, or change. These func-tions vary with regularity as families experience the tensions inherent in relational life.

Cohesion   From the moment of birth, you have been learning how to manage issues of distance and closeness within your family system. You were taught directly or subtly how to be connected to, or separated from, other family members. For example, you received messages about when to solve problems on your own and when you should ask your parents for help. In other words, every family socializes its members about the extent to which closeness is encouraged or discouraged. Cohesion is defined as the emotional bonding that family members experience with each other and includes concepts of "emotional bonding, boundaries, coalitions, time, space, friends, decision-making, interests and recreation" (Olson, 2000, p. 145).

Although differing in terminology, the concept of cohesion has been identified by scholars from various fields as central to understanding family life (Pistole, 1994). Early on, family researchers Kantor and Lehr (1976) viewed "distance regulation" as a major family function; family therapist Salvador Minuchin and colleagues (1967) talked about "enmeshed and disengaged" families; sociologists Hess and Handel (1959) described the family's need to establish a pattern of separateness and con-nectedness. There are four levels of cohesion ranging from extremely low cohesion to extremely high cohesion. These levels are as follows:

1. *Disengaged.* Family members maintain extreme separateness and independence, experiencing little belonging or loyalty.
2. *Connected.* Family members experience emotional independence as well as some sense of involvement and belonging.
3. *Cohesive.* Family members strive for emotional closeness, loyalty, and together-ness with emphasis on some individuality.
4. *Enmeshed.* Family members experience extreme closeness, loyalty, dependence, and almost no individuality (Olson, DeFrain, & Skogrard, 2008).

Through their communication, family members develop, maintain, or change their patterns of cohesion. Because a father may decide that it is inappropriate to continue the physical closeness he has experienced with his daughter now that she has become a teenager, he may limit his playful roughhousing. This nonverbal message may be confusing or hurtful to his daughter. She may become distant, find new ways of being close, develop more outside friendships, or attempt to force her father back into the old patterns. A husband may demand more intimacy from his wife as he ages by asking for more serious conversation, making more sexual advances, or sharing more of his feelings. His wife may ignore this new behavior or increase her intimate behaviors. Balanced families generally are found at connected or cohesive levels; such families tend to be more functional.

In enmeshed families, those with extremely high cohesion, members are so intensely bonded and over-involved that individuals experience little autonomy or fulfillment of personal needs and goals. Total loyalty is expected. Family members appear fused or joined so tightly that personal identities do not develop appropriately; thus, members are highly interdependent, as indicated by the following example:

My mother viewed us as "best friends," a mixed blessing. I relied on her heavily in high school and college when I had a lot of problems with other girls who hated my theatrical successes. She cried on my shoulder about my dad and her hard life. Now that I'm entering the entertainment industry, my mother has positioned me at the center of her life—her dreams and plans are totally intermeshed with mine. This level of "togetherness" has cost me romantic partners and created problems in my career.

In disengaged families, found at the other end of the continuum, members experience extreme emotional separateness; each member has high autonomy and individuality. Individual interests and priorities predominate.

Throughout this book, we will examine ways families deal with issues of coming together or remaining apart and how they communicate in an attempt to manage their separateness and/or togetherness. Families do not remain permanently at one point on the cohesion continuum although some research suggests that more cohesion is better (Segrin & Flora, 2011). Because there are widely varying cultural norms for acceptable or desirable cohesion, what seems balanced for one family may be quite distant for another family. For example, Latino families may find acceptable cohesion at a point that might feel too connected for families with a Northern European background.

Disengaged Families	Cohesion	Enmeshed Families
← Connected		Cohesive →

Cohesion continuum

Flexibility   When you think of the changes in your own family over the past five or ten years, you may be amazed at how different the system and its members are at this point. A family's experience changes as members move through developmental stages and manage stresses that arise in everyday life, such as adapting to an illness or a job transfer of one of its members. Even everyday living involves managing relational tensions.

Flexibility is defined as the amount of change in a family's leadership, role relationships, and relationship rules. It includes concepts of "leadership (control, discipline), negotiation, styles, role relationships and relationship rules" (Olson, 2000, p. 147). Family flexibility, or adaptability, focuses on how family systems manage stability and change. You will note that we use the terms adaptability and flexibility interchangeably.

There are four levels of adaptability ranging from extremely low adaptability to extremely high adaptability. These can be described as follows:

1. *Rigid.* Family members experience very low levels of change, as well as authoritarian leadership and strict roles and rules.
2. *Structured.* Family members experience more moderate levels of change as well as limited shared decision-making and leadership and relatively stable roles and rules.
3. *Flexible.* Family members experience high levels of change, shared decision-making, and shifting rules and roles.
4. *Chaotic.* Family members experience very high levels of change as well as nonexistent leadership, and confused and very variable rules and roles (Olson et al., 2008).

Each human system exhibits both stability-promoting processes (morphostasis, or form maintaining) and change-promoting processes (morphogenesis, or form creating). Family systems need periods of stability as well as change in order to function. Chaotic families are characterized by little structure and few rules and roles. Due to almost total unpredictability, members cannot maintain predictable relationships and common meanings. At the other extreme, rigidity characterizes families that resist change and growth, leaving members continuously repeating old patterns. Balanced families are generally found at structured or flexible levels, meaning that family members do not experience extremes.

Rigid Families	Flexibility	Chaotic Families

Structured   Flexible

Flexibility continuum

Although most scholars consider either an excess or a lack of change to be dysfunctional, they view a system's ability to change its structure as necessary and desirable. So, for example, parents may have strict rules about Internet and social media use for younger children and will monitor their interactions very carefully. As children mature, most parents give children more freedom on the Internet. Again, issues of ethnicity and socioeconomic status affect a family's experience of change. For example, families confronting poverty and relying on social welfare agencies often experience life as more chaotic than those who live in a secure economic situation, which makes it easier to manage outside stresses.

Family systems constantly restructure themselves as they pass through predictable developmental stages, such as pregnancy or when children enter into adulthood. Likewise, when positive or negative stresses arise, involving such issues as money, illness, or divorce, families must adapt. Finally, family systems must adapt both structurally and functionally to the demands of other social institutions as well as the needs of their own members, as evidenced here.

My son and daughter-in-law adopted an older child from foster care and had to adapt their communication patterns to accommodate her. Although lying was forbidden in their family, when they adopted Shirley they had to reassess this position, because she had learned to lie for most of her life in order to fit into the culture of different foster homes. My son and daughter-in-law had to learn to be more tolerant of this behavior, particularly when she first joined the family, or they would have had to send her back to the agency.

Communication is central to the adaptive function of a family. Effective adaptation relies on shared meanings. Through communication, family members learn to regulate their adaptive behaviors, thereby affecting the system as a whole. Olson and his colleagues hypothesize that when families exhibit a balance between change and stability, more mutually assertive communication styles, shared leadership, successful negotiation, role-sharing, and open rule-making and -sharing occur. The functions of cohesion and adaptability represent the two major functions family members continuously manage.

You may have noticed that the term "communication" does not appear on the various visual representations of the cohesion/flexibility model, yet communication is a critical factor in how families manage cohesion and flexibility. Communication serves as the "grease that smooths frictions between partners and family members" (Olson et al., 2008, p. 88). Olson and his colleagues depict the following six dimensions used to assess family communication: listening skills, speaking skills, self-disclosure, clarity, staying on topic, and respect or regard (see Table 2.1). Schrodt (2005) emphasizes the importance of communication to impact the way families manage the dimensions of cohesion and flexibility, saying: "Whereas positive communication skills, including clarity, empathy, and effective problem solving, are believed to facilitate healthy levels of family cohesion and flexibility, lack of communication skills is believed to inhibit the family system's ability to change when needed" (p. 360).

Applying the work of Olson and his colleagues, you can visualize the mutual interaction of flexibility and cohesion within families by placing them on an axis (Figure 2.1a). By adding the extremes of cohesion (disengagement and enmeshment)

TABLE 2.1	Levels of Couple and Family Communication		
Characteristic	**Poor**	**Good**	**Very Good**
Listening skills	Poor listening skills	Appear to listen, but feedback is limited	Give feedback, indicating good listening skills
Speaking skills	Often speak for others	Speak for self more than for others	Speak mainly for self rather than for others
Self-disclosure	Low sharing of feelings	Moderate sharing of feelings	High sharing of feelings
Clarity	Inconsistent messages	Clear messages	Very clear messages
Staying on topic	Seldom stay on topic	Often stay on topic	Mainly stay on topic
Respect and regard	Low to moderate	Moderate to high	High

and flexibility (rigidity and chaos), you can imagine where more or less functional families would appear on the axis (Figure 2.1b).

The central area represents balanced or moderate levels of flexibility and cohesion, seen as a highly workable communication pattern for individual and family development, although there may be instances when a different pattern could aid a family through a particular developmental point or through a crisis. The outside areas represent the extremes of cohesion and flexibility, less workable for consistent and effective long-term communication patterns.

Most well-functioning or balanced families avoid the extremes, except when members are under high levels of stress. In those situations, placement at the extreme may serve a purpose. This idea will be developed in Chapter 11. If a family member dies, for example, a highly cohesive communication pattern may be critical as the family mourns the loss and adjusts to life without this person. At the time of a family death, members

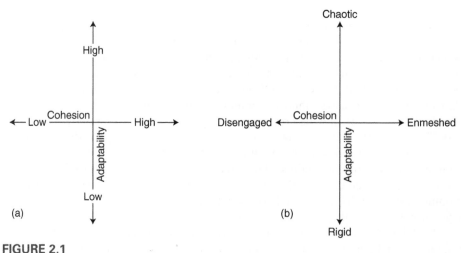

FIGURE 2.1

Family cohesion–adaptability axes

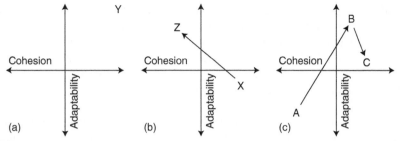

FIGURE 2.2
Application of family cohesion–adaptability

may find themselves at point Y (Figure 2.2a). Such a family may be experiencing extreme closeness among remaining members but chaos in terms of dealing with the changes in roles or in everyday activities. In contrast, a family with a teenager may find itself shifting from point X to point Z on the axis, as the adolescent demands greater freedom and less connectedness from the family, forcing changes in the system (Figure 2.2b).

The situation in the following quotation may be graphed as three moves (Figure 2.2c):

As a small child I lived in an active alcoholic family in which people kept pretty much to themselves. We did not talk about the problems caused by our parents' drinking and we acted as if things were fine. Yet we were very rigid because we never could bring friends into the house, and we never let outsiders know about the drinking. My older sister always took care of me if there was a problem, while my older brother locked himself in his room. Thus, we were at point A. When my parents finally went into treatment, the house was crazy in a different way for a while, since no one knew exactly how to act, but we did get closer and we were all forced to discuss what was going on. I guess we got closer and almost too flexible or unpredictable (point B). Now, five years later, I'm the only child left at home and my sober parents and I have a relatively close and flexible relationship (point C).

If you think about stages in your family life, you should be able to envision how the family shifted from one point to another on the cohesion–adaptability axes at different times. Families at different developmental stages appear more functional in different quadrants of the model, reflecting their life-stage demands. For example, young couples without babies function best in either the upper-right or lower-left quadrants. Families with adolescents function best in the central, or balanced, area; older couples relate best in the lower-right quadrant. Adolescents function best when they have average cohesion, being neither enmeshed with parents or disengaged, and when their adaptability is midway between rigidity and chaos. Obviously, these results indicate adolescents' need for a family system without rigid rules. Older couples function best when cohesion is high but adaptability is low. Possible explanations for these findings will become clearer in the chapter on developmental changes. Although results may differ for families from varying ethnic origins or particular sets of values, these findings support maintaining a flexible attitude toward what it means to function well as a family.

While in the systems perspective we have espoused focusing on the family rather on individuals, we know that when viewing an entire family system, there may be individual members who would be graphed in a different place if they were to be pictured separately. These models attempt to represent the whole family group on the axes. Throughout the text, the cohesion–flexibility framework will be used as a backdrop for understanding family communication.

Dialectical Interplay   Most long-term intimate relationships are built on a history of needing to manage the contradiction and interplay between independence and interdependence and a continued interplay between other often opposing tendencies, such as needing both stability and change (Baxter, 2006). The term **relational dialectics** refers to the "both/and" quality of relationships or the need for partners to simultaneously experience independence and connection or openness and privacy. We will talk about relational dialectics in more detail in Chapter 3.

How much closeness or distance do family members need in order to function effectively? How can family members manage their needs for privacy and openness as they interact with each other too much? These questions are indicators of some of the tensions all relationships face. These are called dialectical tensions and are managed through verbal and nonverbal communication. As family members interact, they encounter struggles while attempting to meet the needs of another as well as one's own needs.

From a dialectical perspective, cohesion and adaptability may be viewed as both family functions and dialectical tensions due to their importance and inescapable presence within the family. At various points in time, partners or parents and children may struggle with how much togetherness and autonomy each person needs. The following quote from a young wife captures the closeness-distance dialectical tension:

> On the one hand it is like, sure, I can go on my own. And on the other hand,
> I want him to go with me…I want to do things with him, and I think it is okay
> if he doesn't want to go and then it actually upsets me a lot if he doesn't go.
> (Hoppe-Nagao & Ting-Toomey, 2002, p. 146)

This is also true for flexibility. Family members struggle with how to enact their needs for routines and spontaneity as they move through a day or a year. Adolescents are more likely to value spontaneity over predictability much of the time, whereas their grandparents may prefer predictability much of the time. Yet, occasionally, grandparents may cherish a spontaneous outing with their grandchildren.

Although the issues related to cohesion and flexibility/change are viewed as the primary functions, these functions do not provide the complete picture. Additional family functions—supporting functions—contribute to an understanding of family interaction.

Supporting Functions

In conjunction with cohesion and adaptability, four supporting functions give shape to family life. Hess and Handel (1959) identified five processes, or family functions, that interact with the development of a family's message system. Because one of these processes relates to cohesion, we will list only the remaining four. The supporting family functions include

1. Establishing a satisfactory congruence of images.

2. Evolving modes of interaction into central family themes.
3. Establishing the boundaries of the family's world of experience.
4. Managing significant biosocial issues of family life, such as gender, age, power, and roles (p. 4).

Each of these processes interacts with a family's point on the cohesion–flexibility axis and influences a family's communication pattern. Each process is based on principles of symbolic interaction, since the underlying linking thread is the role of subjective meanings (White & Klein, 2002).

Family Images   Relationship patterns can be viewed as metaphors, which allow people to understand one element in terms of another. There are simple metaphors and root metaphors. A simple metaphor may be "My sister is a butterfly. You can never get her to settle down." Root metaphors assume a connection between a way of talking about the world and a major analogy or metaphor; they reveal an underlying worldview. A root metaphor captures a family's core value(s). Such root metaphors might include service, competition, spirituality, or achievement. Identifying small and simple metaphors is relatively easy; identifying an overarching root metaphor usually takes a good deal of thought and analysis.

If you had to create a single mental image or a root metaphor for your family, what would it be—a nest, a broken wagon wheel, a corporation, a rowing team, or a rock? Every family operates as an image-making or metaphor-creating entity. These metaphors reflect the family's worldview as they represent the family's collective experience (Pawlowski, 1996). Each member develops images of what the family unit and other family members are like; these images affect his or her patterns of interaction with the others. In well-functioning families, members' metaphors reflect some similarity; highly divergent metaphors indicate a wide range of members' beliefs or experiences. An image of one's family embodies what is expected from it, what is given to it, and how important it is (Hess & Handel, 1959). Thus, the image has both realistic and idealized components that reflect both the imagined and the imaginer. The following root metaphor conveys a good deal of information about this two-parent family with four adolescent children:

My family is like a Navy fleet. In the center are my parents, both upon the carrier. My mother is the executive officer (XO). The XO is the bad guy who runs the ship, keeps things in order, and intercepts messages before they reach the commanding officer. My father is the commanding officer (CO). He decides the general direction the family heads but is more concerned with navigating than maintaining everyday life on board. My three siblings and I are the small ships in the group. We can go off but must return to refuel. I am the cruiser and have more responsibilities and provide services, such as information. Jon and Stephanie are both destroyers, who are freer to range around. Michael is the airplane who sits on top of the mother ship. He has a short range and endurance away from the carrier. The destroyers like to intimidate him but would never really fire on him. We all know our places and positions and defend each other from any threat. We are close, but not too close. We all follow orders from the CO but spend much of our lives interacting more easily with the XO.

A less complicated example follows:

Since my mom passed away, our family has become like a basketball team, with my dad as a player-coach. We all work together for the survival of our team, and we all contribute. Each one of us has strengths and weaknesses, yet there is always that force driving us to achieve more together. As the player-coach, my dad has the responsibility of guiding our performances and our practices; as the scorekeeper, my uncle keeps the records.

Family images differ significantly. One study of college students' family metaphors revealed 138 options for one's family of origin. Images such as rock, tree, circus, security blanket, safety net, and basketball team appeared more often than others (Pawlowski, Thilborger, & Cieloha-Meekins, 2001). Thilborger (1998) reported feminine metaphors for families of origin, emphasizing team/group, nature, and healing/nourishment. Male metaphors emphasize nature, particularly animals, and foundational objects such as brick walls or concrete structures. Sometimes images reflect a family's humor.

My family is like a Ferrero Rocher chocolate. On the outside we are a little bumpy with different personalities, health issues, and minor conflicts. We are also covered in gold foil that shows our respectability and success as a group. We are sweet and supportive and a little nutty.

Relationships within families may be viewed metaphorically. One set of siblings may viewed by the family members as "two peas in a pod"; another set may be "oil and water." If two people's images of each other are congruent and consistent over time, a predictable pattern of communication emerges. For example, if a mother sees her son as dependent, she may exhibit protective behaviors, such as keeping bad news from him. If the son envisions his mother as a protector, the congruence of the images will allow harmonious communication; but if the son sees his mother as a jailer, conflict will occur. If one child sees her mother as a *tyrant* and her siblings see their mother as an *angel*, the inconsistent images may result in strong alliances among those with congruent images. Adult partners will experience conflict if their family images conflict: for example, if one sees the family as a "nest" involving nurturing, and protection, and the other sees it as a "corporation" involving a strong power structure and good organization. Yet, since complete consensus is improbable and change inevitable, the patterns will never become totally predictable. This is particularly true for foster children who may live in multiple families before reaching the age of 18. Paula McLain's (2003) memoir of life as a foster child depicts her experience of living in "multiple hotels" because nothing—towels, books, beds—belonged to her. The family metaphor serves as an indicator of members' collective identity. Because communicating feelings in some families remains difficult, metaphors may serve as an effective way to convey a sense of connection (Pawlowski et al., 2001).

Family Themes   In addition to images, each family shares themes. A theme represents a pattern of feelings, motives, fantasies, and conventionalized understandings grouped around a particular locus of concern, which has a particular form in the personalities of individual members (Hess & Handel, 1959). Essentially, themes capture a fundamental view of reality and a way of living within this worldview. Through its theme, a family responds to the questions "Who are we?" and "What do we do about it?" Sample family values include security, strength, dependability, caretaking, inclusion, separation, and kindness. We view themes in a family as statements that actualize the members' values and collective identity:

> Nielsens play to win.
> We have responsibility for those less fortunate than us.
> You can sleep when you die.
> Happiness is homegrown.
> You can *only* depend on your family.
> You can *always* depend on your family.
> Stick with your own kind
> Garcias never quit.
> Love sees no skin color.
> Always have Plan B.
> You can always do better.
> Seize the moment.
> Liu's are survivors.

Themes capture the beliefs that guide family members' actions; thereby you may predict a family's themes by watching how members live their lives. Living according to a theme necessitates the development of specific behavior patterns for interacting with each other and the outside world. For example, a family with the theme "We have a responsibility for those less fortunate than us" would be open to helping extended family members and those outside the family. Members might donate to charity, raise foster children, or work with the homeless. Yet, it may be difficult for family members to accept help from an outside source because of the caregiving theme. Still, a mother who lives according to this theme may spend hours working at an adolescent drop-in center and remain unaware of the problems her own teenage children face. Cohesive families with prominent themes display a clear family identity. Family themes undergird everyday life, as the following portrays:

I grew up with the theme "We'll love you anyway." This conveys the idea that the family will always forgive you and be there for you regardless of mistakes in judgment or action. Even when it's a shameful situation, such as getting kicked out of school or fired, or thrown in jail, the family stands behind that member. No members are rejected or cut off.

Some families have the theme "Working together keeps us together."

Some family themes may be complex and subtle, involving worldviews that are not immediately obvious. It is important to identify a family's main theme(s) in order to fully understand the meanings and communication behavior of its members. Clearly the opening example of Bruce and Melissa demonstrates how difficult it is to live together with disparate strongly held core themes.

Boundaries   Boundaries exist between and among members and between the family and the outside world. The boundary of a system separates it from its environment. The boundary defines the family system as an entity by creating a permeable separation between its interior (members) and the environment. You can imagine boundaries as physical or psychological limits that regulate family members' access to people, places, ideas, and values. All families establish some external and internal boundaries. Most frequently, family boundaries regulate access to people, places, ideas, and values.

Some family boundaries are highly permeable, or flexible, allowing easy movement across them. These open boundaries support the flow of information or people from the external environment or support an open flow of information among family members. Closed boundaries resist the flow of information and people across them due to their inflexibility (Figure 2.3).

External boundaries establish the level of connections between family members and the rest of the world. Some parents permit or encourage their children to make many different kinds of friends, explore alternative religious ideas, and encounter controversial ideas through media; such permeable boundaries permit

FIGURE 2.3
External boundaries

new people, ideas, and values to enter the family. Other parents retain *complete* control of their children's activities to prevent them from coming into contact with people or ideas considered to be "undesirable." Parental figures expect members to internalize the family boundaries, as does the grandfather in the following example:

My grandfather says, "The family does not end at the front step." When you are a Commastro, you represent the entire family (your aunts, uncles, cousins, grandparents, and your heritage). This means that one must be at one's best whenever in public and never tell family stories or secrets.

Extremes of such expectations result in the creation of rigid boundaries around the family system. Rigid boundaries protect secrets, known to and guarded by family members (Vangelisti & Caughlin, 1997). Most families with an alcoholic member create strong external boundaries in order to prevent outsiders from learning the family secret.

On the other end of the continuum, some families establish few boundaries—members experience little sense of membership identity and no control over other members' contact with people, places, ideas, or values. Such systems provide little sense of "family," due to the lack of a collective identity. These families tend to be chaotic.

Families cannot always control their own external boundaries because many everyday interactions occur between family members and social systems (Socha & Stamp, 2009). Outside agencies, such as schools, may require parents to share private family information, purchase school uniforms, or volunteer as a room parent. Members of families formed through transracial/transnational adoption may confront invasive questions or comments from medical or educational professionals because of the visual dissimilarity of family members (Suter & Ballard, 2009).

Internal family boundaries vary according to members' personalities, the types of experiences to which members are exposed, and the freedom each member has to enact a personal value system. Most adult members appropriately establish boundaries around issues or experiences that belong to adult partners or relatives. Frequently, serious financial concerns or parental sexual issues remain private. Although a parental subsystem may set strong boundaries, a self-assured adolescent may challenge rigid positions on certain issues by rejecting the established traditional boundaries. Conversely, siblings share secrets that are not intended for adult ears.

Functional families establish internal boundaries to protect members' self-identities and the identity of generational groups. If the boundaries between individuals are diffuse, or nonexistent, members may experience psychological problems, such as over-involvement, codependency, or a loss of physical boundaries, such as occurs in incest. If the internal boundaries are too rigid and strong, members will feel disengaged and out of touch.

Generations establish their boundaries based on behaviors appropriate for their age and role. Yet, the term "helicopter parent" describes adults who "hover" over their adolescent or young adult children, resisting the development of age-appropriate boundaries (Lum, 2006). In two-parent families, the adult subsystem represents a significant bounded dyad. Usually, partners share private information as well as sexual and emotional connections. Children are not allowed to share in all aspects of the partnered relationship. Sometimes even adult children can be separated from the marital relationship, as noted in the following:

My parents viewed their illnesses as private. My father had surgery and needed to stay at the hospital for a short visit. My mother decided to keep this a secret and not tell anyone, even their adult children. When we figured it out and called to check in on our parents to see how they were, my father became angry that no one came to see him at the hospital. He refused to speak with us for weeks. All five of us children felt that, because we were not told about any of their illnesses, we were considered outsiders.

Conversely, conflicts arise if the family's internal boundaries, particularly the marital or partnership boundary, are highly permeable. Often children are co-opted into fulfilling some functions of the spousal role. For example, troubled families, such as those with an addicted parent, experience shifts in the marital boundary as the functional parent relies on children for assistance. If a depressed husband cannot provide the interpersonal support needed by his wife, she may co-opt one of the children, expecting the child to act as her adult confidant and emotional partner. When boundaries are inappropriately crossed, roles become confused and pain results for all members.

Internal boundary membership differs across cultural groups. Given the high degree of interdependence among extended family members in many ethnic cultures, the family may have less rigid boundaries, as members are part of multiple households with strong emotional ties and mutual assistance. When new immigrant families face issues such as language barriers or limited outside social support networks, these extended family ties become even more critical and intense (Bush, Bohon, & Kim, 2010).

Boundaries vary according to the level of ties among members. Parent figures and their children serve as first-tier families, with highly established boundaries, whereas aunts, uncles, and cousins serve as second-tier families. Even though the first-tier boundaries may keep such relatives from developing the closeness of the first-tier ties, relatives such as aunts and nieces can experience strongly bounded ties (Segrin & Flora, 2011).

Boundary issues may play-out across generations. Although many adults create family boundaries similar to those in their families of origin, a daughter whose mother invaded her personal life may determine not to act in the same way toward her children, and actually distance herself from them. Her children, in turn, may resolve to develop closeness with their offspring and end up invading thevir children's lives. The physical and psychological boundaries set by each family strongly influence the interpersonal communication that occurs within the system.

Biosocial Issues   Families operate within a larger community and cultural sphere that provides conventional norms for coping with biosocial issues of gender, age, power, and roles. Each family creates its own strategies within this framework. Hess and Handel (1959) identified the following biosocial issues: male and female identity, authority and power, shaping and influencing children, and children's rights. We have adapted these issues of gender, age, and position or role, and these form the basis for much current research today.

Families differ in the extent to which criteria such as gender, age, and position/role in the family, for example, oldest brother, youngest sister, or grandfather, determine the power and responsibilities of members. Position-oriented families allocate rights and responsibilities according to their criteria; person-oriented families tend to rely more on individuals' interests, talents, and availability. In the latter case, a teenage male may choose to cook dinner regularly whereas his twin sister may purchase and maintain the family computers.

The family serves as a primary source of gender identity (Wood, 2013). Gender identity and physical development issues affect styles of interaction and vice versa. A family that assigns responsibilities based on a member's gender differs from one that uses personal interest or preference as the basis for assigning responsibilities. Usually it is more acceptable for girls to act masculine than it is for boys to act feminine: The most fundamental requirement for manhood is not to think, act, or feel like a female because aggression, sexuality, success, and self-reliance are prized (Wood, 2013). But emerging views of masculinity challenge some previously held beliefs. Conversely, females may still feel pressures from expectations regarding appearance, sensitivity, and superwoman powers even as such expectations continue to shift.

Gendered familial expectations may be subtle and surprising. In their study of parental attitudes and infidelity, Fenigstein and Peltz (2002) found that both mothers and fathers regarded sexual infidelity as more distressing when committed by a daughter-in-law than by a son-in-law. In contrast, they found emotional infidelity was more distressing when it involved a son-in-law. Such traditional gender beliefs are often unrecognized but operational.

Gender experiences vary across cultural groups. For example, in Hispanic and African American families, collectivistic values affect gendered family roles. Such a cultural perspective is displayed in the following comment:

My mother has characteristics of both the Korean attitude and the Western point of view toward women. She fulfills the Korean view of what a woman should be by being the primary nurturer of the family. She is the parent who drove us to piano lessons and took care of us when we were sick. She is the parent that we talk to first when we have a relational problem. In addition to being the nurturer of the family, she also meets the western view that women should have careers. She is an equal financial contributor to our family. This helps us relate to her even more.

Other value decisions relate to the use of power within the family structure. To what extent are decision-making and authority issues resolved according to traditional gender and role configurations? Flexible families tend to engage in ongoing negotiations regarding power and decision-making in the system. As many children become more technologically proficient than their parents, the older generation includes members of the younger generation in decisions regarding technology purchases and turn to them for technological assistance (Turkle, 2011).

The social sphere also involves attitudinal issues related to roles and responsibilities that may be exemplified in parent-child relationships. Parent-child interactions reflect members' beliefs and attitudes. If a parent views children as a temporary responsibility, his or her interactions will be immensely different from those of a parent who envisions a prolonged responsibility for offspring, far beyond the adolescent years. Complicated gender issues may arise as new family configurations form as noted in the following quote:

For the first 11 years of life, my stepson, Travis, was raised in a household that catered to his every need. He was encouraged to remain a little boy in many ways. His mother, Martha, could not have more children, so she and her first husband doted on him. When I married Martha, my two daughters came to live with us. They had been raised to be self-sufficient and independent. I have found myself becoming very impatient with Travis and pushing him to act like my children. As a result, Martha and I have had many fights over the children's responsibilities.

Family images, themes, boundaries, and biosocial issues interact with the functions of cohesion and adaptability. Flexible families will experience greater variety in images, themes, boundaries, and responses to biosocial issues than will rigid ones. These factors also affect the family's functional levels of cohesion and adaptability. For example, a family with strong boundaries and themes that support strong family interdependence and strong traditions will develop extremely high cohesion and low adaptability in contrast to the family with flexible boundaries and themes supporting independence. Family members' communication behaviors reflect the family's strongly held values. Communication serves as the means by which families establish their patterns of cohesion and adaptability, and develop their images, themes, boundaries, and responses to biosocial issues.

Family-of-Origin Influences

"My son's a Kaplan, all right. He'll walk up and talk to anyone without a trace of shyness." "My grandparents and parents always fought by yelling at each other and then forgetting about it. My wife doesn't understand this." These statements indicate family-of-origin influences on the communication patterns of the next generation. The term "family of origin" refers to the family or families in which a person is raised. One's family of origin is generally considered to be the earliest and most powerful source of influence on one's personality and a primary source of expectations for how families should function (McGoldrick, Gerson, & Petry, 2008). The opening vignette describing Mark and his father's patterns of discipline provides an example of the power of family-of-origin patterns.

The term "family-of-origin influences" refers to the ways in which current relational experiences and interaction patterns reflect (1) unique **multigenerational transmissions** and (2) the members' ethnic heritages. The multigenerational and ethnic background that each person brings to a partnered relationship significantly influences their interpersonal interactions and, eventually, interactions with any children of that relationship. For example, you may desire to create an adult family life different from the one you experienced as a child, yet you find yourself recreating similar patterns within your adult family.

Parental socialization serves as a major factor in determining children's future romantic relationship and family formation behavior. Adults often create partnerships similar to those of their parents because they unconsciously enact a family pattern. Research indicates that links between family-of-origin experiences of hostility and positive engagement during adolescence are a predictor of later marital hostility and positive behavior of offspring (Whitton, Wakdinger, Schulz, Allen, & Crowell, 2008); research also reveals links between family-of-origin attachment styles and behavior during adolescence with romantic relationship behaviors in young adulthood (Dinero, Conger, Shaver, Widaman, & Larsen-Rife, 2008). In addition, recent research on adolescents indicates that parental aggression and satisfaction in parental relationships when a child was 13 were predictive of the qualities in teenagers' romantic relationships when they were 18 years of age. For example, paternal aggression predicted adolescent aggression (Hare, Miga, & Allen, 2009). Such findings indicate a tendency for subsequent generations to adopt similar behaviors but multiple factors may influence the nature of the transmission. For example, Yoshida and Busby (2012) found that culture impacts such transmissions. In their study of family-of-origin influence on relationship satisfaction, their comparisons of North American-born Asian, Asian-born Asian, and Caucasian American heterosexual couples revealed that males experience greater family-of-origin influence than females in Asian couples whereas females experience greater influence in Caucasian couples.

Multigenerational Transmissions   Families of origin provide blueprints for the communication of future generations. Initially, communication is learned in the home, and, throughout life, the family setting provides a major testing ground for new communication skills or strategies. Each young person who leaves the family of origin to form a new system carries a set of conscious and unconscious ways of relating to others based on the socializing influence of his or her family (DeGenova & Rice, 2005). For example, the idiosyncrasies and culturally based communication patterns of the current Watson family may be passed on to generations of children. Even language may cross generations as the following quote suggests:

My husband gets crazy with all the odd words my family uses, especially around children. I came from a family of 12 kids and there were always words someone couldn't say or codes for things. So I talk to our kids about "Sea Friends" (bath toys), doing a "zipperino" (getting dressed), or "Letter Letter M's" (M&M's). Their cousin calls candy, "M-de-M's."

Just as simple language terms travel across generations, more significant attitudes and rule-bound behaviors move from a family of origin to a newly emerging family system. Essentially, the family of origin serves as the first communication classroom. Differences in family-of-origin experiences can lead to a communication

Messages and meanings pass from one generation to the next.

breakdown between adult partners. In the following example, a wife describes the differences in nonverbal communication in her family of origin from that of her husband:

It was not until I became closely involved with a second family that I became conscious of the fact that the amount and type of contact can differ greatly. Rarely, in Rob's home, will another person reach for someone else's hand, walk arm in arm, or kiss for no special reason. Hugs are reserved for comfort. When people filter into the den to watch television, one person will sit on the couch, the next on the floor, a third on a chair, and finally the last person is forced to sit on the couch. And always at the opposite end! Touching, in my home, was a natural, everyday occurrence. Usually, the family breakfast began with "good morning" hugs and kisses. Even as adults, no one ever hesitated to cuddle up next to someone else, run their hands through another person's hair, or start tickling whoever happens to be in reaching distance.

Models of relationships can act as a guide for children's behavior and influence their interpretation of others' behavior. For instance, if you have lived in a stepfamily, you may have witnessed the stress involved in integrating your step-siblings' family-of-origin influences and more recent adult family relationships into your *family* system's communication patterns.

Family-of-origin patterns have been used to study abusive or harsh parenting. Chen and Kaplan (2001) examined the continuity of supportive parenting across generations and found positive patterns. The results of their longitudinal study report modest intergenerational continuity tied to factors such as interpersonal relations, social participation, and role modeling.

Although family-of-origin issues may be discussed as parent-to-child transmissions, greater emphasis has been placed on transmission across multiple generations. For example, family researchers have focused more directly on the effect of multigenerational systems, indicating some parenting and discipline patterns can be predicted from parental practices (Belsky, Jaffee, Sligo, Woodward, & Sliva, 2005). Following are the basic assumptions inherent in such an approach:

Multigenerational systems:

- Develop mutual influence processes involving individuals born into, or raised within, them
- Appear similar to, but more complex than, other human systems
- Experience developmental changes
- Develop patterns that are shared, transformed, and manifested in future generation
- Develop and transmit issues that may appear only in certain contexts and may be at unconscious levels
- Develop cross-generation and within-generation boundaries
- Develop functional and dysfunctional patterns reflecting the intergenerational patterns and current circumstances (DeGenova & Rice, 2005; Hoopes, 1987)

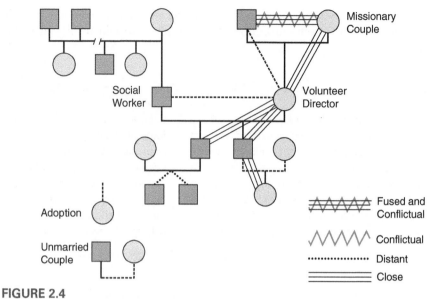

FIGURE 2.4
Multigenerational systems

Genograms provide one way to envision intergenerational transmissions (McGoldrick et al., 2008). A genogram is a multigenerational family tree that depicts familial relationships visually. It records information about social relationships and biological and psychological issues in the family across three or more generations (Galvin, Bylund, & Grill, 2010).

Consider Figure 2.4, a multigenerational system genogram that contains examples of highly connected parent-child relationships, a family theme of service, and flexible boundaries. In a genogram, men are represented by squares and women by circles. The nature of the lines that link certain persons reflects the interactive nature of their relationship. For example, jagged lines imply conflict.

The power of multigenerational transmission is part of a puzzle that is unfolding. In the following passage, a young woman reflects on her painful experiences and insights:

I have come to learn that my behavioral problems were a reaction to my mother's alcoholism, and to her emotional distance during my infancy and childhood. Likewise, my mother's behaviors had a similar origin. Affected by her own mother's chronic depression, my mother never received the affirmation she needed and desired. Yet, having been reared by an alcoholic mother, my grandmother was in no better position to be an effective mother or role model for intimacy. With such unavailable models, the women in my family were perpetually unable to develop this essential capacity. Consequently, my own mother built our relationship from a faulty blueprint.

Family patterns need not be so dramatic. Most relationships that significantly influence family members are of the perpetual but dormant kind: "They are part of the unchallenged and comfortable predictability of lives made up of routine, regular conversation, and assumptions that most of tomorrow will be based on the foundation of today" (Duck, 1986, p. 91). Yet, although patterns do move across generations, some patterns change in the process. Conversely, children also shape their parents' behavior (Olson et al., 2008), reflecting bidirectional interpersonal patterns.

Some of the factors used to examine multigenerational issues include the following: gender roles; losses; patterns of closeness and distance; factors that link individuals, such as names or physical similarities; family themes; boundary management practices; conflict patterns; and parenting styles (McGoldrick et al., 2008). Other issues such as alcoholism (Watt, 2002) and eating patterns (Baker, Whisman, & Brownell, 2000) appear to have some basis in family-of-origin messages. These patterns may emerge, consciously or unconsciously, across three or four generations. Yet, further research needs to address issues such as why some children in problematic families replicate the problematic patterns, while others create well-functioning adult familial relationships. "Some children seem to escape most serious ill effects (although that does not mean that they have been totally unaffected or unscarred), whereas others succumb to lasting psychopathology" (Rutter, 2002, p. 335). Resilience appears to account for some of the variance. Resilient children have the capacity to "develop clear and realistic goals, solve problems, relate comfortably with others and to treat oneself and others with respect" (Goldstein & Brooks, 2013, p. 13). In addition they deal effectively with stress and challenges and exhibit the capacity to bounce back from adversity. In addition, mutual influence between parents and children must also be considered. Because parents and children interact with and influence each other, this occurs in a bidirectional manner as opposed to a unidirectional manner (Saphir & Chaffee, 2002). If parents do not exhibit resilience, children need to find other significant adults in order to function effectively.

The effects of significant traumas impact future generations. Studies of children of Holocaust survivors identified issues faced by some of them, including impaired self-esteem and identity problems, catastrophic expectations and preoccupation with death, anxiety, feelings of loss and increased vulnerability, exaggerated family attachments or exaggerated independence, and difficulty with intimate relationships (Kellerman, 2001). Family scholars Amato and Cheadle (2005) suggest that the effects of divorce may be transmitted across multiple generations.

Biological/Genetic Factors   Current scientific research in biology and genetic studies will influence thinking in family communication over the next decades. Many family problems reflect health and genetic concerns. The following biological topics have direct links to family interaction: (1) behavioral endocrinology, (2) behavioral genetics, (3) evolutionary psychology, and (4) behavioral psychopharmacology (Booth, Carver, & Granger, 2000). The impact of physiology, genetics, and evolution on interaction patterns gained greater attention in the past 15 years due to a renewed focus on biological contributions to individual communication practices and discussion of the communibiological paradigm (Afifi, Davis, & Denes, in press; Floyd & Haynes, 2006). Researchers have been discovering evolutionary and biological influences on communication for example to exchanging affection (Floyd, Judd, & Hesse, 2008), investing in relationships, and ending relationships when trust has been sacrificed (Afifi et al., in press). Negative family behavior and relationships have been shown to have negative psychological health consequences, which are displayed in physiological changes such as lower salivary cortisol (Lueken, Kraft, & Hagan, 2009). Research examining links between interaction patterns and their physiological effects stands to contribute significantly to an understanding of family communication patterns.

Advances in genetic research and its impact on family interactions have only begun to influence family communication. Since the turn of the century "there has been increased interest from family communication scholars in the intersection of family communication and health" (Gaff & Bylund, 2010, p. xv). Although knowledge of the effects of complex sets of genes on behavior remains limited, established lines of research are exploring passive, reactive, and active influences related to behaviors of parents and children. Family communication about genetics involves two major functions—disclosure and discussion. Factors that affect initial disclosure by the first family member identified with the disease (the proband) depends on multiple factors including gender, culture, family role, family structure, relational histories, and privacy rules (Galvin & Grill, 2009). Ongoing family discussion tends to be gendered and reflective of established family communication patterns. Family communication about genetics will be addressed in Chapter 12.

Ethnicity   The role of ethnicity in multigenerational communication patterns often remains overlooked. Its influence can be powerful, because individuals retain ethnic values and identification across many generations after immigration (McGoldrick, Giordano, & Garcia-Preto, 2005b). Ethnicity relates to cultural factors such as common ancestry, language, nationality, and beliefs. Ethnicity also represents the immigrant group's class and occupational skills that link to historically or regionally specific jobs, housing stock, and political conditions (Coontz, 1999).

Ethnic family issues surface in issues such as age, gender, roles, expressiveness, birth order, separation, or individuation. For example, Italian families are known for celebrating, loving, and arguing, with value placed on cleverness, charm, graciousness, and attention to family honor. Italian families function within a network of other relatives, *gumbares* (old friends), and godparents from whom mutual support is expected. This ethnicity stresses parental role distinction, with the father as the undisputed head of the family and mother as the heart (Giordano, McGoldrick, & Klages, 2005).

This generalization about the Italian heritage contrasts sharply with descriptions of Scandinavian family patterns, which generally stress the importance of emotional control and avoidance of open confrontation (Erickson, 2005). Norwegian family members believe that words are to be used sparingly, inner weaknesses are kept secret, and direct conflict is avoided. Aggression reveals itself through teasing, ignoring, or silence. A marriage of persons reflecting these two ethnic backgrounds has the potential for misunderstanding unless partners address their differences. Such differences may never be resolved because of the pattern's strength.

African Americans share a communal sense of identity, expressed as "We are, therefore I am" (McGoldrick, 2003, p. 240), and value extended kinship bonds, African roots, strong three-generation systems, religion, and spirituality (Stewart, 2010). African American parent-child interaction patterns involve parents as cultural advisors and coaches, given their unique need to socialize children to manage situations of racial derogation (Socha, Bromley, & Kelly, 1995). African American parents tend to exhibit the "imperative mode" or directive communication (Chandler, A'Vant, & Graves, 2008) with their children as a protective authority. Many African American women learn from their family and community members to avoid talking about certain health problems, such as cancer risks (Cohen, 2009).

A family's ethnic heritage dictates communication norms, which are maintained for generations. For example, an emphasis on "keeping things in the family," or the way in which sensitive subjects are discussed pass from generation to generation, reflecting individual and cultural influences. An examination of communication patterns through three generations of an extended Irish American family revealed similarities across generations (Galvin, 2007). Whereas Irish families value strong privacy boundaries, the following description of Arabic family life portrays a different picture:

Growing up in an Arab household, our immediate family and our extended family reflected the strong patriarchal influence and a theme of "family is family," which implied active support of many relatives. We lived by the Arabic proverb "A small house has enough room for one hundred people who love each other." We shared joys, sorrows, money, and things among and across generations.

Although a growing number of studies address different ethnic patterns, few studies examine ethnic differences that occur as the result of remarriages and stepfamilies, transnational adoptions (particularly of older children), or transracial domestic adoption or foster care placements. Multiracial/ethnic families are especially discourse dependent and as members must rely on communication as they navigate their identities, family roles, and expectation within the family and externally with others (Galvin & Braithwaite, 2014). Family communication scholars are paying attention to interaction in multiracial/ethnic families as intergroup communication and looking at the influences of interaction on identification across cultural groups (Soliz, Thorson, & Rittenour, 2009). Until recently, "The psychology of marriage as it exists is really a psychology of European American middle class marriage" (Flanagan et al., 2002, p. 109). Increasingly, family communication scholarship privileges ethnic family communication patterns (Buzzanell, Berkelaar, & Kisselburgh, 2011; Song & Zhang, 2012).

The family of origin plays a significant role in creating and developing members' communication patterns, tied closely to the primary functions of cohesion and adaptability and the **secondary functions** of images, themes, boundaries, and biosocial issues. Taken together, all these factors contribute to create a framework for examining family communication.

A Framework for Examining Family Communication

There are numerous ways to analyze the family as a system, such as viewing a family as an economic, political, or biological system. Because our concern lies with members' interactions within and about the family, this text centers on communication within the family system. The following statement provides our framework for examining family communication:

> The family is a system constituted, defined and managed through members ongoing communication patterns. Family members' interactions regulate cohesion and adaptability and enact images, themes and boundaries and biosocial issues in order establish and maintain their collective identity through the flow of patterned, meaningful messages. Such messages exist within a network of evolving interdependent relationships located within a multigenerational and cultural context.

The importance of this definition necessitates that each segment should be explored separately:

> The family is a system constituted, defined, and managed through members ongoing communication patterns.

The family may be understood as a set of individuals and their relationships that, together, form a complex whole; a change in one part results in changes in other parts of the system. Essentially, family members are linked inextricably to each other; each member, and the family as a whole, reflects any change in the system. Communication, the symbolic, transactional process of creating and sharing meanings, is the means by which members co-create and enact the family system.

> Family members regulate cohesion and adaptability and enact images, themes, boundaries and biosocial issues in order to develop a collective identity…

Communication facilitates a family's movement on the cohesion–adaptability axis (Figure 2.1). The way in which people co-create messages influences the form and nature of their relationships. A family's collective identity is formed through the congruence of the **primary functions** and secondary functions.

> …through the flow of patterned, meaningful messages within a network…

Family members co-create their meanings and their relational culture. Based on families of origin and other environmental sources (people and circumstances), each new family develops its own set of meanings that become predictable as members interact with one another using similar communication patterns over and over again. Communication patterns create and reflect members' relationships within networks.

> …of evolving interdependent relationships…

Family life is not static; both predictable and unpredictable changes alter the system. Family relationships evolve over time as members join and leave the system, draw closer or move farther apart. Family members struggle to negotiate dialectical tensions and boundaries internally and externally. Yet, due to the family's systemic nature, members remain interdependent, as they manage relational issues of intimacy, conflict, roles, power, and decision-making.

...located within a multigenerational and cultural context.

Families beget families. The multigenerational lineage includes links across multiple generations and specific family-of-origin patterns that impact two or three generations very directly. Communication patterns move through generations, reflective of unique individual members and their interaction practices, as well as the family's ethnic heritage(s).

Family normality or functionality may be viewed as transactional or process oriented. This perspective emphasizes attention to adaptation over the life cycle and adaptation to various contexts. A family's developmental stages and members' reactions to change combine with contextual issues such as ethnicity, gender, and socioeconomic status to create a culture within which members operate. Norms and expectations vary greatly across groups of families, but may remain relatively similar for families within a given cultural context.

Throughout the following chapters, we will examine the concepts of this framework in order to demonstrate the powerful role communication plays in family life. We will highlight the complexity and systematic nature of family life, an often-overlooked reality as indicated in the following comment:

When you really think about it, family life is extremely complex and most of us just go through the motions every day without much reflection. I usually take for granted that most families are similar to mine. However, the more I look carefully at other family systems, the more aware I am of the differences. Perhaps families are like snowflakes, no two are ever exactly alike.

It seems appropriate to close this chapter with the words of Handel and Whitchurch (1994), who suggest that as members engage in social interaction, they "define their relationships to one another, and to the world beyond the family as they establish individual identities as well as a collective family identity" (p. 1).

Conclusion

This chapter described the communication process while proposing a connection between communication patterns and family functions. Communication was explained as a symbolic transactional process. Systems theory serves as the critical perspective for understanding family communication. It addressed the importance of meaning-making and managing dialectical tensions. The primary functions of cohesion and change were discussed as were the supporting functions of family images, themes, boundaries, and biosocial issues. The chapter concluded with a framework for analyzing family interaction.

In Review

1. Using your own family or a fictional family, identify three areas of "meaning" that would have to be explained to an outsider who was going visit you for a week. What would have to be explained for your houseguest to understand how your family members make sense of the world (e.g., teasing means Dad likes you)?

2. Describe a recurring interaction pattern in a real or fictional family focusing on the predictable verbal and nonverbal messages. Describe the effect of this interaction pattern on the persons involved, or on the family as a whole (e.g., the way a teenager gets permission to take the car for the evening).

3. Describe and give examples of three behaviors that might characterize an enmeshed family and three examples of behavior that might characterize a disengaged family.

4. Using a real or fictional family, give an example of how the family moved from one point on the cohesion–flexibility grid to another point due to changes in their lives. Discuss any changes in their interaction patterns.

5. How might one of the themes in your family, or a family you know, play out in family communication patterns? What image, boundaries, and biosocial issues might support that theme?

6. Identify three communication patterns characterizing a real or fictional step-family. Identify and describe how key communication patterns or themes from a first family moved into the new family configuration or were dropped.

7. Identify significant communication patterns that have been passed from your parents' families of origin. To what extent have you accepted or rejected these patterns? You may also choose to discuss how communication patterns pass through generations in a work of fiction.

Key Words

Cohesion (Primary function)   32

Communication   26

Family images   39

Family themes   41

Flexibility (Primary function)   34

Metacommunication   31

Multigenerational Transmission   47

Primary functions   54

Relational dialectics   38

Secondary functions   53

Transactional communication perspective   26

CHAPTER 3

Family Theories

Cash grew up with two brothers, Carl and Cam, all of whom were star athletes in high school and college. His family valued athletic achievement and held an elaborate "Jackson Family Olympics" each summer for this competitive family. Cash went on to play minor league baseball as a catcher, settling in Minneapolis after marrying Louisa. Now in his mid-thirties, Cash has shoulder and knee problems, not usual for a former catcher, and asthma, which plagued him as a child. Cash manages a health club in Minneapolis and works out regularly. Although in good shape, he has to watch his health carefully.

Cash is very close to his brothers, who both live in LA. Louisa loves Carl and Cam, but she does have concerns for Cash's health when they get together. The brothers party hard and love to tell stories about trying to outdo each other to win the family competition. They plan a vacation each summer they call "The Olympics" and challenge each other to do risky maneuvers while mountain biking, surfing, or riding motorcycles. Cash needed knee surgery after last summer's trip and has had asthma attacks on multiple occasions. Cash is very considerate about calling and texting Louisa during his trips, but he never includes details about what the brothers are doing. However, Cam posts photos online of their sports and partying. Louisa has come to dread Cash's trips to LA.

Cash is in LA now. Before the trip, Louisa overheard the brothers planning the next Olympics while talking on Skype. All Cash told Louisa about the trip was the brothers were going camping. Louisa wanted to talk with Cash about her concerns, but she didn't want him to think she was spying on him. Early in the trip, everything seemed to be fine. Cam posted beautiful photos and Cash texted her regularly. However, on Thursday night Louisa did not hear from Cash, which was strange.

Friday morning Louisa checked her Twitter feed over breakfast. She noticed a tweet from Cam saying he'd spent the night in the emergency room with his brother; Louisa panicked! She grabbed her phone and tried to call and text Cash, but there was no response. Louisa had no idea what hospital he was in. She considered calling his parents, but did not want to worry them. She finally reached Carl who told her Cash had passed out the night before. The doctors thought it was probably his asthma, put him on oxygen, and kept him in the hospital to run a few more tests this morning. Louisa was not sure if she was more scared or more furious. By now, she was yelling and crying, "I cannot believe no one called me and I had to find out on Twitter!" Carl seemed perturbed, "Chill out, Louisa. None of us wanted to worry you until we had some definite answers. I'm on my way to the hospital now and will call you when I know something."

Eunjung, an international undergraduate student from Korea, encounters ongoing surprises as she begins to make American friends in her dormitory. When Eunjung hears other students on her floor talking about their conversations with their mothers, she finds herself amazed by how open they are with each other about what is going on in the family and in their own lives. Growing up in a traditional Korean family, she was taught to respect the distance between a child and her parents as well as the importance of saving face. Eunjung learned to avoid talking about personal family matters with her friends, as well as to withhold information about her immediate family from outsiders, even extended family members. She avoided telling her personal secrets to her friends because it could bring shame to her family members. Therefore, she remains silent if her comments might bring shame to herself or her family.

Although her roommate and friends talk about their parents' divorces or a parent's struggles with alcoholism, such topics are off-limits for Eunjung. In fact, sometimes it is hard to sit through the conversations because they seem so personal. An area of particular discomfort is the way her roommates talk about their grades and test scores. In Korea she learned to talk about such topics with her parents but no member of the family would discuss the topic with outsiders, especially regarding any poor academic performance. Eunjung's greatest surprise came when she heard her friends indicate that they talked about sex with their mothers. Since sexuality was seldom talked about in the Korean families she knew, Eunjung wondered what such a discussion would be like. When her mother calls, sometimes Eunjung will mention the topics her friends discuss just to see how her mother will react. Usually her mother reminds her to avoid joining in those conversations.

There are many ways to make sense of how a family functions, particularly to understand the central role of communication in every aspect of family life. In this chapter we describe a set of theories frequently used by scholars to explore family dynamics. Theories are practical tools that function like a lens on a camera or a filter on photograph software; use a different lens or filter and you see and understand things from a different vantage point and other things fade into the background. The function of theories is to help make understandable a phenomenon or process (Baxter & Babbie, 2004). Although we cannot address all relevant theories, we will introduce some key theories and broad perspectives that influence research and our understanding of family communication. We will focus on systems theory, symbolic interaction/social construction, narrative theory/narrative performance, relational dialectics theory, and communication privacy management. Understanding these theories and related concepts will help you develop your own framework for analyzing family interactions.

The Systems Perspective

When individuals come together to form relationships, what is created is larger and more complex than the sum of the individuals; they create a system. When individuals form families, they create **family systems** through their interaction patterns. The systems perspective provides valuable insights into a family's communication patterns. Family systems theory, an offshoot of general systems theory (GST), provides a framework for understanding the amazing complexities of human organizations, including families (Galvin, Dickson, & Marrow, 2006; Watzlawick, Beavin, & Jackson, 1967). As we discussed in the first chapter, we will focus on family systems theory in greater detail as this theory forms the basis for how we approach family communication in this book. The following example provides insight into how a family operates as a system and reflects the complexity of the task of examining families from a systems perspective.

Family life is incredibly subtle and complex. Everything seems tied to everything else. When our oldest daughter, Marcy, contracted spinal meningitis, the whole family reflected the strain. My second daughter and I fought more, while my husband tended to withdraw into himself, which brought me closer to my son. In their own ways, the three children became closer while our marriage became more distant. As Marcy's recovery progressed, there were more changes that affected how we relate now, even eight years later.

Everyday family behavior patterns often seem almost invisible, buried in apparent predictability, yet powerful in their effects. Individuals get caught up, often unconsciously, into their family patterns, as depicted in the case of the three brothers in the chapter's opening case and the example above. Unless you view individuals, yourself included, within their primary context, you may never fully understand their behaviors. We define a *system* as a set of components that interrelate with one another to form a whole. Due to their interconnections, if one component of the system changes, the others will change in response, which in turn affects the initial component. For families, this means that a change in one individual affects every other family member.

Families do not exist in a vacuum; they live within a time period, culture, and community, and experience other influences that impact them directly such as religion, economic status, or geographic locations. This larger context, or ecosystem, affects a family's life course. From a systems perspective, "Decontexted individuals do not exist" (Minuchin, 1984, p. 2). Persons live their lives as part of groups, not as individuals. Imagine a family photograph in which the members are in the background and their relationships are depicted in the foreground. Their patterns of interaction take precedence over the individuals. Therefore, understanding families involves exploring family communication patterns.

When two or more individuals come together in a relationship, a system is created. It is larger and more complex than the individuals. Communication creates and serves as the centerpiece of the system. Relationships are formed, maintained, and changed through interaction among the individuals (Duncan & Rock, 1993, p. 48). Yerby (1995) stresses the importance of seeing our own behavior as well as that of others as interrelated and somewhat predictable. Most importantly, she asks us to appreciate the significance of **interdependence** between family members and focus on relationships at the level of the family system, rather than seeing problems as the fault of one person or the other. In the opening case, you can understand Cash's choice not to contact Louisa immediately when he went to the hospital because of your knowledge of their family system. An individual's behavior becomes understandable only when viewed within the context of the human system within which he or she functions and within the broader context in which the family is situated (Cowan & Cowan, 1997; Galvin et al., 2006).

We will apply the following systems characteristics to families: interdependence, wholeness, patterns/self-regulation, interactive complexity/punctuation, openness, complex relationships, and equifinality.

Interdependence

Within any system, parts are so interrelated as to be dependent on each other for their functioning. Interdependence serves as the centerpiece of a system. In a system, the parts and the relationship between them form the whole; changes in one part will result in changes in the others. Satir (1988) described a family system as a mobile. Picture a mobile that hangs over a child's crib, with people instead of elephants or sailboats hanging from it. Every movement of one part of the mobile sets the others in motion. As events touch one member of the family, other members reverberate in response to the change in the affected member. If a family member loses a job, wins a scholarship, marries, or joins the military, such an event affects the entire family system; the impact depends on each person's relationship with that individual. For example, a parent's infidelity affects not only the married couple but has a ripple effect throughout the family system to the children and others (Thorson, 2013). In addition, because family members are human beings, not objects, they can "pull their own strings," or make their own moves. If a daughter chooses to withdraw from the family by pulling away, other members may shift into closer relationships. Thus, as members move toward or away from each other, all members are affected.

An evolutionary model of family systems is one that incorporates the possibility of spontaneous or kaleidoscopic change (Hoffman, 1990). No matter what change a family experiences, all members are affected due to their interdependence. You may be able to pinpoint events in your own family, such as a sibling who develops a drug dependency or adopts a child, that have influenced all members in an identifiable way. A behavior that seems problematic to the outside world may serve an important function within the family system. Lerner (1989) provides the following example, which enlightens the process. Seven-year-old Judy exhibits temper tantrums and obnoxious misbehavior. Lerner suggests that Judy acts out when her father seems distant and her mother seems extremely focused on her daughter. Judy's behavior functions to bring her parents back together, and Lerner discussed the outcome of Judy's effects on the system: "Distant Dad is roped back into the family (and is helped to become more angry than depressed), and the parents are able to pull together, temporarily united by their shared concern for their child. Judy's behavior is, in part, an attempt to solve a problem in the family" (p. 3).

From a family systems perspective, the behavior of each family member is related to and dependent on the behavior of the others. Even in a relatively simple family structure of two parents and two children, this becomes complicated. Imagine the complexity of stepfamily configurations when considering the ways members inside the immediate household affect and are affected by members outside the household (Schrodt et al., 2007). The brothers depicted at the beginning of the chapter may just be starting to recognize how the changes in their brother Cash's health will impact their life patterns directly and the choices they make about their extreme sports vacations will certainly affect Cash and Louisa's lives.

Wholeness

A family systems approach assumes that the whole is greater than the sum of its parts. An integration of parts characterizes the systems model. Families exhibit characteristics that reflect individuals and the interplay of family members. Outsiders use these to characterize the family and each member. The parts, or members, are understood in the context of that whole. The Boyer family may be characterized as humorous, religious, and charitable, yet these adjectives need not apply to each family member. Certain group characteristics may not reflect those of each individual. Wholeness characterizes a system because behaviors emerge from the interactions of particular individuals. These are called emergents or emergent properties because they develop or appear only at the systemic level (Whitchurch & Constantine, 1993). Conflict or affection may emerge as an inherent part of communication between specific family members. A certain comment or action may trigger patterns of behavior without members' awareness. A delightful example follows:

Something wonderful and funny happens when my sister and I get together. We tend to play off each other and can finish each other's sentences, pick up the same references at the same time, and create a dynamic energy that leaves other people out. We don't do it on purpose. Rather, we just seem to "click" with each other and off we go!

Patterns/Self-Regulation

Human beings learn to coordinate their actions, creating patterns together that could not be created individually. Although coordination of actions varies dramatically across family systems, each family system develops communication patterns that make life somewhat predictable. Members learn to live within a reciprocal, patterned, and repetitive world. Think about your family's dinner times, holidays, and other family

Families are characterized frequently by activities members share.

events—because you likely have patterns that you repeat, you know what to expect and what you are to do and say. Interaction patterns provide a lens for assessing communication behaviors within a system, because they provide the context for understanding specific behaviors. In the opening case, the more that the brothers talked about their exploits and extreme sports, the more worried Cash's wife Louisa became. Understanding this, Cash told her less and less about their activities, which caused her to worry even more.

Communication rules constitute a special pattern. Rules are relationship agreements, often unconscious, that prescribe and limit a family member's behavior over time; they are capable of creating regularity out of chaos. For example, in Eunjung's family, cultural patterns of privacy created rules about topics she could and could not discuss with her parents. Ongoing communication generates rules and is regulated by rules. Rules will be discussed more fully in Chapter 4.

Human systems attempt to maintain levels of constancy within an overall defined range of acceptable behavior. From a mechanistic viewpoint, a system needs to maintain some type of standard for actions, by noting deviations from the norm and correcting them when they become too significant. The function of maintaining stability in a system is called *calibration*. Calibration involves monitoring and correcting a scale on which to weigh items. In the case of a family system, it implies checking and, if necessary, correcting the range of acceptable behaviors. On occasion, the changes happen too dramatically for a family to exert any control. But everyday life is filled with

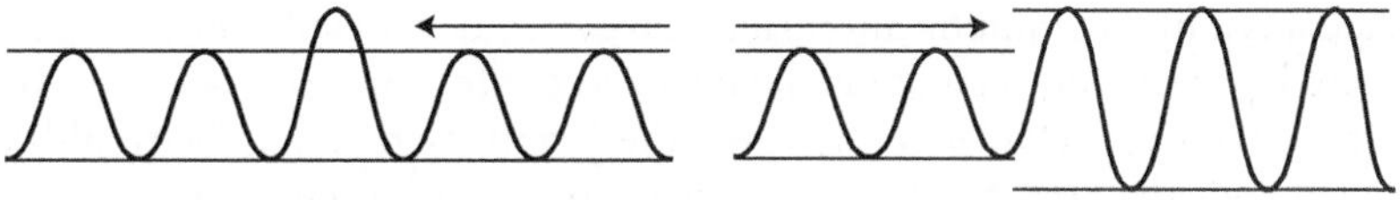

a. Maintenance Feedback
(no change)

b. Change-Promoting Feedback
(change occurs)

FIGURE 3.1
Feedback systems

opportunities to maintain or alter family patterns. A parent may post on a social net-working site what they think is a cute and harmless photo of their teenage son wearing a ballet tutu when he was a toddler assuming that only family members will see it. However, once the photo is tagged and the son's friends can see the photo, the family will need to recalibrate and come to agreement about new rules for sharing family photos (Child & Petronio, 2011). Systems can be compared to mechanical operations, in that human systems are capable of evolving and made to function better.

Systems generate maintenance and change-promoting feedback processes. *Maintenance* feedback processes imply constancy or maintaining the standard while minimizing change. *Change-promoting* feedback processes result in recalibration of the system at a different level. You can visualize this process in the following ways. Figure 3.1a represents a system in which maintenance feedback prevents change from occurring. For example, this may happen when a teenager swears at a parent for the first time, yet the rules themselves are not totally stable.

The parent may threaten, "You swear at me again and I'll ground you," or appeal to the family values, "We show each other respect even in disagreement." If the teenager becomes frightened by the threat, or apologetic for challenging the fam-ily value system, swearing may not occur again.

Figure 3.1b represents a system in which change-promoting feedback occurs. For example, if a wife cannot stop her husband's initial use of physical force, hitting may become part of their long-term conflict pattern. If she threatens to report him to the police, he may refrain from hitting her again.

Change-promoting feedback processes enable the system to grow, create, inno-vate, and change, whereas maintenance feedback processes attempt to preserve the status quo. In the following situation, change-promoting feedback processes operate as a father responds to his son's attempts to reach greater physical closeness:

As an adult, I became very aware of the limited physical contact I had with my father. He never touched the boys in the family, with the exception of a handshake. I determined that I wanted a greater physical closeness with him and consciously set out to change our way of relating. The first time I hugged my father was when I returned from a trip and I walked in and put my arms around him. I was nervous and tentative; he was startled and stiff, but he didn't resist. Over time I continued to greet him with hugs until we reached the point at which both of us could extend our arms to each other. I can now see my brothers developing a greater physical closeness to him also.

When a family's communication rules have been developed over time, the family is calibrated, or "set," to regulate its behavior in conformity to those rules. If one or more family members challenge the rules, the family system may be recalibrated in accordance with the new rules. For instance, an unwritten family rule may be that a seriously ill 14-year-old is not allowed to hear the truth regarding his condition. If anyone should suggest that he has a blood disease, maintenance feedback in the form of a parental nonverbal sign, such as a look of disapproval, or a change of subject may keep the son relatively uninformed. The family is "set" not to discuss the issue with him. Yet, the rules may be changed and the system recalibrated through a variety of change-promoting feedback mechanisms. If the adolescent suspects the severity of his illness, he may confront one or more family members and insist on the truth. Once the truth has been told, the family cannot return to their previous behavior and will recalibrate what they talk about concerning his illness. Sometimes information or feedback from outside the family will lead to change in the system. A doctor may suggest that the young man's condition be discussed with him and request the family to do so. Human systems must change and evolve in order to survive. Families constantly restructure themselves to cope with normal developmental stages and unpredictable crises.

The ongoing **dialectical struggles** of human beings keep a system in some level of flux; for example, parents and children are continually negotiating levels of independence during the adolescent years. In addition, human systems are capable of sudden leaps to new integrations, reflecting a new evolutionary state (Yerby, 1995), such as when a family member reveals they are lesbian or gay or announces they have taken a job overseas. The traditional calibration model needs to be modified and placed within an evolutionary framework, recognizing both types of change.

Interactive Complexity/Punctuation

Understanding families from a systems perspective implies a move away from considering causes and effects of behavior, because systems theory maintains cause and effect are interchangeable. When you function as a member of an ongoing relational system, each of your actions serves as both a response to a previous action and a stimulus for a future action. In one family a mother was very concerned about her young adult son, who was still unemployed six months after college graduation. She gave him lots of advice and offered to help him financially. He greatly reduced calling his mother after he concluded she was overly involved in his life. The more he increased the distance between them, the greater her concern became. She increased the number of e-mails, texts, and calls to her son. The harder she tried, the more the son concluded she was pushy and controlling and kept his distance. The term *interactive complexity* implies that each act triggers new behavior as well as responds to previous behaviors, rendering pointless any attempts to assign cause and effect. In most families, patterns of behavior take on a life of their own because members' behaviors become intertwined. Family problems are seen in light of relational patterns in which all members play a part; one member is not solely to blame.

Humans will make sense of the world, by "punctuating" sequences of behavior. **Punctuation** refers to the interruption of the sequence of behavior at different intervals in order to give it meaning or to indicate "things started here." Alissa starts stressing the positive qualities of father because her mother is complaining about him so much. In turn, her mother starts complaining more because she believes Alissa is not listening to her. Interactions, like sentences, tend to be punctuated, or grouped syntactically, to create meaning. Yet punctuation may serve as a trap, leading people to assign cause and blame to individuals instead of focusing on the problematic pattern of behavior in the relationship.

Confusion occurs when people punctuate behavioral sequences differently, thereby assigning varied meanings to the behaviors. The son in the example above might say, "Our trouble started when my mother started contacting me too much," whereas the mother might indicate that the family problems started when her son remained unemployed after college graduation. Punctuating the cycle according to the son's interpretation implies placing blame on the mother, suggesting that "fixing" her would solve the problem. Punctuating the interaction according to the mother's view implies that the son was at fault for not getting a job, and if he took care of that the family troubles would end. It is pointless to try to locate the "cause" because, even if it could be found, the long-term pattern is what must be addressed, not an individual's past actions. Sometimes family members will "scapegoat" one person, suggesting that he or she is responsible for all the problems and remove themselves from any responsibility. Working from the idea of circular causality within the system, it seems less important to try to punctuate the system by assigning a starting point than it does to look at the act as a sequence of patterns and try to understand this ongoing process. In Figure 3.2, you can imagine the different interpretations that could emerge depending on how the cycle is punctuated. A classic example of punctuation is found in the "nag-withdraw cycle," which demonstrates the pointless nature of looking for cause and effect: "He withdraws because she nags" versus "She nags because he withdraws" (Caughlin & Scott, 2010).

Openness

Just as there are no decontexted individuals, there are no decontexted families. Human systems include individuals, families, communities, and cultures that form nested layers. Human systems need interchange with other people, ideas, and institutions in order to remain physically and psychologically functional. In the second case at the start of the chapter, Eunjung comes to recognize the privacy boundaries in her family that come from her culture. Until she moved to the United States and

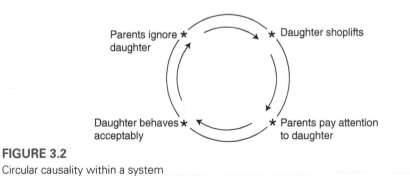

FIGURE 3.2
Circular causality within a system

saw different cultural patterns, she might not have been very aware of her own patterns. Family members maintain an almost continuous interchange, within and across the family boundary within their household, to extended family, and to the larger culture in which they live. Some families will embrace opening their boundaries and others may resist it.

Each family operates within the larger system, which includes legal, educational, political, health, and economic systems, as well as extended family and friendship systems. As a small child, you depended on your family for all your immediate needs, but as you grew older you needed to interact with nonfamily members in order to function in society. Such interchange with and adaptation to the environment is critical. Family boundary strength depends on how the family views the "outside world." A family's immediate physical environment may be experienced as threatening, such as when children can be shot walking to school, or supportive and nurturing, such as when neighbors create a kinship network. Individual circumstances, such as that described in the following, may force a family into active contact with institutions in their environment:

As the parent of a hard-of-hearing child, I am constantly managing our family's boundaries and dealing with outside systems. We deal regularly with the medical community in terms of advances that might affect Melissa's condition. The school counselor and I monitor her classroom placements. I need to keep up with legal changes to ensure that our child's rights are protected in terms of access to special programs. Finally, I am constantly aware of the support of extended family and friends who reach out to help.

For Melissa's mother, by opening the family boundaries to others, she is able to get more assistance for her daughter. At the same time, she may have to deal with unwanted interference from others in her daughter's life.

Few families can insulate themselves, and children especially, because schools and media expose them to a range of values and beliefs, some of which may be contrary to those held by the family. Television, social media websites, and music open worlds to children that parents may not even comprehend or approve. Family system rules include guidelines for maintaining and regulating relationships within the environment. In this rapidly changing and mediated world, families may not be able to keep pace with the technological advances.

Complex Relationships

Systems embedded in systems create a highly complex set of structures and interaction patterns that may only be understood in relation to each other. Frequently, family members' relationships reflect dynamics of power and privilege. A traditional hierarchical view establishes parents as more powerful than children. In almost all cultures, authority, respect, and power go to the older generation, and often to the males of that generation. Appropriate boundaries separate generations; when generational boundaries are blurred, confusion results, such as in the following case:

After my father moved out, I found myself playing surrogate dad to three younger sisters who needed a lot of support. I moved into the role very easily since it seemed to take pressure off my mother, who was severely depressed for almost three years. At the time, I just did it. Now I wish I had not given up my adolescence so easily.

Given today's diverse family forms, the traditional hierarchical structures cannot account for multiple family experiences. Immigrant families in the United States face dramatic structural changes as young members gain power as the only English speakers, or "language brokers," in the family. They gain power by controlling their parents' information and relationships to the schools and larger community.

The complex structure of the family system may be seen through the multiple subsystems that contribute to the whole family's functioning, such as sibling dyads or extended family. In addition, family members interact with institutional systems, such as schools, churches, or governmental agencies. In most cases, interpersonal subsystems change membership over time. Coalitions develop when individuals align in joint action against others. When one parent gambles, other parent and children may form a tight group as a means of coping with the gambler's unpredictable behavior. The coalition may develop strategies for hiding money, supporting the others in arguments, or lying to those outside the system. Following parental divorce and remarriage, stepchildren may find that their grandparents and other extended family members of their nonresidential parent may form a coalition and reduce contact with them (DiVerniero, 2013).

Family triangles, characterized by two insiders and one outsider, represent a powerful type of coalition. Under stress, two-person relationships may become unstable, so they will draw in a third to stabilize their relationship (McGoldrick, Gerson, & Shellenberger, 1999). For example, many stepfamilies struggle with family triangles issues in early years:

My mother and I have always been extremely close, especially during the time after my parents divorced when she was a single mother. When she remarried we still wanted to have time to talk, just the two of us. My stepdad, Frank, didn't like that and wanted to be included in these outings. My mom and I would arrange to meet for lunch and while at the restaurant, I would see Frank driving by the restaurant repeatedly. Mom and Frank would then have a big fight when we arrived home.

Triangles often result in frustration and unhappiness for the "third" person. This is especially difficult when the triangle cuts across generations, thereby violating the appropriate boundaries, such as when a parent is aligned with a child against the other parent or a child forms a close relationship with a grandparent who takes their side with their parent. A couple can triangulate a child into a scapegoat position by deflecting their marital tension onto the parent-child relationship, thereby labeling the child as the source of all family problems.

Equifinality

An open, adaptive family system demonstrates **equifinality**, which means that "a particular final state may be accomplished in different ways and from different starting points" (Littlejohn, 2002, p. 41). There are many ways to reach the same result. Two families may have a theme of "Family members are supportive." Yet, one family may interpret the theme to mean emotional support, whereas the other may view it as economic support. Stepfamilies come to realize that there is more than one way to become a family. Some stepfamilies feel like a family almost from the beginning. Other stepfamilies experience a series of ups and downs before feeling like a family (Braithwaite, Olson, Golish, Soukup, & Turman, 2001). Systems theory helps us realize that there are often many possible ways of reaching the same end point.

Communication and the Systems Perspective

Communication is a key attribute of human systems. As we described in Chapter 2, family systems are constituted in the communication process—communication creates, maintains, and changes the system. Individuals in family systems behave according to the meanings they assign to each other, the family, and aspects of the environment. Communication messages may be viewed as interwoven patterns of interaction that stretch through a family's history rather than as singular events. In most families members share relatively congruent or similar worldviews and interact to update or change the worldviews over time.

While systems theory is a very useful way to understand families, decades of thinking and research on systems theory have revealed some limitations. First, some systems theory has been criticized for ignoring the historical power inequality between males and females in families, given the patriarchal nature of family life (Wood, 2010). A systems view does not adequately address issues such as male violence in the family and underplays the individual level of responsibility for the abuser, suggesting that a victim shares equal responsibility for the abuse (Galvin et al., 2006).

Second, because systems theory focuses on the group, it tends to overlook individual, or psychobiological, issues. The responsibility for problems is placed on the family rather than on individuals who may be ill or be genetically predisposed to certain disorders such as depression or alcoholism (Broderick, 1993; Spotts, Towers, & Reiss, 2006). Researchers are also increasingly looking to biological and evolutionary explanations for individual behavior within the family system and these should not be ignored (Beatty, McCroskey, & Heisel, 1998; Floyd & Afifi, 2011). The assumption of shared or equal responsibility can be devastating to family members who are frustrated by the problems.

We hope that you can see the usefulness of systems theory and why it is the central theory that guides our approach to family communication. The second set of theories to follow guides the approach to communication in family systems we articulated in Chapter 2.

Social Construction/Symbolic Interaction

Social construction and symbolic interaction, both interpretive theories, address the creation of meaning and together represent a broader perspective by which we can understand family communication. Each theory emphasizes the significance of symbols, primarily language and social interaction, by which people co-create meanings. Although these theories are often viewed as interconnected, Leeds-Hurwitz (2006) maintained they are distinct, arguing that "what separates them is that social construction is centrally concerned with how people make sense of the world, especially through language, and emphasizes the study of relationships; whereas symbolic interaction's central concern is making sense of the self and social roles" (p. 233). Each theory emphasizes different issues and they will be discussed separately.

Social Construction

This theory proposes that (1) people make sense of the world by constructing their own model of the social world and how it works, and (2) language is viewed as critical to human society; therefore, conversation serves to create and maintain reality (Leeds-Hurwitz, 2006). **Social construction** places a unique focus on how meanings are created and negotiated in specific contexts, rather than significantly influenced by societal norms or expectations. Identity of individual family members is co-created via communication, and the family co-creates its own culture in interaction (Bergen & Braithwaite, 2009). Nontraditional, discourse-dependent families are formed as members constitute their family identity through language and interaction. For example, voluntary or fictive kin relationships are created as persons come to regard and label nonbiological or nonlegal kin as family or "like a sister to me."

According to Klein and White (1996), "The private understandings constructed by family members are based on their shared history, perspective, and interpretation of events. Dating and marriage are viewed as a process by which separate individuals 'fuse' into a common living arrangement and worldview" (p. 107). In their classic work, Berger and Kellner (1964) captured marital meaning creation, saying, "Each partner's definition of reality must be continually correlated with the definitions of the other" (p. 224). Such correlation occurs in interaction and is continually being negotiated and updated. In order to form a marital system, a couple must negotiate a set of common meanings through interaction and mutual accommodation so that their meanings of marriage are linked with the other. Recently, Holtzman (2008) explored the power of negotiated family definitions ranging from traditional (biological and/or legal) to socially expansive (i.e., nonbiological and nonlegal) relationships.

Families are systems formed and negotiated in communication as we discussed in Chapter 2. As they interact, they co-create meanings about what it means to be a member of the family and what family members are expected to say and do. These meanings are continually negotiated and there are changes within the family system, and the system recalibrates. You can see this in the case of brothers Cash, Cam and Carl at the beginning of the chapter. Over the years they have co-constructed a sibling relationship around competition and fun, which is challenged by Cash's health issues.

In healthy relationships, members develop the ability to recognize and negotiate joint understandings through their interactions. In other families, members struggle constantly with the lack of shared meanings on important issues. In one family the elderly mother is constantly upset that her daughter does not call her on a regular basis. The daughter is perplexed with her mother's disappointment as she bought her mother a computer, e-mails her mother at least twice a week, and posts pictures of the grandchildren on a shared family website that she taught her mother to use. Although most family members co-construct shared meanings, perfect agreement never results. As individuals form new families and as families change over time, the processes of negotiating shared meanings are set in motion.

Symbolic Interaction

This theory is based on the work of George Herbert Mead and also emphasizes the self, meanings, and construction of self through interaction. **Symbolic interaction** places a strong focus on social roles, assuming that (1) humans think about and act according to the meanings they attribute to their actions and social contexts, and (2) humans are motivated to create meanings to help them make sense of the world and we do this through language (Leeds-Hurwitz, 2006). Klein and White (1996) captured this view in the following example:

> A 3-year-old may show no interest in a particular toy doll. But when an older sibling plays with the doll, it suddenly takes on a new interactional and situational meaning. Now, the doll is desired. The meaning of the toy is constructed by the situational interaction of the two siblings. (p. 92)

Symbolic interaction focuses on the connection between symbols, or shared meanings, and interactions, via verbal and nonverbal communication (LaRossa & Reitzes, 1993). This approach views families as social groups in which communication fosters the development of self and group identity. The following assumptions reflect the importance of meaning for human behavior:

1. Human beings act toward things on the basis of the meanings that the things have for them.
2. Meaning arises out of the process of interaction between people.
3. Meanings are handled in and modified through an interpretive process used by the person in dealing with things he or she encounters. (LaRossa & Reitzes, 1993, p. 143)

Essentially, symbolic interaction requires paying attention to how events and experiences are interpreted by the actors (White & Klein, 2002). Meaning is negotiated and co-created through the use of language. This meaning-making process may be voluntary or involuntary, explicit or implicit, but it is always tied to language and discourse. Meanings are created and shared, influenced by larger cultural and social processes that influence groups who share similar contexts, as the Korean Eunjung and her family demonstrate in the second case above. Thus, ethnicity, gender, religion, and socioeconomic status all influence the interpretation process. In her study of "commuter wives," Bergen (2010) found that, unlike the experience of husbands who lived away from home for work, wives experienced much more pressure and disapproval from others, given cultural expectations women should live at home and take care of the family. She found that commuter wives and their husbands needed to interact and come to share meanings concerning how women could be a "commuter wife" and at the same time function as a "good wife."

The importance of symbolic interaction from a family perspective is important for both defining families and making sense out of family interaction. Through communication and shaped by culture, families develop their own unique practices, boundaries, and rules concerning what may be discussed and not. These shared definitions may be challenged at times; for example, before having a family portrait taken, the family may face some difficult negotiations about who will be in the picture. Does the family include dating and cohabiting partners or the children of Grandma's new husband?

Interaction among family members and the interpretation of that interaction serve as the source of meanings for each member. Sometimes partners or siblings do not label the same events as fights, apologies, or invitations. How often have you heard someone say "I apologized to you" and the other reply "I never got an apology from you"? Eventually you may hear, "I did so apologize. I took you to dinner." The issue revolves around one partner's assumption that "taking someone to dinner" means "apologizing." Enduring relationships are characterized by agreements between members as to the meaning of their interconnections. Family members develop a worldview reflecting the members' symbolic interdependence.

Communication undergirds and illuminates the structure of family relationships. Through communication the family creates a social structure and bond based on their interaction patterns. These selected tenets of social construction and symbolic interaction will help guide your thinking about the importance of families as meaning-making systems.

Relational Dialectics

Family relationships are not static; they are constantly in process, sometimes joyful, other times difficult, and always complex. Relational dialectics theory grew from the social theorist Mikhail Bakhtin's view that social life is an open dialogue characterized by multiple systems of meaning or discourses that guide and influence our interaction and relationships with others (Baxter, 2011). The theory highlights the struggles between these systems of meaning in family relationships that emerge from the struggle of different, often opposing discourses. For example, recent research found that adoptive parents talk about their adopted children as both similar and different than children in other families. Parents will say that their children are just like children in any family and a minute later will say that their children are different or special because they come from another culture or because of the adoption experience (Harrigan, 2009).

Relational dialectics theory recognizes that "family life is a both/and experience—families gain their meanings from the give-and-take interplay of multiple competing themes or perspectives ..." (Baxter, 2006, p. 131). From the perspective of relational dialectics, we focus on the process of contradicting (Baxter, 2011). You can see evidence of this in your own family relationships as you and your family members struggle with questions such as the following: How do we stay involved in each others' lives without smothering one another? What information about the family is okay and not okay to tell those outside of the family? How do we handle all the changes that happen when the family moves to a new city and keep a sense of normalcy? Each of these questions potentially involves the process of contradicting. This is not necessarily bad or to be avoided. And one of the choices is not always better than the other. For example, it would not be wise for us to say that we should be totally open with our families and hold no information back. There may be things that your family chooses not to tell young children or your grandfather. There may be a certain thing that as an adult you choose not to discuss with your parents. It is important to understand that the process of contradicting is a normal aspect of life in relationships as it is how we make sense of family relationships.

These discursive struggles come from the wider culture in which we live and they come from interaction in our relationships, or what are called distal and proximal discourses (Baxter, 2011). Imagine the experience of children of lesbian or gay parents whose parent "comes out" to the child. The child knows their parent as heterosexual and at some point the father informs his daughter that he is gay. For this child and her father, they must navigate some cultural discourses that say that homosexuality is wrong, which the daughter may be hearing from religious leaders, the media, and other members of the family. At the same time, she and her father are very close and the discourse of homosexuality as acceptable also characterizes their interaction. Both father and daughter will need to interact and handle these competing discourses in their own relationship (Breshears & Braithwaite, in press). They will come to understand how their relationship is similar to and different from other families and to the time before the father came out. The father may help his daughter figure out what to say or do when someone says negative things about gay people or about him specifically.

Communication researchers have studied the different struggles, or contradictions, that appear in a variety of family relationships. Earlier dialectical scholars identified contradictions in the form of pairs, for example, how family members interact and manage autonomy-connection, openness-closedness, and predictability-novelty (Baxter, 2006; Baxter & Montgomery, 1996). First, the common struggle in almost all relationships revolves around issues of autonomy and connection, as you saw on the cohesion axis in Chapter 2. An adolescent may wish to be independent yet connected to her parents. A parent and young adult daughter may struggle with issues of autonomy-connection when she moves home after college (Vogl-Bauer, 2009). Parents may believe they should have input into her comings and goings as she is living in their house. Issues of autonomy and connection issues need to be renegotiated when children marry and in-laws enter the picture (Prentice, 2009), when couples divorce (Graham, 2003), or when children feel caught in the middle between their divorcing parents (Afifi, 2003). Second, the openness-closedness contradiction refers to family members' conflicting needs to be open and expressive as well as private, as we described above. Third, the predictability-novelty contradiction is reflected in partners' struggles regarding a desire for constancy, ritual, and familiarity as well as a competing need for excitement and change. In your family, cherished family rituals such as how you celebrate holidays or birthdays are comforting in that you can count on what will happen. At the same time, the family may appreciate doing things differently at times. For instance, the Finley family always enjoyed Thanksgiving dinner at Grandma's house. Last year they shook things up and went on a cruise to

Mexico. As much as they enjoyed the cruise, recent postings on the family blog show that they are looking forward to Grandma's turkey and cranberry salad this year.

You have likely noticed that these different dialectical struggles are more complex than the separate pairs would indicate. In fact, contradictions interplay with one another (Baxter & Braithwaite, 2008; Baxter & Montgomery, 1996). For example, when students go away to college they find themselves appreciating the excitement of all the changes happening and enjoy the autonomy of being away from their parents. At the same time they may miss the stability of home life, and want their parents' advice. Parents may realize the need to respect the child's need of new experiences; at the same time they want the child to be open about what they are doing. Researchers have seen this all play out in the use of the social networking site Facebook. In one study, college freshmen and sophomores described how they used Facebook to keep in touch and share their new lives with their parents and family at the same time. They used different strategies, such as privacy controls, to be able to establish their new identity in college and keep some information from their parents (Stephenson-Abetz & Holman, 2012). While the freshman may decide to practice openness and put pictures from last weekend's blowout party on Facebook, she is also thinking about the fact that she will lose some independence from her parents once they learn how she is spending her free time.

In both of the examples of the child of a gay father and for freshmen and their parents, we see two additional aspects of relational dialectics theory. First, the theory highlights that these dialectical struggles are not happening at the level of the individual, but rather the theory focuses at how these struggles occur and are addressed within the relationship. Second, even though this theory focuses on dialectical struggles, this does not mean that family relationships necessarily experience these struggles all the time. In most family relationships, these struggles, while always present, exist in the background and come to the forefront from time to time.

Dialectical struggles are often quite evident during times of change; for example, members of stepfamilies may find themselves pulled by competing forces, when members' significant dialectical dilemmas involve managing the voluntary marital relationship and the involuntary stepparent-stepchild relationship (Baxter, Braithwaite, Bryant, & Wagner, 2004). In their examination of stepparent-stepchild interaction, Baxter and colleagues (2004) found that stepchildren desired open communication with stepparents but at the same time they also resented it. They desired emotional closeness but also valued distance. They also indicated a desire for power to remain with the residential parent, while also wishing the residential parent and stepparent would share authority as the following case shows:

It's been six years and I still can't reach some stability with my stepdaughter. Just when we seem to have made progress and are getting closer, we take four steps backward. One day she asks my advice on how to talk to her dad, and a week later she makes fun of me in front of him. Or she tells me how worried she is about her boyfriend, and the next time I ask about him, she says it's none of my business.

Recent research in relational dialectics theory has taken on a critical approach as has the theory. What this means is we pay attention to "discursive inequality," focusing on power in relationships and the fact that the discourses of our relational lives are not valued equally (Baxter & Norwood, in press). Some discourses occupy a central position and others are pushed toward the margins (Baxter, 2011). In the earlier example, the child may accept her gay father but find that discourse questioned and pushed to the margins by relatives who hold a set of cultural values about homosexuality as wrong. The daughter may feel powerless to respond to a beloved grandparent who criticizes her father or to a friend who makes fun of LGBT people.

Although dialectical struggles are ongoing, partners or family members make efforts to manage them through a set of strategies that include the following: (1) selection, (2) segmentation, (3) neutralizing, (4) cyclic alteration, and (5) reframing (Baxter, 1990). *Selection* implies making choices between opposites. After a husband's stroke left him with speech problems that made him hard to understand, a couple may choose intense togetherness to the exclusion of spending time with family or friends. *Segmentation* involves denying the interdependence of the contrasting elements by uncoupling or separating them. Members of a family business may tease each other and express affection at home but interact in more formal and distant ways in the workplace. *Neutralizing* implies diluting the intensity of the contrasting poles. A grandmother and granddaughter may monitor their personal sharing to keep from being closed off from each other or enmeshed with each other. *Cyclic alteration* occurs when family members choose one of the opposite poles at varying times. During an adult daughter's visit home, she and her mother may set aside time for each other and time to spend with individual friends. *Reframing* involves transforming a perception of the elements so the apparent contradictions are not viewed as polar opposites. An athletic father may reframe his son's passion for video gaming as providing new avenues for mutual sharing as opposed to seeing it as rejection of his interests. Relational dialectics recognizes that partners and families interact and navigate ongoing struggles throughout the life of the relationship. Last, relational dialectics helps us pay attention to the dialectical struggles that occur outside the boundaries of a single household with extended family, friends, workplace relationships, or institutions, such as schools, the medical system, or courts.

Some people might be tempted to ask why we just do not confront and "work out" dialectical struggles in our relationships. Relational dialectics helps us understand that family relationships are a process of contradiction; meanings are always ongoing and in flux as we create and recreate meanings in interaction. On the one hand, this may seem somewhat discouraging if we are looking for family relationships to be stable and predictable. However, the theory is very useful in that it helps us understand that relationships are complex, messy, and sometimes difficult. Relational dialectics theory helps us to understand and appreciate the central role of communication in co-creating and navigating ever-changing family relationships.

Narrative Theory/Narrative Performance Theory

Narrative theory and narrative performance theory represent meaning-centered approaches.

Narrative Theory

"When it comes to human lives, storytelling is sensemaking" (McAdams, 2006, p. 76). We tell each other stories to make sense of our world, construct and alter identities, cope with stress and loss, and help others become part of our experiences and lives—family stories both affect and reflect our family (Koenig Kellas, 2010; in press). Narrative theorist Walter Fisher wrote, "Humans are essentially storytellers" (1987, p. 64). According to narrative theory, humans experience life in narrative form and find personal meanings for their stories through interpretation, not objective observation. Similar stories may have different meanings for various tellers. Narration involves verbal and nonverbal symbolic actions, words, and/or deeds, set within a sequence of events that have meaning for those who create or interpret them. As a narrator you engage in self-discovery and self-creation, and we engage in this process in family groups as well. The following assumptions support Fisher's (1987) narrative paradigm:

- The essential nature of humans is rooted in stories.
- People decide which stories to accept or reject based on what makes sense or on good reasons.
- Good reasons are determined by history, biography, culture, and character.
- The standards for narrative rationality are coherence and fidelity.
- Humans experience the world as a set of stories. As they choose among them, they create and recreate their lives.

Family narrative scholars focus on stories that recount experiences, such as births or adoptions, how we met, memorable events, or ancestors' lives. Current family research explores how families construct and use stories, for example, functions of family stories across ethnic backgrounds (Bylund, 2003), family members' health (Manoogian, Harter, & Denham, 2010), and stories couples tell to cover for each other (Hest, Pearson, & Child, 2006). Painful or "dark side of narratives" (Koenig Kellas, 2010) and stories that serve as accounts for behavior have received less attention.

Narrative researchers do not seek objectivity. Rather they ask, "What interpretations do people construct for their lived experiences? What significance do they assign to the events and moments of their lives?" (Babrow, Kline, & Rawlins, 2005, p. 34). Two criteria determine the rational quality of a narrative and its ability to persuade or teach (Fisher, 1987). First, it must be *cohesive*—realistic, meaningful, and free of inconsistencies. Second, a narrative must display **narrative fidelity**—appear truthful or reliable. **Narrative coherence** implies an internal consistency; all parts of the story are present and fit together. Sections of the story should not contradict each other. Overall coherence includes (1) structural coherence, where elements flow smoothly and they are not confusing or jumbled; (2) material coherence or the degree of congruence between this story and related ones; and (3) characterological coherence or the extent to which the characters appear consistent. You experience narrative coherence when parts of the story work together, this story "fits" with other related stories, and the characters are described in ways that seem consistent with what else you know about them.

Fidelity implies that a story needs direct ties to social reality in order to resonate with listeners' personal experiences and beliefs. The criterion for fidelity is "logic of good reasons." This implies truthfulness and reliability, or the sense that (1) this story appears, on the face of it, to be honest and plausible and (2) it appears to resonate with listeners' personal experiences and beliefs. For example, you find narrative characters believable when they act as you do or as you imagine you would act.

Narratives fall into overarching types: "recounting" or "accounting for" (Fisher, 1987), also described as stories/narratives and accounts (Koenig Kellas, 2010). Recounting provides a history—a retelling of memories of what was experienced; accounting includes explanations or reasons for persons' behaviors or situations. Family narratives may be categorized easily into one of these types. For instance, the story your mother tells of the day of your birth is a recounting story, while the story your grandfather tells of living through the depression may account for his penny-pinching behavior today. We can better understand the relationship and actions of the three brothers at the beginning of the chapter in their retelling of the stories of the "Jackson Family Olympics." We see how that narrative accounted for their risky sports behavior today.

Narrative theorists and researchers often focus on family narratives because of their centrality to human life. For example, Dan McAdams examines narratives of generativity told in adulthood or "the adult's concern for, and commitment to promoting the welfare and development of future generations" (2006, p. 4). He concludes that adults focus most of their generativity on their families and their stories reflect this familial experience.

Narrative Performance Theory

Narrative performance theory focuses on the actual performance or telling of the family stories, exploring the communicative practice of storytelling as one way of "doing family." Theorists explain their attention to the actual performance of storytelling saying, "Storytelling is participatory. In performance terms, family storytelling forms a system of shifting relationships among audiences and storytellers, narrators and characters" (Langellier & Peterson, 2006, p. 102). The strategic function of narrating serves as the theory's central concern. The narration of certain stories changes as children age, becoming an increasingly interactive storytelling performance. In her study of storytelling in families formed through international adoption, Harrigan (2010) found that adoptive parents used artifacts, such as pictures of first meetings or a child's homeland, as an interactive tool and children often participated in family storytelling surrounding their adoption. Over time these stories became more elaborate as the children asked questions or grew old enough to understand certain information.

The interactional work of family storytelling is ordered according to generation and gender (Langellier & Peterson, 2006). Conditions such as context and content constrain narration: for who is present and what is appropriate for the age or gender of those present. In addition, family storytelling operates according to norms of power and knowledge. A parent may forbid the repetition of stories that serve to ridicule a particular relative, or the older generation may tell the family immigration story because they experienced it. The right to perform certain stories may be passed down through generations according to gender.

Many families create explicit or implicit rules for performing narratives. These may determine who may speak or listen on a particular subject (who can tell and who can hear the "Dad got busted for speeding" story) and how such roles are determined (after Grandpa passed away, Aunt Lou and Dad may tell the immigration saga together). Rules may even address the way to present the content (respectfully, humorously), coherence (what details to include so the car accident story makes sense), and consequences (the price that is paid if Pete and Ellen use swearwords in the telling).

Observing jointly told family stories provides insight into family identity construction. Researchers audio or video-record the family members telling narratives; these recordings are analyzed using concepts such as turn-taking, perspective-taking, and engagement. Over time, storytelling experiences may become somewhat scripted or patterned; they may be told jointly by partners, siblings, parents, and children. For example, Dickson (1995) interviewed couples who had been married more than 50 years and, in addition to analyzing the content of their responses, she focused on their storytelling patterns. One couple is described as follows: "They do not talk to each other; they consistently talk to the interviewer ... They rarely talk at the same time like other couples who appear more connected" (pp. 45–46). Jointly shared storytelling occurs when family members construct stories through collaborative interaction. Plot, character, and setting may be developed in a way that helps assign meaning to the event(s) and to their relationships (Koenig Kellas, 2005). As family members co-construct stories, they may agree or disagree, contradict or question each other, add or reject details, and correct or clarify information.

When my Uncle Jake died in Iraq, his youngest son, Jack, was only 18 months old. My aunt decided that the night before his burial we would have a long evening of storytelling about Uncle Jake so all three of his kids, but especially Jack, would remember him. It was really hard, but she collected 22 stories from relatives and friends. We laughed and cried for hours as family members together told their own versions of different stories. Everyone in the family now has a copy of the video and we will all remember Uncle Jake at special times in our lives. Even his future grandchildren will get to know Uncle Jake a little bit.

Tellers develop narrative identities and perform them for actual audiences, other people in the space and internal audiences or those people imagined to be there, a former wife, a hospitalized child, who influence the performance. Narrative performance is a fluid process. Families make sense of events and innovate meanings; they remember, forget, and alter stories as they reinterpret and emphasize what has been marginal or muted (Langellier & Peterson, 2006). Eventually both teller and listener develop their "narrative knowing" or what it is you learn and understand from stories (McAdams, 2006).

Communication Privacy Management Theory

Every family and family member has their private information that is to be shared only with certain persons. Younger members learn the rules for managing family information through directions they receive from parents or other older members, or they learn, usually by making mistakes, what information can be revealed and not. Like individuals, families have privacy orientations—some families are very open with one another and those outside of the family while others are much more closed (Petronio, 2002). Families develop privacy rules with one or more other members as new events occur that affect the family. Some members may choose to keep certain information secret from one or more family members. Communication privacy management (CPM) theory, developed by communication scholar Sandra Petronio, places communication at the core of understanding how family members negotiate private information (Petronio, 2002, 2006, 2010). Using a "boundary" metaphor to identify the border around private information, CPM theory asserts that the regulation of private information depends on the family's system of privacy rules that develop over time.

One of the cornerstones of this theory is that individuals regard information as something that is owned (Petronio & Caughlin, 2006). You likely have information about your romantic relationship that belongs to you and your partner and you do not share it with others. Families also have information they own and may establish rules about, such as talking about the family's finances or mental illness in the family. Information may be owned by a whole family, a pair of siblings, or an individual. Louisa, from the beginning case, believes she should have been called as Cash's wife, once he went to the hospital. Over time, privacy rules may be changed or ignored.

Boundaries are also *permeable*, or flexible, as information may flow freely back and forth or sometimes only in one direction (Petronio, 2002). As children are young, information about their health and bodies flows one way as parents keep track of children's eating habits, bedtime, and health, for example. In most cases, parents do not need to share information about their health with their children. As children age, normally more of this information becomes private and the **privacy boundary** is not permeable—information does not flow from children to parent. Later in life, the adult child caregiving for an elderly parent asks the parent if they are eating well and how their visit with the physician went. Thus, boundaries *change* over time as circumstances lead members to include or exclude others from certain information. Privacy management, a very complex process, addresses the tension between "the need to be connected to family members while retaining a sense of autonomy apart from those members" (Petronio, 2010, p. 175).

CPM identifies four concepts that guide the privacy rule management process: **boundary rule formation**, boundary rule usage, **boundary rule coordination**, and boundary turbulence (Petronio, 2002).

Boundary Rule Formation   Boundary rule formation refers to the factors that regulate the flow of information between and among others. We establish privacy rules based on five criteria: culture, gender, motivation, context, and the risk/reward ratio (Petronio, 2002). First, *culture* encompasses the family's global or ethnic culture. The concept of "saving face" espoused by Asian cultures may limit the negative private information that is shared with persons outside a Korean family, as depicted in the case of Eunjung and her family in the opening case. Second, *gender* may affect how much is shared inside or outside the family. More than males, females are often socialized to create strong relationships through personal conversations; sisters or mother-daughter pairs may share more private information than brothers or father-son pairs.

Third, a family member's *motivation* for revealing or concealing information affects privacy rules. Louisa, the wife in the beginning case, did not reveal her concerns to her husband as she learned about his upcoming trip through overhearing his Skype conversation. Her motivation not to be a snooping wife overpowered normal openness with her husband. Fourth, the *context* (situation or setting) may support revealing or concealing information desirable. A long road trip may be the perfect situation for an older cousin to talk with her teenage cousin about safer sex, or a crowded restaurant may deter a father from discussing the family's economic difficulties with his children. Researchers are in the early stages of trying to understand communication privacy management in the context of computer-mediated communication. For example, Child and Westermann (2013) found that few young adults refused their parent's request to friend them on Facebook or altered their privacy settings when it came to their parents. The researchers concluded that the power differential between parents and even young adult children may contribute to the children's perception that refusing a parent's request for access would be harmful to their relationship.

Fifth, family members consider the *risk/reward ratio* of sharing certain information. A couple may struggle with how to discuss the wife's firm desire to remain child-free and the husband's desire to have children. Continually bringing up the subject creates tension, triggering the risk of disagreement, yet reaching a joint decision would be good for the couple's relationship (Durham & Braithwaite, 2009).

Boundary Rule Usage The five criteria discussed above serve to create boundary access rules that affect (1) decisions about whether to talk about a particular subject or not, (2) how to talk about the topic, and (3) the timing of any discussion. Family members must consider the impact of telling certain information to a particular person. This involves considering and predicting what might be the short-term or long-term implications of the disclosure. Might it hurt another person for no reason? For example, if a woman sees her former brother-in-law holding hands with a woman in the park, should she tell her sister? Sometimes the issue involves how much information is shared. Should a 90-year-old grandparent in a nursing home be told his granddaughter was diagnosed with terminal ovarian cancer or should he be told she received a cancer diagnosis and she is recovering from surgery? Finally, the timing of a disclosure must be considered. If a close cousin has just suffered a miscarriage, another female cousin may postpone announcing her pregnancy for a while in order to be sensitive to the recent loss.

Additional privacy rules may be triggered by new events. A significant drop in income may require telling children about financial problems, even though family finances have seldom been discussed. Whereas adults may control their privacy boundaries rather easily, younger and older family members have more permeable privacy boundaries issues, due to their medical needs or their access to transportation, which may necessitate involving others. Women experiencing infertility reported their privacy boundaries became more permeable as they had to talk about delicate and sensitive topics such as sex and bodily fluids in new ways (Bute & Vik, 2010). Families also need to socialize children and new members into the privacy rules of the family (Petronio, 2002). For example, a woman may let her fiancée know that it would be inappropriate to talk about political beliefs of the family on Twitter.

Boundary Rule Coordination Information may be co-owned by dyads, small groups, or the family as a whole. Once an individual shares his or her private information with another person, that information is co-owned. When that happens, the co-owners may explicitly or implicitly coordinate their private boundaries. Agreements or explicit rules may be established as to how that information may be shared with others, such as when a grandfather sternly reminds his granddaughter that she is never to tell anyone that he entered the country illegally as a small child. Or the teller may assume the hearer will implicitly understand the expected level of privacy, such as when teenagers understand they should not tell others about Mom's drinking problem. Rules regarding co-ownership tend be more effective when the need for secrecy is explicitly stated and the ties between parties are strong.

Boundary Turbulence Boundary turbulence arises when privacy boundaries have not been coordinated properly. Persons may become confused as they attempt to manage multiple boundaries or when situational stresses force persons to reconsider a rule-bound agreement. Sometimes it can be as simple as an individual's assumption that "I tell my spouse everything," but the person sharing the information never imagined such an assumption. Other times people misunderstand the privacy agreement or forget that the information should be kept private. Occasionally people learn another's private information by accident, such as overhearing a phone call or receiving a misdirected e-mail, which can create a dilemma.

Privacy dilemmas develop under a range of conditions. These include the following: (1) The confidant may believe the teller will be harmed if the information is not revealed. A brother's drug use may escalate, and other siblings may feel compelled to tell a parent in order to get treatment for him. (2) The private information may be revealed accidentally. For example, a pediatric oncologist may discuss a child's cancer diagnosis with a parent while a grandparent is in the room (Duggan & Petronio, 2009). (3) Illicit activity may be revealed by accident. A teenager may encounter e-mail information indicating that a parent is having an affair. (4) A family member may encounter information that places him or her in a dilemma. A teenage niece may turn to a favorite aunt for money for an abortion. Her aunt may realize that protecting her niece's privacy could jeopardize her own relationship with her brother and her entire extended family, which strongly opposes abortion.

CPM is a very valuable theory that has important implications for every stage of family life as family members are continually faced with making decisions about revealing and concealing information.

Conclusion

This chapter described some of the major theories that undergird family interaction. It established that a family system consists of members, relationships among them, family attributes, and an environment in which the family functions. Social construction and symbolic interaction theory describe meaning-making processes, which create and reflect family patterns and understandings. Narrative theory and narrative performance theory explore and demonstrate the power of story to family identity construction and meaning-making. The ongoing processes of managing dialectical struggles both within a family and between a family and the system were addressed within relational dialectical theory. Finally, the exploration of communication privacy management theory reflects the power and complexity of family boundary regulation.

In Review

1. Using the systems terminology, describe how a change in one member of a real or fictional family affected the other family members.
2. Using a real or fictional family, describe its calibrated level for acceptable conflict behaviors as described in the systems perspective. Describe attempts to recalibrate conflict communication using the concepts of maintenance or change-promoting feedback processes.
3. Using social construction, describe how a family negotiates what it means to be close to the family at different stages of life.
4. Identify one or more significant narratives that serve to create family meaning (values, identity) and reflect the family to others in a real or fictional family.
5. Reflecting on a couple you know, explain how these partners attempt to communicate and manage two different dialectical contradictions or struggles. Give examples.
6. Describe a situation in which information about a family member who believed she or he owned the information, became known to others outside the family. Explain how the family managed boundary turbulence and altered their privacy rules.

Key Words

Boundary rule coordination   78

Boundary rule formation   78

Communication rules   62

Dialectical struggles   64

Equifinality   68

Family system   59

Interdependence   60

Narrative coherence   75

Narrative fidelity   75

Privacy boundary   78

Punctuation   64

Relational dialectics   71

Social construction   69

Symbolic interaction   70

CHAPTER 4

Communication Patterns and the Creation of Family Identity

LEARNING OBJECTIVES

- Illustrate how language contributes to a family's relational culture
- Differentiate between regulative and constitutive family communication rules
- Illustrate the six functions of family secrets
- Compare and contrast the types of family communication networks
- Explain the seven functions of family stories
- Explain the importance of family stories to family members' everyday lives

---

Simon Greenwald, age 86, sat stone-faced as his 52-year-old daughter, Sarah, made her recurring plea one more time. "Dad, you have to tell us about your childhood in Warsaw and your two years in the concentration camp during WWII. We need to know your story before you are no longer able to tell it. My children and Ari's children need to know that part of their heritage. Ari and I deserve to hear about that part of your life. Mother died before we were old enough to understand the importance of your stories and ask her about it." Simon, appearing anxious and depressed, responded predictably, "I do not talk about that time. It needs to stay in the past." Sara continued, "You need to get beyond the sadness and silence that you have held in all those years." After more discussion Simon finally replied, "I'll think about it. Maybe I'll write about it so I can do it my way." Sara agreed reluctantly, viewing this as one more avoidance strategy.

Four months later Simon handed a sheaf of papers to both Sarah and Ari saying, "I'll answer questions if you have any." The siblings were amazed at what they read. They learned their father and mother had met in the camp as older teenagers and vowed to search for each other, if and when they got out. Ari and Sarah had believed their parents met after the war. Their father depicted a happy childhood in Warsaw before Hitler's rise to power. Simon's older brother was killed in a resistance action. His parents died in the concentration camp. Two days later Sarah indicated that she and Ari had questions and requested he audio-record his responses. Much to her surprise Simon agreed, saying, "As I wrote these words I realized that you and your brother deserved to know the truth and so should my grandchildren." Two days later Simon talked for hours at the kitchen table as the recorder captured every word. Within the next two months his grandchildren began to understand their grandparents and their family heritage in an entirely new way.

Emily wishes she could disappear on Mother's Day. Although Sharon, the woman her father married two years after her mother died, tries to be good to her, on days like this it's hard to even look at her. Emily, age 15, just wants to take a walk with her mother and stop at the bookstore where her mother would select a book for her holiday present and a proud young Emily would pay for it with her babysitting money. Her brother Jake, age 7, has an easier time with holidays because he was quite young when the car accident happened. He doesn't remember all the holiday rituals with their mother's relatives—the Thanksgiving family baseball game, the elaborate Christmas Eve dinner at her grandmother's, or the Fourth of July parade and barbeque. Her uncles told crazy jokes, her aunts told wonderful stories about growing up, and her grandmother taught her many of their Swedish family recipes.

When Sharon and Emily's dad remarried, Emily's family moved into Sharon's big house, about 30 miles away, and the holidays are spent with her father's family or Sharon's relatives, although Dad will drive Emily over to see her grandmother and other relatives on Christmas morning. Sometimes Emily feels as if she is the only person in her family who misses their old life. Even Jake prefers to stay with his stepbrothers to play with their toys. No one talks about Mom on her birthday or on the day she died. Emily reminds her brother but Jake does not remember much about her. Emily fears that she will lose her precious memories of her mother.

Communication patterns serve as the foundation of family identity. Identity is respected in how we answer the question "Who am I?" or "Who are we?" We are challenged in life to understand ourselves as individuals as within our web of relationships, including our family (Bergen & Braithwaite, 2009). The previous chapter examined the family from various theory perspectives; this chapter centers on the patterned meaning-making function of families. It is through communication that family members manage their everyday lives and construct their collective identity. In order to understand the significant role that meaning plays in the relational development of identity, this chapter will address (1) the formation of a family's relational culture through communication and (2) the development of those meanings through four key communication patterns: family communication rules, family secrets, family networks, and family narratives. Selected tenets of systems theory, symbolic interaction theory, and narrative theory will guide your thinking about the importance of families as meaning-making systems constructing their realities through communication.

Relational Cultures

Each of you learns to interpret and evaluate behaviors within your family system while simultaneously creating a set of meanings that may not be understood by an outsider. For instance, one of our students shared a family ritual that started in her childhood wherein their father should shout "carrot time!" and the entire family would go out on the lawn on Christmas Eve and toss carrots onto the roof of their house. This seemed an odd practice to the various boyfriends and later fiancé she brought home for the holidays. While this started as a ritual for young children to provide carrots for Santa Claus' reindeer, continuing this ritual into adulthood had become a way to reflect their unique family culture that valued togetherness and fun. These days they share these pictures on social media for extended family and friends to see. Every family system creates its own world-view that reflects members' shared beliefs and meanings. Members may or may not identify equally with the worldview that undergirds their family's communication patterns.

Communication not only involves interchanges among family members, but also creates, shapes, and alters the structure of the family system, affecting each individual family member and all of them together. Communication serves to create a relational culture, a privately transacted system of understandings reflecting the attitudes, actions, and identities of participants in a relationship. Coordinated understandings emerge from a jointly constructed worldview or relational culture. A relational culture is a "private world of rules, understandings, meanings, and patterns of acting and interpreting that partners create for their relationship" (Wood, 2007, p. 308). **Relational cultures** emerge from ongoing communication patterns as members build, maintain, alter, and sometimes dissolve their connections. Just as close friends and romantic pairs form relational cultures, family members also form powerful relational cultures with long-lasting effects.

Consider partners' behaviors as they develop a family system. Each must undergo a process of mutual accommodation by developing a set of patterned transactions—ways in which each spouse triggers and monitors the behavior of the other and is, in turn, influenced by the previous behavioral sequence. These transactional patterns form "an invisible web of complementary demands that regulate many family situations" (Minuchin, 1974, p. 17). To form a two-partner system, individuals must negotiate a set of common meanings as they interact over time. This negotiation process is both subtle and complex; some couples never effectively accomplish this task. Partners who succeeded are described in the following:

My parents see each other as intelligent, attractive, loving, and genuine. They don't respond well to each other when it is obvious that the other partner is trying to avoid conflict. They openly discuss problems relating to their personal relationship, inner feelings, and children because they desire to grow together through the good times and the bad times. My parents are a highly interdependent couple who value being together and experiencing life as partners yet they enjoy their separate careers and friends outside of the home. Both believe they need each other, plus their sense of independence, to make themselves spiritually whole.

Through language, partners strive to create mutual meanings. Similarities in their physical and social processes assure some generalized common meanings. However, the intent of some behaviors, if not discussed, may be misinterpreted; yet, these behaviors and their interpretations become part of the relational meaning pattern. Usually, the more similar the partners' culture and backgrounds, the less negotiation is needed. Relying on the verbal and nonverbal repertoire available, family members negotiate a set of common meanings reflecting their physical, social, and individual competencies. When behaviors are interpreted in a similar way, little communication is needed, but when it comes to light that behaviors are interpreted in different ways, these interpretations need to be discussed and clarified so that similar meanings emerge and clearer communication results.

Words play a significant role in developing a relational culture; research on distressed and non-distressed partners indicates that nonverbal behavior is also an important contributor to the relational culture. In his early work, relationship researcher John Gottman (1979) found that distressed couples were more likely to "express their feelings, mind read, and disagree, all with negative nonverbal behavior" (pp. 467–468). In some cases they express contempt, powerfully indicated by eye rolling, sarcasm, mocking, name calling, or belligerence (Gottman, Gottman, & DeClaire, 2006), sometimes referred to as "the sulfuric acid of love" (Gottman, 1999, p. 47). When families add members, the relational culture becomes more complex and interaction becomes important to increase understanding.

As a family system evolves, communication among members creates and affects the continuously developing relationships. Over time family members come to have certain meanings within each relationship and families socialize or help new family members understand the family culture.

Our communication patterns tend to join or separate family members from each other. In the following dialogue script Mom and Amy appear joined against Dad, although Mom criticizes Amy when she swears. Another child, Scott, reinforces his sister's position after she brings him into the discussion. Here's a typical example of the family in action:

Mom: *Sam, let's go to the zoo. The kids would love to see the animals.*

Dad: *I'm tired of doing what the kids want. Let's just stay home.*

Sister: *Damn, Dad. You never want to do anything that we like. Right, Scott?*

Mom: *Amy, watch your language. Now, apologize to your father!*

Sister: *No, he doesn't care about us.*

Dad: *That's correct. I don't care! (Very serious facial expression.)*

Brother: *We always have these fights. Why do we bother being a family? (Scott storms to his room.)*

After living within these types of patterns for years, we are so used to the "moves" that, as soon as one person hears the predictable opening line, the entire family starts to move through the usual script, very much like actors in a play.

Well-coordinated meanings do not develop quickly. Partners may struggle for years to reach similarity in interpreting and responding to each other's behaviors. Parents and children may live with serious misunderstandings throughout most of their lives if they do not communicate effectively with one another. For example, if two siblings sense parent favoritism, both may consciously avoid the subject, or one may resist the other's attempt to explore the subject.

Communication Patterns That Influence Family Meanings

Family meanings emerge through the continuous interpretation of, and response to, messages. Over time these interactions become predictable, forming communication patterns or complex sets of "moves" established through repetition that have become predictable without conscious awareness. Through these patterns family members create meanings and define relationships. Communication patterns emerge from reciprocally shared verbal and nonverbal messages, recurring and predictable within family relationships; they may be altered by forces within the ecosystem or the family system itself. To fully understand how these family meanings emerge from patterns, the following areas must be explored: (1) family communication rules, (2) family secrets, (3) family communication networks, and (4) family narratives.

When I was 15, my father had surgery on … to this day I don't know exactly what! When I came home from school my mother said my father had "some hospital procedures and would be home tomorrow."

When my grandmother quickly became very fragile and confused, my parents refused to address it. I got the message loud and clear—never talk about a parent's or grandparent's health issues.

Family Communication Rules

The previous example reflects a common family pattern—the communication rule. *Over time* every family develops rules for acceptable interactions and transmits them to new members explicitly or implicitly. Rules are relationship agreements that prescribe and limit a family's behavior over time. Every family becomes a rule-governed system; family members interact with each other in an organized, repetitive fashion, creating patterns that direct family life. **Communication rules** emerge from "shared understandings of what communication means and what kinds of communication are appropriate in various situations" (Wood, 2007, p. 108) and are maintained through repetitive interactional patterns. Rules serve to create regularity where none exists. In most cases, rules reflect patterns that have become "oughts" or "shoulds." Relational rules develop when people in relationships, implicitly or explicitly, develop rules unique to their connection; eventually these rules become patterned.

Because of their regularities, rules serve a powerful function in coordinating meanings for people. Through rules, family members gain a sense of shared reality and mutual understanding. Family rules may be constitutive or regulative (Trenholm & Jensen, 2013). *Constitutive* rules define "what counts as what" and help family members understand why they should not do or say something as communicators construct meanings. For example, "You should 'friend' your sister on Facebook as she is family" or "You should call Grandfather on his birthday as a sign of respect." Essentially constitutive rules determine meanings because they tell members how to recognize and interpret speech acts, such as "You need to work harder," which may be based on a family rule such as "We should give 100% effort to what we do."

One's family of origin is a primary source of such learning. During the early years, families teach us what counts as affection (in some families, members kiss and hug but in other families, affection is not displayed overtly), and what counts as conflict (families differ in how openly and civilly they manage differences).

Regulative rules prescribe acceptable communication behavior—how, when, where, and with whom to talk. Members of the Rosario family hear, "Text me or your sister whenever your plans change, even if it is a small change"; Williams family members learn, "Always greet older family members directly when you return home" and "Do not disagree with your father about your curfew time." Families may also develop special rules applicable to specific contexts. For example, when a family member is diagnosed with a genetic disease, the family may establish rules about who can talk about this and under what conditions (Forrest et al., 2003).

Development of Rules   How does one learn these communication rules? You learned some rules explicitly, and you learned other rules implicitly. Rule formation varies on an awareness continuum, ranging from a very direct, explicit, and conscious rule that may have been clearly negotiated, to the implicit, unspoken, unconscious rules emerging from repeated interactions. The former are straightforward, while the latter are extremely complex. In some families, particular rules are negotiated directly, such as "We will never go to bed without kissing goodnight" or "We will openly discuss sex with the children." More often rules develop as a result of repeated interactions. Influential invisible rules are so much a part of the family's way of life that they are not recognized or named, but they are enforced, as indicated in the following example:

When I accidentally bring up a subject that is "taboo" when we are around other people, my mother gives me the cold stare, although she would deny it. If we are engaged in a one-on-one conversation, she ignores me or changes the subject. We've never talked about these topics or rules directly. I doubt we ever will.

Rules develop great staying power. Individuals tend to carry their family rules into the families they form, implicitly combining those rules with their partners' family-of-origin rules. The task for newly formed families is to "negotiate rules that will structure interaction in this new family structure" (Rasheed, Rasheed, & Marley, 2011, p. 63). If the old patterns are not questioned, such rules pass from generation to generation. Partners from families with dissimilar rules experience greater struggles, forcing them to address the differences. Consider the difficulties if two people bring to their marriage the following individual rules for behavior during a family argument:

Partner 1: If one person expresses strong negative emotion, the other should consider it carefully and refrain from a spontaneous response. This is considered thoughtful.

Partner 2:   If one person expresses strong negative emotion, the other should respond with emotional supportiveness. To avoid responding would indicate rejection.

You can imagine the process of implicit and explicit rule negotiation needed in order for these two people to develop a disagreement pattern with which both feel comfortable. What makes this especially complicated is that these rules brought in from the family of origin are most likely implicit—something the family did, but never discussed. Implicit rules are hard to deal with as often family members are not aware of them and this comes to light when the taken-for-granted rule is violated.

Ethnic backgrounds influence family rules. When sibling conflict occurs, many Asian parents will admonish the younger child for not respecting the older sibling and admonish the older child for not being a good role model. Essentially, the family rule is to avoid conflict (Lee & Mock, 2005). Members of Irish families learn to "Keep your feelings to yourself" (McGoldrick, 2005), whereas members of Polish families learn that stubbornness works unless you are fighting with a parent (Folwarski & Smolinski, 2005).

Analysis of any rule-bound system requires an understanding of the mutual influence pattern within which the rules function and which create new relational patterns. In order to know how two people will communicate, you need to know each individual's rules and how well they will interface. Once rules are established, changing any one may be complicated and time consuming unless the family has a flexible adaptation process and can recognize that the rule no longer serves a useful function. We also need to realize that we may not always know if all rules are followed. For example, researchers found that parents believed adolescents followed their rules concerning tobacco use and sexual abstinence more than adolescents actually did (Baxter, Bylund, Imes, & Routsong, 2009). While we might be completely surprised to learn this, it is important that family members talk about and follow up on their rule expectations.

Rules are maintained or changed through the negative (maintenance) or positive (growth) feedback processes discussed in systems theory. Rules may be recalibrated explicitly and implicitly as family members pass through certain developmental stages. For example, privacy rules change as children age. We do not expect young children to have much privacy, but parents need to recognize and cope with the fact that an adolescents will expect not to have to tell their parents where they are at all times (Petronio, 1994). On the other hand, rules may be openly negotiated or changed as the result of various factors, such as member dissatisfaction. A teacher's suggestion to "Encourage Patrick to stand up for his own opinions" may affect a parent's willingness to listen to a son's arguments.

Old patterns shift as the family system recalibrates itself to accept a wider variety of behaviors and people. One may comment, "I have broken our family's rule about not discussing sex with my mother when I openly talked about my living arrangement with my boyfriend." Some family rule changes reflect societal shifts. Although adoption used to be highly secretive and adoptees rarely talked with those outside of the family about being adopted, the increase in open adoptions renders it a far more transparent, discussable experience (Galvin & Colaner, 2014).

Most rules exist within a hierarchy. Two families may each establish the rule "Do not swear." In the Parson family, it may be a critical concern, whereas the Coopers may see it as desirable. Once you learn the family rules, you then have to figure out the importance placed on each of them, which rules can be violated or not, and what the consequence of violating rules will likely be.

Conflict occurs when a family member breaks rules that he or she did not realize existed. This may occur when rules are implicit, meaning they are assumed but not discussed. Often, implicit rules are guidelines or expectations from the broader culture that may or may not be understood or followed within a particular relationship (Metts & Cupach, 2007). Such conflicts frequently arise for in-laws or newly formed stepfamilies. For example, a stepchild from a family with very open and flexible boundaries may be chastised by a new stepmother for entering the parent's bedroom without knocking. For the child, who had unlimited access to her parent's bedroom before the divorce, she has broken a rule that she never knew existed. In their study of topic avoidance, Guerrero and Afifi (1995) suggest that the family life cycle influences parent-child communication. For example, teenagers may exhibit verbal avoidance, thus unilaterally establishing a rule. The more transparent the rules, the greater the likelihood that they will be discussed and coordinated at appropriate times.

Importance of Rules   Through rule-bound interaction, families enact their primary and secondary family functions. Rules set the limits of cohesion and adaptability and influence the management of a family's images, themes, boundaries, and positions on biosocial issues such as power and gender. Family development over time impacts further rule development. The interaction of rules and family functions supports the development of a family's self-definition. A rule that the family does not discuss problems with those outside of the family allows the family to protect itself and present the image they want to others. Rules provide stability in interactions and serve to socialize younger members or those who join the family through adoption or partnership/marriage. It is not unusual for a person to clue his fiancée in on family rules as she comes to meet the parents for the first time in an effort to have this meeting go well. Predictable communication patterns allow a family to carry on its functional day-to-day interactions smoothly.

Types of Communication Rules   Key questions provide a framework for looking at types of communication rules: What can be talked about? How can it be talked about? And with whom can it be talked about? (Satir, 1988). Each family's rules differ on the issues of what can be discussed. Can death, sex, salaries, drugs, and serious health problems be talked about in the Martinez family? Are there Adams family skeletons or current relatives who are never mentioned? Some topics may be forbidden under any circumstance. Most communication rules become quite clear, as explained in the following:

At my father's house there are lots of unspoken rules that dictate unsafe topics of conversation. It's clear that I should never mention (1) my mother, (2) the way we used to celebrate holidays, (3) my need for money, (4) my mother, (5) old family vacations, (6) my mother's relatives, (7) (8) (9) (10) my mother!

Decision-making provides a fertile field for family rules. Are children allowed to question parental decisions, or are parents "the law," which cannot be challenged? Some families have rules that allow joint decision-making through discussions, persuasion, or voting.

Over time family members become quite strategic. They learn how to talk about a particular topic or issue either directly or indirectly. In a family with an alcoholic parent, a parent or older sibling may say, "Mom's not feeling well today," but no one says, "Mom is drunk." Many couples never draw up a will because one or both partners cannot find a way to talk directly about death. Thus, the "how" may involve vague allusions to the topic or euphemisms such as "If anything ever happens I know you'll take care of everything."

Circumstances also affect conversational topics. You may learn not to talk about money when your mother had a tough day at work. Some topics seem to be discussed in a certain place, such as the kitchen or the car. One father found excuses to take a drive with his daughter as she seemed more receptive to what he had to say when they were driving around.

Often the rules for who is able to participate in the conversation, either actively or silently, reflect biosocial issues such as age, gender, or family role. When children are small, they may be excluded from financial discussions, but as they grow older or serious financial problems arise, they enter the conversations. Sometimes unforeseen circumstances, such as death or divorce, move a child into conversations on previously off-limits topics. A 14-year-old daughter of a single parent may discuss topics with her parent that would not have arisen if another adult lived in the home.

Sometimes family myths affect communication rules. Messages such as "Don't tell so and so because ..." may create myths that prevail for years. Some grandchildren hear the following rule after the death of a grandparent: "Don't talk to Grandpa about Granny. It will make him depressed." Although this may be true for the first three months after her death, when the rule remains in place three years later, Grandpa may believe that only he misses his wife and no one else cares that she is gone.

In order to form a highly functional stepfamily, members need to "negotiate rules that will structure interaction in this new family structure" (Rasheed et al., 2011, p. 63). A father in a stepfamily may receive complaints from his children and his wife about sharing in household tasks. He may call a family meeting and the family may come to agreement about the importance of saying something directly to the person when they are disappointed or upset about another's behavior. Such negotiations seldom occur prior to the merger; rather, they occur after a period of frustration with those on "the other side."

In order to fully appreciate the "what," "how," and "who" of a family's communication rules, it is necessary to analyze the system to see which rules are enforced in what contexts. The following set of regulative communication rules, developed within one young woman's family, indicates the interpersonal nature of rules:

Don't disagree with Dad unless he's in a good mood.
Don't talk about our family's finances outside the family.
Don't discuss sex with family members, except with siblings.
Don't ask about Grandpa's two previous marriages.
Never mention Aunt Bea's cancer or Tim's hearing problem.
Family deaths are discussed only in terms of religion.

Do not ask your stepbrother about his mother.
Mother's pregnancy at marriage is never acknowledged.

The author of these rules concluded that she had learned to distinguish among people and circumstances but had not experienced very direct and open communication in her family about what was expected.

Metarules   In addition to ordinary rules, some families have metarules, or rules about their rules. As Laing (1972) aptly stated, "There are rules against seeing the rules, and hence against seeing all the issues that arise from complying with or breaking them" (p. 106). When partners do not make a will because one or both refuse to talk about death, they may be living with an unspoken metarule—"Never discuss our rule about avoiding the topic of death." Both pretend they are too busy or too young to meet with a lawyer. The following thoughtful analysis of the rules in the previous young woman's family indicates this meta-level of rule-bound behavior:

The death of my brother has spawned an entire catalog of rules. It is unacceptable to discuss his death with family outsiders. There is a strong rule to mention him in conversation among family members where it would be appropriate. There seems to be a rule that has evolved over the past two years that it is all right for my mother, but not my father and me, to show grief in front of the family. My father and I have a sort of metarule that we ignore the rule about not showing grief to each other. I have the feeling that these rules will change when I go home this summer and help my family clean out my brother's room.

All family members live with powerful rule-bound patterns, giving little conscious attention to most of them. Yet, rules give meaning to each relationship. Rules and metarules evolve as new members enter the family and other members die, thereby increasing the complexity of communication.

Family Secrets

Secrets involve information purposefully hidden or concealed by one or more family members. For example, the issue of family secrets emerges as one considers the link between powerful family rules and taboo topics. A common communication rule in alcoholic families, "Don't talk," provides a way to maintain or deny the problem (Black, 2001). Family secrets create critical communication concerns because family ties are shaped "by what is shared and what is held secret by family members" (Vangelisti & Caughlin, 1997, p. 679). Making, keeping, and revealing secrets all shape a family's interaction patterns. In many cases, "A secret may be silently and unknowingly passed from generation to generation like a booby-trapped heirloom" (Imber-Black, 1998, p. 4). Family members are more likely to keep secrets from one another if they perceive they will be punished for talking about their concerns, and this can have very negative impact on family closeness (Afifi & Olson, 2005). The nature of a family secret may change over time. Whereas certain topics such as adoption, divorce, cancer, and mental illness are less stigmatized now, other issues such as being diagnosed with a genetic disease or using a sperm donor are emerging.

Secrets may establish strong subgroup boundaries.

Secrets and Boundaries   Secrets create or reinforce boundaries—whether between the family and the outside world, or around individuals or subsystems. Communication privacy management theory (Petronio, 2002) portrays control as a boundary issue; people view private information as owned or co-owned with others. Revealing private information may make one vulnerable. Family members control an exterior boundary regulating the flow of private information, such as adoption, to those outside the family (Caughlin & Afifi, 2004), and establish internal boundaries that range from high to low permeability. For example, a study titled "How Much Did You Pay for Her?" describes the adoptive strategies used by Caucasian parents to protect their family privacy when persons outside the immediate family asked questions about their adopted Chinese children (Suter & Ballard, 2009). Some parents indicated they would never answer questions on topics such as adoption expenses, their child's personal story, or their adoption decision. These are viewed as private information. Managing family secrets effectively depends on members' ability to identify who "owns" what information. An individual may believe that certain private information "belongs" to her, and other family members, who know the information, do not have the right to share it with others. If the individual's boundary is ignored, turbulence will result. For example, if a new husband tells his family of origin that his brother-in-law has a serious drug abuse problem, his wife may be very angry because she believes her family "owns" the information about her sibling.

Family secrets may be known to all immediate family members but kept from the outside world (whole family secrets), known to subgroups of the family (intra-family secrets), or known only to an individual family member (individual secrets). Although secrets tend to be associated with something that would hurt or embarrass one or more members, some secrets protect positive information, such as Mom's upcoming 60th surprise party, which reinforce cohesiveness and identity. Family secrets often include funny childhood stories, or financial success.

In the twenty-first century, privacy and secrecy appear anachronistic to younger, westernized generations as evidenced by social media. Society appears biased against secrecy because "open communication is valued and revealing secrets if considered to be healing and morally superior to keeping them" (Rober, Walravens, & Versteynen, 2012, p. 530). Family members must think carefully about how they use social media. A recent study of how college students use Facebook reveals that college students use Facebook as an indirect way to introduce family and old friends to the changes they experienced in college (Stephenson-Abetz & Holman, 2012). At the same time, students would manage their privacy settings in such a way as to use the technology to keep certain information about college life from their parents.

Types of Family Secrets   Secrets may be categorized in a variety of ways. Imber-Black identifies four types of family secrets: sweet, essential, toxic, and dangerous (1998, pp. 13–19). *Sweet* secrets serve the purpose of protecting fun surprises and are usually time limited such as a cousin's surprise baby shower. *Essential* secrets include talk about fears or insecurities, which enhances closeness and fosters the personal relationship. For some partners, self-disclosing conversations serve as an integral part of their relational growth. Many sibling pairs value revealing deep concerns and fears with each other, especially in their late adolescence and early adulthood. **Toxic secrets** poison family relationships; significant family issues and stories remain untold and unaddressed. Maintaining such secrets has chronic negative effects on problem-solving, conversational repertoire, and emotional well-being since, even when a family member is not in immediate danger, "toxic secrets nonetheless sap energy, promote anxiety, burden those who know, and mystify those who don't know" (Imber-Black, 1998, p. 13). The protected alcoholism of one member may shut down vital interaction among other family members and between these members and the outside world. Avoiding issues such as affairs, drug abuse, or imprisonment may inhibit interactions about other topics.

Dangerous secrets put their "owners" in immediate physical jeopardy or cause such severe emotional turmoil that their capacity to function is threatened. These may involve physical or sexual abuse or threats of suicide or harm to others.

Functions of Secrets   Given the commonplace nature of family secrets, a key question arises: What functions do secrets serve? In her early work on whole family secrets, Vangelisti (1994b) reported six functions of such secrets:

1. *Bonding.* Family secrets increase cohesiveness among family members. The sister who intercepts her brother's school absence notices strengthening of the sibling bond. Most couples' sexual rituals remain private to them. Sharing family secrets with new members, such as in-laws, acknowledges their place in the family (Serewicz, 2006).

2. *Evaluation.* Family secrets help members avoid negative judgment. Parents may hide a child's sexual preference or a partner's multiple divorces to avoid negative evaluations of their family.

3. *Maintenance.* Some secrets help keep family members close while protecting them from stressors. Unusual religious practices, reliance on a sperm donor, or an unexpected inheritance may be kept a secret to prevent outside pressures and internal anxieties.

4. *Privacy.* Some secrets appear to be personal and/or irrelevant to others. Family members frequently view income, plans for pregnancy, or payments for major purchases as none of anyone else's business.

5. *Defense. Volatile* secrets protect information from outsiders who might use it against family members. Goodall (2008) discusses a major family secret—his father's experience as a CIA spy. Some health issues become volatile secrets. A parent's diagnosis with Huntington's disease frequently remains secret in order to protect the individual and other members' potential genetic inheritance. Enmeshed families rely more heavily on defense secrets.

6. *Communication.* Secrets reflect a general lack of open communication among family members. In families with low verbal interaction, certain topics may never surface because the family is not perceived as open or no one would know how to talk about them, such as in the following example:

When one of us wants space, we may go into our bedroom, drive to the mall, or take a run alone. None of us really shares too much of our private lives with one another. Our friends, social lives, and romantic lives are rarely disclosed, and if they are, it is done humorously.

The functions of family secrets have direct links to revelation choices because people who were unlikely to reveal their family secrets strongly supported functions associated with evaluation, maintenance, privacy, and defense (Vangelisti & Caughlin, 1997).

In their study of criteria for revealing family secrets, Vangelisti, Caughlin, and Timmerman (2000) identified ten criteria linked to individuals' tendencies to reveal family secrets. Respondents who closely identified with their family secrets, viewing them as intimate or negative, were more likely to support a number of the criteria such as relational security and important reasons. Relational satisfaction interlinks with secret-keeping because persons who are unlikely to reveal personal secrets reported greater satisfaction with their family relationships than those who were moderately or highly likely to disclose their secrets (Vangelisti & Caughlin, 1997).

Secrets and Family Patterns   Secrecy links to family change. Although a secret's creation or dissolution can occur at any moment, many secrets are created or revealed at periods of intense relationship change, such as marriage, divorce, birth of a child, leaving home, or death. Secrets constructed at such key developmental points may affect the natural developmental process. Relationships with the potential to change and grow become frozen, as a significant secret locks people in place (Imber-Black, 1998).

Secrets reinforce boundaries across various family forms. Stepfamily members often share secrets with the members of their family of origin while concealing them from other stepfamily members (Caughlin et al., 2000). Former partners and co-parents face the task of creating joint rules for communicating with their children about their dating and postmarital relationships since former partners often have different expectations for secrecy around this topic (Miller, 2009). A recent study of romantic relationship secrets revealed that sexual orientation impacts secrecy patterns; homosexuals were most willing to keep significantly more secrets than heterosexuals (Easterling, Bauthorsfield, & Knox, 2012). The authors speculate on reasons for this finding including a history of keeping secrets, given respondents' history with prejudice and discrimination. Adult secrets about a family member's approaching death may create a climate in which children feel isolated (Bosticco & Thompson, 2005).

As noted earlier, multigenerational communication patterns frequently involve managing secrets. In a study of three-generation families of Holocaust survivors, Chaitin (2002) found the conspiracy of silence affects what topics survivors and their descendants can and cannot discuss because, when the past is avoided, grandchildren do not need to confront emotionally loaded issues. But, by avoiding the topic, grandchildren may separate themselves from the subject and may create distance from their grandparents.

Family secrets impact immediate family members as well as the multigenerational family. A hidden suicide, abortion, or prison term impacts the communication patterns of future generations. Someone may struggle with questions such as the following: Do I have the right or responsibility to keep this a secret? Who would be injured if I reveal this secret?

Persons affected with HIV confront painful choices as they consider revealing the illness for fear of rejection, isolation, and harassment by coworkers, acquaintances, friends, and other family members (Haas, 2002). Revelation within the family also involves great consequences and challenges. Three reasons mothers decided to disclose their HIV status to their children were trying to educate them, needing their children to hear it from them, and believing the children should know before their mother became very ill. Yet some mothers opted for secrecy because, in addition to reasons of age and maturity level, they did not want their children to bear the emotional burden, to experience rejection, and to fear losing their mother (Schrimshaw & Siegel, 2002).

Family secrets link to family power patterns. Afifi and Olson (2005) examined the chilling effect of family members' concealment of secrets from one another by comparing the direct effects model with the indirect effects model. "Direct effects" suggests power in families has a direct influence—it suppresses the desire to reveal sensitive information for fear of negative consequences. In contrast, "indirect effects" suggests that power diminishes members' closeness and commitment, compelling them to conceal negative secrets. Their findings supported the direct effects model. In other words, coercive power created a pressure to conceal secrets in families. In certain cases, secrets can be kept alive through innuendo, powerful silences, and rumor (Smart, 2011). Family secrets affect how information moves between and among family members within the family's communication network.

Family Communication Networks

Family systems establish patterns for connecting, referred to as family networks. Although multiple interpretations of this term exist, we will focus on family networks that include those who are (1) blood or adoptive; (2) kin such as aunts, uncles, grandparents, or those related through one or more marriages; and (3) those considered as voluntary kin (Schmeeckle & Sprecher, 2013). As we talk about these networks, we include both face-to-face and technological networks that family members create and manage. Such family networks reveal members' connections and disconnections along relatively stable communication pathways.

Family members regulate the direction of message flow throughout the network, as well as the message recipients. Some members participate actively in these networks; others participate infrequently or reluctantly. Horizontal communication occurs when the persons involved represent perceived equal status or power, as when siblings share messages or when parents and adult children work out problems together. Vertical communication occurs when real or imagined power differences characterize the interactions.

Families develop networks to manage members' connections and related relational tasks, such as conveying instructions, maintaining secrets, organizing activities, regulating time, sharing resources, and keeping others up to date on personal thoughts and activities. High member adaptability implies a wide variety of network arrangements; low adaptability implies rigid networks.

Families operate within networks that range from high technological connection to high face-to-face connection. Some families stay in touch primarily through face-to-face interactions because members live in close proximity and, in many cases, technology costs or skill levels limit access. The shift from household phones to personal mobile is part of the shift to networked families (Wellman & Rainie, 2012). In some families, relatives may stay in touch almost exclusively through technology, such as cell phones, including calling, texting, blogging, or Skyping, and Internet resources such as Facebook. These technological connections are particularly important when family members are geographically dispersed, residing across the country or globe so that face-to-face interaction is quite limited. Today most families exist within multigenerational, highly complex networks. Within a family, network use varies among different sets of family members—two sisters may use text messaging as a way to keep in touch with each other about small, daily happenings as well as big life changes. They call their brother if they have big news to share. Today families exist within multigenerational networks of great complexity.

Networks and rules operate with mutual influence—rules may dictate the use of certain networks; networks create certain rule patterns. For example, a young woman may ensure that she and her fiancé call their parents when they became engaged before putting that information up on social media, understanding that their parents would be upset if they did not hear the information first.

High Face/Voice Connection   High Mediated Communication

←——→

Face/Voice Network Interactions   Although mediated connections increasingly impact family interactions, face-to-face and direct voice connections remain critical in family life, especially for families with children at home. These families tend to operate using interpersonal network models that include the chain, the Y, the wheel, and the all-channel.

An operating **chain network** occurs when family members talk along a series of links; chains may be vertical (power-driven hierarchy) or horizontal (equal-power connection). Usually a parent figure heads a hierarchy whereby messages move down the chain from parent to an older child and on to younger ones. Requests from younger children travel up the chain. Horizontal chains, often used for efficiency, occur when one sibling relays information to another sibling who passes it on to a third. Chains keep certain members from interacting directly. In the **Y** network, a key person channels messages from one person on a chain to one or more other family members. An inverted Y might involve a domineering grandmother who rules her son, who relays her wishes to his children.

In the **wheel** network, one family member serves as the clearinghouse, or the hub of the wheel, who relays messages to other family members. This position confers power and control since the key figure can filter and adapt messages positively or negatively. Yet it pressures the central figure to manage multiple messages continually. Because only one person communicates with all the others, this person becomes critical to ongoing family functioning. The Internet has reduced the practical need for such a central figure, although some individuals who thrive in this position attempt to maintain their power. When circumstances change, many central figures pay a price.

Mom was the center of our family network. As kids, we expected her to settle our problems with other family members. She always knew what everyone was doing and, more important, how they felt. When we became adults and left home, Mom digested the family news or members' concerns and conveyed the important issues and relayed the information about what each of us was doing. After her death, my siblings and I have had to find new ways to keep connected. Usually we stay in contact through e-mails directed to everyone but that seems to limit the one-on-one conversations of a more personal nature.

Frequently messages in chain, Y, and wheel networks may become distorted as they pass from one person to another. The **all-channel network** facilitates exchanges between or among the whole family, supporting direct interaction and maximizing immediate feedback. Most families employ a variety of networks. When special circumstances occur, such as a seriously ill child, members may establish formal patterns for keeping others informed. After a divorce, family members must establish new networks, often involving additional members, although former networks may disappear. Aimee Miller (2009) studied how divorced co-parents negotiated telling the former spouse that they were dating. She found that some were very direct and others left it to the children to tell the co-parent. Subgroups and coalitions directly affect the family networks. Observers can frequently locate the family networks by identifying who has access to what information, such as secrets, although revealing a toxic secret may destroy an established network pattern (Petronio, 2002).

Many families maintain active large networks. Working parents rely on grandparents or other relatives to take care of their children; an elderly parent's ill heath triggers ongoing medical information sharing. In the latter case, such circumstances might trigger many phone calls, e-mails, or tweets. Technological innovations have increased the way that family members receive updates when one member becomes ill. For example, families can create websites such as Lotsa Helping Hands (https://www.lotsahelpinghands.com/c/656236/), wherein they can post health updates and family and friends can post encouraging messages or volunteer from a list of tasks needed to help the sick individual.

New Media and Family Communication Networks   In the twenty-first century, family members rely heavily on **mediated interaction** to stay connected. On any given day, family members e-mail, text, tweet, post photos on social media sites, and read one another's blogs. This change reflects technological innovations and, as a result, a shift toward more active family member interactions. These interactions occur within a large network of social connections created on the Internet and through other new media, such as Twitter or Instagram. Therefore, communication occurs in multiple ways—through "intentional connections," such as an e-mail directed to a brother; "assumed connections," such as the belief that your in-laws will read about your China trip on Facebook; and "random connections," when your former sister-in-law or grandmother (*surprise!*) responds to your recent Facebook post after seeing your beach party pictures. Ledbetter (in press) points out that family members may use certain media to communicate with the whole family and more private channels, like a personal text, with family members with whom they have stronger ties.

This digitally connected world changes relational life. Increasingly, adults meet their partners through online social networks; geography and friends or family no longer dominate romantic connections (Christakis & Fowler, 2009). Internet dating sites provide millions of users with access to, communication with, and matching with potential compatible partners (Finkel, Eastwick, Karney, Reis, & Sprecher, 2012). A major study (Kennedy, Smith, Wells, & Wellman 2008) depicted American families as "networked families" because of the wide range of communication media members use to stay in touch. College students rely heavily on such networks to remain connected to home as indicated by this parent:

My partner and I have two sons in the same out-of-state college. I cannot imagine how we would manage without cell phones and e-mail since they are seldom in their dorm rooms and they constantly travel with the tennis team. We often catch them on the bus heading to tournaments or between classes just to check on how they are doing. It's important to keep up with their day-to-day lives—the classes, the tennis demands, and their social lives.

This Pew/Internet Life study also study found that couples report contacting each other regularly during the day to coordinate their lives. More than three-quarters of children and parents connected, usually on a daily basis, through cell phones or landlines. Respondents indicated that such communication tools helped them to stay connected to family members although these contacts often blurred the lines between home and work. Study participants reported that these advanced technologies allowed their current family life to be as close, or closer, than the connections in their families of origin, although those with high levels of technology ownership were less likely to share meals or enjoy leisure time (Wellman & Rainie, 2012). A more recent study of adolescents, "Teens and Technology" (Madden, Lenhart, Duggan, & Gasser, 2013), reported that 78 percent of teens have a phone and 47 percent have a smartphone. Contacting family members through interactional networks provides opportunities for everyday conversations, problem-solving, schedule management, tracking health issues, and sharing affection. The technological advances of the past 25 to 30 years have transformed everyday family interaction patterns.

Narratives and Storytelling

My father was in his early twenties when he came to the United States from Taiwan, leaving behind his parents, three brothers, and two sisters. His first job was as a waiter in a Chinese restaurant. During this time the only thing my father would spend pay on was bread and cheap meats to feed himself on days when he did not work. He earned about $300 a month, of which he sent $200 home to repay the money he borrowed for travel. He sent $50 to his family. He used the rest for chemistry books and English classes.

My father, who became a research chemist, has told this story many times because I think he was trying to instill in us the importance of working hard for your dreams and the importance of helping your family. I will tell my children about their grandfather's struggles, so they understand the importance of hard work and sacrifice.

This **narrative,** a powerful example of how one creates family meanings, provides family members with inspiration while carrying a clear message, "If you work hard enough, you can reach your dream." Wells (1986) writes about "storying" as a way of "making meanings," saying that when storying "is given expression in words, the resulting stories are one of the most effective ways of making one's own interpretation of events and ideas available to others" (p. 194).

Koenig Kellas and Trees (2013) stress that "We are born into family stories" (p. 392). How often have you heard comments in your family that sound something like these: "Uncle Wayne, tell us how Mom drove the car into the lake" or "My grandmother told us stories about the caring teachers who taught in the segregated school she attended while living in Alabama and encouraged her to go to college. She motivated me to become a professor". Such stories give meaning to everyday life: "People grow up and walk around with their stories under their skin" (Stone, 2004, p. 6).

Narratives fall into two broad types—stories/narratives and accounts (Koenig Kellas, 2010). *Stories* tend to provide a history—a retelling of memories of what was experienced; these may include ancestor stories, memories of moments shared by current family members, or recounting of immediate life experiences. *Accounts* provide explanations or reasons for persons' behaviors or situations; they may include explaining why a family member chose to marry or divorce, or decided to join the military or retire at 50.

Many family members share a master narrative—a story of extraordinary proportions, known to all members, that serves to define what it means to be a member. Often these are linked to larger-than-life individuals who took unimaginable risks, or achieved a seemingly unattainable goal. A master narrative, on the grand scale, may include a Holocaust survival story told by grandparents and passed on by grandchildren, a parent's immigration-from-Vietnam story, or the self-made man story of a great uncle who founded the business that today employs 24 family members. In contrast is a less dramatic, but equally compelling, tale of a family member who did the "right thing" by supporting three children whom his wife would not let him see or who exhibited singular motivation by completing a college degree at 86. Such powerful narratives serve as life guides for other members.

Every family develops stories that reflect its collective experience. Some stories remain too painful to voice; others serve as the centerpiece of many family gatherings. Families make their norms known to members and outsiders through **family stories** that emphasize "the essentials, like the unspoken and unadmitted family policy on marriage or illness. Or suicide, or who the family saints and sinners are ..." (Stone, 2004, p. 7).

Stories hold a strong personal power because "one's sense of self is the story that a person has created about herself from the totality of her experiences" (Yerby, 1995, p. 6). Personal stories may "fit" with other family stories or may serve to separate a member from the family.

Once voiced, stories develop a life of their own, taking on additional meanings beyond the first telling. You may embellish a story to turn a member into a hero and alter another one to save a member from embarrassment. Each retelling places a slightly different "spin" on the tale. In essence, stories do not just reflect life; stories shape family life with powerful effects.

Most family members' stories are interconnected. You may be recruited into your brother's story of a childhood prank; your partner may delight in retelling your first Thanksgiving dinner disaster. Sometimes, families revise a narrative in order to create a slightly different perspective. For example, a mother may reframe her son's actions as "cautious" rather than "scared."

Functions of Stories Stories convey important messages to family members while serving the following key functions: (1) to remember, (2) to create belonging and family identity, (3) to teach expected behavior and deeply held values to current and future members, (4) to develop the family culture, (5) to connect generations, (6) to manage stresses, and (7) to entertain (Koenig Kellas & Trees, 2013; Stone, 2004).

Family stories encourage members to remember together. Remembering connects siblings as they age, helping them recall key people or moments in their shared lives. Stories construct and reaffirm the members' identities representing part of a

Some family stories can be told only by one key member.

self-definition. Many identity stories remind members of what it means to be a Shih or a Joravsky. A study of 115 couples revealed that 96 percent occasionally talked to their small children about their childhood; 45 percent of preschool mothers and 38 percent of preschool fathers told childhood stories at least once a week (Fiese, Hooker, Kotary, Schagler, & Rimmer, 1995).

Stories construct bridges connecting generations, creating a sense of history that gives younger members a place in the world. Family stories instruct members in the family values, or themes, and what is expected of them. Such stories contain moral lessons or practical lessons. A study of family legacies identified three themes of positive family legacies—hard work, caring for others, and family cohesion. Participants tended to reject negative stories as family legacies (Thompson et al., 2009). Stories reflecting themes such as care, togetherness, or adaptability are linked to satisfaction, whereas themes such as disregard, hostility, or chaos are negatively linked to feelings about the family (Vangelisti, Crumley, & Baker, 1999). Frequently, stories reflect family themes, such as "Only your best is good enough." Stories socialize new members to the family. The prospective in-law may hear all about the family's journey from Costa Rica to Texas or about eccentric Grandpa Joe. Stepfamily members socialize each "side" to some family history because these stories serve as a connection that holds people together as they begin to create their own joint stories (Collins, 1997).

Family stories help family members to remember the good or bad times that contributed to current situations. Some families tell disaster stories that include surviving floods, bankruptcy, or an earthquake. Survivors of the massive 2013 Moore, Oklahoma, tornadoes will share their stories with their children and grandchildren, about how community members and outsiders bonded together to support their families. Such stories convey the importance of serving others. Family stories also connect people to their cultures. African American parents tell family stories to teach their children how to deal with racism (Bylund, 2003). Members of families formed through international adoption tell stories as a way to provide a straightforward history as well as to discourage fantasies children may have about their birth parents (Harrigan, 2009). Finally, family stories evoke joy or laughter as members remember special times or embarrassing moments; sometimes, these stories can be bittersweet, such as when a cherished member becomes ill.

Now that Mom is in a nursing home and Dad comes to visit, they tell stories about camping trips, birthdays, family moves, and other childhood events. Sometimes they will have very different versions of the same story, or each remembers various pieces, or one won't remember it at all. They joke and say that in old age they "have one brain between them." Together, we get from them a fuller picture of events in our lives.

Studies by narrative researchers reveal the significance of major narratives to a person's life. For example, Kranstuber and Koenig Kellas (2011) studied themes that emerged from adoption entrance stories (how a child joined the family) and the impact of these narratives on the self-concept of the adoptees. After identifying the seven themes of openness, deception, chosen, fate, difference, rescue, and reconnection, the authors concluded that the importance of the narrative themes are associated with the adoptees' levels of generalized trust of others and self-esteem. For instance, someone whose narratives about their adoption highlight the themes of chosen child and difference tended to have a higher level of self-esteem and generalized trust.

As you might imagine, family stories present unique challenges for members of highly complex family forms. Members of stepfamilies tend to avoid telling many of their family-of-origin stories because not everyone shares those stories and, in many cases, the stories serve as reminders of a difficult period. In addition, adoptive, foster, same-sex partners, and stepfamilies often must do extra "narrative work" in order to help children come to terms with the family form and their place in it (Koenig Kellas & Trees, 2013). Members may share some family-of-origin stories in order to explain comments or behaviors that new step-relatives would not easily understand. On the other hand, certain stories about biological extended family members or family events shared before the stepfamily formed may be avoided, because it only has meaning to certain members or it may make members of the new family uncomfortable.

Recent research addresses the role of stories in health management. A study of storytelling in families with histories of diabetes reveals that stories shape the ways patients cope with diabetes depending on which stories are taken seriously and what sense is made of these stories (Manoogian, Harter, & Denham, 2010. The researchers identified two sets of relatives who influenced intergenerational communication patterns about the disease. The *linchpins* conveyed information across generations through their stories targeted to those who appear at risk for the disease, whereas the *buffers* closed down transmission of such information to the next generations. Essentially they maintain or disrupt health legacies. Although the disease may vary, these health communication patterns appear in many families.

Questions Stories Answer   A family develops stories that represent its collective experience. These are frequently tied to primary and secondary family functions. Family stories create responses to questions such as the following:

- *Are parents really human?* Children love to hear stories in which parents struggle with issues of growing up or making decisions—stories that remove a parent figure from a pedestal. Some are humorous, such as when Mom "lost" her baby brother, and some are serious, such as a stepfather's struggle with drug addiction. Some stories may be told for the first time, when a parent self-discloses his or her youthful mistakes at the point a child is old enough to learn from such a story (Miller, Sandel, Liang, & Fung, 2001).
- *How did this family come to be?* Most families tell some version of "creation" stories. These may be first meetings of adult partners, birth stories, the first step-siblings' meetings, or adoption stories. Such stories provide accounts of how the current family came to be. Such a story follows:

We arrived at the airport two hours before the plane from Seoul was due to arrive, because we were too excited to stay at home. We brought Grandma and Poppa and Uncle Allen and Aunt Mary. Your father kept walking up and down the concourse and we could not get him to sit down. Three other couples arrived to wait for their babies. We were all anxious, trying to pass the time through small talk. Finally the plane arrived, 15 minutes late, and one by one all the business passengers filed out. Finally, when it looked like there were no more people left on board, a young woman carrying a baby appeared in the doorway. She was followed by other young people with babies. When I saw the third baby I knew it was you. I started to grab you as the woman carrying you said "Dobbs." You gave me the most beautiful smile and your dad and I started to cry and laugh. We had waited two-and-a-half years for that moment.

Although "family formation" stories create good feelings in the listeners, they can stir up painful feelings in others. On occasions when former and current family members come together, such as weddings, funerals, and special birthdays, many adults find it hard to overhear the "how we met" stories told by an ex-spouse about his second partner. Or for children from a first marriage to hear their step-siblings tell wonderful stories about their stepfather when that father makes little time for his biological children.

- *How does a child become an adult in this family?* These narratives address moments or experiences when a child moves into adulthood by accomplishing some feat—beating a parent at a sport, earning more than a parent, or solving a significant family problem. These stories are poignant because they signal a passage of time and, in some cases, a *parent-child* role reversal. A middle-aged adult may tell of caring for a parent whose recent fall left her unable to live alone or how her grandson translated for the doctors when his mother had a stroke.

- *Will the family stand behind its members?* Some stories depict strong family support, or no family support, when members face stressful times or their behavior violates family norms. You take a risk when you leave the expected path, that you will be disowned. Stories link to family themes and adaptability. Comments such as "No one ever mentions Aunt Hillary because she married outside our religion and Granddad disowned her" serve to answer the question "Why don't you ever talk about Aunt Ginny?" Such stories may be told after a member is convicted of a major crime or violates a strong family value such as entering a same-sex partnership.
- *How does the family handle adversity?* When unpredictable crises arise, such as illness or job loss, does this family pull together or does the family fall apart? Countless immigrant stories depict ancestors battling against great odds to build a new life. Stories of family members facing illness, prejudice, or economic hardships depict aggressive or passive responses. A study of male prostate cancer survivors revealed consistent stories of wives as health monitors, caregivers, and supporters. One man reported, "I remember standing here with my wife and crying, having my bathrobe on in the middle of the day … and saying, 'It's just me and you against the whole world, honey' " (Arrington, 2005, p. 149).
- *What does it mean to be a (family name)?* This is a question of collective identity. There may be a master narrative that captures the essence of being a Lutz or a Watters. Family stories influence family members as they make decisions in accordance with the dominant narratives that tell these members who they are and how they should act. Some families have a "master narrative" *that* captures what it means to be a family member.

Performing Family Stories   As we explore family stories, we also need to think about the performance element—who tells the stories, and when and where are they told? Usually storytelling is a singular experience, but frequently sibling pairs or small groups of family members tell particular stories together. Couple storytelling research identified three types of couples according to their performance style (Dickson, 1995). *Connected* couples tell stories as if they are co-owned. Dialogue overlaps and partners affirm each other's words. *Functional separate* couples demonstrate respect, validation, and support while engaging in individual storytelling, often of unshared experiences. *Dysfunctional separate* couples exhibit contradiction, disagreement, and poor listening as each tells his or her stories. When couples jointly tell more coherent and expressive stories, they tend to have higher marital satisfaction, both at the time the story is told as well as two years later (Oppenheim, Wamboldt, Gavin, Renouf, & Emde, 1996).

In an elaborate study of joint storytelling and perspective-taking among members, Koenig Kellas (2005) videotaped 58 family triads telling stories that they told frequently and that best represented the family. The stories addressed a wide range of themes such as accomplishment, fun, tradition, culture, togetherness/separateness, and child mischief, but the most common theme was dealing with stress. The findings indicated that families whose members attended to and confirmed each other's perspectives during joint storytelling reported "the highest feelings of family cohesion, adaptability, satisfaction, and overall family functioning" (p. 385). In a related study of making sense of difficult experiences through joint storytelling (Trees & Koenig Kellas, 2009), researchers explored how the family relational context relates to jointly enacted behaviors such as engagement, turn-taking, coherence, and perspective-taking. Coherence of the story and perspective-taking emerged as important behavioral predictors of relational qualities. The researchers speculated that members most involved in the difficult situation may engage more actively in storytelling or that telling difficult stories creates a more somber and less interactive environment. In a related study, Fivush (2008) identified two different family narrative styles. When asked to narrate highly emotional events that the family has shared in the past, some families displayed a collaborative style—each person contributed to an emerging coherent narrative as they constructed a shared perspective. Conversely, in other families, members performed independent reminiscing in which each told their part of the story but the parts were not interwoven. In the study of these narrative styles, Fivush (2008) suggests that women's autobiographical narratives tend to focus on issues of care and community whereas men's narratives focused on individual identity and achievement.

Some family members develop performance patterns whereby, on cue, one disagrees or adds the punch line. A parent may ask a sibling to perform the "warning" story about the dangers of drug use. Couples may jointly perform "cover stories" that create an "explanation" to avoid hurting another's feelings, or to make one or both of the partners look good (Hest, Pearson, & Child, 2006). For example, family members learn to cover for each other with narrative explanations designed to save face; a mother may develop an elaborate tale of her son's injuries after falling off his bike in order to avoid attending a family reunion that they did not wish to attend.

Family storytelling varies by gender, although women play a more active role than men (Stone, 2004). Mothers may introduce family stories as a way to control the topic and the timing of the stories (Ochs & Taylor, 1992). Females also hear more family stories and become more familiar with stories of previous generations. Mothers also tell stories with stronger "affiliation themes," whereas fathers tell stories with stronger "achievement" themes (Fiese et al., 1995).

Storytelling occurs in context. Storytelling often occurs at bedtime or in response to a trigger situation, such as a bad grade or a disloyal friend. Yet holidays remain classic contexts for family stories. A study of Thanksgiving rituals suggests members "chronicle" or individually update others on recent events in their lives (Benoit & Associates, 1996). Members of the older generations control the content of talk by encouraging chronicling from younger generations and by acting as narrators. Families tell stories in various locations such as the dinner table, on long car trips, at family parties, or in any event that elicits the recall, such as a wedding or funeral.

Family stories function to develop family solidarity and to enact family structure. Parents and grandparents usually tell the stories; frequently children become the protagonists, creating a sense of solidarity for all involved. Occasionally, the reason for recounting creates tension or heightens emotions. A study of foster family narratives describes how two sets of husbands and wives display degrees of emotion when telling stories about their decisions to become foster parents (Jacob & Borzi, 1996). Women displayed more emotion; men remained more passive until the end of the narrative, when they were active and enthusiastic.

Complexities of Family Storytelling   Although most families tell stories with positive benefits, such as helping them cope with stresses, or the lack of stories thereof, can create stress (Koenig Kellas, Willer, & Kranstuber, 2010). Some families omit or lose certain stories over time. Missing stories result from family rules or painful experiences. Some families develop explicit or implicit rules such as "Never mention that Ashley had a brief marriage before she found Alex." Such rules may occur to protect loved ones from distress or support certain fictions ("This is Ashley's first marriage").

Occasionally painful personal experiences, such as military service in a war zone, or the death of a toddler, "disappear." The story about how Grandma and Grandpa met and fell in love may drop out of the family repertoire after their divorce or after Grandpa dies. Finally, some stories reflect the attempts of one or more family members to piece together fragments of stories into a coherent narrative to try and better understand their experiences. A college student whose parents divorced when he was young may put together parts of stories and photographs trying to picture what his early family life was like. In some cases, piecing together stories results in an inaccurate version that influences members' personal identities, even if they are corrected (McGeough, 2012).

As we close this chapter we would like to share the following narrative, "Sierra's Story," written by Dennis Grady Patrick, who has been an adoptive and foster father for many years. He wrote this story for his first foster daughter, Sierra, because he wanted her to learn about a particular nine-month period in her life which she would be too young to remember. He also wanted her to know she was loved during that time. He wrote this hoping that she will read it sometime in the future. As you read it, imagine under what circumstances Sierra might hear this story.

I'll never forget the night you first came into our lives. It was about five-thirty in the evening. Middle of December. I was at the stove making dinner when the phone rang. It was a case manager from the social service agency. "We're looking for a foster home for a nineteen-month-old girl," she said. She told me about your case and why you were in foster care. "So are you interested in taking her in?" she asked. I put my hand over the receiver and turned to my partner, Tom. "They have a nineteen-month-old girl." I repeated everything I was just told about the case. "Do we want to take her in?" "Wow," Tom said. "Yeah, I think I want to do this," he replied. "What do you think?" he asked. "I think I want to do this too," I answered. We were feeling both excited and nervous at the same time. I got back on the phone. "Yes," I said. "We'll be happy to take her in." The case manager said, "That's great. Can you pick her up at eight o'clock?" I glanced at the clock. It was less than three hours away. I put my hand back over the receiver. "Can we pick her up in a couple hours?" I asked Tom. "Sure," he said. "We can do this," he reassured me. I got back on the phone. "No problem. We'll meet you at eight." I hung up the phone. And then panic set in. We had nothing for a girl your age. Nothing. No car seat. No crib. No high chair. I wasn't even sure I knew how to change a diaper. I remember calling some of our friends who were parents and asking them all kinds of questions. What can she eat? What do we need? The couple of hours flew by and it was soon time for us to leave.

I remember driving in the snow and in the dark to pick you up at the social service agency. We walked through the front door into the lobby. There you were, this tiny little girl, all wrapped up in a big coat with your head peeking out from under the hood. We borrowed a carseat from the agency and put you in the backseat. We took your stuff, which was packed in plastic bags, and put it in the trunk. On the way home I kept glancing at you in the rearview mirror. You were beautiful. The first few days you called both me and Tom "Mama." I never thought I would be a "Mama." It was funny. We would be someplace like the grocery store and you would point to something and say, "Mama, look!" And I could see the other shoppers turning their heads and staring at us. You could tell they were wondering why this little girl was calling this man "Mama." So Tom and I talked it over and decided that I would be "Daddy" and he would be "Papa." That made you the very first one to call me "Daddy." And when you said, "I love you, Daddy" for the first time, my heart melted.

There were so many things to love about you. I really liked picking you up at day care. No matter what you were doing or who you were playing with, you dropped everything when I walked into the room. You just got this big smile on your face. And then you would run over to me and wrap your little arms around my legs. If I was working late and you were already home, you would come running up to me as I walked through the door, yelling, "Daddy! Daddy! Daddy!" There was nothing better to come home to. We had lots of fun together. We wrestled. And jumped up and down on the bed. And played goofy games. You loved playing "Ring Around the Rosie." You called it "Ashes." You wanted to play it again and again and again. "Ashes, Daddy. Ashes," you would say. You loved to be held and you wanted to be carried everywhere. I pretty quickly learned to do everything with one hand while I held you in my other arm. You told great stories. At night we would sit on the couch and you would sit on the little bench. Sometimes you would tell us stories about your friends and what happened at day care. "Sierra BUMP her head. Sierra cry." Most of the time you would make things up. "And I was shopping. And a monster came. And it BIT me." "Where did it bite you, Sierra?" "It bit me RIGHT HERE," you would say, holding up your hand. Half the time your stories didn't make any sense but it was so much fun to just sit there and listen to you talk …

Then one day we got a phone call from the social service agency. You were going back to your mom. "Back home," they said. On one hand we were happy

for you. Your mom loved you a lot and she worked really hard to get you back. We liked her and wanted her to succeed. Many of the kids in foster care never return to their biological families. You were one of the lucky ones. You got to go back. But it was gonna be so hard to say goodbye to you. You had been with us for nine months. 270 days. We were completely in love with you. And the thought of saying goodbye to you and never seeing you again really hurt.

We didn't know how to explain to you what was going to happen. You were only two. I wasn't even sure you remembered a time when you lived with your mom. We kept talking about her. And how much she loved you. And how much fun it was going to be to live with her. We completely spoiled you the last few days you were with us. We let you do pretty much anything you wanted to do. We stayed up late. We ate lots of ice cream. We cherished every moment we had with you. No matter what we were doing I caught myself thinking this would be the last time for us to do it together. The last trip to the grocery store. The last time making popcorn and watching videos. The last time getting you dressed in the morning. On your very last day with us I took you and the other kids out to eat. You were asleep when we got to the restaurant. I picked you up and carried you in. While the other kids ate, I closed my eyes and held you in my arms while you slept. "This is it," I said to myself. "The last time you'll be sleeping in my arms. The last time I'll hold you like this. Just the two of us. Sierra and Daddy. For the last time."

When we dropped you off at your mom's house that night, she had a little party to welcome you back. There were relatives and friends there, and she had ordered a cake and bought balloons. Papa and I thought the best thing for us to do would be to slip out without saying goodbye. We thought it would be easier that way. Easier for you, easier for us, easier for your mom. But you saw us leaving. You ran to the door and you were crying. And you were calling our names. "Daddy! Papa!" And we had to get into the car and drive away. That was so hard. It was the most difficult thing I had to do in my entire life. I kept wondering what was going through your little head. If you had any way of understanding what was happening and why we were leaving you. It still hurts to think about that day.

I don't know if you'll remember us five years from now. Ten years from now. I don't really remember anything from my life when I was two years old. But I hope there's a part of us that will always be with you. Because there's a part of you that will always be with us. Since then we've had other foster kids. And we love them very much. And we even have the opportunity to adopt some of them. But you know what, Sierra? You were our first little girl. You were the first to call me "Daddy." You were the first to win my heart. And I'll never forget you.

Families are formed and maintained through the interactions of their members. Such interactions' patterns emerge from and reflect family communication rules, secrets, networks, and narratives. What seems like everyday conversation serves to construct the foundation of family identity.

Conclusion

This chapter explored how families develop identity through the creation of family meanings. This process involves establishing a relational culture reflective of the interactions of partners and family members. In addition, families need patterns that contribute to members' identity. These include (1) communication rules, (2) family secrets, (3) communication networks, and (4) family narratives and storytelling. Each contributes to unique family meanings and each factor influences the others. As you will see throughout the book, patterns serve as the skeletal structure undergirding family life, both reflecting and determining relationships.

In Review

1. Take a position on the following question: To what extent do family-of-origin patterns influence the communication patterns of future generations? Give examples to support your position.
2. Identify three communication patterns that have been passed down across two generations to your family of origin or in another family you know well. Describe how these patterns play out in the lives of current family members.
3. Describe a turning point or major event in a real or fictional family's development that challenged members to reconsider their family rules. Describe how those rules were maintained or changed due to the turning point circumstance.
4. Identify a family secret that existed in a real or fictional family. Discuss the type of secret, how it was managed communicatively, and the effect of such a secret on family members.
5. Relying on a real or fictional family, describe how the most frequently used communication network(s) have changed over time due to developmental changes.
6. Analyze a commonly told family story and describe its impact on family values or beliefs.
7. Select one of the four major communication patterns discussed in this chapter and describe how these changed after a divorce or a parental death.

Key Words

CHAPTER 5

Relational Maintenance within Families

LEARNING OBJECTIVES

- Explain the concept of relational maintenance and provide descriptive examples
- Distinguish among confirming acts of recognition, dialogue, and acceptance
- Illustrate how respect is conveyed in families
- Explain the ways in which rituals maintain family identity
- Compare and contrast the use of relational currencies in families
- Compare and contrast families with distinctly different relational cultures

When his mother, Emma, married Christopher, Jake was angry. He and his mother had been very close since she adopted him at age four. Nine years later he resented Christopher's appearance in their lives. For two years Jake did his best to avoid him, although Christopher would talk with him about music or sports and invite Jake to go to movies. He even showed up at Jake's school concerts with his mother. Before the wedding Christopher took Jake out to lunch to talk about how much he loved Jake's mother and how he wanted to be part of Jake's life. It was a one-sided conversation; Jake didn't say much. Over the last two years Jake's resistance has broken down. Christopher appears at every music theater event at the high school as well as parent conferences. Christopher takes Jake for blueberry granola pancakes every Saturday while Emma gives piano lessons. During those breakfasts they plan events such as Emma's birthday party or a family camping trip. Last week Jake asked him to chaperone a band trip; Christopher agreed.

When Desmond was deployed to Afghanistan, his wife, Samiera, immediately started to imagine how she and the girls (ages 8, 5, and 3) would be able to stay closely connected to him for the next 18 months. Samiera decided to talk with some of the other mothers living on the army base to learn how they managed the separation. After a week of discussions she collected a list of possibilities. She talked with the girls about what each one might wish to do. Samiera began to plan what she, herself, would do to stay close to her husband. Then she and Desmond discussed what would make him feel connected during the long separation.

Each girl decided to fill a fancy envelope with locks of her hair, photos, and drawings. Desmond decided to video-record himself reading stories that each girl liked to hear at bedtime. Samiera planned to make a small photo book of wedding and family pictures. The girls put a map of Afghanistan and a collage of Daddy pictures on the kitchen wall. Everyone also looked forward to the video chats and e-mail correspondence.

What keeps partners in a close, trusting relationship for years? What explains the importance of strong sibling ties in later life? Members of successful partnerships sustain their ties by enacting the "caring, compassion, and companionship that can sustain a long-lasting relationship" (Brody, 2013, p. D7). The same could be said of many other family ties. Family connections, sometimes solid and sometimes fragile, reflect members' communicative efforts to create and manage their connections. Some relationships are maintained at low to moderate levels of connection for long periods; many family relationships never reach deep levels of intimacy.

This chapter addresses **relational maintenance**. In the first section, the concept of relational maintenance is considered; this is followed by a discussion of specific relational maintenance strategies of confirmation, **respect**, rituals, and **relational currencies**. You may recognize that the topics addressed in the previous chapter on family identity (rules, secrets, networks, and narratives) also contribute to relational maintenance.

Relational Maintenance

Much of the time, family relationships just *are*! We live them rather than analyze them. The ordinary, routine behaviors of life carry us through each day, usually in a patterned and often unreflective way. We *communicatively maintain* our families through everyday interactions, but, on occasion, we stop and focus on a specific relational tie when responding to an unpredictable crisis, strategically crafting a message, or seriously reflecting on the role of a family member in our lives.

Consider all the aspects of our lives that we attempt to maintain through routine and strategic actions—health, cars, homes, computers, gardens, professional pursuits, and much more. Do we give similar attention to our family ties? We maintain our family relationships through both routine and strategic communication. Routine behaviors include driving a child to school each morning or asking about another's day over dinner. More intentional maintenance efforts require planning and the use of strategic behaviors such as selecting a gift to please a partner on her birthday, attending a child's soccer game, or apologizing after a fight.

Exactly what does relational maintenance mean? It encompasses that "huge area where relationships continue to exist between the point of their initial development and their possible decline" (Duck, 1994, p. 45). Relational maintenance involves keeping a relationship (1) in existence, (2) in a state of connectedness, (3) in satisfactory condition, and (4) in repair (Dindia & Canary, 1993; Stafford, 2010). Relational maintenance strategies range from talking about everyone's day at dinner, to planning romantic birthday celebrations, dealing with relational struggles as they occur or supporting the other through a rough time.

What does communication contribute to relational maintenance? Dindia (2003) answered that question saying, "to maintain the quality of a relationship, one must maintain the quality of the communication" (p. 28). Although more is involved, talk is the essence of relational maintenance. Talk may involve discussing individual needs, negotiating new behaviors, or forgiving another. Why does this everyday relational maintenance matter? The answer is that efforts toward maintaining relationships help keep members together and more satisfied (Guerrero, Andersen, & Afifi, 2014).

Relational maintenance differs across partnerships and family forms because adult ties differ from ties between parents and children, or siblings. Marriages or partnerships involve *voluntary* adult relationships, whereas parent-child or sibling relationships are essentially *involuntary*, although most develop depth through voluntary connectedness across the life span. Stepfamily relationships also involve maintaining both involuntary (parent-child) and voluntary (stepparent-stepchild) ties. Adults choose whether to nurture their ties; young children do not have the emotional maturity to consciously "work at" a relationship. Most relational maintenance studies focus on marriages or other adult partnerships because these relationships depend on intentionality.

Marital/Partnership Maintenance

Folk wisdom suggests that "over time, romance moves into reality." In this section we will discuss marriages as well as long-term committed partnerships because of the increasing numbers of unmarried persons involved in romantic, long-term committed relationships. Although most partnerships experience moments or periods of great intimacy, everyday life always intrudes with its pragmatic demands such as managing health and financial issues as well as career demands. Parents of younger children find their time dominated by their needs.

Marital maintenance has received extensive attention from researchers. An early marital study of the first two years of marriage concluded, "Although most spouses start with extraordinarily high levels of satisfaction and love, these feelings dwindle as time passes" (Vangelisti & Huston, 1994, p. 179). Partners develop predictable routines and become more aware of their partners' flaws. Eventually couples face relational reality, including disenchantment. The authors reported that partners who maintained strong positive feelings for each other in the early years had a better chance of maintaining this relationship for many years. Decades later, things have not changed much. A study of couple talk revealed the daily talk behavior of satisfied couples over a week (Alberts, Yoshimura, Rabby, & Loschiavo, 2005). The 13 talk categories included self-report, observations, back-channel comments, talk about another person, TV talk, partner's experiences, miscellaneous comments, household tasks, humor, plans, narratives, positivity, and conflict. Topics even varied across weekdays and weekends.

Because relationships inevitably involve stresses and challenges, partners need to communicate openly and regularly in order to cope with difficulties and maintain their connections (Koenig Kellas & Trees, 2006). Marital resilience implies a process in which couples respond to difficulties and purposefully engage in maintenance behaviors, communication, and actions to repair, sustain, and thereby continue relationships in the ways they want them to be (Canary & Stafford, 1994). Maintenance behaviors help to promote relational resilience since they prevent relationships from decaying and help to repair troubled relationships. Researchers have worked to identify the behaviors couples use to maintain their relationships (Stafford, 2010; Stafford & Canary, 1991). These include the following:

1. *Positivity*. Includes acting positively with the other. Interactions involve cheerfulness and optimism.
2. *Openness*. Includes explicitly discussing the relationship and sharing thoughts and feelings about relational problems.

3. *Assurances.* Includes messages of affection, support, and commitment, implying the relationship has a future.
4. *Understanding.* Includes conveying a nonjudgmental attitude, forgiving, apologizing, being understanding.
5. *Networks.* Includes involving family and friends in activities as well as sharing interconnected networks and social support.
6. *Relationship talks.* Includes discussing the nature and quality of the relationship and sharing feelings about the relationship.
7. *Self-disclosure.* Includes being open about feelings, talking about fears, encouraging the other to share thoughts and feelings.
8. *Tasks.* Includes conveying a sense of equity or jointly performing tasks and performing one's "fair share" of the work.

The importance and intensity of relationship maintenance behaviors varies across relationships. Interactions with a marital or romantic partner may involve more intense use of these strategies than interactions with a sister or nephew may include. On the other hand, assurances tend to endure over time, so the need for constant assurance is not as great as the ongoing need for positivity.

While most of the maintenance research involves heterosexual relationships, scholars who study relational maintenance of same-sex partnerships found very similar maintenance behaviors to those used by heterosexual partners although gay and lesbian partnerships may experience additional stresses (Haas & Stafford, 1998). Most same-sex partners desire to live and work in environments supportive of the relationship, to be "out" in their social network, to be able to introduce the other person as one's *partner*, and to spend time with others who accept these relationships. A comparison of the relational maintenance practices of same-sex partners and marital partners revealed that the range of behaviors reported was quite similar with the most commonly reported behavior being "shared tasks" (Haas & Stafford, 2005).

While we may think that maintaining relationships seems somewhat mysterious, in the end, one of the most important pieces of advice highlights the importance interacting positively—"touching, smiling, pay compliments, laughing, etc." (Gottman, 1999, p. 57). The crucial nature of positivity is supported by the "5 to 1 ratio" of positive to negative messages characteristic of stable marriages (this will be developed in Chapter 6). In one of the only longitudinal examinations of marital maintenance, Weigel and Ballard-Reisch (2001) found that maintenance behaviors sustain desired relational definitions and that effective use of such behaviors should predict future marital satisfaction. In addition, they reaffirmed the importance of positivity, assurances, and similar social networks. More recently, these authors' large study of marital maintenance revealed that partners' use of maintenance behaviors is interdependent; a spouse's perception of satisfaction and commitment is associated with their own and their partner's use of maintenance behaviors (Weigel & Ballard-Reisch, 2008).

Although most studies assume persons engage in maintenance behaviors to support the relationship, this is not always the case. Ragsdale and Brandau-Brown's (2005) marital study focuses on individual communicator characteristics of married partners by examining issues such as self-monitoring and Machiavellianism, such as deceit or cunning. They raise the possibility that men, who are skilled in modifying their self-presentation, tend to emphasize positivity in an attempt to create an advantageous climate. In addition, based on a study of attachment styles of married partners, Guerrero and Bachman (2006) found that secure individuals used more assurance, romantic affection, and openness than did dismissive individuals who were uncomfortable with closeness and commitment.

Long-distance partnerships confront special challenges, such as the military family depicted at the beginning of this chapter. Certain strategies, such as sharing tasks and sharing social networks, may not be highly relevant. If partners' ongoing ties depend almost totally on mediated messages, they may avoid difficult topics, resulting in relational stagnation. Yet Dainton and Aylor (2002) found that when there are at least limited opportunities for face-to-face interaction, partners may experience ongoing relational maintenance needs. The pressure to share "good" times together results in the use of more face-to face positivity, although avoiding problematic topics eventually leads to distancing and dissatisfaction.

Parent and Child Relational Maintenance

Although parents of small children enact most of the consciously chosen affection messages, even a toddler learns how to delight a parent with a hug or a kiss. At a much later point in life, caretaking may be reversed as an adult child brings favorite foods and a grandson's drawings to a nursing home. As parent and child relationships shift from highly vertical to more horizontal, responsibility for relational maintenance becomes shared. Across years and life stages, parents and children learn, through conversation and negotiation, how to stay connected even as children need more independence and develop personal preference expressing connectedness. Conversely, changes in parental lives affect their desires or needs for connection. During adolescence most parents and children express varied needs for autonomy and connection; in later years when adult children become parents, the autonomy-connection struggles with their own parents may intensify. In some cases, midlife adults may find themselves maintaining critical ties with two or three other generations (Shellenbarger, 2005).

My father takes such good care of his mother who has suffered with Alzheimer's for many years. Every Saturday morning he picks her up at the nursing home and takes her to the local Corner Bakery for breakfast. He holds her hand from the car to the restaurant and settles her into a chair. Dad orders oatmeal for her and a muffin for himself plus two coffees in paper cups with lids. He feeds her the oatmeal while she stares into space. He also helps her to manage some of the coffee. Dad talks to Grandma about the family and sometimes he touches her hand. Then, after about 25 minutes, they head back to the car.

Highly complicated family structures require more attention to relational maintenance; this may involve other relatives or step-relatives who assume some or all parental responsibilities for a child. In many cases, the establishment of a relational tie with a stepchild or stepparent involves a set of negotiations, ranging from

"What do I call you?" to "How can we build a tie without hurting my father?" Many stepfamilies are formed through voluntary ties between adults and often involuntary ties between stepparents and stepchildren, resulting in limited efforts to build new ties. Frequently, even the form of address becomes a contested issue as it relates to establishing ties; for instance, a child may resist calling a stepmother "Mom" (Koenig Kellas, LeClair-Underberg, & Lamb Normand, 2008). Finally, in some families, grandparents assume major parental responsibilities that necessitate a renegotiation of roles and relational maintenance activities (Soliz, Lin, Anderson, & Harwood, 2006). Parent-child relational maintenance will be discussed more fully in Chapter 10.

Sibling or Step-Sibling Relational Maintenance

Sibling ties represent the longest lifetime relationships for most people, but, until recently, little was known about how these ties are maintained through communication. Siblings may develop ties with each other before creating strong ties with their peers; at certain life stages, such as middle childhood, they spend more time with each other than with their parents (Stafford, 2013). During adolescence, siblings tend to spend more time with friends, especially if they are not very close in age. In early adulthood, they begin to connect or reconnect, forming adult ties.

The long-term nature of the sibling bond depends on the extent to which individuals engage in relational maintenance efforts. In an examination of the first five of the relational maintenance behaviors noted above, Myers and his colleagues' (2001) exploration of college-age sibling relationships revealed that, although siblings are involuntarily linked, most report having a commitment to this relationship beyond obligatory ties. In their study of 257 persons, ranging in age from 18 to 90, siblings reported using sharing tasks, such as helping each other and sharing duties, most frequently, and openness least frequently. This differs from other familial ties, such as partners or husbands and wives, as noted in the list above. They also found that the greater the sibling liking for each other, the more they tended to use all five maintenance strategies. Sibling liking is predicted by use of positivity and networks. It could also be argued that sibling alliances help maintain relationships because, as the opposite of sibling rivalry, they represent a combination of joint efforts (Nicholson, 1999). In a later study Myers (2008) examined the relational maintenance strategies used by 640 adult siblings ranging in age from 18 to 82; findings revealed 53 maintenance behaviors that represented five strategies: tasks, networks, avoidance of negativity, humor, and confirmation or validation of their involvement in each other's lives.

Overall research in this area supports the following conclusions: (1) female siblings use relational maintenance behaviors at a higher rate than males, (2) more intimate adult siblings use maintenance behaviors more frequently than those in congenial or apathetic relationships, (3) use of maintenance efforts in early or middle adulthood depends on the level of psychological closeness, and (4) maintenance behaviors are used more strategically than routinely. As adult siblings enact relational maintenance strategies, they "provide emotional, moral and psychological support, fulfill familial responsibilities, engage in shared activities, and remain involved in each other's lives" (Myers, 2011, p. 342), as noted in the following:

I have six brothers and sisters, and we are spread across the country from coast to coast. We all make an effort to keep in touch with each other through e-mail, blogging, Facebook, Skyping, phone calls, text messages, and visits. Much of our communication is focused around certain tasks such as going in together on a gift for Mother's Day or planning a family reunion or a visit. We provide each other emotional support through the ups and downs of life, such as acceptance into graduate school, marriage, pregnancy loss, unemployment, and illness. We are also in frequent contact about less monumental things—a text to my sister to see what she thought about the final episode of our favorite TV show or a quick online chat with my brother on his birthday. As far flung as we are geographically, all of these activities help us to feel close emotionally.

Adult siblings frequently confront the challenge of maintaining connections across many miles while raising their own children. Many older siblings pay greater attention to each other, communicating in ways that create positivity (Harwood, Rittenour, & Lin, 2013) as well as strengthening connections and providing counsel. Yet, some siblings drift apart over the years having never recovered from earlier slights or fights.

In certain cases, external factors support overall family relational maintenance. Some relationships continue, in a stagnant state, because geographically close members gather ritualistically for holidays but few maintain meaningful ties or barriers. Frequently an elderly parents' needs prevents the dissolution of sibling ties.

Relational Maintenance Strategies

Maintaining relationships requires attention and effort. When family members consciously focus on keeping their relationships strong, they are rewarded with strong ties. In addition to the identity-building strategies noted in the previous chapter, three major communication strategies serve to strengthen family relationships. These include confirmation, rituals, and relational currencies.

Confirmation

Confirming messages serve as the cornerstone of relational maintenance. Confirmation communicates recognition and acceptance of another human being—a fundamental precondition to intimacy. Sieburg (1973) provided four criteria for such messages: (1) acknowledging the other person's existence, (2) affirming the other's communication by responding relevantly to it, (3) reflecting and accepting the other's self-experience, and (4) suggesting a willingness to become involved with the other.

Confirming responses may be contrasted with two alternative responses: rejecting and disconfirming. Confirming responses imply an acceptance of the other person. Confirming messages do not necessarily suggest one person agrees with the other, but responses such as "I see" display one's regard without expressing agreement (Canary, Cody, & Manusov, 2008). Rejecting responses imply that the other is wrong or unacceptable. Messages include such statements as "That's really stupid" or "Don't act like a two-year-old." Disconfirming responses send an invalidating message telling the other "You do not exist." Disconfirming responses occur when a family member ignores another member, talks about the other person as if he or she is invisible, or excludes another from a conversation, or physical contact (Stafford & Dainton, 1994).

When my sister remarried, she and her new husband tried to pretend they did not have her 12-year-old son, Paul, living with them. Her new husband did not really want him. They would eat meals and forget to call him, plan trips and drop him with us at the last minute, and never check on his work in school. The kid was invisible in that house. Finally, his father took him, and Paul seems much happier now.

Recognition, dialogue, and acceptance characterize confirmation.

Recognition   Recognition indicates a willingness to be involved with the other. One may confirm another's existence verbally by recognition, which includes using the person's name, including him or her in conversation, or just acknowledging the individual's presence. Comments such as "I missed you" or "I'm glad to see you" serve to confirm another person's existence. Nonverbal confirmation is equally important in the recognition process. Touch, direct eye contact, and gestures also may serve to confirm another person within the norms of diverse cultures.

Dialogue   Dialogue implies an interactive involvement between two or more persons. Comments such as "Because I said so" and "You'll do it my way or not at all" do not reflect a dialogical attitude, whereas comments such as "What do you think?" or "I'm upset—can we talk about it?" open the door to dialogue and mutual exploration. Nonverbal dialogue occurs in families *when members share* in appropriate affectionate displays.

Acceptance   Acceptance occurs when we allow others to be themselves. Acceptance avoids interpreting or judging one another. It encourages hearing things you do not want to hear or working to understand another's perspective even if you disagree with it. If you feel accepted in a relationship, disagreements do not challenge how you feel in the relationship.

Confirming behavior in a current relationship often reflects one's family-of-origin patterns. Persons who grew up in an inexpressive family may have trouble satisfying the reassurance and recognition needs of a partner or a child. Cultural differences, in the use of eye contact or touch, may create a sense of disconfirmation for one partner. Family connections develop from each member's sense of acceptance. When family members continuously ignore each other or withhold affirming messages, relational maintenance remains an impossible goal. If one "learns to love by being loved," then one *only* learns to confirm by being confirmed.

Respect

Similar to acceptance, respect involves acting in a way that demonstrates honoring and caring for another and his or her well-being. Sometimes respect involves supporting another's choices, values, and actions, even though you view them as unwise or problematic. Many family members struggle when another member makes decisions that appear to reject family values or expectations, such as becoming a chef rather than a lawyer or choosing to remain childless when other siblings have chosen parenthood.

Respect involves two primary content components: equality/mutuality and caring/supportiveness (Hendrick & Hendrick, 2006). The first component implies a horizontal relationship characterized by respect or treating the other as a valued person. Among adults this implies that family members honor other members' choices and decisions even if they do not fully understand or value those choices. In a parent-child relationship, this would imply encouraging children to make their own decisions and choices, appropriate to their ages. Therefore, respect may mean supporting the child who chooses to become involved in theatre when everyone else in the family pursues athletics. It implies attending this child's plays just as parents attend another child's soccer games. Often this involves honoring another's decision that challenges your expectations. Essentially, "There is no 'one down' position with equality/mutuality" (Hendrick, Hendrick, & Logue, 2010, p. 128).

My parents migrated from the Philippines when my younger sister and I were in elementary school so we grew up in a much wider world, and learned to speak English fluently. We both attended a local college where my sister met her fiancé, Joseph, whose relatives arrived from Ireland in the early 1900s. His parents were accepting of his marriage plans but this was very hard for my parents. They did not forbid the marriage and after a few years, due to his kindness to all of us, my parents came to respect and embrace Joseph and treat him like another son.

The second characteristic implies engaging in "behaviors that are reciprocally thoughtful, considerate and designed to 'lift up' another" (Hendrick et al., 2010, p. 128). Such actions are as simple as visiting a family member in the hospital, although it interferes with holiday plan, or helping your aunt with her computer problems again and again. Although respect often implies honoring elders, the reverse also holds. A teenager witnessing a parent's alcoholism or abuse may find it challenging or impossible to respect that individual because of the pain that results from those circumstances.

Respect overlaps with the concept of relational currencies that is addressed later in the chapter.

Rituals

Rituals convey a variety of messages and meanings in emotionally powerful patterns; they remind family members who they are and how much they care about each other, as they reflect a family's relational culture.

One thing we NEVER do is go to bed alone. Ever. I don't go upstairs and get in bed and then Robert comes up later. Or vice versa. When we go to bed, we both go to bed. Together. (Bruess & Kudak, 2008a, n.p.)

Conscious repetition of actions and words creates meaning and eventually results in ongoing **family rituals**. These special meanings, enacted in repetitive form, contribute significantly to the establishment and preservation of a family's identity or relational culture as they honor something important in the relationship (Baxter & Braithwaite, 2006). Over time rituals serve ongoing maintenance and relational functions. Rituals are more than routine events; they serve a highly significant relational maintenance function. They may cluster around occasions such as dinnertime, errands, vacations, religious celebrations, or rites of passage such as birthdays, graduations, and weddings. Sometimes rituals form around less pleasurable events such as conflicts, discipline, or teasing. Such symbolic activity helps family members make sense of their lives. Thompson and Dickson (1995) asserted that rituals function as communication events; their symbolizing function leads to "sense-making," which involves remembering, belonging, instructing, and providing community.

Family rituals range from those connected to the overall culture, such as celebrating Halloween, to those known only to a few members, such as spiritual rituals or anniversary rituals, to everyday behaviors. Rituals may be categorized in the following manner:

1. Family celebrations, often tied to cultural norms, include the ways holidays are celebrated or that certain special events are recognized.
2. Family traditions, reflecting unique family occasions, embody patterns passed down by family-of-origin members.
3. Patterned family interactions, reflecting everyday connections, emerge out of increasingly patterned interactions usually developed implicitly (Wolin & Bennett, 1984; Baxter & Braithwaite, 2006).

Family ritual involves communication events that are voluntary, recurring, and patterned and "whose jointly enacted performance by family members pays homage to what they regard as sacred, thereby producing and reproducing a family's identity and its web of social relations" (Baxter & Braithwaite, 2006, pp. 262–263). Rituals connect members in meaningful ways. Although many significant family rituals involve highly ritualized holiday events, such as Thanksgiving softball games, we are focusing on repetitive, communicative moments that define everyday life for family members. Therefore, although rituals and routines (patterned behavioral interactions) coexist in families, rituals may be differentiated in that they give an ascribed meaning to ongoing patterned interactions (Crespo, Davide, Costa, & Fletcher, 2008). Thus, going to bed at the same time might be a practical couple routine; consciously deciding to always go to bed together carries significant meaning.

Couple Rituals   Expressions of affection, code words for secrets, and repetitive daily or weekly experiences are signs of a developing relational culture. Carol Bruess extensively researched relationship rituals, identifying rituals both for couples (Bruess & Kudak, 2008a) and for parents with young children (Bruess & Kudak, 2008b). Based on her earlier interview research, she developed the following typology of rituals (Bruess & Pearson, 1997, pp. 33–41):

1. *Couple time.* This frequently enacted ritual includes three types: enjoyable activities, togetherness rituals, and escape episodes. Enjoyable activities are illustrated by the couple who reports "playing volleyball every Tuesday" or watching foreign films. Togetherness refers to times when couples simply spend time being together, such as walks after dinner. Escape episodes include rituals specifically designed to satisfy couples' needs to be alone. Escape rituals, which provide "shared time," such as a monthly overnight stay in a hotel, provide couples with a way to create boundaries around themselves.

2. *Idiosyncratic/symbolic.* These rituals are divided into favorites, private codes, play rituals, and celebration rituals. Favorites include couples' most valued, and often symbolic, places to go, things to eat, items to purchase or give, and activities to do. For example, one woman reported that her husband's favorite cake is her wicky-wacky chocolate cake:

   > So when I really, really, really, really like him, and he's really, really, really, really made me happy, I bake him a wicky-wacky cake. He knows I'm really happy with him when he gets a wicky-wacky cake. (p. 35)

   Private code rituals include the repeated, idiosyncratic use of jointly developed words, symbols, or gestures for communicating. These have a unique and special meaning. Play rituals represent intimate fun in the form of couples' kidding, teasing, silliness, and/or playful bantering.

   Celebration rituals represent the shared practices couples enact when celebrating special holidays, birthdays, anniversaries, or other special events. Most involve established rules. One couple may celebrate every month's anniversary; another may have elaborate birthday surprise rituals.

3. *Daily routines/tasks.* These involve accomplishing ordinary activities, tasks, and chores and shared daily patterns. For instance, one partner will cook while the other cleans up.

4. *Intimacy expressions.* These rituals involve physical, symbolic, and verbal expressions of love, fondness, affection, or sexual attraction. Intimacy rituals link to relational currencies described later in the current chapter.

5. *Communication.* These rituals encompass couple talk time, including the specific times and ways couples establish opportunities for talking, sharing, or staying in touch, such as debriefing conversations, regular cell phone calls, or text messages.

6. *Patterns/habits/mannerisms.* These rituals involve interactional, territorial, and/or situational patterns or habits couples develop. For example, partners may always sleep on the same side of the bed or sit in the same chairs to watch television.

7. *Spiritual.* Certain rituals serve couples' religious needs and include praying or attending worship services together, saying grace before meals, or celebrating Shabbat weekly.

Rituals serve to maintain partners' relationships and signal their *coupleness* to the outside world. Rituals support partners' efforts to create a "marital culture" (Gottman & Silver, 1999). In their study of couples with children, Bruess and Kudak (2008b) identified rituals that keep partners connected while actively involved in parenting: these included examples such as putting the kids to bed together and, after they fall asleep, sitting in the room to talk about their day or current problems, or road-biking together on weekends. Such rituals keep the couples highly connected.

Many daily ritual conversations carry little meaning—"What's for dinner?" or "How's the homework going?" In their study of couples' daily conversations, Alberts, Yoshimura, Rabby, and Loschiavo (2005) found that satisfied couples tend to have more conflicts on the weekends while asking about each other's experiences than during the week. Their research identified 13 categories of couple conversations that might be considered routine, but not necessarily all the time. These authors address the differences in strategic versus routine couple conversations. A leisurely couple Saturday breakfast may become a highly meaningful ritual because it represents "their" time together to catch up.

An infrequent couple ritual involves the renewal of marriage vows. After interviewing couples who participated in such a ritual, Braithwaite and Baxter (1995) suggested that couples use this ceremonial event to "weave together their past, their present and their future commitments to one another" (p. 193). This ritual serves to maintain rather than repair the relationship, while communicating ongoing commitment to each other and a larger network of family and friends. In a later study of individuals engaged in a vow renewal ritual, Baxter and Braithwaite (2002) found the experience allowed couples to link two different idealizations of marriage—the public marriage, experienced with a community, and the private marriage of two expressive people. Countless couple rituals exist, but often their meaning remains overlooked.

Intergenerational Rituals   Rituals serve as a way to bond family members of all ages across generations, providing a sense of family identity and connection. Rituals frequently involve parents and children and, on occasion, grandparents or other relatives. Many working single parents consciously attempt to establish ongoing rituals, often with other single parents and children, to reinforce their family identity.

In a recent study of the variety of family-of-origin rituals experienced by South African young adults and the value attached to such rituals, researchers asked young adults to describe certain rituals and discuss the symbolic meaning or value they attach to these rituals (Smit, 2011). The most significant theme emerging from the narratives involved the importance of the family history or family story and the need to remember "where we came from" as well as to maintain family memories that have been passed from generation to generation through storytelling rituals.

Frequently, grandparents establish rituals with their grandchildren in order to reinforce their special connections. These may include regular phone calls, e-mails, sleepovers, special meals, everyday care, or summer trips, as indicated by this grandchild:

Ever since I was 5 years old, my grandfather has taken me on a trout fishing weekend in the mountains. He rents a cabin at a fishing camp. We spend most of the day in the streams and cook on a grill every night. Then we sit and stare at the stars and talk about life—usually this is really about me. Over the years, the conversations have changed from my baseball games to my career plans, but generally he asks and listens. Hopefully these will go on for a long time.

As families change over time, members discontinue or update their rituals. Sometimes changes in gender roles impact couple satisfaction with family rituals. For example, men appear to be happier when their partners report more family investment in rituals, but the more husbands reported their investment in family rituals, the less happy and close their wives were. This may occur because women view their husbands as intrusive, or find them to be critical of the plans and preparations (Crespo et al., 2008). Rituals reflect societal change, as indicated by divorce recognition greeting cards and divorce ceremonies as well as gay male and lesbian marriages and commitment ceremonies.

Many blended families struggle with the place of ritual in their lives. Their challenge is to selectively embrace certain features of both former families while creating new ones, so that members of both old and new family structures feel connected. As with other family forms, successful family rituals in the blended family "hold both sides" of the contradiction between old and new family systems. A study of stepfamily rituals reveals that (1) some unsuccessful rituals carried from the former family were perceived to threaten the new one and (2) ritual practices help well-functioning stepparents and stepchildren accept the historical roots of their blended family while constructing the new one (Baxter, Braithwaite, & Nicholson, 1999). In her study of post-bereaved stepfamilies (ones formed after the death of a parent), Bryant (2006) identified three different family experiences. *Integrated* families created rituals to memorialize and celebrate the deceased parent's life, such as taking flowers to the grave; *denial* families had no rituals acknowledging the deceased parent; and *segmented* families struggled with the presence-absence tension, often engaging in rituals that avoided direct acknowledgment of the deceased parent. Stepfamily research indicates a need for adapting old ritualized behaviors as well as creating new rituals that bond stepfamily members.

Specialized Circumstances: Health Rituals   Recent studies indicate that rituals may be good for members' physical and emotional health. For example, in a study of children with asthma, Santos, Crespo, Silva, and Canavarro (2012) found that when young people perceive their families as supporting frequent and symbolic events, such as dinnertime or annual celebrations, they experience their family as more cohesive and less conflictual than families without such rituals. In addition, because asthma may increase overall life stress and anxiety, rituals provide a sense of stability.

Family rituals tend to provide socio-emotional support, especially when family members experience high stress (Smit, 2011). In physical health-related stressful situations, cultural rituals may vary. When a family member faces serious illness, various rituals are viewed as normative at different phases; these rituals might include bedside vigils in hospitals and funeral rituals (Rolland, 2012). Latino culture supports frequent visits by extended family members to the patient's hospital room, and in Greek culture, a mother, even of a married son, would be expected to attend to her dying offspring in the hospital. Public family prayer rituals at the bedside and in houses of worship are common when a member is seriously ill or dying.

Family Ceremonials and Celebrations   Family ceremonials, such as weddings, graduations, and funerals, include several rituals (Trice & Beyer, 1984). These serve as major rites of passage. **Ceremonials** involve elaborate preparations. Weddings that include friends and family members serve to remind newlyweds of their support systems as they establish their new identity, yet partners who have cohabitated for multiple years may not strongly emphasize the social components of their marriage (Kalmijn, 2004). In addition, major cultural events such as Thanksgiving or the Fourth of July involve ritualized family celebrations. In their study of Thanksgiving rituals, Benoit and associates (1996) identified "chronicling" as the most frequently occurring verbal behavior. Chronicling refers to "talk about present events or those of the recent past, in which the communicator updates others by providing information about his or her life" (p. 22). Grandparents and older relatives are likely to elicit this news from children; the extended kinship network participates by sharing their news.

Although most family members experience identification and connection through their rituals, these opportunities may not be open to everyone. Participation

Holiday dinners usually involve family rituals.

in ritualistic family celebrations may be limited for members of the gay and lesbian community and those facing multiple problems such as poverty and illness (McGoldrick & Carter, 2003).

Negative Rituals   Although most of the writing and research on family or couple rituals reflects members' attempts to connect and convey caring in a positive manner, some families experience painful negative rituals. Family dinners or holidays may be painful and punishing in a family with alcoholic members. Children in alcoholic families may engage in a Monday morning ritual of watering down a parent's liquor bottles (Black, 2001). Even ordinary circumstances may foster negative rituals; when a younger child mispronounces a word, an older sibling may launch into a list of the child's other verbal mistakes, or when one spouse watches televised sports, the other may complain loudly about being deserted. Partner abuse may also become ritualized such as when a wife goes out with friends and is beaten for her absence and independence (Jacobson & Gottman, 1998). Incest becomes a destructive ritual played out in families when parent-child or sibling boundaries are shattered. Such negative rituals are difficult to identify because few individuals self-report their negative experiences (Bruess, 1997).

Relational Currencies

Affection is an important relational currency in families as it is something of value, as in the following example:

> Affection has always been displayed openly in my household. I remember as a young child sitting on my father's lap every Sunday to read the comic strips with him. I always hugged my father and mother, and still do. We still hang up our phone calls with the words, "I love you."

One partner may make sushi to please the other, or a grandfather may e-mail his granddaughter at college to share family news. Both of these instances represent an attempt to share affection, but the meaning depends on a shared perception of the value of the behavior.

Communication behaviors that carry meaning about the affection or caring dimension of human relationships can be viewed as relational currencies (Villard & Whipple, 1976), or a vocabulary of loving behaviors, sometimes called "love languages" (Chapman, 2004). Relational currencies serve as a symbolic exchange process. As family members share currencies, they form agreements about their meanings that either strengthen or weaken their relationship. Many currencies arise from family-of-origin patterns because every family implicitly and explicitly teaches its members specific ways to show caring for others and to accept caring from others (Wilkinson & Grill, 2011).

Types of Currencies   Certain currencies make a direct statement; the act is the message. For example, a hug can mean "I'm glad to see you" or "I'm sad that you are leaving" depending on the circumstances. Usually, the sender's intent is clear and easily interpreted. Other currencies permit a greater range of interpretation. After a family quarrel, does the arrival of flowers mean "I'm sorry, I was wrong" or

Positive verbal statements	Money
Self-disclosure	Food
Listening	Favors
Nonverbal affect displays	Service
Touch	Staying in touch
Sexuality	Time together
Aggression	Access rights
Gifts	

FIGURE 5.1

Sample relational currencies

"I still love you even if we don't agree on one issue"? Multiple relational currencies exist. The list that follows, and depicted in Figure 5.1, presents common ways family members share affection; you may add to or subtract from this list *based on your experiences*. Each of these currencies represents one way of sharing affection. The use of each currency must be considered within the contexts of gender, ethnicity, class, and a family's developmental stage (McGoldrick, Giordano, & Garcia-Preto, 2005b).

Positive Verbal Statements   Such statements include oral, written, and electronic messages indicating love, caring, praise, or support. In some households people express affection easily, saying "I love you" directly and frequently. Other families view such directness as unacceptable, preferring to save such words for very special situations. In some cultures, children receive little verbal praise (McGoldrick, 2005). Within families, age, gender, culture, and roles affect this currency.

Self-Disclosure   This currency involves self-revelation, or taking the risk of voluntarily telling another individual personal information or feelings that he or she is unlikely to discover from other sources. Johnson (2008) argued that the way to deepen a relationship involves *continually* reestablishing the emotional connection through openness, although, as we discussed in Chapter 3, family members do need to consider when and how to open and close privacy boundaries (Petronio, 2002). Generally self-disclosure serves to deepen understanding between people although occasionally it can be a manipulative strategy to gain information from another. As a relational currency, intentional self-disclosure serves to demonstrate trust and affection in a relationship. This currency is discussed in detail in Chapter 6.

Listening   Effective listening carries a message of involvement with, and attention to, another person. Having a partner or a parent with good listening skills builds relational rapport that result in the development of strong relational bonds and relational satisfaction (Gottman & DeClaire, 2001). Attentive listening may be taken for granted, thus discounting the listener's effort.

Positive Nonverbal Affect Displays   Affect displays involve spontaneous indications of feelings that may be positive or negative. Positive affect may be best characterized as one's eyes lighting up or face breaking into a smile at the sight of another, as well as a vocal shift to squeals of delight or softer, more intimate tones. These nonverbal affect displays indicate joy and comfort at being in the other's presence.

Touch   Touching serves as the language of physical intimacy. Positive physical contact carries a range of messages about caring, concern, love, comfort, or sexual interest. Touch contributes to one's physical and mental well-being. A very powerful currency, touching often conveys feelings that a family member may not be able to put into words.

Sexuality   For adult partners, sexuality provides a unique way to experience intimacy. Partners' discourse surrounding intercourse, as well as the act itself, combines to create a powerful message of affection and bonding. Conversely, inappropriate sexual contact can destroy family members' ties to each other. We discuss sexuality as a form of partner communication in Chapter 6.

Aggression   Aggressive actions, usually thought to be incompatible with affection, may serve to create an important emotional connection between members of certain families. Individuals who are uncomfortable with expressing intimacy directly may rely on verbal or physical aggression as signs of caring. Often children find teasing or poking each other as a way to connect to a sibling. When adults do not know how to express intimacy in constructive ways, they may use bickering, sarcasm, or belittling as their means of contact. For aggression to function as a relational currency, the target of the tease or put-down must be able to interpret these as signs of caring.

In addition to these rather personal verbal and nonverbal currencies that convey caring rather directly, other currencies may require more active interpretation in order to translate the level of caring. These include the following:

Gifts   Gifts serve as a tangible symbol of caring or remembering the other (Chapman, 2004). Viewing presents as currencies may be complicated by issues of cost, appropriateness, and reciprocity. In addition, the process of identifying, selecting, and presenting the gift serves as part of the currency. If partners grow up in families with similar attitudes and practices about gifting, celebrating birthdays or other gift-giving events will be comfortable; if the attitudes were dissimilar, partners may confront times of frustration until they establish a joint agreement about how to manage their gift-giving practices. When members of extended families represent divergent financial circumstances, individuals may have to hold discussions about how to manage gift-giving practices.

Money   Cash or checks serve as relational currencies in many families. When members of wealthy families use money as the major relational currency, a parent may not convey a message of affection by writing a check because others view it as impersonal and predictable. To be a relational currency, money must be given or loaned as a sign of affection and not as *an easy way to* meet a family or spousal obligation. In tough economic times family members experience giving or receiving money either as an obligation or a gift.

Food   A symbol of nurturing in many cultures, food has emerged as an important currency in romantic and immediate family relationships. Preparing and serving special food for a loved one serves as a major sign of affection in many relationships. Even websites reflect this growing trend to sharing caring, whether in dating couples, between partners, or among family members (http://pinterest.com/pinlovermary/food-showing-love/).

Favors   Frequently performing helpful, thoughtful acts for another becomes complicated by norms of reciprocity and equality. To be considered as relational currencies, favors must be performed willingly rather than in response to a spousal or parental order or expectation. The underlying caring message may be missed if the recipient takes the effort required by the favor for granted.

Service   Service implies a caring effort that evolves into a habitual behavior. Driving the car pool to athletic events, making a partner's coffee in the morning, or paying the bills reflect routine currencies. Many adolescents teach their grandparents how to function on the computer (Shellenbarger, 2011) and regularly answer their countless questions. Such services are frequently taken for granted, thus negating the underlying message of affection.

Staying in Touch   This currency implies efforts to maintain important relational ties, often across significant distances. Daily cell phone interaction between parents and college-age students usually conveys caring. Whereas teens are likely to text-message each other, most use cell phones to talk with parents (Lenhart, 2010). Although e-mail is especially useful for connecting with distant relatives, younger relatives are likely to text each other. Even if the conversations are not about intimate topics, the effort to stay in touch reflects caring.

Time Together   Being together, whether it is just "hanging out" or voluntarily accompanying a person on a trip or errand, carries the message "I enjoy being with you." Fathers report great tension between their desire to spend time with their children as a way of showing caring and workplace pressures (Duckworth & Buzzanell, 2009). This is a subtle currency with potential for being overlooked as an effort to show caring.

Access Rights   Allowing another person to use or borrow things you value is a currency when the permission is intended as a sign of affection. This is a currency due to the exclusive nature of the permission that is given only to persons one cares about.

This list of currencies does not represent the "last word" on the subject. You may identify unnamed currencies that you exchange or that you have observed in family systems. For example, Fujishin (2002) suggests that "doing nothing" can be a loving and powerful message in certain relationships because it may convey trust in what the other is doing. For instance, while a mother might want the laundry folded a certain way, she may refrain from saying that to her son who attempted to please her by doing the laundry. Across various cultures, currencies may convey different meanings or values for a specific currency.

Meanings and Currencies   Relational satisfaction is tied to perceptions about the relational currency exchange process. Although an individual may intend to convey affection, some family members may misinterpret that person's intentions. Pipher (1996) captures this idea, saying, "Two of ten people spend their lives searching for one kind of love, when all around them there is love if only they would see" (p. 142). When meanings are shared, rewards are experienced; when meanings are missed, costs are experienced. Over time, intimate partners will create common assumptions about the importance of certain currencies as they develop high levels of symbolic interdependence. Currencies may be exchanged with the best intentions, yet accurate interpretation occurs only when both parties can learn to speak the other's language.

The question remains: Does every partner realize that a favorite dinner or a repaired computer represents an attempt to show love? Perhaps you see others as more loving if they express their affection the same ways you do. Such similarity adds to symbolic interdependence and strengthens your relational culture.

Without common meanings for relational currencies, family members may feel taken for granted or rejected. One partner may place a high value on regular sexual relations. If the other partner holds similar views, their sexual currency will heighten their devotion; if not, these partners will struggle with communicating affection. As another example, fathers report being more affectionate with their sons than sons reported them being (Floyd & Morman, 2005). Such perceptual differences are very common. Therefore, "Understanding each other's love styles may help partners maintain a happy relationship" (Guerrero et al., 2014, p. 165).

Occasionally routine currencies may become strategic, changing their meaning. Holding hands while taking a walk may be routine touching, but reaching for another's hand after a fight may be strategic. Such a shift frequently reflects new attention to the currency, as noted in the following comment:

My mother and I often say "I love you" in a routine way. We take the phrase for granted. But, after a fight or if something bad happens to one of us, we tend to look directly at each other and say "I really do love you" just to make sure the message gets across.

Figure 5.2 provides a way to consider how a currency's meaning might be valued by two people. In quadrant 1, both persons value the currency, which makes communication relatively direct. In quadrants 2 and 3, one party values the currency but the other does not, leading to disappointments and missed messages. In quadrant 4, neither person values the currency; the agreement helps avoid missed messages.

What happens if family members wish to share affection but seem unable to exchange the currencies desired by others? Villard and Whipple (1976) concluded that spouses with more similar affection exchange behaviors were more likely to report (1) high levels of perceived equity and (2) higher levels of relationship satisfaction, thus greater relationship reward. Interestingly, accuracy in predicting (i.e., understanding) how the other spouse used currencies did not raise satisfaction levels.

Other

		Yes	No
Self	Yes	Both value the currency	You value the currency; other does not
	No	You do not value the currency; other does	Neither values the currency

FIGURE 5.2
Dyadic value of specific relational currency

For instance, knowing that your partner shows love through making elaborate meals does not mean that you will be more positive toward this currency if you prefer intimate talks. Individuals who were very accurate at predicting how their spouses would respond to certain currencies still reported low marital satisfaction levels if the couple was dissimilar in their affection behaviors, as indicated in the following:

When my wife went through a very bad time in her work, we bumped into our differences. My caring solution was to give advice, try to help more around the house, and leave some little gifts for her. These were not having much impact. Cyndi wanted someone to listen to her—empathically listen—not provide a list of suggestions. She wanted to be hugged and she needed verbal reassurance. Fortunately, Cyndi let her needs be known, and in the midst of that self-disclosing conversation a crisis was turned into an opportunity. Since that time, as I have worked to provide listening, compliments, and hugs, the bond between us has grown stronger.

Exchanging relational currencies benefits family members. High-affection communicators receive advantages in psychological, emotional, mental, social, and relational characteristics compared to low-affection communicators (Floyd, 2002). Because of their secure attachment style, they receive more affection from others.

A family's levels of cohesion and adaptability interact with its relational currencies. Highly cohesive families may expect high levels of affection displayed with regularity, whereas low-cohesion families may not provide enough affection for certain members. In families near the chaotic end of the flexibility continuum, members may vary the types of currencies valued, whereas more rigid systems may require the consistent use of a few specific currencies. Family themes may dictate currency exchange: The Hatfields' theme "We stick by each other through thick and thin" means that members should provide money to hard-pressed relatives.

Because a family system evolves constantly, the meaning of currencies changes. Some members change their affection strategies because of new experiences or expectations. A lost job may result in fewer gifts but greater sharing and doing favors within a family. The process of sharing relational currencies significantly affects family intimacy.

Conclusion

In this chapter we explored a range of communication practices that maintain partnered and family relationships while leading to closeness among members. It provided an overview of relational maintenance and a discussion of confirmation, respect, rituals, and relational currencies.

Think about the kinds of interactions you observe in the families around you. Under what conditions do members confirm each other? How is respect or disrespect for others conveyed? How do members attempt to connect through rituals and relational currencies? To what extent do these communication behaviors reflective of the family ethnicity? All human beings long for connectedness, but it is a rare family in which the members (spouses, parents and children, siblings, grandparents) consciously strive for greater sharing over long periods of time. Such mutual commitment provides rewards known only to those who put forth their best efforts.

In Review

1. Take a position on the following statement: "If you have to work at a relationship, there is something wrong with the relationship." Give your reasons for the position.
2. Observe the use of confirming behaviors in a particular family relationship and indicate the extent to which the receiver appears to recognize the effort. Explain how some attempts at confirmation might be taken for granted after a while.
3. Interview three individuals to provide you with examples of confirmation and disconfirmation in their families.
4. Identify three everyday face-to-face or mediated rituals that partners use to connect with each other. How effective are their efforts?
5. Reflect on a dyadic family relationship (parent-child, partners, siblings) that you consider as well maintained. Describe two specific relational currencies that convey affection on the part of each individual and explain why they convey affection.
6. Interview someone from another culture to describe (1) the most significant relational strategies in their culture and (2) the relational strategies used in U.S. culture that would not be appropriate in his or her culture.

Key Words

Acceptance   117

Assurances   113

Ceremonials   123

Confirming messages   116

Dialogue   117

Family rituals   119

Negative rituals   124

Openness   112

Positivity   112

Recognition   117

Relational currencies   111

Relational maintenance   111

Respect   111

CHAPTER 6

Intimacy within Partnerships and Families

LEARNING OBJECTIVES

- Assess the importance of communication to partner and family intimacy
- Explain the significance of commitment to members of a real or fictional family
- Illustrate the concepts of sacrifice, forgiveness, and sanctification
- Compare the benefits and costs of total self-disclosure in family relationships
- Explain the challenges of talking about sexuality with children and adolescents
- Create guidelines for parents on how to talk about sex with their children
- Illustrate the barriers to partner and family intimacy

Angela, the oldest of three daughters and a young professional at a major San Francisco bank, lives in a downtown high-rise apartment building, but spends many weekends at home or hanging out with her younger sisters in the city. Her middle sister, Valeria, a star on the basketball team of a local state college, never comes home. Her other sister, Andrea, is completing her junior year in high school while working 15 hours a week as a hostess at a local restaurant. Their mother, Teresa, and alcoholic father, Joseph, work as emergency medical technicians on alternate schedules. Over the past ten years the couple's fights have escalated, leaving the young women frightened and frustrated. They have encouraged their mother to leave their father but instead she copes by working extra hours and going out with friends. When Angela left for college she felt like she was abandoning her younger sisters; after Valeria left for college, Angela determined to save Andrea from the fighting and turmoil at home.

Currently, Angela spends weekends at her parents' home outside the city or invites Andrea to stay at her apartment. Sometimes they will watch Valeria's games and hang out together on her campus; other times they enjoy the coffee shops and events in the city. Angela spends many hours advising Andrea on the college application process; she plans to take her to visit some schools outside California in the next few months. Andrea talks about how lonely she is at home because her parents fight, and when Dad drinks, she wants to run away. Angela listens, reassuring her that, if Dad becomes abusive, Andrea must move in with her. During their hours together these sisters share dreams, plan their futures, and reassure one another that "We will always be there for each other."

Their friends talk about Max and Julie's relationship as incredibly special. Married for nine years to her college sweetheart, Julie still lights up when he enters a room. In turn, Max knows just how to make her laugh. Although Julie worries about her father with Alzheimer's and Max carries the burden of losing his younger brother in a car accident, they find ways to bring joy to each other on a daily basis. Their rule "Never go to bed without a kiss" means that they have to settle any disagreements before going to sleep. Usually, it's easy, but sometimes it takes an hour before that kiss. Each checks in with the other during the day, often texting a love message. When Max travels for business, affectionate notes appear in his suitcase; when Julie goes on her annual "Girls Weekend," flowers appear in her hotel room with a note, "Love, Me."

Life has its complications. After two years of trying to conceive a child, Julie learned that a condition called endometriosis might prevent a pregnancy. This diagnosis led to long discussions about shared dreams and other routes to parenthood, and a decision to wait for a few more years before moving forward with adoption plans. Although stressful, these conversations bring them even closer together as each reaffirms a commitment to their marriage, with or without children. Currently they are planning a wedding anniversary camping trip to the Grand Tetons, where they honeymooned almost a decade ago.

Family connections, sometimes solid and sometimes fragile, depend on members' communicative efforts to create connections and intimacy. Although some relationships are maintained at low to moderate levels of connection for long periods, many family relationships reach a level of intimacy that involves sharing interpersonal emotions including love, warmth, passion, and joy (Guerrero, Anderson, & Afifi, 2014). We can think about intimacy as the glue that holds relationships together.

The word intimacy comes from the Latin term *intimus*, meaning "inner." Most individuals develop a personal sense of what intimacy means but multiple definitions exist. The term presence, or "being there" for another, may be understood as intimacy; it implies physical, emotional, and cognitive presence (Foley & Duck, 2006). Intimacy involves a cluster of interpersonal emotions including love, warmth, passion, and joy that are tied to intimate feelings (Guerrero et al., 2014). Essentially all definitions of intimacy share one important feature, "a feeling of closeness and connectedness that develops through communication between partners" (Laurenceau, Feldman-Barrett, & Rovine, 2005).

Marital partnership and family intimacy reflect many similarities. Marital intimacy involves the following characteristics: (1) a close, familiar, and usually affectionate or loving personal relationship; (2) a detailed and deep knowledge and understanding from close personal connection or familiar experience; and (3) sexual relations (Feldman, 1979). The renowned marital researcher John Gottman (1994b) maintains that stable couples exhibit a 5:1 ratio of positive messages to negative messages, evidenced by indicators such as displaying interest, affection, caring, acceptance, empathy, and joy. Intimacy research tends to focus on marriages or adult partnerships but, with the exception of sexual relations, these same characteristics may apply to all family relationships. Clearly, sibling intimacy differs from intimacy between children and parents or other relatives, but all of them share some characteristics in common. Family intimacy involves interpersonal devotion along intellectual, emotional, and physical dimensions, demonstrated by shared knowledge and understanding of others as well as close loving relationships appropriately reflective of developmental stages and culture. Intimacy becomes a reality through partners' and family members' communication practices.

Family intimacy reflects the interactions of members as they manage dialectical struggles over many years. This intimacy also reflects each member's past intimate experiences, current need for intimacy, perception of the other(s), and desire for maintaining or increasing connections within a particular relationship. Yet, over time, each individual experiences differing needs for and comfort with intimate ties. Schnarch (1991) argued that sometimes expectations of reciprocity promote unrealistic expectations of emotional fusion that are "alien to the acute experience of self and partner as related entities" (p. 116). Therefore, when one member of a couple or another family member feels that the intimacy is becoming too great, he or she will initiate a conflict or withdraw in order to decrease the interpersonal closeness. This is a type of relational calibration.

The same calibration process may be enacted in other family relationships. Each family subsystem sets limits for acceptable expression of intimacy at a given point in time. A small son and his mother may cuddle, tickle, kiss, and hug. A teenager and stepmother may discuss the adolescent's personal hopes or dreams and exchange kisses on occasion. A husband and wife develop limits for acceptable and unacceptable sexual intimacy as well as sharing feelings and showing nonverbal affection. Intimacy expressions change over time; touch may become more or less important whereas the desire to share dreams may reappear at critical life moments. True intimacy occurs most often in two-person relationships, although certain sibling groups or other subgroups may also experience it. The following comment indicates how higher levels of intimacy can emerge after years of partnership:

After 26 years of marriage, my parents seem to have grown closer. They often hold hands. They share common interests in music and theater. They just can't get enough of each other, but each has special friends and interests, which balances their intensity. Life hasn't been all that easy for them, yet each has helped the other cope.

Finally, intimacy is tied to overall family themes, images, boundaries, and biosocial issues. Family themes that stress verbal sharing, such as "There is no need to carry secrets alone," may promote honest disclosure if both or all feel supported; if not, secrets will prevail. Viewing family members as a team may convey closeness. Boundaries influence the extent to which intimacy occurs in family subsystems and how intimacy develops with those outside the immediate family. Gender-related attitudes support or restrict the capacity of members to express intimacy directly. Knowing information about another family member is not sufficient to develop intimacy. Relational growth depends on meaningful communication about that knowledge (Duck, Miell, & Miell, 1984).

The basis for all well-functioning family relationships lies in the members' abilities to co-construct and share meanings through communication. Countless writings on enduring and/or healthy marriages or families emphasize the importance of communication as a hallmark of successful family relationships (Covey, 1997; Foley & Duck, 2006; Gottman, 1994b, 1999). Marital and family intimacy develops from the base of relational maintenance behaviors, discussed in Chapter 5.

In this chapter we will examine major factors that serve to undergird the development of communication-related closeness and intimacy as well as factors that threaten intimate ties. The former include commitment, self-disclosure, and sexual communication. Other factors, such as effort and sacrifice, **forgiveness,** and sanctification also contribute to relational intimacy. **Intimacy barriers** include jealousy and deception. Because closeness is co-constructed in the ongoing management of both interdependence and independence, differences and struggles are inevitable.

Commitment

"If you have to work at a relationship, there's something wrong with it. A relationship is either good or it's not." These words capture a naive but common belief about marital and family relationships. **Commitment,** a complex and sometimes overlooked, relational concept, plays a significant role in relational intimacy over decades. An examination of the concept revealed three types of commitment (Johnson, Caughlin, & Huston, 1999): personal commitment (the rewards inherent from the relationship), moral commitment (an obligation to a partner), and structural commitment (barriers to leaving the relationship and the absence of viable alternatives). Although the following discussion reflects the dynamics of personal commitment, many partners report that, during some rough or painful periods, their promise of commitment held the partnership together. Although lack of funds, religious commitments, values, or family pressures may serve to keep partners together, we do not consider these reasons for staying together as meaningful commitment.

It is only through personal commitment that a loving relationship remains a vital and vibrant part of one's life. Personal commitment implies intense singular energy directed toward sustaining a relationship. As such, it emphasizes a partnership relationship, which limits other possibilities. This dual reality represents the key distinction between "commitment as the intrinsic desire to be with the partner in the future and commitment defined in terms of limits on personal choice" (Fincham, Stanley, & Beach, 2007, p. 280). Baxter and Braithwaite (2002) sought to understand commitment by interviewing couples who took part in a ritual to renew their marriage vows. They found that these couples viewed commitment as a "lifetime promise to stay in the marriage, not a fair-weather declaration to be abandoned when maintaining the relationship became effortful" (p. 103). A study of dating and married couples reveals that the relationships of married couples revolve around upholding the commitment made to their partners (Molden & Finkel, 2010). Other researchers assert that "getting married doesn't merely certify a preexisting love relationship. Marriage actually changes people's goals and behaviors" (Waite & Gallagher, 2000, p. 17). Other family relationships experience commitment differently as these do not rely on a singular tie as marriage does. Siblings and other relatives may experience multiple commitments within the extended family including fictive or chosen kin.

Even the strongest, personal commitment may encounter significant challenges over the life span of the family, such as when one partner becomes disabled or addicted to drugs. In his discussion of adjusting to his wife's progressive neuromuscular disease, hearing loss, and stroke, Piercy (2006) describes how his marriage changed in later life: "When Susan and I talk together with friends, I make sure that she can follow the conversation. When we go out, I make sure she navigates the steps. Our shifting system rebalances, and we move on" (p. F13).

Approaches to relationships based on equity would predict that we put into relationships what we get out of them (Stafford, 2008). Yet mature adult commitment in intimate relationships goes deeper than an equity model of reciprocity. It cannot be measured in amount that one gives to the relationship, because the depth of the commitment is associated with higher relationship satisfaction and stability and with behaviors that maintain and enhance the quality of relationships (Flanagan et al., 2002). In her exploration of a marital life of commitment during a period of geographic separation, Diggs (2001) examined her own 24-year marriage as an African American from inside the relationship. Her writing captures the intensity of connection and the gender differences in emphasizing emotional versus physical presence, and concludes by suggesting that their commitment is characterized by "displays of love, and physical presence (emotional and instrumental), and dialoguing to find a connection (I feel ya; refocus on the person or values that keeps a couple together; and the awareness of levels or areas of unity)" (p. 25).

Intensity, repetition, explicitness, and codification support commitment talk. Certain phrases need to be asserted firmly and then reaffirmed. Explicitness reduces misunderstanding: "I will stand behind you, even if I don't agree." Such a comment makes the commitment quite clear. Codifying means explicit communication and may involve anything from love letters to written rules for fighting, to a marital contract. In the opening vignette of a couple, loving partners Max and Julie continuously reaffirm their love and commitment to each other in everyday meaningful ways. Parental commitment to a child, a one-sided implicit promise, emerges and is codified in the many comments or conversations reassuring one's offspring that "Daddy will always love you" or "I will always be there for you." In many cases it is not just what we say, but how we say it that counts or "The way we enact our commitment talk is at least as important, if not more so, than the content itself" (Knapp & Vangelisti, 2005, p. 297).

One way that we express and celebrate commitment is through a ritual, such as an engagement or marriage ceremony. While this option has been until relatively recently available to only heterosexual couples, an increasing number of same-sex couples are choosing to marry, participate in commitment ceremonies, or enact commitment in different ways. In a study of 20 long-term cohabiting same-sex couples, 60 percent reported forming committed relationships as they moved through the years without a ceremony. Most did not believe the commitment ceremony made a significant difference since it was not legal, but some respondents reported that holding a commitment ceremony was a transition point for the relationships. I recognized their many years together and signaled that they were "out" as a couple to those around them. Yet, the majority of these individuals reported desiring legal same-sex marriage, which is becoming possible in an increasing number of states (Reczek, Elliott, & Umberson, 2009).

Finally, some individuals in long-term marriages report that the legal commitment of a marriage ceremony provided the glue that kept them together at times when things seemed to be falling apart. The family therapist Randy Fujishin asked one of his dearest friends, who had been married for more than 55 years, to what she attributed her long marriage. She answered, "The knowledge that some decades are harder than others" (2002, pp. 3–4). Sometimes a legal or strong personal commitment provides the resolve that moves partners and family members through very difficult periods of time.

Having lived with a partner who struggled with drug addiction for more than a decade, I can honestly say that there were times when the marriage certificate provided the only reason I did not leave. I took a solemn vow including the words "Until death do us part." That, and only that, formed the final link in our relational chain that did not break.

Self-Expression: Disclosure and Nonverbal Affection

Intimacy is an "experiential outcome of an interpersonal, transactional, intimacy process reflecting two principal components: self-revealing and partner responsiveness" (Laurenceau et al., 2005, p. 315). Such self-expression involving self-revelation or **self-disclosure** as well as nonverbal emotional expressiveness represents a highly significant, complex, and sometimes difficult interpersonal communication (Segrin & Flora, 2011). Self-disclosure occurs when one person intentionally tells another person highly personal or private information about himself or herself that the other would not discover in a different manner. Self-disclosure always involves some level of risk on the part of the discloser, as anything you disclose about your experiences or feelings risks misunderstanding or rejection by the other. For the discloser to experience intimacy, the listener must respond verbally or nonverbally in a manner that conveys validation, understanding, and caring (Laurenceau et al., 2005). This creates intersubjectivity, or communicators' access to each other's thoughts and feelings (Foley & Duck, 2006), which is a prerequisite for true sharing. As we discussed in Chapter 3, members of families are continually negotiating privacy boundaries with each other as they understand that knowing what and when to reveal and conceal information is an important choice in close relationships.

Trust, the essence of which is emotional safety, serves as the foundation for disclosure because "trust enables you to put your deepest feelings and fears in the palm of your partner's hand, knowing they will be handled with care" (Avery, 1989, p. 27). High mutual self-disclosure occurs within family relationships characterized by a strong relational culture of trust, confirmation, and affection. Essentially, disclosure serves to create **mental love maps** of "the other" in a relationship (Gottman, 1999): it permits access to deeper parts of another's life. Partners and family members establish and communicate trust by honoring boundary coordination rules and maintaining private information in the relationship (Petronio, 2002). Too much or little information shared in a relationship or consistently high levels of negative disclosure may occur within some close relationships, resulting in boundary turbulence and high levels of conflict, hurt, and anger. In the end, because trust depends on appropriate openness, partners and family members need to pay careful attention to when and how they coordinate revealing information to each other, especially disclosures that involve emotions. Family members build and preserve trust by communicating and managing information within the family and with those external to the family.

In addition, self-expression may be enacted through expressing affection non-verbally, including physical connections, such as reaching for another's hand, holding another person, or an intense visual gaze. These serve as "bids" for affection (Gottman & DeClaire, 2001). Back rubs, hand-holding, intense visual stares, or kisses often accompany or substitute for verbal self-disclosure.

"Even after 23 years I see moments when my mothers signal each other affectionately and I can imagine them as young people falling in love. Mom starts to give Momma a shoulder rub. The next thing I know is that one is sitting in the other's lap and they are laughing."

Parent-adolescent self-disclosure paves the way for strong adult relationships.

In the following subsections, we address disclosure and privacy in greater depth, given how important they are to establishing and maintaining intimacy.

Family Background

Family-of-origin experiences, cultural heritage, and gender set expectations for appropriate management of privacy boundaries (Petronio, 2002). Ethnic heritage sometimes influences the amount and type of self-disclosure appropriate for a given relationship. For example, in many Japanese families, the degree of intimacy is prescribed by position or status; members rely heavily on nonverbal communication to share critical feelings and important messages (Shibusawa, 2005). Whereas Jewish families often exhibit verbal skill and a willingness to talk about trouble and feelings, Irish families may find themselves at a loss to describe inner feelings (McGoldrick, 2005). Verbal emotional disclosure is viewed as a more feminine style of relating, whereas the more masculine style of connecting privileges sharing joint activities. Accordingly, women may initiate and receive more disclosures than do men (Wood, 2013).

Rules for privacy boundary management are influenced by the type of family relationship. For example, intimacy within in-law and stepfamily relationships reflects the willingness and ability of family members to self-disclose outside biological ties and to manage the complex ties. Sometimes a biological mother may need to step out of the middle of the relationship between her children and their stepfather and let them work out and strengthen their relationship (Weaver & Coleman, 2010). When a spouse mediates the relationship between a partner and his or her parents, conflict may be avoided but intimacy between the in-laws remains elusive (Prentice, 2008). These examples demonstrate that it takes moving through periods of interpersonal struggle to reach a point when members disclose directly and manage boundaries appropriate with newer family members.

Partner Relationships

Marital self-disclosure involves not only the disclosure by one partner but the listener's responses perceived as supportive, understanding, accepting, or caring. Marital partners must successfully create and coordinate dyadic privacy boundaries, all of which change over the life of the marriage (Petronio, 2002). Partner responsiveness undergirds the development of satisfying and close relationships. A major study of marital intimacy involving spouses writing diary entries for 42 evenings revealed that "both self-disclosure and partner disclosure significantly predicted rating of intimacy for husbands and wives on a day to day basis" (Laurenceau et al., 2005, p. 321). These researchers found that perceptions of responsiveness to self-disclosures served as an important predictor of experiencing feelings of intimacy daily.

High levels of disclosure of negative feelings contribute to decreased marital satisfaction. Dissatisfied marital partners often invalidate the feelings disclosed by a spouse about relational difficulties, a move that negatively impacts marital satisfaction (Clements, Cordova, Markman, & Laurenceau, 1997). Partners who feel comfortable sharing their emotions and discussing issues in their marriage are more satisfied (Finkenauer & Hazam, 2000). Yet, couples who insist on "No secrets" frequently discover such openness obliterates any sense of individuality (Imber-Black, 1998).

Serious individual health issues raise disclosure concerns for couples, especially if partners differ on whether or how to share certain information. For example, in cases of infertility, Goldsmith (2009) suggested that the partnership context draws attention to their "interdependence as a distinctive feature of uncertainty management" (p. 205) as partners struggle with what to say to each other and to those outside of the dyad. For example, when struggling with infertility issues, individuals or partners confront questions about sharing this information with other family members or friends. A related study discusses multiple ways that women concealed or revealed their infertility struggles including providing minimal details or denying the issue (Bute & Vik, 2010). Such circumstances confront partners with experiencing empathic distress, discussing feelings, engaging in joint problem-solving, and buffering or hiding concerns to protect the other. Decisions about disclosure and managing privacy boundaries have a direct impact on partner intimacy.

Parent-Child Relationships

Parent-child disclosure is central to expressing and maintaining intimacy in this primary relationship. Petronio (2002) points out that rules of disclosure and maintenance of privacy boundaries do not involve all family members equally. In general, mothers receive more disclosure from children than fathers but, in some cases, parents perceived as nurturing and supportive elicit more disclosure. Although older studies indicated that college students were more likely to disclose more information more honestly to same-sex best friends than to either parent, contemporary relationships between many college students and their parents invalidate that claim as many children have very open with their parents. Factors such as smaller families, a desire to remain interconnected, and constant mediated accessibility have contributed to a greater sense of openness, although this does not apply in certain cultures (Galvin, 2008). Unlike earlier generations that had reduced interaction when children went away to college or moved from home, it is not unusual for today's parents and children, who may remain connected through regular phone calls, texts, and social media like Facebook.

For parents and adolescents or young adult, negotiating privacy boundaries can be challenging as parents and children struggle to maintain intimacy at the same time that children are establishing independence. The children may perceive that parental privacy invasion occurs as they struggle with autonomy and closeness-boundary conflicts resulting in secrecy or confrontation. Because adolescents tend to narrow the topics considered legitimate for parents to share, teens will limit the areas they consider legitimate for parents to regulate leading to partial disclosure, distortion, and lying (Darling, Cumsille, Caldwell, & Dowdy, 2006). In her study of mother-daughter pairs, Miller-Day (2004) found significant differences in self-disclosure between pairs that were connected and those that were enmeshed, representing an unhealthy connection. The connected pairs were more comfortable with sharing and managing boundaries appropriately. The enmeshed pairs tended to exhibit great demands for disclosure and a great need for individual secrecy to maintain a sense of personal identity.

The nature of the disclosure topic impacts intimacy as well. While children or parents do not behave or make expected life choices, intimacy can be threatened.

Recognizing how to disclose and talk about these issues is important. Parental reactions to their child's disclosure that they are gay or lesbian can be very challenging for the parent-child relationship. In many cases, common initial parental responses to the disclosure involve sadness, denial, anger, and self-blame; although some mothers were supportive, the majority responded with some degree of negativity, denial, or intolerance (Willoughby, Doty, & Malik, 2008).

Sometimes newly divorced parents turn to children as confidants and comforters, which can increase their intimacy. However, there is a danger when a parent reveals so much personal information that is inappropriate for their child's age or the child feels caught in the middle between the parents. Researchers have found that divorced mothers may believe they need daughters to listen to their negative feelings about their ex-husbands and financial and personal worries, creating distress for the younger women (Koerner, Wallace, Lehman, & Raymond, 2002). Clearly, appropriate disclosure and boundary management is important to establishing and maintaining intimacy and we discuss some strategies in the following subsection.

Managing Privacy Boundaries and Disclosure

Disclosing private information to loved ones can create complications. Clearly we have established the link between appropriate disclosure and intimacy for couples and families and discussed the importance of effective disclosure rules and boundary coordination. Prioritizing spending time and engaging in everyday talk together establishes a pattern of disclosure that is important to building and maintaining relationships. Vangelisti and Banski (1993) reported that if couples hold **debriefing conversations,** or talk about how their day unfolded, they more likely to experience marital satisfaction. You can imagine this kind of talk in Max and Julie's relationship, described in the case at the beginning of this chapter. We believe this is the case for families as well. Everyday conversations set the groundwork for discussing riskier topics when the need arises. In addition, some circumstances, such as long rides in a car or a ritual of taking a walk in the evening, encourage members to share information with one another. If family members rarely talk openly, it will be difficult if not impossible to preserve relationships and navigate difficult situations that arise. As intimacy decreases, so does their ability to interact and work together in difficult situations, such as when they needed to work together when their mother became ill.

Joint living space provides the potential for everyday interaction and establishing privacy rules that encourage, positive, trusting relationships. These days, especially with all of the different communication technologies available, families engage in ongoing communication even when they live apart (Mesch & Frankel, 2011). Think about all of the different ways that you and your adult family members communicate, especially those who do not live together or near one another. You have options to call, text, e-mail, share photos and videos online, and Skype, just to name a few. Until relatively recently, these technologies were unavailable or available only to those with great financial means.

Whether connecting face to face or via technology, family members must navigate private information, establishing shared and workable rules for managing privacy boundaries. For example, a parent may break a child's trust unwittingly by discussing the child's concern with another adult, not respecting the child's privacy. Unless disclosers indicate how private certain information is to them, another person may accidentally reveal that information to others. This, as noted in the following quote, damages the relationship:

I have stopped discussing anything important with my mother because she cannot keep her mouth shut. She has told my aunt and some friends at work all about my relationship with my boyfriend, my use of birth control pills, and some of my health problems. Well, she doesn't have much to tell them now since she doesn't hear about my real concerns anymore.

Sibling disclosure becomes increasingly important as sibling ties represent the longest-lasting relationships across the life span. Even sibling relationships that were fraught with conflict and competition during childhood may become increasingly intimate as young adults learn to share their significant feelings and protect their siblings' confidences. The process of sharing oneself with another tends to emerge in adolescence. Younger adolescents' sibling disclosure occurs based on their perceptions of their relational connection to a brother or sister (Howe, Aquan-Assee, Bukowski, Lehoux, & Rinaldi, 2001). Disclosers felt positively about sharing when warmth and closeness existed in their sibling connection. As discussed in Chapter 3, communication privacy management theory holds that if self-disclosure messages are not carefully coordinated, boundary turbulence occurs. For example, when a brother posts a congratulatory message about his sister's pregnancy on social media before she is able to reveal her own news, she may become angry.

Recent scientific and medical advances, particularly in the area of genetics, raise critical self-disclosure issues for family members. The proband, or first family member identified with a genetic disease, often carries the responsibility of informing other members of their potential risks. Issues such as gender, relationship to certain relatives, privacy rules, the nature of the disease, and culture influence such disclosures (Gaff et al., 2007). When an individual or couple decides to use a sperm donor to achieve parenthood, decisions about disclosing this choice to other relatives or to the child remain controversial (Golombok, MacCallum, Goodman, & Rutter, 2002).

Managing privacy boundaries bears a direct relationship to family levels of cohesion, flexibility, and ultimately intimacy. An extremely cohesive family may resist members' negative self-disclosures, fearing the disclosures would threaten their connectedness, particularly if the family has a low capacity for adaptation. For example, a highly cohesive family with a theme of "We can depend only on each other" would resist negative disclosures. Families with moderate to high adaptation and cohesion capacities may cope relatively well with the effects of high levels of positive or negative self-disclosure. Essentially, "The complex dynamics of individual disclosures can contribute to the construction of a family identity" (Foley & Duck, 2006, p. 193).

Sexuality and Communication

Sexuality within a marriage or committed adult partnership involves far more than just physical performance; it involves the members' sexual identities, their history of sexual issues, their mutual perceptions of each other's' needs, their feelings for their partners, the implicit messages within their sexual expression, and the nature of their **sexual communication**. The quality of the sexual relationship affects, and is affected by, the other characteristics of intimacy—the partners' mutual knowledge and their affectionate/loving relationship. These characteristics influence partners' overall sexual patterns as well as day-to-day sexual expressions (Ridley, Collins, Reesing, & Lucero, 2006).

At the partnership level, "communication plays an important role in the development of intimate sexuality" (Troth & Peterson, 2000, p. 195). Sexual communication involves "people exchanging verbal and nonverbal messages in a mutual effort to co-create meaning about sexual beliefs, attitudes, values, and/or behavior" (Warren & Warren, 2013, p. 5). This definition presents a broader conception than the narrower depiction of sexual communication as the transmission of sexual information. Sexuality, including sexual attitudes and behavior, may be viewed as a topic of communication, a form of communication, and a contributing factor to overall relational intimacy and satisfaction. Sprecher and McKinney (1994) suggested, "Sex is not only an act of communication or self-disclosure. Verbal and nonverbal communication is essential for the accomplishment of rewarding sexual episodes" (p. 206). Although sexuality and intimacy are disconnected in certain relationships, we view sexuality as directly related to partner intimacy and family ties. In the next pages we will explore sexuality in terms of partner communication, parent-child communication, and communication problems within family relationships.

The basis for a mutually intimate sexual relationship reflects each partner's orientation toward sexuality, including what each learned in their families of origin. Personal identities include sexual/gender identity as a core component, which influences later sexual experiences. The sexual dimensions of family life link strongly to gender identities, personal boundaries, and developmental change. Your attitudes about sex, and your own sexual behavior, reflect your biosocial beliefs regarding sexuality learned in your family of origin. Many parents possess a set of gender-specific ideas about males and females developed from their childhood experiences and from "typical" behaviors of girls or boys of similar ages to their children. In addition, cultural background influences expectations about what it means to be a male or female.

Partner Sexual Communication

As an individual develops sexual experiences and a sexual identity, his or her personal background influences these encounters, as does the partner's sexual identity. Partners establish their own patterns of sexual activity early in the relationship, although sexual desire changes over time. For example, a German study revealed that sexual activity and sexual satisfaction decline in men and women, ages 19–31, in steady partnerships (Klusmann, 2002). Researchers also found strong links between sexual desire and interpersonal intimacy. Couples kept diaries for 56 days on their interpersonal affect (feelings for the partner) for one another and sexual desire for one another. The researchers found that mutual lust or desire was influenced by relational affect and current relational state. Partners' lust and positive and negative feelings were associated with the other spouse's lust. On days when partners had relatively positive feelings toward the other, those others were also likely to experience higher lust and vice versa (Ridley et al., 2006).

Open communication becomes critical for both individuals, since a good sexual relationship depends on being able to express what is satisfying to each partner. Therefore we will spend a great deal of space in this chapter discussing the importance of appropriate disclosure. A couple that cannot communicate effectively about many areas of their life will have difficulty communicating effectively about their sexual life. Such direct and honest conversations between partners about their sexual relationship enhance a sense of mutuality. In one of the few studies that address communication during sex, Babin (2012) examined a model in which sexual communication apprehension and sexual self-esteem were expected to predict partners' verbal and nonverbal communication of pleasure during sex. Her study of 207 individuals, the majority of whom were in committed or married relationships, identified only nonverbal communication as a significant predictor of sexual satisfaction.

A combination of self-disclosure and sensitivity to partner desires that are communicated nonverbally is important to understanding the needs and desires of one's partner in order to give sexual pleasure to the other. Put another way, it is important to understand the distinction between *monological* and *dialogical* sex. Monological sex implies that one or both partners attempt to satisfy only their personal needs. Dialogical sex is characterized by mutual concern and sharing of pleasure (Wilkinson, 2006), which can be accomplished only through effective sexual communication.

Partners may find it difficult to talk about their sexual relationship as sex remains a taboo topic for many people. However, compared to a few decades ago, talk about sex and intercourse occurs much more frequently and is less stigmatized than it once was. Slang or euphemisms for sex and body parts may serve partners well in order to promote the desired erotic climate but create disappointment or distance when they replace honest dialogue. Satisfied couples report their ability to directly discuss topics such as feelings about sex, desired frequency of intercourse, who initiates sex, desired foreplay, sexual techniques, or positions. They avoid "mind reading," such as "If she really loved me, she'd know I would like ..." Partners must develop ways to engage in sexual self-disclosure. A study of dating investigated two pathways between sexual self-disclosure and sexual satisfaction—the expressive and instrumental paths (MacNeil & Byers, 2005). The expressive pathway implies reciprocal sexual self-disclosure contributes to relationship satisfaction, which leads to greater sexual satisfaction. The instrumental pathway implies one's own sexual self-disclosure leads to greater partner understanding of one's sexual likes and dislikes, which promotes greater sexual satisfaction. These authors found support "for the expressive pathway for women and for the instrumental pathway for both men and women" (p. 178). They conclude that sexual disclosure by both partners may contribute more to relational and sexual satisfaction in long-term relationships than in dating relationships.

Based on their history of sexual relations in a committed relationship, partners are freer to discuss their desires and understand what is sexually satisfying to each other. But without open conversations, partners may remain stuck in frustrating patterns. For example, some partners report a fear of using any affectionate gesture because the other spouse always sees it as an invitation to intercourse; others say their partners never initiate any sexual activity, while their partners report being ignored or rebuffed for such attempts. Without addressing these issues, these partners will remain distant and frustrated.

Sexual communication in the early years of a partnered relationship may or may not predict sexual communication decades later. Due to longevity and good health practices, many individuals have the potential to remain sexually active into their seventh decade or longer. Life-cycle studies reveal that sexuality remains important, yet sexual expectations are altered due to developmental changes and health issues. Older couples interviewed about the history of their sex lives often report dramatic changes in sexual interest, depending on other pressures in their lives. However, changes in sexual interest and practices may not just happen with age. For example, dual-career couples report a decline in time and desire for sex. In some partnerships, between 10 and 15 percent of females experience a lack of lust and powerful attraction for long-term partners (Klusmann, 2002). In addition, stress and loss, such as a miscarriage, affect a couple's interpersonal and sexual relationships, necessitating ongoing and often difficult conversations. Concerns about sex, such as premature ejaculation or other performance issues, often change sexual patterns. Male reactions include performance anxiety, interpersonal alienation, and a dread of talking about sex; such reactions require couples to discuss the issue using active listening and sexual negotiation (Metz & McCarthy, 2003).

Illness also affects sexual desire or performance and necessitates communication about sex. For example, in the aftermath of prostate cancer treatments or breast cancer surgery, many couples face reduced interest in sexuality, at least temporarily, as well as a heightened need for emotional closeness and reassurance of attractiveness. Both female and male patients may need to adjust to feeling less self-sufficient and sexual, at least in the short term.

At any stage of a couple's relationship, willingness and ability to talk about sex fosters intimacy. Some couples may fear that talking about sex seems less spontaneous and less romantic (Sanders, Pedro, Bantum, & Galbraith, 2006). However, effective communication about sexual needs and desires releases emotions, provides a better sense of the other's needs and feelings, and creates a greater sense of closeness. Thus, for couples desiring an intimate relationship, open and direct communication about sexuality may deepen their intimacy even during times of struggle.

Parent-Child Communication about Sexuality

Parent-child discussions of sexuality support a sense of family connectedness and help prepare children for positive intimate relationships in adult life. In previous generations, parents were often uncomfortable or afraid to talk about sex or misinformed about sex themselves. However, in contemporary families, conversations about sex occur more frequently due to greater societal openness, media treatment of sexuality, concerns about sexual health, and higher levels of parental willingness to discuss sexuality. Even though open conversation about sexuality occurs more frequently, a large majority of parents still express discomfort in talking with adolescents about sex, finding it uncomfortable or embarrassing (Jerman & Constantine, 2010). Think back to your own family experience and the extent to which sex was discussed openly. Family members' cultural backgrounds and religious affiliations also influence the extent to which such discussions occur. Not surprisingly, factors that predict parent-child communication about sex reflect parental beliefs and attitudes about sexuality (Segrin & Flora, 2011).

Parental talk about sexuality tends to influence offspring behavior and appears to buffer adolescents from certain peer or environmental pressures about sexual activity. Growing research establishes a communicative differential between mothers and fathers. Research on parent-child discussions of sex reflects the tendency of mothers to discuss this topic more frequently than fathers, particularly with their daughters. In her study of sexual risk communication, Hutchinson (2002) found that girls who talk to their mothers about sexual topics are more likely to have conservative sexual values and less likely to have initiated sex; girls who talk to parents about when to have sex are less influenced by peer behavior. Culture also plays a role in this communication; for example, Hispanic-Latina women reported less parent-adolescent sexual risk communication than non-Hispanic peers.

Mother-daughter discussions about condoms are associated with greater consistency of condom use (Hutchinson, 2002). Frequently, such mother-daughter conversations present challenges; mothers and daughters may experience a dialectical tension between perceiving sex talk as natural and open, and awkward and private. Another study of mother and late adolescent daughter pair's sexual communication revealed that, although mothers and daughters both described the topic as natural, some viewed it as a challenging topic, especially in earlier years. Mothers reported feeling unsure about when to raise the topic and what sexual information to discuss (Coffelt, 2010).

Issues such as culture and economic status impact parent-child discussions of sexual topics. Results of a study of gender differences in sex-related communication among urban mothers and their teenage children reveal that mothers talked more to their daughters about topics of dating, when to have intercourse, and reasons not to have sex until one is older (Kapungu et al., 2010). In contrast, most males reported discussions with their mothers (48 percent) rather than their fathers (22 percent) about condom use. Adolescents and mothers frequently differed on the topics that were discussed. Such studies highlight the importance of comfortable and open parent-child discussions about sexuality and the important role many mothers play in socializing their adolescents and providing sexual risk information. Of course, studies like these do not always predict communication in any individual family.

Increasingly, fathers play a more significant role in the sexual socialization of their children through the discussions of sociosexual issues with daughters such as "resisting pressure for sex" and "understanding men" (Hutchinson, 2002). Some fathers help daughters understand the communication strategies young males could use to persuade them to engage in sexual behaviors. A study of father-son communication about sexuality found permissive values were a predictor of information sharing but not a predictor of values sharing (Lehr, Dilorio, Demi, & Facteau, 2005). The authors speculate that sharing values could lead a son to inquire about his father's sexual experiences, a topic the father might prefer not to discuss.

In general, sons engage in far less parent-child talk about sex than daughters (Warren, 2006). In his comprehensive review of father-child sexual communication research, Wright (2009) asserts that "fathers play an important role in the sexual development of their children" (p. 223). His findings include the following: fathers are more likely to engage in sexual communication with sons than with daughters; **black** and Latino fathers may engage in more sexual communication than white and Asian fathers; sexual communication varies with the amount and quality of overall father-child communication; if engaging in sexual communication is comfortable, the more likely it is to occur. Fathers are more likely to discuss sex when their children are older and in a romantic relationship. Although fathers remain less involved in such discussions, the good news is that recent research underlines the importance of father-child communication about sex.

Even when both parents become involved in sexual discussions, they are more likely to talk about sex with daughters rather than with sons. Heisler (2005) asked college student-mother-father triads to recall and report on conversations about sexuality. Most participants (77 percent) could remember discussions with their parent or child, particularly on topics of morals, pregnancy, and relationships. Although mothers were predominantly responsible for sexual communication with their children, many children reported that friends were the main source of sexual information, followed by their mothers and then fathers.

Many teenagers report that they are more comfortable discussing sex than their parents. Some parents have difficulty talking with their adolescents about premarital sex because they question their own knowledge and skill, and they worry that bringing the topic up will encourage sexual activity and their children will not take them seriously (Jaccard, Dittust, & Gordon, 2000). Due to their insecurities, parents rate themselves low on the list of influences on children's sexual behaviors, whereas children rated their parents high on the list (Wilson, 2004). In addition, cultural heritage impacts parent-child communication about sex. For example, a study of parental sexual communication reveals that Asian American college students received very little information about a range of sexual topics. Sons reported receiving less sexual information than daughters, and fathers seldom addressed the topic. Asian mothers who did discuss sexuality tended to address menstruation and dating norms rather than sexual activities (Kim & Ward, 2007). Overall, while parents likely understand that it is important to talk with their children about sex, some parents were raised at a time when their own parents were not open about or effective in communicating about sex (Hutchinson, 2002).

For 15 years the communication researchers Clay Warren and Michael Neer conducted a series of studies that explored the quality and content of parent-child communication about sex and developed the FSCQ, or family sex communication quotient (Warren, 2011). This survey tool measures a general orientation to discussions about sex within the family unit along the dimensions of comfort, information, and values. The researchers identified four significant elements that help us summarize effective parent-child communication about sex:

• Satisfaction with family discussions about sex is dependent on the key factor of mutual dialogue. Children report greater satisfaction with family communication about sex when parents facilitate the conversation and help them feel comfortable raising the topic.

- The ability to communicate supportively about sex revolves around an attitude of openness. Teens want parents to talk with them, not at them, and to avoid preachy messages.
- For discussions to have the greatest impact, they should become part of family communication patterns well before children reach age 16. Many parents put off talking about sex; however, raising the topic early facilitates more frequent discussion as well as children's perceptions of their parents as effective communicators.
- Parent-child communication about sex that is frequent and that is regarded as effective tends to facilitates children's open discussion with their own dating partners. Children tend to model patterns found in their home (Warren & Warren, 2013).

While we understand the importance of effective communication about sex, even today families differ greatly in their approach to sexuality. Maddock (1989) described the communication behaviors of sexually neglectful, sexually abusive, and sexually healthy families. First, in **sexually neglectful families**, sex is seldom or never addressed. In these families sexual communication occurs on an abstract level, so direct connection is not made between the topic and the personal experience of family members as in the following example:

My mother explained the act of sex in the most cold, mechanical, scientific, factual way she could. She made a point of saying throughout, "After marriage ..." I was embarrassed and I couldn't look at her face after she finished. I know it was very difficult for her. Her mother had not told her anything at all, and she had let her get married and go on a honeymoon without any knowledge of what was going to happen.

Through their own behavior, parents model sexual messages about sex. These messages, often indirect and veiled or vague comments, communicate an underlying attitude of anxiety or displeasure about sex. When parents have a rigid marital privacy boundary surrounding sexuality, children never see their parents as sexual beings. First, there are no playful jokes, hugging, or kissing in the children's presence. Second, **sexually abusive families** are characterized by boundary confusion between individuals and generations. Members' communication reflects a perpetrator-victim interaction pattern, especially in cross-gender relationships, resulting in marital conflict and lack of emotional intimacy. In both the sexually neglectful and sexually abusive families, sexual attitudes and sexual behavior are seldom addressed directly.

Third, **sexually healthy families** are characterized by (1) respect for both genders; (2) boundaries that are developmentally appropriate and support gender identities; (3) effective and flexible communication patterns that support intimacy, including appropriate erotic expression; and (4) a shared system of culturally relevant sexual values and meanings. These families discuss sex "using language that can accurately cover sexual information, reflect feelings and attitudes of members, and facilitate decision making and problem solving regarding sexual issues" (Maddock, 1989, p. 135).

Sex education is accurate and set in a context of family values that is transmitted across generations. Such families enact Warren's (2006) suggestions for effective family communication about sex: start talking early, include both parents and sons and daughters in the conversation, and establish a supportive environment in which mutual dialogue can occur.

Communicating about Same Sex Partnerships in Families

Research on sexual communication reflects the experiences of married or romantic heterosexual pairs. However, there are important variations based on this partnership type that are worth noting. Discussing one's own homosexuality with a child raises particular issues. Breshears and Braithwaite (in press) describe the challenges children faced when parents they knew as heterosexual "came out" as lesbian or gay to them. While this revelation was often difficult for these children at first, they reported coming to terms with their parents' altered identity and having very positive relationships with parents, even when they received other negative cultural messages about homosexuality. In their study of gay and lesbian foster parents, Patrick and Palladino (2009) found that some case managers had not told the foster children that their new home would have same-sex parents; some of these foster parents chose to discuss this directly with their children if they were old enough to understand. In addition, lesbian mothers must be prepared to respond when their children insist a dad is needed to make a baby (Galvin, Turner, Patrick, & West, 2007). Some same-sex partners include discussion of donor insemination with their children so they are better able to understand where they came from.

We have discussed sexual communication at length in this chapter because this topic is critical to couple and parent-child intimacy and children's abilities to develop healthy and safe sexual practices in their own lives.

Intimacy Factors: Effort, Sacrifice, Forgiveness, and Sanctification

In addition to the influences of commitment, disclosure, and sexual communication, partners and family members develop closeness and intimacy through members' efforts and sacrifices, willingness to forgive, and sanctification.

Effort

Rewarding and intimate couple and family relationships do not happen by accident; they take effort. Many factors compete for attention in life. Workplace demands, homework, school, friendships, family commitments, and community responsibilities take time and effort. Nurturing our marital or family relationships often occurs after everything else has received attention. In most cases, this limited attention spells relational disaster. According to Brody (2013), "Many severed marriages seem to have just withered and died from a lack of effort to keep the embers of love alive" (p. D7). Unless family relationships receive conscious attention, relationships "go on automatic pilot" and eventually stagnate or deteriorate.

Because the family operates within larger systems such as the workplace and school, each system impacts the other. Tensions between work and home obligations often leave partners stressed and overwhelmed. This era of commuter marriages, job losses, and relocations can threaten partner and **family intimacy**. Technological advances such as cell phones and Skype have altered the way we do work, but in many cases they mean that workers are expected to be connected to the office 24 hours a day.

Partners who make significant efforts to remain connected to family members become experts on their loved ones' worlds. John Gottman and Nan Silver (1999) stressed the importance of developing "love maps," or mental maps of a partner's psychological world. Such "mapmakers" can tell you their partner's worries and joys, dreams and hopes, their best friends, favorite movies, food, and books, the names of their partner's work colleagues, and what "pushes their partner's buttons." This deep and detailed knowledge allows partners and family members to support the other in meaningful ways when life turns painful and share celebrations when life brings joy. Such efforts are especially important during life transitions that can be stressful and take focus away from couple intimacy. Gottman (1999) stressed the effects of the shift to parenthood and the importance for couples to go onto this new stage of life knowing one another very well.

Putting this kind of effort into family relationships means that parents listen to their children, remember the names of their best friends and teachers and beloved sports heroes or music stars, and know their current career aspirations, hobbies, fears, and dreams. For all family members, these "cognitive maps" serve as indicators of connection among them. A conscious and mutual determination to focus on the relationships keeps family ties intact. We also want to stress that this is not just the responsibility of parents, but parents do model this behavior for children. Children who see their parents put great effort into interaction and caring for others in the family learn to do this in their own lives as well.

Sacrifice

In addition to making efforts to create and maintain intimacy in families, couples or families often make sacrifices for one another. Sacrifice involves choosing to give up something in order to benefit another person. It involves a high level of commitment and effort, the opposite of self-interest. A willingness to sacrifice for your relationship demonstrates strong commitment, high relational satisfaction, and longer relationships (Flanagan et al., 2002). Marital vows often include words such as "for better or worse" but many brides or grooms have not had to make significant relational sacrifices for their partners before marriage. Marital research supports the value of sacrifice. A recent study of young married couples, average age of 27, found that attitudes about sacrifice predict marital success and relational maintenance in the early years of marriage. The authors speculate that performing sacrifices for the relationship may be a significant symbol of devotion to the partner (Stanley, Whitton, Sadberry, Clements, & Markman, 2006). Conversely, a study of young adult romantic partners reveals that sacrifices can be detrimental to relationship quality when the partners are not able to attend to their own needs also. The levels of satisfaction varied with the nature of partners' attachment orientation; for example, those high in attachment avoidance prefer lower levels of dependence (Ruppel & Curran, 2012). Therefore, partner sacrifice is not always valued.

Other family relationships benefit from relational sacrifices such as canceling a vacation to stay with a sick grandparent, or working a second job to fund a daughter's college tuition. Many immigrant parents have paid a high personal price to raise their children in the United States. A study of Mexican migrant parents found that children of unmarried migrant mothers exhibit strong academic motivation because they view their mothers' migration as a sacrifice (Dreby & Stutz, 2012). The chapter's opening vignette describes an older sister who makes sacrifices for her younger sisters: many siblings build deep intimacy through sharing their burdens and supporting each other when parents cannot fulfill their roles effectively.

Forgiveness

What is the relational impact of saying "I forgive you"? Defining forgiveness is difficult because of multiple meanings. Communication scholars Waldron and Kelley (2008) discuss forgiveness as a relational process in which harm is acknowledged by one or both parties; the harmed party extends mercy to the transgressor, one or both experience a transformation from a negative to positive state, the meaning of the relationship is renegotiated, and reconciliation becomes possible. Frequently, forgiveness implies an explicit renegotiation of the relationship that usually involves metacommunication.

Hurt and the need for forgiveness occur regularly in family interactions given the long-term nature of family ties and the intensity of connections. "Paradoxically, those we love are the ones we are most likely to hurt, and may not always be the ones with whom we communicate most effectively" (Fincham & Beach, 2002, p. 239). While we talked extensively about relationship maintenance in Chapter 5, things do go wrong in families, and families need to repair relationships (Kelley, 2012). In his study of close relationships, Kelley (1998) found that over 70 percent of respondents' motivations for forgiveness included love, restoring the relationship, and well-being of the other. He suggested that the obligatory nature of family relationships creates a sense of stability and resiliency. It seems self-evident that the motivation and ability to discuss forgiveness depend on the severity of the transgressions; family-oriented transgressions range from an affair or physical violence to an insult or revelation of another's secret.

Because marital ties involve high emotional attachment, trust, and interdependence, some transgressions may be emotionally devastating, shaking the relationship's foundation (Waldron & Kelley, 2008). Issues such as incest, physical or mental abuse, or affairs are unforgivable in some relationships. Unwillingness to forgive may be associated with patterns of negative reciprocity because partners often hurt each other and initiate reciprocal negative messages that work against intimacy (Fincham & Beach, 2002). Parent-child forgiveness processes develop over time as the child's ability to comprehend transgressions and forgiveness changes.

Conversely, in some cases, young adults may struggle with forgiving immediate or extended family members. A recent study of college students revealed the following three tensions they struggled with as they decided whether to forgive another family member: choice-obligation, trust-risk, and openness-closedness (Carr & Wang, 2012).

For example, one respondent consciously chose not to discuss the specifics of the hurtful situation again so the wounds would heal.

In certain situations forgiveness does not occur. A study of couples who completed daily diaries reporting partner transgressions, apologies, and perceived apology sincerity revealed that apologies predicted forgiveness only when the injured party was highly satisfied with the relationship and the apology appeared sincere (Schumann, 2012). In extreme cases, an offensive family member may be cut off by many or all family members. Frequently this occurs when the member violates a deeply held family belief or strict rule in areas such as interracial marriage, homosexuality, or incest. Only a proactive attempt to engage a family member in reconciliation provides the possibility for positively increasing constructive communication and intimacy.

Sanctification

We end our list of important relational and family communication behaviors of intimacy by talking about sanctification. **Sanctification** refers to a psychological process "through which aspects of life are perceived as having divine character and significance" (Pargament & Mahoney, 2005, p. 183), which serves as a source of relational connectedness. Sanctification occurs in two ways. First, it may be theistic, or a manifestation of one's images, beliefs, or experience of God; this is more common for believers in a God or deity. Second, without reference to a specific deity, a sense of transcendence, ultimate purpose, and timelessness may create a sense of the spiritual (Mahoney, Pargament, Murray-Swank, & Murray-Swank, 2003). Many couples view marriage as a sacred state endowed with spiritual meaning; parenthood may also be viewed as spiritual in nature. Thus, spiritual beliefs serve to sustain family relationships during difficult times.

Sanctification may serve as an example of embeddedness in broader community-supported systems of meaning (Fincham et al., 2007). Religious affiliations influence how partners or parents perform their relational roles. Many weddings occur within a house of worship, displaying the couple's view of the sacred nature of these vows. Religious leaders may serve as marriage counselors providing theologically grounded guidelines for repairing marriages.

Other familial relationships may gain strength from the spiritual realm. Some parents identify their mother or father role as a sacred duty; their parenting behaviors may reflect these beliefs. For example, mothers who reported higher levels of the sanctification of parenting reported using less verbal aggression (yelling, calling names) with young children (Mahoney et al., 2003, p. 228). Attending and participating in worship services reinforces the importance of a deity to the family members.

Barriers to Intimacy

As we can see throughout this chapter, building marital or familial intimacy involves effort and risk. Many find it more comfortable to maintain a number of pleasant or close relationships, rather than becoming intensely involved with a partner, child, or other relative. Some family members establish barriers to deep relationships as a way to protect themselves from potential pain or loss.

Maintaining closeness takes sensitivity and effort. Lavee (2005) studied daily reports from 94 couples over a week containing checklists of daily hassles, interpersonal conflicts, positive/negative moods, and a measure of the sense of dyadic closeness. A sense of closeness was associated with the other spouse's level of stress. The more stress a person experienced in a certain day, the less closeness (or more distance) his or her spouse reported. The effect was stronger for men than for women. Couples who had high-quality relationships reported more closeness than did those in distressed marriages, regardless of the stress level. However, both happy and distressed couples associated more stressful days with increased dyadic distance. Although many individuals fear deep intimacy, even maintaining a sense of closeness is a complex process.

Jealousy

Although some partners view jealousy as a sign of affection, these feelings can turn violent or obsessive, creating a barrier to intimacy. Jealousy is an aversive emotion that may involve negative thoughts and feelings of insecurity, anger, sadness, and fear induced by the threat or actual loss of a relationship with another person. Jealousy results from the perception that a treasured relationship is threatened, usually by another person. Constantly mulling over jealous concerns heightens relational tension resulting in active distancing, expressions of negative affect, general avoidance/denial, and threats of violence. Jealousy erodes relational connections.

Romantic jealousy is most closely associated with marital and partner relationships, although sometimes one parent feels jealous of the other's connection to a child or to another family member. Sibling jealousy reflects birth order, a redistribution of parental resources, or parental favoritism. One child may believe a parent shows favoritism to a sibling or new family member (Golish, 2000). A teenager may reject a sibling's new "best friend" who interferes with family time. Negative consequences of parental favoritism include sibling rivalry and lowered self-esteem, and perceptions of declining family support.

Deception

Given that trust appears as a hallmark of intimacy, deceiving another violates relational expectations. Most people expect family members and loved ones to tell the truth to loved ones. Deception involves communicating or withholding information intentionally for the purpose of creating a false belief. The suspicion that one partner keeps information from the other may lead to dissatisfaction. When an individual in a heterosexual marriage comes out as gay, lesbian, bisexual, or transgender, the news usually overwhelms an unsuspecting spouse, often shattering the partner's core identity (Buxton, 2006). Sometimes deceptions create accidental privacy dilemmas when an unsuspecting family member discovers problematic information about someone in the family (Petronio, 2002). Some deceptions violate the adult relationship covenant, challenging values that are viewed as sacred, such as sexual exclusivity (Waldron & Kelley, 2008); others attempt to sustain a desirable fiction, such as when parents do not reveal their use of a sperm donor to achieve parenthood (Marquardt, Glenn, & Clark, 2010). Such cases threaten the relationship itself.

Other deceptions, such as persistent secret gambling or drug use, may be resolved if the offender enters a treatment program.

Maintaining Intimacy across Diverse Family Forms

Although many closeness and intimacy studies center on marital couples or parent-child relationships, multiple family types create a range of valued familial connections. When asked about their current relationship, lesbians and gay men reported as much satisfaction with their relationships as did heterosexual couples, the great majority describing themselves as happy. Relational quality for same-sex partners includes feelings of equality, ongoing attraction, and shared decision-making (Kurdek, 2004). A particular issue faced by such partnerships involves supportive networks. Certain gay and lesbian couples experience tremendous pressure to be "everything" to each other due to lack of full family support or strong friendship networks or because one or both of the partners are not "out." In some cases, partners' public expressions of affection are discouraged within the extended family or community network.

Stepfamilies can also be sources of great satisfaction and intimacy, although deep relational connections usually develop slowly. Issues of loyalty, guilt, and loss compound the ability of stepchildren and stepparents to develop intimate ties. Although the first few years in a stepfamily are often complicated in terms of levels of closeness, creating a strong adult bond represents a key developmental task. Eventually many stepparent-stepchild relationships will be characterized by voluntary and meaningful personal interactions. Across multiple studies of stepchild perceptions of family functioning, Schrodt identified five types of stepfamilies; one is the bonded stepfamily characterized by "low levels of dissension and avoidance and relatively high levels of stepfamily involvement, flexibility and expressiveness" (Braithwaite & Schrodt, 2013, pp. 163–164). In such cases, the outcome justifies the effort. In their study of stepfamily development, Braithwaite, Olson, Golish, Soukup, and Turman (2001) cautioned against expecting all stepfamilies to form quickly and without problems, like the Brady Bunch of television fame. In fact, they found that stepfamilies that developed expectation of closeness more slowly were ultimately closer and stronger than those that felt the pressure to love and accept each other from the outset.

Adults raising children without partners need intimacy in their lives as much as anyone else. Because they do not have a partner, they will need to find more intimacy and support within their extended families; this is particularly true for single mothers. However, single parents may report difficulty in sustaining strong, intimate adult relationships due to the pressures and demands of raising children on their own. Some children of single parents, fearing the loss of parental intimacy, may intentionally or unintentionally sabotage a parent's efforts to develop new romantic ties. Without a partner to share their problems, joys, and decision-making, single parents are best off when they can develop and function within strong interactive interpersonal networks.

In the end, "Most marriages, even good ones, are gratifying in some ways and frustrating in others" (Huston, 2009, p. 318). The same holds true for any adult partnership as well as for a range of family forms. One of life's joys and challenges is to learn how to be yourself while you are in a significant long-term couple and family relationship.

Conclusion

This chapter explored a range of communication practices that lead to intimacy within adult partnerships and families. It also addressed the close relationship between intimacy and communication, focusing on specific communication behaviors that encourage intimacy within marital and family systems: commitment, self-disclosure, and sexual communication. Commitment implies creating an unbreakable bond with another person. Family intimacy cannot be achieved unless members nurture their relationships through commitment. Self-disclosure involves intimate sharing of personal and private information with a partner or other family member as a way to build and sustain a valued relational tie. Sexuality serves as a means of communicating affection within a partnered relationship; talking about sexuality provides opportunities for intimate conversations between adult partners and important bonding conversations between parents and children. In addition, factors such as effort, forgiveness, sacrifice, and sanctification contribute to familial intimacy. Finally, barriers to intimacy, such as deception, jealousy, and fear of intimacy, may prevent certain relationships from developing their full potential.

All human beings long for intimacy, but it is a rare relationship in which family members (spouses, parents and children, siblings) consciously strive for greater sharing on significant personal topics over long periods of time. Yet, such mutual commitment provides rewards known only to those in intimate relationships.

In Review

1. Create your own definition of marital and/or committed partnership intimacy and provide two examples of such relationships characterized by intimate communication.
2. Create your own definition of family intimacy and provide two examples of such relationships characterized by intimate communication.
3. Take a position on the following statement and defend it: A marital/partnership commitment should be broken only in cases of partner or child abuse.
4. Under what circumstances, if any, would you recommend withholding full self-disclosure of a very serious issue in a marital and/or family relationship?
5. Relying on personal observation or a media example, discuss ways you have seen an intimate adult relationship overcome jealousy or deception through forgiveness.
6. Assume you are a parent. What qualities would you advise your child to look for in a marital partnership or long-term committed partnership?

Key Words

Commitment   134

Debriefing conversations   140

Family intimacy   149

Forgiveness   134

Intimacy barriers   134

Mental love maps   136

Sanctification   151

Self-disclosure   136

Sexually abusive families   147

Sexually healthy families   147

Sexually neglectful families   147

Sexual communication   142

CHAPTER 7

Communication and Family Roles and Types

LEARNING OBJECTIVES

- Explain the concepts of roles and role functions
- Illustrate the difference between role expectations and role enactment
- Describe how each family role function may be enacted
- Compare the enactment of a specific family role function in different families
- Illustrate the four family types based on the family communication patterns typology
- Explain Fitzpatrick's three major couple types

Rebekah is a married mother of two children, ages four and two. Before her first child, Miriam, was born, she had begun a program as a doctoral student in history at the state university. Both of her parents are professors at a college in a neighboring state and have always been very supportive and proud of their daughter following in their footsteps. Rebekah continued full-time in the program until her second child, Aaron, came along. Following Aaron's birth, Rebekah decided she needed to reduce her studies to part-time until the kids got a little older, given her husband's busy work schedule. Rebekah recognized that she really didn't need to have a career to provide for her children because her husband made enough money to support the family. However, she had such a love of history and felt a real desire to continue the program. She also wanted to be a role model for her daughter in pursuing her dreams. But even part-time has been difficult with Rebekah still taking on full responsibility for child care and managing the household. She has been discussing this with her husband.

Now Rebekah is considering quitting the program altogether, but worries what her family will think of her, especially since she is so close to completion. She feels a lot of conflict about her responsibilities: "When I'm with the kids, I am always thinking about what I should be doing in my studies, and when I'm at school or studying, I always worry that I should be with the kids."

Jarvis, age 46, is a solo parent to his son, Jamal, age 12. Jamal's mother left when he was just two years old, and Jarvis and Jamal have been on their own since then. Jarvis' mother and sister live nearby and have helped as needed, but Jarvis has prided himself for being there for Jamal as much as he can. He had often felt stretched, wondering if he could provide everything Jamal needed. Jarvis is deeply religious, and he and Jamal attend weekly services at their local church. About a year ago, Jarvis began dating Sylvia, a woman he met at a church singles' group. As their relationship has become more serious, he has slowly begun to include Sylvia in activities that were traditionally those that he and Jamal did together, just the two of them. Jamal initially did not take to this well, but over time has seemed to adjust to having Sylvia take on a role in their family. Jarvis has been really grateful to have Sylvia around, as he was never good at what he calls the "touchy, feely stuff." He thinks that Sylvia has a nice way of providing the emotional support for Jamal that he doesn't provide very well. She has also encouraged Jamal to pursue his interest in music, often driving him to piano lessons—something that Jarvis was never able to do due to his busy work schedule.

More recently, Jarvis and Sylvia have been discussing marriage, and Jarvis intends to propose fairly soon. When he explained this to Jamal, he framed the news as "something wonderful"—Jamal was going to finally have a mother! Jarvis was surprised at Jamal's intensely negative response: "She's not my mother! And she never will be my mother!"

T
remendous variability is found in communication across families as members interact with each other, creating patterns of role relationships. To demonstrate the increasing complexity of family roles just consider the emerging language related to roles. Family role terminology includes words such as *co-bread-winners*, *stay-at-home parent*, *noncustodial father*, or *third mother-in-law*, all of which have implications for family interaction. Today opinions differ widely about what it means to enact the roles of partner, mother, stepbrother, ex-sister-in-law, or foster daughter. In order to explore these complex role issues and their implications for communication, this chapter will discuss (1) role definition, (2) role functions, (3) role appropriation, and (4) couple and family typologies.

Within families, roles are established, grown into, grown through, discussed, negotiated, redefined, and accepted or rejected. As members mature or outside forces impact the family, roles emerge, change, or disappear. In order to understand role development, we need to consider role definitions, expectations, and performance.

We define family roles as *recurring patterns of behavior developed through the family members' interactions that family members enact in order to fulfill family functions*. From a communication perspective, these expectations develop as family members create shared meanings and negotiate how roles should be enacted. This perspective contrasts with theories that present a fixed, or unchanging, view of roles. Rather than take a fixed view, we prefer an interactive perspective, emphasizing the emerging aspects of roles and their behavioral regularities developed through social interaction.

Roles emerge through members' dialogue with each other reflecting the transactional nature of communication. Persons with labels such as "father" or "wife" struggle as they manage the reciprocal nature of roles. According to this interactive perspective, you cannot be a stepfather without a stepchild, or a wife without a husband; in fact, you cannot be a companionable father to a child who rejects you. Family members exchange interrelated behaviors over time creating predictable interaction patterns and roles.

Today family roles are less tied to age because of increased longevity and more fluid life stages (Rubin, 2001). A 48-year-old female may parent a preschooler;

a 21-year-old male may do the same. Over time, family members negotiate their mutual expectations of one another, and acquire or share role identifications such as provider or nurturer at different life stages. As circumstances change, or some hopes or expectations fade, members may relinquish certain roles.

Interactive role development reflects (1) the identity background and role models of a person who occupies a social position, such as oldest son or stepmother, (2) the relationships in which a person interacts, (3) the changes each family member experiences as he or she moves through the life cycle or encounters life crises, (4) the effects of each member's role performance on the family system, and (5) the extent to which a person's social/psychological identity is defined and enhanced by a particular role. For example, a woman's behavior in the role of spouse may have been very different in her first marriage than in her second, due to her own personal growth and the **role enactment** of each partner.

Roles are inextricably bound to communication processes. Family roles are developed and maintained through communication. One learns how to assume his or her place within a family from the feedback provided by other family members, such as "I don't think we should argue in front of the children." Children may receive direct instructions about how to enact the role of son or daughter in a particular household or may model their behavior from interactions they observe. Adults tend to use their family-of-origin history as a base from which to negotiate particular mutual roles, such as partner or parent; children develop their roles through a combination of adult direction, family experiences, peer relationships, and societal and cultural norms.

Strong links exist between family roles and communication rules because each contributes to the maintenance or change of the other. Rules may structure certain role relationships, whereas particular role relationships may foster the development of certain rules. For example, such rules as "Do not discuss family finances with our children" or "Solve school problems with your mother" reinforce the roles of family members.

Specific Role Functions

The **McMaster model of family functioning** (Epstein, Bishop, & Baldwin, 1982) focuses on discovering how a family allocates and manages family responsibilities. It examines five essential family functions that serve as a basis for family roles:

1. Providing adult sexual fulfillment and children's gender socialization
2. Providing nurturing and emotional support
3. Providing for individual development
4. Providing for kinship maintenance and family management
5. Providing basic resources

These family functions can be categorized as instrumental (providing the resources for the family), affective (support and nurturing, adult sexual needs), and mixed (life-skill development and system upkeep). When you look at Figure 7.1, imagine a mobile with the system's parts balanced by the multiple role functions operating within the family. These role functions become superimposed on the family system and its members.

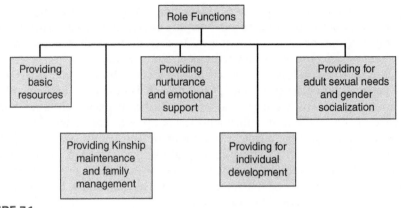

FIGURE 7.1
Family role functions

Although almost all the research in this area presumes two-parent households involving a male and female parent, same-sex partners with children face many similar issues as they confront daily family life (Gianino, 2008) as do single parents, members of multigenerational households and stepfamilies.

Providing for Gender Socialization and Sexual Needs

In a culture that provides multiple possibilities and few clear distinctions, men and women frequently receive mixed messages about what it means to be masculine and feminine. Men may hear that a woman wants a man who is expressive, gentle, nurturing, and vulnerable, yet also successful, assertive, prosperous, and capable. Women may receive similarly conflicting messages regarding dependence and independence. Yet, male and female family roles represent the intertwined social and economic forces impacting family life.

The process of learning what it means to be male or female begins at birth. Think about all of the indirect and direct messages you received in this regard. Even as newborns, males and females are handled differently; most babies receive "gender-appropriate" toys. Studies of kindergarten children show that most boys enact masculine behaviors expected of them and restrict their interests and activities to avoid what might be judged as feminine. Similarly most girls encounter feminine expectations, although society makes room for "tomboys." Family members teach children, both explicitly and implicitly, what is "masculine" and what is "feminine" from their comments about exercise, weight, appearance, and dress (Wood, 2013). Certain religious or cultural traditions support strong male-female distinctions, while such gender-bound distinctions appear repressive to others. Gender socialization often involves same-sex guidance from a parental figure. For example, in their study of male role socialization, Morman and Floyd (2006) reported that young males consistently referenced their fathers, not their mothers, suggesting that sons learned the fatherhood role from male parents.

The childhood gender-based communication directives and modeling you encountered tend to reappear when you become a parent unless you deliberately choose not

Role development involves observing and imitating role models.

to follow such expectations. For example, traditionally men were considered to be less nurturing, to disclose less about themselves than women, and keep more secrets than women. Today many men reject restrictions on their nurturing communication with their children. Current research suggests that males' roles are becoming more flexible as adult partners engage in role renegotiation and fathers become increasingly involved in raising their children (Duckworth & Buzzanell, 2009). Yet, many married fathers who lose their jobs fight to retain their roles as "real men" in a change they view as emasculating, these men cognitively reframe the situation in order to find ways to maintain a breadwinner self-concept (Buzzanell & Turner, 2003).

Two decades ago Wood and Inman (1993) challenged the disclosure research that reported women engaged in greater self-disclosure (more open, expressive communication), suggesting openness privileges one type of intimacy. They indicate that, because male self-disclosure does not reduce stress as much as it does for females, men often regard practical help, mutual assistance, and companionship as better benchmarks of caring. More recently, Wood (2007) captured the differences, suggesting that talk between women tends to be personal and disclosing, whereas men often express closeness through action. Traditionally these differences were enacted in family role behaviors particularly in families headed by a heterosexual couple. Mothers shared more time with daughters in meal preparation and family care projects; fathers shared more time with sons in doing home and car repairs as well as yard work. Today, partners enact gender roles that work for their particular relationships. Same-sex couples, due to a lack of traditional marital role models, must negotiate responsibilities rather than rely on societal expectations or previous gender role models for their answers. In same-sex couples division of household tasks tends to be more equal than in heterosexual couples, with decisions about housework based on skill, interest, and need (Rothblum, 2009).

Ultimately many factors, such as career demands or individual expectations, affect the way couples enact gender roles. Often more flexible roles emerge from interaction within the couple and family, rather than through cultural expectations. One mother of an adult son writes:

I recently received an e-mail from my son that reminded me of how his marriage is so different from mine. He wrote about the meals he cooked for the family and taking the kids shopping for school clothes. This week he was the primary caregiver while his wife, Alyana, was in Los Angeles on business. She loves the outdoors, takes care of the lawn, and coaches the boys' baseball team. Their lifestyle amazes me, and I love to see Brian act as such a caring and active parent to their two sons.

Changes in family life have led to greater androgynous role enactment. Androgynous individuals possess qualities that culture defines as masculine and feminine instead of only assigned to one sex (Wood, 2013). This affects role performance. Androgynous family members evaluate issues on their merits or demerits, without reference to the gender of the persons involved. The androgynous person is flexible, adaptive, and capable of being both instrumental (assertive, competent, forceful, and independent) and expressive (nurturing, warm, supportive, and compassionate) depending on the demands of the situation. Many adult family members have become more androgynous as circumstances, such as a partner's military deployment, or a divorce, challenge the other partner to assume new role responsibilities. Clearly solo parents, male or female, engage in androgynous role enactment.

Yet, not everything changes quickly in terms of gender **role expectations**. For example, young adult women are more likely than young adult men to receive advice from parents that they should stop work after having children and that they should make career choices that will accommodate family (Medved, Brogan, McClanahan, Morris, & Shepherd, 2006). Men who would like to stay at home with children receive negative reactions as do wives and mothers who might need or want to take on a commuter role and be away from family for all or part of the week (Bergen, 2010b; Loscocco & Spitze, 2007). One professional wife and mother reflected:

When my husband and I decided that I should accept a position overseas, we did so not knowing if he would be able to find suitable employment or if he would instead take on a stay-at-home parent role. Before we went, many friends and family asked us what he was going to do there. I think that for many of them, the idea that a man would give up employment for his wife's professional opportunity was hard to believe.

Providing Nurturing, Support, and Empathy

Family members need mutual admiration, support, and reassurance. From a transactional perspective, family satisfaction increases when each member meets the needs and expectations of the others. Children who are nurtured and supported by their parents, social networks, and community, develop the capability to be nurturing and supportive to others in the future.

Nurturing Children This family function, the primary process of transmitting parental caring and family values, occurs via communication. Through advice, directives, and answers to questions, and observing behaviors of others, children learn what parents and society expect of them. Until recently, mothers served as primary nurturers because they had far greater contact with their children than did fathers. This is still true in certain families, but not to the same extent as in the past. A recent study (Golden, 2007) examining the ways in which fathers of preschool children communicatively construct their child-rearing behaviors reveals a "masculine" concept of caregiving reflective of the increasing role of fathers as caretakers. Historically, children usually experienced their fathers as more distant, less empathetic, and less caring, especially in verbal and nonverbal signs of love. However, fathers today spend more time with their children than fathers did in the past (Silverstein, 2002).

Yet, differences continue to exist especially in some contexts. Mothers are typically the primary caregivers of children who have special needs. Schock and colleagues (2002) found that fathers with children with mood disorders have more difficulty accepting the illness and are less likely to participate in therapy efforts. A comparison of mother/father stress when parenting school-aged children with disabilities revealed that, although both experienced similar levels of stress, fathers reported more difficulty establishing an emotionally close relationship with the child (Keller & Honig, 2004).

Although sibling socialization is often overlooked, it plays a significant role for many children in middle childhood (ages 5 to 11), especially when they spend more time with their siblings than with their parents (Stafford, 2013). Many older siblings become important role models, for better or, occasionally, for worse.

No matter what the sources of family role socialization are, in keeping with the bidirectional nature of family member influence, children's behavior can influence how parents enact their roles. In addition, children can resist socialization messages. This frustrates parents, especially those in a rigid family system.

Providing Support and Empathy This function implies a willingness to focus on another's needs, listen to another's problems, and provide emotional support. Empathic listening provides the other with a sense of being understood, and/or the chance to ventilate pent-up feelings of rage, frustration, or exhaustion.

My father's way is to be very calm and patient with his children. When he helped me with my homework, he would never leave until he knew I understood it completely. He would tell me how hard it was to deal with math and science assignments. Now when I explain something, I try to see that my children understand because I remember the good feelings that I had when I finally understood my homework.

Empathy implies conveying nonjudgmental understanding and concern for another. If the communication channels between family members encourage and permit the open expression of feelings, other family members can function therapeutically, which includes listening empathically, offering advice, or questioning others to help them understand their own motives. Several studies indicated not only how providing support and empathy is perceived by children, but how it positively affects them. A study of self-esteem in late adolescence found parental attachment had direct effects on self-esteem and that teens who reported high levels of empathy also reported more pro-social behaviors such as displaying empathy or showing concern for another or assisting another in need (Laible, Carlo, & Roesch, 2004).

Providing for Individual Development

This role function includes those tasks that each individual must fulfill in order to become self-sufficient. Individuals must simultaneously seek to sustain a "sense of uniqueness from other relationships yet the sense of commonality with other relationships" (Baxter, 1990, p. 16), and they work this out in their interactions with family members especially. Young family members, who cannot accomplish that task, can easily become dependent on the family system. A "take care of me" attitude on the part of any member diminishes interdependent aspects of the family system.

Family members must interact in ways that facilitate each other's opportunities for self-discovery and talent development. Parents perform this function in their children's formative years, but from an early age children influence one another's talents. Through their play with one another, children develop the communication strategies they need to assume future family roles. It is very important that both fathers and mothers bond with their children at an early age. In order to avoid enmeshment, younger family members need messages that support or encourage individual decision-making. Recognition of members' ideas, arguments, and decisions creates a context for valuing independence.

Providing for Kinship Maintenance and Family Management

These functions address issues of maintaining relational ties and managing the daily lives and needs of all members.

Kinship Maintenance   One complex and often overlooked maintenance function involves managing and nurturing kinship ties within the extended family network. Kinship maintenance involves sharing in, participating in, and promoting the family's welfare through managing contacts with biological and chosen kin who live outside the family home. Almost all interactions with kin occur in three areas: visiting, recreation, and communication (by letter, phone, e-mail, Facebook, and text messaging).

Essentially kinkeeping involves keeping in touch with other family members and, in some cases, keeping members in touch with each other (Leach & Braithwaite, 1996; Rosenthal, 2009). Family members who specialize in this behavior are called kinkeepers and their work in maintaining family communication takes several forms including providing information and assistance, facilitating rituals, and maintaining family relationships, thus continuing a previous kinkeeper's work (Leach & Braithwaite, 1996). Researchers have found that women are more likely to play this role in families. Frequently aunts take on kinkeeping functions, working to preserve and strengthen family bonds through activities such as facilitating rituals and maintaining communication, particularly long distance (Ellingson & Sotirin, 2010). Women are more likely to talk about genetic issues with extended family members (Wilson et al., 2004) and to be the recipients of such information (Claes et al., 2003).

The kinship maintenance function directly involves and impacts family communication because "kin-work" is the labor that enables families to endure over time (Stack & Burton, 1998). Whether one is included or excluded from family events or hears the latest family gossip signifies one's place within the family system. Although previous research indicated that kinkeepers, usually females, relied heavily on the telephone, today more family members use e-mail, social networking sites, and family members' blogs to create a "new connectedness" (Kennedy, Smith, Wells, & Wellman, 2008). As one mother and wife explained:

I was very reluctant to join a social networking site. I was dragged on one kicking and screaming by my sister but I have to say it's been a terrific tool for staying connected and reconnecting too. I love the playful exchanges and updates on all the little/regular things in daily life that really are our "lives." All of our family is far-flung so it's great to check in daily. An unexpected benefit has been improved communication with a few difficult family members, as it's the perfect tool for light-hearted interactions. It's also the perfect vehicle for me as I've never been a phone person.

Holidays represent a special time for kin-related family maintenance communication. In some families, particularly highly cohesive ones, attendance at get-togethers is mandatory and only illness or great distances are acceptable excuses. In some households holidays evoke sadness or conflict because "cut-off" or divorced members are excluded. Members of low-cohesive families may envy the highly cohesive families' celebrations. Stepfamilies must work to create their own rituals to provide members with a sense of identity even as some members may resist these attempts (Braithwaite, Baxter, & Harper, 1998). At holiday time, women, and increasing numbers of men, share the tasks of shopping, calling, visiting, buying gifts, and attending events, although women still send more greeting cards or letters, online or offline.

Females manage most contacts with extended family members although this is changing in some families. Yet, many husbands maintain fewer kinship contacts with their relatives and actually have more contact with their wives' relatives given that wives take the lead in family maintenance communication (Stack & Burton, 1998). Today, the increase in single fathers and gay male partners, with or without children, contributes to the number of male kinkeepers.

Kinship ties are also affected by external factors, especially in nontraditional family forms. Single-parent and blended family systems encounter special kinship concerns. Single fathers are more likely than married fathers to share breakfast, home activities, and outings with their children. For example, in divorced families, there may be special problems in communication with the ex-spouse and his or her new family. In stepfamilies, the ability to maintain relationships will be affected by the attitudes of step-grandparents and ability to retain ties with biological paternal grandparents (Pasley & Lee, 2010). On occasion, children lose active contact with an entire side of their family heritage. Divorced parents and extended family members need to work to prevent children from becoming pawns and experiencing forced separations. Maintaining supportive contact on significant child-related matters benefits all parties—both parents and children.

Family kinship networking varies according to family of origin and ethnicity. For example, Mexican men and women tend to have equally strong relationships with their relatives. However, Mexican men networked more with other persons outside their families, whereas the women formed their strongest relationship ties within families (Falicov, 2005). In Chicano cultures, godparents (*padrinos*) link families and communities through friends or authorities. Although often not relatives, godparents play key roles in religious activities, such as first communion, confirmation, and marriage. They also provide nurturing and financial aid when needed, as a moral obligation (Garcia-Preto, 2005a).

Because a family consists of people bound by blood, law, and language, kinship ties often include extended family members bound by their caring and commitment.

Since my immediate family is dead, and any other distant relatives on my husband's side or my side live thousands of miles away, we have worked at creating a local family. Over the years, we have developed close friends who serve as honorary aunts and uncles for the children. The highlight of our Christmas is our annual dinner when we all get together to decorate the tree and the children get to see the people they refer to as Uncle Matt and Aunt Mandy within a family context. I feel closer to these people than to many of my blood relatives.

Kinkeeping practices represent a special way to communicate the importance of family. In this age in which relatives are spread across miles and continents, kinkeeping takes on greater meaning. When family members feel comfortable sharing their problems, joys, and family celebrations, they reap the benefits of the kinship function.

Management of Daily Needs   Other role maintenance and management functions include decision-making to facilitate housekeeping, child care, recreation, and managing of family finances. In dual-earner partnerships, men tend to spend more time than their wives working outside the home, while women do more work inside the home (McNeil, 2004). Trends over the past three decades reveal that women's increased earning power has been associated with men participating more in child care, cooking, and cleaning (Galinsky, Aumann, & Bond, 2008).

Division of household chores frequently creates conflict. In the case of married couples, both husbands and wives tend to see the division of household chores as less fair to wives who tend to perform a greater amount of housework, regardless of the presence of children or the woman's employment status. However, in marriages where wives and husbands were both employed full-time, the gap between the amount of housework wives and husbands performed was smaller than when wives worked part-time or not at all (Grote & Clark, 2001).

Ongoing changes in home maintenance reflect active negotiation between partners, since most are creating a housekeeping system different from that in their families of origin. A major partner negotiation task involves coordinating duties and responsibilities with each other; 40 percent report negotiating these details daily and 26 percent indicate such negotiations occur two to three times a week (Halpin, Teixeira, Pinkus, & Daley, 2010). In commuter marriages this can be more complicated. One study revealed that, although commuting wives were resisting cultural expectations by pursuing their own careers, they experienced traditional gendered expectations for housework and other family roles. For instance, wives reported needing to remind or nag their husbands to complete tasks at home (Bergen, Kirby, & McBride, 2007). Changes in family structure, such as divorce, force a redefinition of roles tied to daily routines (Downs, Coleman, & Ganong, 2000).

Recreation management, another role function, is defined as coordinating those things family members do for relaxation, entertainment, or personal development. Whereas athletic activities increasingly involve both genders, other activities may appeal to different ages or genders. Extremely cohesive families encourage much group recreational activity, whereas low-cohesion families do not. Parental behavior telegraphs to children what is appropriate recreational behavior, and conflicts may result if a child does not measure up.

Another type of basic resource role function involves managing family members' health. Women are more likely to enact this role in different ways. For example, studies of Internet use show that women are more likely than men to search the Internet for health information (Rice, 2006).

Providing Basic Resources

Traditionally, men served as the major financial providers in families, although there have always been exceptions, especially for African American women who traditionally worked outside the home to contribute to the economic resources of the family (Boushey, 2009). However, the task of providing basic resources no longer remains a gendered expectation. In fact, in 40 percent of households with children under the age of 18, women are either the sole or the primary source of income (Wang, Parker, & Taylor, 2013). Of these "breadwinner moms," 37 percent are married and 63 percent are single mothers. Some researchers distinguish between dual-career couples and dual-earner couples. Dual-career couple refers to partnerships in which each person pursues a full-time career and expects to advance up the career ladder. By contrast, in a dual-earner couple, both employed partners work at positions that do not offer a career ladder. Obviously some couples represent a blend of these types.

Not surprisingly, the current economic climate and a growing cultural acceptance of both parents acting as caregivers and earners have led to stressful lifestyles.

Negotiating these roles is complicated and often unsatisfactory (Boushey, 2009). In most families today, no one stays at home all day, so there's no one with the time to prepare dinner, be home when the kids arrive home from school, or deal with the little things, such as accepting a package or getting the refrigerator repaired. Families face the challenge of trying to oversee their latchkey kids from afar and worry about what their teenagers are doing after school. Parents are increasingly reliant on technology; for example, children check in via cell phone and some parents have installed cameras to make sure children are home and safe.

Merging the roles of provider/worker and family member creates **spillover**. Spillover is bidirectional; family demands can spill over into work life and work demands can spill over into family life. A divorced woman with primary parenting responsibilities for two elementary school-aged children experiences spillover of her family responsibilities into her work. For example, if one child is sick and needs to be kept home from school, she must stay home from work to care for the child, perhaps videoconferencing in to an important meeting. The same woman also experiences her work demands spilling over into her family life when she gets online to complete some work while her children watch a movie.

Work-family conflict and spillover may be even more of a challenge for low-income, unmarried mothers. Of these women, those who report high levels of work-family conflict are less likely to be employed. Work-family conflict may keep these women unemployed, or if they find jobs, make it difficult for them to maintain employment stability (Ciabatarri, 2007).

A consistent line of research has addressed work and family roles. Barnett, Marshall, and Pleck's (1992) research on men's multiple roles and stress focused on three key roles in men's lives: the job role, the marital role, and the parental role. The same roles and stresses exist in women's lives. Dilworth and Kingsbury (2005) examined how different generations experience spillover. Older respondents (over age 50) were more likely to report home-to-work spillover involving care for elderly parents, while middle to younger generations reported spillover focused on caring for children at home. However, all generations reported more negative work-to-home spillover than home-to-work spillover.

Effective communication is critical to managing the multiple role identities. Relying on the interactive perspective of roles, Golden (2002) suggests that couples create shared meanings for their roles as providers and caregivers through their communicative practices. This involves **role negotiation,** or ongoing role coordination, in addition to constructive conflict management as we discuss in Chapter 9. According to a major study, a majority of both men and women report that they are "sitting down at their kitchen tables to coordinate their family's schedules, duties, and responsibilities, including child care and elder care, at least two to three times a week" (Shriver, 2009).

Some employees manage family-to-work stress through specific strategic workplace interactions. Krouse and Affifi (2007) identified eight communication strategies mothers use for managing family spillover. These include venting with superiors and/or with coworkers, receiving affirmation and assurances from coworkers, seeking advice from coworkers, and seeking instrumental (practical) support from supervisors.

Family forms impact members' ability to manage work-family stress. Some single parents report that providing economic stability has become their primary role. Single mothers report struggling with decreased economic resources, longer work hours, and more limited social support (Berryhill, Soloski, & Adams, 2012). Some stepparents believe that they have lost control of financial or time resources that go toward the stepchildren. Many divorced fathers view providing economic support for their children as a significant and continuing role (Mandel & Sharlin, 2006).

There are times when I feel like a banker rather than some version of a father and husband. I spend much of my time talking or arguing with my two ex-wives, and my current wife, about finances because each "ex" expects that I should provide more tuition money for the two children who are college students and pay a larger share of my oldest daughter's wedding. This leads to painful conversations with my new wife who wants us to plan trips to China and Eastern Europe. All I want to do is find time and money to play golf once a week!

The Combined Functions

Depending on their circumstances, families combine these five role functions in unique ways. If both spouses are highly successful in their careers, they may devote money and time to recreation and travel. Housekeeping functions may be provided by a cleaning service. Single parents often face economic stresses, neighborhood safety concerns, and a need to rely on extended family members for child-care assistance. Parents may emphasize the therapeutic and provider roles (Stewart, 2010), depending on the needs of their children. Recreation may be more individually oriented, while kinship functions may receive limited attention. In some single-parent or dual-earner families, children may take on responsibilities such as sibling supervision or meal preparation. In a single-parent system, children may be expected to provide therapeutic listening that would be expected of a spouse in a two-parent household.

The Role Appropriation Process

The key question remains: How do family members learn, demonstrate, adjust, or relinquish these role functions? The answer requires an understanding of the aspects of role appropriation. Role appropriation is a three-part, overlapping process involves role expectation, role enactment, and role negotiation (Stamp, 1994). Issues of role conflict also emerge. Each of these will be explored in the following subsection.

Role Expectations

Society provides models and norms for how certain family roles should be enacted, thus creating role expectations. Walk into any bookstore or look on a parenting website and you will see print or mediated material on how to be a good parent, partner, grandparent, or stepparent. The media provides many family role models through television specials, situation comedies, movies, or talk shows. Daily life within a community also serves as a source of role expectations. When you were growing up, the neighbors and your friends probably all knew who were the "good" mothers or the "bad" kids on the block or in the community. Religious and educational organizational cultures and school leaders set expectations for how family members should behave. Each of you has grown up with expectations for how people should function in family roles, just as the following example shows:

My mother grew up on a ranch in the Great Uinta Basin in Utah. The women in her family were extremely strong and used to doing "men's work." Again, whatever had to be done would be done by whoever was available. It didn't matter whether one was a girl or boy—all hands were necessary and looked upon as being equal in her family.

Cultural groups convey beliefs about parenting or spousal roles, which are learned by members of their community. In the Jewish tradition, the role of mother is associated with the transmission of culture and primary values; as such, it carries a particular significance and implies certain expectations (Rosen & Weltman, 2005). Historically African American women have worked outside the home, often as the solo or major breadwinner in order to support their families (Hines & Boyd-Franklin, 2005). *Familism* dominates life in Puerto Rican families: whereas women are gaining personal power by contributing financially to the household, men may suffer some loss in status if their wives work (Garcia-Preto, 2005a).

In addition, role expectations also arise from significant others and complementary others. *Significant others* are those persons you view as important and who provide you with models from which you develop role expectations. In addition to family members, a favorite teacher who combined a career with a family may influence your role choices. Thus, part of learning roles occurs by observing and imitating role models, persons whose behavior serves as a guide for others.

Complementary others fulfill reciprocal role functions. During the later stages of romantic relationships, couples spend long periods of time discussing their expectations for a future spouse. "I want my partner to be home with the children until they go to school" or "I need a partner who will help parent my children from my first marriage." A future stepparent may try to explore expectations with a future older stepchild; a parent and college-aged child may discuss expectations for their interaction during summer vacations.

When one parent dies or leaves the family, the other parent may expect a child to fulfill an emotional role of confidant or a task role of household helper. "You're the man of the house now" typifies this lowering of boundaries between parent and child subsystems often resulting in communication breakdowns. Frequently such an expectation places great pressure on the child, alienates the child from other siblings, and eventually interferes with the normal process of separating from the family at the appropriate developmental period.

Dual-career families face constant role negotiation.

© PhotoInc / iStockphoto.com

Additional expectations arise from each person's self-understanding. You may find that, with your skills or personality, you wish to be a certain kind of partner or parent. Sometimes one's role expectations clash with those of significant others.

Colleen and I have disagreements with our parents. They expect us to produce grandchildren, but neither of us wants the responsibility of children. It has taken each of us over a decade to finish our educations by paying for it on our own and working full-time. We love our dog, but that doesn't guarantee we would be nurturing parents!

Finally, role expectations reflect an imagined view of yourself—the way you like to think of yourself being and acting. A father may imagine himself telling his child about the facts of life. A teenager may imagine lecturing a younger sibling on avoiding drug use. Such imaginings are not just daydreams; they serve as a rehearsal for actual performance. No matter what you imagine, until you enact your role with significant others, you remain at the role expectation point.

Role Enactment

Role enactment involves role performance or complementary interactive behavior. As with role expectations, role performance reflects the individual's capacity for enacting the role.

Persons in complementary or opposing roles impact your role performance. Have you ever tried to reason with a parent who sulks, pamper an independent grandparent, or correct a willful child? However, if two complementary family members perceive things in similar ways, it enhances role performance. Young adults living with their parents may believe that they should no longer be subject to curfews and notifying parents of their evening plans; this belief will be reinforced by parents who no longer ask. If a mother's advice to her adult son and his wife about caring for their sick infant is appreciated and followed, the mother will likely continue to give such advice. Thus, the way others assume their roles and comment on your role affects how you enact your role.

Additionally, your background influences your behavior. For example, if certain communication behaviors are not part of your repertoire, they cannot magically appear in a particular situation. A father may wish he could talk with his son instead of yelling at him or giving orders, but he may feel incompetent when discussing controversial subjects with his child. Self-confidence in attempting to fulfill a role also affects behavior. A shy stepmother may not be able to express affection either verbally or nonverbally with her new stepchildren for many months. On occasion, people discover that they can function well in a role they did not expect or desire, as this woman discovered:

I was really furious when my husband quit his sales job to finish his degree. I didn't choose the role of provider and I didn't like being conscripted into it. But after a while, I got to feeling very professional and adult. Here I was supporting myself and a husband. I didn't know I had it in me.

When trying to enact both work roles and family roles, partners' experiences may be somewhat different. Among a predominantly working-class population, women's sense of balance between their work and family roles depends on their gender ideology. Women who enact a more traditional gender ideology perceive more balance in their roles than women who had a less traditional gender ideology, but men's gender ideology did not affect their sense of balance between work and family roles (Marks, Huston, Johnson, & MacDermid, 2001). Some men attempt to enact both work and family fully, resulting in the "superdad" role. In a study of male science and technology workers in Silicon Valley, Cooper (2000) found that "superdads" attended to both the emotional and care needs of their families as well as investing heavily in their work, whereas other male colleagues remained in the traditional male role or chose to invest more in work when work-family pressures arose.

Today increasing numbers of gay male partners choose to become parents. Because this option became available only relatively recently, those in the first generation of partnered "intentional" fathers have few role models (Lewin, 2009). Therefore these men need to negotiate their roles as partners and parents.

Choosing to enact one role may affect a person's ability to assume other roles as well. Hewlett (2002) studied how highly educated women in the top 10 percent of earning power have enacted roles in their lives. At age 40, one-third of these women were childless, most not by choice. Instead, enacting the very demanding role of a consultant, lawyer, doctor, or other professional left these women with very little time to pursue romantic relationships. For male professionals, however, the opposite was true. The more successful they were in their careers, the more likely they were to be married with children. More recently, Sheryl Sandberg (2013), the Chief Operating Officer of Facebook, attempted to publically debunk this perception citing a study of female CEOs of Fortune 500 companies, indicating that of those 28 women, "twenty-six were married, one was divorced, and only one had never married" (p. 110).

Frequently family members hold different perceptions of how other family members enact certain roles. For example, Mikkelson (2008) asked fathers to report their involvement and emotional involvement with their children. Their children's mothers (whether or not they were married to the fathers) were also asked to report on the father's involvement and emotional involvement with their children. Fathers reported spending 17.6 percent more time with their children than the mothers estimated.

Role Negotiation

Effective role enactment involves communication as well as implicit agreement among those in related roles. Individuals enacting their complementary roles, such as stepfather and stepdaughter, experience a process whereby, in communication with others, they socially construct and structure their reality and give meaning to their lives as we discussed in Chapter 2. This is called role negotiation. In describing the move to parenthood, Stamp (1994) found that, when couples become parents, "their ongoing conversation constructs, monitors, and modifies the new reality of their changed existence. Their new roles are appropriated into their overall identities" (p. 91). This critical use of communication applies to assuming and maintaining any family role. In the case of Jarvis and his son Jamal, discussed at the beginning of the chapter, bringing a new family member into the system requires negotiation.

The role enactment process involves implicit or explicit negotiations with those family members in related roles. Discussions may involve reconstructing differences and exploring new ways to act regarding certain expectations, sometimes through direct confrontation or through experimentation and adjustments to discover how the other reacts to a new role behavior. Becoming a new mother is associated with increased housework and more disagreements with spouses as compared to wives without children, although this finding did not hold true for husbands (Nomaguchi & Milki, 2003). Some gay male parents report, that as same-sex couples, they were free of gender role expectations which gave them greater flexibility in choosing responsibilities or allowing responsibilities to evolve, partly based on personality style (Gianino, 2008). Finally, an individual's roles need to be integrated with other members' roles. Occasionally family members must integrate the sometimes-conflicting roles of parent, partner, daughter, aunt, grandmother, and friend, all with their own expectations and demands.

Frequently, role negotiation involves managing conflict. Individual family members may know what is expected of them, but some persons may not enact those expected behaviors. For example, a husband and wife may have agreed early in their marriage to share the provider role. However, after having a child, the wife may decide that she prefers instead to stay home with the baby. When this occurs, the organizational structure in the system changes; this creates a new style of interdependence between partners that must be negotiated. When faced with transitions or stresses, couples often have to renegotiate their previously predictable agreements (Webb & Dickson, 2012). In their study of 90 low-income noncustodial fathers, half of whom had been imprisoned and half of whom had criminal histories, Edin, Nelson, and Paranal (2001) found that fathers with damaged family bonds before imprisonment used prison time as an opportunity to turn their lives around and reconnect to their children—a complicated role renegotiation.

Clearly, the potential for **role conflict** exists; in many cases multiple role conflicts occur simultaneously. When complementary or significant others have different expectations of another's role performance, conflict results. An adult son who has moved to a different country may argue with his mother about how frequently he should e-mail, Skype, or return home to visit.

Role conflict frequently occurs when a divorced parent remarries, bringing a stepparent into the family system as there is a lack of clear and institutionalized roles for stepfamily members (Ganong & Coleman, 2004). One study of successful stepmothers found that role ambiguities and role conflicts were a common experience in the early years as they tried to figure out their different role functions, such as nurturing, protecting, coordinating, and disciplining (Whiting, Smith, Barnett, & Grafsky, 2007). Stepmothers overcame some conflicts if they had an accepting attitude, worked to resolve conflicts, and established good support systems.

Role conflict also occurs when a family member tries to enact two incompatible roles simultaneously that are incompatible or are difficult to enact together, such as in the example of Rebekah at the beginning of the chapter. You have experienced examples of role conflict in your family. For instance, a 14-year-old boy who finds out that his 17-year-old sister is sneaking out of the house at night might experience role conflict between his role as the dependable son, who would tell his parents, and his role as a sibling who wants his sister's approval. Frequently, grandparents who, by necessity, assume parental roles experience role conflict. Most report support groups as beneficial in managing these role conflicts (Smith, Savage-Stevens, & Fabian, 2002).

Work-life balance issues arise in most households. Hochschild (1989) introduced the term "the second shift," suggesting that married women often work at taking care of house and children after putting in a full day's work on the job. Over the ensuing decades, most committed partnerships struggled with a variation of this issue. The schedule of parents' work may also impact family functioning. A study of Canadian families found that parents working evenings, nights, and weekends was associated with lower family functioning and less effective parenting, as compared to families with parents working standard weekday hours (Strazdins, Clements, Korda, Broom, & D'Souza, 2006).

Many factors influence the role conflicts between work and family responsibilities. Campbell Clark's (2000) work-family border theory helps to explain how and why conflict between work and family roles increases or decreases. The theory proposes that when the domains of work and home have similar cultures and weak borders, it is easier to flow back and forth between them, causing less conflict. For instance, a parent's ability to bring work home when a child is ill, and to also work at the office on the weekend, if needed, indicates weak borders. However, in cases where one domain has a strong border and the other has a weak border, work-family balance favors the domain with which a person identifies most strongly. Imagine a woman who identifies primarily as a mother, but works in a field with a very strong border, such as a television producer. This theory explains that the wife and mother in the next entry will experience less work-family balance than her partner.

As the wife of a trial lawyer with a national firm, I ended up with a great number of child-care responsibilities even as I tried to achieve tenure at my college. He left the house before six in the morning so, if one of my young twin children woke up feeling sick, I had to find him in order to teach my classes.

As you will read in later chapters, predictable and unpredictable life crises affect the roles you assume and how you function in them. Unforeseen circumstances may alter life in such a way that roles change drastically from those first planned or enacted. In some cases, state or federal policy determines how roles may be enacted. For example, the Family and Medical Leave Act, signed into law in 1993, requires U.S. large employers and public agencies to provide up to 12 weeks of unpaid leave for the birth or adoption of a child. Most other countries have more flexible legislation (Bernard, 2013).

Mature and functional families set aside time to discuss and try to come to agreement on roles. Couples who take time to debrief and share work experiences greatly increase their relational satisfaction (Vangelisti & Banski, 1993). Like everything else in families, roles are dynamic and continually shift over time. Role conflict can be heightened when we are enacting roles in ways that are outdated for couples and families. Certainly, increasing each partner's sense of worth affects his or her role performance and lessens conflict. The following section addresses how couples and families have been grouped based on research in typologies that are now used for research purpose.

Couple and Family Typologies

Couple or family typologies represent another way to explore how roles develop through family interaction. Many family researchers and therapists believe family behavior and organization can be classified into various typologies, depending on the patterns of the interactions. Typologies are useful to researchers and students of family communication because they help bring order to phenomena studied in family communication. We will discuss two couple typologies and one family typology.

Couple-Oriented Typologies

Fitzpatrick's Couple Types   An extensive attempt to classify couple types is found in Mary Anne Fitzpatrick's research (Fitzpatrick & Badzinski, 1994; Fitzpatrick, Fallis, & Vance, 1982; Noller & Fitzpatrick, 1993). In her early work,

Fitzpatrick (1977, 1988) tested a large number of characteristics to find out which made a difference in maintaining couple relationships. She isolated eight significant factors that affect role enactment: (1) conflict avoidance, (2) assertiveness, (3) sharing, (4) the ideology of traditionalism, (5) the ideology of uncertainty and change, (6) temporal (time) regularity, (7) undifferentiated space, and (8) autonomy. All eight factors affect role enactment. Fitzpatrick designated three **couple types** called traditionals, separates, and independents. She also found six mixed-couple types wherein the husband and wife described their relationship differently. She found that 20 percent are traditionals, 17 percent are separates, and 22 percent are independents (1988). Thus, about 60 percent can be classified as pure types and 40 percent as mixed. As you read this, you can think about how couples you know fit into her typology.

Independent types accept uncertainty and change. They pay limited attention to schedules and traditional values. Independents represent the most autonomous of the types but do considerable sharing and negotiate autonomy. Independents are more likely to conflict and to support an androgynous, flexible sex role (Fitzpatrick, 1988).

Separates differ from independents in greater conflict avoidance, more differentiated space needs, fairly regular schedules, and less sharing. In relationships, separates maintain a distance from people, even their spouses. They experience little sense of togetherness or autonomy. Separates usually oppose an androgynous sexual orientation and tend to avoid conflict (Fitzpatrick, 1988).

Traditionals uphold a fairly conventional belief system and resist change or uncertainty because it threatens their routines. This leads to a high degree of interdependence and low autonomy. They will engage in conflict but would rather avoid it. Traditionals, like separates, demonstrate strong sex-typed roles and oppose an androgynous orientation (Fitzpatrick, 1988).

The other six mixed types have the husband designated by the first term. These are traditional/separate, separate/traditional, independent/separate, separate/independent, traditional/independent, and independent/traditional (Fitzpatrick, 1988). These are not a category of "leftovers," but represent many different couple systems (Fitzpatrick & Ritchie, 1994). In the separate/traditional category, couples had low consensus on a number of relational issues, but they were moderately cohesive. These couples claimed high satisfaction for their relationship and outwardly expressed much affection (Noller & Fitzpatrick, 1993).

Research using the couple types continues. For example, separate couples score lowest on commitment, dedication, and satisfaction among the couple types (Givertz, Segrin, & Hanzal, 2009). Although research indicates that traditional couples tend to be the most satisfied, followed by mixed (traditional/separate) and then by independents and then separates, each couple type has the potential to create satisfactory marriages (Kelley, 2012).

Table 7.1 summarizes the ways in which couple types responded to a variety of relationship measures, including sex roles and gender perceptions. In predicting communication, you might expect that traditional families would demonstrate affection and sharing of the role functions discussed earlier in this chapter, with males and females remaining in defined positions. You could expect male dominance in attitudes and values regarding the providing, recreational, housekeeping, sex, and kinship functions, since the traditional type resists change. Because independents are

TABLE 7.1 Couple Type Differences on Relational Measures

Couple Types	Marital Satisfaction	Cohesion	Consensus	Affectional Expression	Sex Roles	Psychological Gender States (Wives Only)
Traditionals	High	High	High	Moderately high	Conventional	Feminine
Independents	Low	Moderately high	Low	Low	Nonconventional	Sex-typed androgynous
Separates	Low	Low	Moderately high	Low	Conventional	Feminine sex-typed
Separates/ traditionals	Moderately high	Moderately high	Moderately high	High	Conventional	Feminine sex-typed
Other mixed types	Moderately high	Low	Low	Moderately high	Depends on mixed type	Depends on mixed type

more open to change, they might be more open to dual-career marriages and sharing the providing and housekeeping functions. Because independents value autonomy and avoid interdependence, individual partners may be freer in their role functions.

Potential problems when communicating about role functions applies especially to the separates who have not addressed, or cared to address, managing the interdependence/autonomy issue in their marriage. Fitzpatrick uses the label "emotionally divorced" for this type, because separates are least likely to express their feelings to their partners. Baxter (1991), in her explorations of dialectical theory, suggests that Fitzpatrick's traditionals privilege continuity over discontinuity, with independents privileging change over continuity, with separates somewhere in the middle.

Gender-Organized Couple Types   Other researchers have created couple types based on how gender beliefs are used to organize the relationship (Cowdery & Knudson-Martin, 2005; Knudson-Martin & Mahoney, 2005). Imagine how members of the following three couple types can be applied to dual-earner and non-dual-earner couples. *Post-gender* couples are those who have made a conscious effort to move past gender as a way to organize the relationship and tasks associated with it. For example, partners that perceive each other as having equal responsibility and power in all household and child-rearing tasks would be considered post-gender. *Gender-legacy* couples do not overtly recognize gender as the reason for their division of labor, but use it by default to do so. For example, if both spouses work, the wife in a gender-legacy couple may be more likely to organize her schedule to maximize her time at home. A husband, although he says he is an equal partner in child care, may describe his wife as being more "in tune" with others' needs (Knudson-Martin & Mahoney, 2005). Traditional couples use gender as a conscious method of dividing labor in the relationship and see their roles, though different, as equal. Though each takes on different tasks, they view their roles as deserving equal respect.

Such use of gender also affects parenting and the construction of the role of mother. Cowdery and Knudson-Martin (2005) reported that fathers in traditional and gender-legacy couples have an indirect relationship with their children that is moderated by the mother. Instead of caring for children because the children need their care, these fathers report caring for children because the mother needs a break. In contrast, post-gender fathers have direct relational connections with their children, assuming that responsibility is shared. The leading marital researcher John Gottman developed a well-known couple typology based on conflict styles. This typology will be discussed in Chapter 9.

Family Typologies

You will recall from Chapter 1 that families can be understood and classified by their **family communication patterns,** particularly cohesion and adaptation (flexibility). Another model of family communication patterns influences roles. This typology of family communication patterns relies on two dimensions of communication, labeled **conformity orientation** and **conversation orientation** (Koerner & Fitzpatrick, 2006). Some families' communication behavior may be characterized by one of these orientations, while other families may be divided by members who use one while others prefer the opposite. In a family high on conformity, members express similar values and attitudes, which in turn enhances harmony. A family low on conformity expresses more varied values, attitudes, and patterns of interaction. It upholds individuality and brings out the unique personalities of family members. Family members high on the use of conversation have an open family system so that individuals can speak their minds easily on a whole range of conflict issues with little fear of what they say. In families low on this dimension, members speak out less frequently on fewer conflict issues. These dimensions both contribute to and reflect roles that members enact in the family system.

Fitzpatrick and Ritchie (1994) describe four different kinds of families: (1) consensual, (2) pluralistic, (3) protective, and (4) laissez-faire, based on the family's use of either a conformity or conversation orientation in their interactions (see Figure 7.2). This typology recognizes that families can function well with different types of behaviors and that there is not just one functional way to communicate (Koerner & Fitzpatrick, 2006). Consensual families are high in both conversation and conformity strategies with their communication characterized by pressure for agreement, although children are encouraged to express ideas and feelings. Pluralistic families, high in conversation orientation and low in

	High Conversation Orientation	Low Conversation Orientation
High Conformity Orientation	Consensual	Protective
Low Conformity Orientation	Pluralistic	Laissez-faire

FIGURE 7.2

Family types based on family communication patterns

conformity, have open communication and emotional supportiveness. Protective families rank low on the use of a conversational approach and high on conformity dimensions. They stress upholding family rules and avoiding conflict. Laissez-faire families, low on both conformity and conversation dimensions, interact very little. In this kind of family, children may look outside the family for influence and support.

Differences also exist among family types in parenting roles and in the motives parents have for talking to children. For example, in the two family types that are marked by a high conversation orientation (consensual and pluralistic), parents have relational motives for talking with their children, such as for pleasure or relaxation or to show affection. In the protective family types, parents are motivated to communicate with their children to seek control, although these parents also report affection as one reason they communicate with their children (Barbato, Graham, & Perse, 2001). In a recent study examining family communication patterns and adoption, Rueter and Koerner (2008) found that protective families and laissez-faire families were unable to lessen the adolescent adjustment risks that are associated with adoption. However, adopted adolescents in consensual and pluralistic families were no different in adjustment risks than non-adopted adolescents.

Another study examined cross-cultural differences in family communication patterns, finding that the consensual family type was most common in the United States, while the laissez-faire family type was most common in Japan. In both countries, conversation orientation was associated with communication satisfaction, while American participants reported less communication satisfaction when conformity orientation was higher (Shearman & Dumlao, 2008).

It is important to think about family communication patterns and types from a transactional perspective, as family communication patterns are developed through interaction between family members. Family member roles and couple's marriage and parenting styles heavily influence family communication patterns (Koerner & Fitzpatrick, 2004), and adolescent communication also affects these patterns (Saphir & Chaffee, 2002).

Conclusion

This chapter relies on an interactive approach to roles, stressing the effect of family interaction on role development and performance and vice versa. The distinction between position-oriented and person-oriented roles was applied to everyday family communication. The five role functions presented in a mobile model are explained with more emphasis placed on those roles that rely more heavily on communication strategies as the way we develop and enact family roles. The development of roles takes part in a three-step process—role expectation, role enactment, and role negotiation—each of which has communication components.

Finally, the couple and family typologies attempt to render family members' interactions more understandable and predictable. They are viewed as sources for understanding the communication practices that undergird family patterns. When examining family roles or couple/family types, emphasis is placed on their dynamic nature, which is viewed in accordance with the personal developments and unpredictable circumstances faced by the family members in specific families.

In Review

1. Discuss how family roles may change by 2025. How might families be similar or different at that point? What new roles may emerge or disappear?
2. Compare and contrast the communication tasks required to carry out the role functions involved in providing resources and nurturance for the family. Describe how these functions are enacted in a family with which you are familiar.
3. Identify a real or fictional family that changed over time. Note how some family roles may have shifted in the past few years and give reasons for these changes. What has been the effect of these role changes on the family system?
4. Identify two examples of adult partnerships you know that fit Fitzpatrick's couple types. Describe some communication strategies that the partners use.
5. Identify a media character who has been part of two or more serious romantic relationships. How did the character change within this new partnership? Give two examples of changes in communication style.
6. How do different communication technologies affect family roles and communication patterns today? How has this changed over the last 10 to 15 years? What changes do you anticipate by 2025?

Key Words

Complementary others 168	McMaster's family role functions 157
Conflict types 155	Role conflict 172
Conformity orientation 176	Role enactment 157
Conversation orientation 176	Role expectations 160
Couple types 174	Role negotiation 166
Family communication patterns 176	Significant others 168
Family roles 156	Spillover 166

CHAPTER 8

Power, Influence, and Decision-Making in Families

LEARNING OBJECTIVES

- Trace the source of power in families and the transactional nature of power
- Compare and contrast Cromwell and Olson's three aspects of power
- Identify five sources of power in families
- Demonstrate how different influence strategies may be used by individual family members or subgroups
- Analyze the factors affecting family decision-making
- Illustrate communication skills that facilitate family decision-making

---

When Alberto and Michael fell in love four years ago, they had a series of conversations about their future, including whether they would ever become parents together. At that time Michael declared his strong desire to be a father while Alberto indicated he was open to thinking about it. By the time of their commitment ceremony, two years later, they told their guests that parenthood would be in their future—somehow. Since then they have held many conversations on the pros and cons of reaching parenthood through adoption or by using a surrogate. At first Alberto believed it would be important for one of them to have a biological link to the child, although Michael felt so less strongly. But when they learned of the large financial commitment involved, that path to fatherhood seemed closed. After watching two sets of friends adopt children through a local state agency, they started searching the Web about their options. Reading the stories of other couples who had successfully adopted and seeing their friends with their babies made this all seem more possible. They met with the social worker and decided to pursue the adoption. The agency personnel indicated that most birth parents tended to request an open adoption, giving them some contact with the family as the child grows up. After much discussion Michael and Alberto decided to agree to an open or closed adoption and to accept a child of any ethnic or racial background. After many months they were paired with a single pregnant birth mother who desired an open adoption. At this point the two anxious men are waiting for a phone call from the agency inviting them to meet their new son.

These days Alberto and Michael are discussing which of them will be the legal father because state regulations do not permit adoption by same-sex parents. They also need to decide what a child would call each of them. Michael prefers "Daddy," whereas Alberto is considering "Papa" or "Pops". At this point all they want to hear are the words, "Come meet your son!"

Robert groaned when he got the phone call from his mother. His father had "blown up" at his grandfather, and now his parents were not speaking to his grandparents, despite living next door to each other in the town Robert grew up in. Robert's 35 years of life had been peppered with similar fights and splits. He had not seen his aunt and uncle since he was 12 because of a falling out they had with his grandparents, and he had had a similar issue with his grandparents during his college years. Robert had just accepted that this was the way his family was, and had moved across the country when he married to get away from all of this family drama. While he appreciated the convenience of being able to keep in touch and up on what is happening with the family by e-mail and social media, it seemed easy to get drawn into family problems and worry about them constantly. Robert had two young children and was planning a weeklong stay in his hometown this summer. He did not want to bring his wife and his children into this family feud, and he certainly did not want to worry about having to separate time with his parents and his grandparents. He had to do something!

Robert considered many courses of action. He thought about threatening his parents and grandparents that if they couldn't solve their problems, he would not visit. He was the only child, and knew that they would be very sad not to see their grandchildren/great-grandchildren. But he wasn't sure he'd actually follow through on such a threat. He could try reasoning with them and explaining to them why this was going to be so difficult for him. However, he'd tried this when they'd had their last falling out and both sides were just so stubborn it didn't work. Ultimately, Robert decided to appeal to his family's minister, Pastor Michael. He called the pastor and discussed the situation with him, asking him to please help.

W hom do you ask for permission to skip a family reunion? If you believe a family member is not taking care of their health, what do you do or say? When are the times that you yield to the wishes of another person in the family and when do you stand your ground? How do members of your family communicate and make decisions? When you made a choice about where to enroll for college, how involved were your family members in this decision? The answers to these questions tell you something about power, influence, and decision-making in your family, concepts that we address in this chapter. Family members' ability to influence one another is related to power and both affect how families make decisions. Communication is the central process by which power and influence are enacted in the family system and we interact to negotiate decisions. In addition, all three processes influence how we interact within the family and what we discuss or withhold.

As you probably realize from your own experience, the concepts of family power, influence, and decision-making are interrelated. In the second case to open this chapter, Robert has to decide if he will try and insert himself into the conflict between his parents and grandparents by threatening not to let his parents see the grandchildren. The Jamison family's decision to go to Disney World for summer vacation may be the result of 10-year-old Ben's persistent attempts to influence his parents and sisters. Or, a father may decide that because he paid a $400 fee for his son's martial arts class, his son cannot quit the class. Despite how closely these concepts are connected, they need individual attention. Family members use different types of power; one family member's power does not always result in gaining influence for her or having others reach the decision she supports. As you read this chapter, think of the ways in which power, influence, and decision-making have been negotiated and enacted in families that you have observed.

Power

Power is present in all human relationships and interactions. Power has been conceptualized as "the ability (potential or actual) of an individual to change the behavior of other family members" (Noller & Fitzpatrick, 1993, p. 124). While individual family members may enact power in the family, subsets within the family or whole families may enact power to influence other family members. For instance, mothers and fathers have parental power to influence a child, adult siblings may have power to influence an elderly parent, or a branch of a family that has significant economic resources may assert a powerful influence over whole family decisions. Thus we understand that power operates transactionally in a family, meaning that it does not belong to an individual; rather, it is negotiated in a relationship between two or more persons (Dunbar, 2004). In other words, you need other people around to have power; if you lived alone on a desert island you would have no power without other humans with whom you interact. The same is true in families as no one has power without the presence of others.

Power is an inherent part of human relationships and family life—it is simply impossible to live in a family without encountering power negotiations or engaging in them yourself. While at first glance we might think of power as something adults yield, children also enact power in the family (Socha & Yingling, 2010). For instance, a child quickly learns that she can get attention and snap parents into action by claiming to have a stomachache and demanding to stay home from school. The first few times this happens, the family system is thrown into last-minute chaos as the parents negotiate who will stay home from work with the child. Like everything else in families, the negotiation of power is ongoing and is dynamic, as the family recalibrates itself. In the situation above, the parents may realize what is happening and next time tell their daughter she may stay home from school on Friday but because she is ill they will need to cancel her slumber party on Saturday. Within ten minutes she may display a miraculous recovery.

The power dimension in a family system may vary greatly over time, depending on a host of factors, such as family structure, developmental stage, external stresses, and the family's economic, cultural, or intellectual resources. One cannot assume that all families experience and exercise power in similar ways. Family systems are rooted in culture, values, and histories in which **power processes** may operate differently as in the following example:

When my parents separated and Dad left the house, my mom, sister, and I moved in with my grandmother. She quickly became the ruling force in our lives. My mother would go along, out of respect for her age and that fact that she had taken us in. Grandma would yell and scream if something wasn't done the way she wanted. We had no voice in her rulings, and Mom and I would often secretly do what we wanted. We kids left home sooner than we might have in order to escape Grandma's domination.

Within a given culture there will be power differentials based on ethnicity, gender, age, or economic advantage. For example, the older immigrant generation may use religion as a way to cope with powerlessness (McGoldrick, Giordano, & Garcia-Preto, 2005) whereas the younger generation may increase power through education. In some religions, husbands are accorded greater power than wives. Women may have additional power when it comes to making decisions about caring for infants; however, in families in which a husband stays home as the primary caregiver, he may have more power on decisions regarding the child. In any given culture, certain discourses are given a central or powerful position and others are pushed to the margins (Baxter, 2011). In the case of the stay-at-home dad, gendered discourse that holds women as primarily responsible for children's care is dominant and these fathers may be judged outside the family as second-class parent or too weak for the workforce. At the same time, researcher Karla Bergen (2010b) interviewed women who lived away from their families for work and found they received a much harsher judgment as a parent than men who did the same thing.

It is important to understand that power can affect communication in family relationships in non-influence and non-decision-making situations as well. Power appears both in everyday conversations and during intimate self-disclosure (Dunbar, 2004). In order to understand the complexity of power and its communication dynamics within family systems, you need to examine the aspects of power that impact family systems and the development of power in family systems.

Aspects of Power in Family Systems

Power can be conceptualized in multiple ways. Cromwell and Olson (1975) conceptualized power to include (1) power bases, (2) power processes, and (3) power outcomes. We will use their typology as a starting point as we talk about each one, and will highlight the role of family communication and power.

Power Bases   The foundation of family power are resources used by family members that allow them to attempt to exert control in a specific situation. Resources consist of whatever is perceived as rewarding to an individual or a relationship; it is anything that one partner makes available to the other to satisfy needs or attain goals (Socha & Yingling, 2010). McDonald (1980) described five sources from which persons may derive power. They include normative, economic, affective, personal, and cognitive resources.

1. *Normative resources* refer to the family's values and to the cultural or societal expectations of where authority lies. Normative definitions represent the culturally internalized expectations of how family relationships should function, that which are the perceived role expectations and obligations of members; for example, in many cultures, family norms stipulate that the mother have the power in managing the children's daily care and activities. Interestingly, a researcher studying Turkish families found that the higher the level of education a father has, the more decreased is his perceived power in relation to his wife and son (Schonpflug, 2001). The author of this study speculated that fathers with more education operate under a more egalitarian mode in the family. In some cultures, the responsibility and power for caring for parents is given to the adult child, which impacts medical decision-making.

2. *Economic resources* refer to the monetary control exerted by family members as persons designated to make financial decisions. Economic power comes from wages earned and money saved or inherited, and thus family breadwinners often have power over this resource. Historically economic resources have been controlled. For instance, in some families, a breadwinning parent may refer to the household income as "my money." Power differentials can occur due to changes in economic resources. Due to the recent recession, 13 percent of parents reported that a young adult moved back home, placing that person in a less powerful position (Wang & Morin, 2009). In Taiwanese marriages, the wife's resources gained from education and employment help to determine the balance of marital power (Xu & Lai, 2002).

3. *Affective resources* reflect involvement, commitment, nurturing, and the power to give or withhold affection. For instance, a caring foster parent has the power to provide her foster daughter with affection hoping that will result in trust and increased self-esteem, or a father may try and change the behavior of an adolescent who broke curfew by withholding his normal affection.

4. *Personal resources* refer to a family member's individual characteristics such as personality, physical appearance, and role competence (McDonald, 1980). They also include interpersonal factors for which the individual would be perceived as attractive or competent, and therefore accorded power. For example, a grandson may have the ability to make his grandparents laugh by talking in a funny voice. He soon learns that using this voice allows him to say things that otherwise would get him into trouble.

5. *Cognitive resources* refer to perceptions of power that family members have to influence their own and others' actions and affect others. It deals with using intelligence to logically determine what power options are available. Some children learn at a young age what strategies to use when trying to get what they want from different family members. Many immigrant children serve as "cultural brokers" because they speak English better than any adult relative, providing resources to older generations but dismantling the traditional family power structure (Bush, Bohon, & Kim, 2010).

It is likely that no family member possesses all five power bases equally or uses all of them in a given situation or with a given person. Some power bases may never be used, whereas others may be used in combination, in certain situations, or with certain other family members. For instance, June, a partner in a prominent law firm, may use normative and economic power resources in her interactions with her husband, and simultaneously use cognitive and affective resources in her interactions with her young children. This process of engaging multiple power bases is exemplified by the following:

I can influence Uncle Fernando. I simply have to go about it the right way! He states his ideas and expects the rest of us to agree. Then I join with my sisters and together we argue with him. We talk about what we learned in political science or history courses and, because he did not go to college, he has trouble refuting our points. Eventually we wear him down and he gives up.

Power Processes   Power processes regard how power is used in family interactions, in those family communication practices that influence family discussions, arguments, and decision-making (Socha & Yingling, 2010). These include assertiveness, negotiation, and persuasion (discussed later in this chapter) (McDonald, 1980). As you know from your own experience, the longest or loudest talker may not hold the power. Effective communicators understand power processes and how to communicate in ways that are competent, meaning they communicate in ways that are appropriate and flexible, understanding how to make arguments and adapt their communication in different situations (Spitzberg & Cupach, 2002). A family member may have the normative or economic power bases but they also need to communicate effectively to use those power bases. A powerful person may use nonverbal cues to communicate power; for example, they may stand when others are sitting, speak first or most during interactions, or establish more direct eye contact (i.e., "stare someone down") (Burgoon, Guerrero, & Manusov, 2011).

Messages created by ill or dysfunctional members can also influence family power. Families with alcoholic members have learned just how powerful that member can be. Everyone may learn to tiptoe around the drinker and develop strategies to minimize the alcoholic's verbal abuse. This places the alcoholic into a central and powerful position in the family, although he or she may be talked about as weak or helpless. Conversely when an adult alcoholic makes progress toward sobriety, it is not unusual for his or her partner to unconsciously undermine the drinker's recovery in order to maintain the respected position as the competent one (LePoire & Dailey, 2006). Therefore, a family member who acts helpless can control the other's behavior in a relationship just as effectively as another who dominates, as this respondent reports:

My sister, I think, has a great deal of power in my family because she positions herself as dependent and helpless. Everyone is supposed to help Tamika because she can't cope. I think she is highly capable, deliberately or not, of manipulating everyone to meet her needs. She preferred to remain unemployed while she was single! And, now that she has a kid, she has a very good reason not to work and to need help in every way—money, child care, home, car. My mother falls for it all the time.

Power Outcomes   The final area, family **power outcomes**, focuses on who makes decisions and is able to influence others in the family. Cromwell and Olson (1975) talked about this as who wins or gets their way. These outcomes include decisions, solutions, new rules or procedures, emotional effects, and feelings about the decisions (Socha & Yingling, 2010). In this respect, at least one family member gets his or her way or receives rights or privileges of influence.

Power bases influence power outcomes. Family members who hold normative positions of authority wield the greatest power. In the case at the beginning of the chapter, Robert is considering his power bases to "threaten" his grandparents with the potential of not seeing their great-grandchildren, hoping for the outcome of positively influencing family infighting. Often, the balance of power rests with the partner who contributes the greatest economic resources, and we have seen many changes in this aspect of power resources as more women are working outside the home. Women are now the chief source of income in 40 percent of all homes with children, an increase from 11 percent in 1960 (Pew Research Center, 2013). Sources of power may also be tied to rewards. In her dyadic power theory, Dunbar (2004) suggested that satisfaction is tied to perceptions of equality among partners. Satisfaction will be low when one partner views her power as extremely high or extremely low in relation to her partner. When partners view their power differences as moderate or small, satisfaction will be higher. Researchers studying newlywed couples in Singapore reported that couple power tended to become equalized if prioritizing the woman's career encourages men to change role expectations, assume some household tasks, attend to their spouse, and accept partner influence (Quek & Knudson-Martin, 2008). Yet, in this culture, the researchers note that this shift is effective only when men retain the ultimate choice regarding power and their wives can influence them.

Hierarchies in the family system establish guidelines for power processes that avoid conflicts yet affect power outcomes. Family members have orchestration power and/or implementation power (Safilios-Rothschild, 1976). Orchestration power means that only certain family members control family life and make critical decisions. They usually make important decisions that determine the family lifestyle. The person with orchestration power may delegate unimportant and time-consuming decisions to the partner or older child who derives implementation power by carrying out these decisions. For example, a mother may tell her 10-year-old son to find his 6-year-old brother and make sure he cleans his room. In this case, the mother has the orchestration power as she made the decision that the younger child needed to clean the room. But she gave the older child the implementation power by asking him to carry that decision out.

It is important to remember that each family and each family member uses a variety of power sources relevant to their goals and resources. While there are times when a family member has an unshakable power base, in most situations family members must interact and negotiate, attempting to co-create mutually acceptable outcomes. While a parent may believe she or he has the power base to demand an adolescent refrain from driving while texting, in most cases, parents and adolescents will be best served by sharing power via open communication and discussing the issue. In some families and in some cultures, traditional roles, including the biosocial norm of male dominance, are clearly defined. Since no one challenges them, the family operates as if that were the only way to function. For immigrant families that move to another culture with different gender power norms, this can be a challenge, especially as children become part of the new culture, often becoming the language broker for the family. In this role he or she translates for the family in multiple settings including medical appointments, parent-teacher conferences, and business meetings. This role provides them with increased self-esteem and the power to withhold or alter information (Weisskirch, 2006).

Power Development

As we mentioned earlier, due to the systemic nature of family relationships, power develops through a transactional process. For instance, an alcoholic cannot control a spouse unless the nonalcoholic spouse permits it by refusing to detach from the drama (LePoire & Dailey, 2006). A mother relinquishes her own personal control when she gives an "acting-out" child power over her. Only the small child who has limited means of resisting power moves must accept certain power outcomes; for example, an abused child has few means of resisting punishment. In some cultures, gender traditions limit power positions of women in families. To follow, we will look at the power of marital partners, followed by children.

Marriage and Power   Marital power reflects the extent to which one partner loves and needs the other. Marital power is often measured by looking at spouses' dependent love for one another based on the belief that the spouse with the strongest emotional involvement in the relationship is the less powerful (Loving, Hefner, Kiecolt-Glaser, Glaser, & Malarkety, 2004), The spouse with the strongest feelings of attachment emerges in a less powerful position because the person with the least interest more easily controls the one who is more involved. The balance of such power in a relationship can affect how spouses respond physiologically to conflict (Loving et al., 2004). Much of the commonly accepted cultural knowledge about marriage is quite stereotypical when it comes to gender and power. Men are often regarded as more logical objective and more dominant and women as emotional and dependent. However, more current thinking helps us realize that there is greater similarity between the sexes that might see a reversal or more shared characteristics when it comes to power in marriage (Burleson & Kunkel, 2006). In addition we can see power negotiations in the different marital couple types discussed in Chapter 7; for example, we may see a more traditional male-dominated power relationship among traditional couples and more equal power among the independent couple type.

Couples may enter a relationship with unequal power, but the relationship can achieve balance over time, as seen in the following example: Power relationships in marriage may change over time as partners age, become more confident, achieve additional education or economic power, increase trust in one another, or have other experiences that alter the initial power balance and outcomes in the relationship over the years.

In the beginning of our relationship, Jack, who is older, tended to dominate. He had had a previous partner for several years and when that commitment ended, he had made up his mind to be more autonomous in any future relationship. I resented being treated as if I were his former partner and assuming that we would have conflict in similar situations in the same way. Now that we have been together a few years, he realizes that the past is not the present. We can make joint decisions, and both of us are much happier.

In addition, married couples divide authority in different ways across family systems. One model is based on only one spouse having authority, and two models describe couples with more equally divided power (Olson, DeFrain, & Skogrand, 2008):

- *One-spouse dominant.* In one-spouse-dominant families, major areas of activity are influenced and controlled by the dominant spouse, which may be the male or the female. This dominance permeates all areas of family power: the use of resources or bases, power processes, and power outcomes. One spouse demonstrates control in the system, while the other accepts such control. Thus, one spouse often orchestrates and the other implements the power.

- *Syncratic.* A syncratic relationship, characterized by much shared authority and joint decision-making, implies that each partner has a strong say in all important areas. In this relationship both partners may confer and make decisions together, with both partners having input and shared power.
- *Autonomic.* In the autonomic power structure, the couple divides authority; that is, the husband and wife have relatively equal authority but in different areas. Each spouse is completely responsible for specific matters. The wife may have more power over the budget, vacation plans, and choice of new home, while the husband may have more power over the selection of schools, cooking and shopping for food items, and buying appliances and technology. The following example shows how couples negotiate decision-making power:

When Kurt and I married, we agreed never to make big decisions alone, and we've been able to live with that. This way we share the risks and the joys of whatever happens. It just works out best between us if we wait on deciding all important matters until we sound out the other's opinions. It's when we decide over the little things that I know that each of us respects the rights and opinions of the other.

Cultural influences on marital power can also be strong. This is particularly apparent when marital couples immigrate to the United States from a more patriarchal society. In a recent study, researchers compared two groups of Chinese immigrant couples—those in which the husband had been arrested for marital violence and those in which the husband had not. Both groups had experienced a shift in marital power such that the wives had more power following immigration. In the couples where the husband had been violent, wives had gained more education than their husbands as a result of immigration. However, in the couples where there was no history of violence, both spouses had gained education and the husbands had also gained more income than their wives. The researchers concluded that the violent men may have felt the power imbalance favoring their wives more than the nonviolent men, and that they may have used physical violence to regain some of this power (Jin & Keat, 2010).

As we mentioned above, families with ill members will recognize how power transactionally affects all members, and this is especially true in the marital couple. A couple with an alcoholic partner or one with a serious disease will often see shifts in the balance of power. Counselors or support groups can help couples understand and recalibrate relational power in the group and family. For families with addicted members, groups such as Al-Anon help family members learn how to cope with some of the power maneuvers used by the alcoholic member. This includes learning how to ignore power moves that hook family members into nonproductive behaviors. Highly skewed relationships, such as extreme husband or wife dominance, experience greater violence when the partners are unskilled at communication and negotiating these issues (Anderson, Umberson, & Elliott, 2004). Abusive partners aggravate one another through domineering behaviors. If both attempt control and neither submits, conflict escalates.

The degree of violence or abuse a partner experienced in his or her family of origin may relate to the use of coercive power and using force in families. According to Gelles (2010), "While experiencing violence in one's family-of-origin is often correlated with later violent behavior, such experience is not the sole determining factor" (p. 127). Other factors, interpersonal, cultural, and economic, may influence violence patterns. Negative emotions in family relationships can become more intense and irrational than those in other close relationships because families are together longer in an environment with closer and more frequent contact. Because family members assume their relationships have a long future, individual members may see this as a license to violate conversational and relational norms that they would not otherwise violate (Vangelisti, 1993).

Children and Power   Children need to be included in any discussion of family power because they impact family interaction and their words and behaviors affect the development of family rules. Legally and socially, parents are expected to control and be responsible for their children's behavior; yet, although children are often viewed as followers of parental directives, they, are often active power brokers in the family (Socha & Yingling, 2010). Think about the addition of an infant to the family system and you quickly realize that the baby's needs influence when the parents eat and sleep (or not), the family's schedule, and use of economic resources. Children may struggle to establish their position in the family, to gain certain resources, or to establish an identity. Alberto and Michael, the gay couple waiting to adopt in the case at the start of this chapter, are likely well aware of some of the challenges their children may face as children of same-sex parents (Koenig Kellas, & Suter, 2012). In many single-parent families as well as dual-earner families, younger children and adolescents may assume more personal and domestic responsibilities, experiences that not only affect their power but may also enhance their maturity and self-reliance.

Sometimes children influence the interaction and outcomes of power struggles by using power plays such as interruptions or screaming. Children often become adept at playing one parent against the other. "Daddy said I could do it" or "If Mom was here, she'd let me" has echoed through most homes. In some families, one spouse consciously or unconsciously co-opts a child into the role of ally in order to increase the strength of his or her power. Children also gain power by forming alliances with one parent. This may be because children feel they have insufficient power to change other family members' behaviors (Vangelisti, 1994a). In abusive families, children may keep important information about abuse or neglect from other family members or outsiders in order to maintain the family system or because they fear additional abuse (Petronio, Reeder, Hecht, & Mon't Ros-Mendoza, 1996).

Stepfamilies often contend with issues of power and authority in relation to children (Baxter, Braithwaite, Bryant, & Wagner, 2004). Stepparents often found themselves receiving contradictory messages from children wanting their input and direction, but resenting and rejecting it at the same time. Braithwaite and colleagues (2008) learned how children wield power in stepfamilies as they talked with them in focus groups. The young adults talked openly about taking advantage of a co-parent who did not communicate directly or had a lot of conflict. Children gained a lot of power in those families and were able to persuade parents that they had different rules in the other house concerning issues such as curfew, bedtimes, or chores. In fact the stepchildren reported that they dreaded the times their parents would cooperate and find out the truth.

Single-parent families display unique power alliances due to the presence of one adult. A child with a solo parent negotiates directly with only one adult for immediate answers and wields direct personal power. However, the same child cannot form a parent-child alliance to try to change a decision the way a child can in a two-parent family, unless the child creates an alliance with a grandparent, aunt, or uncle.

Children may also form alliances in families that may increase their power, either over a period of time or only for reaching a specific decision. For example, siblings may band together and strategize to persuade parents to buy them their own television for their playroom so they can watch the programs they want. The results of past alliances can obligate family members to believe that they must support another to repay a debt. For example, a child might think, "Leon helped me convince Dad to buy me a new bike. Now I ought to help him argue with Dad to get his own car."

Cultural differences also affect power interactions of children in families. For instance, in Asian families most parents tend to demand filial piety, respect, and obedience from their children (Lee & Mock, 2005). The following remarks describe how the family of origin and cultural background influence power outcomes:

Within our Thai culture, children are taught early to defer and show respect to their elders. Given names are rarely used in conversation, except for older family members talking to younger ones. Respect for relationships is formalized verbally by the use of the term "phi" for older siblings and "nong" for younger siblings. The boy child is very important to Thai families and outranks any girl child.

While young children exercise some power, they usually develop more independent power as they grow older, when they begin to demand and can handle more power within the family structure. A 6-year-old may fight for a new toy, whereas a 16-year-old fights for later curfews and other moves that increase independence. Many children gain expert power through their specialized skills. One mother reported that when her younger child wants to play Wii, she tells him to ask his older brother to set it up, because she does not have those skills.

As families change and move through the life cycle, the original power relationships undergo significant modification as the family network increases, fragments, or solidifies. In addition to developmental issues, other forces affect changes in power, from inflation and environmental factors to changing cultural norms. For example, Child and Westermann (2013) studied how parents and young adults negotiated parental Facebook friend requests. While children may hesitate on granting this access to parents, the researchers believe that the perceived power differential between parents and children made it hard for children to refuse the request. In other situations, especially when a family faces a serious stress such as the death or serious illness of a parent or partner, the other adult may assume greater power or establish new ties with a child that involve sharing power differently.

Communication and Power

Certain family communicative acts may be used to address power issues. Because of the nature of transactional communication, these communicative acts address power only when met with a response that engages them.

Children engage in power struggles at very young ages.

Confirming, disconfirming, and *rejecting* can become a part of power messages when family members attempt to separate and connect in one-up, one-down sub-systems. In a *one-up* position, one family member attempts to exercise more power control over one or more other members. The *one-down* member accepts from the one-up member the control implied in the messages (Escudero, Rogers, & Gutierrez, 1997).

Confirming implies acknowledgment and may be used to gain power when one tries to get another to identify with him or her, or when one tries to give rewards in order to gain power. The careful, nonjudgmental listener may wittingly or unwittingly gain power. The "silent treatment" represents a frequently used *disconfirming* behavior. One family member can put another in a one-down power position with the punishment strategy of disconfirmation. "I'll ignore him; he'll come around" represents such an effort. On the other hand, disconfirming a power message may serve as an effective method of avoiding a power struggle. The child who pretends not to hear "clean up your room" messages effectively deflects the parental power, at least for a while. *Rejecting* messages tie directly to punishment messages and are often used as control in family power plays. "I hate you" or "I don't care what you say" may effectively halt control attempts. Hample and Dallinger (1995) claimed that individuals will avoid argumentative situations when they sense they are being berated and stressed. The negative conflict behaviors of displacement, denial, disqualification, distancing, and sexual withholding can also be used as rejecting power moves.

Self-disclosure serves as a major means of gaining intimacy within a relationship, but it is not without risks. Communication privacy management theory, discussed in Chapter 3, helps us understand that disclosure may also be used as a power strategy when one party attempts to control the other through revealing information (Petronio, 2002). For example, when a self-disclosed affair is thrown back at a spouse during a fight ("Well, you had an affair, so how can you talk?"), the accused person may lose power. Even having to defend an accusation, even if it turns out not to be true, can also result in a loss of power as well. Communicative privacy management theory (Petronio, 2002) sheds light on how couples and families establish boundaries and navigate co-ownership, revealing and concealing information.

Influence

Influence occurs when family members use their power to try to change or modify each other's behavior or beliefs. Family influence involves interpersonal persuasion; it is an intentional attempt to "influence the attitudes, beliefs, and behaviors of others who have some measure of choice about how to respond" (Wilson, Guntzviler, & Munz, 2013, p. 358). Influence in family communication is ever present. Think about your last interaction with a family member and how influence was involved. Were you trying to persuade your father that you indeed understand his position on a given topic and know what you are talking about? Were you trying to influence a sibling to loan you some money? Did one of your parents try to persuade you to join the family for a reunion over a holiday weekend? Were you involved in a debate over an issue, trying to influence a sibling to change his or her opinion? Any parent will tell you of countless attempts to influence a child, whether it is trying to get a teenaged son to clean his room or to convince a toddler to eat her dinner. Influence is a fundamental part of everyday interactions for all family members. In fact, most communication scholars believe that all communicative events can be examined for persuasive qualities (Gass & Seiter, 1999), as we always have influence goals when we interact (Wilson & Morgan, 2006). While sometimes our goals are explicitly persuasive (e.g., trying to persuade an elderly parent to stop driving), in reality all communication involves influence. In what we do and say we are hoping to influence others to see us as knowing what we are talking about, as caring and worthy of love. In the following subsection we discuss the types of influence strategies family members use, who uses which strategies, and which strategies seem to be effective in producing desired change.

Types of Influence Strategies

Influencing other family members requires using interpersonal compliance seeking messages targeted at getting someone to alter his or her behavior or opinions (Canary, Cody, & Manusov, 2008). Family members have goals that they wish to achieve and develop plans to help them achieve their goals (Wilson & Morgan, 2006). For example, you may have a goal of helping your recently widowed grandmother to feel less lonely. You may seek to achieve this goal by developing a plan for you and your cousins to visit her on different weekends over the next three months.

Influence strategies may be characterized as direct or indirect and as a **unilateral influence strategy** or one that is bilateral (Falbo & Peplau, 1980). **Direct influence strategies** include bargaining, reasoning, and asking; **indirect influence strategies** include hinting and withdrawal. Bargaining is an example of a **bilateral influence strategy** or interactive strategy, whereas hinting and withdrawal are examples of unilateral strategies. A number of scholars have developed typologies of **verbal influence strategies**; for example, Guerrero, Andersen, and Afifi (2014) summarized 11 different interpersonal influence strategies and we can see how these would be used in families:

1. **Direct requests:** Asking for what is desired
2. **Bargaining:** Offering to do something in exchange for what is desired
3. **Aversive stimulation:** Behaving in a negative manner (e.g., complain, cry) to achieve what is desired
4. **Ingratiation:** Engaging in positive behaviors to achieve what is desired
5. **Hinting:** Communicating indirectly to achieve what is desired
6. **Moral appeal:** Suggesting what good or moral persons should do to achieve what is desired
7. **Manipulation:** Communicating in ways that elicit negative emotions (e.g., guilt, shame) to achieve what is desired
8. **Withdrawal:** Silence, avoiding, leaving, or other behaviors designed to elicit the desired behavior
9. **Deception:** Exaggeration or lies designed to achieve what is desired
10. **Distributive communication:** Power messages (e.g., bully, antagonize) designed to achieve what is desired no matter what it takes
11. **Threats:** Attempt to intimidate the other via threats that one may or may not intend to carry out

Depending on one's goals, a family member may use one or more of these strategies together or in sequence. An older sister who is trying to get her younger sister to stop taking her clothes without asking may start with hinting ("Has anyone seen my blue shirt, I wanted to wear it tonight?") to direct requests of her sister ("Please stop taking my stuff without asking me first") and proceed to threats ("The next time you take my clothes without asking, I am going to wear your favorite sweater and stretch it out"). In addition, family members will use nonverbal communication as a way to substitute for or back up these verbal strategies. For example, direct eye contact may accompany direct requests, distributive communication, or threats; lack of eye contact may accompany manipulation, deception, or withdrawal; silence may accompany withdrawal.

A study of dual-career couples revealed that both wives and husbands tend to use direct more than indirect strategies and bilateral strategies more than unilateral strategies with their spouses (Weigel, Bennett, & Ballard-Reisch, 2006). Bilateral strategies are also used more often by children who perceive that their parents have higher power than those who perceive their parents to have lower power (Bao, Fern, & Sheng, 2007). A study of Mexican American immigrant women and their partners found that both men and women used direct and indirect strategies, and that both sexes used bilateral strategies more frequently than unilateral strategies (Beckman, Harvey, Satre, & Walker, 1999). The only perceived difference in strategy use between the sexes was that men were more likely than women to buy gifts to influence their partners.

The sender and the receiver of the influence strategy each may perceive the strategy in different ways depending on their perspectives on the relationship (Wilson & Morgan, 2006). For example, Lauren uses a very direct strategy with her younger brother, Joel, to try to get him to carry the garbage to the street: "Joel, take out the garbage!" Lauren thinks that this strategy is perfectly appropriate as she perceives that she has more power over Joel because of her age. Joel, who does not perceive Lauren to have more power over him, finds this strategy to be face threatening and does not comply with it. In their study, Butkovic and Bratko (2007) found that high school students and their parents did not agree when asked to report the types of influence strategies they used on each other, further reinforcing the idea that senders and receivers perceive the strategies differently.

Certain influence strategies tend to be situation specific. For instance, when making joint purchase decisions, marital and cohabiting couples more frequently used influence strategies, such as bargaining and reasoning, than other strategies, such as acting helpless and displaying negative emotions (Kirchler, 1993). Adolescents also use a variety of influence strategies when trying to persuade a parent in a purchasing decision.

Family members may also use influence strategies to persuade each other in specific contexts, for instance to modify health behaviors. In situations where spouses are trying to influence the health behaviors of each other, Tucker and Mueller (2000) found that the most frequently used influence strategies included the following:

- *Engaging in health behavior together.* A wife who thinks her husband needs more exercise might ask him to join her on her nightly walk.
- *Discussing the health issue.* A spouse might give a newspaper or magazine article to the other spouse about a health concern or issue and then request they discuss it.
- *Requesting that the partner engage in the health behavior.* One spouse might use a direct strategy and ask the other spouse to quit smoking.
- *Engaging in facilitative behavior.* A partner may provide help to make behavior easier to achieve; for example, a husband may put a multivitamin on his wife's dinner plate or set aside money each month for her to spend on exercise classes.

You can see several health influence strategies in the following example:

If I didn't cook the broccoli or cut up the cantaloupe for dinner and put it on the table, my husband would certainly revert to his bachelor diet of frozen pizza, macaroni and cheese, and fast food. I also encourage him to make doctor and dentist appointments.

Sometimes I remind him that married men live longer because they have their wives to help them take care of themselves. Although I say it in a lighthearted manner, I really believe that he is healthier since marrying me.

There are a variety of verbal and nonverbal communication behaviors family members can use to influence one another. The more power a person possesses, the more they may succeed with direct or distributive messages. Less powerful members may find indirect strategies less threatening and more successful. One danger with using direct messages is that they are more easily misunderstood or ignored. One may hint around or whine about something they want but these messages can be missed or passed over. On the other hand, a direct request may be clear, but it is much easier to get a "no" in response, which makes achieving influence goals more difficult.

Factors Affecting Influence Strategy Use

As you look at the influence strategies explained in the previous subsection, which ones are you more likely to use with your family members? Most of you would probably answer, "It depends!" It depends on the outcome you are trying to attain, on your closeness to and relational history with a particular family member, and on the power bases that you can use in relation to that family member.

Gender is one factor in social influence that family researchers have attended to, especially as they ask whether husbands and wives use influence strategies differently when trying to persuade their spouse. Traditional stereotypes of a wife nagging her husband come to mind for many people (Soule, 2011). However, in most marriages, the type or amount of persuasion may be similar as spouses try to influence each other. Men and women tend to be quite similar in the types of influence strategies that they use (Baxter & Bylund, 2004). For husbands, marital satisfaction is associated with their use of direct and bilateral/interactive influence strategies (Weigel et al., 2006). Kirchler's (1993) research showed that women are more likely to report using strategies that are more partner oriented, such as offering trade-offs, whereas men are more likely to make autonomous decisions and be less cooperative. When considering persuasion about health issues, wives and husbands are equally likely to use influence strategies on their spouses (Tucker & Anders, 2001).

One challenging area for social influence for women and men surrounds division of labor in the home. Wood (2006) stresses that, despite the significant increase in dual-wage-earner homes or, as we described earlier in the chapter, women who are primary wage earners in families, on average women do more home care than do men. This is an issue over which partners often have conflict and engage in interpersonal persuasion and one that can have very negative effects on partner satisfaction (Alberts, Tracy, & Tretheway, 2011). Wood points out that not only do women tend to do more of the work to maintain the home and children, but the work they do requires greater effort and more psychological responsibility (e.g., remembering everyone's schedules and appointments), and is often less gratifying. Alberts and colleagues (2011) explain some of the challenges couples face; for example, when women attempt to discuss and equalize domestic labor, they may encounter resistance from male partners and negative judgments from others inside and outside the family. At the same time, male partners may become frustrated, as they believe they are making contributions and may believe their partner is being unreasonable and asking them to do something they do not care much about.

It is very important to understand family norms and expectations for the division of domestic labor and how couples communicate and make sense of their practices in this area. Julia Wood (2011) also reminds us to be mindful about the standards that we accept as desirable standards for what our households should look and be like, especially when these standards encourage women to link their identity with a clean house. She points out that these are socially constructed values that can be examined and altered. In addition, it is important to understand norms and expectations for the division of household labor and child care and remember they do not always divide along gender lines. For instance, a male partner who does the cooking may see this as his domain and be very concerned about certain standards of cleanliness in the kitchen and want control over what is done there. Alberts and colleagues recommend that couples have direct discussions of expectations and needs when it comes to domestic labor so as to try and "mitigate conflict/inequities" (2011, p. 34).

Parents and children also engage in influence strategies. The sex of the parent and child and the age of the child make a difference in the types of strategies parents use in an attempt to influence their adolescent children. For example, adolescents were

Engaging in health behaviors together is a good influence strategy.

asked to think of a situation in which their parents were trying to get them to help with spring-cleaning. Older adolescent boys reported their fathers to be more likely to use specific influence strategies, such as pre-giving (e.g., first giving the child permission to stay out late), whereas younger adolescent males reported their mothers would be more likely to use pre-giving (deTurck & Miller, 1983). Conversely, children's persuasion skills depend on their ability to engage in perspective-taking or understand how another might think or feel. By age 4 many children can use multiple strategies and personalize them for a specific parent (Socha & Yingling, 2010). The culture of the family also seems to play a part in determining influence strategy use. In one cross-cultural study, researchers found American mothers to be more likely to use directive statements, such as "Bring me the toy," than did Japanese mothers (Abe & Izard, 1999).

Finally, you may have noticed in this section that we know more about influence strategies in marital couples and in parent-child interactions than we do about other relational forms, such as in same-sex couples, single-parent families, or multiethnic families. For example, how do lesbian or gay-headed families negotiate the division of domestic labor? We can think about how these demands will change for Alberto and Michael as they become parents. Thus is it important to acknowledge that we need more research to understand influence strategies in a wider variety of family forms.

It is important to remember that understanding how to influence another successfully is only one part of the picture. Family members need to know when to accept influence from others as well. Marital researchers who have observed countless couples living temporarily in an apartment in their research lab talked about the importance of knowing when to consent to the influence of another, a "willingness to yield during an argument in order to 'win' in the relationship" (Driver, Tabares, Shapiro, & Gottman, 2012, p. 64). This can be challenging as conflict is normally over differing goals, as we saw in Chapter 7, and accepting influence may mean that we will end up going a different direction than we thought. This does not mean giving up and giving in to everything, but recognizes the value of compromise at times. For the sake of the relationship and partner, knowing when to accept influence may be as important as knowing when to use it.

Decision-Making

Questions such as "Who should talk with Mother about our concerns about her driving?" and "Where should we enroll the twins in preschool?" or "How much should we share with our families about Wei-Lin's history before we adopt her?" represent concerns that require family decision-making. Family members facing family and work conflicts, as discussed in Chapter 7, often face difficult decisions as they manage these tensions. The number of children to have, whether or not one spouse should accept a promotion that requires relocation, and whether money should be spent for private school tuition represent decisions that family members make. Decision-making is the process by which family members make choices, reach judgments, or arrive at solutions. While we are concerned about decision-making in family systems, and families sometimes do make decisions as a whole, in actual practice, most decisions occur within family subgroups, for example, a husband and wife, adult sibling pairs, a parent and two children, or grandparents and a teenage grandson.

Clearly power, influence, and decision-making are closely tied together. Decision-making allows differences between individual family members to be aired and addressed. Decisions are not made as much as they emerge from interactions. Following our perspective on family communication introduced in Chapter 2, this means that decisions are co-constructed in communication. Family members use power resources and influence strategies that we discussed earlier in the chapter to try and meet individual and collective goals. In addition, decision-making processes rely on the repertoire of strategies members have developed to manage conflicting needs and desires as we will discuss in Chapter 9. In addition, in decision-making, family members interact and negotiate their shifting needs for closeness and distance, novelty and predictability, as well as privacy and openness, as we discussed in relational dialectics in Chapter 3. The kind and quality of decisions affect how family roles, rules, or themes are enacted. Today's families struggle to find time to make careful decisions. The pressure on single parents and dual-employed couples or partners with children to set aside time to engage in careful and thoughtful decision-making requires prioritizing among competing demands. The more complex the family system, the more important and potentially complex and challenging are the decision patterns, as demonstrated in this next example:

Both Mom and Dad work overtime. The oldest sibling at home is in charge of decisions that involve those siblings in the house. For example, when my older brother is home, he makes decisions on who can go somewhere or what friend can come over. If he's at work, I take over. My next younger sister does the same for our youngest brother if I have something after school. It's really a problem if the younger two get into arguments because they are close in age.

Decision-making is a process that belongs to the family system, not to an individual. Therefore, decision-making varies greatly among families because each family holds and negotiates about values, dreams, or resources differently. Unlike a small group that comes together to accomplish a particular task, a family has a history of continuous interaction among and between a set of interdependent individuals, and a future that will be impacted by decisions made today. Families tend to remain together even when members disagree. Even if the decision-making process results in turmoil, the family continues, although sometimes as a factional and unhappy one. This is not true of outside groups that often disband when disagreement and lack of shared values and goals become too much for them. For example, a study of parent-adolescent problem-solving reveals that adolescents may vent great anger over decisions on a particular issue, but not be dissatisfied with the overall family relationship (Niedzwiecki, 1997). As family relationships are both involuntary and lengthy, members may use negative messages that ironically function to maintain the family system while reinforcing the separate identities of members rather than focus on communicating ways that bring the family together (Vangelisti, 1993).

Family decisions can be either instrumental or affective. Instrumental decisions require problem-solving rather practical or functional issues, such as getting a job to pay the family bills or providing transportation. Dual-career couples likely engage in instrumental decision-making as they sit down to map out the week's various activities for the children and their own work and travel schedules. Instrumental decision-making may include those outside the family, such as a babysitter or relative who will keep children after school. Affective decisions relate to decisions made about family values or relationships and often rely heavily on emotions or feelings. Clearly, many decisions involve affective and pragmatic arguments. For example, when parents and mental health professionals meet to discuss a child with social emotional disturbance (SED), and the family and professional team hold planning meetings, emotional and research-based arguments arise (Davis, Dollard, & Vergon, 2009).

The location of a family along the adaptability continuum (cohesion to flexibility) discussed in Chapter 2 affects its decision-making behavior. Highly enmeshed, rigid families may pressure members to reach predictable and low-risk decisions, whereas disengaged families may have trouble sharing enough information to make reasonable decisions. The length of time together also influences decision-making. Over the years, partners or families tend to develop highly predictable decision-making styles. Understanding family decision-making involves examining (1) types

Joint decision-making reflects shared family power.

of decision-making processes, (2) styles of decision-making, (3) phases in decision-making, and (4) factors that influence decision-making.

Types of Decision-Making Processes

Each family has its own way of reaching decisions on issues. Decisions can be reached through use of the following levels of agreement: (1) consensus, (2) accommodation, and (3) de facto decisions, each of which involves different degrees of acceptance and commitment.

Consensus Consensus, the most democratic decision-making process, involves discussion that continues until agreement is reached. Because the desired goal is a solution acceptable to all involved, this may require compromise and flexibility. Each family member has a part in the decision and a chance for influence, making it more likely they will share the responsibility for carrying it out. Major purchases, money issues, and vacations are common topics for consensus discussions. The complexity of such decision-making appears in the following example:

Every Tuesday night is family night, and everyone must be present from 7:00 until 8:00. This is the time when we make certain family decisions that affect all of us. We may make a joint decision about vacations and try to find a plan that will please everyone. We talk about who needs to be available to take care of Zak on evenings when Mom works. All six of us have to agree to go ahead with the decision.

Accommodation   **Accommodation** occurs when some family members consent to a decision not because they totally agree but because they believe that further discussion will be unproductive. Consent may be given with a smile or with regret. The accommodation decision requires a great deal of trading, because no one really achieves what he or she desires. For example, you may want to go to a church picnic while someone else wants to play in three ball games that weekend. This type of decision-making occurs when families pressure for high cohesiveness and individual members feel they must "go along," as in the example to follow. We can only imagine what living in this family and trying to make decisions is like:

It's just easier to agree with Dad and let him think his ideas are what we all want than to argue with him. He's bound to win anyway, since he controls the money. Sometimes when we humor his wishes, Mom, my sister, and I can then get our way on what we want to do—sort of a trade-off!

Sometimes family members line up on opposite sides of an issue and vote. The minority views held by losing family members might have genuine merit, but the losers accept majority rule rather than cause trouble. In accommodation, decisions may favor a dominant member, and less aggressive family members may develop a pattern of submitting to their wishes. Accommodative decision-making encourages distance and can also enforce negative family themes and images while implementing stereotyped thinking on biosocial issues, especially in cases of male dominance. As we discussed earlier, couples and families need to understand and accept mutual influence in families as no one member will be able to, or should, have their way or meet their own goals at the expense of others (Driver et al. 2012).

De Facto *Decisions*   What happens when the discussion reaches an impasse? Usually, one member will go ahead and act in the absence of a clear-cut decision. This is a *de facto* decision—one made without direct family approval but nevertheless made to keep the family functioning. A fight over which video game system to buy while on sale may be continued until the sale nears an end and Mom buys one. For smaller, less important decisions like in this example, de facto decisions may be sufficient. We can quickly see the risks in de facto decisions on larger, more important issues, as they really are not family decisions at all. While a family member or subgroup might be able to explain or even justify their actions, commitment to the decision and family satisfaction often suffer when decision-making is not shared among them.

De facto decisions encourage family members to complain about the result, because they played either no part or a passive part in the decision. The family "decided" not to make a decision, and the family member who acts in the vacuum of that decision may have to endure complaints or a lack of enthusiasm from those who have to accept the decision. Although many families, particularly rigid ones, seem to use only one type of decision-making, more flexible families vary their styles according to the issues. Critical issues may require consensus, whereas less important concerns can be resolved by a vote or a de facto decision.

Phases in Decision-Making

Most family decision-making passes through a series of phases to reach satisfactory or unsatisfactory decisions. A valuable way to consider phases is to use the family problem-solving loop developed by Kieren, Maguire, and Hurlbut (1996) (see Figure 8.1). The loop illustrates the phases of decision-making developed in the somewhat circular path families take when they make decisions. It also provides for shortened loops when decision-making falters. It breaks the process down into eight steps that decisions proceed through in solving problems. Remember that we are presenting this as a general model of decision-making. You can certainly see how families making decisions in their everyday lives may not follow this model precisely in this order or follow all of the steps each time.

Each of the model's eight steps marks or identifies the beginning and ending of different patterns of interaction in problem-solving. Note that each of the eight steps that develop the loop can be condensed into four phases based on the similarity of activity family members perform. Phase 1 includes steps 1, 2, and 3 (identification of problem, formulating a goal, and assessing resources) and is labeled identification/clarification. Phase 2, called alternatives, covers steps 4 and 5 (generation of alternatives and assessing their value). Phase 3, designated as consensus-building, involves step 6 (selecting the best option). It includes the attempts individual family members

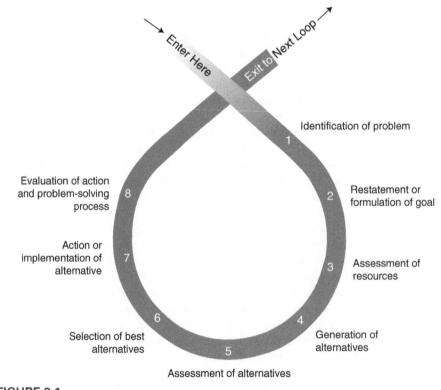

FIGURE 8.1

The family problem-solving loop

make to gain support for a solution. Phase 4 relates to the decision, covering steps 7 and 8 (accepting a decision, acting on it, and evaluating it as an outcome).

Decisions are never as simple as they appear. In examining the four phases in decision-making, it is important to realize that the process may be short-circuited at any point by a family member or subsystem alliance that does not agree with certain choices. A family may reach a decision by skipping some steps. It may be difficult to identify which phases are being used in problem-solving because family members are doing other things simultaneously and discussing decision options intermittently. Some families tend not to be rational or to follow steps in problem-solving. Once problem-solving patterns are learned, either good or bad, they are resistant to change. In their study of 40 families, Kieren et al. (1996) report more support for a rational rather than a random pattern of decision-making. Reflect on how this next family effectively followed decision-making in terms of the loop model:

My siblings and I and our wives actually went through a formal decision-making process as we decided how to take care of our elderly mother after she was unable to live alone. We went through all kinds of hassles on topics such as nursing homes, residential facilities, and social security benefits. We had to set monetary criteria for any solution based on a percentage of our salaries and based on a location that everyone could reach. Our mother had to agree to the solution also.

We agreed we could not force our solution on her. Each couple investigated different options, specific senior citizen housing options, live-in nurses, nursing homes, and specialized group homes. We finally reached two options that we could live with—a particular senior citizen facility or a nursing home. We discussed these with our mother who rejected the nursing home instantly but who agreed to the senior citizen housing facility.

This stepwise approach to decision-making does not just happen naturally in families. Some families become bogged down and never get beyond the first or second phase. Other families may make a tentative decision, but continue to rethink the decision. For instance, Adams (2004) studied cross-national couples and their decision-making processes about where to live. She found that although couples might decide where to live initially, this decision-making process could continue for a long time afterward, as the decision is continually revisited in an ongoing process. Thus, in order to understand the complexity of the process, we need to examine what affects family decision-making.

Factors Affecting Decision-Making

The decision-making process is affected by multiple factors. In this section, we will discuss how the following affect decision-making: (1) children, (2) the role of individual involvement and resources, and (3) outside influences.

The Role of Children and Adolescents   Since family-of-origin experiences affect all areas of your life, your decision-making experiences as a child impact your approach to adult decision-making in ways that you may or may not be aware of. In addition, your own children may affect your family's decision-making processes. In certain circumstances, children share the leadership in decision-making, especially when a child feels support from other members. For instance, Labrecque and Ricard (2001) found that children ages 9 to 12 are influential in family decision-making about choosing a restaurant, and we can see their influence in other areas as well.

Emotions and moods of either parents or adolescents affect decision-making. Niedzwiecki (1997) reported that problem-solving should be postponed until participants' moods are positive or neutral. Children often respond best to positive emotional patterns of communication and perform less well when parents express negative emotions. Although negative feelings need to come out in decision-making, the way in which they are treated will affect the outcomes. The "Let it all hang out" philosophy hinders family problem-solving. When too many negative feelings surface during decision-making, the focus shifts from problem-solving to personalities.

The role of parents in adolescents' decision-making remains a significant research topic. In one study of family decision-making with 76 middle-class African American adolescents and their mothers, researchers found that mothers' involvement in decision-making was consistently higher for conventional decisions (e.g., chores, manners) and prudential decisions (e.g., smoking cigarettes, drinking alcohol) than for other types of decisions (Smetana, Campione-Barr, & Daddis, 2004). Adolescents were more involved in personal decisions (e.g., what time to get up, what clothes to wear) than they were in other types of decisions. In viewing decisions about friends, dating, and social activities, for example, the average adolescent and mother reported that these decisions were jointly made, although adolescents became more involved in those decisions as they aged. The researchers stress the importance of parents being involved in adolescents' decision-making. A decision to move the family overseas may be a difficult one for an adolescent daughter, as shown in the following example:

When my husband and I announced to our daughters that we were considering a move to another country for my job, my older daughter was very upset. She said we would be ruining her life and that she wouldn't come with us. As we visited the country, and made plans to move, we made a consistent effort to involve her in decisions such as which bedroom she would like to have, whether to adopt a pet, and where to travel on our first vacation. Involving her in this way seemed to help her feel she had a little more control over what was happening. And now, six months later, she says she's glad we moved!

One type of family decision that children often influence is purchase decisions. Although children ages 8 to 11 may not perceive themselves as having any right to make family purchase decisions, they do try to influence them through exhibiting their knowledge about a product, using good behavior, and selecting items that they think their parents would endorse. Marketers attempt to influence children to exert influence on their parents' decisions, sometimes called "pester power" (Weintraub-Austin, Hust, & Kistler, 2009). Children's influence over purchasing is particularly influential over technology purchases as children may have greater expertise and knowledge than their parents. The Internet has profoundly changed the way families make purchase decisions and has given the adolescent a more powerful role in these decisions. Belch, Krentler, and Willis-Flurry (2005) introduced a concept of teen Internet mavens. These are teenagers who "receive great personal enjoyment from surfing the Internet and use their virtual market knowledge to contribute significantly to family decision making" (p. 574). Teen Internet mavens influence the early stages of the process (such as search and information provision) more than they do the final decision.

As children perceive they have successfully influenced family purchase decisions, they may expect they will have future favorable outcomes (Flurry & Burns, 2005). Cross-cultural research has shown that adolescents in both Chinese and U.S. cultures perceive themselves as being influential at both the initiation stage of purchase decision-making as well as in the final decision. In comparison with research from the 1980s and 1990s, researchers comment that there may be a shift to more adolescent influence in these decisions in contemporary families (Wang, Holloway, Beatty, & Hill, 2006).

An observational study of parents and children up to 12 years old during supermarket and toy store visits found that the likelihood of children trying to influence their parents to purchase something for them increased until early elementary school years, and then decreased. The researchers also examined the ways in which these children tried to influence the purchase decision-making process through coercive behavior, defined as forceful or persistent verbal or nonverbal influence behavior such as begging, crying, or showing anger (Buijzen & Valkenburg, 2008). They found that coercive behavior was associated with less likelihood of being invited to participate in the purchase decision-making process and to result in purchasing the product.

As parents and children grow older, decision-making processes can take on different meanings. Elderly parents may require caregiving decisions to be made by their adult children, which can be a difficult situation for families. Discussing preferences for caregiving by both parents and adult children or relevant others may be useful to have taken place earlier rather than later in the aging process. For mothers and adult daughters with close relationships, there may be little need to discuss the issues of future caregiving, because mothers believe that daughters already know their preferences or because there is denial about the aging process (Pecchioni & Nussbaum, 2001). Adult children and parents may agree to children keeping close tabs on parents via electronic communication, for example, regular phone calls or Skype sessions, which would have seemed intrusive in earlier stages of life (Ludden, 2010).

Not all families have children, and couples may engage in decision-making that results in choosing to be childless (versus not being able to have children due to infertility challenges). Durham and Braithwaite (2009) interviewed childless adults about how they interacted and made this important decision. They discussed four different decision-making trajectories that lead to the spousal decision not to have children. First, the accelerated-consensus trajectory was present when spouses had similar childless preferences, leading to a quick consensus. Second, mutual negotiation described spouses who were uncertain about family planning and had conversations over time that lead to the decision not to have children. Third, in the unilateral-persuasion trajectory, a spouse who preferred to remain childless attempted to persuade an undecided spouse to come to the childless decision. Fourth, the bilateral-persuasion trajectory involved one spouse wanting children and the other not wanting children. The spouses who wanted children had incorrectly believed that they could persuade their spouse, and they chose their commitment to the spouse over having children, although most of them never wavered from their desire to have children.

Individual Investment and Resources   How many times have you left or avoided a family decision-making session because you did not care about the result? If you do not sense how things affect you, you are not likely to get involved, even though you will probably be affected. Parents' desire and need for a new refrigerator may not be perceived as important to an adolescent. If money, or any shared resource, is scarce, decision-making can become a competitive process for the limited resources. If each family member can become involved in agenda-setting and has the right to raise issues and objections, the decision-making prospers. Agenda-setting power rather than decision-making power better indicates marital satisfaction (Wilkie, Ferree, & Ratcliff, 1998). Discussion may be unimportant to some family members and critical to others. Personal investment in decisions varies over time with the degree of separateness or connectedness within the family system as in the example to follow:

I have learned that the best way to reach my partner with my needs is through persuasion. I suggest he consider the situation and see if he can think of some plan that will accomplish his goals with as little impact on me as possible. With a little charm thrown in, I might even venture an idea. I reveal my feelings, explain the situation as I see it, and listen to what he has to say. Then I ask for time to think about what we've said. Later, either can bring up the subject again and we'll both be better able to discuss it. Other decisions about our relationship, where there is not so much friction, are made by whoever really cares about the issue.

Reiss and Webster (2004) compared how purchase decision-making differed among traditional (married heterosexual) and nontraditional (cohabiting heterosexual, gay, and lesbian) partnerships. They found that across all types of couples, involvement in the purchase decision had a significant effect on the relative influence of each partner in the purchase decision-making. However, the resources an individual brought to the partnership were associated with relative influence in the purchase decision-making for married couples.

Outside Influences   A number of outside factors affect how a family makes decisions. Mom's salary, A. J.'s friends, and Miriam's teacher may all affect how a decision is resolved. Decisions within a family system often represent compromises or adaptations to other societal systems. School, corporate, and government systems impinge on families and influence decisions. For example, think of how a corporation affects family decision-making. If the mother must travel, work overtime, or take customers out in the evening, the family makes decisions differently than if this were not necessary. The school-home interface requires other adjustments in decision-making. Children who are responsible for themselves after school, between the end of the school day and when a parent arrives home, need to make different types of decisions than children greeted by a parent at the door.

Decisions forced on a family by an outside agency, such as a court, restrict individual members' choices. A tumultuous divorce or untimely death can greatly alter the decision-making processes in a family. If separating partners cannot reach decisions about money and property, attorneys and judges intervene. If there are children, decisions must be made regarding custody, visitation rights, and financial arrangements. Similarly, when a family member is seriously ill and has not made known his or her end-of-life preferences, family decisions can be difficult. In many cases, families consult experts, who impact the decision-making, as explained in the following example:

In this age of experts, our family was almost ripped apart as my parents tried to make decisions about how to raise my younger brother, who has a serious attention deficit disorder. My mother always wanted to follow the advice of a doctor or a teacher; my father wanted our family to make the decisions about Marcus' care. My parents were constantly disagreeing with each other and the medical and educational experts.

Health and Illness   Decision-making about issues surrounding health and illness can create major struggles for families. For example, a family in which the mother is diagnosed with breast cancer may face decisions surrounding the woman's treatment—deciding between a more time-consuming treatment with a slightly better prognosis and a less time-intensive treatment that will allow her to continue in her other responsibilities. Parents of male children diagnosed with fertility-threatening cancer face a decision about sperm banking before cancer treatment begins. Parents of female children and adolescents diagnosed with fertility-threatening cancer may face a decision about fertility-preserving ovarian surgery that must occur before the cancer treatment begins. Parents may have hours or days to make these decisions while confronting the overwhelming cancer diagnosis. These represent "high-stakes, emotionally charged, time-sensitive decisions with long-term implications" (Galvin, 2010, p. 98). Today ongoing debates occur within the medical community regarding the decision-making role of seriously ill children (Rosato, 2008).

Decisions to undergo and complete fertility treatment among married couples may be influenced by couples' desires to make sure that they had done everything possible to have their own biological child. As one partner explained, "Because we really tried everything possible, we could let go … you really can't have regrets if you gave it your best shot" (Daniluk & Hurtig-Mitchell, 2003, p. 392). Other families may have to make decisions about work and family balance based on becoming caregivers for their elderly parents (Miller, Shoemaker, Willyard, & Addison, 2008).

With increased technology and medical knowledge, more and more families are facing decisions about genetic testing and the subsequent sharing of that information with other family members. Many factors will influence these decisions, including the family's privacy rules, communication patterns, and attributions and personal theories about disease and genetic risk (Gaff & Bylund, 2010).

Communication Skills in Decision-Making

In one way or another, each family member becomes involved in one or more critical decisions affecting one or more other members. Socha and Yingling (2010) argued that "especially for children, learning to make individual choices is an important part of the process of crafting their identities, discovering their likes/dislikes as well as their signature strengths" (p. 106). The more prepared family members are to engage in thoughtful and well-reasoned decision-making, the more effective the process will be. In this way, decision-making involves a variety of communication skills that we discuss in various chapters across this book. Effective and competent communication forms the basis for responsible family problem-solving and decision-making. These include (1) being open to allowing different family members to speak out; (2) avoiding negative messages, either verbal or nonverbal, that convey hostility; (3) seeking more than one option as a solution; and (4) communicating in clear, positive remarks focused on the problem discussed (Vuchinich & DeBaryske, 1997). These four relate to the phases of problem-solving and styles of decision-making discussed. Adults in families model these communication practices, which positively or negatively affect the development of problem-solving in children (Vangelisti 2013).

Many families have difficulty with disagreements when attempting to manage or resolve problems, especially when hostile messages are sent and received. In her influential research on couple decision-making, as we discuss in Chapter 9, disagreement and conflict are normal family processes. Krueger (1983) reported that disagreements serve as a functional part of the decision-making process, particularly when both partners use positive communication strategies to express their differences. They may acknowledge the validity of another's ideas, indicate a willingness to incorporate part of another's solution, or praise the others' past contributions. In the "give and take" of exchanges over a decision, family members establish trust and a sense of fairness and equality. Disagreeing allows for minority alliances in a family to have an input and function as a source for ideas to include in a compromise decision.

Clearly communication plays a key role in determining the outcomes of family decision-making. The way in which family members use words and nonverbal cues heavily influences decision-making outcomes. The sending of mixed messages by one or more members affects decisions and may alter the cohesion and balance of the family system.

The following principles could help guide family members in their decision-making: (1) create a sense of justice by treating family members equally, regardless of sex or power resources; (2) create a sense of autonomy by respecting each family member's rights to free choices in order to carry out actions that enhance his or her life; (3) create a sense of caring by helping other family members achieve their goals; (4) create an awareness of which decisions lead to actions and behaviors that harm family members or place them at risk; and (5) create a sense of loyalty via keeping promises and carrying out decisions mutually agreed upon. These principles should enhance the self-concepts of each family member. This complex process of decision-making can be aided by family practices of shared power and effective communication, as described in the following:

For 52 years, Lawrence and I made decisions together. We tried to spend our money as we both saw fit and discuss what was important to us. We usually shopped together for groceries, machinery, cars, and so on. Even when buying our tombstone, we looked them over and decided on one we both liked. Now he rests in front of it. We had our differences, but we always tried to see things from the other's point of view and eventually we'd resolve that problem. I miss him. We had a great life together!

Conclusion

This chapter presented an overview of power, influence, and decision-making in the family. We discussed power bases, power processes, and power outcomes as described by McDonald's model and indicated how they affect cohesion and adaptability in family systems. There are many types of influence strategies used by family members. Use of these strategies is predicted by context, age, gender, and personality traits. Effective strategies with spouses are often direct. Through communication interactions, power and influence are employed in decision-making, often using consensus, accommodation, or de facto decisions. Family members need to engage in communication and decision-making practices that help them manage their differences and challenges to strengthen cohesion in the family.

In Review

1. How might power affect a family's cohesion and adaptability?
2. Analyze the power resources used regularly by members of a real or fictional family. Indicate how members use communication to convey their use of these resources.
3. Analyze the types of verbal influence strategies used by a real or fictional family. Do you see any patterns of strategy usage? Which influence strategies seem to be most effective in your example?
4. Give specific examples of how families may use consensus, accommodation, and de facto decision-making processes.
5. To what extent should children be part of the family's decision-making process? How can they develop the communication skills necessary to participate effectively in such discussions?
6. Using the eight phases of the loop model of problem-solving, analyze how a family makes a decision on an important issue. Choose your family of origin if you like, but feel free to select another family you know well or a family in a movie, TV show, or novel.

Key Words

Accommodation   199

Bilateral influence strategy   191

Consensus   198

De facto decision-making
  process   207

Direct influence strategy   191

Indirect influence strategy   191

Power bases   182

Power outcomes   184

Power processes   181

Unilateral influence strategy   191

Verbal influence strategies   191

CHAPTER 9

Communication and Family Conflict

LEARNING OBJECTIVES

- Demonstrate what a conflict is via defining conflict and explaining the role of interdependence, expression, perceptions, goals, and scarce resources
- Analyze an ongoing family dispute using the conflict stages model
- Explain communication and conflict negotiation in different couple types, family communication patterns, and Gottman's conflict types
- Illustrate the role and management of unresolved family conflict
- Compare and contrast destructive and constructive conflict communication

---

Throughout her life Callie has always had close male friends, both straight and gay. Throughout her adult life she related well to her husband Peter's friends, to men at her law firm, and to the friends of her sons. She always felt comfortable talking with guys, and they seemed comfortable confiding in her and seeking her advice about dating, careers, and many other topics. While Callie always had a large group of female and male friends, Peter is much more of an introvert, and she appreciated his calmness and steadiness. He always teased her about her guy friends, such as Jim whom he called Callie's "work husband."

Peter retired three years ago and Callie retired just this last spring. Callie always heard it was important not just to retire from something, but also to something. She immediately joined the planning committee for the city marathon and the board of the local food bank. Peter mostly stays home, is more quiet than usual, and shares few of her interests. Peter and Callie, who argued very little in their marriage, now seem to bicker over small issues they would not have noticed while they were both working.

Callie has been working on the marathon planning with Kirby, a widower. They have done some runs together as they are very evenly matched. Callie and Kirby regularly text and chat online and have sat and talked after their meetings. Callie really enjoys talking with Kirby and both have shared stories about their lives, their hopes and frustrations. Callie tells Kirby things she would have shared with Peter in the past. While their relationship has been completely innocent, Callie feels a bit guilty at the same time. She has not hidden the friendship from Peter, but does not go out of her way to talk about it either. Peter has started commenting when Kirby calls and texts, or when Callie spends a lot of time online. Three nights ago, when Callie came home from a marathon committee meeting, Peter asked her if she is having an affair with Kirby. She was shocked! Peter demanded she drop off the committee and stop having contact with Kirby. They had a big fight and have barely spoken since that evening, Callie now only texts or calls Kirby when Peter is not around.

Chung Ha and Marina Revello met during sophomore year in college as dorm counselors. They became a couple during junior year. After graduation they attended the same law school, graduated, and found positions in the same city. To the joy of their families, Chung and Marina announced their engagement last Fourth of July and their wedding date as July 4 of the following year. Marina's older brother, Anthony, took a different path. He dated seriously and serially throughout college and his years in the U.S. Navy, but he always ended these relationships. Early last fall he fell madly in love with Michelle, a fellow officer, and proposed to her on New Year's Eve; they quickly set a wedding date of June 7th, approximately four weeks before Marina's wedding. Family fireworks followed!

Currently the Revello family is in turmoil. Marina has claimed that she "owns" this year for her wedding and that Anthony and Michelle need to wait a year to marry. She is furious at the idea that they planned to upstage her wedding by marrying first, especially because they only met last fall. Michelle argues that no one can "own a year" for a wedding and, given her age of 31, she wants to marry and start a family as soon as possible. In addition, Michelle will be at sea for months after the wedding so she could not have a wedding between August and November. Chung and Anthony, surprised and overwhelmed by the tensions, are struggling to remain in the background although each tries to support his future wife. The in-laws each support their daughters but worry about the long-term fallout between the couples. The Revello family dreads the negative impact on their tight-knit family unit.

Conflicts in family systems stem from multiple issues and are handled in a variety of ways with different degrees of success. As we will see in this chapter, conflict in families is not necessarily bad; in fact, it is inevitable. Communication plays a central role in family conflict as families navigate conflict in interaction (Sillars & Canary, 2013). A family's themes or images of conflict influence the amount and type of conflict that develops and how they respond to and manage disagreements. For example, in the second case at the start of this chapter, if Marina views conflict as war, she may feel the need to recruit other family members into battle, and winning at any cost becomes the ultimate goal. If Michelle views conflict as inevitable but unpredictable, she may feel powerless when conflict occurs. Both of these examples depict the negative connotations of conflict. However, there are more positive ways of viewing conflict. Understanding conflict is important to the quality of family relationships and the psychological and physical health of family members (Canary & Canary, 2013).

It is important to understand that the mere absence of conflict does not mean that a family functions well. In fact, conflict avoidance can lead to negative long-term consequences (Gottman & Krokoff, 1990). One strong parent or sibling can suppress or avoid conflicts to make the family system appear to be balanced, when that is not the case. Over time, however, such suppression can have negative effects. Dysfunctional families may get stuck in a powerful conflict cycle that devastate one or more family members, as the following quote indicates:

In our family we were not allowed to fight. My mother wouldn't tolerate it! She would say, "God only gave me two little girls and they are not going to kill one another." Arguments were cut off and we were sent to our rooms. After she died we fought most of the next ten years! We each had so many old resentments to settle. For over two years we didn't speak to one another. Fortunately, we finally broke the ice and relearned how to relate to one another.

It is important to consider the family context when considering conflict avoidance. Sillars, Canary, and Tafoya (2004) explained, "Avoidance of conflict has a different meaning and consequence when it occurs in the context of a generally positive and affectionate relationship, as opposed to a context in which avoidance masks latent hostility that leaks out in various ways" (p. 423).

Although both functional and dysfunctional families experience conflict, functional families engage in conflict in more constructive and positive ways (Gottman, 1994a). In other words, functional family members engage in conflict in ways that make their differences more tolerable. The ways in which family members agree are important, and the more agreement there is among members, the less likely it is that disastrous conflict will result. The ways in which family members disagree are equally important. Some battle openly, whereas others covertly harm each other. What is accepted as rational in one family may be perceived as irrational in another (Vangelisti, 1993). All members of a family system contribute, negatively or positively, to the regulation of tensions created by conflict. For example, one young adult reported that when she and a sibling would argue as kids, her mother would make them sing their arguments to each other, which quickly turned the arguments into peals of laughter. Thus, it is less important to strive for conflict-free relationships and families and more important to understand the nature of conflict and communicate and manage it well.

Conflicts are present in many successfully functioning marriages as well as dysfunctional marriages (Gottman, 1994a). Even though all relationships have problems, successful ones include partners who have learned how to interact and successfully negotiate conflicts. Gottman and Krokoff (1990) found that some forms of confrontation during marital conflict precede increases in marital satisfaction. By exploring the process of conflict and how it can develop realistically or unrealistically, and by becoming aware of better communication practices to use during that process, understanding of the development and management of family conflict situations improves.

In this chapter we examine the conflict process, factors related to the conflict process, unresolved conflicts, and destructive conflicts, including violence, and close with a section on constructive conflict, including communication strategies for managing inevitable and often necessary family conflicts.

The Process of Conflict

Family members who confront their differences are more likely to improve their relationships and experience more joint benefits that increase love and caring. One of the values of conflict is that it may provide opportunities for openness and valuable feedback leading to innovations that enhance adaptability and cohesiveness. The intensity of the conflict determines the kinds of messages produced, the patterns the confrontations follow, and the interpretations placed on the communication cues (Roloff, 1996).

Conflict Defined

It is human nature to notice how others' behavior affects us, and from this perspective conflict has an element of self-orientation to it. One could hardly go through a day and not feel some sorts of negative emotions in relation to the other people in our lives. We may be upset that a partner does not wash the dirty dishes, a sibling forgets our birthday, or an uncle talks incessantly about his own interests. Negative emotions are very real, but from a communication perspective, we do not have an interpersonal conflict until certain conditions are met. Hocker and Wilmot (2014) help us understand that interpersonal conflict may be viewed as "an expressed struggle between at least two interdependent parties, who perceive incompatible goals, scarce resources, and interference from the other party in achieving their goals" (p. 9). This definition is very useful to help you understand your own family conflict, and we will explore each part of the definition. First, conflict is an *expressed struggle*, meaning that it is not an interpersonal conflict if all parties are not aware of its existence. You may feel frustrated or angry about something, but if you have not communicated this to your family members, you experience negative emotions but it is not an interpersonal conflict. In the beginning case, Peter may have been frustrated or concerned with Callie's relationship with Kirby, but until that was expressed, there was no interpersonal conflict.

Second, in line with systems thinking, the parties need to be *interdependent*. You cannot have interpersonal conflict if the outcomes do not affect other members of the system. Third, conflicts involve *perceptions*. Conflict may arise as the result of a perception, such as an individual's belief that the degree of intimacy expected of him either smothers him or requires more of him than he wants to provide. Conflict may also develop over a difference in attitudes or values. For instance, Latricia, a full-time working mother, does not enjoy cooking and would prefer to go out with the family to eat pizza rather than fix dinner. Her partner values home-cooked meals and believes these are one way a mother shows she cares about her family. Fourth, conflicts concern *goals* and *scarce resources*. It is inevitable in family relationships for family members to have different goals at different times. An adolescent's goal may be to establish independence; at the same time a parent wants to become closer. A husband at midlife who has achieved many of his career ambitions may want to spend more quality time with his wife, just as her career is peaking. In addition, conflict is often about control over scarce resources (Ingoldsby, Smith, & Miller, 2004). A scarce resource could be time, such as the year of a wedding as in the opening vignette about Marina and Anthony's family, or resources of money, attention, and even physical space. Conflict occurs when one person's behavior or desire blocks the goals of another, resulting in a "showdown" over values and resources, as each family member seeks to satisfy his or her needs—usually at some expense to the other.

The process of conflict is very complex, consisting of both individual and relational dimensions. An individual family member's frustrations or problems can lead to conflict throughout the family system. A frustrated mother who is unhappy at work may act out the tensions at home and create struggles in family. A son's drug use may create conflict between his parents as they struggle to figure out the best ways to help him. One parent wants to send him to rehab while the other wants to keep his problems private within the family. Relating back to relational dialectics theory from Chapter 3, family members may use conflicts in a dialectical sense to gain autonomy when they feel trapped and need to reduce connectedness. It is important to understand that not all dialectical contradictions involve conflict; those that do are referred to as **antagonistic discourses**, where one person articulates one discourse and another an opposing discourse. For example, upon the death of a child, one parent may want to express their grief and the other parent may not want to talk about it (Toller & Braithwaite, 2009). Other discourses are **nonantagonistic discourses**; they do not lead to conflict (Baxter & Norwood, in press). Antagonistic contradictions often result from an explicit mismatching of interests and goals of individual family members.

Although we will stress conflict management and conflict resolution throughout this chapter, some conflicts, referred to as *deep disagreements*, cannot be managed or resolved. A deep disagreement is a situation in which "there is no shared framework that can serve the arguers as a common standard of point of reference" (Zarefsky, 2012, p. 2). Essentially the conflict is irresolvable. Issues that may be perceived as irresolvable in certain families include a member's interracial or same-sex marriage or religious affiliation. In some cases deep disagreement leads to distancing, as seems to be the situation for Callie and Peter in the case at the start of the chapter. In the most extreme situations, conflict may lead to disowning a family member.

Conflict and Family Systems

When considering family conflict, it is important to remember that families act as systems, as discussed in Chapter 3. Because of their interdependence, a conflict between any two members of the family will affect other members. As we recall from Chapter 3, systems thinking focuses on the level of the group or family and not at the level of the individual. Canary and Canary (2013) stress that we understand conflict in a family system by focusing on the interaction between family members. Of the various subsystems in a family, the way in which marital conflict affects children has received the most attention. A review of 39 studies found that parents' conflicts influence their parenting behaviors, consequently affecting their children (Krishnakumar & Buehler, 2000). These researchers explained that "the emotions and tensions aroused during negative marital interactions are carried over into parent-child interactions" (p. 30). For instance, parents who express high hostility within their marriage also use more harsh discipline with their children and show less sensitivity, support, and love to their children. Other researchers have found that when spouses have conflict one day, the likelihood that they will have tense interactions with their children the next day increases (Almeida, Wethington, & Chandler, 1999). Even infants have observable reactions to parental conflict (Du Rocher Schudlich, White, Felishchhauer, & Fitzgerald, 2011).

The effects of family conflict and the way in which parents communicate and manage conflict can have profound effects on children and their relationships with family members and others, particularly as they grow older and develop their own intimate relationships. A longitudinal study of parents and adolescents found that parents' marital conflict resolution styles were related to conflict resolution styles between the parents and adolescents two years later (Van Doorn, Branje, & Meeus, 2007). A study of a racially diverse sample of families demonstrated that high levels of marital conflict in a family are related to both overt and relational aggression of young adolescents (Lindsey, Chambers, Frabutt, & Mackinnon-Lewis, 2009). In another study, Darling and colleagues (2008) found that parents who use more positive conflict behaviors and less negative conflict behaviors have adolescents who use similar patterns with their own romantic partners. Similarly, a study of college students in dating relationships revealed that students who perceived higher levels of verbal aggressiveness from their parents were more likely to report higher levels of involvement as instigators and recipients of violence in their dating relationships (Palazzolo, Roberto, & Babin, 2010). This finding was particularly strong for same-sex parent-child dyads, suggesting that the strongest role model of aggressive behavior for a son is his father and for a daughter is her mother. Finally, college students with secure attachment styles in their romantic relationships reported parents with lower verbal aggressive tendencies (Roberto, Carlyle, Goodall & Castle, 2009).

Conflict varies across family forms. Conflicting cohabiting couples are more likely to be abusive than dating couples of the same age. In fact, they experience conflict more often on a larger range of topics and are twice as abusive, particularly in longer-term relationships (Magdol, Moffitt, Capsi, & de Silva, 1998). Same-sex couples with serious conflicts or in abusive relationships may have less access to social support from others, since living in what may be considered a nontraditional lifestyle tends to limit access to help from family members and others who do not approve of their lifestyle. To disclose problems may lead to rejection and ridicule. Another type of conflict often arises in gay and lesbian families when they have children from previous marriages, especially in the early years after divorce. This stepfamily form does not have universal acceptance, which may cause conflicts at holiday times and vacations or during visits from the children, or arguments over which biological parent should have custody. Children in single-parent families and stepfamilies may be exposed to intra-household fighting within their homes and to inter-household conflicts with the biological parent living in another home. Children of divorced parents may feel caught in the middle between their parents; one daughter reflected that she felt like a bone caught between two dogs (Braithwaite, Toller, Daas, Durham, & Jones, 2008). Children become talebearers who carry stories from one home to another, which can cause conflicts.

Cultural background influences family members' attitudes toward conflict. In some cultures, open struggle is commonplace and comfortable; in other cultures, verbal expression of differences is avoided at all costs. In many Asian families, "saving face" is a priority, and preserving harmony as a social group ranks over an individual's needs to express strong feelings and inner thoughts. For example, a study of Chinese parent-child conflict styles found that children avoided competing as too confrontational and avoiding as too passive. Instead, they preferred collaborating, which appears more constructive and face saving (Zhang, 2007).

In contrast, in Iranian families, "fighting ensues and overt communication stops for days, weeks, or months" (Jalali, 2005), such that eventually a mediator may be required to bring about resolution. Latino families may have a strong culture of familism within which children are expected to show support and obedience to their parents, particularly their fathers (Crean, 2008). In a study of conflict in low-income Mexican families, the more supportive the mothers and the closer the children felt to their mothers, the less depression they experienced as a result of frequent parental conflicts (Dumka, Roosa, & Jackson, 1997). Furthermore, in a study of Mexican-origin adolescent siblings, researchers found that those who reported higher familism values (e.g., felt obligated to help their family and relied on their family) were more likely to use solution-oriented and nonconfrontational conflict resolution strategies (Killoren, Thayer, & Updegraff, 2008). Ultimately, individual family characteristics may account more for differences in conflict styles than culture (Oetzel et al., 2003).

Types of Conflict

Families experience conflict over many issues. Gottman and DeClaire (1997) discovered that couples have conflict over the same issues 69 percent of the time. They concluded that, since many conflicts arose over insolvable problems, "We need to teach couples that they'll never solve most of their problems" and that couples need to "establish a dialogue" about the problems (p. 20).

If you have siblings, or have been around siblings, you probably realize that they can quarrel with each other over many issues—who gets the front seat in the car, whose turn it is to take out the trash, who can use the iPad, and which game to play for family game night. More serious issues in families such as a teenager using drugs, the perception that one sibling is getting more resources or attention, a spouse's infidelity, or a parent's alcohol addiction also lead to conflict. Technology has provided even more opportunities for communication but also more opportunity for family conflict. For example, in one family, conflict ensued between the parents and an adult son over the division and sale of some family property and this conflict grew to involve other adult siblings and extended family members. E-mails and texts sent were kept and turned into evidence as legal cases against other family members were developed. The son's wife posted descriptions and photos of family birthday parties on social networking sites so the parents and others could see the parents were not invited. E-mails and text messages are especially prone to misunderstandings as the nonverbal behaviors that provide clues to the meaning of a message are missing. Jon's quick reply to his wife Allison's text message that seemed humorous to him may be construed by Allison as him not taking her request seriously, when Jon has just been having a stressful day at work.

Stepfamilies are especially prone to struggles that are unique to this family form (Coleman, Fine, Ganong, Downs, & Pauk, 2001). Conflicts over resources, space, privacy, and finances may emerge as members try to develop a family identity. Divorced co-parents need to negotiate how they will parent, stepparents and stepchildren may have conflict over the stepparent's authority, and step-siblings may struggle over sharing bedrooms and parents' attention. Not all stepfamily conflict is negative, however, and may result in discussion and compromise that can often lead to positive change (Coleman et al., 2001).

In any family form, change may trigger uneasiness and consequent conflict. Adding a new family member, a job loss, the trauma of a divorce, or the loss of income all impact the family system. Even positive events like inheriting a large sum of money, retirement, or having a baby can lead to disturbances in family equilibrium and conflict as the family struggles to adjust to changes. Given that families are always in process, family systems experience an ongoing low-level friction, since they continually change to survive and cope with conflict, either realistically or unrealistically.

Families that own a business together experience additional occasions for conflict (Klein, 2002). More importantly, the quality of communication in family-run businesses affects the quality of the work they do (Sciascial, Clinton, Nason, James, & Rivera-Algarian, 2013). The following comment reflects some of the challenges family businesses can create:

My grandfather used some money he had earned selling a patent to open his own business. A very controlling and intelligent man, he spent a lot of time putting his business together and thus did not spend a great deal of time nurturing his relationship with my grandmother. The overwhelming control that my grandfather had over his family created an immense amount of conflict, even though my grandfather, my uncle, my aunt, and my father all work at the family business. My uncle and my father have a great deal of conflict with my aunt because they think she does not work as hard as they do and that she (and her family) get a lot of special favors from my grandparents.

Finally, whatever the topic, some issues result in deep, seemingly intractable or unsolvable conflicts that reappear over time to create painful and frustrating points of struggle in ongoing relationships.

Conflict Styles Model

Every family dyad or triad disagrees differently. For example, your mother and brother exhibit a conflict style different from the one you and your mother exhibit. As you grew up, you learned how to manage or survive conflicts; this learning influenced the style of the conflict strategies you tend to use. These conflict styles are patterned behaviors that family members use in conflicts, and we often turn to these patterns without much thought (Hocker & Wilmot, 2014). The authors make the important point that one conflict style is not necessarily better than another and what is more important is that family members find the right style that works best for the particular situation they are in. Kilmann and Thomas (1975) developed a classic **model of conflict styles** (Figure 9.1) and a way to measure conflict (Thomas, 1992). They demonstrate that conflict style consists of two partially competing goals: concern for others (or cooperativeness) and concern for self (or assertiveness). Conflict contains elements of both cooperation and assertiveness.

Competition and collaboration are at the top of the model. *Competitiveness* requires high assertiveness and going after what you want. Your concern for self is high; thus, you see conflict as a way to get what you need, regardless of another's

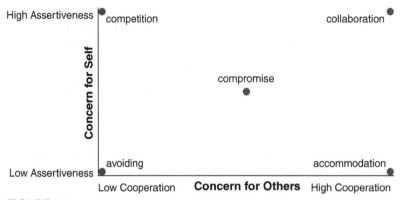

FIGURE 9.1
Conflict styles

needs or concerns. Competition becomes highly selfish if it is your only relational conflict style. It can mean "I win, you lose" too often and destroy cohesion within a family. The challenge is to compete to achieve personal goals without taking unfair advantage of other family members.

Collaboration occurs when you show concern for other family members as well as high concern for self. It often means finding an alternative or a creative solution that satisfies all parties. Collaborating depends on high trust levels and self-disclosure on the part of all members. Conflicting members must seek a solution that enables all parties to feel they have won without compromising issues vital to individual needs.

Compromise represents a solution that partially meets the needs of each member involved in the conflict. In some families, the motto is "Be wise and compromise." Such a family theme supports giving in or giving up some of one's needs. Usually it implies an equal win and loss for each member.

At the lower right of the model is *accommodation*, which occurs when you are unassertive but cooperative. It is the opposite of competition, because you meet the demands or needs of the other person but deny your own.

Finally, *avoiding* implies an unassertive and uncooperative style in which at least one member refuses to engage the issue. This may leave one partner highly frustrated because he or she cannot involve the other partner in any resolution efforts. Sometimes it is wise to use a "pick your battles" approach; other times avoiding is a powerful passive aggressive response.

This conflict style model provides a way to understand how one family member's conflict strategy affects another's response pattern. Where do you think the following example would fall on the model?

My father left my mother last year to live with someone else. I have become my mother's main support. She calls me at college almost every day demanding that I come home for all kinds of silly reasons. It's a three-hour round-trip! Right now I can't seem to tell her to back off. So, I do whatever she wants and hope this stage will pass quickly.

The conflict style model based on Kilmann and Thomas' research provides one view of how families use conflict; other strategies will be discussed later.

Stages of Ongoing Conflict

Understanding how conflict develops allows you to unravel some of the complexity and position a disagreement or fight in a larger context. Families tend to experience many recurring and **unresolved conflicts** as certain issues arise triggered by reoccurring events or circumstances. We developed the following six **conflict stages** as a model for analyzing the ongoing and repetitive conflict process: prior conditions; frustration awareness; active conflict; solution or nonsolution; follow-up; and resolution stage. These are represented in Figure 9.2. As you read through this model, think about a recent conflict in your family. Did each of these stages emerge as a distinct entity or was it difficult to know when one ended and the next began?

Prior Conditions Stage Ongoing conflict does not emerge from a vacuum. It is rooted in the history of the relationship. Prior conditions are present in the absence of active conflict but, under pressure or stress, come into play. Prior conditions that may trigger a clash including ambiguous limits on each family member's responsibilities and role expectations, ongoing competition over scarce resources such as money or affection, unhealthy dependency of one person on another, and problematic decision-making patterns. Holiday times, income tax time, drunken episodes, or the arrival of in-laws may all serve as prior conditions. Past experiences set the groundwork for tension arousal. Kelley (2012) indicates that the stage may be set for conflict by mindlessness, or going through relational life on autopilot, without paying much attention to the present state of the relationship or the perceptions of others.

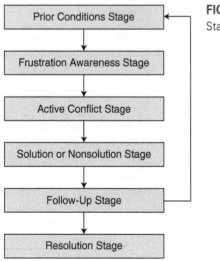

FIGURE 9.2

Stages of ongoing family conflict

Frustration Awareness Stage   As a response to sensing a prior condition event, this stage involves one or more family members becoming frustrated because someone or something blocks them from satisfying a need or concern. One or more parties become aware of snappy answers, nonverbal messages in the form of slammed doors, or avoidance of eye contact. In most ongoing repetitive conflicts, it is common for nonverbal cues to appear before verbal ones. As you nonverbally become aware of the conflict, you might think, "He's really getting upset" or "I can feel myself getting tense." Certain code words or phrases also heighten tensions. For example, "You're not going to have another drink (piece of cake, cigarette), are you?" or, "Why don't I ever have any clean clothes?"

Inaccurate perceptions can create conflict where none exists because they can trigger tensions. An incipient conflict may end at this point if one person perceives that the negative consequences outweigh the possible advantages. "Backing off" from the issue ends the immediate tension but does not remove the causes or satisfy the needs that provoked it. Sometimes tension ends through self-disclosure as one recognizes the potential for conflict: "I'm really just upset about the test tomorrow and I'm taking it out on you," or "You're right—I was selfish and I'm sorry." Also, during this stage, labeled "agenda-building" by Gottman (1993), cross-complaining may begin via a series of negative messages that the involved family members are unwilling to stop. Cross-complaining involves meeting another's complaint or criticism with one of your own while ignoring the other's point.

Active Conflict Stage   At this point, the conflict manifests itself in a series of direct overt verbal and nonverbal messages. This symbolic interchange may resemble a battleground or a calm, pointed discussion, depending on the family's rules and style of fighting. In some families, yelling signals a major fight, while yelling is commonplace in others, as noted in the following:

Unfortunately, my husband is the type who would rather yell. He is not always a fair fighter. When I want to talk and explain my feelings, and then give him a chance to explain his, he either goes into moody silence or explodes. I find both approaches useless.

Typically, active conflict escalates from initial statements and queries to overt fighting, bargaining, or giving an ultimatum. This may be characterized by a discernible strategy, or game plan, when one or more family members try to maneuver and convince others of the merits of an issue. The longer the conflict continues, the more the participants' behavior may raise frustrations, encourage active arguing, and increase resistance to change. Problematic couples usually escalate their conflicts by continued cross-complaining, accusations, and blaming. Functional couples tend to match positive remarks or coordinate negative with positive remarks. In one study of engaged couples, researchers found that during discussions about problems, more satisfied couples were characterized by the female's domineering statement being followed by the male's submissive statement (Heatherington, Escudero, & Friedlander, 2005).

Wives tend to have more other-directed and relationship-sensitive concerns during active conflict; husbands are more likely to be concerned with the content of the message, their conversational role, and themselves (Sillars, Roberts, Leonard, & Dun, 2000). Thinking about the conflictual interaction in terms of a dyad (e.g., "We're getting more and more irritated" [Sillars et al., 2000, p. 490]) is uncommon for husbands and wives. Wives and husbands also view their own communication during the conflict interaction as more favorable than the communication of their partner. One study of couples married three years or less found that a husband's or wife's expectations about the spouse's understanding and negative communication was associated with their own communication. For example, if a wife expected that during conflict her husband would not try to understand her feelings, she was more likely to use negative communication (such as complaints and criticism) and less likely to use positive communication such as compliments and displays of affection (Sanford, 2006).

The ability of each spouse to accurately understand the emotions of the other plays an important role during active conflict. Spouses infer how the other is feeling during active conflict based on their observations of their spouse as well as their own feelings and thoughts. The presence of depressive symptoms in either husband or wife during the active conflict stage can make it difficult for the spouse to accurately assess their partner's anger (Papp, Kourous, & Cummings, 2010).

Solution or Nonsolution Stage   The active conflict stage evolves into either the temporary solution or the nonsolution stage. The solution may range from creative, constructive, and satisfactory to destructive, nonproductive, and disappointing. The solution may represent a compromise or adjustment of previously held positions. In this stage, how the conflict is managed or solved determines the outcome and whether positive or negative results follow in the immediate future. It does not *resolve* the issue.

Solutions may be considered as *conflict management*. For example, partners who struggle continually over the wife's work as an undercover police officer may argue over her inability to stay in touch with her husband while on duty. He becomes upset because he gets frightened when she does not return calls within a few hours, something that happens regularly, and he resents always being the go-to parent for problems at their son's school. The times that she has access to a safe phone or can pick up her son from school provide a short-term solution. But when the next phone call comes and she has to remain in her role, even into overtime hours, he becomes angry once again. So, although occasionally a conflict can be defused and managed with vacation days or less dangerous assignments, it is never resolved. However, if she took a desk job, the conflict would disappear.

Some conflicts move into ongoing nonsolutions: The active conflict stops but nothing is resolved. Family members live with the frustrations or angry feelings. Nonsolution brings the conflict to an impasse. In the opening vignette about Callie and Peter, this couple may enter into the nonsolution stage when each of them just stops talking about their problems, which has a negative impact on family cohesion and adaptability (Schrodt, 2005). Obviously, communication problems can develop if too many conflicts end with nonsolutions. However, every family lives with some unresolved conflicts because the costs of an acceptable solution outweigh the advantages to one or more family members. In some families, these unresolved conflicts may become major problems, but other families may live with irresolvable disputes without a negative impact on their relationships (Roloff & Miller, 2006).

Follow-Up Stage   This stage could also be called the aftermath stage. It includes the reactions that follow the active conflict and affects future interactions, such as avoidance or conciliation without acceptance. Grudges, hurt feelings, or physical scars may fester until they lead to the beginning stage of another conflict. The house may be filled with long silences, avoidance, or formal politeness. On the other hand, the outcomes may be positive, such as increased intimacy and self-esteem or honest explorations of family values or concerns. The members may exchange apologies or communicate about the fight. This aftermath stage is linked by a feedback chain to the initial stage, because each conflict in a family is stored in the prior conditions "bank." In ongoing, unresolved conflicts, whenever the trigger or the prior conditions reoccur, the entire conflict process occurs again. This may go on for years or decades.

Resolution Stage   This stage signals that a certain recurring conflict no longer exists; it no longer affects the family. For example, a husband and wife may conflict over priorities on bills to be paid. They negotiate and compromise on demands, and then stick to their agreement. Time and developmental stages of each family member also affect solutions to conflicts. For example, parental conflicts over who will take Wei-Lin to school decrease or disappear after she becomes old enough to walk there by herself; the same will be true of parental conflicts over dating rules and curfews when she becomes a young adult. Conflicts over space and territory among six children competing for three bedrooms no longer require solutions when some have left home.

It is important to remember that in the model (Figure 9.2) participants may "exit" at any stage. A visitor may interrupt the frustration awareness stage and defuse the tension, at least temporarily. One or the other party may disengage from the issue, give in, or shift the focus.

Factors in Family Conflict

Family members fight with each other in different ways. Over time, most families develop rules for conflictual situations, and each pair or small group stays within their calibrated argument levels, except in unique situations when an argument may drive them beyond acceptable fighting levels or reconciling behaviors. A tearful embrace may jolt the family pattern far more than a flying frying pan. Dialectical tension generated in conflicts is not a negative force but rather a part of the ongoing dynamic interaction between opposite views and needs of family members. It can be a positive force because the "interplay of opposing tendencies serves as the driving force or catalyst of ongoing change in relationships" (Werner & Baxter, 1994, p. 351).

Patterns of Family Conflict

Conflict will play out in a unique way within unique family and relational cultures (Kelley, 2012). In their groundbreaking study of conflict in early marriage, Raush, Barry, Hertel, and Swain (1974) found that although specific partners make individual contributions to the marital unit, the couple is considered a system. Their analysis revealed that the marital unit was the "most powerful source in determining interactive events" (p. 201). Couples developed their own styles of conflict, which were unique to them. Soon after marriage, the system develops its own fight style, one that often persists throughout the marriage.

In another classic study, Feldman (1979) viewed a couple's conflictual behavior as part of an intimacy-conflict cycle. Couples move away from a state of intimacy when one member becomes anxious or fearful, leading to conflict and separation. Eventually, one partner makes an attempt to patch up the differences. The desire for intimacy draws them back together. The need to be touched, reaffirmed, comforted, and valued is a powerful conciliatory force in conflicts. At first, one partner might reject attempts to resume more positive communication, but the need for intimacy provides the motivation for repeated efforts to achieve it.

The couple's reconnection does not mean the problem between them has been resolved. Quite often, the issue has not been satisfactorily discussed or even fairly treated in the best interests of one or the other. Intimacy issues will again erupt into conflict when one partner feels threatened by the issue or aggressive enough to challenge the other. Have you heard people fighting and had the feeling you were hearing a rerun or rehearsed battle? The degree and limits of acceptable intimacy and acceptable conflict are important dimensions of normal calibration within a marital system. When these limits are violated, the intimacy-conflict cycle starts again.

Parts of Feldman's intimacy-conflict theory can be related to Baxter's views that individuals respond to contradictory demands by seeking to fulfill each demand separately. They do this through either cyclic alternation or segmentation responses. In *cyclic alternation*, first one partner complains or yells and the other responds. In conflict, husband and wife can "cycle or spiral between the two poles of contradiction, separating them temporally with each contradictory demand gaining fulfillment during its temporal cycle" (Werner & Baxter, 1994, p. 363). In *segmentation*, the family members try to verbally group their complaints around a conflicting point. Segmentation involves separate arenas for dealing with contradictions. A couple may fight about their household finances, but when it comes to making financial decisions for the family business, the husband has complete control. These authors report that cyclic alternation and segmentation are the most frequently used responses couples enact to manage the dialectical struggles in their relationship.

One common pattern of conflict that couples engage in is called the **demand/withdraw pattern** (Caughlin & Scott, 2010). In this pattern, one spouse enacts a complaining or nagging behavior, while the other spouse withdraws, trying to avoid conflict. This can happen in a particular conflict episode, but it can also become a pattern of behavior in the relationship. One spouse might nag the other about a chore that needs to be done. The more the spouse nags, the more the other withdraws, by ignoring or not answering the spouse. Substantial research has shown the association between this pattern and undesirable outcomes, including current and future marital dissatisfaction (Caughlin & Huston, 2002). Researchers have also examined the pattern of demand/withdraw in terms of parent-adolescent dyads. The most common pattern here is the parent demanding and the child withdrawing (Caughlin & Ramey, 2005).

Caughlin and Scott (2010) identify four distinct types of the demand/withdraw pattern:

1. *Discuss/exit.* In this type of demand/withdraw, one partner seeks discussion of a topic and the other partner exits—either physically (by leaving the room) or communicatively ("Next topic!").
2. *Socratic question/perfunctory response.* This type of demand/withdraw is characterized by one person asking a series of questions and the other giving expected responses. It is most often seen in parent-adolescent dyads.
3. *Complain/deny.* In this type of demand/withdraw, one partner complains about a relational issue, and the other denies the legitimacy of the issue—in a sense, avoiding or denying the conflict.
4. *Criticize/defend.* This type of demand/withdraw occurs when one person states a criticism of the other, who is defensive in response.

Relational dissatisfaction has been linked with the presence of the demand-withdrawl conflict pattern, so it is important to understand how this unfolds (Caughlin & Malis, 2004).

Rules for Family Conflict

In Chapter 4 we discussed the development of rules that govern interaction and behavior in the family system. Members of family systems also develop implicit and explicit practices and rules governing the communication of conflict messages. Think about the implicit (stated) and implicit (unstated) conflict rules that govern conflict in your own family. You can compare your own rules to those that appear to be operating in the cases opening this chapter. Jones and Gallois (1989) reported that couples generate or employ four kinds of rules in managing their differences: (1) rules governing consideration (e.g., don't belittle me; don't blame the other unfairly; don't make me feel guilty); (2) rules governing rationality (e.g., don't raise your voice; don't get me angry; don't be so aggressive); (3) rules governing specific self-expression (e.g., let's keep to the point; let's be honest; don't exaggerate); and (4) rules governing conflict resolution (e.g., explore alternatives; make joint decisions; give reasons for your views). Rules governing conflicts differ when couples or families are in public or in private. The rationality rules are used more in public settings as one may not expect a partner to "make a scene" and they are also more important to husbands than to wives. However, both husbands and wives agree that rationality rules are less important than the other types of rules. These rules can become a part of coping strategies in both private and public settings on how to vent negative feelings, how to avoid conflicts, and how to find support in others.

Rules for conflicts in families with children have great variation. In some families, children cannot "talk back" to parents and other adults. In other families, children are encouraged to speak up about their feelings. In disciplining children for conflicts, the rules again vary. Some parents have rules that prohibit any hitting or verbal abuse while others believe spanking or screaming are appropriate. Couple roles frequently influence the conflict behaviors of their children, as in the following example:

As a child I remember my parents referring to their rules for fighting, such as "Never go to bed mad" or "Never call the other person names." It seemed a bit silly at the time but, after the kinds of fighting I experienced in my first marriage, I made sure that my fiancé and I discussed fighting and set some rules for disagreeing before we married.

Couple and Family Types and Conflict

Couple and family types, as discussed in Chapter 7, can also affect conflict patterns. Over time the family system develops conflictual behaviors that characterize the group, if not the individuals.

Fitzpatrick's Couple Types Fitzpatrick's (1988) couple types, discussed in Chapter 7, demonstrate distinctive conflict behaviors. Her continued research with colleagues has strengthened her conclusions about types and conflict (Fitzpatrick & Badzinski, 1994; Fitzpatrick & Ritchie, 1994; Koerner & Fitzpatrick, 2002; Noller & Fitzpatrick, 1993). Traditional couples seek stability and resist change by confronting rather than avoiding conflict. However, they may avoid conflicts more than they realize. Traditionals more often collude with one another to avoid conflicts; for example, a husband may not interfere with how his wife wants to run their home even if there are things he would like to change. Independents more readily accept uncertainty and change by confronting societal views on marriage in a much more direct communication style than traditionals. This is important as they do not have as many cultural models, especially if raised by traditional-style parents. So they need to interact and develop their own conflict style and rules. Independents do not run away from conflicts and, in fact, they resent a spouse who withdraws. Separates often avoid engaging in conflict.

Family Communication Patterns Family conflict depends on how much family members use two types of communication labeled *conformity orientation* and *conversation orientation* (Koerner & Fitzpatrick, 2004). Remember in Chapter 7 we referred to four types of families that are created with these two orientations (see Figure 7.2). In which kind of family did you grow up? Did your family use a conformity or conversation orientation in its conflicts? For example, if your family type was pluralistic, then children's views were heard in family disputes. There was a conversational quality about your disagreements. You could argue with Dad or your obnoxious sister. This way, all siblings could develop verbal competence. Your parents would listen and not avoid conflicts, like a conformity-oriented family would. The interplay of these two orientations affects how family members engage in conflicts.

As you might expect, families' conversation orientation and conformity orientation affect how they deal with conflict. Families high on conformity orientation focus on avoiding conflict while families high on conversation orientation do not avoid conflict (Koerner & Fitzpatrick, 2004). In one family with conformity orientation the father dictated their family norm of avoiding conflicts. When conflicts arose Dad would pronounce, "'Nuff said," and discussion about that issue would cease. More than other family types, consensual families frequently express their negative feelings and seek outside support from friends and relatives to deal with conflicts, enabling them to better cope with negativity. Conversely, protective families avoid outside social support but regularly vent negative feelings expressed in emotional outbursts (Koerner & Fitzpatrick, 1997). From these studies we can better understand that not all families will experience and express conflict in the same way.

Figuring out a person's family-of-origin family type may also help one understand that person's conflict behavior in romantic relationships (Koerner & Fitzpatrick, 2002). For the most part, young adults seem to approach conflict in their own romantic relationships in ways they experienced in their families of origin. For example, persons from families with a high-conformity orientation are more likely than persons from low-conformity families to resist their romantic partners' aggressive moves and to engage in mutually negative behaviors with their romantic partners. Koerner and Fitzpatrick concluded that families of origin play an important role in socializing their children to conflict behavior. Understanding the approach to conflict you bring with you from your own family of origin may help you learn to manage conflict more effectively in adult life.

Gottman's Conflict Types   Relationship researcher John Gottman classified different types of couples according to the style of the conflict interactions the couple experiences. He found clues to lasting marriages in the communication of the couple and how they managed conflict. Gottman's three couple types are (1) validating, (2) volatile, and (3) conflict avoiders. In the *validating* type, partners respect one another's point of view on a variety of topics and, when they disagree, try to work out a compromise. This couple type agrees on most basic issues of sex, money, religion, and children. When they disagree about roles, they listen to one another and refrain from shouting or "hitting below the belt." The *volatile* type of couple is comfortable with disagreement and lack of harmony. Any question over roles and who does what and when leads to open conflict. They fight often and not always fairly—even so, the conflict tends to be productive and energizes the relationship. The third type, *conflict avoiders*, abhors negative messages and goes to any length to keep from engaging in conflicts. Partners placate and please one another rather than meet their own needs. They walk away from arguments, often giving family members the silent treatment. They are comfortable with standoffs, and uncomfortable with rage or protest. Gottman and colleagues (2002) capture the communication differences, suggesting that volatile couples are high on immediate persuasion attempts and low on listening or validation before persuading. Validating couples listen efficiently and reflect feelings before persuading. Conflict-avoidant couples avoid attempts at persuasion.

According to Gottman (1994a), a central contributing factor in marriages that do not end in divorce is the "couple's ability to resolve the conflicts that are inevitable in any relationship" (p. 28). Conflict is going to occur in marriage, and Gottman argued that expressing anger, disagreeing, and airing complaints is a very healthy activity for spouses. Gottman and colleagues proposed that validating, volatile, and conflict-avoidant couples can all have lasting marriages; the most important factor is not a couple's style but that the couple has a five-to-one ratio of positive to negative messages during interactions. This means that couples can and should express their frustrations and disagreements, but it is important that these are not the types of messages that dominate their interactions. It is challenging to think about your own couple and family interactions and see if you can stick to Gottman's suggested positive-to-negative ratio.

One challenge for family systems is that members do not always have conflict styles that complement one another. For example, researchers studied 1,983 couples in committed relationships and found that about one-third of the people perceived that their personal conflict style did not match their partner's conflict style. Of all the couple types, the mismatch between volatile and conflict-avoiding partners in a relationship was associated with more relationship problems and lower levels of relationship satisfaction and stability than other mismatches (Busby & Holman, 2009).

Two types of couples whose relationships do not tend to last are hostile/engaged and hostile/detached; again, notice that damaging conflict communication was central to their demise. The *hostile/engaged* couple is one that argues often, using sarcasm, insults, and name-calling. The *hostile/detached* couple also argues often, but individuals do not listen to one another, and stay detached and uninvolved emotionally (Gottman, 1994b). Gottman's years of research have resulted in the ability to predict with a great deal of accuracy which marriages are in danger of moving toward separation or divorce by observing their communication. One clue is the ratio of positive to negative messages we discussed above. Distressed relationships were also marked by what he called "**The Four Horsemen of the Apocalypse.**" These are four communication practices that have very negative outcomes for the particular interaction and for the relationship. Listed from least to most destructive communication behaviors, these are as follows:

- *Criticism.* Criticism is sometimes confused with complaining. Complaining can be healthy for a marriage if directed toward the partner's behavior rather than toward personal characteristics (Alberts, 1988). When a spouse complains productively, he or she is focused on behaviors that can be changed. When a spouse criticizes, the focus is on the person's character. For instance, Bridget and Liam have an ongoing disagreement about the amount of time Bridget spends working, both at the office and when she is home with the family. Bridget really likes her work and believes she can advance very quickly if she outproduces her colleagues. Liam may start out with complaints about her behavior, "You worked most of the weekend again, leaving me no time to relax or do anything I enjoy." By focusing on the behavior, Liam and Bridget can talk about how any hours would be reasonable to work over the weekend. If Liam's complaints turn into criticisms, he would attack her character, "You are so selfish, working all the time." It is much more productive to try and manage a conflict over acceptable number of hours to work versus what it means to be unselfish.

- *Contempt.* Contempt is considered criticism with the intention to insult and psychologically abuse the other person. Contempt may be displayed through verbal and nonverbal communication. If Bridget and Liam's conflict about the former's work hours is not resolved, an argument exhibiting contempt may include Liam yelling at Bridget face to face or sending an e-mail all in capital letters, "SO YOU'RE THE BIG SUCCESS AT THE OFFICE, HUH? ENJOY IT, BECAUSE YOU'RE THE

BIG FAILURE AT HOME!" Gottman proposed that we can recognize messages of contempt when mockery, hostile humor, insults, and nonverbal behaviors such as eye-rolling are present. Liam might exhibit contempt in digital form by texting Brigit at work repeatedly, saying nothing but announcing the time, "9:15 PM," "9:45 PM," "10:30 PM." When contempt is present, spouses have a difficult time identifying anything positive in their partner or saying anything positive.

- *Defensiveness.* Defensiveness is a natural response to criticism and contempt. When being attacked, spouses may use defensive techniques such as denying responsibility, making excuses, responding with a complaint about the spouse, or whining. To Liam's contempt, Bridget may respond: "Shut up! All I am doing is trying to keep up with your spending habits! If you didn't want to always buy new things, I wouldn't have to work so hard!" The major problem with defensiveness is that it prevents partners from trying to understand each other's perspective. In addition, once one partner is defensive, it is very easy for negative emotions and defensive communication to well up in the other partner as well (Kelley, 2012).

- *Stonewalling.* Stonewalling means the partner removes him or herself either emotionally or physically from interaction. Spouses often believe that stonewalling is a way of trying to keep things calm and not make them worse. However, in reality stonewalling is akin to giving up on trying to communicate and manage conflict productively. Husbands are more likely to use this technique, and this can be particularly difficult on their wives, whose heart rates go up when their husbands stonewall them.

While withdrawing from one conversation or even flying off the handle once in a while does not signal the end of a marriage or family, when the behavior sequence of the Four Horsemen becomes a communication pattern, the relationship is headed toward disaster. Gottman pointed out that even if these behaviors are present, couples can still turn their marriages around. These are to be seen as warning signs that changes need to be made.

Unresolved Conflict

Just because a family is not actively arguing about an issue does not necessarily mean the issue over which they have had conflict is resolved (Roloff & Miller, 2006). In fact, experts in conflict often talk about "conflict management" rather than conflict resolution, as so many conflicts are ongoing. For example, a daughter-in-law may have an ongoing conflict with her mother-in-law who gives unwanted advice that is perceived as intrusive by the daughter, especially if she perceives the motivation to undermine her own marriage or parenting (Rittenour & Soliz, 2009).

Families are not able to resolve interpersonal conflicts when "at least one of the individuals involved believes the conflict is impossible to resolve" (Miller, 2011, p. 241) What happens in the family if conflict cannot be resolved? The answer to this may depend on the family. Some families are able to cope and live with unresolved conflicts in ways that do not hurt their relationships (Roloff & Miller, 2006). However, in other families unresolved conflict is associated with low relationship satisfaction (Cramer, 2002). One factor will be how important or central the issue is to the family's identity or functioning. If a critical issue cannot be resolved, some or all members of the family may suffer psychological and/or physical estrangement and separation. If a child will not accept his father's remarriage or a parent will not accept a child's religious conversion, psychological and/or physical distance or separation follows. Young family members may remain in the home but withdraw from family activities and find connection with others via the Internet. Some members may be cut off from all contact with the family and may be treated as nonexistent, as in the following example:

When I came out of the closet and told my family I am gay and had been in a romantic relationship with Joe for three years, I knew I was essentially making a choice between my parents and Joe. While I don't agree with them on this issue, I understand that for my parents being homosexual is not acceptable within their religious values. I guess I had hoped that maybe somehow we would be able to resolve this. When Joe and I held a commitment ceremony, I invited my parents but they refused to come. My brother and sister have been to see me, but I am "dead" as far as my parents are concerned. Joe and I are talking about adopting a child. I would hope Mom and Dad would come around as this would be their first grandchild, but I seriously doubt this will be the case.

When irresolvable conflict occurs over issues that are central to the identity of individuals or the family system, pessimism and frustration result (Roloff, 2009). In certain relationships, unresolved conflict may lead to interpersonal violence (Olson, 2002). Serious unresolved partner conflicts result in dissolution of the relationship. In a couple, one or both members withdraw, seeing the ending of their formal relationships as the only logical solution. Yet, when children are involved, spouses are divorced from each other, not from their children. This means some level of ongoing interaction will continue as former spouses remain as co-parents, which can be very challenging to navigate as the couple did not handle conflict well during the time they were married.

Some couples with unresolved conflicts stop short of separation because the cost of the final step may be too great; yet, the rewards of continuing to live together are few. In these cases unresolved conflict may add great tension to the entire family system. When an issue is unresolvable, it may be more functional for the family to avoid the issue and direct its communication to areas that bring cohesion (Fitzpatrick, Fallis, & Vance, 1982). Yet, over time, family members may learn to live with topics that are avoided because the pain of addressing them is too great.

When I asked my wife what she wanted for our 25th anniversary, she said, "Marriage counseling. The next 25 years have to be better than the first." I knew we had many fights, but I never knew she was that unhappy. I agreed to the counseling, and we really worked on our differences and ways of resolving them. After a few months, we were able to talk rationally about things we always fought over—money, my schedule, our youngest son. Next month we will celebrate our 28th anniversary, and I can say that the last 3 years were a lot better than the first 25.

Destructive Conflict

Some conflicts have enormously destructive outcomes. We divide destructive conflict into two types—covert (hidden) and overt (open)—and we discuss how families use these types to cope with conflicts. Conflict styles may range from the very covert (purposefully burning dinner, not showing up for a family dinner, or leaving a family member out of vacation photos posted on Facebook) to the very overt (hostile words, pots or fists flying). In addition, partners with highly problematic conflict patterns may be confronting many problems having no direct connection to the disagreement; these include mental disorders, drug addiction, chronic illness, and serious employment concerns (Roloff, 2009). These individual problems actively contribute to conflict escalation within the family system. Violence, whether in the form of verbal aggressiveness that emotionally abuses family members or physical attacks, fits under destructive conflict. It represents the worst kind of conflict. Communication is tied closely to family violence, as it affects and is affected by violence. "Violence is a form of interactive communication. It is motivated by a desire to communicate a message—often a demand for compliance" (Anderson, Umberson, & Elliott, 2004, p. 630). Destructive conflict is illustrated in the following example:

One member of our family, my 20-year-old stepson, enters the house with a barrel full of hostilities and problems. He overwhelms my wife with yelling and screaming and a string of obscenities. My reaction is to tell him to shut up and not to have anything to do with him—certainly not to do anything for him. My wife seethes until she can no longer cope; then she explodes. After a litany of verbal attacks, she retreats behind a closed bedroom door and seals herself off from the problem.

Covert Destructive Conflict

In covert conflict, sometimes called "guerrilla warfare," emotions are hidden and messages are often unclear, sometimes intentionally. Sometimes family members cover up hurt or express anger indirectly in order to preserve equilibrium in the system and keep relationships intact. To cope with verbal and physical attacks during conflicts, members often use covert hidden, conflict strategies while usually relying on one of the following five communication strategies: denial, disqualification, displacement, disengagement, and pseudomutuality. *Denial* occurs most frequently when one hears "No problem; I'm not upset" or "That's OK, I'm fine" accompanied by contradictory nonverbal signals. Sometimes acquiescence strategies such as apologizing, pleading, crying, or conceding are ways that family members discount stronger feelings and deny their deeper levels of hurt (Vangelisti & Crumley, 1998). *Disqualification* describes situations in which a person expresses anger and then discounts, or disqualifies, the angry reaction: "I'm sorry, I was upset about the money and got carried away," or "I wouldn't have gotten so upset except the baby kept me awake all night." Admittedly, these messages are valid in certain settings, but they become a disqualification when the person intends to cover the emotion rather than admit to it.

Displacement implies anger that is directed to an inappropriate person. Displacement is depicted in the story of the man whose boss yelled at him but the man could not express his anger at the boss. When he arrived home, he yelled at his wife, who grounded the teenager, who hit the fourth-grader, who tripped the baby, who kicked the dog. When a person believes anger cannot be expressed directly, the individual finds another way to vent the strong emotions. Dangerous displacement occurs when parents who cannot deal emotionally with their own differences turn a child into a scapegoat for their pent-up anger; over time he or she becomes the "acting-out" child. Relational members judge messages as more hurtful and distance themselves from the relationship when they perceive that a message was intentionally hurtful and part of a pattern of hurtful messages, rather than an isolated instance (Vangelisti & Young, 2000).

Disengaged family members live within the hollow shell of relationships that used to be functional. Disengaged members avoid each other and express their hostility through their lack of interaction. Instead of dealing with conflict, they keep it from surfacing. Some families go to extremes to avoid conflicts, as depicted in the following:

My wife and I should have separated 10 years before we did. I was able to arrange my work schedule so that I came home after 11 o'clock and slept until Carmen and the kids had left in the morning. That was the only way I could remain in the relationship.

We agreed to stay together until Luis graduated from high school. Now I feel as if we both lost 10 years of life, and I'm not sure the kids were any better off just because we all ate and slept in the same house.

Pseudomutuality represents the opposite of disengagement. This style of anger characterizes family members who appear to be perfect and delighted with each other because no hint of discord is ever allowed to dispel their image of perfection. Anger remains below the surface to the point that family members lose all ability to deal with it directly. Pretense remains the only possibility. Only when one member of the "perfect" group develops ulcers, exhibits a nervous disorder, or acts in a dysfunctional manner do the relational cracks begin to show and members may use covert strategies to express conflict.

Frequently, sexual interaction links to covert strategies. For some couples, sex is a weapon in guerilla warfare. Demands for, or avoidance of, sexual activity may be the most effective way of covertly expressing hostility. Sexual abuse, put-downs, excuses, and direct rejection wound others without the risk of exposing one's own strong anger. Such expressions of covert anger destroy rather than strengthen relationships.

Covert behavior links to family themes that discourage conflict or independence. Themes such as "We can depend only on each other" or "Never wash your dirty linen in public" encourage family members to hide conflicts. These covert strategies of conflict relate to the belief that conflict equals powerlessness (Buzzanell & Burrell, 1997). Family members who view themselves as victims, powerless to change or influence others, use less-threatening covert techniques to reduce conflicts. When family members become insular and hide conflicts from others, they also miss out on the opportunity to get help or social support from extended family, friends, or even professionals who might be able to assist them.

Overt Destructive Conflict

Overt destructive conflict behaviors include hostile verbal aggression and physical aggression that can lead to violence. Domestic violence occurs when one family member imposes his or her will on another through the use of verbal and emotional abuse and often physical force. In this situation the violent family member intends to inflict pain, injury, or suffering, either psychological or physical, on other family members (Cahn & Lloyd, 1996). What is violence would seem to be cut and dry and would seem to violate acceptable social norms, but different forms of behavior may be tolerated within a particular culture and not in others (Dailey, Leen & Spitzberg, 2013). Threats are violent messages that warn family members that they will be punished now or later if they do not comply with the wishes of the aggressive member (Roloff, 1996). While the causes, forms, and outcomes of family violence are indeed complex, scholars conclude that "intimate partner violence results from a combination of various biological, psychological, social, contextual, and interactional factors" (Dailey et al., 2013, p. 485). Research on family violence indicates that partner abuse and parent-child abuse become a part of ongoing role relationships. In physically combative families, such behaviors occur frequently enough for children, husbands, wives, or partners to experience it as normative. Evidence suggests that when children are exposed to destructive conflict between adults, it affects their own conflict-handling behavior (Davies, Myers, Cummings, & Heindel, 1999).

Think back to the previous chapter in which we discussed power, influence, and decision-making. Our discussion of overt destructive conflict is tied to those issues. Lloyd and Emery (1994) wrote that if the purpose of conflict is to meet

Sometimes partners exaggerate nonverbally as part of their fight style.

one's own needs, and that if aggression adds to the chance of getting those needs met, the emotional and physical health of a partner become secondary. Some family members will win at any cost, or use aggression as power to attain the goal at the emotional expense of other family members. This power extends beyond physically abusive behaviors. Violent husbands seem to assume more of the power of decision-making in their families than do nonviolent husbands (Frieze & McHugh, 1992). If the power dimensions are not equal between the sexes in the family, especially in the marital dyad, the conflicts that involve negative strategies could be attempts to more equitably balance the power domains. There are inconsistencies between men and women regarding reporting abuse. "Women often do not label their violent experiences as abusive" (Hamby, Poindexter, & Gray-Little, 1996, p. 137). Conflicts that include anger, physical abuse, and alcohol and drug use definitely do have long-term effects on women's health (Ratner, 1998). Thus, negative words and actions in conflicts can lessen family harmony. Sometimes power moves are expressed during talk about the most mundane activities, as in the next example, in which the mother asserts her expertise in shopping:

My mother always seemed to think that my father had some type of problem carrying out simple tasks. Every once in a while she would give him the shopping list to pick up a few things. When he would return home, my mother would find something that he did "wrong." For example, my dad did not get the exact meat that was on sale; he got four bags of grapefruit instead of three, or bought the wrong brand of napkins. Verbally aggressive comments such as "What is wrong with you? Are you stupid or something? Why can't you follow simple directions?" served as a spark to really set him off.

This conflict appears to address more than shopping. It may address the couple's overall inability to communicate positively with one another. Often, what couples fight about is a cover-up for larger issues.

The terms *violence* and *aggression* are often used to generally define both physical attacks and verbal attacks. Physical violence such as hitting, screaming, kicking, teasing, grabbing, and throwing objects characterizes some family conflicts. Men are more likely to bully, drive dangerously, hold and shake, or roughly handle a child or partner than women and children, who more often endure these painful behaviors (Marshall, 1994). Women, because they are smaller in size and often have fewer options for leaving relationships, are at greater risk for physical injuries (Whitchurch & Pace, 1993).

Verbal attacks also can characterize family conflicts and are significant. "Words hit as hard as a fist," according to Vissing and Baily (1996, p. 87). One particular type of verbal attack is called *gunnysacking*. It implies storing up grievances against someone and then dumping the whole sack of anger on that person when he or she piles on the "last straw." People who gunnysack store resentments and wield their gunnysack when a family member does that "one more thing." The offender usually retaliates, and the battle escalates. Families handle verbal attacks in different ways, one of which is described in the next example:

My husband is a workaholic. I resent that my husband does not share in child raising. In fact, it really bothered me when he referred to his staff as his "family." It bothered me even more when his paralegal became more involved with him than we were. They went to play golf and to ball games. I held my anger in for over a year and finally dumped all my resentments. We are at a standstill. Now he never talks about work; I resent him even more, and so the cycle goes.

In the following subsections, we discuss violence and aggression in the contexts of intimate partner relationships and parent-child relationships:

Partner Destructive Conflict   Destructive conflict between romantic partners is widespread. Approximately three-fourths of all couples have admitted making threats of violence to one another (Cahn & Lloyd, 1996). According to the National Research Council's Panel on Research on Violence against Women (National Advisory Committee on Violence Against Women, 2012), up to 2 million women are battered by an intimate partner each year (Crowell & Burgess, 1996), and 84 percent of spouse abuse victims are female (American Bar Association, 2010). But violence may be even more prevalent in couples than these numbers indicate. **Common couple violence** is defined as "the dynamic in which conflict occasionally gets 'out of hand,' leading usually to 'minor' forms of violence, and more rarely escalating into serious, sometimes even life-threatening, forms of violence" (Johnson, 1995, p. 285), and researchers have found that about half of all couples have engaged in these behaviors (Olson, 2002).

Olson (2004) emphasized the diversity of intimate aggression. Her research demonstrated that there are different types of violent couples: abusive, violent, aggressive, and combative. Abusive couples have frequent (weekly) and severe types of violence, while violent couples display very high levels of aggression bimonthly. Aggressive couples exhibit moderate levels of violence about once a month, and combative couples have episodic low-level violent episodes that are infrequent (once a year). Each of these types can be further defined by being particular to an individual or to both members of the couple.

Intimate violence involves persons of all ages. In the past decade, researchers have become more aware of intimate violence in later life or "late-onset domestic violence." This occurs when a long marriage that has been free of physical abuse unexpectedly turns violent. Triggers for this might include retirement, health problems, or disability (France, 2006).

Conflict about certain emotionally charged topics is more likely to be accompanied by physical or verbal aggression between intimate partners. When asked to describe situations in which conflict resulted in aggression, participants in one study most frequently reported situations in which the behavior of the partner was problematic, such as drug/alcohol use, lack of motivation, or not coming home (Olson & Golish, 2002). Participants also reported life change events and the involvement of a third party (such as a past partner) to be accompanied by physical or verbal aggression. There also appear to be several different patterns in which aggressive events occur over time. For example, some respondents reported that aggression became more severe during the course of the relationship. Others explained that aggression in their intimate relationship began as severe and declined over time. Stable patterns, cyclical patterns, and oscillating patterns (up and down) also were reported.

The language used by family members influences conflict outcomes. Word choice reflects the degree of emotion and reveals the amount of respect the conflicting individuals have for one another. Kelley (2012) points out that when people are highly emotionally aroused in conflict situations, this negatively affects their ability to process information and respond appropriately. It is sometimes easy to underestimate the very real damage that verbal aggression can bring to individuals and to family systems. In Marshall's (1994) study of verbal attacks, he found that 77 percent of the males and 76 percent of the females had expressed threats of violence to their partners and received almost the same percentages of threats Emotional hate terms ("You idiot!" or "Liar") quickly escalate conflicts. In some families, swearing is an integral part of venting rage. In others, the rules do not permit swearing, but name-calling replaces it. Put-downs heighten conflicts and slow the solution process by selecting words that describe and intensify bad feelings. The use of one-up messages represents attempts to dominate or control others. These verbal stances used by dominant family members occur whenever they feel threatened. They overreact to neutral messages if challenged (Rogers, Castleton, & Lloyd, 1996). These attacks are usually accompanied by screaming or other negative nonverbal cues. Men more often blame their wives for using verbal attacks that get out of control, whereas wives more often make excuses for their spouses being violent (Sabourin, 1996). In their study of emerging adult (18–25-year-old) siblings' verbally aggressive messages, Myers and Bryant (2008) found that seven types of verbal aggression, namely insults, name-calling, withdrawal, physical acts or threats, repudiation of the relationship, negative affect (conveying hatred or dislike), and unfair comparisons, were used between two siblings. The researchers found that the messages did not differ in their perceived hurtfulness, intensity, and intent.

Infante, Sabourin, Rudd, and Shannon (1990) discovered that abusive couples exhibited significantly more reciprocity in verbally aggressive exchanges than did distressed, nonabusive control groups. For the majority of couples that used verbal aggression, conflict did not lead to physical aggression, but when it did, couples attributed it to previous verbal aggression (Roloff, 1996). Stress also increases the likelihood of verbal aggressiveness between marital or intimate partners. The ability of individuals and dyads to cope with stress is associated with less verbal aggressiveness (Bodenmann, Meuwly, Bradbury, Gmelch, & Ledermann, 2010).

Increasing numbers of studies have explored abuse in same-sex couples. Gay male and lesbian couples may also use physically aggressive or occasionally violent tactics in relationship conflicts. Although some patterns of conflict may be similar between heterosexual and same-sex couples, this is not always the case. The simplistic abuser-victim split observed by most professionals trained to deal with violent couples is more complicated by lesbian dynamics since certain negative behaviors may be considered more or less aggressive (Ristock, 2002). When lesbian couples have children, their decisions to remain together after abuse is affected by whether or not the children were born into the relationship (Hardesty, Oswald, Khaw, Fonseca, & Chung, 2008). Thus, conflict and abuse plague same-sex as well as heterosexual couples.

A power imbalance may affect how partners express or deal with conflict. A "*chilling effect*," described by Cloven and Roloff (1993), occurred when one partner had more punitive power and the other believed they had less relational power. The less powerful partner was hesitant to complain or express grievances. This chilling effect increased when the less aggressive partner felt that the more aggressive partner was less committed to the relationship, had more alternatives, or had less dependent needs regarding the love continuing. Undoubtedly, the chilling effect exists in many marriages and leads to destructive conflict.

Unfortunately, divorce from a physically violent partner may not mark the end of the relationship, especially in cases where there are children. The typical case is the mother with custody of the children who is expected to facilitate the children's visits with the father. The mother continues to be at risk of violence and the children will undoubtedly be affected by exposure to the violence. The history of intimate violence is not always known by the courts, and even when it is, it is not often considered an important factor in visitation and custody decisions (Hardesty & Chung, 2006).

Parent-Child Destructive Conflict   In 2008, approximately 772,000 children were shown to have been victims of child abuse and neglect in the United States. Seventy-one percent of the 772,000 were neglected, 16 percent were physically abused, and 9 percent were sexually abused (United States Department of Health and Human Services, 2010). According to Wilson and Whipple (1995), "Physical child abuse is a societal tragedy of immense proportion" (p. 317). They argue that abusive parents view their children as more difficult, and therefore needing more power-assertive forms of punishment, such as threats, reprimands, whippings, and orders to comply, rather than suggestions for altering their behaviors. Abusive mothers rank the value of punishment higher than abusive dads and nonabusive couples. Abusive parents send mixed messages by failing to enforce rules consistently and then hitting or kicking children for disobeying. "Child abuse has devastating psychological and interpersonal effects on children both while they are young as well as later in life when they are at heightened risk for abusing their own children" (Segrin & Flora, 2011, p. 369). The effects of physical conflict in families take a severe toll on members' relationships, as indicated in the following example:

As I got older and more mischievous, I became more and more familiar with the sting of my father's belt and the resultant welts and bruises that were not only across my legs and backside, but around my wrists where my father held me so I couldn't get away. Finally, when I was about 11 and tired of being embarrassed to wear shorts in gym class, and of making up stories to explain my welts, I turned on my father as he brought down the belt, caught it and tried to yank it from his hand. I was never spanked again. In fact, we have never spoken of his whippings of me. As an adult, my relationship with him is very superficial; we talk just once a year.

An analysis of eight observational studies of parent-child interactions revealed that families with a documented history of child abuse or neglect had different interaction patterns than did families with no history of child abuse or neglect. Specifically, parental physical negative touch (e.g., hitting, slapping, spanking) was more frequent in families with documented histories of child abuse or neglect. In addition, child non-compliance was less frequent in the families with no history of child abuse or neglect (Wilson, Shi, Tirmenstein, Norris, & Rack, 2006). A social-interactional explanation for child abuse is that physically abusive parents react in an inconsistent and ineffective manner to children's noncompliance, thus using physical discipline more quickly than nonabusive parents (Wilson, Xiaowei, Tirmenstein, Norris, & Rack, 2006).

Even in situations where there is no physical abuse, mothers have more of a tendency to interact with their children in negative ways. For instance, a mother's level of child abuse potential was found to be related to how much she used affirming or soliciting behavior in interacting with her child; women who had a higher child abuse potential were less likely to use such behaviors (Wilson, Morgan, Hayes, Bylund, & Herman, 2004). Clearly, child abuse is a large societal problem that has implications for the present and the future. Cahn and Lloyd (1996) reported that children who see their parents hit one another are also hit, that sons who have violent fathers become abusive to their wives, and that one in five who were sexually abused as kids repeat the abuse with their own children. However, Segrin and Flora (2011) caution that there are multiple ways of interpreting the research findings that suggest that abused children become abusers. Although this section focuses primarily on negative things that family members *do* to each other, it is also important to note that child neglect, or what parents *fail to do* for their children, can be just as severe (Segrin & Flora, 2011).

Verbal abuse or verbal aggressiveness directed from a parent to a child represents another form of child abuse. In one study, mothers who tended to be more verbally aggressive in their behaviors were also more likely to vocalize negative thoughts about their children (Wilson, Hayes, Bylund, Rack, & Herman, 2006) and to use directives to control the choice, rate, and duration of activities (Wilson, Roberts, Rack, & Delaney, 2008).

Incest represents a very extreme form of family violence. Usually cloaked in a family secret only held by the victim and the perpetrator, incest is often not revealed until adulthood, when the victim has left the family home. In their study of sexual abuse in children and adolescents, Petronio and colleagues (1996) found that victims are bound by rules enforced by those who violate them. The victims were vigilant about guarding the release of information about the abuse; they wanted to be in control of what would happen if they disclosed the truth. The authors concluded that "trust is so central in their decision to tell" (p. 196). Too many children fear they will be held accountable for any legal action, such as parental arrest, or be beaten for their disclosure of parental abuse.

Children are not always the victims, however. Sometimes parents are the recipients of physical or verbal abuse from their adolescent children. Parents in such situations often feel powerless to stop the abuse. They feel that they have lost the power to be a parent and that they cannot turn to the legal system for help. A parent being abused by an adolescent may disengage from that child. Following a family systems perspective, it is not surprising that adolescent-parent abuse affects the parents' marital relationship as well as other family relationships (Eckstein, 2002). Finally, it should be noted that what is considered to be family physical or verbal abuse in the United States may be viewed as acceptable disciplinary behaviors in other parts of the world (McGoldrick, Giordano, & Garcia-Preto, 2005a).

Constructive Conflict

Learning skills to deal constructively with conflict can have an optimal effect on family relationships for years to come. We seem to know more about what makes conflict destructive and less about what makes it **constructive conflict** (Canary & Canary, 2013). Indeed, a couple's ability to handle conflict well can have benefits for their children. "Children who see their parents successfully resolve conflicts and share affection might be expected to feel secure about the future of their family and about their own relationships" (Cox & Harter, 2002, p. 172). When children witness constructive conflict management practices, it may affect their responses to future conflicts that they encounter (Davies et al., 1999). Additionally, among engaged couples in which male partners had experience with parental violence, there was more negative communication and negative affect expressed in their interactions (Halford, Sanders, & Behrens, 2000) than in couples where the male partner had not experienced parental violence.

In successful conflict management experiences, happy couples or children go through sequences that lead to conflict management. Kelley (2012) points to the important role of managing strong negative emotions and forgiveness. Family members learn they can either agree or disagree and bring out their ideas and feelings during an argument. If family members can listen to one another, they can better understand motives, opinions, and feelings. Because children are younger and have less vocabulary to use, they must have a climate in which they can participate in the disagreement, if the conflict relates to them. Children's responses to harsh messages vary greatly: some children are sensitive and will suffer immediately; others do not show any harm for a long time (Vissing & Baily, 1996). Parents can effectively model conflict management, as illustrated by the following example:

One of the things that characterizes both my parents is their willingness and ability to listen. They may not always agree with us or let us do the things we want, but no one feels like they don't care. At least we feel like they heard us, and usually they explain their responses pretty carefully if they don't agree with us. As a teenager, I was always testing my limits. I can remember arguing for hours to go on a camping trip with my male and female friends. My mother really understood what I wanted and why I wanted to go, but she made it clear that she could not permit such a move at that time. Yet I really felt that she shared my disappointment, although she stuck to her guns.

Researchers reported that romantic partners who had more displays and experiences of love also dealt with conflict more constructively than romantic partners without as many displays and experiences of love (Gonzaga, Keltner, Londahl, & Smith, 2001).

As we discussed earlier based on his research with 2,000 couples, Gottman (1994b) concluded that satisfied couples maintain a five-to-one ratio of positivity to negativity (1994a). He found that it was not the way couples handled their compatibilities that prevented divorces, but how they communicated about their incompatibilities. This single positivity-to-negativity factor determined longevity, despite fighting styles that ranged from openly combative to passive-aggressive. Additionally, couples exhibiting a collaborative conflict management style (Figure 9.1) had higher marital satisfaction than couples who did not use a collaborative style (Greeff & de Bruyne, 2000). This is good news for those of us wanting to manage conflict in our own relationships—even when hard to put into practice, knowing the importance of this positive-to-negative messages ratio gives us something tangible to shoot for. Sillars and Canary (2013) summarize the research by indicating that when it comes to conflict, family members tend to respond "in kind" and will reciprocate both positive and negative messages.

Family members appear to manage conflict creatively by recognizing that they have a twofold responsibility: (1) to meet their individual needs and wants, as well as (2) to further the family system. This requires communicative give-and-take, resulting in collaboration. These beliefs enhance flexibility and help to avoid conflicts that result from being too rigid or assuming that one family member's views must be followed. In a comparison of abusive and non-abusive mothers, Wilson and Whipple (1995) reported that non-abusive mothers exhibited flexibility by introducing more topics into discussions, giving more verbal and nonverbal instructions, and utilizing more signs of verbal and nonverbal affection. These non-abusive parents used more inductive or indirect strategies—such as time-outs, withdrawing privileges, explaining consequences, and so on—to discipline their children. If the system is flexible and differentiated, family members can more readily accommodate one another, learn new ideas from other members and themselves, and change. In a study of gay and lesbian couples and heterosexual couples, Kurdek (1994) found relationship satisfaction depended on the degree of investment in the partnership and the use of positive strategies to problem-solve and resolve conflicts. Thus, a climate of validation or confirmation establishes the tone for constructive interaction.

Strategies for Constructive Conflict

Although Chapter 12 describes specific methods of improving family communication, three constructive conflict behaviors will be briefly discussed here: listening, fair fighting, and managing the physical environment.

Listening   Empathic listening serves as the cornerstone of constructive conflict. Attentive listening serves to defuse conflict and helps clarify and focus the issues being debated. Sometimes just asking the other to "tell me more" indicates an interest in learning their perspective and gives us an opportunity to make sure we understand what they are thinking and feeling. Empathic listening requires that one listens without judging while attempting to recognize the feelings and attitudes behind the other's remarks. A comment such as "You're really angry" or "That had to bring up all the sadness again" indicates to a family member that the other has listened, yet not become trapped within his or her own emotions. Restating what one has heard another person say can be most helpful in clarifying a point or slowing the escalation of conflict. "Alex, are you saying …?" Asking Alex to repeat his point is another helpful approach. Some partners will go so far as to switch roles in a conflict and repeat the scene to check out the accusations. It gives one partner a chance to experience the other's feelings.

Although it may not always be a conscious strategy, the capacity to use humor and affection in the midst of a disagreement has the power to defuse the power of the argument. In their study of newlywed couples' daily interactions, Driver and Gottman (2004) found that one couple's fleeting moment of shared laughter and positive emotion "turned out to be one of the most important moments in the couple's discussion" (p. 302). The authors depicted a moment when, in the midst of an argument, the wife asked her husband about his blackened white socks and he replied with a comment about having to chase a raccoon out of the yard without having the time to find shoes. The partners' ability to use positive affect in such a moment predicted the future health of the relationship. After studying videotapes of 130 couples the researchers concluded that it would be difficult to teach partners to use positive affect during conflict but suggested that one partner's enthusiasm in daily moments impacts the other partner's affection during conflict.

Fair Fighting   Many bitter family conflicts result from the use of unfair tactics by various members; this can be changed with a commitment to what has been called "fair fighting." In a fair fight, equal time must be provided for all participants; name-calling or "below-the-belt" remarks are prohibited. In this process, family members agree on how they will disagree, including specifying shared speaking time and topic limitations. Such strategies can be used only with the mutual consent of the parties involved and the assurance that each will listen to the other's messages. Distressed couples have great difficulty in fighting fairly. They readily exchange one-for-one negative remarks and cannot cycle out of negative-feedback loops. They continue blaming and fail to build on remarks that would lead to change and solve the conflict (Weiss & Dehle, 1994). An example of unfair fighting and the use of name-calling to "hit below the belt" are demonstrated in the following:

My mother always used a lot of verbal attacks to "handle" conflict. Put-downs definitely intensified bad feelings. My mother knew the exact names to call me that really hurt. She used to call me Chubby, Fatso, and other similar words. These words only made me angrier and never settled any argument.

My mother rarely used swearwords when she was yelling, but if she called me those names, I would usually start swearing at her. When she went into treatment for drug abuse, the whole family got involved and through counseling we learned to avoid the "red flag" words that would set each other off.

In fair fighting, family members try to stay in the present and not bring up past fights or grievances. They specify what it is that they feel caused the conflict. Each family member takes responsibility for his or her part in the fight and does not blame the others. Jim tells Michelle, his wife, "I really felt angry this evening when you told Rebecca that she didn't have to go to the church program with us. I worry that you give her more freedom than she can handle." In this approach, Jim continues to release his anger during the time granted to him by his wife. According to the rules of fair fighting, he can express his anger only verbally—no hitting or throwing things. Michelle can deny the charges Jim makes, which can lead to a careful recounting of what was said and with what intended meanings. This often helps clear the air. She can also ask for a break until later if she becomes angry and cannot listen.

Sometimes flexibility and compromise will not resolve conflicts. An individual's self-image may be more important than family expectations of flexibility. Some families permit members to decide what is negotiable and nonnegotiable for them.

Stating "This is not negotiable for me at this time" enables one to own his or her position and part of the problem. Speaking tentatively and including a phrase such as "at this time" leaves the door open for future discussion. The following is an example of a partner who works hard to resolve conflicts:

If I feel like Italian food and Roger, my husband, has his heart set on Chinese food, Chinese it is. I have never thrived on conflict, and will avoid it by settling for less, especially on "little things." In the case of a more serious conflict, I try to problem-solve. I believe that two people in conflict should never go to bed mad at each other. If the problem is big enough to cause conflict, it is worth the time and effort to solve it, for the sake of the relationship.

It goes without saying that cross-complaining defeats the purposes of fair fighting. In cross-complaining, one partner ignores the complaint of the other and counters with his or her own complaint. Both parents and children can get caught up in an endless cycle of "You did this!" followed by "But you did the same thing yesterday!"

Whatever rules or methods couples and families use in their fighting, the nonverbal aspects of conflict need special attention. Careful monitoring of nonverbal cues often reveals the true nature of conflict (Gottman, 1994b) in ways that words themselves cannot. Threatening gestures, rolling one's eyes, or refusals to look at others indicate the intensity of the conflict. Gottman observed that "nonverbal behavior discriminates distressed from nondistressed couples better than verbal behavior" (p. 469). Sometimes nonverbal cues contradict verbal statements. A receiver of such mixed messages must decide "Do I believe what I hear or what I see?" Supportive nonverbal cues may drastically reduce conflict; a soothing touch or reassuring glance has great healing power.

Managing the Physical Environment   Choice of space may dampen certain conflicts. Sitting directly across from someone makes for easy eye contact and less chance for missing important verbal or nonverbal messages. Conflicting family members need to be aware of all the factors that can escalate a fight. Choosing an appropriate and private space lessens distractions or related problems.

One thing I have learned about fighting with my teenaged son is never to raise an argumentative issue when he is in his bedroom. Whenever we used to fight, I would go up to talk to him about school or about his jobs in the house, and five minutes after we started arguing, I would suddenly get so upset about his messy room that we would fight about that also. By now I've learned to ask him to come out of his room or wait until he is in another part of the house before I voice a complaint.

It is important to think carefully about the role of technology in family conflict and you have likely encountered various issues in your own family. Technology is a part of the physical and social environment of the family, as families communicate with and about technology. They must deal with issues such as where to put computers in the home and what level privacy users can expect. They may have conflict over who owns and has access to cell phones, laptops, tablets, and other technology and struggle over time spent on technology versus in interaction with the family. We know that technology has expanded family boundaries exponentially, making it possible to import more information and people into the system, which can be both positive and negative in families, and researchers are just starting to understand the effects on family interaction (Ledbetter, in press). Technology also has the potential to increase conflicts at all life stages, but especially between parents and adolescents (Mesch & Frankel, 2011) as families navigate the need for rules for Internet access and use that were unnecessary just a few years ago. Technology is challenging for families as children, adolescents particularly, have advanced skills parents do not have and parents need to find ways to protect children and monitor Internet use, which is an additional source of conflict (Galvin, 2013). Families will continue to benefit from technology and also struggle and navigate conflicts over its use and influence.

The rewards of better-managed family conflicts are numerous. Use of positive communication and constructive conflict practices slows the cumulative aspect of conflicts. A series of minor conflicts left unresolved can escalate into separation, divorce, or emotionally punishing relationships. Successful communication and conflict management leads to emotional health and reconciliation in families. Effective conflict skills lead to greater appreciation for each family member. The following summary of strategies for constructive conflict reflects integration of many pieces of prescriptive advice. As you will note, certain strategies are valued, but across different cultures, other strategies may be seen as more critical.

Elements of Constructive Conflict

The following descriptors characterize successful conflict management:

1. An exchange takes place in which each participant perceives they have equal and ample time to express their point of view.
2. Feelings are identified appropriately, not suppressed.
3. People listen to one another with empathy and without constant interruption.
4. The conflict remains focused on the issue and does not get side-tracked into other previously unresolved conflicts.
5. Family members respect differences in one another's opinions, values, and wishes.
6. Members believe that solutions are possible and that growth and development will take place as a result of healthy conflict.
7. Functional rules for disagreement have evolved from past conflicts.
8. Members have experience with problem-solving as a process to settle differences and build on past successes.
9. One or more family members do not exercise control over the actions of others.

Constructive conflict management and resolution strategies seldom emerge if older family members do not model them and young people fail to learn these communication and problem-solving skills. Also, guidelines for disagreement must be culture sensitive to be effective.

After years of researching conflict and social influence, Roloff (2009) identified practical points of conflictual practice including the following:

- Do not assume lack of argument indicates agreement.
- What you do not do matters as much as what you actually do.
- Silence does not mean the conflict is over.
- Some conflicts are intractable and serial arguing will occur.
- Serial arguments create predictable and dysfunctional repetitive patterns.

Conclusion

Given the many stresses families face in today's world, conflict management becomes an important critical skill for families. In this chapter, we have presented a variety of ideas about conflict. We view conflicts as inevitable, potentially rewarding, and contributing to the management of differences within families. From a dialectical perspective, the potential for conflict is always present in families, part of the normal struggles of residing in relationships within the family system. As families are in a continual state of fluctuation, adjustment, and change, conflict will always be a part of the human experience and an important communication challenge.

In Review

1. Take a position and discuss whether conflict is inevitable and necessary for family relationships to develop and grow.
2. Using the stages of family conflict, describe a recurring conflict in a real or fictional family.
3. Interview three persons about their attitudes or practices toward conflict communication they learned in their family of origin and how they perceive those attitudes and practices influence how they manage conflict today.
4. Relate examples from your own experiences with families that might agree or disagree with Gottman's conclusion that couples can encounter conflict, but the ratio needs to be five positive messages to one negative over time if a relationship is to last.
5. Give an example of destructive conflict in a real or fictional family. What makes it destructive? How could the family communicate and manage the conflict more effectively?
6. Give an example of constructive conflict in a real or fictional family. What makes it constructive? How does the family communicate and manage the conflict more effectively?

Key Words

Antagonistic discourses   212

Collaboration   216

Common couple violence   232

Conflict stages   217

Constructive conflict   236

Demand/withdraw pattern   221

Four Horsemen of the Apocalypse   225

Kilmann and Thomas model of conflict styles   215

Nonantagonistic discourses   212

Unresolved conflict   217

CHAPTER 10

Communication and Family Developmental Stresses

LEARNING OBJECTIVES

- Explain the developmental stages and life-course approaches to family development
- Characterize the role of communication in the family stress model
- Illustrate major communication tasks and challenges in the different stages of family life course
- Analyze the function of communication in the family's transitions between stages

Ashley and Tom Rybecki, parents of three teenagers, never imagined spending time in the Dean of Students' office at Emerson High School. Last year Grace graduated with high honors, having spent her four years intensely involved with the debate team and the student council. She represented the school at a national debate tournament for three years and won the Best Speaker award as a senior. Currently she is studying in Spain before starting college. Dan, a senior, has played on the varsity basketball team since the middle of freshman year and is president of the high school's community outreach program. Holly, a freshman, is in danger of failing four classes due to attendance problems, poor exam scores, and missing homework. Although Holly was supposed to be involved in chorus and her church group, she seldom attends, choosing to hang out at her boyfriend's house or at the park with her friends. When Holly is at home, it hardly seems like she is there. She is in her room, surfing the Internet or talking with or texting her boyfriend. Today's discussion with the parents and the vice principal centers on how to reengage Holly and prevent her from failing freshman year.

As part of the discussion, Ashley recounted some experiences of the past year to Vice Principal Ricardo. Tom's manager assigned him to oversee a big account for a client on the out of state for six months, necessitating weekly travel. Ashley returned to full-time work as a nurse in order to earn additional money for college tuition, and Tom's mother, who lives nearby, broke her hip and still requires many hours of attention and care each week. Tom and Ashley return home from the meeting at the school and end up having a painful conversation with Holly, raising questions such as "Why didn't you tell us you were in such trouble?," "Why didn't we see what was going on?," and "What can we do to help?" Holly refuses to talk about any of this, telling her parents that she is not one of their "star" children and that they expect too much from her.

At age 71, after 48 years of marriage, Bobby Ashford was diagnosed with stage 4 lung cancer seven months ago. A smoker since his teenage years, Bobby fought the addiction for the past 30 years, always falling back into old patterns when tough times arose at the automotive garage he owned with his brother. Although he worked six days a week and sometimes on Sunday, he and his wife Sandra managed to raise three sons, and, at this point, they have eight grandchildren, some of whom worked at the garage part-time while they were in school. "Gramps" is very special to everyone in the family. Since learning of his diagnosis the family has struggled with the news and their emotions as they contemplate what lies ahead as it is clear that time is running out.

With their doctor's guidance, Bobby and Sandra investigated using hospice home care rather than having Bobby die in a hospital because they thought this would be easier on the family. The hospice staff has been coming regularly for the past three weeks, providing support to Bobby and his relatives. The grandchildren come by every day to play cards or listen to music with their grandfather. Sometimes they go through some of the old family photographs from their childhood to remember the good times, especially the vacation week at the beach each year. Sandra wanders in and out until the children and grandchildren leave. Then she sits in bed next to Bobby while knitting a blanket for their ninth grandchild who will be born next month. It's clear that Bobby is struggling more each day and that the end is near. Bobby tells her she will be alright because she is a strong woman with many people who love her.

Families change continually as time and events alter their lives. Some events are predictable as passing years lead to normal **developmental changes;** for example, children are born and mature, and family members retire and become elderly. Many of these developmental changes are positive and bring happy times in families, for example, births, graduations, engagements, parenthood, and retirements. Most of these events bring with them stresses; for example, the **transition to parenthood** or retirement is likely to be joyous and stressful at the same time. While some stressors are predictable across the life span, unpredictable events and crises also occur, including unemployment, losing the family home to fire, divorce, or severe illness. Major unpredictable stresses alter family developmental patterns in important ways; we discuss unpredictable stress in Chapter 11.

Communication is at the center of family development. First, anytime a family system or a specific family member experiences a transition, whether expected or not, communication plays a critical role in negotiating the transitions involved (Yingling, 2004). Second, family communication itself is part of what brings about change at different developmental stages. For instance, when a parent hears an adolescent interact in a mature way or an aging parent's responses are jumbled and confused, this may also move the family to the next stage of life. Each change in the family system influences the following one, like a great chain of connections from previous generations, to the present, and into the future, and families experience these changes differently depending on cultural influences. Every family experiences stress at different points across the years, and those stresses differ depending on the family's culture. For instance, the pressures that adolescents can place on a family system are illustrated in the following example:

"Jesus, Mary, and Joseph, save my soul!" can be heard from the lips of my mother at least once a day. Mom thought three kids in diapers was bad but since has decided three teens are worse. Presently, we have three teens in Driver's Ed, three teens on their phones constantly when not tying up the family computer, three teens falling in and out of love. Mom jokingly threatens to run away once a day. Dad says we drive him crazy and should be locked up until we go away to college.

What has marked your family's changes? Most families acknowledge **marker events**, or the transition points in human development. Families regularly experience internal and external stresses growing out of both positive and negative marker events such as child's first steps, a bar mitzvah, a teenager's driver's license, a wedding, or the birth of a baby. Family worldviews affect members' perceptions of different developmental stages and the stresses they bring. If one or more family members perceive the world as chaotic, disorganized, and frequently dangerous, any change may be upsetting. Conversely, if other family members view the world as predictable, and reasonably ordered, change may be perceived as manageable. How a family understands and responds to change and stress depends on its organizational structure prior to the stress, its position on the cohesion-flexibility continuum (discussed in Chapter 2), and its images, themes, boundaries, and biosocial beliefs.

In this chapter we are highlighting developmental and life-course perspectives on family systems. These perspectives focus on the changes that occur throughout our lives as we interact and co-create relational meanings. The family system shifts according to the winds of developmental change and outside stressors. We discuss here family communication patterns related to developmental and life-course changes that are reasonably predictable; the following chapter focuses on a range of unpredictable stresses. Throughout we focus on how communication plays a central role in how individuals and family members experience, understand, and adapt across the life span.

Overview of Family Change

Developmental Stage and Life-Course Approaches

Developmental stages and **life-course** issues are central to understanding the role of communication in change and challenges in family life. Individual developmental stages refer to one's experience of critical periods of change, or life stages, from birth until death (Carter & McGoldrick, 2005b; Erickson, 1968; Levinson, 1978; Rogers & White, 1993; Yingling, 2004). Think about writing a book about your life—how would you divide your life into chapters? What chapters do you anticipate you would write in the future? These chapters would undoubtedly represent different developmental stages in your life.

The original research on developmental stages started by focusing on individuals at different life stages from birth, childhood, and adolescence, and all the way to aging and death. A first limitation of this view came when family theorists realized the importance of focusing on the family system and created developmental stage models of families. Early writings about the family life cycle reflected the position that "normal" families remained intact from youthful marriage through child rearing to death in later years. In other words, developmental stage models most often reflect the lives of middle-class, intact, white families (Carter & McGoldrick, 2005b). Because of this, the models were relatively simple and the communication components of these developmental stages were viewed as reasonably predictable.

A second limitation of developmental stage models is that they are usually applied to whole families such that the entire system could be thought of as moving through particular stages at the same time. Yet we know that families consist of multiple individuals in different life stages at the same time. For instance, in one family a 45-year-old divorced man with children who are 10, 15, and 20 marries a 24-year-old woman who has never lived away from home. All at the same time, different members of this family are experiencing stages of leaving home, marriage of new couple, family with adolescents, and launching children into adulthood. Thus we need to keep in mind that developmental stage frameworks provide broad categories that capture the experience of many families, but they cannot always account for the experience of individual families that follow a different set of patterns, for example single-parent families or those with children widely spaced by age as they go through the middle stages of development. Other family types, for example, couples who are childless by choice or lesbian and gay families, remain overlooked.

However, as we are stressing throughout the book, families that follow "nontraditional" patterns such as stepfamilies, those with different cultural backgrounds, or those experiencing unpredictable events, such as untimely death or divorce, are not abnormal (McGoldrick & Shibusawa, 2012). However, the diversity of family experience tells us that creating simple models of family development is extremely challenging. What does it mean to say that a family is developing "normally" or experiencing events at the "right time"? Today, family theorists consider variation in family experiences, such as divorce and solo parenting, as part of a wider view of stages (Carter & McGoldrick, 2005b). This view of family development conceptualizes family life as a path with forks in the road along the way, rather than as a "straight-line" model of family development. This places the experience of nontraditional families as not abnormal; rather, in the language of systems theory from Chapter 3, equifinality is in play and there is no one accepted or normal family experience.

A *life-course approach* focuses on transitions and trajectories and provides another valuable way to understand change because the life trajectories of individuals are linked with others' trajectories, especially family members (Bianchi & Casper, 2005). It is likely hard for you to think about who you have become to this point in your life without thinking about members of your family, for example, your parents, siblings, grandparents, or cousins. The life-course perspective includes understanding changes in individuals, families, and social organizations over historical time (Aldous, 1990). From this perspective we recognize that individuals and families living in the new millennium are dealing with stresses reflecting this particular historical period, such as the influences of digital media, economic uncertainties, environmental concerns, globalization, new reproductive technologies, and terrorism. In addition, as we have been stressing, families are constantly changing and developing over the life course, and we never reach a plateau when we are done developing (Price, Price, & McKenry, 2010).

Like individuals, whole family systems also pass through various "seasons" of their lives.

Digital technology provides one lens through which to view how current life-course issues impact the family. Members' stress levels can be affected instantaneously via cell phones, laptops, tweets, e-mail, and IM. Posts on Facebook or other social networking sites carry instantaneous news of events and people. These ever-evolving technologies provide a plethora of information we might not otherwise have and force attention to concerns as they occur. Technology can contribute to stress if family members are forced to be "on call" 24 hours a day. Laptops extend the workday, parents learn of children's school experiences and performance before they might even arrive home from school, and cell phones link parents and adolescents continuously. This high level of connectivity and information may increase stress, but may be positive as well. For example, one study of 500 adolescents found that those who used social media with their parents felt closer to their parents (Walker & Coyne, 2012). Digital technology has dramatically altered family life over the past decade and rapid changes will only continue.

A *life-course perspective* focuses on three types of *time*: individual time, generational time, and historical time. *Individual time* refers to chronological age, *generational time* refers to "family time" or the positions and roles individuals hold in families (grandmother, breadwinner), and *historical time* refers to events that occur during the era in which one lives (e.g., the Civil Rights Movement; the creation of the Internet; September 11, 2001; or the Boston Marathon bombing in 2013). From a life-course perspective, events tend to be thought of as "*on time*" or "*off time.*" Yet, these conceptions of when life events "should" be happening are in flux. Whereas most individuals marry in their twenties (traditionally viewed as on time), today individuals may marry for the first time in their forties or choose to cohabit in a committed relationship for decades. Increasing numbers of women are becoming mothers, single or partnered, biologically, through adoption or new technologies, well into late forties or early fifties. Many individuals will experience three or four careers before leaving the workforce, return to college multiple times to earn multiple degrees, or work until they are in their eighties. Such variations are considered "off time" compared to historical norms but they are certainly not unique today.

One way to connect the developmental-stage perspective and the life-course perspective is by adding greater diversity of stages to the developmental perspective. For example, imagine a subcategory for 18–29-year-olds who remain living at home because jobs are scarce or because they returned home after failed marriages. In fact, some scholars have suggested that the later teenage years through most of the next decade should be considered a separate developmental stage labeled emerging adulthood (Arnett, 2004). Taking a life-course perspective suggests that when unexpected changes or crises occur in important arenas such as family members' education, income, occupation, or values, satisfaction or dissatisfaction with life may be more significant than his or her placement within a particular family stage. In addition, certain families encounter quite different experiences from other families because "life course perspectives and historical accounts of the lives of ethnic/minority families suggest that, in fact, the developmental pathways of African Americans, Hispanics, Native Americans and recent Asian American immigrants may be quite different from those of mainstream individuals" (Dilworth-Anderson & Burton, 1996, p. 326).

Future generations of families will be represented by elongated generational structures due to the recent changes in population growth in industrialized nations, another life-course factor. Bengston (2001) reported that due to increases in longevity and decreases in fertility, the population age structure in these nations has changed from a pyramid, with few older family members to a larger younger generation, to a rectangle, creating "a family structure in which the shape is long and thin, with more family generations alive but with fewer members in each generation" (p. 5). In some countries, such as China, the effect will be an inverted pyramid as four grandparents may have only one grandchild due to the one-child policy started in the late 1970s (Greenhalgh, 2008). This creates shifts in relational interaction as elder generations compete for connections to limited numbers of grandchildren and great-grandchildren. Multigenerational bonds grow in significance as the length of life spans increases, and this longevity will result in an increase in shared years together. We may have relationships with grandparents, great-grandparents, and great-great-grandparents where this would have been rare in previous generations. These elders can bring great strengths to families as well as increased caregiving responsibilities. No single model can reflect the complexities of all the possible family systems structures. The life-course approach allows for more variation in understanding family strengths and stresses and depicts differentiation as normal rather than as a deviation. The following represents some perspectives on family development with recognition of life-course issues, while drawing implications for family communication.

Sources of Family Stress: A Model

In their work on change in the family life cycle, Carter and McGoldrick (2005b) present a model depicting the flow of stress through the individual and the family by identifying stressors that reflect family anxiety and affect the family system

(Figure 10.1). Stressors reflect two time dimensions. The **vertical stressors** bring past and present issues to bear on the family; **horizontal stressors** represent issues that are developmental and unfolding. The vertical stressors include unique family patterns of relating that are transmitted across generations, including family attitudes, values, expectations, secrets, rules, societal pressures, and individual makeup. The authors argue that within the same family, individual members experience and react to these stresses differently as we see in the following example:

My brother and I were both adopted from different families as infants. While I always thought being adopted was positive—I figured my parents had to work very hard to get me—from the beginning my brother always thought about adoption as being rejected by his birth mother. When our mother died, our father remarried within the year. Those years were very tough, but somehow it made me stronger as an adult. My brother went the opposite direction, became even more depressed, and escaped into drugs and alcohol. It was like he gave up. I've often wondered why two people raised in the same situation responded so differently.

Stress varies with the position and age of each family member. Many of these communication-related stressors were discussed earlier as the images, themes, myths, rules, boundaries, and expectations that come from the family of origin. The horizontal flow in the system includes the anxiety produced by the stresses on the family as it moves across time—both the predictable (developmental stressors) and unpredictable events that disrupt the life cycle, and major historical events. Current life-event stressors interact with one another and with the vertical stressors to cause disruption in the family system. The greater the anxiety generated in the family at any transition point, the more difficult the transition.

The past and present family stresses are affected by all levels of the larger systems in which the family operates. These are the life-course concerns—social, cultural, economic, and political contextual factors. One's community, family, and personal resources also contribute to the process of moving through life. The scholars have continued to develop the model and look at the multicultural factors that influence families at all different points in the life cycle (McGoldrick & Shibusawa, 2012). This model is too complex for us to develop fully here, yet when you look at it, the model gives you a sense of the enormous number of life influences and variations experienced in the everyday world.

The developmental approach emphasizes stages, focusing on the linear progression of families moving through the life cycle; increasingly more families experience a nonlinear sequence reflecting the life-course approach. Families are influenced by social and structural forces such as technology, religion, racism, unemployment, education, and poverty. As you move through the chapters of the book that is your life, the phases of your individual and family existence, these forces will positively or negatively influence the process. Thus, these three major factors—vertical stressors, horizontal stressors, and system levels—taken together put a family's life cycle and its life-course position into perspective.

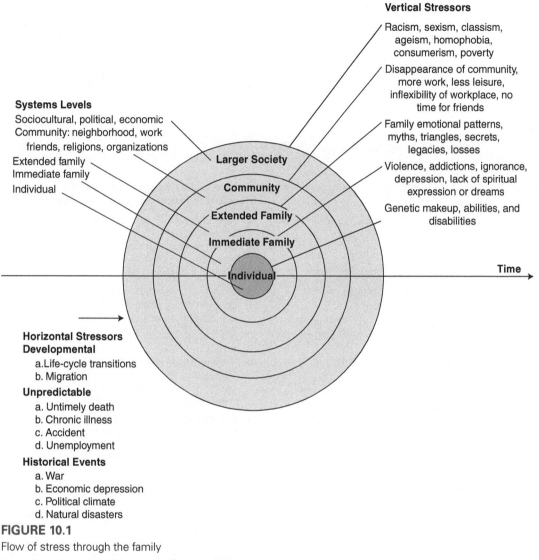

Vertical Stressors

Racism, sexism, classism, ageism, homophobia, consumerism, poverty

Disappearance of community, more work, less leisure, inflexibility of workplace, no time for friends

Family emotional patterns, myths, triangles, secrets, legacies, losses

Violence, addictions, ignorance, depression, lack of spiritual expression or dreams

Genetic makeup, abilities, and disabilities

Systems Levels
Sociocultural, political, economic
Community: neighborhood, work
   friends, religions, organizations
Extended family
Immediate family
Individual

Larger Society
Community
Extended Family
Immediate Family
Individual

Time

Horizontal Stressors
Developmental
   a. Life-cycle transitions
   b. Migration
Unpredictable
   a. Untimely death
   b. Chronic illness
   c. Accident
   d. Unemployment
Historical Events
   a. War
   b. Economic depression
   c. Political climate
   d. Natural disasters

FIGURE 10.1
Flow of stress through the family

Source: From Carter, B. & McGoldrick, M. *The Expanded Family Life Cycle,* 3/e, © 2005. Published by Allyn and Bacon, Boston, MA. Copyright © 2005 by Pearson Education. Reprinted by permission of the publisher.

Family Stages and Life-Course Issues

In this section we will examine some of the findings about family communication in different developmental stages across the life course. We have already stressed the limitations of trying to draw a complete portrait of all families by focusing on traditional developmental stages. At the same time, these stages are shared by a wide variety of families, for example, marriage of a couple, families with adolescents, and leaving home. To help meet our goal of recognizing diverse family types, we will integrate aspects of the life-course approach in order to broaden the discussion and highlight familial variations that affect family communication.

Those creating developmental models of family life have included anywhere from 6 to 12 stages. In this section we feature a model of the stages of the family life cycle (Table 10.1) by Carter and McGoldrick (2005b) to highlight the diversity of stages that families can experience. Traditionally, family researchers applied the stage concept to whole families so that the entire system could be thought of as moving through particular stages. Such analysis has difficulties because families consist of multiple individuals

TABLE 10.1 The Stages of the Family Life Cycle

Family Life Cycle Stage	Emotional Process of Transition: Key Principles	Second-Order Changes in the Family Status Required to Proceed Developmentally
Leaving home: single young adults	Accepting emotional and financial responsibility for self	a. Differentiation of self in relation to family-of-origin b. Development of intimate peer relationships c. Establishment of self in respect to work and financial independence
The joining of families through marriage: the new couple	Commitment to new system	a. Formation of marital system b. Realignment of relationships with extended families and friends to include spouse
Families with young children	Accepting new members into the system	a. Adjusting marital system to make space for children b. Joining in child rearing, financial, and household tasks c. Realignment of relationships with extended family to include parenting and grandparenting roles
Families with adolescents	Increasing flexibility of family boundaries to permit children's independence and grandparents' families	a. Shifting of parent-child relationships to permit adolescents to move into and out of system b. Refocus on midlife marital and career issues c. Beginning shift toward caring for older generation
Launching children and moving on	Accepting a multitude of exits from and entries into the family system	a. Renegotiation of marital system as a dyad b. Development of adult-to-adult relationships between grown children and their parents c. Realignment of relationships to include in-laws and grandchildren d. Dealing with disabilities and death of parents (grandparents)
Families in later life	Accepting the shifting generational roles	a. Maintaining own and/or couple functioning and interests in face of physiological decline: exploration of new familial and social role options b. Support for more central role of middle generation c. Making room in the system for the wisdom and experience of the elderly, supporting the older generation without overfunctioning for them d. Dealing with loss of spouse, siblings, and other peers and preparation for death

in different life stages at the same time. Such frameworks provide simplicity but seldom effectively account for families with numerous children or children widely spaced by age as they go through the middle stages of development. Other family types, for example, childless partners or lesbian and gay families, often remain overlooked.

No matter which framework is adopted, communication emerges as a critical issue across the life span. As we established in Chapter 2 and highlight throughout the book, communication is the central influence across the life course as individual and family identities are co-created and altered in interaction (Bergen & Braithwaite, 2009). In the following subsections we examine some of the different stages of the life course.

Independent Life Stage

Young adulthood or what is often called emerging adulthood (Arnett, 2004) has received more attention in the past decade because the life experiences are more diverse than in previous generations. Although this **independent life stage** seldom appears on earlier life-cycle lists, Carter and McGoldrick (2005a) add it as an essential stage, recognizing that the young adult must come to terms with his or her family of origin and separating from or leaving home to enter a new stage. The unattached young adult faces developmental tasks in areas of work and relationships. Arnett (2011) views this as an age of identity exploration, instability, self-focus, feeling in between, and possibilities. These play out differently, depending on social class and ethnicity. For example, in recent years this stage has been confounded by economic stresses that keep many young adults financially dependent on their parents temporarily or indefinitely (Vogt, 2009). These shifts are occurring differently in Western Europe and in westernized nations such as Japan, New Zealand, South Korea, and Australia (Arnett, 2011). In addition, the traditional process of parental separation has been affected by changes in the separation/individuation process reflecting cultural changes. Increasing numbers of Mexican and other Latino families deemphasize offspring independence in favor of close family ties (Falicov, 2005). Many of us have experienced that during the early independent life stage, young adults are making important decisions but are often reluctant to make many long-term or lifetime commitments, and this is likely a good idea, as they will be experiencing many changes in the next years.

Communication is central to managing the transition to young adulthood successfully and preventing problems from developing in the stages that follow. Young people need to negotiate sufficient autonomy to separate and achieve their goals of healthy independence from parents, completing their education, establishing careers, and creating close adult friendships and peer networks. Establishing the "self" as separate and yet a part of the family of origin remains the objective for most people. Ideally, the young adult feels free to achieve his or her own goals and command the respect and encouragement of his or her parents, even if they might have hoped for other outcomes. Parents and children move through this stage successfully when they learn to accept separation and independence while remaining connected, tolerating difference and ambiguity in an adult child's career choice and accepting a range of intense emotional attachments and lifestyles outside the family (Willoughby & Arnett, 2013). Most young people and their parents find their communication improves during this stage and adult-to-adult communication patterns emerge more fully, as seen in the following example:

My older stepbrothers cannot believe that I talk with my mother at least once a day, but I've learned to treat her like a friend and I rely on her for advice. There are some things I don't talk about since she would not approve of some of my choices, but generally she serves as a good sounding board and sometimes she asks me for advice.

Willoughby and Arnett (2013) point out that technology can both help and hinder communication during the emerging adult stage. The quantity of communication may increase given the many interactional choices afforded by technology, and today's emerging adults are the highest technology users of any group. However, communication can also be stilted as users turn away from interaction with family and friends and establish online relationships.

Because of years of advanced schooling and a reluctance to marry early, many young adults invest in intimate peer relationships, some of which may be romantic, and begin the process of exploring deep interpersonal connections. Increasing numbers cohabit with a romantic partner without a commitment to marry. In many cases this results in "sliding" into marriage (Stanley, Rhoades, & Markman, 2006). Researchers argue that inertia, or feeling stuck, impacts the decision of long-term cohabitors to marry since it is harder to end a cohabiting relationship than a non-cohabiting dating relationship (Stanley & Rhoades, 2009); thus they slide into marriage, which may account for the data that indicate that those who cohabit have exhibited poorer marital quality (Priem & Surra, 2013). Conversely, noncohabitors and those who cohabit after becoming engaged make a proactive decision to marry. However, for other couples cohabiting may be a choice due to convenience, financial circumstances, or a normal course of the relationship in preparation for marriage (Rhoades, Stanley, & Markman, 2009a).

There are an increasing number of diverse family types that begin in the young adult stage (Rosenfeld, 2007), for instance, interracial same-sex, childless by choice, and single-parent families. For example, interracial marriages continue to rise, as more diverse educational systems bring young people of varied backgrounds into contact. The timing of "coming out" has changed in the gay and lesbian communities. Although "coming out" often occurs gradually, about two-thirds of gay or lesbian individuals report having first come out and revealed their status to others by age 18 (Kaiser Family Foundation, 2001). Most family members are unaware that their children are not heterosexual and may provide messages of nonacceptance of LGBT people that discourage children revealing their status (Green, 2012).

Partners

Although some young people move quickly into a marital relationship, other remain single or cohabit serially for years before deciding to marry (Surra, Gray, Cottle, & Boettcher, 2004). While a small number of people remain single throughout their lives, that number is rising. DePaulo (2006) argues that, although often stigmatized, many who are single by choice are living very satisfying lives and maintain close ties with their families of origin and/or develop fictive or chosen family relationships.

Marriage or committed partnership is not only a relationship of two, but also one of extended families, social networks, as well as future generations. The couple negotiates a new relational definition, within many other subsystems: parents, siblings, grandparents, nieces and nephews, and friends. Marriage, however, is no longer the defining marker of entering adulthood nor is it the highly predictable event it used to be.

Partners creating a long-term committed relationship must interact and address three developmental challenges in order to achieve satisfaction in later stages: commitment, power, and closeness. *Commitment* requires each to make the other his or her primary partner and loosen their ties to parents, siblings, and friends. *Power* reflects the dialectical tension between full self-determination and the sharing of power to a partner to strengthen the relationship. *Closeness* involves managing competing needs for separation and attachment that is mutually satisfying for the couple. In this early stage, partners communicate and negotiate rules for distance regulation as they negotiate a mutually satisfying level of interpersonal togetherness. Over time partners revisit the issue of what is an acceptable or unacceptable interpersonal distance, as the following example illustrates:

Sometimes I feel like a piece of Swiss cheese—full of holes. I grew up in a non-touching, often violent family. I realize I hunger for touch and affection. I can cuddle and hold my partner for long periods of time, but he gets uneasy after a while and wants to move away. We have struggled to reach a point where both of us are comfortable and feel our needs are met.

Based on their review of premarital relationship stability, Cate, Levin, and Richmond (2002) developed a commitment model that includes intimacy-oriented relationship behaviors of self-disclosure, frequency of interaction, diversity of interaction, impact of interaction, and sexual intimacy. Involvement over time leads to deeper levels of connection. As we discussed in Chapter 3, couples must establish privacy boundaries and rules governing their communication patterns. This can be challenging as partners may have different views of privacy based on their culture, gender, and previous experience (Petronio, 2002). As intimacy develops, communication both affects and reflects the closeness developing. Couples adopt relational terminology; for example, "girlfriend" may be replaced with "partner" or "fiancée." Nonverbal artifacts may signal the relationship, for example, rings or other jewelry, and the couple participating in family rituals such as holiday dinners. As you read the following example, think of the way relationship commitment would be signaled in your family:

In my family, we always knew that relationships were serious when the annual family reunion time arrived. If you brought someone, you were expected to formally introduce this person to each member of the clan. However, you didn't choose to go through this ritual, and take all the teasing that followed, unless an engagement was imminent.

We also note that same-sex couples may find acceptance in their families of origin or may conceal their relationship from relatives or coworkers. If they believe they will not be accepted, they may not reveal their commitment to other family members.

The act of bonding, or institutionalizing, the relationship changes the nature of many relationships. Some parents may not be prepared for the separation issues involved. Each family faces the questions of realignment wondering: "How willing are we to accept this new person as an in-law?" Couples must confront the following issues that need to be discussed: spending time with friends, desires for children, sexual needs, career goals and related educational plans, religious participation, money management, housing, in-laws, and acceptable conflict behaviors. Extended family members may become involved. In some cultures, such as Asian, Indian, Muslim and Christian, marriage brings together families, not just individuals. Many of these young couples' lives involve extensive involvement within a strong hierarchical extended family (Almeida, 2005). The communication event—the actual ritualized wedding or partnership ceremony—serves as a sign of formal bonding to the outside world. For some couples, a wedding ceremony, representing ethnic customs, also serves as a symbol of negotiating intercultural differences (Leeds-Hurwitz, 2002).

Marriages between young adults involve certain predictable tasks such as (1) separating further from the families of origin; (2) negotiating roles, rules, and relationships; and (3) investing in a new relationship. This is a period of unconscious negotiation between the couple and their families of origin regarding how the old and new systems will relate to each other. Sometimes marriage holds surprises even when couples have known each other a long time and lived together, as noted in the following example: In some cultures, the task of separating from one's family of origin does not occur. In Mexican families, parent-child connectedness may remain more powerful than the marital bond; the eldest son and mother bond is particularly strong. Therefore, mothers may remain an integral figure in a young couple's life (Falicov, 2005).

I had known my husband since childhood, and we dated since our junior year. Our parents knew each other and we attended the same church, yet we had some real difficulties in the first years of our marriage. We had lived together for six months but I had difficulty in the following areas: First, still learning to live with my husband's habits; second, trying to be a full-time employee and a homemaker; third, deciding at which family's house to celebrate holidays; fourth, telling my husband when I was angry; and fifth, dealing with my husband's mother who kept dropping in unexpectedly.

The initial stage of marriage involves negotiating the roles of "husband" and "wife" or "partner"—a shift even for those who cohabited for a long time and who may have worked out a set of roles that change once the couple encounters tradition-laden marital expectations. Even a formal commitment ceremony represents a new way of conceiving the partnership; many couples report a deeper sense of "we-ness." Social networks may shift as partners renegotiate issues of time together, with joint friends, and with individual friends. Newly married couples also must negotiate relationships with extended family, particularly in-laws. The mother-in-law and daughter-in-law relationship tends to be viewed as the most turbulent tie, although sons-in-law have potentially problematic in-law relationships also (Rittenour & Soliz, 2009). These now-formal links require attention and discussion on issues ranging from negotiating couple and family privacy to autonomy and unwanted advice. After entering a committed relationship, formally or informally, same-sex partners often struggle with similar extended family issues, which can be compounded if one or both families of origin are not comfortable or accepting of the relationship.

Partners' ability to negotiate a new relationship relates directly to the quality of their communication. This is a time of investing in their relationship through deeper self-disclosure and open sexual communication as we described in Chapter 6. Time, energy, and risk-taking nourish the relationship and establish a range of acceptable intimacy for the system. Couple conflict tends to increase during engagement and early stages of marriage (Canary & Canary, 2013) as couples are negotiating their expectations for the balance of power between partners, decision-making, and role performance. Communication patterns tend to establish themselves within the first two years of marriage and demonstrate great stability; a greater proportion of communication is devoted to marital conflicts that gradually surface (Sillars & Wilmot, 1989).

The previous descriptions assume starting out parenthood as part of a couple relationship. Increasingly marriages involve couples bringing children from previous relationships or from their single life. In such cases, beginning the marital relationship becomes more complicated because the partners are starting out as a group of three or more. A life-course approach recognizes that marriage may be delayed, follow the birth of one or more children, or never occur. Because of legal restrictions, racism, unemployment, welfare rules, and poverty, many couples follow a nonlinear path of relationship development. Such families construct "developmental pathways in which the timing and ordering of life course transitions such as marriage and childbearing are not comparable to mainstream patterns" (Dilworth-Anderson & Burton, 1996, p. 328).

Most couples eventually become a three-person system, with pregnancy heralding the transition to a new stage. Whether married or not, this example highlights the importance of the period before parenthood:

The period before the children began to arrive was a critical point. If we had not established a really strong, trusting relationship in those first two years, we would have drifted totally apart in the next 23 years of child rearing. We lost most of our time together. If I had it to do over, I would have waited five years before having children, to share who we really were before we tried to deal with who the four new people in our lives were.

Yet the past decade witnessed the "decoupling" of marriage and childbearing and a continuing increase in nonmarital childbearing (Smock & Greenland, 2010), as increasingly children are born prior to marriage of the parents. Same-sex partners face a complicated road as they consider adoption or biological parenthood. When gay males and lesbians choose parenthood they face unique decisions. For example, lesbian partners confront questions such as the following: "How will we become parents, or if we use donor insemination, who will be the biological mother?" (Chabot & Ames, 2004). Gay males must decide to use one man's sperm or mix their sperm so it is unknown which one is the biological father (Berkowitz & Marsiglio, 2007). In addition, increasing numbers of single women in their thirties and forties are choosing solo parenthood by means of adoption or known or unknown sperm donors (Hertz, 2006).

Families with Children

The transition to parenthood presents both opportunities for relational growth and closeness, and also challenges for most new fathers and mothers. Partner communication shifts dramatically as the new role requires significant time and energy (Holmes, Huston, Vangelisti, & Guinn, 2013; Stamp, 1994; Stamp & Banski, 1992).

In addition to navigating couple communication at the transition to parenthood and beyond, the parents are also learning to communicate with children. A key dynamic characterizing parent-child interaction is the bidirectional nature of this relationship—parents and children experience a mutual influence process (Saphir & Chaffee, 2002). Parents grow and change as a result of their new roles while their children learn and grow from their interactions with their parents. Given the complexities of parent-child interactions, in the following subsections we are able to only highlight a limited number of communication issues.

Parents play a major role in developing a child's communication competence.

Family with First Child   Parenthood occurs later in life than in earlier decades because the age at first marriage has steadily increased. Couples who entered parenthood before marriage or soon after marriage reported lower marital quality prior to becoming parents than couples who had their baby "on time" or "delayed" (Helms-Erickson, 2001). As noted in Chapter 1, an increasing number of children are born to single mothers. Some youths go from adolescence right into adult status as parents, thus speeding up their whole life-course trajectory. Pregnant teens turn their mothers into grandmothers as young as age 30. Typical adolescent communication issues of dating or choosing the right college are replaced with talk about breast-feeding, how to manage school, and supporting the baby. Such stresses complicate partnerships.

No matter when a first pregnancy occurs, significant changes in a couple's relationship follow the birth of the child. When a couple desires a child and the pregnancy is uncomplicated, this time may involve much intimate communication and long-range planning, yet subtle communication changes occur, particularly in conflict patterns. Three factors that influence couples during the transition to parenthood are their views on parental responsibilities and restrictions, the gratification child rearing holds for them as a couple, and their own marital intimacy and stability. In their earlier study of the transition to parenthood, Stamp and Banski (1992) found that a couple, who may have had quite a bit of autonomy before the arrival of children, is especially challenged to negotiate the dialectic of autonomy and connection. For instance, one spouse cannot easily call the other and announce they are working late. New parents facing this transition "need to renegotiate the reality of their marriage due to both the presence of the child and to their transformed presence with one another with the addition of a new role" (Stamp, 1994, p. 109), and this highlights the important role of communication in negotiating expectations. To date, much more is known about the role of mothering across childhood and adolescence; less is known about what characteristics of fathers matter most (Crosnoe & Cavanagh, 2010), although the study of fathers is a growth area.

If you have ever lived with a newborn baby, you are well aware how one extremely small person can change an entire household. "There is a gradual decline from the emotional high experienced initially to a state more tempered by negative as well as positive feelings" (Sillars & Wilmot, 1989, p. 233). New parents must deal with the following communication-related tasks: (1) renegotiating roles, (2) transmitting culture while establishing a community of experiences, and (3) developing the child's communication competence. Moderately flexible families are likely to weather this period more easily than do rigid or chaotic family systems.

Partners' ability to focus on each other normally declines during early parenthood. New parents may feel inept or exhausted. Whereas women traditionally have assumed the major responsibility for baby care, increasingly fathers are sharing part of the efforts, as indicated in Chapter 7. Even so, mothers may become depressed or overwhelmed with caring for an infant and recovering from childbirth. Dual-career partners must assess and develop ways to manage work, such as planning child care or developing new working hours: for instance, one partner works days and the other nights (Holmes et al., 2013). In their study of new parenting, Huston and Holmes (2004) reported that parenthood expands the workload at home. The arrival of a child increased the number of family-related activities carried out on any given day. For example, new fathers increased their participation in tasks from 1.9

to 2.4 a day and new mothers increased from 3.9 to 5.3 a day. The more husbands thought their wives viewed them as competent, the more husbands contributed to both housework and child care. Increasingly, couples with careers tend to delay parenthood. The timing of parenthood is also a factor. There may be both advantages and disadvantages to having children later rather than earlier in their marriages. For instance, mothers and fathers may be able to be more active parents if they have children later because their careers are more established and they may have more flexibility at work.

Couple intimacy certainly changes with the birth of a child. Female sexual desire remains low for a period of time; both partners tend to be exhausted from the added responsibilities. Yet, although these parents have limited time for maintaining their adult connections, Huston and Holmes (2004) found that new parents tended to laugh together, hug and kiss, and discuss feelings about as often as comparable nonparent partners.

The first child represents a link to posterity and continuation of the family name and heritage—a potentially heavy burden. Naming the child becomes a communication event. Names may serve to link family generations or reflect parental dreams. Although all families face a decision regarding what a child will call his or her parents and grandparents, gay and lesbian couples face the more complicated decision of what their child should call each of them, such as Daddy and Papa or Mommy and Ema (Chabot & Ames, 2004).

When you think about your future children, or the children you have, what aspects of your family background would you wish to pass on to them? Do you wish they could experience the same type of Passover Seders or Christmas dinners you did as a child? Would you want them to have a strong Pakistani or Chinese identity? What games, songs, or stories would you teach them? An example of struggling with transmission of culture follows:

The birth of our first child revived our ties to our childhood. I suddenly recited nursery rhymes and sang songs I forgot I even knew. I started to talk about sending him to camp because everyone in my family went to camp every summer. My partner, Onyi, began to make fancy decorated cookies and little cakes that she remembered from her childhood. We both had many Christmas rituals from childhood that we wanted our son to experience.

For many people, a child represents a link to the past and the future and a sense of immortality. Young parents who develop an independent lifestyle often feel a sudden urge for greater connections with parents, grandparents, and other relatives. Appropriate family and friend boundaries usually require careful negotiation. Once a couple becomes a triad, certain dormant issues may arise—particularly unresolved ones. The child's future religious affiliation may become a contentious issue. A father's unfulfilled dreams may be transferred to his son. Spousal conflicts arise over what is to be "passed down." The transmission of both the cultural heritage and the family's own heritage may create a complicated communicative task, as this observer reports:

It was AMAZING for me to watch my sister and her husband with their first child. After almost 25 years, my sister could remember so many of the songs that our mother sang to us as little ones. She and Lee took great pleasure in creating new words and expressions from things that Jonathan did. They set certain patterns for birthday parties, established Friday nights as "family night," and began to take Jonathan to museums, children's theater, and library storybook programs together. They created their own three-person world.

Some young unmarried mothers depend on their parents for providing housing and sharing child care. These unmarried mothers and their parents follow different life-course trajectories than a traditional couple with occasional help from the child's grandparents. Some grandparents welcome this; others feel guilty that their own children cannot take care of themselves or "their kids." Often, the unmarried mother at ages 14 to 16 has a working mother somewhere between the ages of 30 and 35 and the great-grandparents have to shoulder the child-care responsibilities. Some new parents remain "on the margins" of their child's life. In her study of low-income black fathers, Hamer (2007) distinguished between two types of fathers—those who were just "fathers," or baby-makers who did not care for their children, and those who were "daddies" and "expressed love, provided social support and companionship, and made their children a central part of their lives" (p. 439). Most of her respondents fell somewhere in the middle of these parental types. Their ability to parent actively was affected by circumstances such as substance abuse, illegal employment, incarceration, and contention between themselves and the baby's mother.

Parents serve as their children's first communication models, eliciting babies' responses over time. The moment of birth exposes the child to the world of interpersonal contacts, beginning a powerful parent-child bonding process through physical contact, facial/eye contact, and reciprocal vocal stimulation. Most new parents respond to crying babies intuitively by cradling, rocking, or soothing the child (Socha & Yingling, 2010). Parental warmth, support, sensitive responses, and children's temperament and signaling interrelate to create parent-child connections (Peterson, Madden-Derdich, & Leonard, 2000).

A child makes its first contact with the world through touch, and this becomes an essential source of comfort, security, and warmth. The first few months mark the critical beginning of a child's interpersonal learning. A child's personality is being formed in the earliest interchanges with nurturing parents. Children begin to respond to words at age 6 or 7 months; by 9 or 10 months, they can understand a few words and will begin to use language soon thereafter. Parents set the stage for positive interpersonal development by verbally and nonverbally communicating to a child the feeling of being recognized and loved. From a communication perspective, "Couples do not become parents just by virtue of having a child: parenthood is constituted and maintained through conversation" (Stamp, 1994, p. 109). Such conversations occur between partners and between parent and child. Eventually, conversations include stories: birth narratives for biological children and entrance narratives for adopted children (Harrigan, 2010) that reveal a child's identity and family events surrounding his or her arrival.

The changes that accompany the transition to parenthood are profound for parents as the birth of a first child affects virtually every area of their relationship as well as their individual identities and behaviors (Yingling, 2004). Most partners experience significant life changes. Mothers tend to experience a dramatic transition after a child's birth; fathers may experience a more dramatic transition to parenthood after the first six months. Whereas fathers expected changes in the early period, such as changes in a partner's body or availability, they are faced with a different reality when things do not shift back as easily as they expected (Huston & Holmes, 2004). Fathers are more likely to confront pressures to remain consistent in their workplace commitments than mothers who may have maternity leaves and, in many cases, reduced or altered work expectations. Same-sex partners need to negotiate role responsibilities because they are not presented with strong societal expectations. In cases of open adoption, the adoptive parents will begin to establish the patterns of contact with their child's birth mother or family.

Family with Small Children   The preschool family (2–6-year-old child) experiences less pressure than in the previous period. Parents have learned to cope with a growing child. Barring physical or psychological complications, the former baby now walks, talks, feeds, and entertains himself or herself for longer periods of time.

Three- and four-year-olds exhibit well-developed language skills. A 4-year-old may produce well over 2,000 different words, probably understands many more, and can identify tasks and expectations according to gender. Children at this age begin to develop more sophisticated persuasive strategies for gaining such ends as later bedtimes or favorite foods; in many cases children can use multiple strategies to reach their goals (Socha & Yingling, 2010). And most children over 18 months use negation quite effectively, starting with NO! As children become more independent, parents may directly influence their language acquisition skills through enrichment activities such as reading, role-playing, and storytelling. Media increasingly impact children at this age. Small children watch television, play with computerized toys, and spend time on the computer at home or at day-care. Computer activities might include educational games or participating in social media with a grandparent or other members of the family. Family economic resources directly affect access to these opportunities.

Communication with children differs according to the family's use of restricted or elaborated speech codes, reflecting whether the family tends to be position oriented or person oriented, as described in Chapter 1. A child in a position-oriented family learns to rely on a prescribed, or restricted, range of communication behaviors; the child in a person-oriented family is encouraged to use a greater, or elaborated, range of communicative behaviors. These families differ in the degree to which the child is provided with verbalized reasons for performing or not performing certain functions at certain times with certain individuals. Persons growing up in a household where things are done "because I am your father and I say so" do not gain experience in extended conversation or adapting to the unique individuals involved. Elaborated speech codes also prepare children to interact with a wider range of persons outside the family.

Eventually, first-born children may have to incorporate siblings into their world. The arrival of a second or third child moves the triad to a four- or five-person system and places greater stress on the parents. Additional children trigger a birth-order effect, which interacts with sex roles to affect parent-child interaction. You may have heard characteristics attributed to various people because "She is the middle child" or "He is the baby of the family." There appear to be differences in parent-child communication based on sex and position (Sulloway, 1996). Further, each additional child limits the amount of time and contact each child has with the parents and the parents have with each other. Single parents experience many different challenges and often struggle to find time for themselves. These years set the foundation for a child's ties to many extended family members. For example, children may begin to interact regularly with aunts and uncles, establishing a connection that may increase in depth as the years pass or that may be reinvented when the child is closer to young adulthood (Milardo, 2009; Sotirin & Ellingson, 2006).

Sibling competition develops as the family grows. It is more prevalent when children are close in age and the same gender because they have to share parental attention. The sibling relationship is predictably the longest shared familial relationship and it is not uncommon to see siblings close in early and later life and less close in the middle years as they have their families and careers to attend to (Nussbaum, Pecchioni, Baringer, & Kundrat, 2002). This next example illustrates why parents need direct communication with an older child or children before the next baby's birth or adoption and during the months that follow:

Angie was 3 years old when Gwen was born, and it was a very hard period for her and therefore for us. Angie changed from being a self-sufficient, happy child to a whining clinger who sucked her thumb and started to wet her pants again. Jimmy and I had to work very hard to spend "special" time with her, to praise her, and to let her "help" with the baby when she wanted to. Luckily, Gwen was an easy baby, so we could make the time to interact with Angie the way she needed us to.

Siblings 3 or more years older are more likely to treat the baby with affection and interest, because they are more oriented to children their own age and less threatened by the new arrival. A sibling closer in age may engage in aggressive and selfish acts toward the baby.

In the 3–6-year-old stage, children begin to communicate on their own with the outside world. Some attend preschool. At 5 or 6 years old, most enter kindergarten. From their young peers, children learn about friendship and establish relationships outside the family. Children's interactions with one another vary in response to each other's gender and social characteristics such as dominance or shyness. By age 2 most children distinguish boys from girls, and within two more years they identify behaviors and tasks according to gender (Garcia-Preto, 2005b).

Cultural differences impact communication development. A study of Mexican and African American working mothers reported the difficulty in finding day-care providers who do not racially insult their children or put them down for their cultural differences. Speaking Spanish was often not permitted by the caretakers (Uttal, 1998). This reality affected communication and required the mothers to reduce stress by explaining to their children "about race relations with white society and how to navigate them" (p. 605). African American parents have an additional task of preparing children to deal with racial derogation (Noguera, 2002). These parents will often find themselves relying on an imperative communication style to protect their children from racism (Daniel & Daniel, 1999), and this is especially true for young African American males whose parents must teach them about the dangers they face (Robinson, 2013). Finally, how parents talk about play differs across cultures. Whereas European mothers use talk to describe their play with a child ("Push the green tractor back to Daddy"), African mothers focus more on social relationships than objects ("Your Daddy will get that for you") (Socha & Yingling, 2010).

Family with School-Aged Children   The school-aged family experiences new communication struggles as children become even more connected to the outside world. The family system overlaps continuously with other social systems—educational, religious, and community. Even families with strong boundaries experience increasing outside influences. Schools introduce children to a wider world of ideas, beliefs, and values, while potentially challenging their families' ways. Some parents find communicating with school personnel in support of a child's learning to be highly stressful; the amount and type of homework can create nightly stress, especially for working parents (Wingard, 2009). Parents from diverse cultural backgrounds may face special challenges; school personnel vary in their perceptions of how Hispanic and African American parents can become involved with their children's education (Cooper, 2006). An educator's lack of cultural sensitivity may result in family alienation or lack of direct involvement in a child's education. Some schools and communities will welcome the diverse family forms represented by their local students; if that is not the case, children will be faced with messages that discount or challenge their family experiences.

Given that one in five children in the United States is an immigrant or child of an immigrant, special demands are placed on both parents and children to mediate the family-school relationship. Parents must strive to overcome the language barrier because "without the ability to communicate parents felt helpless, alienated, and unable to advocate on behalf of their children" (Perreira, Chapman, & Stein, 2006). On the other hand, many school-aged children have become "family translators" or "cultural brokers," a role that creates a significant power shift.

School-aged children spend many hours away from family influences. In addition to school-related activities, religious organizations provide educational and recreational events. Organizations such as those for scouting, dance, sports, clubs, and after-school activities compete for family members' time; some organizations may encourage or mandate parental involvement whereas others may attempt to set clear parental boundaries. In their study of parent communication and child athletic involvement, Turman, Zimmerman, and Dobesh (2009) interviewed parents about their experience. Respondents talked about how other parents tried to "butter up" the coaches for favoritism, and how coaches tried to set boundaries on the coach-parent relationships.

During this period children develop many of their formative communication skills. Negotiation and priority-setting become important aspects of child-parent communication. Children's use of persuasive message strategies increase as they age. Kline and Clinton (1998) reported that children ages 5 to 8 use one to two different arguments in beginning to create persuasive messages; children ages 9 to 12 create two to four arguments; and children ages 13 and older used three or more arguments. Summarizing studies of children's speech, they report 5–6-year-olds used more pleading, sulking, threats, and requests. Between 3rd grade and 11th grade, children increasingly use more compromises, arguments that advance their views, more appeals to what they think society expects, and more deliberation about competing alternatives. "Second and third graders use unilateral or coercive strategies such as threats, punishments or appealing to adult authority. Fourth and fifth graders are more likely to use reciprocal strategies such as interpersonal bribes, coordinated teamwork or attempts to convince the other that he/she is wrong" (p. 121). Children become increasingly competent at producing messages adapted to their listeners and creating counterarguments. During this period, a child's communication competence increasingly impacts parental decision-making.

During this period of growth, most children experience strong peer pressures, which may conflict with parental views. Often, family conflict develops because the child feels compelled to please friends rather than parents. Mothers who take time to communicate with their children and listen empathically to them when disciplining or comforting tend to have children who are less rejected by their peers and more frequently chosen as companions (Burleson, Delia, & Applegate, 1992).

During the school years, the family identity as a unit reaches its peak. Members can enjoy a range of joint activities, bringing richness to the intimacy of the family relationship. Children living in two households due to parental separation or divorce experience unique challenges as they navigate custody arrangements and careful planning as they must ensure that all school materials are in the right household. Schrodt and colleagues (2006) examined how parents co-raising children in different households interacted and negotiated the details of the divorce decree. They found that some couples operated strictly by the letter of the law, some took a more flexible approach, and some used the details of the divorce decree to punish each other. In one family the co-parents of young children continually argued over who would have the children at certain times on holidays. They went to court and the judge declared that one parent would have the children until 11:59 PM on Christmas Eve and would need to deliver the children to the other house. After a holiday of exhausted and crying children, the parents made the effort to interact and negotiate a more workable solution (which is likely what the judge hoped would happen).

Media use impacts member role reversals in families with school-aged children because "new media and technologies are often introduced through the younger generations, whose swift adoption of these technologies and wholesale reliance on them in their daily communication behaviors forces older family members to adopt the technologies to maintain communication ties" (Bryant & Bryant, 2006, p. 300). This can be especially problematic if older family members cannot adapt. A recent national Pew study of families and technology revealed that in married-with-children households, 89 percent own multiple cell phones, 55 percent own two or more computers, and 65 percent contain a husband, wife, and child (aged 7 to 17) who all use the Internet (Kennedy, Smith, Wells, & Wellman, 2008). Other family configurations reported lower levels of involvement with technology. These scholars found that "a majority of adults say technology allows their family life today to be as close, or closer than their families were when they grew up" (p. v).

Although the life course differs for single parents, gays or lesbians with children, and unmarried cohabiting couples, each will go through variations of these same phases of experience. Therefore, single parents will tend to rely on relatives or hired child-care resources in order to remain employed. Gay male partners find themselves attempting to identify significant female figures to serve as female role models for their children; lesbian couples tend to seek out significant males to play a role in children's lives (Galvin & Patrick, 2009).

Families with Adolescents

Most family systems change significantly as younger members enter adolescence. Some parents send the message to their teenagers to "hurry up and grow up," promoting this agenda by allowing early dating, relaxed curfews, and dressing like adults. Other parents encourage the opposite, with an attitude "You're only young once; enjoy it." Adolescents experience dramatic physical, sexual, and emotional changes. Physical maturation experiences differ biologically; some children begin puberty very early while others are **off-time**. Some adolescents become pregnant, drop out of school, or become involved in drugs, essentially shortening the adolescent development phase. A 15-year-old school dropout without a job or a 16-year-old mother face different stresses than those who do not confront such complications. Although previous research characterized this period as tumultuous for parents and children, current research takes a more nuanced approach; "cultural factors and socioeconomic forces greatly affect how families define this stage of development" (Garcia-Preto, 2005b, p. 274).

Child and parent bidirectional influence processes become particularly obvious during adolescence. Hormonal changes impact moods, aggression, and feelings of self-worth, all of which affect parental interaction processes. In his review of adolescents' impact on parental development, Farrell (2000) asserted that adolescent development affects immediate states such as mood, distress level, or well-being as well as sense of identity and generativity. At least in some cases, a child's adolescence coincides with parental midlife issues, a challenging combination. For example, in a study of family bonds and emotional well-being in families with teenagers, fathers reported higher emotional well-being when together with other family members than when being alone, whereas mothers did not report the same experience (Vandeleur, Jeanpretre, & Perrez, 2009). At a time when children may need less connection, fathers appear to benefit from strong connections.

Highly functional parent-teen relationships depend on successfully navigating privacy boundaries (Petronio, 1994). Teenagers experience struggles as they cope with change and individuation, particularly in areas of sexuality, identity, autonomy, and friendships. For most adolescents, prior interest in same-sex friendships switches to a growing interest in the opposite sex: "Keep out" signs appear on doors; phone calls become private. Teenagers establish strong boundaries around certain topics in relation to parents (Guerrero & Afifi, 1995). Stronger physical and psychological boundaries, which thereby limit communication with some or all family members, are established.

Teenagers who view their parents positively are more likely to be open in their communication about topics that are sexually risky and are likely to discuss sensitive issues more frequently (LePoire, 2006). However, even today many parents are hesitant, embarrassed, or unprepared to talk with their adolescents about sex (Jerman & Constantine, 2010). This is important as effective parental communication about sex is the greatest predictor for safer sex and delaying sexual activity. Timing of interactions is important, and researchers have found that the more parents are aware of their adolescents' moods and refrain from forcing discussions or decisions during a negative period, the more positive are the eventual outcomes (Niedzwiecki, 1997). Family communication that supports mutual sensitivity and a gradual separation eases the transition.

Adolescent self-esteem affects family relationships. Teenagers care greatly about what peers, parents, and other adults think of them. Through communication interactions, adolescents gain a sense of their own identity. Teens express concerns about identity protection and managing the outcomes of their remarks (Manning, 1996). They trust people who keep personal information private. For African American children and adolescents, racial esteem is the primary predictor of self-esteem and parental communication is important in shaping their self-worth (Daniel & Daniel, 1999).

Based on her experiences counseling adolescents, Garcia-Preto (2005b) concluded that "girls are more likely to let parents know what they are feeling by yelling, while boys are more avoidant and tend to deal with situations by leaving the field" (p. 280). Fink, Buerkel-Rothfuss, and Buerkel (1994) reported fathers' negative behaviors of verbal aggression, high control, lack of involvement with their families, and personal dysfunction can damage father-son communication. Obviously, the relational dialectics of closeness and distance with parents affect stress. The need for privacy often accompanies the search for identity, as illustrated here:

I grew up in a home where doors were always open, and people knew each other's business. I remember going through a terrible period starting at the end of junior high when I hated sharing a room with my sister. I would spend hours alone sitting on my bed listening to music with the door shut, and if anyone came in, I would have a fit. I even locked my sister out a number of times.

A major task of adolescence involves loosening family bonds while strengthening bonds with peers. If the family atmosphere is warm and supportive, adolescents successfully negotiate differences with their parents (Reuter & Conger, 1998). If the atmosphere is hostile and coercive, adolescents are more likely to rebel, conflicts escalate, and disagreements remain unresolved. Reuter and Conger's four-year study of adolescents found that behaviors affecting family communication in the first year escalated by year four. Negative strategies increased in negative families and positive strategies increased in positive families. Stress was much higher and more frequent in families with overly dominant, demanding, and coercive parents. The quality of parent-child relationships prior to adolescence foreshadowed their behaviors during adolescence. The authors concluded, "families entering adolescence showing a straightforward communication, attentive listening, and warmth tended to remain at highest levels of warm interaction one year later" (p. 446). Using data from the Sloan 500 Family Study, Snyder (2007) analyzed responses of parents of adolescents to the question "What does quality time mean to you?" Their responses fell into three categories according to parent types: structured planning parents, time-available parents, and child-centered parents. Those in the last category described quality time as "the intimate heart-to-heart talks they had with their children" (Synder, p. 331). Whether parents talked about sharing moments during errands or having an evening conversation routine, the interactions needed to be personal, nurturing, and focused. As revealed in the opening vignette, the availability of parents, such as the Rybeckis, may differ across time. A need to care for an aging parent or to return to work may result in less time for one child than for other children.

Adolescence is characterized by higher conflict than earlier stages: teens report that 40 percent of their daily conflicts occur with a sibling or a parent (Roloff & Miller, 2006). The process of creating a self-identity leads to increased conflict and decreased closeness with parents, especially for girls (Lauer & Lauer, 2009). Canary and Canary (2013) explain that increased conflicts between parents and adolescents should not come as a big surprise as both are navigating developmental changes and issues surrounding autonomy at this stage. Parents and teens frequently interpret the conflicts differently, with finances becoming a more important issue. Conflicts with girls tend to be less difficult to resolve than those with boys (Roloff & Miller, 2006). Conflicts occur most frequently over simple items, such as chores and appearance, rather than over bigger issues, such as drugs and sex. If a child has a positive perception of parental communication, there is a greater likelihood of a positive relationship and positive self-image (Bollis-Pecci & Webb, 1997). The more time parents spend with adolescents, the more frequent but shorter the conflicts (Vuchinich, Teachman, & Crosby, 1991).

Personal decision-making provides a sense of autonomy for teenagers. Between the ages of 13 and 19 adolescents undergo an individuation process leading to self-reliance accompanied by a desire to make up their own minds. By asserting their developing talents to speak out, work, or perform tasks without constant help and supervision, adolescents signal their maturity and competence.

The adolescent's struggles to work through developmental tasks of sexuality, identity, and autonomy send reverberations throughout the family system. The sexual awakening of their children has a powerful effect on many parents. The upsurge in sexual thoughts and feelings serves as an undercurrent to many interactions that may make parents uneasy because they are forced to consider their child as a sexual being. Opposite-gender parents and children may experience a new distance between them as a response to the power of the incest taboo in society. Unfortunately, in many families this results in the end of nonverbal affection, as illustrated in the following example:

I will never forget being hurt as a teenager when my father totally changed the way he acted toward me. We used to have a real "buddy" relationship. We would spend lots of time together; we would wrestle, fool around, and I adored him. Suddenly, he became really distant, and I could not understand whether I had done something. But I did not feel I could talk about it either. Now that I am older, I can see the same pattern happening with my two younger sisters. Obviously, he has a personal rule that when your daughter starts to develop breasts, you have to back off. Now I can understand that it hurts him as much as it hurts us.

Parents and children may face internal conflicts if they perceive a major contrast between their children's budding sexuality and their own sexual identity. Such conflicts are tied to the parents' stages of development and negative self-evaluations. Because facing this issue would be uncomfortable, such perceptions may result in conflict over more "acceptable" issues such as friends, money, independence, or responsibility. For gay and lesbian adolescents, this is the time they are likely to label and understand their sexual orientation and face questions and fears about the coming-out process. Estimates suggest that 40 to 75 percent of young gay men and lesbians have disclosed their sexual identity to their mother and 30 to 55 percent to their father (Savin-Williams & Esterberg, 2000).

When considering adolescents raised by same-sex parents, Patterson's research (2009) revealed that female teenagers raised in same-sex partner households reported that factors such as adolescent adjustment and qualities of peer and family relationships did not differ significantly from adolescents raised in opposite-sex parent homes. For such adolescents, the quality of parent-adolescent relationships, rather than family form, is associated with positive adjustment.

Opportunities for time spent together between parents and children decrease in a linear form during the period from preadolescence through adolescence. Although perceptions of warm and supportive relationships continue over that time, "both adolescents and parents report less frequent expressions of positive emotions and more frequent expressions of negative emotions" (Laursen & Collins, 2004, pp. 338–339). In stepfamilies, a close, nonconflictual stepfather-stepchild relationship improves adolescent well-being, especially when the teenager has a nonconflictual relationship with his or her mother (Vogt Yuan & Hamilton, 2006).

Adolescents and parents struggle with open communication. Parents report difficulty detecting deceptions by their children, partly because children vary in their communication strategies that include lies. Sometimes it is a "no-win" experience, since some parents will perceive incomplete answers as lying while others see complete information as a sign of deception (Grady, 1997). Adolescents are more likely to accept parental guidelines when they have clear, open lines of communication and feel that their parents respect their values. Only after some adolescents achieve adulthood and independence do they feel close to their parents again.

Economic concerns place significant stress on families, affecting members' communication. In recent years these stresses have escalated. An increasing number of adolescents have experienced homelessness; many older adolescents are postponing their college careers in order to earn money to help out at home. Many families are living apart because the primary breadwinner found a job in a different location but the family cannot move. Countless serious family conversations accompanied these changes. Family culture also interacts with economics. For example, in dual-earner Puerto Rican families when both parents are at work, young adolescent daughters may be required to take over household responsibilities, including the care of siblings (Toro-Morn, 1998). The teenagers experience an abbreviated adolescence because they must communicate as adults in order to manage the house and protect their siblings.

Finally, adolescents may be drawn into parental conflicts. In their study of adolescent triangulation into parental conflict, Fosco and Grych (2010) revealed, "when interparental conflict is persistent, hostile, and unresolved, adolescents are more likely to be drawn into the arguments" (p. 264). This leads adolescents to blame themselves for the conflict or to feel responsible for solving their parents' problems. Neither alternative serves a teenager well. Children of divorced parents often find themselves caught in the middle between parents and want to see parents work out their own difficulties and center the child in their attention (Afifi, 2003; Braithwaite, Toller, Daas, Durham, & Jones, 2008).

Launching Children and Midlife

The period when older children leave home often coincides with parental midlife, signaling another family system recalibration. Although midlife definitions very greatly, it is likely to encompass the late thirties to the mid-fifties (Fingerman, Nussbaum, & Birditt, 2004). Midlife experiences include at least five adaptations. For couples with children these include (1) transition of parent-child relationships to adult-adult relationships; (2) changes in partnership functioning or single-parent experiences; and (3) expansion of the family to include new in-laws and grandchildren, biological, adopted, or stepchildren. All couples will likely experience the last two adaptations: (4) opportunities to resolve relationships with aging parents; and (5) opportunities to revitalize sibling ties. We negotiate these transitions in interactions, and these transitional tasks impact the entire family system.

The "launching" of children into adulthood is a transition for both parents and children (Anderson & Sabatelli, 2007). During this period parents move from being responsible for their children to a sense of mutual responsibility between caring adults. In highly communal role-bound cultures in which parents and children retain a more position-oriented relationship, the parent-child relationship will experience minimal change. When young adults live on their own, especially if they are self-supporting, they assume the responsibilities of adulthood, including significant decision-making and financial responsibility. For some young adults this process actively begins with a move to the college campus; for others, it may occur later as they enter the workplace or attend a local college while living at home. The launching stage becomes a time of clearing out the childhood bedrooms, sending along the extra coffeepot or dishes, and letting go of the predictable daily interactions at breakfast or bedtime that tied parents and siblings into a close, interactive system. Specific conversational topics involve managing money, negotiating living space, making career decisions, maintaining good health habits, or staying in contact. When this separation takes place without significant struggle, parent-child communication usually becomes more open and flexible. Frequent contact with parents and siblings via cell phones, texts, e-mails, or visits maintains family links, and the development in technology has increased the amount of interaction for many parents and young adults at this stage.

Since I've been in college, I call home nearly every day. If I sense that my mother is upset about something and I ask about it, she will say, "Oh, don't you worry about it. It's not your problem; you don't live here anymore." That upsets me, because I still feel I am part of the family. Other times she will call me three times a day because of something my brother did.

By this point in time, parents and their adult children have negotiated, and may continue to negotiate, issues such as privacy rights and the management of intergenerational boundaries (Cooney, 1997). While many parents and adult children experience an improvement in their communication and relationship as the children become independent, that is not the case in all families. Adult children and parents may continue to engage in conflict. Adult children reported that most conflicts with their elderly parents resulted from the parents' unwillingness to provide assistance and accept the child's autonomy, whereas parents may resist their self-assigned authority (Dickson, Christian, & Remmo, 2004).

The high cost of living, underemployment, or unemployment make leaving home difficult. As noted in Chapter 1, many college students are living at home or returning home to live after college due to economic pressures, a process referred to as "renesting" (Anderson & Sabatelli, 2007). Many married children who are divorcing return home as single parents for the same reason. The countertrend involves young people leaving home to live independently prior to marriage, with increasing numbers entering cohabiting relationships. More midlife adults are intimately involved with their children's lives than in the previous generation. Parental support of grown children appears ongoing in many cases; this includes listening and emotional support, advice, and practical financial assistance (Fingerman, Miller, Birdett, & Zarit, 2009).

In addition to negotiating their relationships with children, adults at midlife experience other anticipated and unforeseen stresses. Many adults are engaging in generational juggling as they serve as caregivers to both their older children and one or both of their aging parents or their partner's parents (Fingerman, Birditt, Nussbaum, & Ebersole, 2013). These scholars noted that the communication demands at this stage may be the most complex of any during the life course as adults are juggling so many different roles at home, at work, in the community, and with a wide variety of family and social network members, along with relevant professionals in the education and health care systems, for example. While the task of ongoing caretaking of both generations can be overwhelming, many adults in this stage also encounter crisis situations, such as a health crisis of a partner or one or more of their parents. The competing needs at this stage may become overwhelming, especially if the caretaker is employed. As the elongated generational structure becomes the norm, grandparents and even great-grandparents may rely on the two younger generations for emotional, physical, or financial support.

Major changes occur in many husband-wife relationships or partnerships after children leave home as there are opportunities for increased adult intimacy. Other couples that focused intensively on their children for so many years may find themselves unconnected as the children depart. Partners sensing a distance may feel unable, or unwilling, to attempt a reconnection. For many couples, the readjustment to a viable, two-person entity requires hard work. Separations and divorces occur frequently in this midlife transition period. The challenge for some spouses is reflected in the following example:

When the children left, I discovered myself living with essentially a mute man. We hadn't realized that for years we had talked little to one another—that most of our communication was with or about the children. Since we both worked, we always took vacations with the kids, and kept busy chasing after kids' activities; we never had time for ourselves. Now I've got time to talk, and I have to compete with TV—that's the "other woman" in my house.

Active and extended grandparenting is becoming more common, given increased longevity and the rise in single parents and same-sex parents. Today, grandparents may range in age from 30 to 90-plus; grandchildren range in age from newborns to retirees. A 30-year-old adult has a 75 percent chance of having at least one living grandparent (Soliz, Lin, Anderson, & Harwood, 2006). Children in blended families may experience up to eight grandparent figures, or even more, depending on how many relationships the parents have. Given the reality of a mobile society, some grandparents and grandchildren experience limited face-to-face contacts. Many among the current generation of grandparents are also tech-savvy, and young adults may have more contact with grandparents in previous generations. In addition, an increasing number of grandparents take on participatory roles in modern families, particularly in situations of divorce and caregiving when their children have dual-career marriages.

While assuming the title and role of grandparent is certainly an identity shift for most people, it can open the door for positive family communication experiences. Grandparents may play many different roles depending on geographic location, amount of available time, connections to the parents, and the level of responsibility they have for their grandchildren. Their role contributions include spending pleasurable time with the child, providing financial support for grandchildren or their parents, extending emotional support during divorce or parental separation, or assisting with the caretaking of a child with special needs (Soliz et al., 2006). These interpersonal roles may vary across the years, family situation, and the health and willingness of the grandparent.

Grandparents and grandchildren who interact frequently express feelings of closeness; grandparents can help the family experience continuity, and grandchildren develop increased self-identity through storytelling and oral history. Grandparents provide access to a grandchild's ancestry and the family's roots. Through conversation and storytelling, the intergenerational transmission of family lore and history is passed down. Grandparenthood provides an opportunity for meaningful interaction, while it usually does not entail the responsibilities, obligations, or conflicts of parenthood. Stress can result if grandparents are drawn into parental conflicts. Occasionally, grandparents act as an emotional refuge for children in a strife-torn family, serving as supporters and listeners. Geographically separated grandparents and grandchildren have greater opportunities to communicate regularly today due to technology; many seniors' prime motivation for going online is to connect with their children and grandchildren, rather than with friends (Wired Seniors, 2001). Video conferencing permits grandparents and grandchildren to interact face to face on a daily basis. Multiple factors affect how grandparents play their roles, such as age, gender, and culture.

Off-time grandparents have varied experiences: those who are young may resist the title and role, whereas very old grandparents may not be capable of active engagement in the role (Soliz et al., 2006). Maternal grandparents tend to have closer relationships and more communication with their grandchildren than paternal grandparents (Williams & Nussbaum, 2001). Although most communication research focuses on what family stories grandparents pass down, Fowler and Soliz (2010) examined how young adult grandchildren react when grandparents engage in painful disclosures with them. They found that less satisfying grandparent-grandchild relationships are predicted by the discomfort such disclosures produce for some grandchildren. Again, this raises the issue of significant bidirectional communication between a much older adult and a young adult. Family storytelling also helps families understand difficulties and uncertainties in later life such as health challenges, increased caregiving needs, and dementia of a grandparent (Aleman & Helfrich, 2010).

Cultural expectations affect grandparent involvement. In certain cultures, grandparents are expected to assume a major role in child rearing. In most African American families, older family members play many roles—adviser, mediator, financial supporter, health resource, and transmitter of culture. "Grandparents often have relationships with their grandchildren that are as close as, if not closer than, the relationships they have with their own adult children" (Hines, 1999, p. 339). A study of African American, Latina, and white grandmothers raising or helping to raise grandchildren revealed that Latina grandmothers had higher satisfaction than the other grandmothers when they co-parented with a parent in the household; African American grandparents experienced higher life satisfaction when they had custodial rather than co-parenting situations (Goodman & Silverstein, 2006). Such cross-generational contact provides opportunities for extended transmission of culture and for development of a sense of family history.

The performance of the grandparent role reflects the connections between the grandparent and parent generation. When adult children become parents, this may serve as an opportunity for reconnection and healing in some families; the younger generation may have a new understanding and appreciation of what parents do (Walsh, 2005). Ties to in-laws may be impacted by the arrival of children. In fact, in some families children may form very close relationships with their grandparents (Videon, 2005). Grandparents can be a very positive relationship for children and adolescents, as they can listen and give advice without all of the control issues that parents and children face. Some parents at midlife appreciate this relationship and understand its benefits. Others may be threatened by the close relationship between grandparents and their children and perhaps even be envious at times.

Midlife brings its challenges and its joys. In spite of the decisions about major life changes and the pressures of launching children, this period can be a time of happiness and growth. Children entering adulthood are often wonderful companions and supporters as adult-to-adult sharing increases. Partners and single parents have the opportunity to focus on renewing old relationships or creating new ones.

Families in Later Life

Family relationships continue to be significant throughout later life. During this time approximately one-third of men and over one-half of women live alone, due to divorce or death of a spouse. Given longevity and better health in later years, many people choose to remain single in later life and live fulfilling lives. Most persons who are in later life who are parents live near at least one adult child and total isolation is rare. As family members grow older, they tend to rank their happiness higher the more frequently they interact with relatives (Ishii-Kuntz, 1994). Because people live longer today, more adults over age 65 now work because they wish to do so, and others will continue working to mange expenses such as health-care costs. If they have to work and care for their grandchildren, stress increases for these older adults.

Older family members face self-identity issues related to retirement, health concerns, decreasing physical strength, changes in living arrangements and alterations in interpersonal needs, especially if they lose a spouse, and facing mortality (Williams & Nussbaum, 2001). Some couples experience "reentry" problems when one or both retire, and the couple must negotiate issues such as increased togetherness, autonomy, use of space, and privacy. The increased contact may lead to a deepening of the relationship or result in friction. A survey of over 900 couples revealed that marital conflict is unaffected by husbands' and wives' transition to retirement but wives' continued employment appears associated with greater conflict (Davey & Szinovacz, 2004). In a large study of Dutch retirees, Van Solinge and Henkens (2005) found that preretirement concerns about marital conflict predicted the problems that developed as partners entered retirement. Many men adapt less well to unstructured time and rely on their wives for regular companionship; many women report a frustration at their loss of independence in these circumstances. As reflected in the adage "For better or worse but not for lunch," many women resent male intrusion into their established social life with female friends. Women reach out during midlife and beyond; thus this communication helps extending and multiplying friendships, whereas men rarely make new friends. As a result men tend to become more emotionally dependent on their wives (Yogev, 2002). Some retired persons undergo significant losses of professional identities and self-definitions, such as that of doctor or provider. Losing the social communication network of the workplace places increased pressure for intimacy on retirees' partners or children.

For some, the later years serve as a time of rejuvenation. Established couples now have time to enjoy each other and, if financially secure, to enjoy hobbies and travel. Individuals who put their lives on hold to raise children may find new partners. Although many older individuals show little interest in forming a new partner relationship, an increasing number seek committed companionship in nonmarital unions. In many cases such individuals choose not to marry for pragmatic reasons, such as losing a deceased spouse's pension. Additionally, "living apart together" (LAT), or living a partnered life while maintaining both residences, represents a growing trend among widowed, divorced, separated, and ever-single men and women in their sixties into their nineties (Levaro, 2009). For some, maintaining separate residences allows them to balance their involvement with adult children and grandchildren with also having a loving adult relationship.

During old age, many family relationships are emotionally important even if there is limited face-to-face contact, as these ties are sustained by memories of intense interaction (Bedford & Blieszner, 1997). New technologies provide greater opportunities to bridge the distance gap. For example, 34 percent of Americans aged 65 and over go online; by age 70 only 28 percent go online (Fox, 2006), and these numbers are increasing. Many Internet-skilled seniors will stay in touch with family members and longtime friends, form new relationships, shop, and search for health information online. The Internet can meet practical, social, and emotional needs at a time when mobility and transportation become challenging.

Family members' health and declining strength further impacts family communication. Ill health strains a couple's physical, mental, and financial resources, creating a need for nurturing communication and caregiving from other family members. Many of the physical changes in aging adults can contribute to communication challenges, such as declines in vision and hearing loss (especially the ability to detect higher-pitched tones and, later in life, low tones), and, in some cases, language-processing skills decline (Weiss, 1997; Williams & Nussbaum, 2001). Health and physical declines contribute to a loss of self-esteem, increased stress, and communication frustrations, making individuals reluctant to initiate personal contacts. Listeners may become impatient with an older person's infirmities and reduce or avoid interaction, especially face to face. However, it is important to stress that every person experiences the physical symptoms of aging differently and it is important not to assume that everyone suffers from age-related afflictions in the same way.

Later-life conversations and communication contribute to an individual's well-being.

Communication among family members becomes increasingly important at this stage. Many older family members engage in the "elder function," or the sharing of the accumulated wisdom of their lives with younger people, usually family members. For many older persons, satisfaction comes from imparting historical information or spinning stories designed to guide the younger generations. Reminiscence, recalling events that happened in the past, serves as a coping mechanism, to maintain self-esteem, to feel loved, to gain self-awareness, or to see oneself in a larger historical context. Reminiscence is generally healthy for older adults as long as it does not become obsessive, which is a sign of extreme stress or grief (Nussbaum, Pecchioni, Robinson, & Thompson, 2000). Sharing family stories and collecting oral histories can enrich a family, especially its members' sense of their family of origin, while giving elderly members a chance to communicate to those they love, helped raise, or even hurt at some point in time. Some need to "set the record straight" or to let go of past marital disappointments in order to make peace with previous life events (Dickson et al., 2004). More older people are writing their memoirs, not for publication but because they "want to leave a record of their lives for future generations" (Harker, 1997, p. 32), and families are creating electronic newsletters and blogs that collect and archive this information. The importance of this storytelling is demonstrated in the following:

I'm glad my dad, Bill, lived past 75. Only then did we come to terms with one another. Long after he retired, he mellowed, had a stroke, and became approachable. He talked about the depression, the war years, and the struggle to pay for the farm. Finally I better understood what had made him so tough and noncommunicative.

Many elderly couples confront the serious illness of one of the partners. In some cases full or partial recovery is a strong possibility; in other cases, one member faces a terminal disease or chronic decline due to dementia. Either situation alters their marital interaction. In her study of couples in which one partner is dealing with cancer, Imes (2006) reported the development of a "new normal" status, a term her respondents use to describe the relational status. They reported that things went back to "normal," but their use of this term indicated an acceptance of the cancer event and a return to many routine behaviors, at the same time recognizing their new roles and altered communication behaviors. These couples struggled with role shifts in areas of partnership, health, identity, health awareness, and managing community support. They also negotiated the extent to which they avoided or discussed the cancer-related topic as well as the manner in which they did so. Similarly, wives of elderly husbands with adult dementia confront living in the ambiguous state of "married widowhood" (Baxter, Braithwaite, Golish, & Olson, 2002). These women faced a loss and redefinition of their marital relationships as they watched the husbands they knew slip away; they were present physically but not emotionally or mentally. The wives developed a range of coping mechanisms, such as relying on nonverbal communication, working hard to interpret the limited communication cues, relying on the nursing home staff for information, or limiting contact with their partner. In other cases, a partner may "overfocus on the other's disability to avoid facing his or her own vulnerability, anxiety, or longing to be taken care of" (Rolland, 2005, p. 314). Single elderly adults who become ill need more support than some elderly partnered adults when one of them is a reasonably healthy spouse. When needed, elder care is most often carried out by daughters rather than sons. The caregiving daughter is more likely to be divorced, widowed, or never married in order to be able to meet caregiving demands (Weldon, 1998).

The death of an elderly family member may not be unexpected, or may be seen as on time within the life course, but this does not diminish the family's grief. Functional families find ways to acknowledge death as a normal and appropriate topic throughout life; therefore, an aging member's potential death can be openly addressed in these families. The death of an elderly relative frequently forces family members to communicate and make decisions about end-of-life issues (Hoppough & Ames, 2001). Families participate in approximately 70 to 80 percent of end-of-life decisions in hospital intensive care units (Pochard et. al., 2001). In many cases, one designated member has been prepared to make do-not-resuscitate orders, if appropriate, and to engage in discussions with other members and the health-care team (Galvin & DiDomenico, 2009). As depicted in the second opening case of the Ashford family in this chapter, more individuals and families are choosing a hospice approach to death, which permits family members to interact with a loved one in a setting that supports the natural process of letting go without a continuation of heroic measures to keep the loved one alive (Nussbaum et al., 2000). Although death remains a difficult or taboo topic in many families, others, particularly those with strong ties to an ethnic heritage, are able to confront the issue directly and realistically. For example, within Mexican American families, events surrounding death bring a family together to express emotions freely, reinforce family cohesiveness, and involve members of all ages sharing support for each other and participating in related rituals with each other (Martinez, 2001).

After the death of a spouse or partner, the grieving other must face the reality of living as a single person. Working through the grief period, such individuals may make great demands on friends or family members who are resentful of, or unprepared for, such pressures. The surviving member of a couple has to renegotiate roles and boundaries as he or she attempts to create or maintain interpersonal contacts. It is important that older family members have a say in decisions on their care and be a part of all communication that concerns them as long as possible.

Much to the surprise of their adult children, after a couple of years, many former partners enter new relationships, although remarriage occurs more frequently for men than for women (Walsh, 2005). Interpersonal motives for dating include meeting possible mates, exchanging intimacies, remaining socially active, interacting with the opposite sex, engaging in sex, and maintaining a stable identity. The importance of dating or living apart together is growing, but not necessarily as a prelude to marriage. Remarriages are relatively rare, although more common for those of a younger age and experiencing greater unhappiness as a single person.

Eventually, an elderly person must confront his or her own death. Many families resist addressing the issue directly with an elderly member, yet relationships that include discussion of death and that provide direct emotional support are more helpful. Family members—particularly adult children—may face their own crises as they try to (1) acknowledge the loss of the generation separating them from death, (2) make sense of the experience, (3) anticipate shifts in the family formation, and (4) deal with their own feelings of impending loss. Often, these concerns get in the way of saying farewell in a direct and meaningful manner. True "final conversations" involving talk, interactions, or nonverbal messages may occur when it is understood that one person is dying (Keeley & Yingling, 2007). Such moments help to convey love, caring, gratitude, and forgiveness that bring comfort and closure to the family members engaged in such interactions.

Transitions between Stages

Although each developmental stage offers life-changing experiences and opportunities for functional and meaningful communication, it is important to highlight the importance of transitions between these developmental stages because the instability of these periods often triggers highly meaningful, and sometimes challenging, family interactions. Stress occurs naturally at transitions between different stages of life and when unexpected events occur (McGoldrick & Shibusawa, 2012). Functional families manage these predictable changes through ongoing conversations about their expectations and experiences as well as finding ways to recognize and support each other, navigating the contradictions of life at any given stage. Most families experience the transitions with temporary, but not permanent, stress resulting from the transition. Functional families try and offset the challenges of transitions while focusing on the positive aspects of any given stage. Transitions into marriage or the birth of a child, for example, affect family functioning, but usually the family progresses through them as a normal maturation process. Transitions out of marriage—such as divorce, desertion, or death, or the loss or serious illness of a member—have negative effects and cause higher stress over longer periods of time. Functional families exhibit adaptive capacities that support them through very rough times.

Individual transitions tend to involve periods of oscillations, movements forward and backward, until the new behavior becomes more routine (Breunlin, Schwarts, &

Kune-Karrer, 2001) as people interact and co-create new meanings for themselves and with others. Just as a child does not suddenly stop crawling when she begins to walk, a father may not stop trying to set rules even when children enter adulthood. Family relationships are characterized by variability as each shift is negotiated. Only after a new pattern has begun to take hold can one let go of an old pattern. Even well into adulthood, moments of significant change or crisis arise when a young adult female reverts to being a little girl or a midlife male acts like a teenager for a short time. Variations on typical transitions are increasingly common. Such variations include gay or lesbian marriage or formal commitments, family formation through reproductive technologies, adoption of older children, foster parenting, remarriage to a former spouse, or the termination of cohabiting partnerships. These moments need their own adapted rituals symbolizing family connectedness and support (Imber-Black, 1999).

Dysfunctional families tend to include members who fail to make these transitions at the appropriate times in their lives, thus creating imbalance in their family systems. These members, often confronting serious psychological or physical issues, may remain stuck at a certain developmental stage, unable to move on. They are "off course" in proceeding through expected changes in the life-cycle stages. These affected families experience a piling-up effect, with one or more members stuck at the same stage. Sometimes these same family members experience external stresses (crime, bankruptcy, or devastating divorce) and, as a result of these circumstances, they become even less able to cope.

The changes in family life over decades are accompanied by changes in the communication characteristics of each stage as the family system recalibrates. In some families, communication among members remains vibrant across the years; in other families, communication fulfills a sense of obligation. A recent survey of 500 British couples found that after one year of marriage couples engaged in 40 minutes of conversation during a one-hour dinner. After 20 years, they spent 21 minutes talking, and after 30 years, only 16 minutes. Those married for 50 years spent three minutes in conversation (Zaslow, 2010). Clearly the amount or type of communication diminishes over time in many relationships, but that does not mean meaningful interaction cannot continue.

There are great variations in how families cope with developmental stresses. Some families experience a roller-coaster effect with little relief, especially when multiple stressors accumulate. As they struggle with change and transitions, most persons experience life in its immediate moments, often losing sight of the larger process. Eventually, the movement across the life span becomes lost in its moments.

Conclusion

This chapter provided an overview of the effects of developmental stresses on communication within families and how these affect the life course. Some stresses may come from outside the family system, while others are created within the family system, but all affect the family. After indicating how individuals move through a life cycle, the chapter focused on a stage model for intact U.S. families. The stages included are (1) single young adults, (2) partners, (3) families with children, (4) families with adolescents, (5) launching children and midlife, and (6) families in later life. As families move through the years, each generation faces predictable developmental issues as couples marry, beget children, and live through stages of child development superimposed on their own adult developmental changes. As children leave home to form new systems, their parents face the middle years and adjustment issues. The cohesion-adaptability axis overlays each family system's personal growth, while themes, images, and biosocial beliefs may be challenged as the years pass. Throughout the chapter, research has been included on how the individual's life course can be altered by the **on-time** or off-time sequencing of life cycle or developmental stages.

The entire family developmental process is extremely complex and challenging. Achieving the developmental tasks in each stage represents accomplishment and psychological growth for each family member in his or her life course. Stress gets expressed in the intrapersonal and interpersonal communication that follows as the family member struggles for balance in the dialectical tension between self needs and family system needs.

In Review

1. Reflecting on your own family or one you know well, compare and contrast how the traditional stages of development were affected by life-course issues. Cite three examples of on-time and off-time events that altered the life course.
2. Discuss what impact different cultural backgrounds have on the communication in various stages of development on children and parents. To what extent might an Asian American, Hispanic, African American, or Native American heritage (or pick another) influence two or three developmental issues?
3. Imagining your own family or a family you know well, provide examples of verbal or nonverbal communication patterns that seemed commonplace at different developmental stages in the family life cycle in parent-child, committed partner, and sibling communication.
4. Relying on your own family or a family you have observed, describe how a couple or partners have dealt with the communication tasks of incorporating a child into their system and dealing with the following communication-related issues: (a) renegotiating roles, (b) transmitting culture, (c) establishing a community of experiences, and (d) developing the child's communication competence.
5. What key qualities appear to characterize family communication during the period when one or more adolescents are living within the household?
6. Describe three ways in which communication is affected by the departure of young adults during the launching stage in either two-parent systems or single-parent systems.
7. Compare and contrast communication patterns you have observed in the interactions between middle-aged and older family members in two families. To what extent were reminiscing, reflection, and sorting out important to members at these stages?

Key Terms

Developmental changes   243

Developmental stages   244

Horizontal stressors   248

Independent life stage   251

Life course   244

Marker events   244

Off-time   264

On-time   277

Transition to parenthood   243

Vertical stressors   248

CHAPTER 11

Family Communication and Unpredictable Stress

LEARNING OBJECTIVES

- Understand unpredictable stress that families face and how they cope
- Describe specific types of crises and how family communication is affected by these crises

Erin and Luke Johnson were excited to be expecting their third child. On the day they went for their 20-week ultrasound, they had no idea how profoundly everything would change. They were shocked to learn that their unborn daughter had spina bifida, a birth defect that involves the incomplete development of the spinal cord. Erin was devastated. Every dream she had for her life and her children had changed. She couldn't eat, she couldn't sleep, and she couldn't stop crying. Erin and Luke wanted to hope for the best, but there were so many unanswered questions and terrifying statistics. All of a sudden, the Internet became the scariest place in the world.

As time went on, Erin and Luke found hope. They talked to family members and friends, relied on their faith, and came to believe that their daughter was going to come to them exactly how God wanted her to come to them. They found support online from other parents, and learned about a clinical trial for prenatal surgery that gave them purpose as they moved forward through the next few weeks. Three years later, their daughter is a happy preschooler and doing much better than anyone had expected.

Adelina Perez had just started her junior year of college when she received a phone call from her mother stating that she had left her father and was planning to file for divorce. Adelina was devastated and particularly sad for her mother, who she knew had always tried her best to make the marriage work. She'd known that her parents had problems—both Adelina and her brother Ethan had heard their parents fighting on many occasions. But she always thought they would work it out and stay together. Ethan had just started his freshman year of college. Adelina realized that her parents had stayed together until she and her brother were out of the house.

Adelina had many talks with her mother over the next few months, and became, in a sense, her mother's confidant. There were many things her mother told her about that she wished she hadn't, such as her father's infidelity, his emotional abuse toward her mother, and their financial problems. Her relationship with her father, which was never good to begin with, became more and more distant. Ethan continued to keep in contact with both their father and mother. Adelina's relationship with her own boyfriend of two years, Elliott, also began to deteriorate as Adelina began to have doubts of whether she could trust Elliott.

“ **I** never thought we would have to deal with something like this.” These words have been spoken by countless family members as they faced unexpected challenges, such as home foreclosures, loss of employment, loss of property in natural disasters, and the illness or death of a loved one. Just as difficult are feared events such as losing a father to a stroke, hearing a mother has relapsed into alcoholism, dealing with a parent's military deployment, or having a young son experience a recurrence of his cancer. This chapter addresses what happens to a family system when events occur for which the members have little or no warning and how communication functions in such circumstances.

Unpredictable stresses are brought about by events or circumstances that disrupt life patterns but cannot be foreseen from either a developmental or life-course perspective. Usually they result from significant negative occurrences, such as untimely death, divorce, economic challenges, or serious illness or injury, much like the case of Adelina Perez at the start of the chapter. Some positive events, referred to as “eustress”—such as a large inheritance, wedding, promotion, or the rediscovery of long-lost relatives—may also stress the family system. For instance, Mmari and colleagues (2009) have noted how the return of a parent from war, seemingly a positive event, can be confusing for adolescents as they adjust to having two parents again and become reacquainted with the parent who was deployed. Some theorists have distinguished between stress and trauma, suggesting that stresses can be managed whereas trauma “is a stress so great and unexpected that it cannot be defended against, coped with or managed” (Boss, 2006, p. 35). For example, a mother's breast cancer surgery may be considered a serious stressor whereas a brother's suicide is traumatic, devastating the family. Yet, it is difficult to predict with accuracy the effect of major stressors on a particular family; what may be a stressor for one family is traumatic for another.

Crises occur when a family lacks the resources to cope or when “family demands significantly exceed their capabilities” (Patterson, 2002, p. 351). All families undergo some degree of strain or stress. *Strain* can be defined as that tension or difficulty sensed by family members which indicates that change is needed in their relationships and their family environment. **Stressor events**, discussed in this chapter, are characterized by unexpectedness, greater intensity, longer duration, and their undesirability and serious effects (Lavee, Sharlin, & Katz, 1996).

Sometimes family members experience **ambiguous loss**, one characterized by high uncertainty regarding personal relationships (Boss, 1999). There are two types of ambiguous loss: The first type occurs when “people are perceived by family members as physically absent but psychologically present” (pp. 8–9). This includes soldiers missing in action and kidnapped children. Couples who want to have children but have failed attempts at pregnancy may also experience ambiguous loss (Amason, Wilson, & Rusinowski, 2012).

The second type of ambiguous loss occurs when “a person is perceived as physically present but psychologically absent” (pp. 8–9). This includes people with addictions, closed head injuries, or Alzheimer's disease. In the latter case, Baxter, Braithwaite, Golish, and Olson (2002) found that wives whose husbands had Alzheimer's disease experienced a state called "married widowhood" as they could visit their husband, but many felt like widows as the husband they knew was lost to them. Such losses are often referred to as causing "frozen grief" because they limit the grieving process due to the uncertainties involved. Families of those killed in the September 11, 2001 World Trade Center collapse struggled with the physical loss of a member without verification of their death and no body to bury. The absence of a body delayed or altered the usual ceremonies, such as a funeral mass or sitting shiva, and loved ones found it difficult to start grieving because it might be considered disloyal (Boss, 2001). Another example of ambiguous loss is the premature birth of a child, where the parents manage the dialectical contradiction of grief and joy (Golish & Powell, 2003). Ambiguous loss is considered the most stressful type of loss because "It defies resolution and creates long term confusion about who is in or out of a particular couple or family" (Boss, 2006, p. xvii).

Chapter 10 contains a model of family stressors (Figure 10.1) and a description of the developmental stresses a family faces. The current chapter focuses on those stressors that are unpredictable and which may appear as either horizontal or vertical stressors. It examines (1) coping with unpredictable stress (including the stressors), a model for coping, and the stages of crisis, and (2) communication patterns for coping with stresses such as death, illness, disability, divorce, and remarriage. It also links these stressors to the systems or the life-course frame of the model.

Unpredictable Stress and Family Coping Patterns

Stress involves a physiological response to stressors—events or situations that are seen as either powerful negative or positive forces. Individuals or family members under stress experience physiological and psychological changes as their heightened anxiety affects their coping patterns. Family systems under stress tend to fall into predictable patterns, some functional and some dysfunctional, as the members try to cope individually and collectively. As you might imagine, what is a major stressor to one family may be a minor stressor to another. What one family or family member does to reduce tension differs greatly from another family's or individual's strategies. In order to understand the processes of coping, the family stressors, models of coping, and *stages of crisis* must be examined.

Stressors

Family researchers have examined stresses and crises for more than 60 years. In his classic longitudinal study of families of World War II soldiers, Hill (1949) identified family disruptions that cause crises. These include (1) the coming apart of the family due to the death of a member; (2) the addition of new or returning family members; (3) the sense of disgrace, which may result from infidelity, alcoholism, or nonsupport; and (4) a combination of the above, which could include suicide, imprisonment, homicide, or mental illness. Other stressors such as drug abuse, handgun violence, school shootings, job loss, and natural disasters are also prevalent today. Major stresses throw a family system out of its normal balance and precipitate long-term change. When a stress arises that affects members at multiple stages of the life span or multiple stressors occur at once, the stress is compounded (Afifi & Nussbaum, 2006). The new stepfather who is trying to develop ties to a hostile stepdaughter while managing the early stages of a parent's dementia will experience severe stress, which will affect other family members. Although everyone knows that untimely death is possible, that accidents happen daily, and that serious illnesses can affect anyone, the actual occurrence of these events brings challenges that test the limits of endurance or the ability to cope. These struggles affect all family members.

How well a family copes depends on several factors. In his early, classic work, Bain (1978) claimed a family's coping capacity was tied to four factors: (1) the number of previous stressors the members had faced in recent years, (2) the degree of role change involved in coping, (3) the social support available to members, and (4) the institutional support available to members. Past experiences with crises prepare family members to understand new crises when they occur, but they may also retraumatize family members. The piling up of sad, unpredictable events affects coping, as does the amount of recovery time between shocks to the family system. For example, the severe illness of a child is likely to be very difficult for a family who has recently dealt with major financial or marital problems. It may cause greater strain if a parent has to change roles, such as giving up a career to care for the child, which also affects the family system economically, bringing about further stress. Support from friends and family members who assist physically or offer empathy lessens the stress. Also at risk are the siblings of children with cancer as they are at risk for reduced emotional support (Barrera, Fleming, & Khan, 2004). Yet, often a family or one of its members must acknowledge the need for support and not assume people will know what is needed or how to respond (e.g., is babysitting more desirable than flowers?). The following observation by a teacher attests to the importance of support at the time of crisis:

As a teacher, I watch a few students' families undergo divorce each year. The ones that seem to cope reasonably well are those that have some resources to bring to the process. Usually this is the family that has strong extended family members or neighborhood friends and the family that tells the school or church what is going on. In short, this family lets others in on the pain—and asks for some help.

It is possible to have productive outcomes of dealing with stress as well as the difficulties inherent in such a process. Certainly some families fare better during stressful situations than others. Researchers use the word *resilience* to refer to a family's ability to "do well in the face of adversity" (Patterson, 2002, p. 350). Couples who suffer through the loss of a child, and are able to build intimacy during the grieving process, rather than growing more distant, would be considered a resilient family. Quality-of-life factors affect resilience (Patterson, 2002). Living in poverty or in a violent neighborhood affects a family's ability to be resilient. Resilient low- to

The unexpected death of a key family member sends a family into shock and role confusion.

middle-income families are characterized by internal strengths complemented by community support services, religious programs, and a sense of belonging to the community. It is important to understand the importance of communication for individual and family resilience as we make sense of and deal with stressors through interactions with others (Koenig Kellas & Trees, 2006).

Family Stress Model

Each family exhibits unique coping behaviors. **Coping** implies "the central mechanism through which family stressors, demands, and strains are eliminated, managed, or adapted to" (McCubbin, Patterson, Cauble, Wilson, & Warwick, 1983, p. 359). The primary model currently used to understand family crises evolved from Hill's (1949) original model, which proposed that

> A [the stressor event], interacting with B [the family's crisis-meeting resources], interacting with C [the family's definition of the event], produces X [the crisis]. (McCubbin & Patterson, 1983b, p. 6)

In this model, the stressor, *a*, represents a life event or transition that has the potential to change a family's social system—indeed, its life course. Such events as the loss of a job, untimely death, unexpected military deployment, serious illness, or a major win in the lottery may fall into this category. A stressor event itself is not positive or negative; it is neutral until the family members place their interpretations on it (Ingoldsby, Smith, & Miller, 2004). The *b* factor represents the resources a family can use to manage the stressor and avoid creating a crisis; these include money, friends, time and space, or problem-solving skills. A family's levels of cohesion and adaptability influence their access to, and use of, resources. Resources may come from individuals, family members, and the community (McCubbin & Patterson, 1985). For example, if a child wanders away from home, community and family member resources are needed to conduct thorough searches of the area. If a mother is diagnosed with colon cancer, the cancer hospital becomes a key resource. The *c* factor represents the importance a family attaches to the stressor. For example, in one family, a diagnosis of a member's juvenile diabetes might overwhelm the entire system, whereas another family might cope relatively well, perceiving the diabetes as a manageable disease, one not likely to alter their lives drastically. The extended family members' view of the stressor may also influence the perception of crisis. For example, a three-generation family that has never experienced a divorce may define a granddaughter's marital separation as a severe crisis. A multigenerational system with a history of divorce may see the separation as sad, but not as a crisis. Together, *a*, *b*, and *c* contribute to the experience of stress that is unique to each family, depending on its background, resources, and interpretation of the event. The *x* factor represents the amount of disruptiveness that occurs to the system. It is characterized by "the family's inability to restore stability and by the continuous pressure to make changes in the family structure and patterns of interaction" (McCubbin & Patterson, 1983b, p. 10).

Hill's groundbreaking ABCX model, described above, focused on the precrisis state of the family. However, how a family copes over time is also important from a family communication perspective. McCubbin and Patterson (1983a) developed a **double ABCX model** based on Hill's original work that incorporates these post-crisis variables (Figure 11.1), or the next stages of coping. In this model, the *aA* factor includes not only the immediate stressor (e.g., death) but also the demands

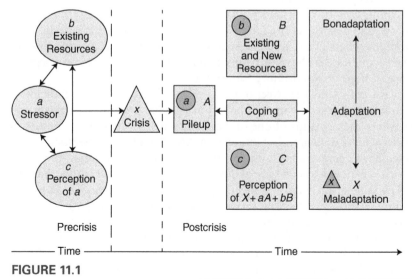

FIGURE 11.1
The double ABCX model

or changes that may emerge from individual system's members, the system as a whole, and the extended system. McCubbin and Patterson suggest that the *aA* factor includes (1) the initial stressor and its hardships, (2) normative transitions, (3) prior strains, (4) the consequences of the system's coping attempts, and (5) ambiguity. Imagine, for example, the death of a 36-year-old man who was the sole breadwinner for his family: a wife and three daughters, ages 6, 10, and 14. When a young father dies, the system must deal with the immediate loss as well as potential economic uncertainty and changes in the mother's role. In addition, a child's developmental stage may require the family to cope with an adolescent's need for independence. The new stress is compounded by any prior strains, such as mother-daughter conflicts. A consequence of the family's attempts to cope may lead to new stresses. For example, if the mother takes a full-time job, it may keep her from meeting her daughters' needs for support at home. Finally, ambiguity might be caused by the confusion of new roles now that the father has died. In the future the mother may remarry, bringing further change. Thus, *aA* is broader than the original conception of *a*.

The *bB* factor represents the family's ability to meet its needs. Over time a family relies on existing and new resources. Existing resources reflect a family's background. In the case of the death of a young father/sole breadwinner, these may include the ways in which a family coped in the past when the father was gone on long business trips. The expanded family resources emerge from the crisis itself. The young widow may create new resources by studying accounting, which leads to a well-paying position, or by joining a self-help group for those who have lost partners to death. The emerging social systems are a critical element in the *bB* factor.

The *cC* factor refers to the ways in which a family interprets a crisis, including the meaning the family gives both to the stressor event and to the added stressors caused by the original crisis. When a young father dies, a family must cope with that event and its meaning. If the mother believes she has lost her only chance at happiness in life, her perceptions will strongly influence her recovery and the attitudes of her children. Family members must also interpret the changes in finances, changes in the mother's role, and how the entire family is affected. In families that manage such a situation well, members adapt to changes in responsibilities and provide support to one another. Families that have difficulty coping find themselves overwhelmed, with little sense of hope or opportunity for growth.

The *xX* factor represents the effect of the family's adaptation on the individual, family, and community levels. Family adaptation is achieved "through reciprocal relationships where the demands of one of these units are met by the capabilities of another so as to achieve a 'balance' of interaction" (McCubbin & Patterson, 1983a, p. 19). If a member's demands are too great for the family's capabilities, there will be an imbalance. There will also be imbalance if the family demands more than the community is capable of providing. Conversely the family and workplace demands may create an imbalance by expecting too much of one person. The positive end of the outcomes continuum, called **bonadaptation**, is characterized by balance between (1) member and family and (2) family and community. The negative end, or **maladaptation**, reflects imbalance or severe losses for the family. Disruptions may be resolved eventually in positive or negative ways. The whole family system reacts to the crisis as shown in the following story:

As a single father, I relied heavily on my own mother to help me with my young children. After my wife left us, Mom helped me get back on my feet. She watched the kids after school and when I had to work late. She supported me in every way as I tried to maintain some sense of normalcy for my children. Mom's sudden and unexpected death was almost too much to bear. This was a crisis not only for me and my children, but for my father, who was in poor health, and for my two sisters and their families as well. Turns out, Mom had been supporting all of us in so many ways. We had to find someone to help Dad a few times a week, I had to hire a sitter for the kids, and my sisters spent many hours going through and organizing Mom's belongings. We still miss her so much, but we are getting by. I have grown closer to my sisters, and we now have a weekly family dinner with the three families and Dad.

Many variations on this model have developed over the years. Olson (1997) refined this stress model by developing a multisystem assessment of stress and health (MASH), which focused on four areas of life (individual, work, couple, and family), creating a biopsychological approach that measures the relationships between stress, coping, system variables, and adaptation in the four areas of life. Other approaches to understanding stress in families include the risk and resiliency theoretical perspective and the family strengths or asset-based approach to understanding coping (Afifi & Nussbaum, 2006).

All unpredictable stresses affect cohesion and adaptability. A family with a high capacity for adaptation and above-average cohesion is likely to weather stressor events more easily than families who are rigid and disengaged. Adaptable and open families are more likely to use and benefit from social supports in their community. In their study of how army families adapted when a member was deployed to a war zone, Pittman, Kerpelman, and McFayden (2004) found that greater unit support was strongly tied to a sense of community, which was linked to family adaptation to the stress. Families who adapt easily have the capacity to discover alternative ways of relating and can adjust their communication behavior to encompass a stressor. Families with rigid boundaries may be unable to cope adequately when severe external stresses occur. By limiting open communication with friends, neighbors, and schools, family members deprive themselves of information and emotional support. Boundaries that prevent friends or extended family from knowing about the problem reduce the number of resources available to support a family through a critical period.

Seemingly positive events can create great stress. For example, a partner's long worked for promotion may bring with it increased salary and benefits, but also the need to relocate, and the couple may need to learn to manage investments and savings. Most immigrants in the United States chose to move to a new country, viewing it as a positive change for their family. A survey of over a thousand immigrants to the Minneapolis–St. Paul area found that most experienced significant stresses over a long period of time, including adapting to a new language, separation from family and friends, health problems, financial problems, finding and keeping a job, and homesickness and isolation (Mattessich, 2001). As we discussed in Chapter 8, even developmental changes create stress. For instance, family members may find it painful to cope with a much-loved child's departure for college.

Communication can improve when the family manages a major crisis. In her study of dialectical tensions in families with a stroke survivor, Pawlowski (2006) found that survivors experienced more open communication with their family members and believed these relationships were closer now than before the stroke. Families of childhood cancer survivors reported positive outcomes from the experience in addition to the stresses and anxiety. The study of childhood cancer survivors an average of 16 years away from treatment and their parents revealed that talking about the experience was emotionally beneficial and healing. Communicating with each other helped them move on (Galvin, Grill, Arntson, & Kinahan, 2012).

Communication plays a central role in the management of such stresses and contributes specifically to the family's movement through stages of stress reaction. In some families, members use direct verbal messages to explore options, negotiate needs, express feelings, and reduce tension. In other families, members' stress may be apparent through the nonverbal messages that indicate their anxiety, fear, or anger. As part of the family's coping pattern, members constantly interpret each other's verbal and nonverbal messages, which inform their responses.

Maguire (2012) proposed a **communication-based coping model** that puts communication at the center of the family coping process in times of crises. This model is grounded in the components of the double ABCX model that we discussed earlier and other coping models. Maguire outlines how communication is central to five major factors of stress and coping as follows:

1. Communication as a source or symptom of stress: Poor family communication or extended, harmful conflictual communication may be the negative stressor on the family. Alternatively, poor communication may be the symptom of a major stressor on the family.
2. Communication as meaning-making: The cC factor listed above, how the family perceives the stressor, is done in large part through family communication about the stressor. How they make sense of the stressor may be seen in families' stories.
3. Communication as a resource: Social support through family communication can be an important coping resource for families during a crisis.
4. Communication as a coping strategy: Numerous forms of communication may help family members cope with a crisis including journaling, humor, relational maintenance, and disclosure.
5. Communication as an indication of the status of individual, relational, or family health: Family communication can also be a measure of how well a family has adapted to the crisis.

Family stress models help us predict and understand the kinds of stress-related issues families face and the role of communication in co-creating stressors and strategies for managing family stress.

Stages of Family Crisis

In any crisis situation, members go through a process of managing loss, grief, or chaos. Depending on the circumstance, these stages may last from a few days to several months or years. Stages may be evident in the case of a death, or news of an incurable illness, but in any crisis, most family members experience a progression of feelings from denial to eventual acceptance. Sometimes a member becomes stuck in the coping process, never reaching the final stage. In the case of Adelina Perez at the start of the chapter we see her in the early stages of this process as her parents have announced their divorce, and at the same time, we see the potential longer-term effects on her ability to establish trust in her own marriage. Yet, since equifinality suggests that no two families view and approach a crisis in the same way, each family will move through the process in a different way. The following stages approximate the process of grieving significant losses. These stages were developed as a response to understanding losses surrounding death, but have since been applied to a range of losses, because all changes involve loss and all losses require change (Goldsworthy, 2005). Although the stages may follow one another, they may overlap, and some may be repeated a number of times.

1. Shock resulting in numbness, disbelief, or denial
2. Recoil resulting in anger, confusion, blaming, guilt, and bargaining
3. Depression
4. Reorganization resulting in acceptance and recovery (Kubler-Ross, 1970; Mederer & Hill, 1983)

After a critical life event, moving through such stages usually results in transformation of the family system. Persons may find themselves more separated from, or connected to, different members and experience a shift in adaptability patterns. Members' communication reflects and aids progress through the stages. Understanding the process allows an individual to analyze others' progress through the stages or to be more understanding of one's own behavior and personal progress.

Shock/Denial   At the *shock stage*, family members tend to deny the event or its seriousness. Comments such as "It can't be true," or "It's a mistake," are accompanied by nonverbal behavior, such as awkward attempts at smiles and encouragement with a terminally ill person or spending money lavishly when the paycheck has been cut off. Most persons move from this stage, exhibiting behaviors that indicate a recognition of reality. Family members acknowledge their grief and feel the pain of the loss. Withdrawal or quietness characterizes the communication of those who find it hard to cry. The news of the crisis begins to take on fuller meanings, such as "Mom will never be the same" or "I can't believe that our home and everything in it is just gone." Denial is transformed into an intense desire to recapture what has been lost, especially in the case of a family death, illness, or severe injury. It tends to occur more powerfully after a shock rather than an expected loss. This may lead to actions that deny reality: for example, "I picked up my phone to text Alex before remembering he's not there" or "I still automatically set the table for five people and then I catch myself."

Recoil   After the initial blow, family members may move into the *recoil stage* of blaming, anger, and bargaining. Blaming often takes place as the grieving family members seek reasons for what has happened. This may include blaming the self ("I was too trusting" or "I never should have left town") or blaming others ("It's his own fault" or "The doctors didn't tell us the truth soon enough"). Such reactions may be interspersed with feelings of "It's not fair." Anger may be directed at the event or person most directly involved or may be displaced onto others, such as family members, friends, or coworkers. Attempts at real or imagined bargains may occur ("If I take a cut in pay, they could hire me back" or "If you come back, I'll stop gambling forever"). Thoughts that the world is unfair or that God has been cruel to let this happen, fill the minds of individual family members and may be communicated to one another.

Depression   Frequently members experience some level of depression; an overwhelming sadness permeates the family members' thinking. Whereas anger is directed outward, depression is directed inward. Usually, family members need to talk about what has happened. In fact, they often retell the crisis story over and over. This represents a normal and healthy response, especially for families experiencing a long period of suffering because of death, incurable illness, permanent injuries, a long jail sentence, or mental breakdown. People outside the family often fail to understand the sad person's need to talk and may attempt to avoid the subject, not recognizing that being supportive may involve just listening.

Reorganization   Family members who have faced crises usually move on to what is described as a "turning point." It may be a moment of recognizing the finality of the event or of realizing one must move ahead with life. Graham (1997) studied communication between divorced spouses and identified 11 turning points in which it changed, usually from negative to more positive over time. From a systems perspective, this is the stage where the family recalibrates the system and moves to a new or altered set of behaviors. Graham found that over time and in a pattern of trial and error divorced couples learned how to move ahead in their relationship with one another. Usually, a decision marks the turning event. It may be to sell a failing business, put away the pictures that serve as daily reminders, go on a date, or join a self-help group. This decision signals that the individual has moved into the fourth crisis stage—reorganization of events in his or her life to effect a recovery. This stage is characterized by family members' taking charge of their lives and making the necessary changes forced on them by the crisis.

If crisis emotions could be diagrammed, the line would descend to the lowest point with depression. The descent begins with the impact of the news and continues the decline with some upward movement in the recoil stage that diminishes as reality returns. After a descent into depression, most people move upward toward recovery (Figure 11.2).

Throughout this process, communication is the way that family members co-create new meanings, and it serves to link family members as they share their reactions. It also links one or more family members to outside sources of institutional or social

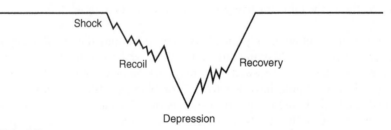

FIGURE 11.2
Linear scale of emotions during crisis

support. If family members become cut off from support or cannot talk about their loss, they may become stuck, unable to complete the process and reach acceptance.

When a family experiences an ambiguous loss, these stages cannot be fully completed. For example, Braithwaite (2002) interviewed wives whose husbands live in a nursing home due to Alzheimer's disease. She called this a state of "married widowhood" as these wives were married but not able to function as wives as their husband was physically present but not able to function as a husband. Many times the wives described visiting their husband who might not even recognize her, or think she was his daughter or mother. Sadly these married widows might be in this situation for several more years, until their husband passes away. In other situations, family members struggle with how to move on because a long-term coma victim may wake up or a missing soldier may return. Eventually most members learn to normalize the ambivalence in order to move on. "Resiliency depends on knowing that the ambivalence from the ambiguous loss is normal and can be managed" (Boss, 2006). The next section we will consider some common types of family crises and communication issues involved with each.

Communication and Specific Crises

Communication patterns and networks shift dramatically when members face major life crises. Interaction becomes unpredictable as individuals withdraw into silence, explode into anger, or resort to constant talking as a way to handle stress or grief.

The remainder of this section focuses on major crises that have been studied extensively. Remember that events that are less dramatic than those discussed here, such as moving, losing a job, or surviving a natural disaster, also disrupt the family system by altering dreams or plans and introducing new tensions into the family. A crisis may force parents and their children to rely on different relationship maintenance strategies as dialectical contradictions shift and the strategies that worked previously no longer address the situation (Baxter & Dindia, 1990). The crisis event can force open discussion among members or expose a family to public scrutiny or media attention, as in the case of a suicide, cyberbully attack, drug arrest, or school shooting. The triggering event may create closeness and connection as the family attempts some sort of a united front in order to cope and support one another, or members may withdraw from each other due to disagreements or pain. Variations in the predictability-novelty dialectical contradictions in individual family members' communication may be exacerbated when the crisis demands a response from each family member. In the following, we discuss four types of specific crises: untimely death, disability, separation and divorce, and separation in military families.

Untimely Death

The finality of death is an emotionally overwhelming crisis for most families. Although the death of any family member carries with it a sense of grief, the death of an elderly person who has lived a full life does not generate the anger aroused by **untimely death**, nor does it carry the potential for major role changes for most family members. However, the untimely death of a younger or middle-aged family member is a major crisis for many families. Surviving partners or children are not prepared for the loss or the role changes. Sudden death, such as in a car accident, provides family members no opportunity to say farewell or resolve relationship issues with the individual. Untimely death throws a family into severe shock, often resulting in prolonged mourning across many years (McGoldrick & Walsh, 2005).

Communication patterns range from the highly intense and emotional to the very superficial and denial oriented. Communication rules influence how members talk to each other about the loss. Religious beliefs and cultural patterns affect the grieving practices; grief may be unrestrained, as in Greek families, where women may express intense sorrow at funeral ceremonies (Killian & Agathangelou, 2005). Irish families may experience a mix of celebration and sorrow, reflecting the deceased's move to a better world (McGoldrick, 2005). Dying persons and their family members, in order to protect each other, often resort to acting as if "everything is going to be all right." Critically ill persons or their family members may search for and continue to enroll in clinical trials, hoping to find something that will save the loved one. Family members in their own grief may deny the diagnosis of a terminal illness. This has been called "conspiracies of silence," where family members avoid talking about the prognosis because they fear it will result in a loss of hope and worsen the illness (Gueguen, Bylund, Brown, Levin, & Kissane, 2009). They shield the dying person from such knowledge and develop communication rules to support this fiction. Sometimes family rules block the dying family member from dealing with all his or her feelings, as well as with immediate fears and loneliness. Some dying members resent the dishonesty involved, as explained here:

I will never forget my uncle complaining bitterly two days before he died about his family treating him like a helpless child and insisting he would recover whenever he started to talk about dying or his fear of never leaving the hospital. I was only 14 and did not fully understand what he was trying to tell me at the time, but I never forgot his pain or anger as he tried to explain the feeling of dying without emotional support.

In her pioneering study of death and dying, Elizabeth Kübler-Ross (1970) suggested that death should be regarded as an "intrinsic part of life" and discussed openly like other events in family life, especially since almost all terminally ill patients are aware of it. The question should change from "Do I tell?" to "How do I share the information?" If a family confronts the issue openly, all members can go through preparatory grief together, which facilitates the later bereavement process. As the process continues, patients and loved ones may attempt to strike bargains—silently or openly. Finally, the loneliness, fears, and practical concerns may be addressed; these may range from "What is really on the other side?" to "How will they cope in school without my help?" Dying persons need empathic listeners who do not deny their reality. Although watching a person die can be devastating to the family members, terminal illness (unlike sudden death) does provide the family members with an opportunity to address relationship issues and to say final good-byes.

Frequently, family members have a chance to talk with the dying member following confirmation of a terminal illness. These **"final conversations"** include "all the moments of talking, touching, and spending time with the Dying" (Keeley &

Yingling, 2007, p. 2). Based on interviews with 55 individuals who had experienced the death of a loved one, Keeley (2007) identified five types of messages that seemed to be important to the survivors and that served a relational purpose. These are love, identity, religion/spirituality, routine/everyday content, and difficult relationship issues. These final conversations may have a very powerful impact on the surviving family member, particularly as they help the member to cope with their loss (Keeley, in press). These conversations may serve an important purpose throughout the survivor's life. Keeley tells of one young daughter who recounted years later the story of her final conversation with her father:

> Ruth (#3) who was not quite five when her father died remembers vividly that "he made eye contact with me and that was important 'cause he was talking to me like I was a real person not like I was his little 4-year old. It was like [my daddy was telling me that] you're going to be alright." She went on to say that that look made all the difference in the world. (Keeley, 2009, p. 237)

When persons choose their own death through suicide, many of their preparatory messages are denied; their attempts to communicate suicide plans go unrecognized until after the event. Parents of young people are advised to watch for behaviors such as talking about suicide, giving away possessions, acting abnormally cheerful after depression, and losing appetite. Suicidal elderly family members may exhibit depression, withdrawal, isolation, changes in sleep patterns, lower self-image, and prolonged bereavement. However, many relatives refuse to interpret these messages as they are intended.

After the death of a family member, the remaining relatives experience an ongoing bereavement process. An unexpected death, either by accident or illness, throws a family into an initial state of shock. Eventually, the shock wears off and the bereavement process begins. The event traumatizes the family, even in cases in which members know of an impending death. The survivors may experience anger and depression. Approximately 5 percent of widows or widowers become severely depressed, while 10 to 17 percent become depressed to a clinically significant degree following the death of their spouse (Walsh, 2005, p. 316). Adolescents may withdraw from family and friends after a sibling's death and refuse to discuss their feelings (McGoldrick & Walsh, 2005). Family members may express regrets about unspoken issues: "If only I had told him how much I loved him." Unforeseen circumstances may arise that present communication challenges. A member's death may become a family secret because it is too painful to address; stories of the deceased may be excluded from conversation, or answering a question about the number of children in the family may confound a grieving parent (Bosticco & Thompson, 2005). These all affect the bB factor of coping.

The coping process varies according to the position that the deceased filled in the family system. The death of a young parent with children leaves a surviving partner or parent yearning for the missing family member, while at the same time assisting the children through the crisis without total withdrawal into personal grief. Parents who have lost a child to an accident, suicide, or homicide most frequently report using private prayer and church attendance to help them grieve (Murray, Tapper Johnson, & Lohan, 2003). A death by homicide appears to be most directly related to posttraumatic stress disorder (PTSD), grief, and despair (Murray, Toth, Larsen, & Moulton, 2010), and is a particularly critical issue given the number of young people who encounter multiple shooting deaths of relatives or witness shootings in their own neighborhoods or schools. Also, many military families experience the untimely death of a loved one. "The impact of a dad's or mom's death in the military can be so traumatically disturbing that the terror involved with the death and the way the parent died may override a child's ability to grieve in a natural way, and share sadness and frustration" (Goldman, 2008, p. 1). The extended family system also experiences stress when a child dies. This young mother was bothered by her older brothers' response after the death of her infant daughter:

When they came to visit at Christmas, they didn't even ask to see her grave. I wanted them to go and be a part of it. I guess I don't know how I would be if it happened to someone else and I didn't experience it, but it just frustrated me a lot because it was like she never existed to them. I think it took them by surprise that we talked about her so openly. I guess that scared them because they didn't know how to react.

The death of a child devastates a family. It carries with it the loss of parental dreams of their child graduating, marrying, and having children, thus violating the natural order of life—the belief that children outlive parents. "A child's death affects every aspect of a parent's life and the marital relationship in particular" (Toller & Braithwaite, 2009, p. 257). The grieving process can be seen as both a personal and a social journey (Titus & de Souza, 2011). In a study of the dialectical contradictions faced by bereaved parents, Toller and Braithwaite found that they experienced a dialectical contradiction between trying to grieve the child's death together and separately. Although wishing to help the other, each parent grieved differently, complicating a very difficult process. Over time, and painfully, couples learned to accept their differences and to compromise on each other's needs. Although both parents experienced needs for openness and closeness, these needs differed in terms of valuing verbal or nonverbal communication, the role of others in the process, and acceptance of each other's way of communicating about the child's death. In a related study, Toller (2008) examined how parents constructed their identities following the death of a child. Respondents faced issues of being "a parent without a child to parent" and being "an insider and an outsider." Over time, some parents chose to tend the grave site and celebrate the child's birthday as a way to continue to nurture the lost child. Parents also had to negotiate with other family members and friends on issues, such as talking about their child, as they moved on. In one study, most mothers who had a child die report that their communication with surviving children changed. Dialectical contradictions present for these mothers included wanting to mourn the dead child while continuing to care for the living children and expressing grief and sorrow about death but also joy for the living (Johnson & Webb, 2012). Parents also report communication difficulties when they are asked in social situations, "How many children do you have?" (Titus & de Souza, 2011).

Adolescents who lose their siblings in a sudden, violent death experience a painful and complex grieving process for up to two years (Lohan & Murphy, 2002). In some cases, members experience disenfranchised grief—grief that exists although society may not recognize the relationship—at the death of a former spouse, a foster parent, or a stepparent (Murphy, Tapper, Johnson, & Lohan, 2003). Many family members experience a return of sadness or withdrawal on the anniversaries of deaths. The anniversary date of a family member's death, as well as significant holidays often act as markers of loss, with memories surfacing with great force.

Stillborn birth and miscarriage are special cases of child death. Among women who have experienced stillborn birth and miscarriage, distress is greater when the pregnancy had been planned, when they know the medical reason for the loss, and when they place a high value on motherhood (Shreffler, Greil, & McQuillan, 2011). Researchers in Sweden studied parents who experienced a stillborn birth at three months, one year, and two years after the birth. They found parents' grieving to be complex and intertwined with their relationship as partners. There were times of *movement toward togetherness*, with the relationship becoming stronger, as well as *movement toward withdrawal*, where parents may need to grieve in their own ways. The majority of parents reported that overall their relationship became closer; the majority also reported that they grieved in different ways than their partner (Avelin, Radestad, Safulnd, Wredling, & Erlandsson, 2013). The intensity of grief following miscarriage can be similar to other losses. Unlike other deaths there is "no publicly acknowledged person to bury or established rituals to structure mourning and gain support" (Brier, 2008, p. 451). Family therapists and counselors often have not been trained to help women and their partners deal with miscarriage (Sperry & Sperry, 2004). Women and men may not have ample opportunities to discuss their loss and feelings about the miscarriage, as early pregnancies are often kept secret. Research has shown that grief decreases over time and with a subsequent pregnancy (Brier, 2008). Although grief may subside over time, it may never really go away completely, as experienced by the following mother:

When my daughter was two years old, I became pregnant again. My husband and I were thrilled to be adding another child to our family. A miscarriage at eight weeks followed and we were very distressed. Since that time, I was able to become pregnant and have two more children.

About a month ago, I was watching a movie in which the main character has a miscarriage. I immediately started crying uncontrollably and had to stop watching the movie. Both my husband and I were surprised at the intensity of my sadness. Here it was, four years later, and I was still mourning the loss of the pregnancy.

Culture plays a significant role in how a family deals with death. In general, African American families, Irish families, and Italian families believe in a "good" send-off. White Anglo-Saxon Protestant families may limit their emotional expression. Puerto Rican families, especially the female members, suffer publicly. Jewish families, reflecting a tradition of shared suffering, tend to deal openly and directly with death. Chinese families believe a "good death" includes relatives surrounding the dying person. Cultures with rituals for dealing with death, a strong sense of community, and tolerance of verbal expressions provide members with greater support. In addition, religion or spirituality can offer meaning about death and provide comfort and support (Imber-Black, 2012; Walsh, 2012).

Illness or Disability

Members of families with a seriously ill or disabled member confront the need for meaningful coping processes. Coping with a family member's disability, disease, or serious accident requires major adjustments involving physical and emotional energy. The immediate disruption of the family in no way equals the long-term drain on family resources and energies required to help the affected family member deal with what may be a lifelong situation.

The mourning process that families may undergo when a member is diagnosed with a serious illness or disability may be similar to stages of coping with death. These include impact, denial, grief, focusing outward, and closure, each with a communication condition. At the *impact* stage the family learns of a member's condition. Anxiety and tension characterize this period; family members respond in a disorganized manner. The family can absorb very little information and has very limited responses. Husbands of women diagnosed with breast cancer have reported feeling "struck by lightning" or wondering "why God would single her out?" (Zahlis & Lewis, 2010). Usually, the *denial* stage follows, carrying with it a sense of disbelief and distorted expectations. Parents may reject the diagnosis of a child's cancer, finding themselves unable to hear what others are saying about the problem. Anger and sadness characterize the *grief*. Parents do not dream of giving birth to a child with health difficulties, and adult children may be devastated at their mother's loss of memory as Alzheimer's disease sets in. Parents question why this happened to their child. Children question why their sibling has to suffer. They may blame each other for the difficulty and isolate themselves from interacting with friends or extended family, effectively preventing open and supportive communication.

Eventually, family members move toward the *focusing outward* stage, beginning a process of seeking information, discussing options, asking for help, expressing feelings, or forming a support group. The *aA* factor of existing and new resources from the double ABCX model is relevant here. In the case of Erin and Luke Johnson at the beginning of the chapter, this happened as they began to work to get Erin admitted to a prenatal clinical trial. Signs of relief are evident as the family moves toward dealing with the issues. The *closure* stage represents reconciliation with reality and a sense of adaptation to the family member's needs. The family pulls together and adjusts in ways that allow the members of the altered system to move forward and to communicate directly about its concerns. A study of family caregivers of cancer patients showed that they had returned to normal levels of quality of life at two years postdiagnosis (Kim & Spillers, 2010). In one Swiss study, the majority of couples reported that the diagnosis of cancer brought them closer together (Drabe, Wittman, Zwahlen, Buchi, & Jenewein, 2013). However, things most often do not return to the way they were, but instead families face a new, altered reality. Parents of children with cancer in Great Britain reported that the end of treatment is not really the end of the crisis, as the threat of cancer remains and the process of role adaptation continues (Mckenzie & Curle, 2012). Similarly, Galvin et al. (2012) reported that even many years later after a child's cancer treatment, the topic of cancer is still present in family communication, primarily because of the need for continued health maintenance.

Illness impacts the entire family system. Family caregivers of ill relatives often experience negative mental and physical health issues as a result of caregiving

(Mosher, Bakas, & Champion, 2013). Following the onset of a chronic disease, it is typical for a patient to assume a central position in the family. This shift in focus, if continued over a longer period of time, affects the marital relationship and other parent-child relationships. Parents who are forced to focus on a sick and demanding child have little time or energy to deal with each other. In two-parent homes, a mother's disability leads to less parental school involvement and a less enriching home environment (Hogan, Shandra, & Msall, 2007). Even when a child develops a disease that can be managed effectively, parents and siblings are impacted. A study of siblings of a diabetic young person revealed that their sisters and brothers evidenced specific diabetes knowledge, awareness of related medical terminology, and diabetes management skills. In addition, their sense of immortality was affected (Pavlik, 2004). In many situations, families must spend a great deal of time with a child in the hospital or in doctors' offices. Many adults who become ill also have older parents who are affected by their adult child's condition. These parents do not get the same help in coping with their child's illness as the child's spouse and children do, often being left to cope with their feelings alone (Gilbar & Refaeli, 2000).

Research reveals a high divorce rate among people with children with disabilities (Braithwaite & Thompson, 2000). In cases where a partner has been diagnosed with lung cancer, the other spouse's blaming of the partner for behaviors which led to the lung cancer was significantly associated with depressive symptoms for both the patient and the caregiver (Siminoff, Wilson-Genderson, & Baker, 2010). However, and as also illustrated in the case of Erin and Luke Johnson, some marriages do well despite the stress of illness or disability. One study examined marriages in which one spouse had chronic heart failure, a life-threatening condition where the body has limited ability to maintain normal blood circulation (Benazon, Foster, & Coyne, 2006). Researchers found that in these marriages, there were high levels of satisfaction and infrequent occurrences of criticism or hostility. In another study, some husbands reported that their wives' breast cancer had strengthened their relationship, while others found it negatively affected their relationship (Zahlis & Lewis, 2010). Those who found it to negatively affect their relationship cited communication difficulties such as the wife not wanting to talk about it, talking being difficult because of the serious nature of the illness, and feeling that talking didn't get them anywhere. In marriages where the wife has advanced breast cancer, sexual relationships are often negatively affected. Constructive communication about sexual issues and concerns has been found to lessen the depressive effects of sexual problems (Milbury & Badr, 2013).

Siblings are significantly affected by a brother's or sister's illness or disability. Research on sibling response indicates that siblings may have a surprising lack of information about the disability. This lack of information may confuse siblings in the following ways: They may feel responsible for the condition, wonder if they are susceptible to it, experience confusion about how to talk about it with others, and feel overwhelmed by anger, hurt, or guilt (Seligman & Darling, 2007). A study of the siblings of children with Down syndrome revealed that many siblings have a positive experience in living in such a family. These siblings had above-average self-concepts, were socially competent, and had low numbers of behavior problems. Siblings did better in families that had less demands, more resources, and better coping and problem-solving skills. The siblings in the study stated that they had

A child with special needs significantly alters family communication patterns.

learned patience, love, and courage from their siblings with Down syndrome (Van Riper, 2000). Parents attribute about twice as much of their stress to a child with a disability than they attribute to the youngest sibling in the family without a disability (Baxter, Cummins, & Yiolitis, 2000). Siblings may have to adjust to whole new interaction patterns, as shown here:

A year and a half ago, my brother, Steve, suffered a paralyzing head injury when he swerved his motorcycle to miss a dog. He dreams of driving his Chevy pickup again but he knows he might live the rest of his life in a nursing home. When asked when he expects to get out, his eyes go blank. "Never," he says. My father discourages such talk. "Now if you work real hard you might get your legs going again, right?" he says. Steve's eyes grow red. "OK," he replies and stares at the wall. It pains me to see him like this.

As in the double ABCX model described earlier, in response to the stressor of illness or disability, the family organizes its current resources at the outset of the crisis and then attempts to develop new resources to carry them through the crisis. Those with less economic resources may struggle the most. One study documented how single, low-income, and immigrant fathers who were primary medical caretakers for their children may be at highest risk for difficulty-coping (Wolff, Pak, Meeske, Worden, & Katz, 2002).

The ability of family members to communicate in a direct and supportive manner directly influences the coping process. The availability of support from the extended family members varies greatly, especially when the family with a severely ill member lives miles or states away. Researchers have found that families with disabled children that were able to communicatively reframe the situation to be a learning experience were able to function effectively (Canary, 2012). Also affecting the coping process may be the social support the family perceives that it has. In a study of families with a child who is diagnosed with congenital heart disease, the more social support a parent perceived, the higher level of coping he or she reported (Tak & McCubbin, 2002).

A few common types of illness that families face are Alzheimer's disease, addiction, cancer, and mental illness. The type of illness affects the ability to cope. A particularly difficult situation that many families encounter is when a family member is diagnosed with Alzheimer's disease. Spouses of men and women who are in nursing homes and have Alzheimer's make sense of their marriage to the affected spouse in different ways. Some continue to strongly view their relationship with their spouse as a couple, while some spouses may move on with their lives as if widowed (Braithwaite, 2002). Others fall in various places on the continuum between those two (Kaplan, 2001). Adult mothers and daughters may need to negotiate how they are going to cope with one member's breast cancer diagnosis, due to varying developmental stages. For example, in one study, young adult women diagnosed with breast cancer reported increased interaction with their mothers to be negative (Fisher & Nussbaum, 2012).

Another form of illness that impacts the family is addiction to drugs or alcohol. Alcoholism distorts a family's patterns of behavior and communication, affecting all members (Hudak, Krestan, & Bepko, 2005). If one or more members are addicted, the entire family tends to develop a verbal pattern to cope with the problem. Such families are characterized by the rules "Don't talk, don't trust, don't feel" (Black, 2001). The questions arise—What do you tell? When do you openly seek help and end the secrecy? How do you communicate with a family member who is in an altered mental state while under the influence of alcohol or drugs? The stress in such families is monumental.

Mental illness can also have a profound effect on family functioning. Research has examined how both children's and parents' mental illness affects family functioning. For instance, families of adolescents with bipolar disorder have been found to have lower levels of cohesion and adaptability and more conflict than families with healthy adolescents (Sullivan & Miklowitz, 2010). Adolescent children of parents with a history of depression are more likely to use coping strategies that allow them to adapt to the environment, rather than to avoid or try to change the reality of their parents' illness. These coping strategies include positive thinking, acceptance, and distraction (Jaser et al., 2007). The effect on children may be more profound when the parent with mental illness is a mother rather than a father. A recent study examined cases where either a mother or father of a young adult had a mental illness. Young adults with mentally ill mothers reported more mental health symptoms, more loneliness, and less overall psychological well-being than young adults without parents with mental illness. There was no difference between young adults with mentally ill fathers and those with mentally healthy parents (Abraham & Stein, 2010).

Separation and Divorce

Separation and divorce, variations in the family life course, are transitional crises that create emotional and practical upheaval. In most cases, there tend to be two phases—the separation and legalization phase and the settling into the single-parent family form. These phases usually overlap to some degree (Carter & McGoldrick, 2005a). Divorce tends to be the result of unhappiness and problems that have developed over time, not just the result of one negative occurrence in the marriage (Hetherington & Kelly, 2002). A systemic view of divorce assumes that both parents contributed to the dissolution of the marriage, although specific individual issues such as addiction, abuse, or severe mental or physical health problems may be presented by one partner. In many cases, divorce may be the result of long-term communication difficulties. Self-reported negative communication before marriage is associated with a higher likelihood of divorce five years later (Markman, Rhoades, Stanley, Ragan, & Whitton, 2010).

Parents remain linked through their children and must find ways to function as an ongoing altered family system in which former partners function as co-parents. Increasingly, the resulting binuclear family reflects three key qualities that contribute to the well-being of children: a child's basic psychological and economic needs are met; extended family or pre-divorce close friendship relations are maintained; and parents exhibit mutual cooperation and support around child-oriented concerns (Ahrons, 2005). Communication researchers have studied these "parent teams" and looked at how the co-parents and other adults, usually new partners, form a family system for parenting children. Sometimes these systems are quite functional and other times they are rife with conflict (Braithwaite, Toller, Daas, Durham, & Jones, 2008).

Separation and divorce processes resemble a mourning pattern. At some point, each partner mourns the loss of the relationship, although one may have emotionally separated from the other years before the divorce became a reality. Initially, spouses may deny that anything is really wrong and communicate to children or others that "Our problems aren't all that serious" or "Daddy will be back soon, so don't tell anyone he's gone." As the reality of separation takes hold, anger, bargaining, and depression intermingle. Attempts at reconciliation may occur. Social integration helps to minimize divorce rates; membership in religious groups and having children serve as integrating factors (Lauer & Lauer, 2009). Painful accusations and negative conflict are often heightened by the adversarial positions required in legal divorce proceedings. Many individuals experience depression, which reflects the sense of loss and/or rejection, often accompanied by great loneliness and a sense of failure (Hetherington & Kelly, 2002). Divorce pressures are intensified by the predictable and problematic withdrawal of social support; a "community divorce" occurs when each of the partners leaves one community of friends and relations and enters another, a process that may include loneliness and isolation for a period of time (Lauer & Lauer, 2009, p. 342). Old friends may be afraid to "take sides," or they act as if divorce might be contagious.

Divorce and remarriage tend to have adverse effects on children (Amato, 2001; Waite & Gallagher, 2000) although some display not serious difficulties and some benefit from it (Greene, Anderson, Forgatch, DeGarmo & Hetherington, 2012). However, researchers point out that children are better off when not living in households characterized by ongoing conflict between their parents (Amato, Loomis, & Booth, 1995). Although divorce is often a badly needed fresh start for the parents, divorce is a much different experience for the child (Wallerstein, Lewis, & Blakeslee, 2000). Children are often affected by their parents' marital problems long before and long after the divorce; detrimental psychological and academic effects on children may occur from about three years before to three years after the divorce (Sun & Li, 2002). Over time, the family system recalibrates itself to establish an altered course, including the development of new communication patterns. Siblings often become closer after a divorce, acting as resources for each other (the *aA* factor from the double ABCX model), and their close relationships frequently carry over into adulthood (Wallerstein et al., 2000). More negative sibling relationships tend to occur when there are higher levels of conflict between parents and between parents and children (Green et al., 2012).

Most children experience confusion and chaos when parents divorce. The following example illustrates what may happen if those fears are not addressed:

When my parents divorced, although it was a relief from the fighting and constant tension, I experienced a sense of loss and many new fears about their future as well as my own. As a child who experienced divorce, I was expected to "bounce back." I was just expected to adapt, but without being given time to express grief. I repressed these feelings and fears, and since they were never really addressed, they resurfaced years later.

Wallerstein and colleagues (2000) studied the long-term effects of divorce on children, which carry into adulthood. In their study of adults, whom they had first met during their parents' divorces many years earlier, the authors found the following. First, children who grew up in divorced families did not have happy memories of play as did those who grew up in intact families. "Instead of caring about who finds who in a game of hide-and-seek or who is at bat in the local softball game, children of divorce have other, more pressing concerns. Is Mom all right? Is Dad going to pick me up tonight?" (p. 19). Second, those who grew up in intact families were much more likely to be able to tell the story of their parents' courtship than those from divorced families. Third, children from intact families also received more financial support through their college years. Wallerstein and colleagues concluded that growing up is harder in a divorced family than in an intact family. However, the researchers described adult children of divorce who created good lives for themselves with happy marriages, children, and successful careers.

Divorcing parents do not always have appropriate conversations with their children about the divorce for a variety of reasons. The parents often do not have information about how to have such a conversation, they may be angry, and they are often overwhelmed. "This means that the child, especially the preschool child, often learns about the divorce in the most traumatic way possible when she wakes up one morning to find that her father and his belongings have vanished into thin air" (Wallerstein et al., 2000, p. 47). Parents who felt they did not have control over the divorce stressors (e.g., the other parent's behavior) are more likely to make inappropriate disclosures to a child about the divorce than parents who felt they did have control (Afifi, McManus, Hutchinson, & Baker, 2007).

Frequently children are informed about the divorce but not encouraged to discuss their concerns. Whereas loss through death involves a socially expected mourning period, there is no sanctioned mourning period for the loss of the "family that was." Children need support at the time of divorce and during the post-crisis period. Divorce forces a division of parental assets, and messages about the availability of money suddenly become frequent. Children who have never been concerned about family resources may be faced with new realities—a smaller home, sharing rooms, moving, fewer vacations, less clothing, and so on.

In one recent study participants were asked to recall their experiences of being told about their parents' divorce and how they felt about these experiences (Gumina, 2009). Five themes of good communication about the decision to divorce emerged:

1. Both parents should talk about the decision with the child/children.
2. Parents should avoid negative communication about the other in front of the children.
3. Emphasize that it is not the child's/children's fault.
4. Do not give unnecessary or specific details about the reasons for divorce.
5. Invite the children to respond or ask questions.

Usually one parent, most often the mother, is named the custodial parent, although increasing numbers of fathers receive custody of children or the couple is awarded joint custody. The term **co-parenting** is used to describe what has been thought to be the ideal parenting relationship after divorce and is seen to involve both parents in decision-making about children. "Coparents maintain a cooperative and constructive relationship with their former partner and opt to prioritize their children's welfare over their own discord" (Gasper, Stolberg, Macie, & Williams, 2008, p. 273). Co-parenting has been shown to be an important factor in young adult adjustment outcomes (Gasper et al., 2008). Some researchers have written about children of divorced parents feeling caught, or being put in the middle of conflict, between their parents. The experience of feeling caught leads to the need to feel protected, which leads to higher anxiety and physiological symptoms (Afifi, Afifi, Morse, & Hamrick, 2008). Mothers' confirming communication to their young adult children lessened the negative effects of feeling caught on family satisfaction (Schrodt & Ledbetter, 2011).

Usually, communication between former spouses becomes less conflictual in the years following a divorce. There are many models for postdivorce partners. Ahrons (2000) identified five types of arrangements: perfect pals, cooperative colleagues, angry associates, fiery foes, and dissolved duos; over time about half the divorced parent pairs become part of the cooperative colleagues group. Braithwaite, McBride, and Schrodt (2003) had parents co-raising children keep a record of all communication with the other household for two weeks. What they found is that after the initial hurts of divorce passed, most parents were able to develop a working relationship and communicate in a more businesslike manner. These co-parents were most successful when they kept messages focused on the children rather than on issues related to their former spouse.

Divorce is seen as a risk to preserving a strong father-child bond. The importance of the nonresidential father's relationship with his children should not be overlooked. Stone (2006) found three important influences on the quality of the father-child relationship after divorce. These are (1) a father's view of his own role as being important; (2) a father's belief in his abilities to be an effective parent; and (3) the belief that the mother is not an effective parent. Young adults whose parents divorced when the children were between the ages of 8 and 15 reported lower levels of father involvement, father nurturance, and less frequent verbal and physical contact with fathers compared to young adults from intact families (Peters & Ehrenberg, 2008). Children of divorced parents are very clear that they want their parents to communicate in ways that keep the children from feeling caught between the parents, in ways that center the child in their parents' attention. Children want enough information to know what is going on (and the communication should be age appropriate), and do not want to be the conduit by which parents pass along messages, for example, being asked to tell their father that he owes his child support (Braithwaite et al., 2008). *Parental alienation* occurs when one parent tries to distance a child from the other parent, such as in the opening case of Adelina Perez, although this can occur in both intact and divorced families and is associated with negative feelings toward the parent who is attempting the alienation (Mone & Biringen, 2006).

The communication between adolescents and their parents can have an effect on adolescents' coping. Researchers in one study asked adolescents and their custodial parents regarding their communication about divorce-related stressors (Afifi, Huber, & Ohs, 2006). The researchers found that adolescents who were more skilled or comfortable having discussions with their custodial parent about divorce-related stressors were able to cope more positively with the divorce. Further, the custodial parents' communication was associated with children's ability to cope with the divorce, such that parents who did not communicate well with the adolescent were more likely to have adolescents who were not coping positively. A second study examining conversations about divorce-related stressors found that when young adult children perceived their parents being vague or ambiguous in discussing these stressors with them, this was associated with young adults reporting less relational satisfaction (McManus & Nussbaum, 2011). Siblings can also provide support for each other following parental divorce, and have a positive effect on adjustment (Jacobs & Sillars, 2012).

Eventually many of these divorced parents and their children find themselves as members of a stepfamily, married, or cohabiting. Just as there are many variations on living as divorced partners, there are many variations of stepfamily life. Multiple pathways are represented in the quest to reach the point of "feeling like a family"; the five developmental trajectories that have been identified represent diverse communicative patterns and include variations in openness and rituals. These trajectories are accelerated, prolonged, declining, stagnating, and high-amplitude turbulent (Braithwaite, Olson, Golish, Soukup, & Turman, 2001). The researchers pointed out that there was no one right way to become a family, which is good news for stepfamilies. The systems concept of equifinality, introduced in Chapter 3, tells us that successful postdivorce and stepfamily life, while complex and not free from problems, can form strong families in which children feel supported and secure.

Military Families: A Special Case of Separation and Stress

A different, but profound, type of separation and stress exists when a member of a family is deployed to war. More than half (53 percent) of military personnel are married and 44 percent of military personnel have children. Research on deployment has focused mostly on spousal relationships as well as parent-child relationships (Department of Defense, 2012). Family communication and relationship maintenance continue during deployment but these must happen through different mediums than face-to-face interactions. Communication may be *delayed* (letters, care packages, and e-mails) or *interactive* (phone calls, instant messaging, video calls) (Carter et al., 2011). Technology has improved the frequency of communication between a deployed family member and his or her family; however, this can have its downside as well, as a family member might worry if contact does not happen every day (Hall, 2008).

Couples who are separated by war learn to enact relational maintenance strategies that help them cope with the separation and uncertainty. Indeed, some romantic partners report that deployment strengthened their relationship and allowed them to appreciate their relationship more (Knobloch & Theiss, 2012). One study of wives of deployed U.S. service members found three different types of relational maintenance strategies used by the couples. First, intrapersonal maintenance strategies included journaling, positive thinking, and prayer. Mediated partner strategies were the second type of maintenance strategies and included activities such as e-mail, webcam, care packages, future talk, and affection and intimacy. Third, wives reported that social and family support helped in maintaining relationships (Merolla, 2010). Other research has applied dialectical theory to couples' separation during deployment. Couples' dialectical contradictions when the husband is deployed include certainty-uncertainty during pre-deployment, autonomy-connection during deployment, and openness-closedness after the husband returns home (Sahlstein, Maguire, and Timmerman, 2009).

Carter and colleagues (2011) found that among male soldiers with higher marital satisfaction, the frequency of delayed, as opposed to interactive, communication was associated with less PTSD symptoms. However, among those with lower marital satisfaction, the frequency of delayed communication was associated with more PTSD symptoms.

When communication does occur, both the deployed solider and family members at home may have difficulties with disclosure. Soldiers in a combat environment may feel that they are unable to share their true feelings when communicating with family members at home, because they do not want to worry them and because they are not supposed to share certain types of information (Durham, 2010). In a study of wives of deployed husbands, with at least one child at home, researchers found that wives sometimes used protective buffering techniques to keep stressful information from their husbands, perhaps as they did not want to increase their husbands' stress. Such protective buffering was more common when the wife perceived greater risks to the husband's safety and was associated with negative health symptoms. True to the transactional nature of communication, women were more likely to disclose their stressors when they perceived that their deployed husbands were receptive to the stressful disclosures. Finally, more disclosures by the wives were related to wives' higher marital satisfaction (Joseph & Afifi, 2010).

Although deployment can be difficult, return from deployment (often called post-deployment) and the reintegration stage can also be challenging. Knobloch and Theiss (2012) surveyed military members and partners where return from deployment had occurred in the past six months. They found challenges of reintegration to include problems reconnecting, difficulty communicating, heightened conflict, and problems reintegrating into everyday life. The following mother's comment illustrates these issues:

We are living with a different man since Carl returned from his deployment. He used to tell funny stories, joke around, and chase after the boys. We would all play flag football in the yard. Now he sits and ruminates or goes running alone. My oldest boy complains that his father treats him the same way he did over a year ago when he was much more immature.

Following return from deployment, military personnel may avoid certain topics of discussion with their romantic partners. In a study of military personnel who had returned from deployment in the past six months, Knobloch and colleagues found that a little over half reported topics that they avoided communicating about with their romantic partners. These included deployment-related issues such as dangers experienced, confidential military information, and sexual fidelity, and reintegration issues such as household stressors, the member's emotions, and future deployment (Knobloch, Ebata, McGlaughlin, & Theiss, 2013). Military members who reported higher relational uncertainty also reported more topic avoidance. Another study found that spouses reported lower quality of communication with each other post-deployment, as compared to during deployment and before deployment (Houston, Pfefferbaum, Sherman, Melson, & Brand, 2013). Reintegration is made more difficult when one of the spouses has depressive symptoms (Knobloch, Ebata, McGlaughlin, & Ogolsky, 2013).

Military deployment also affects parent-child relationships. Parents are often absent for very important events in children's lives, such as a graduation or sports events (Hall, 2008). One study of children from military families found that the children reported emotional difficulties at higher levels than in the general population (Chandra et al., 2009). The longer a parent was separated from the family due to deployment, the more severe were the children's emotional difficulties. Sibling communication during this time becomes more important to coping (Houston et al., 2013).

Youth reported challenges the family faced during deployment, such as increased responsibilities and family conflict (Knobloch et al., in press-B). During the reintegration phase of a parent, some youth reported difficulties with the parent integrating back into everyday routines (Knobloch et al., in press-A). However, Knobloch and colleagues point out that there are also opportunities that children have during a parent's deployment and reintegration. During deployment these included increased family cohesion and developing more independence (Knobloch et al., in press-B). During the reintegration phase of a parent, many positives have been reported by youth including spending time together, emotional tranquility, and returning to pre-deployment patterns (Knobloch et al., in press-A). However, Knobloch and colleagues also point out that there are also opportunities that children have during a parent's deployment and reintegration. During deployment these may included increased family cohesion and developing more independence. During the reintegration phase of a parent, many positives have been reported by youth including spending time together, emotional tranquility, and returning to pre-deployment patterns (Knobloch et al., in press B).

Applying a family systems perspective to deployment and reintegration helps to make sense of the challenges faced by families. When a military parent is deployed, the remaining family unit must adjust and make changes. A spouse may need to work fewer hours or more hours; older children may take on more responsibility and household chores; and extended family members may be relied on for help. When the military parent returns, he or she will find things have changed, and it may be a difficult adjustment (Hall, 2008). Roles need to be renegotiated, and things can never be exactly the same as they once were. Children have matured and families' needs have changed. In one study a participant reported: "I had my own way of doing things with our kids while he was gone and he wanted to come in and change it all" (Knobloch & Theiss, 2012, p. 439).

In addition to the cycle of deployment and reintegration, military families face other stresses such as frequent relocations. When not deployed, military members may spend long hours working with their teams. This can lead to family conflict as well (Hall, 2008).

Support and Communication

Throughout any of the crises we have discussed in this chapter, the family's capacity for developing healthy communication patterns and rules, reflective of its levels of cohesion and adaptation and its images, themes, boundaries, and biosocial beliefs, determines how the system will weather the strain. As we discussed in Chapter 2, a family with low cohesion may fragment under pressure, unless such pressure can link the unconnected members. A family with limited adaptability faces a painful time, since such crises force change on the system and the lives of each member. A family whose images and themes allow outside involvement in family affairs may use its flexible boundaries to find institutional and social support. A family with rigid biosocial beliefs faces difficult challenges if key family figures are lost or injured and others are not permitted to assume some of their role responsibilities. How much social support family members receive in crises depends on how much support they have given one another prior to the crises. One lesson here is that families need to develop functional communication practices in the family system that will carry them through crises and hard times. It is very difficult, if not impossible, to develop functional communication patterns while in crisis.

Some family members may use **protective buffering** to try to reduce distress in other family members by protecting them from becoming upset or being burdened. Protective buffering is achieved through hiding worries and concerns and avoiding disagreements (Manne et al., 2007). In a study of couples where the wife has breast cancer, the use of such techniques has been shown to cause more distress, but only in relationships where marital satisfaction is reported.

Coping Strategies

Every family undergoes periods of unpredictable stress. Many of these stresses are not as immediately critical as death, illness, or divorce, but they do eat away at members' resources and affect coping strategies. Burr, Klein, and Associates (1994) view all kinds of family stress as a multifaceted phenomenon with multiple causes and coping strategies. Their research indicates that families deal with stress in a sequential process, trying Level I coping strategies first, and if these fail, moving on to Level II and III strategies (see Table 11.1).

When a stress occurs, a family will first try to use a Level I process by perhaps changing the family rules or role expectations. In a case where a child is consistently wetting the bed, this might include meeting with a therapist. Or, if one partner takes on new responsibilities at work, the other may need to increase responsibilities at home. If any of these changes work, the family proceeds into a period of recovery.

Level	Strategy
I	Change or adapt existing rules, ways of doing things, rearranging responsibilities to address the stress.
II	Change metarules (rules about rules) so that new areas of rules are created to address the stress.
III	Change the basic assumptions about life; reorder value structure to address stress.

TABLE 11.1 Coping Strategies Sequence

If changing the rules and more superficial aspects of the family's operation fail, then the family seeks more basic or metalevel changes at Level II.

Level II changes involve a middle level of abstraction, one that alters the system in fundamentally different ways. For example, at Level II, the family may need to change metarules about how their rules are made and by whom. For instance, in a family where the parents have divorced, a Level II strategy would include talking about decision-making in the family, changing the way Mom as a single parent directs the family now, modifying the way the family makes and changes rules, and replacing competitive strategies with cooperative ones.

If Level II strategies fail to reduce the stresses to a comfortable point for the family's well-being, the need arises for more abstract Level III coping strategies—ones that entail attempts to change the fundamental values or philosophies of life that govern the family. Changes at this level require communication about what being a member in a particular family means and how members can enhance one another's lives by participating more effectively within the system they have created. Level III refers to highly abstract processes that seek to make changes in the family's beliefs, paradigms, and values to reduce stress. At Level III, the family will question its basic beliefs and try to decide if these beliefs can change in any way to accommodate the negative effects of stress. For instance, a family may strongly believe that children should be raised by a father and mother. When a single, 40-year-old female family member makes the decision to use a sperm donor to become pregnant, her parents may initially react with disapproval. However, as the pregnancy and subsequent birth take place, they may gradually accept their daughter's wishes and realize that their role as grandparents will be important to the child, ultimately giving emotional support to the daughter and baby.

Many predictable and unpredictable stresses will be handled easily by families using Level I coping strategies. Some significant stresses will force the family system to adopt new, creative, and possibly painful ways. Members have less experience in creating new coping strategies, and thus creating Levels II and III strategies is difficult and requires trial and error.

Family members, immediate and extended, may serve as critical supports when one or more members face a crisis. Family members may also create voluntary or fictive kin relationships to supplement the support they need but are not receiving from their family. Most often these voluntary kin relationships do not replace the family of origin, but provide important social support during crises, or over the long term, that the family of origin does not provide (Braithwaite et al., 2010).

Support Groups

Negative stresses—such as alcoholism, drug abuse, child abuse, economic reversals, job transfers, and suicides—take their toll on a family's emotional resources. A stress, such as divorce, reduces the family's support systems at the same time that the family members' pain is increasing. Without a strong communication network, the individuals—forced to rely on themselves—may become alienated or severely depressed. Even seemingly positive experiences such as raising a gifted child, achieving a high-powered position, adopting a child, moving overseas, or receiving a large sum of money through an inheritance can stress the system. In order to understand a family's coping capacity, a family's immediate and post-crisis resources, especially support networks, must be understood.

In a society characterized by mobility and smaller families, individuals increasingly receive interpersonal support from others who share similar experiences and pain. Groups such as Alcoholics Anonymous or support groups for parents who have lost a child can make a real difference in coping. The Internet has increased the possibilities for persons and families to find support. Internet-based support groups can be particularly important to those dealing with rare diseases or who are uncomfortable with face-to-face disclosures (Albrecht & Goldsmith, 2003). Participation in social support groups for cancer patients has been shown to reduce social isolation and negative moods, including depression and cancer-related trauma (Im et al., 2007). In all cases, self-help groups rely on members' communication as a healing process, an important way to share and receive information and comfort.

Conclusion

This chapter examined communication and unpredictable life stresses. Specifically, it focused on (1) the process of dealing with unpredictable stresses and (2) communication during certain major stressful life events, such as death, illness or disability, and divorce. Over the years, every family system encounters external stress from crisis situations as well as stress from developmental change. The system's ability to cope effectively with stress depends on a number of factors, such as the number of recent stresses, role changes, and social and institutional support. The double ABCX model provides an effective explanation of family coping through its focus on precrisis and postcrisis variables. Stressors such as death, illness, divorce, and military deployment necessarily alter family systems over long periods of time. Communication may facilitate or restrict a family's coping procedures. In most families, sharing of information and feelings can lower the stress level. The family with flexible boundaries has the capacity to accept support and the potential for surviving crises more effectively than families who close themselves off from others. Many family members find support outside their family, through friends or support groups.

In Review

1. Using a real or fictional family, analyze the effects on the family of a severe stress that impacted one member (e.g., drug problem, serious car accident, or severe illness).
2. Using the same example of family stress, compare and contrast an analysis of the problem according to the ABCX model and the double ABCX model.
3. Describe how a "happy event" has brought high levels of stress to a family with which you are familiar.
4. How do different cultural and/or religious attitudes toward death aid or restrict the mourning process for surviving family members?
5. What guidelines for communication would you recommend to spouses who have children and are about to separate?
6. Using Baxter's concepts of dialectical contradictions in relationships, discuss with examples how you think crises affect openness-closedness, predictability-novelty, and autonomy-connectedness in a family system.
7. Give examples of Level I, II, and III coping strategies that reflect how families cope with crises.

Key Words

Ambiguous loss   279

Bonadaptation   284

Communication-based
   coping model   286

Co-parenting   300

Coping   282

Double ABCX model   283

Final conversations   290

Maladaptation   284

Protective buffering   304

Stages of family crisis   286

Stressor events   279

Unpredictable stresses   279

Untimely death   289

CHAPTER 12

Family Communication and Well-Being

LEARNING OBJECTIVES

- Describe the association between family communication and physical well-being
- Understand family communication about difficult topics, including genetic risk, money, financial stress, and new technology challenges
- Explain approaches for improving family communication
- Understand the authors' final perspectives on family communication

After two years of specialist visits and misdiagnoses, 38-year-old Drew's doctor suggested he get tested for hemochromatosis, a little-known genetic disease that attacks the organs but, if caught in time, can be managed indefinitely by getting ongoing blood transfusions. After the diagnosis, the genetic counselor recommended that Drew inform his family members, particularly his two siblings, about his diagnosis because they were at an increased risk for being affected by it also. His sister Alisha lived in the same city and he saw her regularly; his brother lived across the country and they seldom were in contact. Although telling them about his diagnosis seemed to be a straightforward task, Drew hesitated for months, worrying about how to tell them without alarming them. Finally, his partner, Molly, began to pressure him to alert his siblings.

After more weeks of stalling, Drew finally sent his sister a short e-mail, although he did not go into much detail on the subject. Alisha immediately called Molly, as they have always been close, to ask if this weird-sounding disease was serious. Molly provided information about hemochromatosis, sent Alisha to a medical website, and explained that if Alisha tested positive, she could control the disease indefinitely. The next week, upon Alisha's request, Drew met Alisha for lunch, and they talked about hemochromatosis and the process of testing. During this lunch, Drew asked Alisha to call their sister-in law, Charlene, to inform their brother Kevin about the disease. Within a day Alisha passed on the news.

After nine years of marriage, two full-time jobs, and two small children, Angeli and Dante had fallen into a set of everyday rhythms that kept the household and family running. Every weekday started at 6:00 AM. with packing lunches, getting the kids dressed, driving to daycare, and heading to the warehouse or office. In the evenings things went in reverse, with dinner, baths, and bedtime stories carrying the couple into an hour of staring at the television until they started dozing off. Every Saturday meant cleaning, shopping, playing with the kids and a Netflix movie. Sunday morning involved church attendance before spending the afternoon with Angeli's parents. Angeli and Dante rarely had time alone, and they saved going out without the children for birthdays or anniversaries.

Despite feeling like she had everything she had wanted—two children, good employment, a nice home, two cars, and a couple of family vacations each year—Angeli found herself growing increasingly dissatisfied with her life and her marriage. After a number of conversations in which Angeli claimed she hardly knew Dante anymore, the couple decided to go on a Marriage Encounter weekend with other church couples in order to find some time to be together and talk about their relationship and their lives. Angeli's parents agreed to watch the children. On Friday evening the couple arrived at a retreat center for the opening session. By Saturday evening Dante and Angeli had heard five leader-couples talk about how they learned to make positive changes in their marriages. The Marriage Encounter approach also included private writing sessions shared with the other to spur conversations on a series of issues that affected their marriage. Both partners were looking forward to the final Sunday sessions. One year later, Dante and Angeli have made strides to improve their marriage. They set aside a monthly date night where they go out alone, take a few minutes every night for debriefing conversations, and try to be more affectionate with each other.

H ow do members of well-functioning families live, grow, and relate to each other year after year? How do they cope with problems and changes? To what extent can family members create new communication patterns and develop healthy ways of loving, fighting, or making decisions? How do these communication practices contribute to family well-being?

In the previous chapters, we have introduced and described many of the important theories and models that help to explain family communication concepts and processes. Throughout these chapters we have referred to outcomes associated with family communication, particularly relationship maintenance and satisfaction. This final chapter explores the connections between family communication and family members' well-being. Defined broadly, the term "well-being" has to do with family members' quality of life (Segrin, 2006).

Many people believe that life happens *to* them: that they have no ability to improve their relationships. Such individuals are *reactors*, taking no responsibility for their contribution to problems in a relationship or for their responsibility to improve relationships. Other persons serve as *actors*, believing they can make personal changes and co-create desirable relational change. Viewing all family members as actors reflects an understanding that communication and relationships are a co-creation rather than focusing on individual experience as we discussed in Chapter 2 (Stewart, 1999). The differences between being a reactor and an actor are captured in the following example:

"That's the way I am. Take me or leave me" was the common comment of my first husband. He believed that if you had to work on a relationship there was something wrong with it. Needless to say, after a few years we dissolved the marriage. Now I am engaged to a man who wants to talk and think about how to keep a relationship growing over a lifetime. We have even had some premarital counseling to explore important issues before the marriage. Life is very different when both people are open to change.

Family members have the potential to grow in chosen directions, although such growth may require great risk, effort, and pain. From a family systems perspective, we know that whenever change is attempted by some members, it may be resisted by other members who wish to keep their system in balance no matter how painful that balance is. In the first case at the start of the chapter, Drew seemed willing to withhold important medical information from his siblings rather than upset the family system. It is difficult, although not impossible, for an individual to initiate lasting change in the system; however, change is more easily accomplished when most or all members are committed to an alternative way of relating. Also, it is a challenge for members of the system to recognize certain negative patterns in which they play a part. It may take a third party or clearheaded, objective analysis to recognize a destructive pattern that needs to be changed. Change depends on one's ability to discover the meanings underlying one's own actions and those of other family members. According to Gottman's "sound marital house theory," change is a process of creating shared, symbolic meaning through dreams, narratives, myths, and metaphors (Gottman, Ryan, Carrère, & Erley, 2002). Because there is no "one right way" for all families to behave, the members of each family have to discover what works well for their system by sharing dreams and stories.

Throughout this book we have focused primarily on functional families, rather than severely troubled ones, recognizing that every functional family experiences alternating periods of ease and distress. Therefore, families fall on a continuum ranging from severely dysfunctional to optimally functional. Although few families remain at the optimally functional point indefinitely due to tensions caused by developmental or unpredictable stresses, many do remain within the functional to optimal range over long periods of time. How do these families maintain their state of well-being? The following sections will explore: (1) the interrelationship of family members' physical health status and health practices and communication; (2) family capacity for holding difficult conversations; (3) personal, instructional, and therapeutic approaches for creating and maintaining effective communication within families; and (4) final perspectives on family communication and well-being.

Family Communication and Physical Well-Being

Think about the family in which you grew up. What were the rules about health behaviors communicated in your family? Perhaps your parents said, "Clean your plate if you want dessert." Maybe yours was a household in which you were expected to try new types of food. Or perhaps your parents let you eat what you wanted. Your parents may have let you stay home from school if you said you did not feel well; perhaps your friend's parents required a fever to stay home from school. As you reached adolescence, your parents may have established a new set of rules focused on reducing health risk behaviors, possibly including rules about alcohol and drug use, smoking, and sexual activity. Over the years, you have also likely experienced the illness and perhaps the death of a family member. The communication in your family that surrounded these events likely has helped to shape your thinking and behavior about health and illness.

These are just a few examples of the interrelationships between family communication and health. As Bylund and Duck stated: "Throughout the lifespan, the everyday interactions among family members have the potential to have a tremendous impact on individuals' construction of health, talk about health, participation in health care systems, enactment of healthy or unhealthy behaviors, and health status" (2004, p. 5). To this we add that individuals' health, illness, and healthy or unhealthy behaviors also have an impact on family members' communication. There is a mutual influence between health and family communication.

Health Status

Family researchers have been particularly interested in marital relationships and marital partners' health status for many years. In general, married adults are healthier than unmarried adults and have lower mortality rates. This is likely in part because people who are healthier are more likely to get married and stay married (Waite & Gallagher, 2000). It also may be due to two protective factors: married persons have less risky health behaviors and they benefit from spousal support and companionship (Segrin & Flora, 2011). The benefit of being married is not equal, though. Husbands gain greater health benefits from marriage than do wives, in part because of wives' greater tendencies to attempt to manage their husbands' health habits. Also, wives are likely to have more people in their support system, whereas husbands usually name their wives as their primary confidant and rely heavily on this one person (Kiecolt-Glaser & Newton, 2001).

Despite the overall benefit of marriage on health, it is important to recognize that marital quality also plays an important role (Segrin & Flora, 2011). Unhappily married persons are generally less healthy than those who are unmarried. The quality of married couples' interactions can have a profound effect on their health. Factors such as spousal conflict, spousal over-involvement, and inequality in decision-making can contribute to poorer health. Conflict in particular seems to have more of a negative effect on wives' health than on husbands' health. In studies where researchers have asked husbands and wives to have a discussion about a topic that they have conflict over, spouses' blood pressure and heart rates tend to increase, with the wives having the greater increases (Kiecolt-Glaser & Newton, 2001). When both spouses in a marriage have a tendency to suppress their anger, their mortality risk for poor health may be greater (Harburg, Kaciroti, Gleiberman, Julius, & Schork, 2008). Family distress and conflict can affect the health and health habits of both adults and children in families (Jones, Beach, & Jackson, 2004; Michael, Torres, & Seeman, 2007).

The fact that a good-quality marriage provides a health benefit makes sense when you consider that those persons who are socially isolated have worse health than those who have meaningful relationships. Marriage frequently provides a stable and consistent guard against social isolation, bringing with it the health-enhancing benefits of a relationship. Whether or not someone is married, however, they can still be healthy and have meaningful relationships with partners, family, and friends (DePaulo, 2006).

Family relationships are also closely linked to mental health. After reviewing the research on family interactions and mental health issues, including mental illnesses such as depression, schizophrenia, and eating disorders, Segrin and Flora (2011) assert that "there is an undeniable connection between abnormal and problematic family interaction patterns and family members' mental health" (p. 317) and indicate whether the poor family interactions cause the mental illness or the mental illness causes the poor family interactions is not always clear; however, it is likely that both are true.

Parents' communication style can also affect how adolescents react physiologically after a difficult discussion with their parents. Adolescents who perceived their parents had better communication were able to better recover from these stressful discussions than those who perceived their parents to have worse communication (Afifi, Granger, Denes, Joseph, & Aldeis, 2011). Furthermore, a recent Dutch study indicated that the effect of family communication on family members may be different by gender. Daughters were found to have less depressive symptoms when their mothers disclosed more to them; sons were found to have more depressive symptoms when their mothers disclosed more. Socialization of daughters versus sons and higher intimacy levels between daughters and mothers may help to explain this difference (Lichtwarck-Aschoff, Finkenauer, van de Vorst, & Engels, 2012).

Influencing Health Behaviors

Family communication may impact family members' health through communication about health-promoting behaviors (e.g., nutrition, exercising) and health risk reduction behaviors (e.g., quitting smoking, practicing safe sex). For example, farmers are at a particular risk for developing skin cancer because of the time they spend in the sun, and communication from their families can be an important factor in their health risk prevention behaviors (Parrott & Lemieux, 2003). Chapter 8 contained examples of how spouses might use influence strategies to modify the other's health behaviors. Here we focus on other ways that family communication might affect family members' health behaviors.

The content of health promotion and risk reduction communication is tied closely to developmental issues in the family. For example, when a couple becomes new parents, one health-promoting behavior for the infant can be how long the mother breast-feeds. Researchers found that how strongly the male partner believes that his partner should breast-feed influences the mother's breast-feeding behaviors. They point out, "These women behaved more in accordance with what their partners thought they should do than with what they had originally intended to do" (Rempel & Rempel, 2004, p. 107).

As children grow older, health promotion and risk reduction discussions may change. For adolescents and young adult children, parents' communications about health issues often focus on risky behaviors such as smoking, drinking alcohol, using other drugs, and engaging in sexual activity. They may use "abstinence rules" (sometimes called "no-tolerance rules") or "contingency rules" (Baxter, Bylund, Imes, & Routsong, 2009; Bourdeau, Miller, Vanya, Duke, & Ames, 2012). An example of an abstinence rule is "Don't drink alcohol until you are 21," while a contingency rule is "But if you do drink, don't drive." In examining specifically rules about alcohol use among teens and parents, Bordeau et al. (2012) found many to have a "call-me" rule that could be present with abstinence or contingency rules. This rule meant that the child should call the parent if they were in a dangerous situation because of their alcohol use and generally that the child would not get into trouble. Baxter and colleagues (2009) found that parents and their adolescent offspring reported abstinence and contingency rules were used for both alcohol and risky sexual behaviors. However, very few contingency rules about tobacco were reported. Miller-Day (2008) found that using a strategy of "no tolerance" may be the most effective in

Parents teach their children about health-promoting behaviors in many ways.

preventing substance abuse. Parents also play an important role in encouraging adolescents to use health-promoting behaviors such as exercise, good nutrition, and sun protection (Bylund, Baxter, Imes, & Wolf, 2010).

One way to view family health communication is to look at the rules that families have about health behaviors and how these rules guide family members' actions. In families that are considered to have high expressiveness, members experience a lot of freedom to express opinions and room for individuality. Families that rate high on expressiveness (similar to the conversation orientation discussed in Chapter 7) rate lower on compliance to health rules, articulation of health rules, and consequences of violating health rules. Parents in these families seem to value individual decision-making, with less focus on a rule-based system. So they may be less likely to interfere in the health decisions of other members. However, in families that emphasize conformity to authority (similar to conformity orientation), adolescents and parents recall **family health rules** in similar ways. These families seem to have a shared understanding of health rules. For example, parents and adolescents may independently report that a nutrition rule in their family was to "try at least one bite of a new food." Finally, families that are conflict avoidant (similar to conformity orientation) tend to hold all children in a family accountable to the same health rules, perhaps to avoid claims of favoritism from siblings (Baxter, Bylund, Imes, & Schieve, 2005).

Family health rules are seldom stated explicitly in a one-time sit-down conversation between parent and child. Two-thirds of parents and offspring report not having those types of conversations, but instead they have ongoing conversations about alcohol and drug use. Content in such discussions may include expressions of disapproval, warnings about the dangers of use, and the potential health consequences

(Miller-Day & Dodd, 2004). When parents make a point to have targeted and frequent conversations with their children about alcohol, this has been associated with less likelihood of alcohol use (Miller-Day & Kam, 2010). One study showed that young adults were more likely to disclose their own risky health behaviors to parents when the parents are more challenging (e.g., encouraging children to improve themselves) and less disconfirming (Aldeis & Afifi, 2013).

Overall parent-child communication may have a more indirect influence on children's substance use. Families with regular conflict tend to have children who are more likely to use drugs. Adolescents who engage in demand/withdraw conflict patterns, which we discussed in Chapter 9, with their parents are more likely to have lower self-esteem and high alcohol and drug use. This is true whether the conflict is about allowance, cleaning one's room, or alcohol and drug use (Caughlin & Malis, 2004).

In some families, persuasive messages about health behaviors may increase after a cancer diagnosis. These persuasive messages might come from the person diagnosed with cancer or from a family member. For example, 94 percent of patients recently diagnosed with skin cancer reported having at least one or two discussions with family members about skin cancer risk since their diagnosis (Hay et al., 2005). Another study showed that in families in which one member had been diagnosed with melanoma, those that were characterized by high cohesiveness and adaptability reported more frequently discussing melanoma with family members (Harris et al., 2010). In addition, melanoma patients may make decisions about which family members they think are at risk, and then target their discussions toward those family members (Hay et al., 2009). Patients with cancer might be particularly well positioned to help family or friends quit smoking (Garces et al., 2010). In one study, researchers interviewed prostate cancer patients and their wives three different times across an eight-month period following prostate cancer treatment. Surprisingly, wives' attempts to influence their husbands to engage in certain health behaviors were associated with less healthy behaviors and lower psychological well-being. There are a couple of possible reasons for this: husbands may react negatively to these influence attempts by not enacting the behaviors or wives may be more likely to attempt to influence less healthy husbands (Helgeson, Novak, Lepore, & Eton, 2004).

Family Communication and Health-Care Interactions

Think about your own experiences when going to the doctor as a child. There was a socialization process happening as your parents or older siblings taught you how to communicate with doctors, nurses, and other health-care professionals. While you were quite young, your parents probably did most of the communicating with health-care professionals, but as you grew older, you probably have become more active in communicating your complaints and symptoms to the doctor. Many young adults can recall when they were first allowed to go to the doctor alone and slowly became responsible for their own health-care communication. In the end, parents help set the stage for children's interaction with health-care providers. For example, a study of African American women found that most sought gynecological health care as an adolescent based upon their mother's recommendation (Warren-Jeanpiere, Miller, & Warren, 2010).

Throughout the life span, members often act as informal **health-care advocates** for each other by attending each other's doctor's appointments at critical times.

When patients are seriously ill, these family members serve an important function by asking questions and helping patients to recall information later. In one study of consultations with an oncologist where bad news about cancer was given, 86 percent of patients had at least one companion (family member or friend) present with them. These companions asked more questions than the patient did on average (Eggly et al., 2006). Sometimes family members must act as an interpreter for the patient and doctor, for example for an elderly family member who may not understand medical terms or medical practices. As noted previously, in certain immigrant families, children are usually the bilingual members of the family and frequently have to take on this role, creating a generational reversal.

Although having a companion present in a health interaction may be helpful for information recall and emotional support, some issues of privacy also can emerge (Petronio, Sargent, Andea, Reganis, & Cichocki, 2004). For example, a hospitalized parent may be embarrassed to have his or her health information revealed in front of their child, even if that child is an adult. Or, imagine two adolescent brothers who went to a party they were not supposed to attend when their parents were out of town. The younger brother, Rob, got in a fight at the party and sprained his wrist. When his older brother Mark took him to the family doctor the next day, Mark told the doctor how Rob sprained his wrist, even though Rob wanted to come up with a different explanation, as he was worried the family doctor would tell his mother.

As children reach adolescence, privacy issues may emerge when the pediatrician asks the adolescent about health risk behaviors while the parent is in the room and the adolescent is faced with lying to the doctor or revealing private information about her behaviors. In some cases, physicians request time alone with adolescent patients to discuss making life-healthy choices and to provide the patient with privacy to raise personal concerns.

Illness and Family Communication

As discussed in Chapter 11, illness of a family member can have a profound effect on the family system. Family communication patterns and practices are often affected by such illness. The content of conversations, the rules for communicating, and frequency of conflict may be drastically altered when a family member becomes seriously ill. How information about illnesses is communicated has a profound effect on health and well-being in families. The theory of health-related family quality of life helps to frame the discussion of illness and family communication (Radina, 2013). There are five main tenets of this theory, which are as follows:

1. When a family member is diagnosed with breast cancer, or another illness with potential long-term survivorship, the entire family is affected.
2. Families comprise multiple actors who interact on the basis of established patterns of functioning that are governed by rules that can be both explicit and implicit.
3. New or revised patterns of functioning can result when the family encounters a stressor (e.g., illness).
4. The introduction of a stressor (e.g., illness) to the family allows for established patterns of functioning to become more apparent when they otherwise might not be so.
5. Quality of family life is subjective and situation dependent.

In each of these five tenets of the theory, we can see the central role of communication in navigating serious illness.

To follow, we briefly present some of the family communication issues that emerge when a family member is diagnosed with a serious disease or suffers a stroke. Every year, hundreds of thousands of families are affected by cancer. Children whose parents are diagnosed with advanced cancer are affected in all aspects of their lives (Kennedy & Lloyd-Williams, 2009). As these families face a diagnosis of cancer in one of their family members, their conversations may focus on describing, explaining, and informing others about the cancer status. Some family members find themselves serving as an intermediary between other family members and doctors, explaining what the doctors have told them. In doing so, they learn to speak the "language of uncertainty regarding cancer" (Beach & Good, 2004, p. 28). Young or adolescent children may find this new language of cancer to be difficult, as the following quote indicates:

We found out that my mom had cancer the same day that the orthopedist removed a cast from my leg after eight long weeks. As a 16-year-old, I was already walking a fine line between teenager and adult in all aspects of my life, but that distinction became even more blurry when "the Big C" entered my house. That afternoon, the conversation in our family room shifted from talk of celebratory ice cream to medical appointment-making with no end in sight. It was clear in that moment that life had changed. I had always prided myself on the fact that my parents treated me like an adult, sharing family news and decisions with me, but when they tried to do this with my mom's disease, I think we were all surprised that there were many things I just wasn't ready to hear. This made it hard for my parents to decide what to share with me and hard for me to decide what of my "normal" life to share with them.

Many families are faced with the diagnosis of a chronic or life-threatening disease of a child, such as childhood cancer. Communication surrounding this disease can be very difficult but can also have a tremendous impact on the child's well-being. For example, parent-child communication seems to impact a child's experience of pain and distress during cancer treatments. Children whose parents used normalizing and supportive communication with them during potentially painful cancer treatments had less pain and distress than those whose parents used invalidating communication with them (Cline et al., 2006).

Helping children to understand and make sense of illness (whether their own or another family member's) is important to effective family communication. Discussing illness with children needs to be tailored to their developmental stage. Children's ideas about the causes of disease mature over time and are correlated with a child's developmental stage. A very young child (two years old) would not even consider the how or why of disease. A child who is three to seven years old may begin to think in terms of disease being contagious, realizing that if Dad has a cold, you might have a cold too. So a child this age may think that since Grandpa has cancer, he might "catch" cancer too. Children who are 8 to 11 years of age begin to understand that the source of an illness can be external or from within the body. By 12 years of age, children are able to understand the cause of disease as a body's process and explain it in terms of organs (Koopman, Baars, Chaplin, & Zwinderman, 2004).

Often, family members are required to take on the role of the caregiver. Having family members who provide supportive communication and care can lessen the burden of being ill. It may also benefit family relationships. For example, stroke survivors reported spending more time with spousal caregivers and having more open communication and greater appreciation for family relationships after their stroke (Pawlowski, 2006). However, becoming a caregiver can be a stressful situation, as the caregiver may feel ill equipped to handle the time demands, physical demands, emotional burdens, and financial costs (Pecchioni, Thompson, & Anderson, 2006). Older caregivers of a sick spouse face an increased risk of death (Christakis & Allison, 2006). In many cases, caregivers become so overwhelmed that it is important for them to seek support as well. Researchers have found that effective communication and joint decision-making about caregiving, when possible, can help both the caregiver and the person who is ill (Harwood, Rittenour, & Lin, 2013). Interventions for caregivers can be helpful and appreciated as they learn how to take better care of themselves and interact with others in similar situations (Schure et al., 2006).

If you think about this change in roles that happens during times of illness from a family systems perspective, it is easy to see the impact that an illness requiring a family caregiver can have on the family system. Open and frequent communication about the changes taking place in the family may be helpful in absorbing some of the shock to the family system.

Difficult Conversations on Current Issues

In a world characterized by the explosion and dissemination of new knowledge, family members confront the challenge of talking with each other about new, complex, and sometimes emotionally charged topics, as we saw in the cases at the start of this chapter. Although each past generation has experienced such challenges, the ongoing knowledge explosion in the twenty-first century requires that family members need to be able to discuss new complicated and challenging issues as they arise. They need to be able to engage in difficult conversations on current concerns. The following subsections explore three topics that have emerged in recent years that have major significance for everyday life and well-being in many families. The first one, talking about genetics in families, focuses specifically on disclosing and discussing genetic disease, a topic made possible only by advances in scientific research, including the groundbreaking Human Genome Project. The second one, talking about money, has long been a topic of conversation in some families. However, in many families serious discussions of money do not usually include young or even adult children. The recent economic downturns and worldwide financial instability makes understanding and discussions of family finances a critical subject. The third topic involves a reversal of the traditional parent-dominated information model: discussions of cutting-edge advances in digital technology belong more to the younger generations. Children and adolescents may enter technological worlds that their parents and older family members do not fully comprehend and are unable to discuss. These new and exciting technological advances as well as related safety concerns that accompany them necessitate that family members hold conversations about members' use of digital technology.

Genetic Heritage and Family Risk

Recent technological advances make it possible for family members to be tested for multiple hereditary genetic diseases. The Human Genome Project, completed in 2003, opened the door to a wealth of genetic information available to individuals and families. Increasingly, family members will be faced with the delicate task of communicating with each other about their genetic heritage, and in stepfamilies or adoptive families multiple or unknown genetic heritages must be acknowledged. These often-difficult conversations, unimaginable 20 years ago, will continue to become more critical in managing family members' health. Family discussions about genetic risk may center on identifying who is at risk, deciding whether and how to disclose this risk to family members, and supporting family members who are dealing with undesirable or painful genetic knowledge (Galvin, 2006). In addition, genetics influence specific family interactions in areas such as parenting and sibling relationships. An example of this might include that an adolescent's behavior often reflected the genetic history from one or both biological parents (Spotts, 2012).

Testing   Genetic counselors frequently interact only with one individual, or sometimes with a small number of family members. Given their professional code of conduct, they are seldom in a position to alert other members about the family's genetic inheritance and the risks other family members may face as in the first case with Drew and his siblings who were at risk for the same condition. The **proband**, or the first person in the family to be diagnosed with the genetic condition, has a major impact on when or if family members learn about their risk and, furthermore, if they decide to get tested. Similarly, members of resilient families are more likely to get tested (Katapodi, Northouse, Milliron, Liu, & Merajver, 2013).

Disclosure   Following testing, the proband may choose to disclose results of his or her test to encourage relatives to get tested, obtain emotional support, and get advice about medical decisions. Sometimes probands deliberately avoid conversation, choosing instead to send an e-mail or post the news to a family website. Avoiding disclosure altogether frequently occurs when the disease is perceived as highly devastating or deadly, the relational history with the person to be informed has been problematic, or the disease is not manageable (Galvin & Grill, 2009). A recent summary of research in this area found the following six factors that affected whether or not the proband discloses genetic information to family members (Seymour, Addington-Hall, Lucassen, & Foster, 2010):

1. How the proband feels about the role of informing relatives: Individuals who underwent testing specifically for the purpose of finding out information for their relatives may not have trouble disclosing while other probands may not accept this role of informant. Mothers at risk for a *BRCA1* or *BRCA2* genetic mutation (measuring risk for breast cancer) report uncertainty about how to communicate with their daughters about this risk (Bylund et al., 2012).
2. The perceived relevance of the information to another family member and the anticipated reactions of the family members: Probands in one study reported not telling some family members due to their lack of emotional and developmental readiness (Dancyger et al., 2011). Probands also may avoid sharing

genetic information when they believe this might lead to a difficult encounter. Such a situation appears in the opening vignette in which Drew attempts to avoid direct conversation with his brother, and instead relies on his partner to convey the news of his diagnosis of hemochromatosis.

3. Closeness of the relationship: Emotionally distant relationships and little contact may prevent genetic information from being passed on (McGivern et al., 2004).

4. Family rules and patterns: Prior agreements and expectations for communication will influence what and how family members disclose. For example, a study on family communication about hereditary hemochromatosis found that a contributing factor in getting tested was an affected sibling's or other family member's communication (Bylund, Galvin, Dunet, & Reyes, 2011). Disclosure is also difficult if the genetic information must be conveyed within already-problematic family relationships, which compounds decision-making about revealing information. A family's communication patterns and norms become set from years of interaction. Cohesive families may respond better to these discussions (McCann et al., 2009), whereas families with significant rifts may struggle with such news. Some family members may refuse to listen to the proband or give subtle cues that they do not want to discuss this topic (Gaff et al., 2007).

5. Timing: Family members need to consider the proper time and place for disclosure. Two main styles of disclosing genetic testing information are **pragmatism** and **prevarication**. A proband who uses a pragmatic style will disclose the information actively and practically. Someone who calls or sends an e-mail to his siblings to tell them of his recent genetic test and suggests that they get tested enacts the pragmatic style. On the other hand, a proband who uses a prevarication style would try to find the "right moment" to disclose the information. Such a person using this style would look for opportunities within normal events, such as a family gathering. However, this attempt to find the right moment may take months or even years (Forrest et al., 2003).

6. The role of health-care professionals: Health care professionals can aid family members in telling relatives, as well as legitimizing the information to be disclosed. Mothers at risk of the *BRCA1* or *BRCA2* mutation have suggested that having a daughter attend a health-care visit to discuss issues surrounding risk could be helpful (Fisher et al., in press).

Finally, when the news could be devastating, such as a diagnosis of hereditary forms of breast or ovarian cancer, a proband may be reluctant to pass on the news as it will be so upsetting to affected individuals and the family system. In the case of Huntington's disease, which affects the nervous system and motor control, a proband may remain silent, choosing instead to monitor family members, scanning the environment for threatening clues of the disease in a relative, before choosing to address the issue.

High proportions of patients going for genetic testing report an intention to tell their family members (Clarke et al., 2005). For example, in a study of 329 women being tested for the *BRCA1* or *BRCA2* mutations for hereditary breast cancer, 98 percent reported before their genetic test that they intended to tell at least one of their adult first-degree relatives (e.g., sibling, parent, or offspring) about their test result; 63 percent reported that they would tell all of these relatives (Barsevick et al., 2008).

However, in reality, this information is not always passed on, resulting in *passive nondisclosure* (Gaff, Collins, Symes, & Halliday, 2005). Why does passive nondisclosure happen? Gaff and colleagues (2007) suggested that nondisclosure needs to be examined on a case-by-case basis, recognizing the many possible causes that may prevent disclosure, some of which are discussed above. Probands find themselves in a very difficult position; they must find a balance between causing the potential psychological harm the information may inflict on a family member and providing critical information that could have important health consequences (Gaff et al., 2007).

Experts recommend that probands follow certain steps when communicating genetic risk information to family members. First, probands should start by identifying whom, how, and where to tell. Second, they should find out how much these family members already know about this genetic risk and how much they want to know. Third, probands should then share the genetic test information and respond to family members' emotions. Finally, they should refer family members to a genetic counselor and share other materials with them (Daly et al., 2001). Family members need each other's support throughout the process of testing (Koehly et al., 2008). Genetic counselors and other health-care providers have been urged to explore and address family communication issues in their meetings with clients (Gaff, Galvin, & Bylund, 2010).

Discussion   Family members' ongoing discussions about genetic risk are difficult and may not occur for several reasons. Some types of diseases may be more difficult to discuss than others. For example, one study compared families' experiences talking about genetic testing for Huntington's disease, a condition that causes brain cells to degenerate, with other families' experiences talking about genetic testing for hereditary breast and ovarian cancer (HBOC). Findings revealed that family members tested for Huntington's disease were less forthcoming with information than family members being tested for HBOC (Hamilton, Bowers, & Williams, 2005). In their study of the impact of genetic testing for Huntington's disease on a particular family and members' interactions, Sobel and Cowan (2003) reported that members experienced significant loss and grief. Siblings found themselves split along lines of those who carried the gene and those who did not. Members who learned they did not carry the gene felt as if they had lost membership in the family because they were excluded from meaningful and emotional conversations. The diversity of members' responses to their test results led to distancing and silence.

Talking to children about genetic testing can be difficult for many reasons (Sullivan & McConkie-Rosell, 2010). In cases of genetic risk for breast and ovarian cancer, the offspring usually are not encouraged to be tested until they are 25 years old. Those who get tested may react differently—some may find the tests confirm what they already thought, while others may be devastated by their diagnosis. Some may search for more information on the Internet, from other family members, or through health-care providers. Offspring report both positive and negative aspects of knowing. For instance, advantages include being able to change health behavior and being aware of future genetic testing and surgical opportunities. Disadvantages include worrying about or developing a fatalistic attitude toward developing cancer (Bradbury et al., 2009).

Issues of privacy and conflict may arise when one member of the family gains genetic information and another wants to remain unaware. Imagine a family with Lynn, a 58-year-old mother diagnosed with early-stage breast cancer. After discussing her family history of breast cancer with her oncologist, Lynn decides to be tested for a genetic condition that is often present in women with family histories of breast cancer. Lynn discusses this decision with her daughters, Julianne, 28 and Meg, 32, and invites them to meet with the genetic counselor and be tested as well. Meg agrees, but Julianne declines saying she would rather not know. Both Lynn and Meg test positive for the genetic condition, which means the possibility that Julianne has the genetic condition is increased. Lynn and Meg are now faced with the conflicting desires of wanting to respect Julianne's wishes by not disclosing this information and wanting to give Julianne information about cancer prevention.

As studies on the results of the Human Genome Project continue to unfold, and more family members choose to receive their genetic profile, family discussion of genetics will increase. Partners will share genetic information with each other in order to determine what, if any, genetic disorder may present itself in their biological child. They may also discuss the use of in vitro fertilization (IVF) to create embryos that can be tested for certain genetic disorders. The future holds the potential for many difficult family conversations related to genetic inheritances.

Money and Financial Stress

"Bankruptcy, short sale, foreclosure"—such terms have entered conversations in many homes. Traditionally, the topic of family finances has been viewed as an adult topic, one to be discussed between husbands and wives, adult partners, or household adults such as a mother and grandmother. Many adolescent or adult children do not know how much money their parents make or how much money the family has in savings. According to Jellinek and Beresin (2008), "Virtually every interpersonal dynamic—controlling, restrictive, aggressive, secretive, guilt-inducing, ambivalent, generative, altruistic—can be manifested in how money is used in families" (p. 251). This lack of disclosure or shared knowledge about a family's financial situation may happen for a few reasons. First, money tends to be equated with power, self-esteem, and success and failure. Money is used as a "way of showing off, wielding power, and creating an image—a persona for an individual" (Jellinek & Beresin, 2008, p. 249). Second, parents may perceive that they need to protect their children from feeling worried or concerned by not talking about financial difficulties (Romo, 2011). Particularly in cases where family finances are compromised by layoffs or debt, parents may choose to not disclose this to their children so that their children can go on with their everyday activities without worry. Third, some parents believe that talking in detail about finances is a cultural taboo (Romo, 2011). This may be something that they learned in their own families of origin. Talking about money both within and outside the family becomes complicated; children may learn a communication rule, "Don't ask Mom or Dad their salaries," or "Do not talk about our family's money outside the family." All of these reasons are related to the family's rules and the criteria for making the decision to reveal or conceal information from communication privacy management theory discussed in Chapter 3.

Until the last quarter of the twentieth century, family money was a highly gendered issue; an adult male's family identity was linked to the breadwinner and financial decision-making role. In recent decades, however, female careers and earning power have changed. Sixty-three percent of women are either the primary breadwinner or a co-breadwinner, earning at least a quarter of the family's income. Additionally, 38 percent of wives earn as much or more than their husbands (Boushey, 2009). Today, couples' ability to adapt to a situation in which the man earns less than the woman depends a great deal on the examples set by their parents.

The meaning of money varies across ethnicity and culture. In more individualistic cultures, money is managed within nuclear households with limited expectations of sharing with extended family members. In more collectivist cultures, money is viewed as an extended family resource; wealthier members have responsibilities to share some of their earnings with other relatives, such as when a niece needs money for college or medical treatment. In many African American families, resources are shared within social networks providing direct and in-kind assistance that softens financial strain (Lincoln, 2007). These different approaches may create tension in intercultural partnerships such as the one depicted in the following:

My husband grew up in a middle-class white family with parents who provided well for them. I grew up in an African American extended family in which everyone helped everyone out. In addition to providing for their own children, those who succeeded were expected to help nieces or nephews whose families were less well-off. Carl and I argue a lot about how much of "our" money or "my" money goes to my younger relatives for tuition or special educational programs. His nieces and nephews get Christmas and birthday presents but we do not take any financial responsibility for their education.

Over the past decade many families have experienced multiple economic challenges. You may have heard friends or relatives expressing anxiety about their financial state, lowered property values, and plummeting retirement funds. Perhaps your family suffered serious financial setbacks. The media reported the rising number of homeless families, the return of young adults to their parents' homes, the loss of employment by parents in well-established careers, the struggles of recent college graduates to find employment, and the additional workplace stresses faced by those fortunate enough to remain employed. Many families were totally unprepared for an economic downturn; members who had never talked with each other about family finances or family financial planning were confronted with challenging conversations.

Adult family members confronted issues such as sending children to less expensive colleges and universities, setting ground rules for twenty-something adults moving back home, assessing whether to help a brother's family with the mortgage, and trying to cut out "extras" ranging from giving up the second car to eating out. Conversations included topics such as closing out credit cards, living without health insurance, and going on a "staycation" rather than a vacation (Mckee-Ryan, Song, Wanberg, & Kinicki, 2005). In some cases, family members discussed whether to declare bankruptcy.

Because economic stress affects individual well-being and indirectly and directly influences family interaction (Conger et al., 1990), such conversations tend to address multiple family stresses. Partner or parental unemployment frequently results in depression, role anxiety, strained family relationships, and low self-esteem. Social networks change as resources diminish, altering social activities and social support. Increasing economic stress raises family tensions, which lead to diminished family relational quality and family disruption (Bartholomae & Fox, 2010). The recent financial difficulties, in the United States and abroad, impacts young people from working-class backgrounds particularly hard. They confront an erosion of the traditional markers of adulthood such as a good job, a house, and marriage, leaving them with insecure intimacies and an absence of choice (Silva, 2013). The adulthood and financial circumstances they imagined growing up are likely to elude many of these emerging adults (Arnett, 2012).

Gender stresses tend to complicate the issues. When unemployment occurs, traditional gender socialization may be upended. Losing the role of breadwinner or co-breadwinner leaves many males upset and depressed; conversely, females, even those with employment, may find themselves stressed at assuming the sole breadwinner role (Gudmunson, Beutler, Israelsen, McCoy, & Hill, 2007).

Financial strain also increases the incidence of couple disagreements and fighting, and decreases their quality time together. A study of the link between financial strain and marital instability involving almost 5,000 married couples revealed that "couple financial strain contributed strongly and *evenly* to increases in husband's emotional distress and wife's emotional distress" (Gudmunson et al., 2007, p. 371). Although couples were quite similar in terms of how they assessed their financial situation, their disagreements were strongly linked to increased couple fighting and decreased quality time together. The lack of couple quality time, compounded by the need to work extra hours or work nontraditional hours, was significantly linked to marital instability.

Not only does partner interaction suffer during times of economic instability but the quality of parenting tends to decline. When parents are stressed by economic threats and losses they exhibit lower levels of involvement with, and supportiveness of, their children (Gudmunson et al., 2007). In these circumstances parents are more likely to suffer from exhaustion, often from working extra hours, or depression leading to low energy and high distractibility. In these difficult economic circumstances, parental warmth and affective support declines (Mistry, Lowe, Remers, & Chien, 2008), as depicted in spousal warmth and affective support.

My father was laid off from his position as a computer engineer over a year ago. My parents resisted talking about it with us but we watched as he went on interview after interview with no luck. Eventually my mother went back to heavy drinking because of the worry and pressure on her to be the primary breadwinner. They began to have terrible fights after we went to bed. Right now he is in a final round of interviews for an administrative position. If he does not get it, I don't know how they will cope.

Throughout the past decade media and family professionals stressed the need for adult family members to talk with each other and their children about financial matters. You may have participated in such discussions. Depending on a family's life stage, discussions might involve middle-aged adults talking with their older parents about their financial status and needs; middle-aged parents sharing their financial status with their young adult or adolescent children as well as providing guidance about ways to manage their money; or young adult parents talking with children about saving and the importance of managing money and using debt wisely.

Although celebrity experts, television shows, blogs, listservs, and trade books provide countless suggestions on managing money, these ideas need to be discussed openly by family members, sometimes in conjunction with a financial adviser. Additionally, many adults seek professional advice about communicating with family members about financial issues. Some suggestions for partners' discussions include talking about feelings such as fear, loss, and guilt, and talking about your experience without blaming a partner or an individual family member. Middle-aged persons are advised to talk with their older parents about their financial status, asking questions such as "How much do you have—and is it enough?" and "Have you made long-term care arrangements?" (Max, 2009). In most cases, when the family can approach financial problems from the perspective of "we" have a challenge to solve, rather than blaming an individual, communication will be more productive.

Parents need to discuss financial matters and practices directly. A 2007 study by the Michael Cohen Group of the perceptions of teenagers regarding the nation's economy revealed that two-thirds of the respondents believed the economic crisis is having or will have a negative impact on their families (Tugend, 2008). A study of 420 college students revealed that parents had a moderately significant influence on their financial attitudes and behaviors but did not have an effect on their financial knowledge (Jorgensen & Savla, 2010), indicating a need for parents to learn how to discuss, teach, and model financial principles to their children. When talking with children, parents are advised to answer children's questions with as much information as they can handle. Popular advice to parents from work-family expert Ellen Galinsky includes avoiding using certain terminology with small children such as "fired," because it may raise images of guns and shooting, and when telling children the difficulties, also discuss the coping strategies that will be used (Abel, 2010).

Most experts remind adult family members that money does not determine a child's happiness. When asking adults in family workshops to go on a "journey of happy memories" from childhood, John DeFrain, an expert in family strengths, found that "adults rarely recall something that cost a lot of money" (Olson, DeFrain, & Skogrand, 2008, p. 345). Instead, they remember holiday traditions, Friday night rituals, doing chores together, or vacations. Serious discussions about family money are often difficult but they are necessary for the financial education of children and the management or resolution of family financial issues.

As parents age and adult children take on caregiving roles, the privacy boundaries that parents have around their finances may need to be reexamined. In a study of adult caregivers and their parents, Plander (2013) found that triggers for greater financial disclosure include physical or cognitive decline as well as the death of one of the spouses. Applying communication privacy management theory discussed in Chapter 3, the boundary linkages between parents and adult children about financial issues may be handled in one of three ways: explicitly (e.g., a parent bringing out all the documents for the adult child to see); implicitly (e.g., starting to write checks for the parent and slowly gaining more financial information); or through a crisis (e.g., a parent has a stroke and an adult child has to take over).

New Technology Challenges

Individuals living in a networked world can be categorized as digital natives, digital settlers, and digital immigrants (Palfrey & Gasser, 2008). The concept of digital natives and digital immigrants, labels coined by Marc Prensky (2001), emerged from conversations on generational differences and the digital world. **Digital Natives** are continuously connected by technology; they think and process information differently from previous generations because they are native speakers of the language of technology. These are toddlers who know how to start their favorite video on their parents' touch-screen smartphone; they are kids who text their parents from the backseat on a family trip, "Are we there yet?" Although **Digital Settlers** grew up in an analog world, they have become sophisticated in their use of technology though they also rely heavily on analog communication. These are parents who wonder how they could juggle so many responsibilities without the ability to work from home, pay bills online, and text a spouse to coordinate family activities. **Digital Immigrants** are those who were not born into the digital age and who have not adapted easily to new technologies. They may have learned to use e-mail or to go to social networking sites, but live much or all of their lives offline. These may be the grandparents who go onto e-mail on a weekly basis to send out a family e-mail update, but expect a handwritten thank-you note for a birthday gift. Although not all younger people are digital natives, a culture defined by age and interaction with information technologies, the number of such natives is increasing exponentially. Many families have members who represent each category of digital connection, which may lead to communication challenges or generational competence reversals.

Some scholars argue that we are moving into an interpersonal world in which we are "alone together," foregoing the benefits of direct human interaction as well as solitude. Turkle (2011) suggests that our use of technology replaces interpersonal connections. We are offered such substitutes as robots and machine-mediated relationships. Family members may text each other when one is another part of the house, or sit together in the living room interacting with others and each other on social media. While digital media use is certainly changing family interaction, we want to be careful not to assume all of the changes are negative; for instance, a parent may text an adolescent, even while at home, as this form of communication can at times reduce conflict.

Risky online behavior may include disclosing personal information, meeting up offline with online acquaintances, sharing photos with strangers, or bullying peers. However, Palfrey and Gasseer (2008) argue that "the more often 'significant adults' talk to young people about their experiences online (and occasionally monitor what they are doing), the less likely the youth are to engage in risky behavior" (p. 101). In many homes those conversations do not occur because parents are unprepared to discuss these issues. In the following discussion, we focus on cyberbullying, sexting, and sharing private information.

In today's world many children are at risk of being a victim of cyberbullying (Palfrey & Glasser, 2008), but parents often feel helpless to prevent it. **Cyberbullying**, or deliberate and repeated harm inflicted through phones and computers, presents serious challenges to young people and their families. Willard (2007) has identified seven cyberbullying behaviors. These include the following: *flaming*, online fighting with angry language; *harassment*, repeated sending of nasty and insulting messages; *denigration*, spreading rumors or gossip about someone; *impersonation*, pretending to be someone else with negative effects on that person; *outing*, sharing someone else's private, embarrassing information online; *exclusion*, intentionally excluding an individual; and *cyberstalking*, intense and repeated harassment that is threatening or creates fear (pp. 1–2).

In recent years the media has provided numerous examples of adolescent suicides attributed to cyberspace bullying; the phenomenon has become so prevalent that the term "cyberbullicide" was coined to describe "suicide directly or indirectly influenced by experiences with online aggression" (Hinduja & Patchin, 2009, n.p.). Cyberbullying represents a particularly dangerous form of harm because, in contrast to former decades when home provided sanctuary from taunting peers, cyberbullying has become a 24/7 experience for many preadolescents and adolescents. A study of 2,000 middle school students reported that 20 percent of respondents indicated seriously thinking about attempting suicide due to cyberbullying (Hinduja & Patchin, 2009). The students reported the most frequent form of cyberbullying involved posting "something online about another person to make others laugh," whereas cyber victims chose receiving "an upsetting e-mail from someone you know." Cyberbullying victims were almost twice as likely to have attempted or

Parents can monitor their children's online activities.

considered suicide compared to youth who had not experienced cyberbullying. In many cyberbullying cases parents expect schools to provide justice and protection for their children, although school district discipline codes seldom address authority over student cell phones or home computers (Hoffman, 2010). Parental discussions about cyberbullying can be important. In a recent study, researchers surveyed middle and high school students about their experiences with cyberbullying. They found that when students believed their parents would punish them, they were less likely to participate in these bullying activities (Hinduja & Patchin, 2012). However, many parents do not discuss these issues with their children or ask their children if they have witnessed or experienced such interactions.

Another technology-related issue with dangerous implications for younger family members involves **sexting,** or the sending of text messages with pictures of children or teens who are naked or engaged in sexual acts (American Academy of Pediatrics, 2009). Sexting has emerged as a serious problem for many young people and their families. In addition to causing emotional pain, and cited as the cause of suicide for a few young people, this activity has serious legal consequences. Conflicting information exists about how prevalent this behavior is. One online panel study (AP-MTV Digital Abuse Study, 2009) found that three in ten young people have been involved in some type of naked texting (the overall incidence is higher among 18- to 24-year-olds and 14- to 17-year-olds). Researchers found that 29 percent reported receiving messages "with sexual words or images" by text or on the Internet. One in ten had shared a naked image of themselves. Nearly one in five recipients of such texts reported passing them on to someone else. Approximately 30 percent reported sharing sexts as a joke or to be funny. Most reported not considering the risks and implications of such behavior. However, a different national study of youth who use the Internet found that only about 10 percent have been involved in some sort of sexually suggestive imaging transfers (Mitchell, Finkelhor, Jones, & Wolak, 2012). Youth's sexting behavior is related to their sexual behaviors, substance use behaviors, and emotional health behaviors (Dake, Price, Maziarz, & Ward, 2012). It appears that many parents do not know about this practice or do not believe their children would participate in such a practice. Little is known about actual parent-child communication regarding sexting.

Another important, but less dramatic, concern involves sharing personal and family information through new technologies. In traditional face-to-face communication, conversations are relatively secure, but that level of privacy does not exist in an Internet-connected world (Grill, 2011). Family members run the risk of sharing each other's news, or violating their communication privacy, as e-mails are forwarded, posts are shared, and members of every generation use social networking sites. The size of the potential audience for private family information is staggering. For example, Facebook has more than 400 million active users; an average user has 130 friends, some of whom are family members (Facebook.com, 2010). In recent years increasing numbers of older people have joined Facebook, often requesting to friend grandchildren or other younger relatives. In many cases this results in younger relatives changing their privacy settings. A family's offline privacy rules are associated with how children respond to their parent's Facebook friend request (Child & Westermann, 2013).

In their national survey of parental mediation of children's Internet use, Livingstone and Helsper (2008) examined parental attempts to regulate their children's media use in order to maximize the advantages of the online environment by using strategies such as rule-making, restrictions, co-viewing, or co-using. They found that co-use was widespread; two-thirds of parents discuss Internet use with their children, almost half watch the screen, and about a third remain physically close when a child is online. Although parental involvement had some impact, one major exception was the ban on giving out personal information online involving buying, filling out forms, and taking quizzes. The study reported that the characteristics of the children determined the incidence of their online risks. Older boys with high skill levels were at the greatest online risk. The authors concluded, "the relative ineffectiveness of parental mediation in reducing risks is consistent with other recent research on children's Internet use" (n.p.).

Not all parents, grandparents, or guardians are able to use the technology well enough to understand these issues or hold meaningful conversations about dangerous online behavior. In some families, older siblings or cousins go online to see what a young relative posted, such as looking at a Facebook page to see if any information could be used to cyberbully them (Hinduja & Patchin, 2010). A family that owns multiple devices that access the Internet may find it difficult to monitor them consistently, as shown in the following example:

One Saturday morning, my young son was sitting on the couch with an iPod and headphones. I just assumed he was watching an approved video or playing a game. His older brother walked by and notified me that in fact he was watching pornographic videos. A school friend had told him to search a certain term online. What a wake-up call that was for his mother and me! We had always followed the rule of having the family computer in a shared area of the house, but it hadn't even crossed our minds he would access these kinds of videos on an iPod.

Parents need to communicate with their children and adolescents about their online lives. They need to see their children's profiles on Facebook or other social networking sites as well as stay abreast of cyber trends, such as bullying or sexting. Only then will parents be able to talk with their children and provide guidance regarding digital experiences. As more parents become digital natives and digital settlers, more family conversations about these difficult topics will occur.

Approaches for Improving Family Communication

If you believed that communication in your family should be improved, what would you do or say? As families go through predictable developmental stresses as well as unpredictable stresses, frequently members do not know how to move forward effectively. When communication problems exist in your family, perhaps you would be willing to talk with other family members about the communication problems or perhaps have your family participate in a structured improvement program. Strategies designed to support positive family change include personal, instructional, and therapeutic approaches. Most of the personal and instructional approaches are designed for functional partnerships or families whose members wish to make changes in their relationships or to find ways to manage a particularly stressful situation. Therapeutic approaches are designed to aid a couple or a family to cope with a serious problem or repair a troubled relationship.

Personal Approaches

Many partnerships or whole family systems attempt to change their relational communication patterns through personal efforts. Personal approaches include (1) seeking education, such as that found through books or the media; (2) engaging in conscious negotiation with partners or family members; (3) establishing ongoing time commitments with family members; and (4) obtaining support from friends or members of a supportive network.

Personal Education　A perusal of bookstore shelves, videos, or websites reveals countless resources devoted to improving family relationships, parenting skills, and the ability to deal with relational change. There are checklists, rules, and prescriptions for improving family meetings, sexual communication, and approaches to conflict. The "checkup" stands as a cornerstone concept of the personal approach to improving partner or family communication. Family members are encouraged to call for a conversation on the question "How are we doing?" Taking a family communication course, as most readers of this book are doing, can be a helpful first step.

Personal Negotiation　In many families, members discuss new ways to communicate or to manage problems. Identifying recurring "trouble spots" in their relationship and planning how to avoid them is a first step. Members may learn to recognize predictable situations when intimacy or conflict becomes threatening and find ways to name it and adapt. Some couples create and practice their own rules for effective decision-making and conflict management and to develop best practices for relationship maintenance, as discussed previously in Chapters 5, 8, and 9.

Parents may consciously attempt to defuse high-anxiety moments by engaging in emotion coaching, trying to listen empathically, or helping a child verbally label his or her emotions (Gottman & DeClaire, 1997). Parents and children learn to share their feelings when silence would be more comfortable but less effective. Significant change involves ongoing communication efforts. One discussion seldom results in permanent change, as demonstrated in the following example:

In my own marriage, my wife and I have been using two mechanisms to serve as a kind of checkup on our marital relations. First, we have learned to communicate both the negative and the positive feelings we have. Second, we sit down together with no outside distractions and, while maintaining eye contact, express our innermost feelings or our current concerns. We each try very hard to listen rather than judge the other. This ritual is a special part of our relationship.

How do conversations about addressing problems and changing family communication patterns actually start? Sometimes one or more family members express their nagging feelings that things could be better. They may have discovered new ideas for partner or family interaction through the media, friends, or religious or educational experiences. They decide to risk trying out new behaviors and evaluating their effectiveness, an approach that involves ongoing mutual cooperation.

Instead of discussing a concern, an individual family member may start by choosing to change his or her behavior, hoping that this change will affect another family member's behavior. From a systems perspective, you can imagine how one member's change in communication may result in another family member's change as well. We do need to realize that these individual efforts may be met with initial suspicion or even strong resistance. The following example from a young adult illustrates how she and her sister used this strategy to change communication in her family:

My father, although being very caring and supportive, has always been the type to only rarely express his love verbally. While in college, my younger sister and I realized that maybe we didn't say "I love you" very often to him. So we decided to see if we could encourage some change. Whenever we talked on the phone with Dad from then on, we would end our conversation with "Love you!" or "I love you." At first Dad would just respond with a pause followed by "Goodbye," but soon he began saying, "We love you" (meaning he and Mom) before hanging up. Still, that was a good change, and we were happy to hear it. He still rarely says, "I love you," but according to our other siblings he ends phone calls with "Love you" to them as well.

Ongoing Time Commitments One relational change strategy involves instituting "couple time," or "family meetings." Members agree to come together regularly in order to discuss and address concerns and problems. Members at all stages of family development agree to reserve times to listen to one another and "really talk." Some families find their topics emerge easily and directly, such as during regular debriefing conversations; others prefer to use a guidebook that prescribes topics or provides questions or discussion material. Sometimes just planning to spend time together makes a difference. Researchers have consistently found that meals together, with both parents especially, is related to the emotional well-being of adolescents (Offer, 2012).

Family meetings or family councils create opportunities for all members to address concerns. Such experiences provide children with important practice in discussion and decision-making. Many religious groups recommend such meetings. Within the Family Home Evening program developed by the Church of Jesus Christ of Latter-Day Saints, church members are encouraged to set aside one night a week to be together as a family, spending time in religious study and family activities (Building a Strong Family, 2010). Topics of discussion include strengthening family bonds, honesty, and compiling family history, as well as religious subjects. Other groups, many of them religion based, support similar programs.

Support Networks In an era when many family members live at great distances from each other, individuals, couples, and families are creating support systems to help them face family problems. Informal support networks, such as friends or members of a faith community, provide adequate support for some families. People are developing voluntary or chosen families that may include persons who are not related but who stand in or supplement for family who are physically or emotionally unavailable. Less commonly, these voluntary families take the place of family of origin when that family has rejected a family member or following the death of key family members (Braithwaite et al., 2010). Talking about family issues may help put things into perspective, serve as a point of emotional release, or help rebuild a marriage (Faith and Marriage Ministries, 2010). Sometimes the support groups become a kind of extended network of friends who provide the caring that biological families cannot or will not provide (Weston, 1993). A personal testimonial to such a group follows:

For eight months I have participated in a divorce recovery group through our church and it has helped me with parenting my three sons and coping with my ex-husband's remarriage. This group has saved my sanity more than once and I have reached some important insights about loss and change.

Instructional Approaches

There has been a significant growth in marital and family enrichment programs designed to instruct individuals, couples, and whole family systems on more productive ways to interact and function. Generally their purpose is educational, not counseling. Couples may participate in marriage and family enrichment programs that attempt to assist relatively healthy couples to develop interpersonal skills that will enhance their relationship and help them to develop relational strengths and strategies for coping with difficulties (Cole & Cole, 1999).

Instructional programs provide families without major problems with facts, skills, and information to help prevent serious relational difficulties. Countless national and local programs assist married or cohabiting partners as well as parents and children to improve their relational lives, including their communication skills and practices (Smart Marriages, 2010).

Marital/Partner Enrichment Programs Multiple national organizations offer **marriage enrichment programs**. These programs, which began in the 1950s and 1960s, are designed to enhance couple or partner growth. Most programs insist that partners attend together, although, increasingly, versions of these programs are offered online. Communication skills appear as the core of most of these marital enrichment efforts. Most persons who attend enrichment programs are self-referred and self-screened, and most programs discourage partners facing serious difficulties from attending. The Internet makes it possible for individuals to have access to quality education through online clearinghouses such as the National Healthy Marriage Resource Center (www.healthymarriageinfo.org).

Although numerous systems-oriented marital and family enrichment programs emphasize communication, only a few representative ones will be described here, just to give you an idea about what is available. The most well known and frequently attended marital enrichment programs include the Marriage Encounter programs, the Prevention and Relationship Enhancement Program (PREP), and PREPARE/ENRICH.

The Marriage Encounter, a weekend program sponsored by Worldwide Marriage Encounter and conducted by a leadership team consisting of three couples and a religious leader, follows a simple pattern. Team members provide the information and modeling designed to facilitate each participating couple's private dialogue. Through a series of talks, team members reveal personal and intimate information to encourage participants to do the same when alone. After each talk, couples separate to write individual responses to the issues raised by the talk. Each partner must write his or her feelings about the topic before they come together for a private dialogue using each other's written responses as a starting point. Although the program began within the Catholic faith, almost all religious traditions offer a version (WWME, 2010). This is a face-to-face workshop; however, the program also offers online support after completing the workshop. The second opening vignette depicts Angeli and Dante who spent so much time involved in working and taking care of their children that they had little time or energy to focus on their marriage. Their decision to attend a Marriage Encounter weekend was one step toward taking care of their relationship.

The Prevention and Relationship Enhancement Program (PREP) represents a research-based skills approach. The program is designed to teach couples better communication and conflict strategies, assist them in clarifying and evaluating expectations, promote understanding of their choices reflecting commitment, and enhance the positive bonding in the relationship (Jakubowski, Milne, Brunner, & Miller, 2004). Recently an online version of PREP has been piloted (Braithwaite & Fincham, 2009, 2011), as well as a version for couples having their first child (Trillingsgaard, Baucom, Heyman, & Elklit, 2012).

Finally, PREPARE/ENRICH provides a customized couple assessment designed to reveal a couple's strengths and areas of growth as well as facilitator-led offline guidance and online programs. The program reflects a Christian perspective. This program, developed by David Olson and colleagues, is grounded in the circumplex model of family functioning and includes inventories and guidelines for counselor/leader training as well as a research team. The program's national survey of over 50,000 married couples reveals that the areas most predictive of happy versus unhappy couples are communication, flexibility, closeness, personality, compatibility, and conflict resolution (Olson, Olson-Sigg, & Larson, 2012). The Couple Checkup (Olson, Olson-Sigg, & Larson, 2008) provides communication-oriented couples' enrichment guidance.

In addition, the Gottman Institute provides multiple enrichment programs. One two-day program, the Art & Science of Love, offers couples the opportunity to learn practical strategies to improve their relationships. This workshop is based on more than 40 years of research by Gottman and colleagues, as cited throughout this textbook (www.gottman.com).

Family Life Education   Family life education programs are defined as "any educational activity ... designed to strengthen relationships in the home and foster positive individual, couple, and family development" (Duncan & Goddard, 2011, p. 4). As with couple education, family life education is offered face to face, via video, and via the Internet as well.

One widely known program is Systematic Training for Effective Parenting (STEP), a set of eight-week online classes, which was developed by the American Guidance Service (AGS). Based on Adlerian psychology, STEP focuses on the goals of children's behavior, the natural and logical consequence of the behavior, and good versus responsible parenting practices. The program stresses active listening, I-messages, and family meetings in its workbook materials (www.steppublishers.com). There are specialized programs for stepfamilies aimed at normalizing their experiences and developing communication skills to enhance family life.

Government and educational institutions have entered the family enrichment area in response to divorce rates and child neglect or abuse. However, whether and how such government programs impact families and family structures is not well understood. A recent analysis of government-supported marriage enrichment initiatives in the United States found little support for the impact of these programs on marriage (Hawkins, Amato, & Kinghorn, 2013).

Secondary prevention efforts are also increasing as more schools, communities, and therapists offer their services, in both in-person and online formats. Such programs are able to reach a wider audience, but need to be designed effectively to engage participants (Hughes, Bowers, Mitchell, Curtiss, & Ebata, 2012).

Military Family Education Interventions   As discussed in Chapter 11, military families face many relational challenges when a family member is deployed. Due to the tremendous strain this puts on these family systems, clinicians and researchers have developed family education programs specifically to help military families. One such program is entitled FOCUS (Families OverComing Under Stress). This program offers education, including skills training for military families, with the goal of enhancing coping with experiences related to deployment, and it has been shown to demonstrate positive impacts on emotional and behavioral adjustment (Lester et al., 2012). Another program, ADAPT (After Deployment, Adaptive Parenting Tools), is specifically focused on helping parents and children following deployment. This program builds on the resilience of military families, helps parents to address family stress within the context of the deployment cycle, and helps parents use emotion regulation to effectively parent (Gewirtz, Erbes, Polusny, Forgatch, & DeGarmo, 2011).

Appraisal of Enrichment Programs   Given the range and type of programs, as well as the diversity of communication content and skills built into these programs, questions have been raised regarding their effectiveness. A review of 13 specific marital enrichment programs (Jakubowski et al., 2004) led the authors to conclude that "only four programs could be considered 'efficacious'." Another evaluative review (Balswick & Balswick, 2007) covered a wide range of programs for their quality and research base concerning issues such as program content, user friendliness, teaching materials, exercises, gender roles, and the degree to which the program reflects a biblical or theological perspective. These authors concluded that much variation existed among programs. A key unifying focus was learning good communication and conflict resolution skills. Typical programs addressed issues including children, sex, money, in-laws, religion, roles, and personality differences. Researchers have also recently been interested in understanding the effectiveness of "self-directed" programs—programs that are either entirely or in part done in a couple's home without an educator present. Many of these self-directed portions of programs are Internet based. In reviewing these studies, researchers concluded that combining in-person and self-directed programs may be of the most benefit to participants (McAllister, Duncan, & Hawkins, 2012). Finally, analyses of enrichment programs focused on stepfamilies found that these programs do have some positive impact on stepfamily functioning and parenting (Lucier-Greer & Adler-Baeder, 2012).

Therapeutic Approaches

Partners or families experiencing severe relational pain or crisis are most effectively served by therapy. A vast body of family-oriented therapeutic literature exists (Nichols, 2008; Pinsof & Wynne, 1995). In this section we are only able to introduce the concept of **family therapy**, but we do want to stress that it is an important avenue for families to consider when their problems go beyond what problem-solving or educational efforts can address. Individual therapy has long been an established approach to dealing with personal problems or illnesses. The one-to-one, counselor-client relationship remains one valid therapeutic approach that can give an individual insights and strategies for managing problems. However, when a relational system encounters a severe crisis or long-term dysfunctional patterns, family or systems counseling presents an appropriate approach.

Exactly what does family therapy entail? The goal of family therapy is to identify family patterns that contribute to a behavior disorder or mental illness and help family members break those habits. Family therapy involves discussion and problem-solving sessions with the family. Some of these sessions may involve group, couple, or one-on-one sessions. In family therapy, the web of interpersonal relationships is examined and, ideally, communication is strengthened within the family. A description of a family therapy experience follows:

Two years ago, my family went into therapy because my younger brother was flunking school and shoplifting and his treatment center required the entire family to become involved in the treatment program. The therapist stressed that Chris' acting out was a family problem, not just Chris' problem. After a few months we were able to understand our patterns of family interaction that "fed" Chris' problem. The therapy forced my mother and stepfather to deal with some problems in their marriage that they had ignored and allowed us to make enough changes that Chris could return to high school and control the shoplifting.

Communication issues emerged as a key feature of the family therapy movement because many of the pioneers, most notably Virginia Satir, focused explicit attention on communication patterns. Early family therapy practices relied heavily on systems theory's assumptions about change and context. Once therapists encountered the whole family system, they realized that often the difficulties of the "problem" member served to stabilize the system and deflect attention from key family issues and that increased parental collaboration served as an effective strategy for breaking up the strong parent-child coalition (Olson, 2000, p. 163). Therefore, problems of individual

A couple often gains insight into their problems when a third party helps to clarify issues.

members must be examined within their family context. Furthermore, attention must be paid to how communication among family members affects members' alliances.

Family communication practices and patterns frequently play a role in therapy. After interviewing counselors about couples' communication problems, Vangelisti (1994a) reported that the most frequently noted communication problems included failing to take the other's perspective when listening, blaming the other for negative occurrences, and criticizing the other. Counselors believed that communication problems resulted from patterns taught to individuals by their families of origin. A majority of counselors viewed communication as a manifestation of more fundamental difficulties; only one-quarter viewed communication as the central issue. Olson (2000) argued that although increasing positive communication skills of couples and families can facilitate change, it is a necessary but not sufficient condition to alter a family's cohesion and adaptability. An important therapeutic goal is to provide members with skills to negotiate system change over time.

Currently family therapists also focus on challenging issues of culture and gender and their effects on the treatment process. The growing number of culturally diverse families that need the services of family therapists has led to increasing interest in cross-cultural family norms and treatment approaches (McGoldrick, Giordano, & Garcia-Preto, 2005a). Cross-cultural family relationships encounter differences in such areas as attitudes toward marriage, male-female roles, and the significance of extended family. Although few therapists can demonstrate expertise in communication patterns of multiple cultures, it is essential for therapists to be open to cultural variability and the relativity of their own values (Hines, Preto, McGoldrick, Almeida, & Weltman, 2005).

Some critics suggest that family therapy has been grounded in beliefs about gender and sexual orientation that limit relational flexibility. Knudson-Martin and Laughlin (2005) argued that family therapy should use a relationship model that is founded on equality, not gender. Therapists are encouraged to examine myths that partners hold about male and female roles. For example, a heterosexual couple may present with the husband's complaint that his wife is too busy to give him attention, whereas she asserts that her responsibilities at home and for her aging parents take all her time and energy. A therapist who operates from an equality model (a post-gender approach) would focus on the value of the wife's responsibilities and how the husband might also make contributions more equally in that realm. This type of approach would make the problem the couple's problem, rather than just the wife's problem (Knudson-Martin & Laughlin, 2005).

The past decades witnessed an increase in research addressing the overall effectiveness of family therapy and specific issues of unique approaches (Goldenberg & Goldenberg, 2008; Gottman et al., 2002). Gottman and colleagues (2002) argued that marital therapy remains relatively uninformed by empirical research, relying instead on clinical history. Research revealed that although marital therapy creates significant short-term effects, there is a high relapse factor over time. Those who show improvement are likely to be less distressed and more emotionally engaged, and show less negative affect. Ongoing research in family therapy will continue to inform therapeutic practice.

In order to change the current communication patterns within your family system, many options are open to you, ranging from individual approaches to the involvement of all members. Communication can be improved; families can grow through effort, time, and struggle. Relationships take work to maintain, and communication stands at the core of that process. The effort required is worthwhile since ultimately it is our loving connections that give life meaning (Wallerstein & Blakeslee, 1995). Intimate relationships encourage members to enlarge their visions of life and diminish their preoccupation with self. We are at our most considerate, most loving, and most selfless within the orbit of a well-functioning family.

Final Perspectives

Just as there is no one right way to be a family, there is no one family scholar who has all the answers on effective family communication. Each scholar reflects his or her own professional and personal orientation to family life. Historical perspectives tend to be descriptive, reflecting few cultural or structural variations. Henry (1973), in his classic work on family functioning, identified seven characteristics of family psychopathology. A reversed wording of his findings would lead to the following characteristics of well-functioning families: (1) interactions are patterned and meaningful, (2) there is more compassion and less cruelty, (3) persons are not scapegoats because problems are identified with the appropriate persons, (4) members exhibit appropriate self-restraint, (5) boundaries are clear, (6) life includes joy and humor, and (7) misperceptions are minimal. Virginia Satir (1988) maintained that untroubled and nurturing families demonstrate the following: "Self-worth is high; communication is direct, clear, specific, and honest; rules are flexible, human, appropriate, and subject to change; and the linking to society is open and hopeful" (p. 4). Bochner and Eisenberg (1987) suggested that the following features are characteristic of optimal family functioning: trust, enjoyment, lack of preoccupation with themselves, and the maintenance of conventional boundaries.

As we have described, families can find advice on healthy relationships and happy families from countless sources. There is popular advice literature, based on expert opinion and research, which supports the positions of academic researchers but presents the ideas in a more readable and prescriptive language. The challenge for families is how to locate sound and high-quality information and advice, with all of the resources out there. It can be overwhelming at times to evaluate the quality of different materials.

There are now sources that target information toward different family forms, for example, adoptive single parents, stepfamilies, and, more recently, same-sex families. You can recognize the value of these ideas as well as the need to be more inclusive of family diversity. Well-functioning families must be understood within their cultural and structural contexts. Communication patterns in a well-functioning Hispanic stepfamily may differ from that in an African American single-parent family system. Open communication may not be possible or desirable for every family, as noted here:

My family struggles with the concept of openness because although my two siblings and I were born in China, our parents moved to Michigan when we were young. We grew up in a western culture surrounded by families who talked about everything and expressed differences directly. My parents were raised to honor the wishes of their elders and not to question or argue about adult decisions. It has been very hard for them to adjust to open and direct communication patterns. We all struggle between the "new" way and the "old" way.

Low-income families, an often overlooked population in academic studies of well-functioning families, face challenges such as existing on public assistance, struggling with health problems, and dangerous living conditions. In spite of these challenges, however, many low-income families demonstrate family strengths, including good communication and problem-solving skills. These skills lead to positive outcomes such as meeting needs and providing activities for children that will help them succeed (Orthner, Jones-Sanpei, & Williamson, 2004).

As the authors of this book, we hold strong beliefs about well-functioning families. Our beliefs may be summarized as follows:

A healthy family recognizes the interdependence of all members and attempts to provide for the growth of the system as a whole, as well as the individual members involved. These families develop a capacity for communication, adaptation, and cohesion that avoids functioning at an extreme level. Members welcome each life stage and attempt to adapt to variations in their family forms. Individuals seek to find joy while living in the present and creating a personal and familial support network. Healthy families exhibit levels of connection that permit members to feel cared for but not smothered. Family members make an effort to understand the central role of communication in co-creating family relationships and the underlying meanings of other members' communication. All members find a sense of connection in the family's stories, rituals, and cultural heritages.

Our beliefs have been influenced by our research, counseling, and teaching experiences, where we are repeatedly reminded of families that lack the necessary understanding of the central role of communication and the skills to negotiate their difficulties and an inability to understand the perspective of other family members. Meaningful family connections require consistent nurturing. In most families, day-to-day routines easily overwhelm members' lives, resulting in primarily functional rather than nurturing communication patterns. Families profit from taking time to ask "How are we doing as a family?" and "How can we improve our communication?" Well-functioning families are able to engage in metacommunication—they are able to talk about how members relate to each other and how, if necessary, the current communication patterns could be strengthened. Finally, strong families have learned the values of communication, commitment, caring, and change.

We leave you with the following jazz-ensemble metaphor, which captures the dynamics of a well-functioning family:

> I like to think of the family as a jazz ensemble, where members move with the flow of what's happening around them, looking for a harmony of sorts, playing off one another, going solo at times, always respecting the talents and surprises surrounding them. Standards, yes. Expectations, always. But everyone moving with the "feel" of the moment and one another. Anyone at anytime can say or shout, "This isn't working!" and can challenge other members toward a different beat or movement or settle into a silence that regenerates spontaneous creativity and energy. We do know "family" isn't a lonely drum in the distance or a plaintive flute on an empty stage. Family is found in the creative energy and interplay of its members. (Wilkinson, 1998)

Conclusion

This chapter explored perspectives and research addressing family communication and well-being. We think of well-being here as including family members' ability to communicate about physical health, capacity to hold difficult conversations on challenging topics, and willingness to engage in individual or structured enrichment experiences or couple or family therapy to strengthen their relationships. These family members have the capacity to profoundly affect each other's health through their attempts to persuade each other to adopt healthy behaviors, their interactions with health-care providers, and their family communication when a member is ill. Such families exhibit the capacity to engage in difficult conversations in order to ensure the health and well-being of members. It is imperative that members learn to talk about tough topics such as their shared genetic heritage, their economic challenges, and members' risky involvement in digital participation in dangerous practices. Finally, family members must be willing to consider engaging in strategies for improving marital and family communication, including personal actions, instructional programs, and therapeutic interventions. Such willingness demonstrates a level of commitment and openness to change, forcing participants to move beyond daily life patterns in order to reflect on and improve their family experience.

In Review

1. In what ways should family communication about health change over one's lifespan?
2. Identify and explain three effective and three ineffective ways for family members to influence each other's health.
3. How would you describe communication in a well-functioning family? Answer within a context of a specific developmental stage, culture, and family form (e.g., a two-parent, Chinese family with adolescents).
4. Analyze the prescriptions for marital or parent-child communication found in a popular book or magazine article. Evaluate the effectiveness of the advice based on your understanding of family systems and communication patterns.
5. What goals and criteria would you establish for a successful marriage or family enrichment program with a communication focus? Briefly describe the audience you envision (e.g., a stepfamily with school-aged children).
6. Take a position on the following question: To what extent should couples or parents be required by religious or civic institutions to engage in family enrichment workshops or family therapy?
7. In what ways would you predict that family therapy would differ across two ethnic groups?
8. Select a specific issue within the difficult conversation areas of genetics or money. Explain how you might suggest to a family you know how an adult member could address the topic meaningfully with other members.
9. Identify strategies that parents might use to stay abreast of digital media advances and ways they can effectively address their concerns with their children.

Key Words

Cyberbullying   325

Digital immigrant   325

Digital native   325

Digital settler   325

Family health rules   313

Family therapy   334

Health-care advocate   314

Marriage enrichment programs   331

Pragmatism   319

Prevarication   319

Proband   318

Sexting   327

REFERENCES

Abe, J. A. A., & Izard, C. E. (1999). Compliance, noncompliance strategies, and the correlates of compliance in 5-year-old Japanese and American children. *Social Development, 8,* 1–20.

Abel, K. (2010). When parents lose a job: Talking to kids about layoffs. *Family education network.* Retrieved from http://life.familyeducation.com/money-and-kids/communication/29623.html.

Abraham, K. M., & Stein, C. H. (2010). Staying connected: Young adults' felt obligation toward parents with and without mental illness. *Journal of Family Psychology, 24,* 125–134.

Adams, J. (2004). "This is not where I belong!" The emotional, ongoing and collective aspects of couples' decision making about where to live. *Journal of Comparative Family Studies, 35,* 459–484.

Addy, S., Engelhardt, W., & Skinner, C. (2013, January). Basic facts about low-income children. *National center for children in poverty.* Retrieved May 25, 2013, from http://www.nccp.org.

Afifi, T. D. (2003). "Feeling caught" in stepfamilies: Managing boundary turbulence through appropriate privacy coordination rules. *Journal of Social and Personal Relationships, 20,* 729–756.

Afifi, T. D., Afifi, W. A., Morse, C. R., & Hamrick, K. (2008). Adolescents' avoidance tendencies and physiological reactions to discussions about their parents' relationship: Implications for postdivorce and nondivorced families. *Communication Monographs, 75,* 290–317.

Afifi, T. D., Davis, S., & Denes, A. (in press). Biological and evolutionary theory. In D. O. Braithwaite & P. Schrodt (Eds.), *Engaging theories in interpersonal communication: Multiple perspectives* (2nd ed.). Thousand Oaks, CA: Sage.

Afifi, T. D., Granger, D. A., Denes, A., Joseph, A., & Aldeis, D. (2011). Parents' communication skills and adolescents' salivary α-amylase and cortisol response patterns. *Communication Monographs, 78,* 273–295.

Afifi, T. D., Huber, F. N., & Ohs, J. (2006). Parents' and adolescents' communication with each other about divorce-related stressors and its impact on their ability to cope positively with the divorce. *Journal of Divorce and Remarriage, 45,* 1–30.

Afifi, T. D., McManus, T., Hutchinson, S., & Baker, B. (2007). Inappropriate parental divorce disclosures, the factors that prompt them, and their impact on parents' and adolescents' well-being. *Communication Monographs, 74,* 78–102.

Afifi, T. D., & Nussbaum, J. (2006). Stress and adaptation theories: Families across the life span. In D. O. Braithwaite & L. A. Baxter (Eds.), *Engaging theories in family communication: Multiple perspectives* (pp. 276–292). Thousand Oaks, CA: Sage.

Afifi, T. D., & Olson, L. (2005). The chilling effect in families and pressure to conceal secrets. *Communication Monographs, 72,* 192–216.

Ahrons, C. R. (2000). Divorce: An unscheduled family transition. In B. Carter & M. McGoldrick (Eds.), *The expanded family life cycle: Individual, family and social perspectives* (3rd ed., pp. 381–398). Boston, MA: Allyn & Bacon.

Ahrons, C. R. (2005). Divorce: An unscheduled family transition. In B. Carter & M. McGoldrick (Eds.), *The expanded family life cycle: Individual, family and social perspectives* (3rd ed., pp. 381–398). Boston, MA: Allyn & Bacon.

Alberts, J. K. (1988). An analysis of couples' conversational complaints. *Communication Monographs, 55,* 184–196.

Alberts, J. K., Tracy, S. J., & Tretheway, A. (2011). An integrative theory of the division of domestic labor: Threshold level, social organizing and sensemaking. *Journal of Family Communication, 11,* 21–38.

Alberts, J. K., Yoshimura, C. G., Rabby, M., & Loschiavo, R. (2005). Mapping the topography of couples' daily conversation. *Journal of Social and Personal Relationships, 22,* 299–322.

Albrecht, T. L., & Goldsmith, D. J. (2003). Social support, social networks, and health. In T. L. Thompson, A. M. Dorsey, K. I. Miller, & R. Parrott (Eds.), *Handbook of health communication* (pp. 263–284). Mahwah, NJ: Lawrence Erlbaum.

Aldeis, D., & Afifi, T. D. (2013). College students' willingness to reveal risky behaviors: The influence of relationship and message type. *Journal of Family Communication, 13,* 92–113.

Aldous, J. (1990). Family development and the life course: Two perspectives on developmental change. *Journal of Marriage and Family, 52,* 571–583.

Aleman, M. W., & Helfrich, K. W. (2010). Inheriting the narratives of dementia: A collaborative tape of a daughter and mother. *Journal of Family Communication, 10,* 7–23.

Almeida, D. M., Wethington, E., & Chandler, A. L. (1999). Daily transmission of tensions between marital dyads and parent-child dyads. *Journal of Marriage and the Family, 61*(1), 49–61.

Almeida, T. (2005). Asian Indian families. In M. McGoldrick, J. Giordano, & N. Garcia-Preto (Eds.), *Ethnicity and family therapy* (3rd ed., pp. 377–394). New York, NY: The Guilford Press.

Amason, P., Wilson, M. L., & Rusinowski, J. (2012). Communication and management of the family crisis of infertility. In L. M. Webb & F. Dickson (Eds.), *Communication and family crisis* (pp. 29–58). New York, NY: Peter Lang.

Amato, P. R. (2001). Children of divorce in the 1990's. *Journal of Family Psychology, 15,* 355–370.

Amato, P. R., & Cheadle, J. (2005). The long reach of divorce: Divorce and child well-being across three generations. *Journal of Marriage and the Family, 67,* 191–206.

Amato, P. R., Loomis, L. S., & Booth, A. (1995). Parental divorce, marital conflict, and offspring well-being during early adulthood. *Social Forces, 73,* 895–915.

American Academy of Pediatrics. (2009). Help kids with cell phones get the message: Say no to "sexting." *AAP News, 30*(26). Retrieved from http://aapnews.aappublications.org/cgi/content/full/30/8/26-d.

American Bar Association, Commission on Domestic Violence. (2010). *Survey of recent statistics.* Retrieved from http://new.abanet.org/domesticviolence/Pages/Statistics.aspx#prevalence.

American Community Survey. (2009). *Same-sex couples in the 2008 American community survey.* Retrieved from http://www.law.ucla.edu/williaminstitute/pdf/ACS2008_WEBPOST_FINAL.pdf.

American Society for Reproductive Medicine. (2013). *Five million babies born with help of assisted reproductive technologies.* Retrieved December 16, 2013, from http://www.asrm.org/Five_Million_Babies_Born_with_Help_of_Assisted_Reproductive_Technologies/

Anderson, K. L., Umberson, D., & Elliott, S. (2004). Violence and abuse in families. In A. Vangelisti (Ed.), *Handbook of family communication* (pp. 629–649). Mahwah, NJ: Lawrence Erlbaum.

Anderson, S. A., & Sabatelli, R. M. (2007). *Family interaction: A multigenerational developmental perspective* (4th ed.). Boston, MA: Allyn & Bacon.

Angier, N. (2013). The changing American family. *New York Times.* Retrieved December 6, 2013, from http://nyti.ms/18TEgrp.

AP-MTV digital abuse study. (2009). *A thin line.* Retrieved from http://www.athinline.org/MTV-AP_Digital_Abuse_Study_Executive_Summary.pdf.

Arnett, J. J. (2004). *Emerging adulthood: The winding road from the late teens through the twenties.* New York, NY: Oxford University Press.

Arnett, J. J. (2011). Emerging adulthood(s): The cultural psychology of a new life stage. In L. A. Jensen (Ed.), *Bridging cultural and developmental approaches to psychology: New synthesis in theory, research, and policy.* Oxford, UK: Oxford University Press.

Arnett, J. J. (2012). New horizons in research on emerging and young adulthood. In A. Booth, S. L. Brown, N. S. Landale, W. D. Manning, & S. M. McHale (Eds.), *Early adulthood in a family context* (pp. 231–244). New York, NY: Springer.

Arrington, M. I. (2005). "She's right behind me all the way": An analysis of prostate cancer narratives and changes in family relationships. *Journal of Family Communication, 5,* 141–162.

Avelin, P., Radestad, I., Safulnd, K., Wredling, R., & Erlandsson, K. (2013). Parental grief and relationships after the loss of a stillborn baby. *Midwifery, 29,* 668–673.

Avery, C. (1989). How do you build intimacy in an age of divorce? *Psychology Today, 23,* 27–31.

Babin, E. A. (2012). An examination of predictors of nonverbal and verbal communication of pleasure during sex and sexual satisfaction. *Journal of Social and Personal Relationships, 30,* 270–292.

Babrow, A. S., Kline, K. N., & Rawlins, W. K. (2005). Narrating problems and problematizing narratives: Linking problematic integration and narrative theory in telling stories about our health. In L. M. Harter, P. M. Japp, & C. S. Beck (Eds.), *Narratives, health and healing: Communication, research and practice* (pp. 31–52). Mahwah, NJ: Lawrence Erlbaum.

Bain, A. (1978). The capacity of families to cope with transitions: A theoretical essay. *Human Relations, 31,* 675–688.

Baker, C. W., Whisman, M. A., & Brownell, K. D. (2000). Studying intergenerational transmission of eating, attitudes and behaviors: Methodological and conceptual questions. *Health Psychology, 19,* 376–381.

Balswick, J., & Balswick, J. (2007). *Marriage enrichment program evaluation*. Retrieved from www.baylor.edu/content/services/document.php/41412.pdf.

Bao, Y., Fern, E. F., & Sheng, S. (2007). Parental style and adolescent influence in family consumption decisions: An integrative approach. *Journal of Business Research, 60*, 672–680.

Barbato, C. A., Graham, E. E., & Perse, E. M. (2001, April). *Communication in the family: An examination of the relationship of family communication climate and interpersonal communication motives*. Paper presented at the meeting of the National Communication Association, Atlanta, GA.

Barnett, R., Marshall, N., & Pleck, J. (1992). Men's multiple roles and their relationship to men's psychological distress. *Journal of Marriage and the Family, 54*, 358–367.

Barrera, M., Fleming, C. F., & Khan, F. S. (2004). The role of emotional social support in the psychological adjustment of siblings of children with cancer. *Child: Care, Health and Development, 30*, 103–111.

Barsevick, A. M., Montgomery, S. V., Ruth, K., Ross, E. A., Egleston, B. L., Bingler, R., …, Daly, M. B. (2008). Intention to communicate BRCA1/BRCA2 genetic test results to the family. *Journal of Family Psychology, 22*, 300–312.

Bartholet, E. (1993). *Family bonds: Adoption and the practice of parenting*. New York, NY: Houghton Mifflin.

Bartholomae, S., & Fox, J. (2010). Economic stress and families. In S. J. Price, C. A. Price, & P. C. McKenry (Eds.), *Families and change: Coping with stressful events and transitions* (4th ed., pp. 185–209). Los Angeles, CA: Sage.

Baxter, C., Cummins, R. A., & Yiolitis, L. (2000). Parental stress attributed to family members with and without disability: A longitudinal study. *Journal of Intellectual & Developmental Disability, 25*, 105–118.

Baxter, L. (1990). Dialectical contradictions in relational development. *Journal of Social and Personal Relationships, 7*, 69–88.

Baxter, L. A. (1991, November). *Bakhtin's ghost: Dialectical communication in relationships*. Paper presented at the annual meeting of the Speech Communication Association, Atlanta, GA.

Baxter, L. A. (2004). Relationships as dialogues. *Personal Relationships, 11*, 1–22.

Baxter, L. A. (2006). Relational dialectics theory: Multivocal dialogues of family communication. In D. O. Braithwaite & L. A. Baxter (Eds.), *Engaging theories in family communication: Multiple perspectives* (pp. 131–145). Thousand Oaks, CA: Sage.

Baxter, L. A. (2011). *Voicing relationships: A dialogic perspective*. Thousand Oaks, CA: Sage.

Baxter, L. A., & Babbie, E. (2004). *The basics of communication research*. Belmont, CA: Wadsworth.

Baxter, L. A., & Braithwaite, D. O. (2002). Performing marriage: Marriage renewal rituals as cultural performance. *Southern Communication Journal, 67*, 94–109.

Baxter, L. A., & Braithwaite, D. O. (2006). Family rituals. In L. H. Turner & R. West (Eds.), *The family communication sourcebook* (pp. 259–280). Thousand Oaks, CA: Sage.

Baxter, L. A., & Braithwaite, D. O. (2008). Relational dialectics theory: Crafting meaning from competing discourses. In L. A. Baxter & D. O. Braithwaite (Eds.), *Engaging theories in interpersonal communication: Multiple perspectives* (pp. 349–361). Thousand Oaks, CA: Sage.

Baxter, L. A., Braithwaite, D. O., Bryant, L., & Wagner, A. (2004). Stepchildren's perceptions of the contradictions in communication with stepparents. *Journal of Social and Personal Relationships, 21*, 447–467.

Baxter, L. A., Braithwaite, D. O., Golish, T. D., & Olson, L. N. (2002). Contradictions of interaction for wives of husbands with adult dementia. *Journal of Applied Communication Research, 29*, 221–247.

Baxter, L. A., Braithwaite, D. O., & Nicholson, J. H. (1999). Turning points in the development of blended families. *Journal of Personal and Social Relationships, 16*, 291–313.

Baxter, L. A., & Bylund, C. L. (2004). Social influence in close relationships. In J. S. Seiter & R. H. Gass (Eds.), *Perspectives on persuasion, social influence, and compliance gaining* (pp. 317–336). Boston, MA: Allyn & Bacon.

Baxter, L. A., Bylund, C. L., Imes, R., & Routsong, T. (2009). Parent-child perceptions of parental behavioral control through rule-setting for risky health choices during adolescence. *Journal of Family Communication, 9*, 251–271.

Baxter, L. A., Bylund, C. L., Imes, R. S., & Schieve, D. M. (2005). Family communication environments and rule-based social control of adolescents' healthy lifestyle choices. *Journal of Family Communication, 5*, 209–227.

Baxter, L. A., & Dindia, K. (1990). Marital partners' perceptions of marital maintenance strategies. *Journal of Social and Personal Relationships, 7*, 187–208.

Baxter, L. A., & Montgomery, B. M. (1996). *Relating: Dialogues and dialectics*. New York, NY: Guilford Press.

Baxter, L. A., & Norwood, K. (in press). Relational dialectics theory. In D. O. Braithwaite & P. Schrodt (Eds.), *Engaging theories in interpersonal communication* (2nd ed.). Thousand Oaks, CA: Sage.

Beach, W. A., & Good, J. S. (2004). Uncertain family trajectories: Interactional consequences of cancer diagnosis, treatment, and prognosis. *Journal of Social and Personal Relationships, 21*, 8–32.

Beatty, M. J., McCroskey, J. C., & Heisel, A. D. (1998). Communication apprehension as temperamental expression: A communibiological paradigm. *Communication Monographs, 64*, 197–219.

Beckman, L. J., Harvey, S. M., Satre S. J., & Walker, M. A. (1999). Cultural beliefs about social influence strategies of Mexican immigrant women and their heterosexual partners. *Sex Roles, 40*(11/12), 871–892.

Bedford, V. H., & Blieszner, R. (1997). Personal relationships in later-life families. In S. Duck (Ed.), *Handbook of personal relationships* (2nd ed., pp. 523–539). New York, NY: John Wiley & Sons.

Belch, M. A., Krentler, K. A., & Willis-Flurry, L. A. (2005). Teen Internet mavens: Influence in family decision making. *Journal of Business Research, 58*, 569–575.

Belsky, J., Jaffee, S. R., Sligo, J., Woodward, L., & Silva, P. A. (2005). Intergenerational transmission of warm-sensitive-stimulating parenting: A prospective study of mothers and fathers of 3-year-olds. *Child Development, 76*, 384–396.

Benazon, N. R., Foster, M. D., & Coyne, J. C. (2006). Expressed emotion, adaptation, and patient survival among couples coping with chronic heart failure. *Journal of Family Psychology, 20*, 328–334.

Bengston, V. L. (2001). Beyond the nuclear family: The increasing importance of multigenerational bonds. *Journal of Marriage and the Family, 63*, 1–16.

Benoit, P. J., Kennedy, K. A., Waters, R., Hinton, S., Drew, S., & Daniels, F. (1996, November). *Food, football, and family talk: Thanksgiving rituals in families*. Paper presented at the meeting of the Speech Communication Association, San Diego, CA.

Bergen K. M. (2010a). Accounting for difference: Commuter wives and the master narrative of marriage. *Journal of Applied Communication Research, 38*, 47–64.

Bergen, K. M. (2010b). Negotiating a "questionable" identity: Commuter wives and social networks. *Southern Communication Journal, 75*, 35–56.

Bergen, K. M., & Braithwaite, D. O. (2009). Identity as constituted in communication. In W. F. Eadie (Ed.), *21st Century communication: A sourcebook* (pp. 165–173). Thousand Oaks, CA: Sage.

Bergen, K. M., Kirby, E., & McBride, M. C. (2007). "How do you get two houses cleaned?": Accomplishing family caregiving in commuter marriages. *Journal of Family Communication, 7*, 287–307.

Berger, P., & Kellner, H. (1964). Marriage and the construction of reality: An exercise in the microconstruction of knowledge. *Diogenes, 46*, 1–25.

Berkowitz, D., & Marsiglio, W. (2007). Gay men: Negotiating procreative, father, and family identities. *Journal of Marriage and the Family, 69*, 366–381.

Bernard, T. S. (2013, February 22). In paid family leave, U.S. trails most of the globe. *New York Times*. Retrieved July 1, 2013, from http://www.nytimes.com./2013/02/23/your-money/us-trails-much-of-the-world-in-providing-paid-family-leave.html?_r=0.

Berryhill, B., Soloski, K., & Adams, R. (2012, June 19). Power of playtime: Single mothers can reduce stress by playing, engaging with children. *Science Daily*. Retrieved July 1, 2013, from http://www.sciencedaily.com.

Bianchi, S. M., & Casper, L. M. (2005). Explanations of family change: A family demographic perspective. In V. L. Bengston, A. C. Acock, K. R. Allen, P. Dilworth-Anderson, & D. M. Klein (Eds.), *Sourcebook of family theory & research* (pp. 93–117). Thousand Oaks, CA: Sage.

Black, C. (2001). *It will never happen to me* (2nd ed.). Center City, MN: Hazelden.

Blumenthal, R. G. (2012). *Multigenerational households: Together again*. Barron's. Retrieved May 2, 2013, from http://online.barrons.com.

Bochner, A. P., & Eisenberg, E. (1987). Family process: System perspectives. In C. Berger & S. Chaffee (Eds.), *Handbook of communication science* (pp. 540–563). Beverly Hills, CA: Sage.

Bodenmann, G., Meuwly, N., Bradbury, T. N., Gmelch, S., & Ledermann, T. (2010). Stress, anger, and verbal aggression in intimate relationships: Moderating effects of individual and dyadic coping. *Journal of Social and Personal Relationships, 27*, 408–424.

Bollis-Pecci, T. S., & Webb, L. M. (1997, November). *The Memphis family perceptions instrument: Tests for validity and reliability*. Paper presented at the meeting of the National Communication Association, Chicago, IL.

Booth, A., Carver, K., & Granger, D. (2000). Biosocial perspectives on the family. *Journal of Marriage and the Family, 62,* 1018–1034.

Boss, P. (1999). *Ambiguous loss: Learning to live with unresolved grief.* Cambridge, MA: Harvard University Press.

Boss, P. (2001, December). Ambiguous loss: Frozen grief in the wake of the WTC catastrophe. *Family Focus* (pp. F12–F13). Minneapolis, MN: National Council of Family Relations.

Boss, P. (2006). *Loss, trauma and resilience: Therapeutic work with ambiguous loss.* New York, NY: W. W. Norton.

Bosticco, C., & Thompson, T. (2005). The role of communication and story telling in the family grieving process. *Journal of Family Communication, 5,* 255–278.

Bourdeau, B., Miller, B., Vanya, M., Duke, M., & Ames, G. (2012). Defining alcohol-specific rules among parents of older adolescents: Moving beyond no tolerance. *Journal of Family Communication, 12,* 111–128.

Boushey, H. (2009). The new breadwinners. *The Shriver report: A study by Maria Shriver and the Center for American Progress.* Retrieved from http://www.awomansnation.com/economy.php.

Bradbury, A. R., Patrick-Miller, L., Pawlowski, K., Ibe, C. N., Cummings, S. A., Hlubocky, F., …, Daugherty, C. K. (2009). Learning of your parent's BRCA mutation during adolescence or early adulthood: A study of offspring experiences. *Psycho-Oncology, 18,* 200–208.

Braithwaite, D. O. (2002). "Married widowhood": Maintaining couplehood when one spouse is living in a nursing home. *Southern Communication Journal, 67,* 160–179.

Braithwaite, D. O., Bach, B. W., Baxter, L. A., DiVerniero, R., Hammonds, J. R., Hosek, A. M., …, Wolf, B. (2010). Constructing family: A typology of voluntary kin. *Journal of Social and Personal Relationships, 27,* 388–407.

Braithwaite, D. O., & Baxter, L. A. (1995). "I do" again: The relational dialectics of renewing marriage vows. *Journal of Social and Personal Relationships, 12,* 177–198.

Braithwaite, D. O., Baxter, L. A., & Harper, A. (1998). The role of rituals in the management of dialectical tensions of "old" and "new" in blended families. *Communication Studies, 48,* 101–120.

Braithwaite, D. O., McBride, M. C., & Schrodt, P. (2003). Parent teams and the everyday interactions of co-parenting children in stepfamilies. *Communication Reports, 16,* 93–111.

Braithwaite, D. O., Olson, L. N., Golish, T. D., Soukup, C., & Turman, P. (2001). "Becoming a family": Developmental processes represented in blended family discourse. *Journal of Applied Communication Research, 29,* 221–247.

Braithwaite, D. O., & Schrodt, P. (2013). Stepfamily communication. In A. L. Vangelisti (Ed.), *Handbook of family communication* (pp. 161–175). New York, NY: Routledge.

Braithwaite, D. O., Schrodt, P., & Baxter, L. A. (2006). Understudied and misunderstood: Communication in stepfamily relationships. In K. Floyd & M. T. Morman (Eds.), *Widening the family circle: New research on family communication* (pp. 153–170). Thousand Oaks, CA: Sage.

Braithwaite, D. O., & Thompson, T. L. (2000). Communication and disability research: A productive past and a bright future. In D. O. Braithwaite & T. L. Thompson (Eds.), *Handbook of communication and people with disabilities* (pp. 507–515). Mahwah, NJ: Lawrence Erlbaum.

Braithwaite, D. O., Toller, P., Daas, K., Durham, W., & Jones, A. (2008). Centered, but not caught in the middle: Stepchildren's perceptions of contradictions of communication of co-parents. *Journal of Applied Communication Research, 36,* 33–55.

Braithwaite, S. R., & Fincham, F. D. (2009). A randomized clinical trial of a computer based preventive intervention: Replication and extension of ePREP. *Journal of Family Psychology, 23,* 32–38.

Braithwaite, S. R., & Fincham, F. D. (2011). Computer based dissemination: A randomized clinical trial of ePREP using the actor partner interdependence model. *Behavior Research and Therapy, 49,* 126–131.

Breshears, D., & Braithwaite, D. O. (in press). A dialectical analysis of discourses surrounding children's experiences of parental disclosures of homosexuality. *Journal of Family Communication.*

Breunlin, D. C., Schwartz R. C., & Kune-Karrer, B. M. (2001). *Metaframeworks: Transcending the models of family therapy* (2nd ed.). San Francisco, CA: Jossey-Bass.

Brier, N. (2008). Grief following miscarriage: A comprehensive review of the literature. *Journal of Women's Health, 17,* 451–464.

Broderick, C. B. (1993). *Understanding family process: Basics of family systems theory.* Thousand Oaks, CA: Sage.

Brody, J. E. (2013, January 14). That loving feeling takes a lot of work. *New York Times*, D7.

Bruess, C. J. (1997). *Interview in family communication*. Teleclass, available from PBS Adult Learning Satellite Service, 1320 Braddock Pl., Alexandria, VA.

Bruess, C. J., & Kudak, A. D. H. (2008a). *What happy couples do: The loving little rituals of romance*. Minneapolis, MN: Fairview Press.

Bruess, C. J., & Kudak, A. D. H. (2008b). *What happy parents do: The loving little rituals of a child-proof marriage*. Minneapolis, MN: Fairview Press.

Bruess, C. J., & Pearson, J. C. (1997). Interpersonal rituals in marriage and adult friendship. *Communication Monographs, 66*, 25–46.

Bryant, J. A., & Bryant, J. (2006). Implications of living in a wired family: New directions in family and media research. In L. H. Turner & R. West (Eds.), *The family communication sourcebook* (pp. 297–314). Thousand Oaks, CA: Sage.

Bryant, L. E. (2006). Ritual (in)activity in postbereaved stepfamilies. In L. H. Turner & R. West (Eds.), *The family communication sourcebook* (pp. 281–293). Thousand Oaks, CA: Sage.

Buijzen, M., & Valkenburg, P. M. (2008). Observing purchase-related parent-child communication in retail environments: A developmental and socialization perspective. *Human Communication Research, 34*(1), 50–69.

Building a strong family. (2010). Retrieved from http://lds.org/hf/display/0,16783,4209-1,00.html.

Burgoon, J. K., Guerrero, L. K., & Manusov, V. (2011). Nonverbal signals. In M. L. Knapp & J. A. Daly (Eds.), *The handbook of interpersonal communication* (3rd ed., pp. 239–280). Thousand Oaks, CA: Sage.

Burleson, B. R., Delia, J., & Applegate, J. (1992). Effects of maternal communication and children's social-cognitive and communication skills on children's acceptance by the peer group. *Family Relations, 41*, 264–272.

Burleson, B. R., & Kunkel, A. (2006). Revisiting the different cultures thesis: An assessment of sex differences and similarities in supportive communication. In K. Dindia & D. Canary (Eds.), *Sex differences and similarities in communication* (2nd ed., pp. 137–159). Mahwah, NJ: Erlbaum.

Burr, W. R., Klein, S., & Associates. (1994). *Reexamining family stress*. Thousand Oaks, CA: Sage.

Busby, D. M., & Holman, T. B. (2009). Perceived match or mismatch on the Gottman conflict styles: Associations with relationship outcome variables. *Family Process, 48*, 531–545.

Bush, K. R., Bohon, S. A., & Kim, H. K. (2010). Adaptation among immigrant families: Resources and barriers. In S. J. Price, C. A. Price, & P. C. McKenry (Eds.), *Families and change: Coping with stressful events and transitions* (4th ed., pp. 285–310). Los Angeles, CA: Sage.

Bute, J. J., & Vik, T. A. (2010). Privacy management as unfinished business: Shifting boundaries in the context of infertility. *Communication Studies, 61*, 1–20.

Butkovic, A., & Bratko, D. (2007). Family study of manipulation tactics. *Personality and Individual Differences, 43*, 791–801.

Buxton, A. P. (2006). When a spouse comes out: Impact on the heterosexual partner. *Sexual Addiction and Compulsivity, 13*, 317–332.

Buzzanell, P. M., Berkelaar, B. L., & Kisselburgh, L. (2011). From the mouths of babes: Exploring families' career socialization of young children in China, Lebanon, Belgium & the United States. *Journal of Family Communication, 11*, 148–164.

Buzzanell, P. M., & Burrell, N. A. (1997). Family and workplace conflicts: Examining metaphorical conflict schemas and expressions across context and sex. *Human Communication Research, 24*(1), 109–146.

Buzzanell, P. M., & Turner, L. H. (2003). Emotion work revealed by job loss discourse backgrounding-foregrounding of feelings, construction of normalcy, and (re)instituting of traditional masculinities. *Journal of Applied Communication Research, 31*, 27–57.

Bylund, C. L. (2003). Ethnic diversity and family stories. *Journal of Family Communication, 3*, 215–236.

Bylund, C. L., Baxter, L. A., Imes, R. S., & Wolf, B. (2010). Parental rule socialization for preventive health and adolescent rule compliance. *Family Relations, 59*, 1–13.

Bylund, C. L., & Duck, S. (2004). The everyday interplay between family relationships and family members' health. *Journal of Social and Personal Relationships, 21*(1), 5–7.

Bylund, C. L., Galvin, K. M., Dunet, D. O., & Reyes, M. (2011). Using the extended health belief model to understand siblings' perceptions of risk for hereditary hemochromatosis. *Patient Education and Counseling, 82*, 36–41.

Bylund, C. L., Fisher, C. L., Brashers, D., Edgerson, S., Glogowski, E. A., Boyar, S. R., ..., Kissane, D. (2012). Sources of uncertainty about daughters' breast cancer risk that emerge during genetic counseling consultations. *Journal of Genetic Counseling, 21,* 292–304.

Cahn, D. D., & Lloyd, S. A. (1996). *Family violence from a communication perspective.* Thousand Oaks, CA: Sage.

Canary, H. E. (2012). Children with invisible disabilities: Communicating to manage family contradictions. In F. C. Dickson & L. M. Webb (Eds.), *Communication for families in crisis: Theories, research, strategies* (pp. 155–178). New York, NY: Peter Lang.

Canary, H. E., & Canary D. (2013). *Family conflict.* Malden MA: Polity Press.

Canary, D. J., Cody, M. J., & Manusov, V. L. (2008). *Interpersonal communication: A goals-based approach* (4th ed.). Boston, MA: Bedford/St. Martin's Press.

Canary, D. J., & Stafford, L. (1994). Maintaining relationships through strategic and routine interaction. In D. J. Canary & L. Stafford (Eds.), *Communication and relational maintenance* (pp. 3–22). San Diego, CA: Academic Press.

Cancer Facts & Figures. (2010). *American Cancer Society.* Atlanta, GA: American Cancer Society.

Carr, K., & Wang, T. R. (2012). "Forgiveness isn't a simple process: it's a vast undertaking": Negotiating and communicating forgiveness in nonvoluntary family relationships. *Journal of Family Communication, 12,* 40–56.

Carter, B., & McGoldrick, M. (2005a). The divorce cycle: A major variation in the American family life cycle. In B. Carter & M. McGoldrick (Eds.), *The expanded family life cycle: Individual, family and social perspectives* (3rd ed., pp. 373–398). Boston, MA: Allyn & Bacon.

Carter, B., & McGoldrick, M. (2005b). Overview: The expanded family life cycle: Individual, family, and social perspectives. In B. Carter & M. McGoldrick (Eds.), *The expanded family life cycle: Individual, family and social perspectives* (3rd ed., pp. 1–26). Boston, MA: Allyn & Bacon.

Carter, S., Loew, B., Allen, E., Stanley, S., Rhoades, G., & Markman, H. (2011). Relationships between soldiers' PTSD symptoms and spousal communication during deployment. *Journal of Traumatic Stress, 24*(3), 352–355.

Cate, R. M., Levin L. A., & Richmond, L. S. (2002). Premarital relationship stability: A review of recent research. *Journal of Social and Personal Relationships, 19,* 261–284.

Caughlin, J. P., & Afifi, T. D. (2004). When is topic avoidance unsatisfying? A more complete investigation into the underlying links between avoidance and dissatisfaction in parent-child and dating relationships. *Human Communication Research, 30,* 479–513.

Caughlin, J. P., Golish, T. D., Olson, L. N., Sargent, J. E., Cook, J. S., & Petronio, S. (2000). Intrafamily secrets in various family configurations: A communication boundary management perspective. *Communication Studies, 51,* 116–134.

Caughlin, J. P., & Huston, T. L. (2002). A contextual analysis of the association between demand/withdraw and marital satisfaction. *Personal Relationships, 9,* 95–119.

Caughlin, J. P., & Malis, R. S. (2004). Demand/withdraw communication between parents and adolescents: Connections with self-esteem and substance abuse. *Journal of Social and Personal Relationships, 21*(1), 125–148.

Caughlin, J. P., & Ramey, M. E. (2005). The demand/withdraw pattern of communication in parent-adolescent dyads. *Personal Relationships, 12,* 337–356.

Caughlin, J. P., & Scott, A. M. (2010). Toward a communication theory of the demand/withdraw pattern of interaction in interpersonal relationships. In S. Smith & S. R. Wilson (Eds.), *New directions in interpersonal communication* (pp. 180–200). Thousand Oaks, CA: Sage.

CCAI, Congressional Coalition on Adoption Institute. (2011). *Facts and statistics.* Retrieved May 1, 2013, from http://www.ccainstitute.org.

CDC. (2009). *Assisted reproductive technology: Home.* Retrieved from http://www.cdc.gov/art/.

CDC. (2010). *Health, United States, 2009.* Retrieved from http://www.cdc.gov/nchs/pressroom/10newreleases/hus09.htm.

Chabot, J. M., & Ames, B. D. (2004). It wasn't "Let's get pregnant and go do it": Decision making in lesbian couples planning motherhood via donor insemination. *Family Relations, 53,* 348–356.

Chaitin, J. (2002). Issues and interpersonal values among three generations in families of Holocaust survivors. *Journal of Social and Personal Relationships, 19,* 379–402.

Chandler, D., A'Vant, E. R., & Graves, S. L. (2008). Effective communication with Black families and students. Communique Online. *NASP Communique, 37*(3). Retrieved June 12, 2013, from http://www.nasponlin.org.

Chandra, A., Lara-Cinisomo, S., Jaycox, L. H., Tanielian, T., Burns, R. M., Ruder, T., & Han, B. (2009). Children on the homefront: The experience of children from military families. *Pediatrics, 125*, 16–25.

Chapman, G. (2004). *The five love languages: How to express heartfelt commitment to your mate.* Chicago, IL: Northfield Press.

Chen, Z., & Kaplan, H. B. (2001). Intergenerational transmission of constructive parenting. *Journal of Marriage and the Family, 63*, 17–31.

Cherlin, A. (2010). Demographic trends in the United States: A review of research in the 2000s. *Journal of Marriage and Family, 72*, 403–419.

Child, J. T., & Petronio, S. (2011). Unpacking the paradoxes of privacy in CMC relationships: The challenges of blogging and relational communication on the Internet. In K. B. Wright & L. M. Webb (Eds.), *Computer-mediated communication in personal relationships* (pp. 21–40). New York, NY: Peter Lang.

Child, J. T., & Westermann, D. A. (2013). Let's be Facebook friends: Exploring parental Facebook friend requests from a communication privacy management (CPM) perspective. *Journal of Family Communication, 13*, 46–59.

Christakis, N. A., & Allison, P. D. (2006). Mortality after the hospitalization of a spouse. *New England Journal of Medicine, 4*, 2190–2191.

Christakis, N. A., & Fowler, J. H. (2009). *Connected: The surprising power of our social networks and how they shape our lives.* New York, NY: Little, Brown.

Ciabatarri, T. (2007). Single mothers, social capital, and work-family conflict. *Journal of Family Issues, 28*, 34–60.

Claes, E., Evers-Kiebooms, G., Boogaerts, A., Decruyenaere, M., Denayer, L., & Legius, E. (2003). Communication with close and distant relatives in the context of genetic testing for hereditary breast and ovarian cancer in cancer patients. *American Journal of Medical Genetics Part C, 116*, 11–19.

Clark, S. C. (2000). Work/family border theory: A new theory of work/family balance. *Human Relations, 53*(6), 747–770.

Clarke, A., Richards, M., Kerzin-Storrar, L., Halliday, J., Young, M. A., Simpson, S. A., ..., Forrest, K. (2005). Genetic professionals' reports of nondisclosure of genetic risk information within families. *European Journal of Human Genetics, 13*(5), 556–562.

Clements, M. L., Cordova, A. D., Markman, H. J., & Laurenceau, J.-P. (1997). The erosion of marital satisfaction over time and how to prevent it. In S. R. Sternberg & M. Hojjat (Eds.), *Satisfaction in close relationships* (pp. 335–355). New York, NY: Guilford Press.

Cline, R. J. W., Harper, F. W. K., Penner, L. A., Peterson, A. M., Taub, J. W., & Albrecht, T. L. (2006). Parent communication and child pain and distress during painful pediatric cancer treatments. *Social Science and Medicine, 63*(4), 883–898.

Cloven, D. H., & Roloff, E. I. (1993). The chilling effect of aggressive potential on the expression of complaints in intimate relationships. *Communication Monographs, 60*, 199–219.

Coffelt, T. A. (2010). Is sexual communication challenging between mothers and daughters? *Journal of Family Communication, 10*, 116–130.

Cohen, E. L. (2009). Naming and claiming cancer among African American women: An application of problematic integration theory. *Journal of Applied Communication Research, 37*, 397–417.

Cohen, S. P. (2002). Can pets function as family members? *Western Journal of Nursing Research, 24*(6), 621–638.

Cohn, D., Passel, J., Wang, W., & Livingston, G. (2011, December 14). Barely half of U.S. adults are married—A record low. *Pew Research Social and Demographic Trends.* Retrieved April 30, 2013, from www.pewsocialtrends.org.

Cole, C. L., & Cole, A. L. (1999). Marriage enrichment and prevention really works: Interpersonal competence training to maintain and enhance relationships. *Family Relations, 48*, 273–275.

Coleman, M., Fine, M. A., Ganong, L. H., Downs, K. J. M., & Pauk, N. (2001). When you're not the Brady Bunch: Identifying perceived conflicts and resolution strategies in stepfamilies. *Personal Relationships, 8*, 55–73.

Collins, R. (1997). *Interview in family communication.* Teleclass, available from PBS Adult Learning Satellite Service, 1320 Braddock Pl., Alexandria, VA.

Conger, R. D., Elder, G. H., Jr., Lorenz, F. O., Conger, K. J., Simons, R. L., Whitbeck, L. B., ..., Melby, J. N. (1990). Linking economic hardship to marital quality and instability. *Journal of Marriage and Family, 52*(2), 643–656.

Cooney, T. M. (1997). Parent-child relations across adulthood. In S. Duck (Ed.), *Handbook of personal relationships: Theory, research and interventions* (pp. 451–468). New York, NY: John Wiley & Sons.

Coontz, S. (1999). Introduction. In S. Coontz, M. Parson, & G. Raley (Eds.), *American families: A multicultural reader* (pp. ix–xxxiii). New York, NY: Routledge.

Cooper, M. (2000). Being the "go-to-guy": Fatherhood, masculinity, and the organization of work in Silicon Valley. *Qualitative Sociology, 23*, 379–405.

Cooper, P. J. (2006). Family-school relationships: Theoretical perspectives and concerns. In L. H. Turner & R. West (Eds.), *The family communication sourcebook* (pp. 405–423). Thousand Oaks, CA: Sage.

Copen, C. E., Daniels, K., & Mosher, W. D. (2013). First premarital cohabitation in the United States: 2006–2010 National Survey of Family Growth. *National health statistic reports, 64*. Hyattsville, MD: National Center for Health Statistics.

Covey, S. R. (1997). *The 7 habits of highly effective families*. New York, NY: Golden Books.

Cowan, C. P., & Cowan, P. A. (1997). Working with couples during stressful transitions. In S. Dreman (Ed.), *The family on the threshold of the 21st century*. Mahwah, NJ: Lawrence Erlbaum.

Cowdery, R. S., & Knudson-Martin, C. (2005). The construction of motherhood: Tasks, relational connection, and gender equality. *Family Relations, 54*, 335–345.

Cox, M. J., & Harter, K. S. M. (2002). The road ahead for research on marital and family dynamics. In J. P. McHale & W. S. Grolnick (Eds.), *Retrospect and prospect in the psychological study of families* (pp. 167–188). Mahwah, NJ: Lawrence Erlbaum.

Cramer, D. (2002). Linking conflict management behaviours and relational satisfaction: The intervening role of conflict outcome satisfaction. *Journal of Social and Personal Relationships, 19*(3), 425–432.

Crean, H. F. (2008). Conflict in the Latino parent-youth dyad: The role of emotional support from the opposite parent. *Journal of Family Psychology, 22*, 484–493.

Crespo, C., Davide, I. N., Costa, M. E., & Fletcher, G. J. O. (2008). Family rituals in married couples: Links with attachment, relationship quality, and closeness. *Personal Relationships, 15*, 191–203.

Cromwell, R. E., & Olson, D. (1975). *Power in families*. New York, NY: Wiley.

Crosnoe, R., & Cavanagh, S. E. (2010). Families with children and adolescents: A review, critique, and future agenda. *Journal of Marriage and Family, 72*, 594–611.

Crowell, N. A., & Burgess, A. W. (1996). *Understanding violence against women*. Washington, DC: National Academies Press.

Dailey, R. M., Lee, C. M., & Spitzberg, B. H. (2013). Charting dangerous territory: The family as a context of violence and aggression. In A. L. Vangelisti (Ed.), *Handbook of family communication* (2nd ed., pp. 479–493). New York, NY: Routledge.

Dainton, M., & Aylor, B. (2002). A relational uncertainty analysis of jealousy, trust, and maintenance in long-distance versus geographically close relationships. *Communication Quarterly, 49*, 172–188.

Dake, J. A., Price, J. H., Maziarz, L., & Ward, B. (2012). Prevalence and correlates of sexting behavior in adolescents. *American Journal of Sexuality Education, 7*, 1–15.

Daly, M. B., Barsevick, A., Miller, S. M., Buckman, R., Costalas, J., Montgomery, S., & Bingler, R. (2001). Communicating genetic test results to the family: A six-step, skills-building strategy. *Family Community Health, 24*, 13–26.

Dancyger, C., Wiseman, M., Jacobs, C., Smith, J. A., Wallace, M., & Michie, S. (2011). Communicating BRCA1/2 genetic test results within the family: A qualitative analysis. *Psychology and Health, 26*(8), 1018–1035.

Daniel, J., & Daniel, J. (1999). African-American child rearing: The context of the hot stove. In T. H. Socha & R. C. Diggs (Eds.), *Communication, race and family: Exploring communication in black, white, and biracial families* (pp. 25–43). Mahwah, NJ: Lawrence Erlbaum.

Daniluk, J. C., & Hurtig-Mitchell, J. (2003). Themes of hope and healing: Infertile couples' experiences of adoption. *Journal of Counseling and Development, 81*, 389–399.

Darling, N., Cohan, C. L., Burns, A., & Thompson, L. (2008). Within-family conflict behaviors as predictors of conflict in adolescent romantic relations. *Journal of Adolescence, 31*, 671–690.

Darling, N., Cumsille, P., Caldwell, L. L., & Dowdy, B. (2006). Predictors of adolescents' disclosure strategies and perceptions of parental knowledge. *Journal of Youth and Adolescence, 35*(4), 667–678.

Davey, A., & Szinovacz, M. E. (2004). Dimensions of marital quality and retirement. *Journal of Family Issues, 25*, 431–464.

Davies, P. T., Myers, R. L., Cummings, E. M., & Heindel, S. (1999). Adult conflict history and children's subsequent responses to conflict: An experimental test. *Journal of Family Psychology, 13*(4), 610–628.

Davis, C. S., Dollard, N., & Vergon, K. S. (2009). The role of communication in child-parent-provider interaction in a children's mental health system of care. In T. H. Socha & G. H. Stamp (Eds.), *Parents and children communicating with* society: *Managing relationships outside of the home* (pp. 133–153). New York, NY: Routledge.

DeFrain, J. D., & Stinnett, N. (2007). Creating a strong family: American Family Strengths Inventory, NEBGuide G1881. Institute of Agriculture and Natural Resources. University of Nebraska—Lincoln, Lincoln, NE.

DeGenova, M. K., & Rice, F. P. (2005). *Intimate relationships, marriages, and families* (6th ed.). New York, NY: McGraw-Hill.

DeParle, J. (2012, July 15). Two classes, divided by "I do": Marriage, for richer; single motherhood, for poorer. *New York Times*, sec 1, 1, 18–19.

Department of Defense. (2012). *Demographics: Profile of the military community*. Retrieved July 5, 2013, from http://www.militaryonesource.mil/12038/MOS/Reports/2011_Demographics_Report.pdf.

DePaulo, B. M. (2006). *Singled out: How singles are stigmatized, stereotyped, and ignored and still live happily ever after*. New York, NY: St. Martin's Press.

deTurck, M. A., & Miller, G. R. (1983). Adolescent perceptions of parental persuasive message strategies. *Journal of Marriage and the Family, 45*(3), 543–552.

Dickson, F. C. (1995). The best is yet to be: Research on long-lasting marriages. In J. T. Wood & S. Duck (Eds.), *Understudied relationships* (pp. 22–50). Thousand Oaks, CA: Sage.

Dickson, F. C., Christian, A., & Remmo, C. J. (2004). An exploration of the marital and family issues of the later-life adult. In A. L. Vangelisti (Ed.), *Handbook of family communication* (pp. 153–174). Mahwah, NJ: Lawrence Erlbaum.

Diggs, R. C. (2001, November). *Searching for commitment with a radical(izing) method: The experiences of an African-American long-distance married couple*. Paper presented at National Communication Association Convention, Atlanta, GA.

Dilworth, J. E. L., & Kingsbury, N. (2005). Home-to-job spillover for generation X, boomers, and matures: A comparison. *Journal of Family and Economic Issues, 26*(2), 267–281.

Dilworth-Anderson, P., & Burton, L. M. (1996). Rethinking family development: Critical conceptual issues in the study of diverse groups. *Journal of Social and Personal Relationships, 13*, 325–334.

Dindia, K. (2003). Definitions and perspectives on relational maintenance communication. In D. J. Canary & M. Dainton (Eds.), *Maintaining relationships through communication: Relational, contextual and cultural variations* (pp. 1–28). Mahwah, NJ: Lawrence Erlbaum.

Dindia, K., & Canary, D. J. (1993). Relational maintenance: Definition and theoretical perspectives on maintaining relationships. *Journal of Social and Personal Relationships, 10*, 163–173.

Dinero, R., Conger, R., Shaver, P., Widaman, K., & Larsen-Rife, D. (2008). Influence of family of origin and adult romantic partners on romantic attachment security. *Journal of Family Psychology, 22*, 622–632.

DiVerniero, R. (2013). Children of divorce and their nonresidential parent's family: Examining perceptions of communication accommodation. *Journal of Family Communication, 13*, 301–320.

Downs, K. J., Coleman, M., & Ganong, L. (2000). Divorced families over the life course. In S. J. Price, P. C. McKenry, & M. J. Murphy (Eds.), *Families across time: A life course perspective* (pp. 24–36). Los Angeles, CA: Roxbury.

Drabe, N., Wittmann, L., Zwahlen, D., Büchi, S., & Jenewein, J. (2013). Changes in close relationships between cancer patients and their partners. *Psycho-Oncology, 22*, 1344–1352.

Dreby, J., & Stutz, L. (2012). Making something of the sacrifice: Gender, migration and Mexican children's educational aspirations. *Global Networks, 12*(1), 71–90.

Driver, J. L., & Gottman, J. M. (2004). Daily marital interactions and positive affect during marital conflict among newlywed couples. *Family Process, 43*, 301–314.

Driver, J., Tabares, A., Shapiro, A. F., & Gottman, J. M. (2012). Couple interactions in happy and unhappy marriages. In F. Walsh (Ed.), *Normal family processes: Growing diversity and complexity* (pp. 57–77). New York, NY: Guilford Press.

Duck, S. (1986). *Human relationships: An introduction to social psychology*. London, UK: Sage.

Duck, S. (1994). Steady as (s)he goes: Relational maintenance as a shared meaning system. In D. J. Canary & L. Stafford (Eds.), *Communication and relational maintenance* (pp. 45–60). San Diego, CA: Academic Press.

Duck, S., Miell, D., & Miell, D. (1984). Relationship growth and decline. In H. Sypher & J. Applegate (Eds.), *Communication by children and adults* (pp. 292–312). Beverly Hills, CA: Sage.

Duckworth, J., & Buzzanell, P. (2009). Constructing work-life balance and fatherhood: Men's framing of the meanings of *both* work *and* family. *Communication Studies, 60*(5), 558–573.

Duggan, A., & Petronio, S. (2009). When your child is in crisis. In T. J. Socha & G. H. Stamp (Eds.),

Parents and children communicating with society: Managing relationships outside of the home (pp. 117–132). New York, NY: Routledge.

Dumka, L. E., Roosa, M. W., & Jackson, K. M. (1997). Risk, conflict, mothers' parenting, and children's adjustment in low-income, Mexican immigrant, and Mexican American families. *Journal of Marriage and the Family, 59,* 309–323.

Dunbar, N. E. (2004). Dyadic power theory: Constructing a communication-based theory of relational power. *Journal of Family Communication, 4,* 235–248.

Duncan, B. L., & Rock, J. W. (1993, January–February). Saving relationships: The power of the unpredictable. *Psychology Today, 46–51, 86, 95.*

Duncan, S. F., & Goddard, H. W. (2011). *Family life education: Principles and practices for effective outreach* (2nd ed). Thousand Oaks, CA: Sage.

Durham, S. D. (2010). In their own words: Staying connected in a combat. *Military Medicine, 175*(8), 554–559.

Durham, W., & Braithwaite, D. O. (2009). Communication privacy management within the family-planning trajectories of voluntarily child-free couples. *Journal of Family Communication, 9,* 43–65.

Du Rocher Schudlich, T. D., White, C. R., Fleischhauer, E. A., & Fitzgerald, K. A. (2011). Observed infant reactions during live interparental conflict. *Journal of Marriage and Family, 73,* 221–235.

Easterling, B., Knox, D., & Brackett, A. (2012). Secrets in romantic relationships: Does sexual orientation matter? *Journal of GLBT Family Studies, 8*(2), 196–208.

Eckstein, N. J. (2002). Adolescent-to-parent abuse: A communicative analysis of conflict processes present in verbal, physical, or emotional abuse of parents (Unpublished doctoral dissertation). University of Nebraska—Lincoln, Lincoln, NE.

Edin, K., Nelson, T., & Paranal, R. (2001). Fatherhood and incarceration as potential turning points in the criminal careers of unskilled men. Institute for Policy Research, Northwestern University, Evanston, IL. WP-01-02.

Edwards, T. (2009). As baby boomers age, fewer families have children under 18 at home. *U.S. Census Bureau News.* Retrieved from http://www.census.gov/Press-Release/www/releases/archives/families_households/013378.html.

Eggly, S., Penner, L. A., Greene, M., Harper, F. W. K., Ruckdeschel, J. C., & Albrecht, T. L. (2006). Information seeking during "bad news" oncology interactions: Question asking by patients and their companions. *Social Science and Medicine, 63*(11), 2974–2985.

EHRC. (2009). *Working better: Fathers, family and work—Contemporary perspectives.* Retrieved from http://www.equalityhumanrights.com/media-centre/2009/october/fathers-struggling-to-balance-work-and-family/.

Ellingson, L. L., & Sotirin, P. (2010). Aunting: Cultural practices that sustain family and community life. Waco, TX: Baylor University Press.

Epstein, N. B., Bishop, D. S., & Baldwin, L. M. (1982). McMaster model of family functioning. In F. Walsh (Ed.), *Normal family processes* (pp. 115–141). New York, NY: Guilford Press.

Erickson, B. M. (2005). Scandinavian families: Plain and simple. In M. McGoldrick, J. Giordano, & N. Garcia-Preto (Eds.), *Ethnicity and family therapy* (3rd ed., pp. 641–653). New York, NY: Guilford Press.

Erickson, E. H. (1968). *Identity, youth, and crisis.* New York, NY: W. W. Norton.

Escudero, V., Rogers, L. E., & Gutierrez E. (1997). Patterns of relational control and nonverbal affect in clinic and nonclinic couples. *Journal of Social and Personal Relationship, 14,* 5–29.

Evan B. Donaldson Institute. (2011). *Never too old: Achieving permanency and sustaining connections for older youth in foster care.* Retrieved June 6, 2013, from www.adoptioninstitute.org.

Facebook.com. (2010). Retrieved from www.facebook.com.

Faith and Marriage Ministries. (2010). Retrieved from http://faithandmarriageministries.org.

Falbo, T., & Peplau, L. A. (1980). Power strategies in intimate relationships. *Journal of Personality and Social Psychology, 38,* 618–628.

Falicov, C. J. (2005). Mexican families. In M. McGoldrick, J. Giordano, & N. Garcia-Preto (Eds.), *Ethnicity and family therapy.* (3rd ed., pp. 229–241). New York, NY: Guilford Press.

Farrell, M. P. (2000). Adolescents' effects on the psychological functioning and adult development of their parents. *Family Science Review, 13,* 10–18.

Federal Interagency Forum on Child and Family Statistics Forum. (2013). *Family structure and children's living arrangements.* Retrieved December 16, 2013, from http://www.childstats.gov/americaschildren/famsoc1.asp.

Feldman, L. B. (1979). Marital conflict and marital intimacy: An integrative psychodynamic-behavioral systemic model. *Family Process, 18,* 69–78.

Fenigstein, A., & Peltz, R. (2002). Distress over the infidelity of a child's spouse: A crucial test of evolutionary and socialization hypotheses. *Personal Relationships, 9*, 301–312.

Fiese, B. H., Hooker, K. A., Kotary, L., Schagler, J., & Rimmer, M. (1995). Family stories in the early stages of parenthood. *Journal of Marriage and the Family, 57*, 763–770.

Fincham, F. D., & Beach, S. R. (2002). Forgiveness in marriage: Implications for psychological aggression and constructive communication. *Personal Relationships, 9*, 239–251.

Fincham, F. D., & Beach, S. R. (2010). Of memes and marriage: Toward a positive relationship science. *Journal of Family Theory and Review, 2*, 4–24.

Fincham, F. D., Stanley, S. M., & Beach, S. R. H. (2007). Transformative processes in marriage: An analysis of emerging trends. *Journal of Marriage and Family, 69*, 275–292.

Fingerman, K. L., Birditt, K., Nussbaum, J., & Ebersole, D. S. (2013). Generational juggling: Family communication at midlife. In A. L. Vangelisti (Ed.), *Handbook of family communication* (2nd ed., pp. 97–111). New York, NY: Routledge.

Fingerman, K. L., Miller, L., Birditt, K., & Zarit, S. (2009). Giving to the good and needy: Parental support of grown children. *Journal of Marriage and Family, 71*, 1220–1233.

Fingerman, K. L., Nussbaum, J., & Birditt, K. S. (2004). Keeping all five balls in the air: Juggling family communication at midlife. In A. L. Vangelisti (Ed.), *Handbook of family communication* (pp. 135–152). Mahwah, NJ: Lawrence Erlbaum.

Fink, D. S., Buerkel-Rothfuss, N. L., & Buerkel, R. A. (1994, November). *Father-son relational closeness: The role of attribution-making in reducing the impact of bad behavior.* Paper presented at the meeting of the Speech Communication Association, New Orleans, LA.

Finkel, E. J., Eastwick, P. W., Karney, B. R., Reis, H. T., & Sprecher, S. (2012). Online dating: A critical analysis from the perspective of psychological science. *Psychological Science in the Public Interest, 13*(1), 3–66.

Finkenauer, C., & Hazam, H. (2000). Disclosure and secrecy in marriage: Do both contribute to marital satisfaction? *Journal of Social and Personal Relationships, 17*, 245–263.

Fisher, C. L., Maloney, E., Glogowski, E., Hurley, K., Edgerson, S., Lichtenthal, W., Kissane, D., & Bylund, C. (in press). Talking about familial breast cancer risk: Topics and strategies to enhance mother-daughter interactions. *Qualitative Health Research.*

Fisher, C. L., & Nussbaum, J. F. (2012). "Linked lives": Mother-adult daughter communication after a breast cancer diagnosis. In F. C. Dickson & L. M. Webb (Eds.), *Communication for families in crisis: Theories, research, strategies* (pp. 179–204). New York, NY: Peter Lang.

Fisher, W. R. (1987). *Human communication as narration: Toward a philosophy of reason, value and action.* Columbia, SC: University of South Carolina Press.

Fitzpatrick, M. A. (1977). A typological approach to communication in relationships. In B. Rubin (Ed.), *Communication yearbook I* (pp. 263–275). New Brunswick, NJ: Transaction Press.

Fitzpatrick, M. A. (1988). *Between husbands and wives.* Beverly Hills, CA: Sage.

Fitzpatrick, M. A. (1998). Interpersonal communication on the Starship Enterprise: Resilience, stability, and change in relationships in the twenty-first century. In J. S. Trent (Ed.), *Communication: Views from the helm for the 21st century* (pp. 41–46). Boston, MA: Allyn & Bacon.

Fitzpatrick, M. A., & Badzinski, D. M. (1994). All in the family: Interpersonal communication in kin relationships. In M. L. Knapp & G. L. Miller (Eds.), *Handbook of interpersonal communication* (2nd ed., pp. 726–771). Thousand Oaks, CA: Sage.

Fitzpatrick, M. A., Fallis, S., & Vance, L. (1982). Multifunctional coding of conflict resolution strategies in marital dyads. *Family Relations, 31*, 61–70.

Fitzpatrick, M. A., & Ritchie, L. D. (1994). Communication schemata within the family: Multiple perspectives on family interaction. *Human Communication Research, 20*, 275–301.

Fivush, R. (2008). Remembering and reminiscing: How individual lives are constructed in family narratives. *Memory Studies, 1*(49), 49–58.

Flanagan, K. M., Clements, M. L., Whitton, S. W., Portney, M. J., Randall, D. W., & Markman, H. J. (2002). Retrospect and prospect in the psychological study of marital and couple relationships. In J. P. McHale & W. S. Grolnick (Eds.), *Retrospect and prospect in the psychological study of families* (pp. 99–128). Mahwah, NJ: Lawrence Erlbaum.

Floyd, K. (2002). Human affection exchange: V. Attributes of the highly affectionate. *Communication Quarterly, 50*, 135–152.

Floyd, K., & Afifi, T. D. (2011). Biological and physiological perspectives on interpersonal communication.

In M. Knapp & J. Daly. (Eds), *The handbook of interpersonal communication* (4th ed., pp. 87–130). Thousand Oaks, CA: Sage.

Floyd, K., & Haynes, M. T. (2006). The theory of natural selection: An evolutionary approach to family communication. In D. O. Braithwaite & L. A. Baxter (Eds.), *Engaging theories in family communication: Multiple perspectives* (pp. 325–340). Thousand Oaks, CA: Sage.

Floyd, K., Judd, J., & Hesse, C. (2008). Affection exchange theory: A bio-evolutionary look at affectionate communication. In L. A. Baxter & D. O. Braithwaite (Eds.), *Engaging theories in interpersonal communication: Multiple perspectives* (pp. 325–340). Thousand Oaks, CA: Sage.

Floyd, K., Mikkelson, A. C., & Judd, J. (2006). Defining the family through relationships. In L. H. Turner & R. West (Eds.), *The family communication sourcebook* (pp. 21–39). Thousand Oaks, CA: Sage.

Floyd, K., & Morman, M. T. (2005). Fathers' and sons' reports of fathers' affectionate communication: Implications of a naïve theory of affection. *Journal of Personal and Social Relationships, 22,* 99–109.

Flurry, L. A., & Burns, A. C. (2005). Children's influence in purchase decisions: A social power theory approach. *Journal of Business Research, 58,* 593–601.

Foley, M. K., & Duck, S. (2006). "That Dear Octopus": A family-based model of intimacy. In L. H. Turner & R. West (Eds.), *The family communication sourcebook* (pp. 183–199). Thousand Oaks, CA: Sage.

Folwarski, J., & Smolinski, J. (2005). Polish families. In M. McGoldrick, J. Giordano, & N. Garcia-Preto (Eds.), *Ethnicity and family therapy* (3rd ed., pp. 741–755). New York, NY: Guilford Press.

Food showing love. (n.d.). *Pinterest.* Retrieved June 11, 2013, from http://www.pinterest.com.

Forrest, K., Simpson, S. A., Wilson, B. J., van Teijlingen, E. R., McKee, L., Haites, N., & Mathews, E. (2003). To tell or not to tell: Barriers and facilitators in family communication about genetic risk. *Clinical Genetics, 64,* 317–326.

Fosco, G. M., & Grych, J. H. (2010). Adolescent triangulation into parental conflicts: Longitudinal implications for appraisals and adolescent-parent relations. *Journal of Marriage and Family, 72,* 254–266.

Fowler, C., & Soliz, J. (2010). Responses of young adult grandchildren to grandparents' painful self-disclosures. *Journal of Language and Social Psychology, 29.* Retrieved from http://jlsp.sagepub.com.

Fox, S. (2006, April). *Data memo.* Retrieved from the Pew Internet and American Life Project website http://www.perinternet.org/pdfs/PIP_Wired_Senior_2006,memo.pdf.

France, D. (2006, January–February). And then he hit me. *AARP Magazine, 61–63,* 76–77, 81–83.

Frieze, I. H., & McHugh, M. C. (1992). Power and influence strategies in violent and nonviolent marriages. *Psychology of Women Quarterly, 16,* 449–465.

Fujishin, R. (2002). *Gifts from the heart* (2nd ed.). New York, NY: Routledge.

Gaff, C. L., & Bylund, C. L. (Eds.). (2010). *Family communication about genetics: Theory and practice.* New York, NY: Oxford University Press.

Gaff, C. L., Clarke, A. J., Atkinson, P., Sivel, P., Elwyn, G., Iredahl, R., ..., Edwards, A. (2007). Process and outcome in communication of genetic information within families: A systematic review. *European Journal of Human Genetics, 15,* 999–1011.

Gaff, C. L., Collins, V., Symes, T., & Halliday, J. (2005). Facilitating family communication about predictive genetic testing: Probands' perceptions. *Journal of Genetic Counseling, 14,* 133–140.

Gaff, C. L., Galvin, K. M., & Bylund, C. L. (2010). Facilitating family communication about genetics. In C. L. Gaff & C. L. Bylund (Eds.), *Family communication about genetics: Theory and practice* (pp. 243–272). Oxford, UK: Oxford University Press.

Galinsky, E. (1999). *Ask the children.* New York, NY: William Morrow.

Galinsky, E., Aumann, K., & Bond, J. T. (2008). *The times are changing: Gender and generation at work.* Retrieved from Families and Work Institute website www.familiesandwork.org.

Galvin, K. M. (2006). Diversity's impact on defining the family: Discourse dependence and identity. In L. H. Turner & R. West (Eds.), *The family communication sourcebook* (pp. 3–19). Thousand Oaks, CA: Sage.

Galvin, K. M. (2007). It's not all blarney: Intergenerational transmission of communication patterns in Irish American families. In P. Cooper, C. Calloway-Thomas, & C. Simonds (Eds.), *Intercultural communication: A text with readings* (pp. 172–192). Boston, MA: Allyn & Bacon.

Galvin, K. M. (2008, September). *Helicopter parents.* Presentation to Lake County Counselors Association, Grayslake, IL.

Galvin, K. M. (2010). Deliberation in a contested medical context: Developing a framework to aid family decision making when an adolescent son faces fertility-threatening cancer. In D. S. Gouran (Ed.), *The functions of argument and social context* (pp. 98–106). Selected papers from the 16th biennial conference on argumentation, National Communication Association, Washington, DC.

Galvin, K. M. (2013). The family of the future: What do we face? In A. L. Vangelisti (Ed.), *Handbook of family communication* (2nd ed., pp. 531–545). New York, NY: Routledge.

Galvin, K. M., & Braithwaite, D. O. (2014). Family communication theory and research from the field of family communication: Discourses that constitute and reflect families. *Journal of Family Theory and Review, 6*, 97–111.

Galvin, K. M., Bylund, C. L., & Grill, B. (2010). *Genograms: Constructing and interpreting interaction patterns.* Retrieved from http://www.genograms.org/.

Galvin, K., & Colaner, C. W. (2014). Created through law and language: Communicative complexities of adoptive families. In K. Floyd & M. T. Morman (Eds.), *Widening the family circle: New research in family communication* (2nd ed., pp. 191–209). Thousand Oaks, CA: Sage.

Galvin, K. M., Dickson, F. C., & Marrow, S. K. (2006). Systems theory: Patterns and (w)holes in family communication. In D. O. Braithwaite & L. A. Baxter (Eds.), *Engaging theories in family communication: Multiple perspectives* (pp. 309–324). Thousand Oaks, CA: Sage.

Galvin, K. M., & DiDomenico, S. (2009, November). *High stakes, emotionally charged health decisions: New directions for family communication and group communication scholars.* Paper presented at the National Communication Association Conference, Chicago, IL.

Galvin, K. M., & Grill, L. H. (2009). Opening up the conversation on genetics and genomics in families: The space for communication scholars. In C. S. Beck (Ed.), *Communication yearbook* (Vol. 33, pp. 213–257). New York, NY: Routledge.

Galvin, K. M., Grill, L. H., Arntson, P. H., & Kinahan, K. E. (2012). Beyond the crisis: Communication between parents and children who survived cancer. In F. C. Dickson & L. M. Webb (Eds.), *Communication for families in crisis: Theories, research, strategies* (pp. 229–248). New York, NY: Peter Lang.

Galvin, K. M., & Patrick, D. (2009, November). *Gay male partners achieving parenthood: Stories of communicative complexities and challenges.* Paper presented at the National Communication Association Conference, Chicago, IL.

Galvin, K. M., Turner, L. H., Patrick, D. G., & West, R. (2007, November). *Difficult conversations: The experience of same-sex partners.* Paper presented at the National Communication Association Convention, Chicago, IL.

Ganong, L. H., & Coleman, M. (2004). *Stepfamily relationships: Development, dynamics, and interventions.* New York, NY: Kluwer Academic/Plenum.

Garces, Y., Pattern, C. A., Sinicope, P. S., Decker P. A., Offord, K. P., & Brown, P. D., ..., Hurt, R. D. (2010). Willingness of cancer patients to help family members to quit smoking. *Psycho-oncology.* Retrieved from www.interscience.wiley.com.

Garcia-Preto, N. (2005a). Puerto Rican families. In M. McGoldrick, J. Giordano, & N. Garcia-Preto (Eds.), *Ethnicity and family therapy* (3rd ed., pp. 242–255). New York, NY: Guilford Press.

Garcia-Preto, N. (2005b). Transformation of the family system during adolescence. In B. Carter & M. McGoldrick (Eds.), *The expanded family life cycle: Individual, family and social perspectives* (3rd ed., pp. 274–286). Boston, MA: Allyn & Bacon.

Gasper, J. A. F., Stolberg, A. L., Macie, K. M., & Williams, L. J. (2008). Coparenting in intact and divorced families: Its impact on young adult adjustment. *Journal of Divorce and Remarriage, 49*(3), 272–290.

Gass, R. H., & Seiter, S. J. (1999). *Persuasion, social influence, and compliance-gaining.* Boston, MA: Allyn & Bacon.

Gelles, R. J. (2010). Violence, abuse, and neglect in families and intimate relationships. In S. J. Price, C. A. Price, & P. C. McKenry (Eds.), *Families and change: Coping with stressful events and transitions* (4th ed., pp. 119–139). Los Angeles, CA: Sage.

Gewirtz, A. H., Erbes, C. R., Polusny, M. A., Forgatch, M. S., & DeGarmo, D. S. (2011). Helping military families through the deployment process: Strategies to support parenting. *Professional psychology: Research and practice, 42*(1), 56–62.

Gianino, M. (2008). Adaptation and transformation: The transition to adoptive parenthood for gay male couples. *Journal of GLBT Family Studies, 4*(2), 205–243.

Gilbar, O., & Refaeli, R. (2000). The relationship between adult cancer patients' adjustment to the illness and that of their parents. *Families, Systems and Health: Journal of Collaborative Family Healthcare Association, 18*(1), 5–17.

Giordano, J., McGoldrick, M., & Klages, J. G. (2005). Italian families. In M. McGoldrick, J. Giordano, & N. Garcia-Preto (Eds.), *Ethnicity and family therapy* (3rd ed., pp. 616–628). New York, NY: Guilford Press.

Givertz, M., Segrin, C., & Hanzal, A. (2009). The association between satisfaction and commitment differs across marital couple types. *Communication Research, 36,* 561–584.

Golden, A. G. (2002). Speaking of work and family: Spousal collaboration on defining role-identities and developing shared meanings. *Southern Communication Journal, 67,* 122–141.

Golden, A. G. (2007). Fathers' frames for childrearing: Evidence toward a "masculine concept of caregiving." *Journal of Family Communication, 7,* 265–285.

Goldenberg, I., & Goldenberg, H. (2008). *Family therapy: An overview* (7th ed.). Belmont, CA: Thomson, Brooks/Cole.

Goldman, L. (2008). Helping military kids with traumatic death. *Tragedy assistance program for survivors.* Retrieved June 6, 2013, from http://www.taps.org.

Goldsmith, D. J. (2009). Uncertainty and communication in couples coping with serious illness. In T. D. Afifi & W. A. Afifi (Eds.), *Uncertainty, information management, and disclosure decisions: Theories and applications* (pp. 203–225). New York, NY: Routledge.

Goldstein, S., & Brooks, R. B. (Eds.). (2013). Why study resilience? *Handbook of resilience in children* (pp. 3–14). New York, NY: Springer.

Goldsworthy, K. K. (2005). Grief and loss theory in social work practice: All changes involve loss, just as all losses require change. *Australian Social Work, 58,* 167–178.

Golish, T. D. (2000). Changes in closeness between adult children and their parents: A turning point analysis. *Communication Reports, 13,* 79–97.

Golish, T. D., & Powell, K. A. (2003). "Ambiguous loss": Managing the dialectics of grief associated with premature birth. *Journal of Social and Personal Relationships, 20*(3), 309–334.

Golombok, A., MacCallum, F., Goodman, E., & Rutter, M. (2002). Families with children conceived by donor insemination: A follow-up at age twelve. *Child Development, 73,* 952–968.

Gonzaga, G. C., Keltner, D., Londahl, E. A., & Smith, M. D. (2001). Love and the commitment problem in romantic relations and friendship. *Journal of Personality and Social Psychology, 81*(2), 247–262.

Goodall, H. L., Jr. (2008). *A need to know: The clandestine history of a CIA family.* Walnut Creek, CA: Left Coast Press.

Goodman, C. C., & Silverstein, M. (2006). Grandmothers raising grandchildren: Ethnic and racial differences in well-being among custodial and coparenting families. *Journal of Family Issues, 27*(11), 1605–1626.

Gottman, J. M. (1979). *Marital interaction: Experimental investigations.* New York, NY: Academic Press.

Gottman, J. M. (1993). The roles of conflict engagement, escalation of avoidance in marital interaction: A longitudinal view of five types of couples. *Journal of Consulting and Clinical Psychology, 61,* 6–15.

Gottman, J. M. (1994a). *What predicts divorce?* Hillsdale, NJ: Lawrence Erlbaum.

Gottman, J. M. (1994b). *Why marriages succeed or fail?* New York, NY: Simon & Schuster.

Gottman, J. M. (1999). *The marriage clinic: A scientifically based marital therapy.* New York, NY: W. W. Norton.

Gottman, J. M., & DeClaire, J. (1997). *The heart of parenting.* New York, NY: Simon & Schuster.

Gottman, J. M., & DeClaire, J. (2001). *The relationship cure.* New York, NY: Crown Publishers.

Gottman, J. M., Gottman, J. S., & DeClaire, J. (2006). *Ten lessons to transform your marriage: America's love lab experts share their strategies for strengthening your relationship.* New York, NY: Crown.

Gottman, J. M., & Krokoff, L. J. (1990). Complex statistics are not always clearer than simple statistics: A reply to Woody and Costenzo. *Journal of Consulting and Clinical Psychology, 58,* 502–505.

Gottman, J. M., Ryan, K. D., Carrere, S., & Erley, A. M. (2002). Toward a scientifically based marital therapy. In H. A. Liddle, D. A. Santisteban, R. F. Levant, & J. H. Bray (Eds.), *Family psychology: Science-based interventions* (pp. 147–174). Washington, DC: American Psychological Association.

Gottman, J. M., & Silver, N. (1999). *The seven principles for making marriage work.* New York, NY: Three Rivers Press.

Grady, D. P. (1997, November). *Conversation strategies for detecting deception: An analysis of parent-adolescent child interactions.* Paper presented at the meeting of the National Communication Association, Chicago, IL.

Graham, E. E. (1997). Turning points and commitment in post-divorce relationships. *Communication Monographs, 64*, 350–368.

Graham, E. E. (2003). Dialectical contradictions in postmarital relationships. *Journal of Family Communication, 3*, 193–214.

Grall, T. (2009). Custodial mothers and fathers and their child support: 2007. *In Current population reports*. Washington, DC: U.S. Census Bureau.

Greeff, A. P., & de Bruyne, T. (2000). Conflict management style and marital satisfaction. *Journal of Sex and Marital Therapy, 26*, 221–224.

Green, R. (2012). Gay and lesbian family life: Risk, resilience and rising expectations. In F. Walsh (Ed.), *Normal family processes: Growing diversity and complexity* (pp. 172–195). New York, NY: Guilford Press.

Greene, S., Anderson, E., Forgatch, M. S., DeGarmo, D. S., & Hetherington, E. M. (2012). Risk and resilience after divorce. In F. Walsh (Ed.), *Normal family processes: Growing diversity and complexity* (4th ed., pp. 102–127). New York, NY: Guilford Press.

Greenhalgh, S. (2008). *Just one child: Science and policy in Deng's China*. Berkeley, CA: University of California Press.

Grill, B. D. (2011). From telex to Twitter: Relational communication skills for a wireless world. In K. M. Galvin (Ed.), *Making connections: Readings in relational communication* (5th ed., pp. 89–96). New York, NY: Oxford University Press.

Grote, N. K., & Clark, M. S. (2001). Perceiving unfairness in the family: Cause or consequence of marital distress? *Journal of Personality and Social Psychology, 80*, 281–293.

Grzywacz, J. G., Almeida, D. M., & McDonald, D. A. (2002). Spillover and daily reports of work and family stress in the adult labor force. *Family Relations, 51*, 28–36.

Gudmunson, C. G., Beutler, I. F., Israelsen, C. L., McCoy, J. K., & Hill, E. J. (2007). Linking financial strain to marital instability: Examining the roles of emotional distress and marital interaction. *Journal of Family Economic Issues, 28*, 357–376.

Gueguen, J. A., Bylund, C. L., Brown, R. F., Levin, T., & Kissane, D. W. (2009). Conducting family meetings in palliative care: Themes, techniques and preliminary evaluation of a communication skills module. *Palliative and Supportive Care, 7*(2), 171–179.

Guerrero, L. K., & Afifi, W. (1995). What parents don't know: Topic avoidance in parent-child relationships. In T. J. Socha & G. H. Stamp (Eds.), *Parents, children and communication* (pp. 219–245). Mahwah, NJ: Lawrence Erlbaum.

Guerrero, L. K., Andersen, P. A., & Afifi, W. A. (2014). *Close encounters: Communication in relationships* (4th ed.). Thousand Oaks, CA: Sage.

Guerrero, L. K., & Bachman, G. F. (2006). Association among relational maintenance behaviors, attachment-style categories, and attachment dimensions. *Communication Studies, 57*, 341–361.

Gumina, J. M. (2009). Communication of the decision to divorce: A retrospective qualitative study. *Journal of Divorce and Remarriage, 50*(3), 220–232.

Haas, S. M. (2002). Social support as relationship maintenance in gay male couples coping with HIV or AIDS. *Journal of Social and Personal Relationships, 19*, 87–111.

Haas, S. M., & Stafford, L. (1998). An initial examination of maintenance behaviors in gay and lesbian relationships. *Journal of Social and Personal Relationships, 15*, 846–855.

Haas, S. M., & Stafford, L. (2005). Maintenance behaviors in same-sex and marital relationships: A matched sample comparison. *Journal of Family Communication, 5*, 43–60.

Halford, W. K., Sanders, M. R., & Behrens, B. C. (2000). Repeating the errors of our parents? Family-of-origin spouse violence and observed conflict management in enraged couples. *Family Process, 39*(2), 219–235.

Hall, L. K. (2008). *Counseling military families: What mental health professionals need to know*. New York, NY: Routledge.

Halpin, J., Teixeira, R., Pinkus, S., & Daley, K. (2010). Battle of the sexes gives way to negotiations. *The Shriver Report: A study by Maria Shriver and the Center for American Progress*. Retrieved from http://www.awomansnation.com/americanPeople.php.

Hamby, S. L., Poindexter, V. C., & Gray-Little, B. (1996). Four measures of partner violence: Construct similarity and classification differences. *Journal of Marriage and the Family, 58*, 127–139.

Hamer, J. (2007). What it means to be Daddy: Fatherhood for black men living away from their children. In S. J. Ferguson (Ed.), *Shifting the center: Understanding contemporary families* (3rd ed., pp. 431–446). Boston, MA: McGraw-Hill.

Hamilton, R. J., Bowers, B. J., & Williams, J. K. (2005, first quarter). Disclosing genetic test results to family members. *Journal of Nursing Scholarship, 37*, 18–24.

Hample, D., & Dallinger, J. (1995). A Lewinian perspective on taking conflict personally: Revision, refinement, and validation of the instrument. *Communication Quarterly, 43*, 297–319.

Handel, G., & Whitchurch, G. (Eds.). (1994). *The psychological interior of the family*. Hawthorne, NY: Aldine de Gruyter.

Harburg, E., Kaciroti, N., Gleiberman, L., Julius, M., & Schork, A. (2008). Marital pair anger-coping types may act as an entity to affect mortality: Preliminary findings from a prospective study (Tecumseh, Michigan, 1971–1988). *Journal of Family Communication, 8*, 44–61.

Hardesty, J. L., & Chung, G. H. (2006). Intimate partner violence, parental violence, parental divorce, and child custody: Directions for intervention and future research. *Family Relations, 55*, 200–210.

Hardesty, J. L., Oswald, R. F., Khaw, L., Fonseca, D., & Chung, G. C. (2008). Lesbian mothering in the context of intimate partner violence. *Journal of Lesbian Studies, 12*, 191–210.

Hare, A. L., Miga, E. M., & Allen, J. P. (2009). Intergenerational transmission of aggression in romantic relationships: The moderating role of attachment security. *Journal of Family Psychology, 6*, 808–818.

Harevan, T. (1982). American families in transition: Historical perspective on change. In F. Walsh (Ed.), *Normal family processes: Growing diversity and complexity* (pp. 446–465). New York, NY: Guilford Press.

Harker, C. (1997, Autumn). Life-saving stories. *Iowa Alumni Quarterly*, 32–34.

Harrigan, M. M. (2009). The contradictions of identity-work for parents of visibly adopted children. *Journal of Social and Personal Relationships, 26*, 634–658.

Harrigan, M. M. (2010). Exploring the narrative process: An analysis of the adoption stories mothers tell their internationally adopted children. *Journal of Family Communication, 10*, 24–39.

Harris, J. N., Hay, J., Kuniyuki, A., Asgari, M. M., Press, N., & Bowen, D. J. (2010). Using a family systems approach to investigate cancer risk communication within melanoma families. *Psycho-Oncology, 19*, 1102–1111.

Harwood, J. J., Rittenour, C. E., & Lin, M. C. (2013). Family communication in later life. In A. L. Vangelisti (Ed.), *Handbook of family communication* (2nd ed., pp. 112–126). New York, NY: Routledge.

Hawkins, A. J., Amato, P. R., & Kinghorn, A. (2013). Are government-supported healthy marriage initiatives affecting family demographics? A state-level analysis. *Family Relations, 62*(3), 501–513.

Hay, J., Ostroff, J., Martin, A., Serle, N., Soma, S., Mujumdar, U., & Berwick, M. (2005). Skin cancer risk discussions in melanoma-affected families. *Journal of Cancer Education, 20*, 240–246.

Hay, J., Shuk, E., Zapolska, J., Ostroff, J., Lischewski, J., Brady, M., & Berwick, M. (2009). Family communications patterns after melanoma diagnosis. *Journal of Family Communication, 9*, 209–232.

Heatherington, L., Escudero, V., & Friedlander, M. L. (2005). Couple interaction during problem discussions: Toward an integrative methodology. *Journal of Family Communication, 5*(3), 191–207.

Heisler, J. M. (2005). Family communication about sex: Parents and college-aged offspring recall discussion topics, satisfaction, and parental involvement. *Journal of Family Communication, 5*, 295–312.

Helgeson, V. S., Novak, S. A., Lepore, S. J., & Eton, D. T. (2004). Spouse social control efforts: Relations to health behavior and well-being among men with prostate cancer. *Journal of Social and Personal Relationships, 21*(1), 53–68.

Helms-Erickson, H. (2001). Marital quality ten years after the transition to parenthood: Implications of the timing of parenthood and the division of housework. *Journal of Marriage and the Family, 63*, 1099–1110.

Hendrick, S. S., & Hendrick, C. (2006). Measuring respect in close relationships. *Journal of Social and Personal Relationships, 23*, 881–899.

Hendrick, S. S., Hendrick, C., & Logue, E. M. (2010). Respect and the family. *Journal of Family Theory and Review, 2*, 126–136.

Henry, J. (1973). *Pathways to madness*. New York, NY: Vintage Books.

Hertz, J. (2006). *Single by chance, mothers by choice: How women are choosing parenthood without marriage and creating the new American family*. New York, NY: Oxford University Press.

Hess, R., & Handel, G. (1959). *Family worlds*. Chicago, IL: University of Chicago Press.

Hest, T. L., Pearson, J. C., & Child, J. T. (2006). Cover stories as family communication practice. In L. H. Turner & R. West (Eds.), *The family communication sourcebook* (pp. 129–142). Thousand Oaks, CA: Sage.

Hetherington, E. M., & Kelly, J. (2002). *For better or for worse: Divorce reconsidered*. New York, NY: W. W. Norton.

Hewlett, S. A. (2002). *Creating a life: Professional women and the quest for children*. New York, NY: Talk Mirimax Books.

Hill, R. (1949). *Families under stress: Adjustment to the crises of war separation and reunion*. New York, NY: Harper & Brothers.

Hill, L. (2011). English proficiency of immigrants. Public Policy Institute of California. Retrieved May 2, 2013, from http://www.ppic.org.

Hindjua, S., & Patchin, J. W. (2009). *Cyberbullying and suicide*. Cyberbullying Research Center. Retrieved from www.cyberbullying.us.

Hinduja, S., & Patchin, J. W. (2010). *Ten ideas for youth to educate their community about cyberbullying*. Cyberbullying Research Center. Retrieved from www.cyberbullying.us.

Hinduja, S., & Patchin, J. W. (2012). Cyberbullying: Neither an epidemic nor a rarity. *European Journal of Developmental Psychology, 9*(5), 539–543.

Hines, P. M. (1999). The family life cycle of African-American families living in poverty. In B. Carter & M. McGoldrick (Eds.), *The expanded family life cycle* (3rd ed., pp. 327–345). Boston, MA: Allyn & Bacon.

Hines, P. M., & Boyd-Franklin, N. (2005). African American families. In M. McGoldrick, J. Giordano, & N. Garcia-Preto (Eds.), *Ethnicity and family therapy* (3rd ed., pp. 77–100). New York, NY: Guilford Press.

Hines, P. M., Preto, N. G., McGoldrick, M., Almeida, R., & Weltman, S. (2005). Culture and the family life cycle. In B. Carter & M. McGoldrick (Eds.), *The expanded family life cycle* (pp. 88–105). Boston, MA: Allyn & Bacon.

Hochschild, A. (1989). *The second shift*. New York, NY: Avon Books.

Hocker, J. L., & Wilmot, W. W. (2014). *Interpersonal conflict* (10th ed.). Boston, MA: McGraw-Hill.

Hoffman, J. (2010, June 28). Online bullies pull schools into the fray. *New York Times,* A1, A12–A13.

Hoffman, L. (1990). Constructing realities: The art of lenses. *Family Process, 29*(1), 1–12.

Hogan, D. P., Shandra, C. L., & Msall, M. E. (2007). Family developmental risk factors among adolescents with disabilities and children of parents with disabilities. *Journal of Adolescence, 30*, 1001–1019.

Holmes, E. K., Huston, T. L., Vangelisti, A., & Guinn, T. D. (2013). On becoming parents. In A. L., Vangelisti (Ed.), *Handbook of family communication* (2nd ed., pp. 80–96). New York, NY: Routledge.

Holson, L. M. (2011, July 4). Who's on the family tree? Now it's complicated. *New York Times*. Retrieved May 1, 2013, from http://nytimes.com.

Holtzman, M. (2008). Defining family: Young adults' perceptions of the parent-child bond. *Journal of Family Communication, 8*, 1–6.

Hoopes, M. (1987). Multigenerational systems: Basic assumptions. *American Journal of Family Therapy, 15*, 195–205.

Hoppe-Nagao, A., & Ting-Toomey, S. (2002). Relational dialectics and management strategies in marital couples. *Southern Communication Journal, 67*(20), 142–159.

Hoppough, S. K., & Ames, B. (2001). Death as normative in family life. In *Family focus on … death and dying* (pp. F1–F2). Minneapolis, MN: National Council on Family Relations.

Houston, J. B., Pfefferbaum, B., Sherman, M. D., Melson, A. G., & Brand, M. W. (2013). Family communication across the military deployment experience: Child and spouse report of communication frequency and quality and associated emotions, behaviors, and reactions. *Journal of Loss and Trauma: International Perspectives on Stress and Coping, 18*(2), 103–119.

Howe, N., Aquan-Assee, J., Bukowski, W. M., Lehoux, P. M., & Rinaldi, C. M. (2001). Siblings as confidants: Emotional understanding, relationship warmth, and sibling self-disclosure. *Social Development, 10*, 439–454.

Hudak, J., Krestan, J. A., & Bepko, C. (2005). Alcohol problems and the family life cycle. In B. Carter & M. McGoldrick (Eds.), *The expanded family life cycle: Individual, family and social perspectives* (3rd ed., pp. 455–469). Boston, MA: Allyn & Bacon.

Hughes, R., Bowers, J. R., Mitchell, E. T., Curtiss, S., & Ebata, A. T. (2012). Developing online family life prevention and education programs. *Family Relations, 61*(5), 711–727.

Huston, T. L. (2009). What's love got to do with it? Why some marriages succeed and others fail. *Personal Relationships, 16*, 301–327.

Huston, T. L., & Holmes, E. K. (2004). Becoming parents: An exploration of the marital and family issues of the later-life adult. In A. L. Vangelisti (Ed.), *Handbook of family communication* (pp. 105–133). Mahwah, NJ: Lawrence Erlbaum.

Hutchinson, M. K. (2002). The influence of sexual risk communication between parents and daughters on sexual risk behaviors. *Family Relations, 51,* 238–247.

Hymowitz, K., Carroll, J. S., Bradford, W. B., & Kaye, K. (2013). Knot yet: The benefits and costs of delayed marriage in America. *National Marriage Projects at the University of Virginia.* Retrieved June 2, 2013, from http://nationalmarriageproject.org/.

Im, E., Chee, W., Liu, Y., Lim, H. J., Guevara, E., Tsai, H. M., ..., Kim, Y. H. (2007). Characteristics of cancer patients in Internet cancer support groups. *Computers, Informatics and Nursing, 25,* 334–343.

Imber-Black, E. (1998). *The secret life of families.* New York, NY: Bantam Books.

Imber-Black, E. (1999). Creating meaningful rituals for new life cycle transitions. In B. Carter & M. McGoldrick (Eds.), *The expanded family life cycle* (3rd ed., pp. 202–214). Boston, MA: Allyn & Bacon.

Imber-Black, E. (2012). The value of rituals in family life. In F. Walsh (Ed.), *Normal family processes: Growing diversity and complexity* (4th ed., pp. 483–497). New York, NY: Guilford Press.

Imes, R. S. (2006, April). *"Everything's the same, except it's different": Communicatively negotiating the new normalcy in the post-treatment cancer stage of long time marriages.* Paper presented at the Kentucky Conference on Health Communication, Lexington, KY.

Infante, D. A., Sabourin, T. C., Rudd, J. E., & Shannon, E. A. (1990). Verbal aggression in violent and nonviolent marital disputes. *Communication Quarterly, 38,* 361–371.

Ingoldsby, B. R., Smith, S. R., & Miller, J. E. (2004). *Exploring family theories.* Los Angeles, CA: Roxbury.

Ishii-Kuntz, M. (1994). The Japanese father: Work demands and family roles. In J. C. Hood (Ed.), *Men, work and family* (pp. 45–76). Thousand Oaks, CA: Sage.

Jaccard, J., Dittust, P. J., & Gordon, V. V. (2000). Parent-adolescent communication about premarital sex: Factors associated with the extent of communication. *Journal of Adolescent Research, 15,* 187–208.

Jacob, A., & Borzi, M. G. (1996, April). *Foster families and the co-construction of shared experiences: A narrative approach.* Paper presented at the meeting of the Central States Communication Association, Chicago, IL.

Jacobs, K., & Sillars, A. (2012). Sibling support during post-divorce adjustment: An idiographic analysis

of support forms, functions, and relationship types. *Journal of Family Communication, 12,* 167–187.

Jacobson, N. S., & Gottman, J. M. (1998). *When men batter women: New insights into ending abusive relationships.* New York, NY: Simon & Schuster.

Jakubowski, S. F., Milne, E. P., Brunner, H., & Miller, R. B. (2004). A review of empirically supported marital enrichment programs. *Family Relations, 53,* 528–536.

Jalali, B. (2005). Iranian families. In M. McGoldrick, J. Giordano, & N. Garcia-Preto (Eds.), *Ethnicity and family therapy* (3rd ed., pp. 451–467). New York, NY: Guilford Press.

Jaser, S. S., Champion, J. E., Reeslund, K. L., Keller, G., Merchant, M. J., Benson, M., & Compas, B. E. (2007). Cross-situational coping with peer and family stressors in adolescent offspring of depressed parents. *Journal of Adolescence, 30,* 917–932.

Jellinek, M. S., & Beresin, E. (2008, March). Money talks: Becoming more comfortable with understanding a family's finances. *Journal of the American Academy of Child and Adolescent Psychiatry, 47*(3), 249–253.

Jerman, P., & Constantine, N. A. (2010). Demographic and psychological predictors of parent-adolescent communication about sex: A representative statewide analysis. *Journal of Youth and Adolescence, 39,* 1164–1174.

Jin, X. C., & Keat, J. E. (2010). The effects of change in spousal power on intimate partner violence among Chinese immigrants. *Journal of Interpersonal Violence, 25,* 610–625.

Johnson, K. B., & Webb, L. M. (2012). Death of a child: Mothers' accounts of interactions with surviving children. In F. C. Dickson & L. M. Webb (Eds.), *Communication for families in crisis: Theories, research, strategies* (pp. 129–151). New York, NY: Peter Lang.

Johnson, M. P. (1995). Patriarchal terrorism and common couple violence: Two forms of violence against women. *Journal of Marriage and the Family, 57,* 283–294.

Johnson, M. P., Caughlin, J. P., & Huston, T. L. (1999). The tripartite nature of marital commitment: Personal, moral and structural reasons to stay married. *Journal of Marriage and the Family, 61*(1), 160–177.

Johnson, S. (2008). *Hold me tight: Seven conversations for a lifetime of love.* Boston, MA: Little, Brown.

Jones, D. J., Beach, S. R., & Jackson, H. (2004). Family influences on health: A framework to organize research and guide intervention. In A. Vangelisti (Ed.), *Handbook of family communication* (pp. 647–672). Mahwah, NJ: Lawrence Erlbaum.

Jones, E., & Gallois, C. (1989). Spouses, impressions of rules for communication in public and private marital conflicts. *Journal of Marriage and the Family, 51,* 957–967.

Jones, N. A., & Bullock, J. (2012, September). The two or more races population: 2010. *U.S. Census Bureau.* Retrieved May 1, 2013, from http:// www.census.gov.

Jorgensen, B. L., & Savla, J. (2010). Financial literacy of young adults: The importance of parental socialization. *Family Relations, 59*(4), 465–478.

Joseph, A. L., & Afifi, T. D. (2010). Military wives' stressful disclosures to their deployed husbands: The role of protective buffering. *Journal of Applied Communication Research, 38*(4), 412–434.

Kaiser Family Foundation. (2001). *A report on the experiences of lesbians, gays and bisexuals in America and the public's views on issues and policies related to sexual orientation.* Retrieved from http://www.kff.org.

Kalmijn, M. (2004). Marriage rituals as reinforcers of role transitions: An analysis of weddings in the Netherlands. *Journal of Marriage and Family, 66,* 582–594.

Kantor, D., & Lehr, W. (1976). *Inside the family.* San Francisco, CA: Jossey-Bass.

Kaplan, L. (2001). A couplehood typology for spouses of institutionalized persons with Alzheimer's disease: Perceptions of "We"-"I." *Family Relations, 50*(1), 87–98.

Kapungu, T. K., Bartiste, D., Holmbeck, G., McBride, C., Robinson-Brown, M., Sturdivant, A., …, Paikoff, R. (2010). Beyond the "birds and the bees": Gender differences in sex-related communication among urban African-American adolescents. *Family Process, 49*(2), 251–264.

Katapodi, M. C., Northouse, L. L., Milliron, K. J., Liu, G., & Merajver, S. D. (2012). Individual and family characteristics associated with BRCA1/2 genetic testing in high-risk families. *Psycho-Oncology, 6,* 1336–1343.

Keeley, M. P. (2007). "Turning toward death together": The functions of messages during final conversations in close relationships. *Journal of Social and Personal Relationships, 24*(2), 225–253.

Keeley, M. P. (2009). Comfort and community: Two emergent communication themes of religious faith and spirituality evident during final conversations.

In M. Wills (Ed.), *Speaking of spirituality: Perspectives on health from the religious to the numinous,* pp. 227–248. Creskill, NJ: Hampton Press Health Communication Series.

Keeley, M. P., & Yingling, J. M. (2007). *Final conversations.* Acton, MA: Vander-Wyk & Burnham.

Keller, D., & Honig, A. S. (2004). Maternal and paternal stress in families with school-aged children with disabilities. *American Journal of Orthopsychiatry, 74*(3), 337–348.

Kellerman, N. P. (2001). Transmission of Holocaust trauma: An integrative view. *Psychiatry, 64,* 256–267.

Kelley, D. L. (1998). The communication of forgiveness. *Communication Studies, 49,* 255–271.

Kelley, D. L. (2012). *Marital communication.* Malden, MA: Polity Press.

Kennedy, T. L. M., Smith, A., Wells, A. T., & Wellman, B. (2008). *Networked families.* Retrieved from the Pew Internet and American Life Project website www.pewinternet.com.

Kennedy, V., & Lloyd–Williams, M. (2009). How children cope when a parent has advanced cancer. *Psycho-Oncology, 18,* 886–892.

Kids Count Data Center. (2013). *The Annie E. Casey Foundation.* Retrieved April 12, 2013, from http://datacenter.kidscount.org.

Kiecolt-Glaser, J. K., & Newton, T. L. (2001). Marriage: His and hers. *Psychological Bulletin, 127*(4), 472–503.

Kieren, D. K., Maguire, T. O., & Hurlbut, N. (1996). A marker method to test a phasing hypothesis in family problem-solving interaction. *Journal of Marriage and the Family, 58,* 442–455.

Killian, K. D., & Agathengelou, A. M. (2005). Greek families. In M. McGoldrick, J. Giordano, & N. Garcia-Preto (Eds.), *Ethnicity and family therapy* (3rd ed., pp. 573–585). New York, NY: Guilford Press.

Killoren, S. E., Thayer, S. M., & Updegraff, K. A. (2008). Conflict resolution between Mexican origin adolescent siblings. *Journal of Marriage and the Family, 70,* 1200–1212.

Kilmann, R., & Thomas, K. (1975). Interpersonal conflict handling behavior as reflections of Jungian personality dimensions. *Psychological Reports, 37,* 971–980.

Kim, J. K., & Ward, L. M. (2007). Silence speaks volumes: Parental sexual communication among Asian American emerging adults. *Journal of Adolescent Research, 22*(3), 3–31.

Kim, Y., & Spillers, R. L. (2010). Quality of life of family caregivers at 2 years after a relative's cancer diagnosis. *Psycho-Oncology, 19,* 431–440.

Kirchler, E. (1993). Spouses' joint purchase decisions: Determinants of influence tactics for muddling through the process. *Journal of Economic Psychology, 14*(2), 405–438.

Klein, D. M., & White, J. M. (1996). *Family theories: An introduction.* Thousand Oaks, CA: Sage.

Klein, K. E. (2002). When it's all in the family. *Business Week Online.* Retrieved December 31, 2013 from http://www.businessweek.com/stories/2002-03-19/when-its-all-in-the-family.

Kline, S. L., & Clinton, B. L. (1998). Developments in children's persuasive message practices. *Communication Education, 47*, 120–136.

Klusmann, D. (2002). Sexual motivation and the duration of partnership. *Archives of Sexual Behavior, 31*(3), 275–287.

Knapp, M. L., & Vangelisti, A. L. (2005). *Interpersonal communication and human relationships* (5th ed.). Boston, MA: Allyn & Bacon.

Knobloch, L. K., Ebata, A. T., McGlaughlin, P. C., & Ogolsky, B. (2013). Depressive symptoms, relational turbulence, and the reintegration difficulty of military couples following wartime deployment. *Health Communication, 28*, 754–766.

Knobloch, L. K., Ebata, A. T., McGlaughlin, P. C., & Theiss, J. A. (2013). Generalized anxiety and relational uncertainty as predictors of topic avoidance during reintegration following military deployment. *Communication Monographs, 80*, 452–477.

Knobloch, L. K., Pusateri, K. B., Ebata, A. T., & McGlaughlin, P. C. (in press B). Experiences of military youth during a family member's deployment: Changes, challenges, and opportunities. *Youth and Society.*

Knobloch, L. K., Pusateri, K. B., Ebata, A. T., & McGlaughlin, P. C. (in press A). Communicative experiences of military youth during a parent's return home from deployment. *Journal of Family Communication.*

Knobloch, L. K., & Theiss, J. A. (2012). Experiences of U.S. military couples during the post-deployment transition: Applying the relational turbulence model. *Journal of Social and Personal Relationships, 29*(4), 423–450.

Knudson-Martin, C., & Laughlin, M. J. (2005). Gender and sexual orientation in family therapy: Toward a postgender approach. *Family Relations, 54*, 101–115.

Knudson-Martin, C., & Mahoney, A. R. (2005). Moving beyond gender: Processes that create relationship equality. *Journal of Marital and Family Therapy, 31*, 235–246.

Koehly, Laura M., June A. Peters, Natalia Kuhn, Lindsey Hoskins, Anne Letocha, Regina Kenen, Jennifer Loud, and Mark H. Greene (2008). Sisters in hereditary breast and ovarian cancer families: Communal coping, social integration, and psychological well-being. *Psycho-Oncology, 17*, 812–821.

Koenig Kellas, J. (2005). Family ties: Communicating identity through jointly told stories. *Communication Monographs, 72*, 365–389.

Koenig Kellas, J. (2010). Narrating family: Introduction to the special issue of narratives and storytelling in the family. *Journal of Family Communication, 10*, 1–6.

Koenig Kellas, J. (in press). Narrative theories: Making sense of interpersonal communication. In D. O. Braithwaite & P. Schrodt (Eds.), *Engaging theories in interpersonal communication* (2nd ed.). Thousand Oaks, CA: Sage.

Koenig Kellas, J., LeClair-Underberg, C., & Lamb Normand, E. (2008). Stepfamily address terms: "Sometimes they mean something and sometimes they don't." *Journal of Family Communication, 8*, 238–263.

Koenig Kellas, J., & Suter, E. (2012). Accounting for lesbian families: Lesbian mothers respond to discursive challenges. *Communication Monographs, 79*, 475–498.

Koenig Kellas, J., & Trees, A. R. (2006). Finding meaning in difficult family experiences: Sense-making and interaction processes during joint family storytelling. *Journal of Family Communication, 6*, 49–76.

Koenig Kellas, J., & Trees, A. R. (2013). Family stories and storytelling: Windows into the family soul. In A. L. Vangelisti (Ed.), *Handbook of family communication* (2nd ed., pp. 391–406). New York, NY: Routledge.

Koenig Kellas, J., Willer, E., & Kranstuber, H. (2010). Family tale and tragedies: Narratively making sense of (and the dark side of making sense) of personal relationships. In B. H. Spitzberg & W. R. Cupach (Eds.), *The dark side of close relationships* (2nd ed., pp. 63–93). New York, NY: Routledge.

Koerner, A. F., & Fitzpatrick, M. A. (1997). Family type and conflict: The impact on conversation orientation and conformity orientation on conflict in the family. *Communication Studies, 48*, 59–74.

Koerner, A. F., & Fitzpatrick, M. A. (2002). You never leave your family in a fight: The impact of families of origins on conflict-behavior in romantic relationships. *Communication Studies, 53,* 234–251.

Koerner, A. F., & Fitzpatrick, M. A. (2004). Communication in intact families. In A. Vangelisti (Ed.), *Handbook of family communication* (pp. 177–195). Mahwah, NJ: Lawrence Erlbaum.

Koerner, A. F., & Fitzpatrick, M. A. (2006). Family communication patterns theory: A social cognitive approach. In D. O. Braithwaite & L. A. Baxter (Eds.), *Engaging theories in family communication: Multiple perspectives* (pp. 50–65). Thousand Oaks, CA: Sage.

Koerner, S. S., Wallace, S., Lehman, S. J., & Raymond, M. (2002). Mother-to-daughter disclosure after divorce: Are there costs and benefits? *Journal of Child and Family Studies, 11,* 469–483.

Koopman, H. M., Baars, R. M., Chaplin, J., & Zwinderman, K. H. (2004). Illness through the eyes of a child: The development of children's understanding of the causes of illness. *Patient Education and Counseling, 55,* 363–370.

Kranstuber, H., & Koenig Kellas, J. (2011). "Instead of growing under her heart, I grew in it": The relationship between adoption entrance narratives and adoptees' self-concept. *Communication Quarterly, 59,* 179–199.

Kreider, R. M. (2012). A look at interracial and interethnic married couple households in the U.S. in 2010. *Random Samplings: Official Blog of the U.S. Census Bureau.* Retrieved June 10, 2013, from http://blogs.census.gov.

Kreider, R. M., & Elliot, D. (2009). America's families and living arrangements: 2007. In *Current population reports.* Washington, DC: U.S. Census Bureau.

Kreider, R. M., & Ellis, R. (2011). Number, timing and duration of marriages and divorces: 2009. *U.S. Census Bureau.* Retrieved April 12, 2013, from http://www.census.gov.

Kreider, R. M., & Simmons, T. (2003, October). Marital status: 2000. In *Census 2000 brief.* Washington, DC: U.S. Census Bureau. Retrieved from http://www.census.gov/prod/2003pubs/c2kbr-30.pdf.

Krishnakumar, A., & Buehler, C. (2000). Interparental conflict and parenting behaviors: A meta-analytic review. *Family Relations, 49,* 25–44.

Krouse, S. S., & Afifi, T. D. (2007). Family-to-work spillover stress: Coping communicatively in the workplace. *Journal of Family Communication, 7,* 85–122.

Krueger, D. L. (1983). Pragmatics of dyadic decision making: A sequential analysis of communication

patterns. *Western Journal of Speech Communication, 47,* 99–117.

Kübler-Ross, E. (1970). *On death and dying.* New York, NY: Macmillan.

Kurdek, L. A. (1994). Conflict resolution styles in gay, lesbian, heterosexual nonparent and heterosexual parent couples. *Journal of Marriage and the Family, 56,* 705–722.

Kurdek, L. A. (2004). Are gay and lesbian cohabiting couples *really* different from heterosexual married couples? *Journal of Marriage and the Family, 66,* 880–900.

Kurdek, L. A. (2009). Pet dogs as attachment figures for adult owners. *Journal of Family Psychology, 23*(4), 439–446.

Labrecque, J., & Ricard, L. (2001). Children's influence on family decision-making: A restaurant study. *Journal of Business Research, 54*(2), 173–176.

Laible, D. J., Carlo, G., & Roesch, S. C. (2004). Pathways to self-esteem in later adolescence: The role of parent and peer attachment, empathy, and social behaviors. *Journal of Adolescence, 27*(6), 703–716.

Laing, R. D. (1972). *The politics of the family.* New York, NY: Vintage Books.

Langellier, K. M., & Peterson, E. E. (2006). Narrative performance theory: Telling stories, doing family. In D. O. Braithwaite & L. A. Baxter (Eds.), *Engaging theories in family communication: Multiple perspectives* (pp. 99–114). Thousand Oaks, CA: Sage.

LaRossa, R., & Reitzes, D. (1993). Symbolic interactionism and family studies. In P. G. Boss, W. J. Doherty, R. La Rossa, W. R. Schumm, & S. K. Steinmetz (Eds.), *Sourcebook of family theory and methods* (pp. 135–163). New York, NY: Plenum Press.

Lauer, R. H., & Lauer, J. C. (2009). *Marriage and family: The quest for intimacy* (7th ed.). Boston, MA: McGraw-Hill.

Laurenceau, J.-P., Feldman-Barrett, L., & Rovine, M. J. (2005). The interpersonal process model of intimacy in marriage: A daily-diary and multilevel modeling approach. *Journal of Family Psychology, 13,* 314–323.

Laursen, B., & Collins, W. A. (2004). Parent-child communication during adolescence. In A. L. Vangelisti (Ed.), *Handbook of family communication* (pp. 333–348). Mahwah, NJ: Lawrence Erlbaum.

Lavee, Y. (2005). Couples under stress: Studying change in dyadic closeness and distance. In V. L. Bengston, A. C. Acock, K. R. Allen, P. Dilworth-Anderson, & D. M. Klein (Eds.), *Sourcebook of family theory and research* (pp. 281–283). Thousand Oaks, CA: Sage.

Lavee, L., Sharlin, S., & Katz, R. (1996). The effect of parenting stress on marital quality: An integrated mother-father model. *Journal of Family Issues, 17,* 114–135.

Leach, M. S., & Braithwaite, D. O. (1996). A binding tie: Supportive communication of family kinkeepers. *Journal of Applied Communication Research, 24,* 200–215.

Ledbetter, A. M. (in press). Media multiplexity theory: Technology use and interpersonal tie strength. In D. O. Braithwaite & P. Schrodt (Eds.), *Engaging theories in interpersonal communication: Multiple perspectives* (2nd ed.). Thousand Oaks, CA: Sage.

Lee, E., & Mock, M. R. (2005). Asian families: An overview. In M. McGoldrick, J. Giordano, & N. Garcia-Preto (Eds.), *Ethnicity and family therapy* (3rd ed., pp. 269–289). New York, NY: Guilford Press.

Leeds-Hurwitz, W. (2002). *Wedding as text: Communicating cultural identities through ritual.* Mahwah, NJ: Lawrence Erlbaum.

Leeds-Hurwitz, W. (2006). Social theories: Social constructionism and symbolic interactionism. In D. O. Braithwaite & L. A. Baxter (Eds.), *Engaging theories in family communication: Multiple perspectives* (pp. 229–242). Thousand Oaks, CA: Sage.

Lehr, S. T., Dilorio, C., Demi, A. S., & Facteau, J. (2005). Predictors of father-son communication about sexuality. *Journal of Sex Research, 2,* 119–129.

Lenhart, A. (2010, September 2). Cell phones and American adults. *Pew Internet Research Center.* Retrieved June 5, 2013, from http://pewinternet.org.

LePoire, B. A. (2006). Commentary on Part C. In K. Floyd & M. T. Morman (Eds.), *Widening the family circle: New research on family communication* (pp. 189–192). Thousand Oaks, CA: Sage.

LePoire, B. A., & Dailey R. M. (2006). Inconsistent nurturing as control theory: A new theory in family communication. In D. O. Braithwaite & L. A. Baxter (Eds.), *Engaging theories in family communication: Multiple perspectives* (pp. 82–98). Thousand Oaks, CA: Sage.

Lerner, H. (1989). *The dance of intimacy.* New York, NY: Harper & Row.

Lester, P., Saltzman, W. R., Woodward, K., Glover, D., Leskin, G. A., Bursch, B., …, Beardslee, W. (2012). Evaluation of a family-centered prevention intervention for military children and families facing wartime deployments. *Journal Information, 102*(S1).

Levaro, L. B. (2009). Living together or living apart together: New choices for old lovers. *National Council on Family Relations Report: Family Focus on Cohabitation, 54,* 9–10.

Levinson, D. (1978). *The seasons of a man's life.* New York, NY: Ballantine Books.

Lewin, E. (2009). *Gay fatherhood: Narratives of family and citizenship in America.* Chicago, IL: University of Chicago Press.

Lichtwarck-Aschoff, A., Finkenauer, C., van de Vorst, H., & Engels, R. C. M. E. (2012). Being mum's confidant, a boon or bane? Examining gender differences in the association of maternal disclosure with adolescents' depressive feelings. *Journal of Youth and Adolescence, 41,* 449–459.

Lincoln, K. D. (2007). Financial strain, negative interactions, and mastery: Pathways to mental health among older African Americans. *Journal of Black Psychology, 33*(4), 439–462.

Lindsey, E. W., Chambers, J. C., Frabutt, J. M., & Mackinnon-Lewis, C. (2009). Marital conflict and adolescents' peer aggression: The mediating and moderating role of mother-child emotional reciprocity. *Family Relations, 58,* 593–606.

Littlejohn, S. W. (2002). *Theories of human communication* (7th ed.). Belmont, CA: Wadsworth/ Thomson Learning.

Livingston, G., & Cohn, D. (2012, November 29). U.S. birth rate falls to a record low; Decline is greatest among immigrants. *Pew Research Social and Demographic Trends.* Retrieved from http://www.pewsocialtrends. org/2012/11/29/u-s-birth-rate-falls.

Livingstone, S., & Helsper, E. J. (2008, December 1). Parental mediation of children's Internet use. *Journal of Broadcasting and Electronic Media.* Retrieved from http://www.allbusiness.com/ society-social-families-children-family/11764547-1.html.

Lloyd, S., & Emery, B. (1994). Physically aggressive conflict in romantic relationships. In D. Cahn (Ed.), *Conflict in personal relationships* (pp. 27–46). Hillsdale, NJ: Lawrence Erlbaum.

Lofquist, D. (2011, September). Same-sex households. American Community Survey Briefs, American Community Survey data on same sex couples. *U.S. Census Bureau.* Retrieved April 14, 2013, from www.census.gov.

Lohan, J. A., & Murphy, S. A. (2002). Parents' perceptions of adolescent sibling grief responses after an adolescent or young adult child's sudden, violent death. *Omega, 44*(3), 195–213.

Loscocco, K., & Spitze, G. (2007). Gender patterns in provider role attitudes and behavior. *Journal of Family Issues, 28*, 934–954.

Loving, T. J., Hefner, K. L., Kiecolt-Glaser, J. K., Glaser, R., & Malarkety, W. B. (2004). Stress hormone changes and marital conflict: Spouses' relative power makes a difference. *Journal of Marriage and Family, 66*, 595–612.

Lucier-Greer, M., & Adler-Baeder, F. (2012), Does couple and relationship education work for individuals in stepfamilies? A meta-analytic study. *Family Relations, 61*, 756–769.

Lucier-Greer, M., Adler-Baeder, F., Ketring, S. A., Harcourt, K. T., & Smith, T. (2012). Comparing the experiences of couples in first marriages and remarriages in couple and relationship education. *Journal of Divorce and Remarriage, 53*(1), 55–75.

Ludden, J. (2010). Wired homes keep tabs on aging parents. *National Public Radio*. Retrieved August 10, 2013, from http://www.npr.org/templates/story/story.php?storyId=129104664.

Lueken, L. J., Kraft, A., & Hagan, M. J. (2009). Negative relationships in the family-of-origin predict attenuated cortisol in emerging adults. *Hormones and Behavior, 55*, 412–417.

Lum, L. (2006). Handling "helicopter parents." *Diverse Issues in Higher Education, 23*(20), 43–46.

Luo, Y., Lapierre, T. A., Hughes, M. E., & Waite, L. (2012). Grandparents providing care to grandchildren: A population-based study of continuity and change. *Journal of Family Issues, 33*, 1143–1167.

MacNeil, S., & Byers, E. S. (2005). Dyadic assessment of sexual self-disclosure and sexual satisfaction in heterosexual dating couples. *Journal of Social and Personal Relationships, 22*, 169–181.

Madden, M., Lenhart, A., Duggan, M., & Gasser, U. (2013, March 13). *Teens and technology 2013.* Pew Research Center's Internet & American Life Project. From http://www.pewinternet.org/Reports/2013/Teens-and-Tech.aspx. Retrieved May 27, 2013.

Maddock, J. (1989). Healthy family sexuality: Positive principles for educators and clinicians. *Family Relations, 38*, 130–136.

Madianou, M. (2012). Migration and the accentuated ambivalence of motherhood: The role of ICTs in Filipino transnational families. *Global Networks, 12*(3), 277–295.

Magdol, L., Moffitt, T. E., Caspi, A., & Silva, P. A. (1998). Hitting without a license: Testing explanations for differences in partner abuse between young adult daters and cohabitors. *Journal of Marriage and the Family, 60*, 41–55.

Maguire, K. C. (2012). *Stress and coping in families.* Cambridge, UK: Polity Press.

Mahoney, A., Pargament, K. I., Murray-Swank, A., & Murray-Swank, N. (2003). Religion and the sanctification of family relationships. *Review of Religious Research, 22*(3), 220–236.

Mandel, S., & Sharlin, S. A. (2006). The non-custodial father: His involvement in his children's lives and the connection between his role and the ex-wife's, child's, and father's perception of that role. *Journal of Divorce and Remarriage, 45*, 79–95.

Manne, S. L., Norton, T. R., Ostroff, J. S., Winkel, G., Fox, K., & Grana, G. (2007). Protective buffering and psychological distress among couples coping with breast cancer: The moderating role of relationship satisfaction. *Journal of Family Psychology, 21*, 380–388.

Manning, L. M. (1996, November). *Adolescent's communication concerns.* Paper presented at the meeting of the National Communication Association, San Diego, CA.

Manoogian, M. M., Harter, L. M., & Denham, S. A. (2010). The storied nature of health legacies in the familial experience of type 2 diabetes. *Journal of Family Communication, 10*, 40–56.

Markman, H. J., Rhoades, G. K., Stanley, S. M., Ragan, E. P., & Whitton, S. W. (2010). The premarital communication roots of marital distress and divorce: The first five years of marriage. *Journal of Family Psychology, 24*(3), 289–298.

Marks, S. R., Huston, T. L., Johnson, E. M., & MacDermid, S. M. (2001). Role balance among white married couples. *Journal of Marriage and Family, 63*, 1083–1098.

Marquardt, E., Glenn, N. D., & Clark, K. (2010). *My daddy's name is Donor*. New York, NY: Institute for American Values.

Marshall, L. L. (1994). Physical and psychological abuse. In W. R. Cupach & B. H. Spitzberg (Eds.), *The dark side of interpersonal communication* (pp. 281–311). Hillsdale, NJ: Lawrence Erlbaum.

Martinez, E. A. (2001). Death: A family event for Mexican-Americans. In *Family focus on … death and dying* (Issue FF12). Minneapolis, MN: National Council on Family Relations.

Mattessich, P. (2001, June). Pressure points: Factors related to stress in a survey of immigrants. *Family focus on … stress* (pp. F14–F15). Minneapolis, MN: National Council of Family Relations.

Max, S. (2009, September). How to talk money with Mom and Dad. *Money*, 31–32.

McAdams, D. P. (2006). *The redemptive self: Stories Americans live by*. New York, NY: Oxford University Press.

McAllister, S., Duncan, S. F., & Hawkins, A. J. (2012). Examining the early evidence for self-directed marriage and relationship education: A meta-analytic study. *Family Relations, 61*(5), 742–755.

McCann, S., MacAuley, D., Barnett, Y., Bunting, B., Bradley, A., Jeffers, L., & Morrison, P. J. (2009, November). Family communication, genetic testing and colonoscopy screening in hereditary non-polyposis colon cancer: A qualitative study. *Psycho-Oncology, 18*(11), 1208–1215.

McCubbin, H. I., & Patterson, J. (1983a). The family stress process: The double ABCX model of adjustment and adaptation. In H. McCubbin, M. Sussman, & J. Patterson (Eds.), *Social stress and the family: Advances and developments in family stress theory and research* (pp. 7–37). New York, NY: Haworth Press.

McCubbin, H. I., & Patterson, J. M. (1983b). Family transitions: Adaptation to stress. In H. I. McCubbin & C. R. Figley (Eds.), *Coping with normative transitions* (Vol. 1, pp. 5–25). New York, NY: Brunner/Mazel.

McCubbin, H. I., & Patterson, J. M. (1985). Adolescent stress, coping, and adaptation: A normative family perspective. In G. K. Leigh & G. W. Peterson (Eds.), *Adolescents in families* (pp. 256–276). Cincinnati, OH: South-Western.

McCubbin, H. I., Patterson, J. M., Cauble, A. E., Wilson, W. R., & Warwick, W. (1983). CHIP—Coping Health Inventory for Parents: An assessment of parental coping patterns in the case of the chronically ill. *Journal of Marriage and the Family, 45*, 359–370.

McDonald, G. W. (1980). Family power: The assessment of a decade of theory and research, 1970–1979. *Journal of Marriage and the Family, 42*, 841–852.

McGeough, D. D. (2012). Family stories: Fragments and identity. *Storytelling, Self, Society, 8*, 17–26.

McGivern, B., Everett, J., Yager, G. G., Baumiller, R. C., Hafertepen, A., & Saal, H. M. (2004). Family communication about positive BRCA1 and BRCA2 genetic test results. *Genetics in Medicine, 6*(6), 503–509.

McGoldrick, M. (2003). Culture: A challenge to concepts of normality. In F. Walsh (Ed.), *Normal family processes: Growing diversity and complexity* (3rd ed., pp. 235–259). New York, NY: Guilford Press.

McGoldrick, M. (2005). Becoming a couple. In B. Carter & M. McGoldrick (Eds.), *The expanded family life cycle: Individual, family and social perspectives* (3rd ed., pp. 231–248). New York, NY: Allyn & Bacon.

McGoldrick, M., & Carter, B. (2003). The family life cycle. In F. Walsh (Ed.), *Normal family processes: Growing diversity and complexity* (pp. 375–398). New York, NY: Guilford Press.

McGoldrick, M., Gerson, R., & Petry, S. (2008). *Genograms: Assessment and interventions* (3rd ed.). New York, NY: W. W. Norton.

McGoldrick, M., Gerson, R., & Shellenberger, S. (1999). *Genograms: Assessment and intervention*. New York, NY: W. W. Norton.

McGoldrick, M., Giordano, J., & Garcia-Preto, N. (2005a). *Ethnicity and family therapy* (3rd ed.). New York, NY: Guilford Press.

McGoldrick, M., Giordano, J., & Garcia-Preto, N. (2005b). Overview: Ethnicity and family therapy. In M. McGoldrick, J. Giordano, & N. Garcia-Preto (Eds.), *Ethnicity and family therapy* (3rd ed., pp. 1–40). New York, NY: Guilford Press.

McGoldrick, M., & Shibusawa, T. (2012). The family life cycle. In F. Walsh (Ed.), *Normal family processes: Growing diversity and complexity* (4th ed., pp. 375–398). New York, NY: Guilford Press.

McGoldrick, M., & Walsh, F. (2005). Death and the family life cycle. In B. Carter & M. McGoldrick (Eds.), *The expanded family life cycle: Individual, family and social perspectives* (3rd ed., pp. 185–201). Boston, MA: Allyn & Bacon.

McKee-Ryan, F. M., Song, Z., Wanberg, C. R., & Kinicki, A. J. (2005). Psychological and physical well-being during unemployment: A meta-analytic study. *Journal of Applied Psychology, 90*(1), 53–76.

McKenzie, S. E., & Curle, C. (2012). "The end of treatment is not the end": Parents' experiences of their child's transition from treatment for childhood cancer. *Psycho-Oncology, 21*, 647–654.

McLain, P. (2003). *Like family: Growing up in other people's houses*. New York, NY: Back Bay Books.

McManus, T. G., & Nussbaum, J. (2011). Ambiguous divorce-related communication, relational closeness, relational satisfaction, and communication satisfaction. *Western Journal of Communication, 75*(5), 500–522.

McNeil, D. G., Jr. (2004, September 19). Culture or chromosomes? Real men don't clean bathrooms. *New York Times*, sec. 4, 3.

McQuillan, J., Greil, A. L., Shreffler, K. M., Wonch-Hill, P. A., Gentzler, K. C., & Hathcoat, J. D. (2012). Does the reason matter? Variations in childlessness concerns among U.S. women. *Journal of Marriage and Family, 74*, 1166–1181.

Mederer, H., & Hill, R. (1983). Cultural transitions over the family span: Theory and research. In H. McCubbin, M. B. Sussman, & J. M. Patterson (Eds.), *Social stress and the family* (pp. 39–60). New York, NY: Haworth Press.

Medved, C. E., Brogan, S. M., McClanahan, A. M., Morris, J. F., & Shepherd, G. J. (2006). Family and work socializing communication: Messages, gender, and ideological implications. *Journal of Family Communication, 6*, 161–180.

Merolla, A. J. (2010). Relational maintenance during military deployment: Perspectives of wives of deployed U.S. soldiers. *Journal of Applied Communication Research, 38*(1), 4–26.

Mesch, G., & Frankel, M. (2011). Family imbalance and adjustment to information and communication technologies. In K. B. Wright & L. M. Webb (Eds.), *Computer-mediated communication in personal relationships* (pp. 285–301). New York, NY: Peter Lang.

Metts, S., & Cupach, W. R. (2007). Responses to relational transgressions: Hurt, anger and sometimes forgiveness. In B. H. Spitzberg & W. R. Cupach (Eds.), *The dark side of interpersonal communication* (2nd ed., pp. 243–273). Mahwah, NJ: Erlbaum.

Metz, M. E., & McCarthy, B. W. (2003). *Coping with premature ejaculation: How to overcome PE, please your partner and have great sex.* Oakland, CA: New Harbinger.

Michael, K. C., Torres, A., & Seemann, E. A. (2007). Adolescents' health habits, coping styles and self-concept are predicted by exposure to inter-parental conflict. *Journal of Divorce and Marriage, 48*, 155–174.

Mikkelson, A. C. (2006). Communication among peers: Adult sibling relationships. In K. Floyd & M. T. Morman (Eds.), *Widening the family circle: New research on family communication* (pp. 21–35). Thousand Oaks, CA: Sage.

Mikkelson, K. S. (2008). He said, she said: Comparing mother and father reports of father involvement. *Journal of Marriage and Family, 70*(3), 613–624.

Milardo, R. M. (2009). *The forgotten kin: Aunts and uncles.* Cambridge, MA: Cambridge University Press.

Milbury, K., & Badr, H. (2013). Sexual problems, communication patterns, and depressive symptoms in couples coping with metastatic breast cancer. *Psycho-Oncology, 22*, 814–822.

Miller, A. E. (2009). Revealing and concealing postmarital dating information: Divorced co-parents' privacy rule development and boundary coordination processes. *Journal of Family Communication, 9*, 135–149.

Miller, C. W. (2011). Irresolvable interpersonal conflicts: Students' perceptions of common topics, possible reasons for persistence, and communication patterns. In K. M. Galvin (Ed.), *Making connections: Readings in relational communication* (5th ed., pp. 240–247). New York, NY: Oxford University Press.

Miller, K. I., Shoemaker, M. M., Willyard, J., & Addison, P. (2008). Providing care for elderly parents: A structurational approach to family caregiver identity. *Journal of Family Communication, 8*, 19–43.

Miller, P. J., Sandel, T. L., Liang, C., & Fung, H. (2001). Narrative transgressions in Longwood: The discourses, meanings, and paradoxes of an American socialization practice. *Ethos, 29*, 159–186.

Miller-Day, M. (2004). *Communication among grandmothers, mothers, and adult daughters: A qualitative study of maternal relationships.* Mahwah, NJ: Lawrence Erlbaum.

Miller-Day, M. (2008). Talking to youth about drugs: What do late adolescents say about parental strategies? *Family Relations, 51*, 1–12.

Miller-Day, M., & Dodd, A. H. (2004). Toward a descriptive model of parent-offspring communication about alcohol and other drugs. *Journal of Social and Personal Relationships, 21*(1), 69–91.

Miller-Day, M., & Kam, J. A. (2010). More than just openness: Developing and validating a measure of targeted parent-child communication about alcohol. *Health Communication, 25*, 293–302.

Minow, M. (1998). Redefining families: Who's in and who's out? In K. V. Hansen & A. I. Garey (Eds.), *Families in the U.S.* (pp. 7–19). Philadelphia, PA: Temple University Press.

Minuchin, S. (1974). *Families and family therapy.* Cambridge, MA: Harvard University Press.

Minuchin, S. (1984). *Family kaleidoscope.* Cambridge, MA: Harvard University Press.

Minuchin, S., Montalovo, B., Guerney, B. G., Rosman, B. L., & Schumer, F. (1967). *Families of the slums: An exploration of their structure and treatment.* New York, NY: Basic Books.

Mistry, R. S., Lowe, E. D., Remers, A. D., & Chien, N. (2008). Explaining the family economic stress model: Insights from a mixed methods approach. *Journal of Marriage and Family, 70,* 196–209.

Mitchell, K. J., Finkelhor, D., Jones, L. M., & Wolak, J. (2012). Prevalence and characteristics of youth sexting: A national study. *Pediatrics, 129*(1), 13–20.

Mmari, K., Roche, K. M., Sudhinaraset, M., & Blum, R. (2009). When a parent goes off to war: Exploring the issues faced by adolescents and their families. *Youth and Society, 40,* 455–475.

Molden, D. C., & Finkel, E. J. (2010). Motivations for promotion and prevention and the role of trust and commitment in interpersonal forgiveness. *Journal of Experimental Social Psychology, 46,* 255–268.

Mone, J. G., & Biringen, Z. (2006). Perceived parent-child alienation. *Journal of Divorce and Remarriage, 45*(3), 131–156.

Morman, M. T., & Floyd, K. (2006). The good son: Men's perceptions of the characteristics of sonhood. In K. Floyd & M. T. Morman (Eds.), *Widening the family circle: New research on family communication* (pp. 37–55). Thousand Oaks, CA: Sage.

Mosher, C. E., Bakas, T., & Champion, V. L. (2013). Physical health, mental health, and life changes among family caregivers of patients with lung cancer. *Oncology Nursing Forum, 40*(1), 53–61.

Murphy, S. A., Johnson, L. C., Lohan, J., & Tapper, V. J. (2002). Bereaved parents' use of individual, family, and community resources 4 to 60 months after a child's violent death. *Family and Community Health, 25*(1), 71–82.

Murphy, S. A., Tapper, V. J., Johnson, L. C., & Lohan, J. (2003). Suicide ideation among parents bereaved by the violent deaths of their children. *Issues in Mental Health Nursing, 24,* 5–25.

Murray, C. I., Toth, K., Larsen, B. L., & Moulton, S. (2010). Death, dying, and grief in families. In S. J. Price, C. A. Price, & P. C. McKenry (Eds.), *Families and change: Coping with stressful events and transitions* (4th ed., pp. 73–95). Thousand Oaks CA: Sage.

Myers, S. A. (2008, November). *An investigation of relational maintenance across the adult sibling lifespan.* Paper presented at the meeting of the National Communication Association, San Diego, CA.

Myers, S. A. (2011). Adult siblings' use of relational maintenance behaviors across the sibling lifespan. In K. M. Galvin (Ed.), *Making connections* (5th ed., pp. 334–352). New York, NY: Oxford University Press.

Myers, S. A., & Bryant, L. E. (2008). Emerging adult and siblings' use of verbally aggressive messages as hurtful messages. *Communication Quarterly, 56,* 268–283.

Myers, S. A., & Members of COM 200. (2001). Relational maintenance behaviors in the sibling relationship. *Communication Quarterly, 49,* 19–34.

National Advisory Committee on Violence against Women. (2012). *National Research Council's panel on research on violence against women.* Retrieved July 11, 2013, from http://www.ovw.usdoj.gov/docs/nac-rpt.pdf.

National Health Statistics Report. (2013). *Infertility and impaired fecundity in the United States, 1982–2010: Data from the National Survey of Family Growth.* Retrieved December 16, 2013, from http://www.cdc.gov/nchs/data/nhsr/nhsr067.pdf.

NCMFR Family Profiles. (2012). Remarriage rate in the U.S., 2010. *National center for marriage and family research.* Retrieved May 1, 2013, from http://ncmfr.bgsu.edu.

Nichols, M. P. (2008). *Family therapy: Concepts and methods* (8th ed.). Boston, MA: Allyn & Bacon.

Nicholson, J. H. (1999, November). *Sibling alliance rules.* Paper presented at the annual meeting of the National Communication Association, Chicago, IL.

Niedzwiecki, C. K. (1997, November). *The influence of affect and attribution on the outcome of parent-adolescent communication in decision-making.* Paper presented at the meeting of the National Communication Association, Chicago, IL.

Noguera, P. A. (2002, May 13). The trouble with black boys. *Motion Magazine.* Retrieved July 20, 2013, from http://www.inmotionmagazine.com/er/pntrouble1.html.

Noller, P., & Fitzpatrick, M. A. (1993). *Communication in family relationships.* Englewood Cliffs, NJ: Prentice Hall.

Nomaguchi, K. M., & Milki, M. A. (2003). Costs and rewards of children: The effects of becoming a parent on adults' lives. *Journal of Marriage and Family, 65,* 356–374.

Nussbaum, J. F., Pecchioni, L. L., Baringer, D. K., & Kundrat, A. L. (2002). Lifespan communication. In W. B. Gudykinst (Ed.), *Communication yearbook* (Vol. 26, pp. 366–389). Mahwah, NJ: Lawrence Erlbaum.

Nussbaum, J. F., Pecchioni, L. L., Robinson, J. D., & Thompson, T. L. (2000). *Communication and aging* (2nd ed.). Mahwah, NJ: Erlbaum.

Ochs, E., & Taylor, C. (1992). Family narrative as political activity. *Discourse and Society, 3*(3), 301–340.

Oetzel, J., Ting-Toomey, S., Chew-Sanchez, M. I., Harris, R., Wilcox, R., & Stumpf, S. (2003). Face and facework in conflicts with parents and siblings: A cross-cultural comparison of Germans, Japanese, Mexicans, and U.S. Americans. *Journal of Family Communication, 3,* 69–93.

Offer, S. (2012). Family time activities and adolescents' emotional well-being. *Journal of Marriage and Family, 75,* 26–41.

Olson, D. H. (1997). Family stress and coping: A multisystem perspective. In S. Dreman (Ed.), *The family on the threshold of the 21st century* (pp. 259–282). Mahwah, NJ: Lawrence Erlbaum.

Olson, D. H. (2000). Circumplex model of marital and family systems. *Family focus on … death and dying* (p. F4). Minneapolis, MN: National Council on Family Relations.

Olson, D. H., DeFrain, J., & Skogrand, L. (2008). *Marriage & families: Intimacy, diversity and strengths* (6th ed.). New York, NY: McGraw-Hill.

Olson, D. H., Olson-Sigg, A. K., & Larson, P. J. (2008). *The couple checkup.* Nashville, TN: Thomas Nelson.

Olson, D. H., Olson-Sigg, A. K., & Larson, P. J. (2012). PREPARE/ENRICH program: Overview and new discoveries about couples. *Journal of Family and Community Ministries, 25,* 30–44.

Olson, D. H., Russell, C., & Sprenkle, D. (Eds.). (1983). *Circumplex model: Systematic assessment and treatment of families.* New York, NY: Haworth Press.

Olson, D. H., Sprenkle, D., & Russell, C. (1979). Circumplex model of marital and family systems: Cohesion and adaptability dimensions, family types, and clinical applications. *Family Process, 18,* 3–28.

Olson, L. N. (2002). Exploring common couple violence in heterosexual romantic relationships. *Western Journal of Communication, 66,* 104–128.

Olson, L. N. (2004). Relational control-motivated aggression: A theoretically-based typology of intimate violence. *Journal of Family Communication, 4,* 209–233.

Olson, L. N., & Golish, T. D. (2002). Topics of conflict and patterns of aggression in romantic relationships. *Southern Communication Journal, 67*(2), 180–200.

Oppenheim, D., Wamboldt, F. S., Gavin, L. A., Renouf, A. G., & Emde, R. N. (1996). Couples' co-construction of the story of their child's birth: Associations with marital adaptation. *Journal of Narrative and Life History, 6*(1), 1–21.

Orthner, D. K., Jones-Sanpei, H., & Williamson, S. (2004). The resilience and strengths of low-income families. *Journal of Customer Services, 53,* 159–167.

Palazzolo, K. E., Roberto, A. J., & Babin, E. A. (2010). The relationship between parents' verbal aggression and young adult children's intimate partner violence victimization and perpetration. *Health Communication, 25,* 357–364.

Palfrey, J., & Gasser, U. (2008). *Born digital: Understanding the first generation of digital natives.* New York, NY: Basic Books.

Papp, L. M., Kourous, C. D., & Cummings, E. M. (2010). Emotions in marital conflict interactions: Empathic accuracy, assumed similarity, and the moderating context of depressive symptoms. *Journal of Social and Personal Relationships, 27,* 367–387.

Pargament, K. I., & Mahoney, A. (2005). Sacred matters: Sanctification as a vital topic for the psychology of religion. *International Journal for the Psychology of Religion, 15*(3), 179–198.

Parker, K. (2012). The boomerang generation: Feeling OK about living with Mom and Dad. *Pew Research Center.* From http://pewsocialtrends.org. Retrieved April 15, 2013.

Parrott, R., & Lemieux, R. (2003). When the worlds of work and wellness collide: The role of familial support on skin cancer control. *Journal of Family Communication, 3*(3), 95–106.

Pasley, K., & Lee, M. (2010). Stress and coping within the context of stepfamily life. In S. Price, C. Price, & P. McKenry (Eds.), *Families and change: Coping with stressful events and transitions* (4th ed., pp. 235–262). Los Angeles, CA: Sage.

Patrick, D., & Palladino, J. (2009). The community interactions of gay and lesbian foster parents. In T. J. Socha & G. H. Stamp (Eds.), *Parents and children communicating with society: Managing relationships outside of the home* (pp. 323–342). New York, NY: Routledge.

Patterson, C. J. (2009). Lesbian and gay parents and their children: A social science perspective. In D. A. Hope (Ed.), *Contemporary perspectives on lesbian, gay, and bisexual identities* (pp. 141–182). New York, NY: Springer.

Patterson, J. M. (2002). Integrating family resilience and family stress theory. *Journal of Marriage and Family, 64,* 349–360.

Pavlik, L. (2004). The effect of a sibling's diabetes on a non-diabetic sibling: A communicative approach (Unpublished honors thesis). Northwestern University, Evanston, IL.

Pawlowski, D. R. (1996, April). *Jelly beans and yo-yos: Perceptions of metaphors and dialectical tensions within the family*. Paper presented at the meeting of the Central States Communication Association, Minneapolis, MN.

Pawlowski, D. R. (2006). Dialectical tensions in families experiencing acute health issues: Stroke survivors' perceptions. In L. H. Turner & R. West (Eds.), *The family communication sourcebook* (pp. 468–489). Thousand Oaks, CA: Sage.

Pawlowski, D. R., Thilborger, C., & Cieloha-Meekins, J. (2001). Prisons, old cars, and Christmas trees: A metaphoric analysis of familial communication. *Communication Studies, 52*, 180–196.

Pecchioni, L. L., & Nussbaum, J. F. (2001). Mother-adult daughter discussions of caregiving prior to dependency: Exploring concepts among European-American women. *Journal of Family Communication, 1*, 133–149.

Pecchioni, L. L., Thompson, T. L., & Anderson, D. J. (2006). Interrelations between family communication and health communication. In L. H. Turner & R. West (Eds.), *The family communication sourcebook* (pp. 447–468). Thousand Oaks, CA: Sage.

Perreira, K. M., Chapman, M. V., & Stein, G. L. (2006). Becoming an American parent overcoming challenges and finding strength in a new immigrant Latino community. *Journal of Family Issues, 27*, 1383–1414.

Peters, B., & Ehrenberg, M. F. (2008). The influence of parental separation and divorce on father-child relationships. *Journal of Divorce and Remarriage, 49*(1), 78–109.

Peterson, G., Madden-Derdich, D., & Leonard, S. A. (2000). Parent-child relations across the life course. In S. J. Prece, P. C. McKenry, & M. J. Murphy (Eds.), *Families across time: A life course perspective* (pp. 187–203). Los Angeles, CA: Roxbury.

Petronio, S. (1994). Privacy binds in family interactions: The case of parental privacy invasion. In W. R. Cupach & B. Spitzberg (Eds.), *The dark side of interpersonal communication* (pp. 241–258). Hillsdale, NJ: Lawrence Erlbaum.

Petronio, S. (2002). *Boundaries of privacy: Dialectics of disclosure*. Albany, NY: SUNY Press.

Petronio, S. (2006). Impact of medical mistakes: Navigating work-family boundaries for physicians and their families. *Communication Monographs, 73*, 462–467.

Petronio, S. (2010). Communication privacy management theory: What do we know about family

privacy regulation? *Journal of Family Theory and Review, 2*, 175–196.

Petronio, S., & Caughlin, J. P. (2006). Communication privacy management theory: Understanding families. In D. O. Braithwaite & L. A. Baxter (Eds.), *Engaging theories in family communication: Multiple perspectives* (pp. 35–49). Thousand Oaks, CA: Sage.

Petronio, S., Reeder, H. M., Hecht, M. L., & Mon't Ros-Mendoza, T. (1996). Disclosure of sexual abuse by children and adolescents. *Journal of Applied Communication Research, 24*, 181–199.

Petronio, S., Sargent, J., Andea, L., Reganis, P., & Cichocki, D. (2004). Family and friends as healthcare advocates: Dilemmas of confidentiality and privacy. *Journal of Social and Personal Relationships, 21*(1), 33–52.

Pew Research Center. (2013). *Breadwinner Moms*. Retrieved August 12, 2013, from http://www.pew-socialtrends.org/2013/05/29/breadwinner-moms/.

Pew Research Social and Demographic Trends. (2011, January 13). A portrait of stepfamilies. *Pew Research Social and Demographic Trends*. Retrieved May 5, 2013, from http://www.pewso-cialtrends.org.

Piercy, F. (2006). Disability and marital interaction: A few personal reflections. *Family focus on … special needs and disabilities* (Issue FF31). Minneapolis, MN: National Council on Family Relations.

Pinsof, W. M., & Wynne, L. C. (1995). The effectiveness and efficacy of marital and family therapy: Introduction to the special issue. *Journal of Marital and Family Therapy, 21*, 341–343.

Pipher, M. (1996). *The shelter of each other: Rebuilding our families*. New York, NY: Ballantine Books.

Pistole, M. C. (1994). Adult attachment styles: Some thoughts on closeness-distance struggles. *Family Process, 33*(2), 147–159.

Pittman, J. F., Kerpelman, J. L., & McFadyen, J. M. (2004). Internal and external adaptation in army families: Lessons from operations Desert Shield and Desert Storm. *Family Relations, 53*, 249–260.

Plander, K. L. (2013). Checking accounts: Communication privacy management in familial financial caregiving. *Journal of Family Communication, 13*, 17–31.

Pochard, F., Azoulay, E., Chevret, S., Lemaire, F., Hubert, P., Canoui, P., …, French FAMIREA Group. (2001). Symptoms of anxiety and depression in family members of intensive care unit patients: Ethical hypothesis regarding decision-making capacity. *Critical Care Medicine, 29*, 1893–1897.

Powell, B., Bolzendahl, C., Geist, C., & Steelman, L. C. (2010). *Counted out: Same-sex relations and American's definitions of family*. New York, NY: Russell Sage Foundation.

Prensky, M. (2001, October). On the horizon. *MCB University Press, 9(5)*. Retrieved from http://facebook.com/pages/Not-posting-personal-problems-or-family-issues-in status-updates.com.

Prentice, C. M. (2008). The assimilation of in-laws: The impact of newcomers on the communication routines of families. *Journal of Applied Communication Research, 36*(1), 74–97.

Prentice, C. M. (2009). Relational dialectics among in-laws. *Journal of Family Communication, 94*, 67–89.

Price, S. J., Price, C. A., & McKenry, P. C. (2010). Families coping with change: A conceptual overview. In *Families and change: Coping with stressful events and transitions* (4th ed., pp. 1–23). Los Angeles, CA: Sage.

Priem, J. S., & Surra, C. A. (2013). A communication perspective on cohabitation and contemporary dating relationships. In A. L. Vangelisti (Ed.), *Handbook of family communication* (2nd ed., pp. 49–64). New York, NY: Routledge.

Quek, K. M.-T., & Knudson-Martin, C. (2008). Reshaping marital power: How dual-career newlywed couples create equality in Singapore. *Journal of Social and Personal Relationships, 25*, 511–532.

Radina, M. E. (2013). Towad a theory of health-related family quality of life. *Journal of Family Theory and Review, 5*, 35–50.

Ragsdale, J. D., & Brandau-Brown, F. E. (2005). Individual differences in the use of relational maintenance strategies in marriage. *Journal of Family Communication, 5*, 61–75.

Rasheed, J. M., Rasheed, M. N., & Marley, J. A. (2011). *Family therapy: Models and techniques*. Thousand Oaks, CA: Sage.

Ratner, P. A. (1998). Modeling acts of aggression and dominance as wife abuse and exploring adverse health effects. *Journal of Marriage and the Family, 60*, 453–465.

Raush, H. L., Barry, W. A., Hertel, R. K., & Swain, M. A. (1974). *Communication conflict and marriage*. San Francisco, CA: Jossey-Bass.

Reczek, C., Elliott, S., & Umberson, D. (2009). Commitment without marriage: Union formation among long-term same-sex couples. *Journal of Family Issues, 30*, 738–756.

Reiss, M. C., & Webster, C. (2004). An examination of established antecedents of power in purchase decision making: Married and nontraditional couples. *Journal of Applied Social Psychology, 34*, 1825–1845.

Rempel, L. A., & Rempel, J. K. (2004). Partner influence on health behavior decision-making: Increasing breastfeeding duration. *Journal of Social and Personal Relationship, 21*, 92–111.

Rhoades, G. K., Stanley, S. M., & Markman, H. J. (2009a). Couples' reasons for cohabitation: Associations with individual well-being and relationship quality. *Journal of Family Issues, 30*, 233–258.

Rice, R. E. (2006). Influences, usage, and outcomes of Internet health information searching: Multivariate results from the Pew surveys. *International Journal of Medical Informatics, 75*, 8–28.

Ridley, M. C., Collins, D. M., Reesing, A. L., & Lucero, A. A. (2006). The ebb and flow of marital lust: A relational approach. *Journal of Sex Research, 43*(2), 144–153.

Ristock, J. L. (2002). *No more secrets: Violence in lesbian relationships*. New York, NY: Routledge.

Rittenour, C. E., & Soliz, J. (2009). Communicative and relational dimensions of shared family identity and relational intentions in mother-in-law/daughter-in-law relationships: Developing a conceptual model for mother-in-law/daughter-in-law research. *Western Journal of Communication, 73*, 67–90.

Rober, P., Walravens, G., & Versteynen, L. (2012). "In search of a tale they can live with": About loss, family secrets, and selective disclosure. *Journal of Marital and Family Therapy, 38*, 529–541.

Roberto, A. J., Carlyle, K. E., Goodall, C. E., & Castle, J. D. (2009). The relationship between parents' verbal aggressiveness and responsiveness and young adult children's attachment style and relational satisfaction with parents. *Journal of Family Communication, 9*, 90–106.

Robinson, E. (2013, July 15). Black boys denied the right to be young. *Washington Post*. Retrieved August 16, 2013, from http://articles.washingtonpost.com/2013-07-15/opinions/40581519_1_trayvon-martin-george-zimmerman-martin-s.

Rogers, L. E., Castleton, A., & Lloyd, S. A. (1996). Relational control and physical aggression in satisfying marital relationships. In D. D. Cahn, D.

D. Loyd, & S. A. Lloyd (Eds.), *Family violence from a communication perspective* (pp. 218–239). Thousand Oaks, CA: Sage.

Rogers, R., & White, J. (1993). Family development theory. In P. Boss, W. Doherty, R. LaRossa, W. Shumm, & S. Steimmetz (Eds.), *Sourcebook of family theories and methods* (pp. 225–254). New York, NY: Plenum Press.

Rolland, J. S. (2005). Chronic illness and the family life cycle. In B. Carter & M. McGoldrick (Eds.), *The expanded family life cycle: Individual, family, and social perspectives* (3rd ed., pp. 492–511). Boston, MA: Allyn & Bacon.

Rolland, J. S. (2012). Mastering family challenges in serious illness and disability. In F. Walsh (Ed.), *Normal family processes: Growing diversity and complexity* (4th ed., pp. 452–482). New York, NY: Guilford Press.

Roloff, M. E. (1996). The catalyst hypothesis: Condition under which coercive communication leads to physical aggression. In D. Cahn & S. Floyd (Eds.), *Family violence from a communication perspective* (pp. 20–36). Thousand Oaks, CA: Sage.

Roloff, M. E. (2009). Links between conflict management research and practice. *Journal of Applied Communication Research, 37,* 339–348.

Roloff, M. E., & Miller, C. W. (2006). Mulling about family conflict and communication: What we know and what we need to know. In L. H. Turner & R. West (Eds.), *The family communication sourcebook* (pp. 143–164). Thousand Oaks, CA: Sage.

Romo, L. K. (2011). Money talks: Revealing and concealing financial information in families. *Journal of Family Communication, 11,* 264–281.

Rosato, J. L. (2008). Foreword. *Houston Journal of Health, Law and Policy, 8,* 195–205.

Rosen, E. J., & Weltman, S. F. (2005). Jewish families: An overview. In M. McGoldrick, J. Giordano, & N. Garcia-Preto (Eds.), *Ethnicity and family therapy* (3rd ed., pp. 667–679). New York, NY: Guilford Press.

Rosenfeld, M. J. (2007). *The age of independence: Interracial unions, same-sex unions, and the changing American family.* Cambridge, MA: Harvard University Press.

Rosenthal, C. J. (2009). Kinkeeping. In H. T. Reis & S. Sprecher (Eds.), *Encyclopedia of human relationships* (pp. 950–952). Thousand Oaks, CA: Sage.

Rothblum, E. D. (2009). An overview of same-sex couples in relation ships: A research area still at sea. In D. A. Hope (Ed.), *Contemporary perspectives on lesbian, gay, and bisexual identities* (pp. 113–139). New York: NY: Springer.

Rubin, L. (2001). Getting younger while getting older: Building families at midlife. In R. Hertz & N. L. Marshall (Eds.), *Working families* (pp. 58–71). Berkeley, CA: University of California Press.

Rueter, M., & Koerner, A. (2008). The effect of family communication patterns on adopted adolescent adjustment. *Journal of Marriage and Family, 70*(3), 715–727.

Rueter, M. A., & Conger, R. D. (1998). Reciprocal influences between parenting and adolescent problem-solving behavior. *Developmental Psychology, 34,* 1470–1482.

Ruppel, E. K., & Curran, M. K. (2012). Relational sacrifices in romantic relationships: Satisfaction and the moderating role of attachment. *Journal of Social and Personal Relationships, 29,* 508–529.

Rutter, M. (2002). Family influences on behavior and development: Challenges for the future. In J. P. McHale & W. S. Grolnick (Eds.), *Retrospect and prospect in the psychological study of families* (pp. 321–351). Mahwah, NJ: Lawrence Erlbaum.

Sabourin, T. (1996). The role of negative reciprocity in spouse abuse: A relational control analysis. *Journal of Applied Communication Research, 4,* 271–283.

Safilios-Rothschild, C. (1976). A macro- and micro-examination of family power and love: An exchange model. *Journal of Marriage and the Family, 37,* 355–362.

Sahlstein, E. (2010). Communication and distance: The present and future interpreted through the past. *Journal of Applied Communication Research, 38,* 106–114.

Sandberg, S. (2013). *Lean in: Women, work, and the will to lead.* New York, NY: Albert A. Knopf.

Sanders, S., Pedro, L. W., Bantum, E., & Galbraith, M. E. (2006). Couples surviving prostate cancer: Long-term intimacy needs and concerns following treatment. *Clinical Journal of Oncology Nursing, 10,* 503–508.

Sanford, K. (2006). Communication during marital conflict: When couples alter their appraisal, they change their behavior. *Journal of Family Psychology, 20,* 256–265.

Santos, S., Crespo, C., Silva, N., & Canavarro, M. C. (2012). Quality of life and adjustment in youths with asthma: The contributions of family rituals and the family environment. *Family Process, 51,* 557–569.

Saphir, M. N., & Chaffee, S. H. (2002). Adolescents' contributions to family communication patterns. *Human Communication Research, 28*(1), 86–108.

Satir, V. (1988). *The new peoplemaking*. Mountain View, CA: Science and Behavior Books.

Savin-Williams, R. C., & Esterberg, K. G. (2000). Lesbian, gay, and bisexual families. In D. H. Demo, K. R. Allen, & M. Fine (Eds.), *Handbook of family diversity* (pp. 197–214). New York, NY: Oxford University Press.

Schmeeckle, M., & Sprecher, S. (2013). Widening circles: Interactive connections between immediate family and larger social networks. In A. L. Vangelisti (Ed.), *Handbook of family communication* (2nd ed., pp. 302–317). New York, NY: Routledge.

Schnarch, C. M. (1991). *Constructing the sexual crucible: An integration of sexual and marital therapy*. New York, NY: W. W. Norton.

Schock, A. M., Gavazzi, S. M., Fristad, M. A., & Goldberg-Arnold, J. S. (2002). The role of father participation in the treatment of childhood mood disorders. *Family Relations, 51*, 230–237.

Schönpflug, U. (2001). Decision-making influence in the family: A comparison of Turkish families in Germany and in Turkey. *Journal of Comparative Family Studies, 29*, 219–230.

Schrimshaw, E. W., & Siegel, K. (2002). HIV-infected mothers' disclosure to their uninfected children: Rates, reasons, and reactions. *Journal of Social and Personal Relationships, 19*, 19–43.

Schrodt, P. (2005). Family communication schemata and the circumplex model of family functioning. *Western Journal of Communication, 69*, 359–376.

Schrodt, P., Baxter, L. A., McBride, C., Braithwaite, D. O., & Fine, M. A. (2006). The divorce decree, communication, and the structuration of co-parenting relationships in stepfamilies. *Journal of Social and Personal Relationships, 23*, 741–759.

Schrodt, P., Braithwaite, D. O., Soliz, J., Tye-Williams, S., Miller, A., Normand, E. L., & Harrigan, M. M. (2007). An examination of everyday talk in stepfamily systems. *Western Journal of Communication, 71*, 216–234.

Schrodt, P., & Ledbetter, A. M. (2011). Parental confirmation as a mitigator of feeling caught and family satisfaction. *Personal Relationships, 19*, 146–161.

Schumann, K. (2012). Does love mean never having to say you're sorry? Associations between relationship satisfaction, perceived apology sincerity, and forgiveness. *Journal of Social and Personal Relationships, 29*, 997–1010.

Schure, L. M., van den Heuvel, E. T. P., Stewart, R. E., Sanderman, R., de Witte, L. P., & Meyboom-de Jong, B. (2006). Beyond stroke: Description and evaluation of an effective intervention to support family caregivers of stroke patients. *Patient Education and Counseling, 62*, 46–55.

Sciascial, S., Clinton, E., Nason, R. S., James, A. E., & Rivera-Algarian, J. O. (2013). Family communication and innovativeness in family firms. *Family Relations, 62*, 429–442.

Segrin, C. (2006). Family interactions and well-being: Integrative perspectives. *Journal of Family Communication, 6*(1), 3–21.

Segrin, C., & Flora, J. (2011). *Family communication* (2nd ed.). New York, NY: Routledge.

Seligman, M., & Darling, M. B. (2007). *Ordinary families, special children: A systems approach to childhood disability* (2nd ed.). New York, NY: Guilford Press.

Serewicz, M. C. M. (2006). Getting along with the in-laws: Relationships with parents-in-law. In K. Floyd & M. K. Morman (Eds.), *Widening the family circle* (pp. 101–116). Thousand Oaks, CA: Sage.

Seymour, K. C., Addington-Hall, J., Lucassen, A. M., & Foster, C. L. (2010). What facilitates or impedes family communication following genetic testing for cancer risk? A systematic review and meta-synthesis of primary qualitative research. *Journal of Genetic Counseling, 19*(4), 330–342.

Shearman, S. M., & Dumlao, R. (2008). A cross-cultural comparison of communication patterns and conflict between young adults and parents. *Journal of Family Communication, 8*, 186–211.

Shellenbarger, S. (2005). *The breaking point: How female midlife crisis is transforming today's women*. New York, NY: Henry Holt.

Shellenbarger, S. (2011, January 12). Teens take elders to tech boot camp. *Wall Street Journal*. Retrieved June 5, 2013, http://online.wsj.com/news/articles/SB100 01424052748704515904576075763253410454.

Shibusawa, T. (2005). Japanese families: An overview. In M. McGoldrick, J. Giordano, & N. Garcia-Preto (Eds.), *Ethnicity and family therapy* (3rd ed., pp. 339–348). New York, NY: Guilford Press.

Shin, H., & Kominski, R. (2010). Language use in the United States: 2007. *American Community Survey Reports*. Washington, DC: U.S. Census Bureau.

Shreffler, K. M., Greil, A. L., & McQuillan, J. (2011). Pregnancy loss and distress among U.S. women. *Family Relations, 60*, 342–355.

Shriver, M. (2009). Times are changing: Gender and generation at work and home. *The Shriver*

Report: A study by Maria Shriver and the Center for American Progress. Retrieved from http://www.familiesandwork.org/site/research/reports/Times_Are_Changing.pdf.

Sieburg, E. (1973). Interpersonal confirmation: A paradigm for conceptualization and measurement. Paper presented at the meeting of the International Communication Association, Montreal, QC (ERIC document no. ED 098 634 1975).

Sillars, A. L., & Canary, D. J. (2013). Conflict and relational quality in families. In A. L. Vangelisti (Ed.), Handbook of family communication (2nd ed., pp. 338–357). New York, NY: Routledge.

Sillars, A. L., Canary, D. J., & Tafoya, M. (2004). Communication, conflict, and the quality of family relationships. In A. Vangelisti (Ed.), Handbook of family communication (pp. 413–446). Mahwah, NJ: Lawrence Erlbaum.

Sillars, A. L., Roberts, L. J., Leonard, K. E., & Dun, T. (2000). Cognition during marital conflict: The relationship of thought and talk. Journal of Social and Personal Relationships, 17, 479–502.

Sillars, A. L., & Wilmot, W. (1989). Marital communication across the life span. In J. Nussbaum (Ed.), Life-span communication: Narrative processes (pp. 225–254). Hillsdale, NJ: Lawrence Erlbaum.

Silva, J. M. (2013, June 23). Young and isolated. New York Times, SR7.

Silverstein, L. B. (2002). Fathers and families. In J. P. McHale & W. S. Grolnick (Eds.), Retrospect and prospect in the psychological study of families (pp. 35–64). Mahwah, NJ: Lawrence Erlbaum.

Siminoff, L. A., Wilson-Genderson, M., & Baker, S. (2010, December). Depressive symptoms in lung cancer patients and their family caregivers and the influence of family environment. Psycho-Oncology, 19(12), 1285–1293.

Simms, M., Fortuny, K., & Henderson, E. (2009). Racial and ethnic disparities among low-income families. Retrieved from Urban Institute website www.urban.org.

Smart, C. (2011). Families, secrets and memories. Sociology, 45(4), 539–553.

Smart Marriages. (2010). Retrieved from www.smart-marriages.com.

Smetana, J. G., Campione-Barr, N., & Daddis, C. (2004). Longitudinal development of family decision making: Defining healthy behavioral autonomy for middle-class African American adolescents. Child Development, 75, 1418–1434.

Smit, R. (2011). Maintaining family memories through symbolic action: Young adults' perceptions of family rituals. Journal of Comparative Family Studies, 42(3), 355–367.

Smith, G. C., Savage-Stevens, S. E., & Fabian E. S. (2002). How caregiving grandparents view support groups for children in their care. Family Relations, 51, 274–281.

Smock, P. J., & Greenland, F. R. (2010). Diversity in pathways to parenthood: Patterns, implications, and emerging research directions. Journal of Marriage and Family, 72, 576–593.

Snyder, K. A. (2007). A vocabulary of motives: Understanding how parents define quality time. Journal of Marriage and Family, 69, 320–340.

Sobel, S., & Cowan, B. C. (2003). Ambiguous loss and disenfranchised grief: The impact of DNA predictive testing on the family as a system. Family Process, 42(1), 47–57.

Socha, T. J., Bromley, J., & Kelly, B. (1995). Invisible parents and children: Exploring African-American parent-child communication. In T. J. Socha & G. H. Stamp (Eds.), Parents, children and communication: Frontiers of theory and research (pp. 127–145). Mahwah, NJ: Lawrence Erlbaum.

Socha, T. J., & Stamp, G. H. (2009). Parents and children communicating with society: Managing relationships outside of the home. New York, NY: Routledge.

Socha, T. J., & Yingling, J. (2010). Families communicating with children. Malden, MA: Polity Press.

Soliz, J. E., Lin, M., Anderson, K., & Harwood, J. (2006). Friends and allies: Communication in grandparent-grandchild relationships. In K. Floyd & M. T. Morman (Eds.), Widening the family circle (pp. 65–79). Thousand Oaks, CA: Sage.

Soliz, J. E., Thorson A. R., & Rittenour, C. E. (2009). Communicative correlates of satisfaction, family identity, and group salience in multiracial/ethnic families. Journal of Marriage and Family, 71, 819–832.

Song, Y., & Zhang, Y. B. (2012). Husband's conflict styles in Chinese mother/daughter-in-law conflicts. Journal of Family Communication, 12, 57–74.

Sotirin, P. J., & Ellingson, L. L. (2006). The "other" women in family life: Aunt/niece/nephew communication. In K. Floyd & M. T. Morman (Eds.), Widening the family circle (pp. 81–99). Thousand Oaks, CA: Sage.

Soule, K. P. (2011). The what, when, who, and why of nagging in interpersonal relationships. In K. M.

Galvin (Ed.), *Making connections* (5th ed., pp. 193–199). New York, NY: Oxford University Press.

Sperry, P., & Sperry, L. (2004). The family experience of loss associated with miscarriage and ectopic pregnancy. *Family Journal, 12*, 401–404.

Spitzberg, B. H., & Cupach, W. R. (2002). Interpersonal skills. In M. L. Knapp & J. A. Daly (Eds.), *The handbook of interpersonal communication* (3rd ed., pp. 564–612). Thousand Oaks, CA: Sage.

Spotts, E. L. (2012). Unraveling the complexity of gene-environment interplay and family processes. In F. Walsh (Ed.), *Normal family processes: Growing diversity and complexity* (4th ed., pp. 530–552). New York, NY: Guilford Press.

Spotts, E. L., Towers, H., & Reiss, D. (2006). Behavior genetics, families and mental health. In S. M. Miller, S. H. McDaniel, J. S. Rolland, & S. L. Feetham (Eds.), *Individuals, families, and the new era of genetics; Biopsychosocial perspectives* (pp. 197–227). New York, NY: W. W. Norton.

Sprecher, S., & McKinney, K. (1994). Sexuality in close relationships. In A. Weber & J. Harvey (Eds.), *Perspectives in close relationships* (pp. 193–216). Boston, MA: Allyn & Bacon.

Stack, C., & Burton, L. (1998). Kinscripts. In K. V. Hansen & A. I. Garey (Eds.), *Families in the U.S.* (pp. 431–445). Philadelphia, PA: Temple University Press.

Stafford, L. (2008). Social exchange theories: Calculating the rewards and costs of personal relationships. In D. O. Braithwaite & L. A. Baxter (Eds.), *Engaging theories in interpersonal communication: Multiple perspectives* (pp. 377–389). Thousand Oaks, CA: Sage.

Stafford, L. (2010). Measuring relationship maintenance behaviors: Critique and development of the revised relationship maintenance behavior scale. *Journal of Social and Personal Relationships, 28*(2), 278–303.

Stafford, L. (2013). Parent and sibling interactions during middle childhood. In A. L. Vangelisti (Ed.), *Handbook of family communication* (2nd ed., pp. 256–270). New York, NY: Routledge.

Stafford, L., & Canary, D. J. (1991). Maintenance strategies and romance relationship type, gender and relational characteristics. *Journal of Social and Personal Relationships, 8*, 217–242.

Stafford, L., & Dainton, M. (1994). The dark side of normal family interaction. In W. R. Cupach & B. Spitzberg (Eds.), *The dark side of interpersonal communication* (pp. 259–280). Hillsdale, NJ: Lawrence Erlbaum.

Stamp, G. H. (1994). The appropriation of the parental role through communication during the transition to parenthood. *Communication Monographs, 61*, 89–112.

Stamp, G. H., & Banski, M. H. (1992). The communicative management of constrained autonomy during the transition to parenthood. *Western Journal of Communication, 56*, 281–300.

Stanley, S. M., & Rhoades, G. K. (2009). "Sliding vs. deciding": Understanding a mystery. *Family focus on … cohabitation* (Issue FF42, pp. F1–F4). Minneapolis, MN: National Council on Family Relations.

Stanley, S. M., Rhoades, G. K., & Markman, H. J. (2009). Sliding vs. deciding: Inertia and the premarital cohabitation effect. *Family Relations, 55*, 499–509.

Stanley, S. M., Whitton, S. W., Sadberry, S. L., Clements, M. L., & Markman, H. J. (2006). Sacrifice as a predictor of marital outcomes. *Family Process, 45*(3), 289–303.

Steier, F. (1989). Toward a radical and ecological constructivist approach to family communication. *Journal of Applied Communication Research, 17*, 1–26.

Stepfamily Solutions. (2010). *The 21st century family: The stepfamily.* Retrieved from http://www.stepfamilysolutions.com/statistics.asp.

Stephenson-Abetz, J., & Holman, A. (2012). Home is where the heart is: Facebook and the negotiation of "old" and "new" during the transition to college. *Western Journal of Communication, 76*, 175–193.

Stewart, A. J., Copeland, A. P., Chester, N. L., Malley, J. E., & Barenbaum, N. B. (1997). *Separating together: How divorce transforms families.* New York, NY: Guilford Press.

Stewart, J. (1999). Interpersonal communication: Contact between persons. In J. Stewart (Ed.), *Bridges not walls* (7th ed., pp. 13–43). New York, NY: Random House.

Stewart, P. E. (2010). Stress and coping in African American families. In S. J. Price, C. A. Price, & P. C. McKenry (Eds.), *Families and change: Coping with stressful events and transitions* (4th ed., pp. 311–331). Los Angeles, CA: Sage.

Stone, E. (2004). *Black sheep and kissing cousins: How our family stories shape us.* New Brunswick, NJ: Transaction.

Stone, G. (2006). An exploration of factors influencing the quality of children's relationships with their father following divorce. *Journal of Divorce and Remarriage, 46,* 13–28.

Strazdins, L., Clements, M. S., Korda, R. J., Broom, D. H., & D'Souza, R. M. (2006). Unsociable work? Nonstandard work schedules, family relationships, and children's well-being. *Journal of Marriage and Family, 68,* 394–410.

Sullivan, A. E., & Miklowitz, D. J. (2010). Family functioning among adolescents with bipolar disorder. *Journal of Family Psychology, 24*(1), 60–61.

Sullivan, J., & McConkie-Rosell, A. (2010). Helping parents talk to their children. In C. L. Gaff & C. L. Bylund (Eds.), *Family communication about genetics: Theory and practice* (pp. 227–242). Oxford, UK: Oxford University Press.

Sulloway, F. J. (1996). *Born to rebel: Birth order, family dynamics, and creative lives.* New York, NY: Pantheon.

Sun, Y., & Li, Y. (2002). Children's well-being during parents' marital disruption process: A pooled time-series analysis. *Journal of Marriage and Family, 64*(2), 472–488.

Surra, C. A., Gray, C. R., Cottle, N., & Boettcher, T. M. J. (2004). In A. L. Vangelisti (Ed.), *Handbook of family communication* (pp. 53–82). Mahwah, NJ: Lawrence Erlbaum.

Suter, E. A., & Ballard, R. L. (2009). "How much did you pay for her?": Decision-making criteria underlying adoptive parents' responses to inappropriate remarks. *Journal of Family Communication, 9,* 107–125.

Tak, Y. R., & McCubbin, M. (2002). Family stress, perceived social support and coping following the diagnosis of a child's congenital heart disease. *Journal of Advanced Nursing, 39*(2), 190–198.

Taylor, P., & Cohn, D. (2012). A milestone en route to a majority minority nation. *Pew Research & Social Demographic Trends.* Retrieved December 16, 2013, from http://www.pewsocialtrends.org/2012/11/07/a-milestone-en-route-to-a-majority-minority-nation/.

The National Center on Family Homelessness. (2013, March). *Pressing issues facing families who are homeless.* Retrieved April 15, 2013, from http://www.familyhomelessness.org.

Thilborger, C. (1998, April). *Metaphorical perceptions of familial communication: Where gender differences are really more than skin deep.* Paper presented at the meeting of the Central States Communication Association, Chicago, IL.

Thomas, K. W. (1992). Conflict and conflict management: Reflections and update. *Journal of Organizational Behavior, 13,* 265–274.

Thompson, B., Koenig Kellas, J., Soliz, J., Thompson, J., Epp, A., & Schrodt, P. (2009). Family legacies: constructing individual and family identity through intergenerational storytelling. *Narrative Inquiry, 19,* 106–134.

Thompson, D. C., & Dickson, F. (1995, November). *Family rituals as communicative events: A grounded theory.* Paper presented at the annual meeting of the Speech Communication Association, San Antonio, TX.

Thorson, A. R. (2013). Adult children's discovery of their parents' infidelity. *Qualitative Communication Research, 2,* 61–80.

Titus, B., & de Souza, R. (2011). Finding meaning in the loss of a child: Journeys of chaos and quest. *Health Communication, 26,* 450–460.

Toller, P. W. (2008). Bereaved parents' negotiation of identity following the death of a child. *Communication Studies, 59,* 306–321.

Toller, P. W., & Braithwaite, D. O. (2009). Grieving together and apart: Bereaved parents' contradictions of marital interaction. *Journal of Applied Communication Research, 37,* 257–277.

Toro-Morn, M. (1998). Gender, class, family and migration: Puerto Rican women in Chicago. In K. Hansen & A. Garey (Eds.), *Families in the U.S.* (pp. 190–199). Philadelphia, PA: Temple University Press.

Trees, A. R., & Koenig Kellas, J. (2009). Telling tales: Enacting family relationships in joint storytelling about difficult family experiences. *Western Journal of Communication, 73,* 91–111.

Trenholm, S., & Jensen, A. (2013). *Interpersonal communication* (7th ed.). New York, NY: Oxford University Press.

Trice, H. M., & Beyer, J. M. (1984). Studying organizational cultures through rites and ceremonies. *Academy of Management Review, 9,* 653–669.

Trillingsgaard, T., Baucom, K. J., Heyman, R. E., & Elklit, A. (2012). Relationship interventions during the transition to parenthood: Issues of timing and efficacy. *Family Relations, 61*(5), 770–783.

Troth, A., & Peterson, C. C. (2000). Factors predicting safe-sex talk and condom use in early sexual relationships. *Health Communication, 12,* 195–218.

Tucker, J. S., & Anders, S. L. (2001). Social control of health behaviors in marriage. *Journal of Applied Social Psychology, 31*(3), 467–485.

Tucker, J. S., & Mueller, J. S. (2000). Spouses' social control of health behaviors: Use and effectiveness of specific strategies. *Personality and Social Psychology Bulletin, 26*(9), 1120–1130.

Tugend, A. (2008, November 8). Breaking financial bad news to the children. *New York Times,* B5.

Turkle, S. (2011). *Alone together: Why we expect more from technology and less from each other.* New York, NY: Basic Books.

Turman, P. D., Zimmerman, A., & Dobesh, B. (2009). Parent-talk and sport participation: Interaction between parents, children, and coaches regarding level of play in sports. In T. J. Socha & G. H. Stamp (Eds.), *Parents and children communicating with society: Maintaining relationships outside of home* (pp. 171–188). New York, NY: Routledge.

United States Census Bureau. (2013). *Quick facts.* Retrieved December 16, 2013, from http://quickfacts.census.gov/qfd/states/00000.html.

United States Department of Health and Human Services. (2010). *Child Welfare Information Gateway.* Retrieved June 9, 2010, from http://www.childwelfare.gov/can/prevalence/.

Uttal, L. (1998). Racial safety and cultural maintenance: The child care concerns of employed mothers. In K. V. Hansen & A. I. Garey (Eds.), *Families in the U.S.* (pp. 597–618). Philadelphia, PA: Temple University Press.

Vandeleur, C. L., Jeanpretre, N., Perrez, M., & Schoebi, D. (2009). Cohesion, satisfaction with family bonds, and emotional well-being in families with adolescents. *Journal of Marriage and Family, 71,* 1205–1219.

Van Doorn, M. D., Branje, S. J. T., & Meeus, W. H. J. (2007). Longitudinal transmission of conflict resolution styles from marital relationships to adolescent-parent relationships. *Journal of Family Psychology, 21,* 426–434.

Vangelisti, A. L. (1993). Communication in the family: The influence of time, relational prototypes, and irrationality. *Communication Monographs, 60,* 42–54.

Vangelisti, A. L. (1994a). Couples' communication problems: The counselor's perspective. *Journal of Applied Communication Research, 22,* 106–126.

Vangelisti, A. L. (1994b). Family secrets: Forms, functions, and correlates. *Journal of Social and Personal Relationships, 11,* 113–135.

Vangelisti, A. L. (2013). Introduction. In A. L. Vangelisti (Ed.), *Handbook of family communication* (2nd ed., pp. 1–8). New York, NY: Routledge.

Vangelisti, A. L., & Banski, M. A. (1993). Couples' debriefing conversations: The impact of gender, occupation and demographic characteristics. *Family Relations, 42,* 149–157.

Vangelisti, A. L., & Caughlin, J. (1997). Revealing family secrets: The influence of topic function and relationships. *Journal of Social and Personal Relationships, 14*(5), 679–705.

Vangelisti, A. L., Caughlin, J. P., & Timmerman, L. (2000, November). *Criteria for revealing family secrets.* Paper presented at the meeting of National Communication Association, Seattle, WA.

Vangelisti, A. L., & Crumley, L. (1998). Reactions to messages that hurt: The influence of relational contexts. *Communication Monographs, 65,* 173–196.

Vangelisti, A. L., Crumley, L. P., & Baker, J. L. (1999). Family portraits: Stories as standards for family relationships. *Journal of Social and Personal Relationships, 16,* 335–368.

Vangelisti, A. L., & Huston, T. L. (1994). Maintaining marital satisfaction and love. In D. J. Canary & L. Stafford (Eds.), *Communication and relational maintenance* (pp. 165–186). San Diego, CA: Academic Press.

Vangelisti, A. L., & Young, S. L. (2000). When words hurt: The effects of perceived intentionality on interpersonal relationships. *Journal of Social and Personal Relationships, 17,* 393–424.

Van Riper, M. (2000). Family variables associated with well-being in siblings of children with Down syndrome. *Journal of Family Nursing, 6*(3), 267–286.

Van Solinge, H., & Henkens, K. (2005). Couples' adjustment to retirement: A multi-actor panel study. *Journal of Gerontology, 60,* 511–520.

Videon, T. M. (2005). Parent-child relations and children's psychological well-being: Do dads matter? *Journal of Family Issues, 26,* 55–78.

Villard, K., & Whipple, L. (1976). *Beginnings in relational communication.* New York, NY: John Wiley & Sons.

Vissing, Y., & Baily, W. (1996). Parent-to-child verbal aggression. In D. Cahn & S. Lloyd (Eds.), *Family violence from a communication perspective* (pp. 85–107). Thousand Oaks, CA: Sage.

Vogl-Bauer, S. M. (2009). When the world comes home: Examining internal and external influences on communication exchanges between parents and their boomerang children. In T. J. Socha & G. H. Stamp (Eds.), *Parents and children communicating with society: Managing relationships outside of the home* (pp. 285–304). New York, NY: Routledge.

Vogt, P. (2009). Live with your parents after graduation? *Monster 2009 annual entry-level job outlook.* Retrieved from http://career-advice.monster.com/job-search/getting-started/live-with-parents-after-graduation/article.aspx.

Vogt Yuan, A. S., & Hamilton, H. A. (2006). Stepfather involvement and adolescent well-being: Do mothers and nonresidential fathers matter? *Journal of Family Issues, 27,* 1191–1213.

Vuchinich, S., & DeBaryske, B. D. (1997). Factor structure and predictive validity of questionnaire reports on family problem solving. *Journal of Marriage and the Family, 59,* 915–927.

Vuchinich, S., Teachman, J., & Crosby, L. (1991). Families and hazard rates that change over time: Some methodological issues in analyzing transitions. *Journal of Marriage and the Family, 53,* 898–912.

Waite, L. J., & Gallagher, M. (2000). *The case for marriage.* New York, NY: Doubleday.

Waldron, V. R., & Kelley, D. L. (2008). *Communicating forgiveness.* Thousand Oaks, CA: Sage.

Walker, L. P., & Coyne, S. M. (2012). Getting a high speed family connection: Associations between family media use and family connection. *Family Relations, 61,* 426–440.

Wallerstein, J. S., & Blakeslee, S. (1995). *The good marriage: How and why love lasts.* New York, NY: Houghton Mifflin.

Wallerstein, J. S., Lewis, J. M., & Blakeslee, S. (2000). *The unexpected legacy of divorce: A 25 year landmark study.* New York, NY: Hyperion.

Walsh, F. (1993). Conceptualization of normal family processes. In F. Walsh (Ed.), *Normal family processes: Growing diversity and complexity* (2nd ed., pp. 3–69). New York, NY: Guilford Press.

Walsh, F. (2005). Families in later life: Challenges and opportunities. In B. Carter & M. McGoldrick (Eds.), *The expanded family life cycle: Individual, family and social perspectives* (3rd ed., pp. 307–326). Boston, MA: Allyn & Bacon.

Walsh, F. (2009a). Human-animal bonds I: The relational significance of companion animals. *Family Process, 48,* 462–480.

Walsh, F. (2009b). Human-animal bonds II: The role of pets in family systems and family therapy. *Family Process, 48,* 481–499.

Walsh, F. (2012). The spiritual dimension of family life. In F. Walsh (Ed.), *Normal family processes: Growing diversity and complexity* (4th ed., pp. 347–372). New York, NY: Guilford Press.

Wamboldt, F., & Reiss, D. (1989). Defining a family heritage and a new relationship identity: Two central tasks in the making of a marriage. *Family Process, 28,* 317–335.

Wang, S., Holloway, B. B., Beatty, S. E., & Hill, W. W. (2006). Adolescent influence in family purchase decisions: An update and cross-national extensions. *Journal of Business Research, 60,* 1117–1124.

Wang, W., & Morin, R. (2009). Home for the holidays … and every other day. *Pew Research Center.* Retrieved from Pew Research Center website http://pewsocialtrends.org.

Wang, W., Parker, K., & Taylor, P. (2013). Breadwinner moms. *Pew Research Social and Demographic Trends.* Retrieved June 28, 2013, from http://www.pewsocialtrends.org.

Warren, C. (2006). Communicating about sex with parents and partners. In K. M. Galvin & P. J. Cooper (Eds.), *Making connections: Readings in relational communication* (4th ed., pp. 319–326). New York, NY: Oxford University Press.

Warren, C. (2011[Q5]). Family sex communication quotient. In T. D. Fisher, C. M. Davis, W. Yarber, & S. L. Davis (Eds.), *Handbook of sexuality-related measures* (3rd ed., pp. 140–142). New York, NY: Routledge.

Warren, C., & Warren, L. K. (2013). Talking about sex with parents and partners. (Unpublished update of Warren, C., Communicating about sex with parents and partners). In K. M. Galvin & P. J. Cooper (Eds.), *Making connections: Readings in relational communication* (3rd ed., pp. 319–326). New York, NY: Oxford University Press.

Warren-Jeanpiere, L., Miller, K., & Warren, A. (2010). African American women's retrospective perceptions of the intergenerational transfer of gynecological health care information received from mothers: Implications for families and providers. *Journal of Family Communication, 10,* 81–98.

Watt, T. T. (2002). Marital and cohabiting relationships of adult children of alcoholics: Evidence from the National Survey of Families and Households. *Journal of Family Issues, 23,* 246–265.

Watzlawick, P., Beavin, J., & Jackson, D. D. (1967). *Pragmatics of human communication.* New York, NY: W. W. Norton.

Weaver, S., & Coleman, M. (2010). Caught in the middle: Mothers in stepfamilies. *Journal of Social and Personal Relationships, 27,* 305–326.

Webb, L. M., & Dickson, F. C. (2012). Effective family communication for coping with crises. In F. C. Dickson & L. M. Webb (Eds.), *Effective family communication for coping with crises* (pp. 1–26). New York, NY: Peter Lang.

Weigel, D. J., & Ballard-Reisch, D. S. (2001). The impact of relational maintenance behaviors on marital satisfaction: A longitudinal analysis. *Journal of Family Communication, 1,* 265–279.

Weigel, D. J., & Ballard-Reisch, D. S. (2008). Relational maintenance, satisfaction, and commitment in marriages: An actor-partner analysis. *Journal of Family Communication, 8,* 212–229.

Weigel, D. J., Bennett, K. K., & Ballard-Reisch, D. (2006). Influence strategies in marriage: Self and partner links between equity, strategy use, and marital satisfaction and commitment. *Journal of Family Communication, 6,* 77–95.

Weintraub-Austin, E., Hust, S. J. T., & Kistler, M. E. (2009). Arming parents with strategies to affect children's interactions with commercial interests. In T. J. Socha & G. H. Stamp (Eds.), *Parents and children communicating with society: Managing relationships outside of the home* (pp. 133–153). New York, NY: Routledge.

Weiss, R. (1997, November 10). Aging: New answers to old questions. *National Geographic, 31.*

Weiss, R., & Dehle, C. (1994). Cognitive behavioral perspectives on marital conflict. In D. Cahn (Ed.), *Conflict in personal relationships* (pp. 95–116). Hillsdale, NJ: Lawrence Erlbaum.

Weisskirch, R. S. (2006). Emotional aspects of language brokering among Mexican American adults. *Journal of Multilingual and Multicultural Development, 27,* 332–343.

Weldon, M. (1998, January 11). Elderly care usually falls to daughters. *Chicago Tribune,* sec. 13, 3.

Wellman, B., & Rainie, L. (2012, July 9). If Romeo and Juliet had mobile phones. *Pew Internet and American Life Project.* From http://networked.perinternet.org/2012/07/09fi-romeo-and-juliet-had-mobile-phones/. Retrieved July 17, 2013.

Wells, B. (1986). *The meaning makers.* Portsmouth, NH: Heinemann.

Werner, C., & Baxter, L. A. (1994). Temporal qualities of relationships: Organismic, transactional, and dialectical views. In M. L. Knapp & G. R. Miller (Eds.), *Handbook of interpersonal communication* (2nd ed., pp. 323–379). Thousand Oaks, CA: Sage.

Weston, K. (1993). *Families we choose.* New York, NY: Columbia University Press.

Whitchurch, G. G., & Constantine, L. (1993). Systems theory. In P. Boss, W. J. Doherty, R. LaRossa, W. R. Schumm, & S. K. Steinmetz (Eds.), *Sourcebook of family theories and methods* (pp. 325–352). New York, NY: Plenum Press.

Whitchurch, G. G., & Dickson, F. C. (1999). Family communication. In M. B. Sussman, S. K. Steinmetz, & G. W. Peterson (Eds.), *Handbook of marriage and the family* (2nd ed., pp. 687–704). New York, NY: Plenum Press.

Whitchurch, G. G., & Pace, J. L. (1993). Communication skills training and interspousal violence. *Journal of Applied Communication Research, 21,* 96–102.

White, J. M., & Klein, D. M. (2002). *Family theories* (2nd ed.). Thousand Oaks, CA: Sage.

Whiting, J. B., Smith, D., Barnett, T., & Grafsky, E. (2007). Overcoming the Cinderella myth: A mixed methods study of successful stepmothers. *Journal of Divorce and Remarriage, 47,* 95–109.

Whitton, S. W., Waldinger, R. J., Schulz, M. S., Allen, J. P., Crowell, J. A., & Hauser, M. A. (2008). Prospective associations from family-of-origin interactions to adult marital interactions and relationship adjustment. *Journal of Family Psychology, 22*(2), 274–286.

Wilcox, W. B. (Ed.), & Marquardt, E. (Assoc. Ed.). (2009). *The state of our unions: Marriages in America 2009. Social indicators of marital health and wellbeing.* University of Virginia: The National Marriage Project. Retrieved May 12, 2013, from http://www.stateofourunions.org.

Wilkie, J. R., Ferree, M. M., & Ratcliff, K. S. (1998). Gender and fairness: Marital satisfaction in two-earner couples. *Journal of Marriage and the Family, 60,* 577–594.

Wilkinson, C. A. (1998). *Family communication* (Video class). University Park, IL: Governors State University.

Wilkinson, C. A. (2006). Expressing affection: A vocabulary of loving messages. In K. M. Galvin & P. J. Cooper (Eds.), *Making connections: Readings in relational communication* (4th ed., pp. 155–163). New York, NY: Oxford University Press.

Wilkinson, C. A., & Grill, L. H. (2011). Expressing affection: A vocabulary of loving messages. In K. M. Galvin (Ed.), *Making connections* (5th ed., pp. 164–173). New York, NY: Oxford University Press.

Willard, N. (2007). *Educator's guide to cyberbullying and cyberthreats* (pp. 1–2). Eugene, OR: Center for safe and responsible use of the Internet.

Williams, A., & Nussbaum, J. F. (2001). *Intergenerational communication across the lifespan*. Mahwah, NJ: Lawrence Erlbaum.

Willoughby, B. J., & Arnett, J. J. (2013). Communication emerging adulthood. In A. L. Vangelisti (Ed.), *Handbook of family communication* (2nd ed., pp. 287–301). New York, NY: Routledge.

Willoughby, B. L. B., Doty, N. D., & Malik, N. M. (2008). Parental reactions to their child's sexual orientation disclosure: A family stress perspective. *Parenting: Science and Practice, 8*, 70–91.

Wilson, B. J., Forrest, K., Van Teijlingen, E. R., McKee, L., Haites, N., Matthews, E., & Simpson, S. A. (2004). Family communication about genetic risk: The little that is known. *Community Genetics, 7*, 15–24.

Wilson, P. M. (2004). 1994: Forming a partnership between parents and sexuality educators: Reflections of a parent advocate. *SIECUS Report, 32*, 6–8.

Wilson, S. R., Guntzviler, L. M., & Munz, E. A. (2013). Persuasion and families. In A. L. Vangelisti (Ed.), *Handbook of family communication* (2nd ed., pp. 359–376). New York, NY: Routledge.

Wilson, S. R., Hayes, J., Bylund C., Rack, J., & Herman, A. (2006). Mothers' trait verbal aggressiveness and child abuse potential. *Journal of Family Communication, 6*, 279–296.

Wilson, S. R., & Morgan, W. M. (2006). Goals-plans-action theories: Theories of goals, plans and planning processes in families. In D. O. Braithwaite & L. A. Baxter (Eds.), *Engaging theories in family communication: Multiple perspectives* (pp. 66–81). Thousand Oaks, CA: Sage.

Wilson, S. R., Morgan, W. M., Hayes, J., Bylund, C., & Herman, A. (2004). Mothers' child abuse potential as a predictor of maternal and child behaviors during play-time interactions. *Communication Monographs, 71*, 395–421.

Wilson, S. R., Roberts, F., Rack, J. J., & Delaney, J. E. (2008). Mothers' trait verbal aggressiveness as a predictor of maternal and child behavior during playtime interactions. *Human Communication Research, 34*, 392–422.

Wilson, S. R., Shi, X., Tirmenstein, L., Norris, A., & Rack, J. J. (2006). Parental physical negative touch and child noncompliance in abusive, neglectful, and comparison families: A meta-analysis of observational studies. In L. H. Turner & R. West (Eds.), *The family communication sourcebook* (pp. 237–258). Thousand Oaks, CA: Sage.

Wilson, S. R., & Whipple, E. E. (1995). Communication, discipline, and physical child abuse. In T. Socha &

G. Stamp (Eds.), *Parents, children, and communication: Frontiers in theory and research* (pp. 299–317). Hillsdale, NJ: Lawrence Erlbaum.

Wilson, S. R., Xiaowei, S., Tirmenstein, L., Norris, A., & Rack, J. J. (2006). Parental physical negative touch and child noncompliance in abusive, neglectful, and comparison families: A meta-analysis of observational studies. In L. H. Turner & R. West (Eds.), *The family communication sourcebook* (pp. 237–258). Thousand Oaks, CA: Sage.

Wingard, L. (2009). Communicating about homework at home and school. In T. J. Socha & G. H. Stamp (Eds.), *Parents and children communicating with society: Maintaining relationships outside of home* (pp. 81–104). New York, NY: Routledge.

Wired seniors: A fervent few, inspired by family ties. (2001, September 9). Retrieved from the Pew Internet and American Life Project website www.pewinternet.org.

Wolff, J., Pak, J., Meeske, K., Worden, J. W., & Katz, E. (2002). Challenges and coping styles of fathers as primary medical caregivers: A multicultural qualitative study. *Journal of Psychosocial Oncology, 28*(2), 202–217.

Wolin, S. J., & Bennett, L. A. (1984). Family rituals. *Family Process, 23*, 401–420.

Wood, J. T. (2006). Critical feminist theories: A provocative perspective on families. In D. O. Braithwaite & L. A. Baxter (Eds.), *Engaging theories in family communication: Multiple perspectives* (pp. 197–212). Thousand Oaks, CA: Sage.

Wood, J. T. (2007). *Interpersonal communication: Everyday encounters* (6th ed.). Belmont, CA: Thomson Wadsworth.

Wood, J. T. (2010). *Gendered lives: Communication, gender, & culture* (9th ed.). Belmont, CA: Wadsworth-Cengage.

Wood, J. T. (2011). Which ruler do we use? Theorizing the division of domestic labor. *Journal of Family Communication, 11*, 39–49.

Wood, J. T. (2013a). *Gendered lives: Communication, gender, and culture* (10th ed.). Boston, MA: Cengage Learning.

Wood, J. T. (2013b). *Interpersonal communication: Everyday encounters* (7th ed.). Belmont, CA: Thomson Wadsworth.

Wood, J. T., & Inman, C. (1993). In a different mode: Recognizing male modes of closeness. *Journal of Applied Communication Research, 21*, 279–295.

Worldwide Marriage Encounter. (2010). Retrieved from http://www.wwme.org/.

Wright, P. J. (2009). Father-child sexual communication in the United States: A review and synthesis. *Journal of Family Communication, 9,* 233–250.

Xu, X., & Lai, S. (2002). Resources, gender ideologies and marital power. *Journal of Family Issues, 23*(2), 209–245.

Yerby, J. (1995, November). *Co-constructing alternative stories: Narrative approaches in the family therapy literature.* Paper presented at the meeting of the Speech Communication Association, Miami, FL.

Yingling, J. (2004). *A lifetime of communication: Transformations through relational dialogues.* Mahwah, NJ: Erlbaum.

Yogev, S. (2002). *For better or worse ... but not for lunch.* New York, NY: Contemporary Books.

Yoshida, K., & Busby, D. M. (2012). Intergenerational transmission effects on relationship satisfaction: A cross-cultural study. *Journal of Family Issues, 33,* 202–222.

Zahlis, E. H., & Lewis, F. M. (2010). Coming to grips with breast cancer: The spouse's experience with his wife's first six months. *Journal of Psychosocial Oncology, 28*(1), 79–97.

Zarefsky, D. (2012, June). *On deep disagreement.* Paper presented at the Biennial Conference on Argumentation, Casa Artom, Venice, Italy.

Zaslow, J. (2010, June 3). 'Til 40 years do us part. *Wall Street Journal,* D1.

Zhang, Q. (2007). Family communication patterns and conflict styles in Chinese parent-child relationships. *Communication Quarterly, 55,* 113–128.

CREDITS

NAME INDEX

SUBJECT INDEX